The Spanish Atlantic World in the Eighteenth Century

This volume elucidates Bourbon colonial policy with emphasis on Madrid's efforts to reform and modernize its American holdings. Set in an Atlantic world context, the book highlights the interplay between Spain and America as the Spanish empire struggled for survival amid the fierce international competition that dominated the eighteenth century. The authors use extensive research in the repositories of Spain and America, as well as innovative consultation of the archives of the French Ministry of Foreign Affairs to bring into focus the poorly understood reformist efforts of the early Bourbons, which laid the foundation for the better-known agenda of Charles III. As the book unfolds, the narrative puts flesh on the men and women who, for better or worse, influenced colonial governance. It is the story of power, ambition, and idealism at the highest levels.

An *académico correspondiente* of the Spanish Royal Academy of History and *acedémico correspondiente* of the Royal Academy of Buenas Letras of Seville, Allan J. Kuethe has published extensively on eighteenth-century Spain and America both in the United States and in Europe. His work began with monographs on military reform, then extended to commercial policy and, as expressed in the present volume, has advanced to a comprehensive overview of Bourbon Madrid's struggle to modernize and to sustain its vast holdings in the Western hemisphere. He is Paul Whitfield Horn Professor at Texas Tech University, to which he has dedicated his entire academic career.

Kenneth J. Andrien specializes in colonial Latin American history, focusing specifically on the Andean region from the sixteenth to the nineteenth centuries. Most recently he has broadened his focus to place the history of colonial Latin America within the context of the early modern Atlantic world. He is author of *Crisis and Decline: The Viceroyalty of Peru in the Seventeenth Century* (1985); *The Kingdom of Quito, 1690–1830: The State and Regional Development* (1996); and, most recently, *Andean Worlds: Indigenous History, Culture, and Consciousness Under Spanish Rule, 1532–1825* (2001). He has also published numerous articles in journals such as *Past and Present, Hispanic American Historical Review, Colonial Latin American Review,* and *Journal of Latin American Studies.* He is the Edmund J. and Louise W. Kahn Chair in History at Southern Methodist University.

NEW APPROACHES TO THE AMERICAS

Edited by Stuart Schwartz, Yale University

Also Published in the Series:

The Spanish Atlantic World in the Eighteenth Century

Century

War and the Bourbon Reforms, 1713–1796

ALLAN J. KUETHE

Texas Tech University, Lubbock, TX

KENNETH J. ANDRIEN

Southern Methodist University, Dallas, TX

CAMBRIDGE
UNIVERSITY PRESS

CAMBRIDGE
UNIVERSITY PRESS

32 Avenue of the Americas, New York, NY 10013–2473, USA

Cambridge University Press is part of the University of Cambridge.

It furthers the University's mission by disseminating knowledge in the pursuit of
education, learning, and research at the highest international levels of excellence.

www.cambridge.org
Information on this title: www.cambridge.org/9781107672840

© Allan J. Kuethe and Kenneth J. Andrien 2014

First published 2014

Printed in the United States of America

A catalog record for this publication is available from the British Library.

Library of Congress Cataloging in Publication Data
Kuethe, Allan J., 1940–
The Spanish Atlantic world in the eighteenth century : war and the Bourbon reforms,
1713–1796 / Allan J. Kuethe, Texas Tech University, Kenneth J. Andrien, Southern
Methodist University.
pages   cm. – (New approaches to the Americas)
ISBN 978-1-107-04357-2 (hardback)
1. Bourbon, House of.   2. Spain – Politics and government – 18th century.   3. Spain
– Colonies – America – Administration.   4. Spain – History – Bourbons,
1700–   I. Andrien, Kenneth J., 1951–   II. Title.
DP192.K84   2014
946'.054–dc23   2013045694

ISBN 978-1-107-04357-2 Hardback
ISBN 978-1-107-67284-0 Paperback

Contents

Color plates section appears between pages 40 and 41.

Introduction: War and Reform in Spain and Its Atlantic Empire

THE CONTESTED BOURBON INHERITANCE

War and reform developed a symbiotic relationship in the Spanish Atlantic world during the eighteenth century. The series of eighteenth-century military conflicts began with the War of the Spanish Succession, fought between 1702 and 1713 over disputed claims to the Spanish throne. When the childless king of Spain, Charles II, lay on his deathbed, he bequeathed his throne to the French Bourbon claimant Philip of Anjou, grandson of Louis XIV of France. The British, Dutch, and later Portuguese allied to support the rival claim of the Hapsburg, Archduke Charles of Austria, fearing the prospect of a powerful Bourbon family dynasty ruling over both France and Spain.[1] Hostilities began in 1702 with an unsuccessful allied attack on Cádiz; but Philip, with a bankrupt treasury and his armed forces in shambles, relied largely on French troops and money to defend his inheritance. The anti-Bourbon alliance attacked next in the Mediterranean theater, seizing Gibraltar in 1704, with Barcelona, Valencia, and Zaragosa falling to the allies in 1706. Once in possession of the whole of the Kingdom of Aragon, Archduke Charles established his court in Barcelona. The next year, an allied force invading from Portugal captured Madrid, but a Bourbon victory at Almansa in 1707 rescued Philip's cause. The war continued badly for Philip in Iberia, and French defeats in Italy and the Netherlands led Louis XIV to remove his troops from Spain in 1709 as a prelude to opening peace negotiations with the allies.

Philip continued the fight with his inadequate Spanish forces, but when diplomatic efforts at peace failed, an emboldened Louis XIV reintroduced

---

[1] When it became apparent that Charles II was gravely ill, the major European powers made a pact to partition the Spanish monarchy, with the throne of Spain passing to the Duke of Bavaria, Joseph Ferdinand, while France would receive some strategic Spanish possessions in Italy and the empire would take over Milan. The treaty was signed in October 1698. See Henry Kamen, *Philip V of Spain: The King who Reigned Twice* (New Haven: Yale University Press, 2001), p. 2.

French troops into Spain in 1710, commanded this time by a grizzled veteran general, the Duke of Vendôme. The duke's Franco-Spanish army defeated first the English army at Brihuega and then forced the Austrians to abandon Zaragosa after their losses in the Battle of Villaviciosa. These setbacks apparently convinced Archduke Charles and his allies that they could not win a clear military victory. As a result, when the Austrian Emperor Joseph died in 1711 and his throne passed to Charles, it raised the possibility of uniting the Austrian and Spanish thrones under Habsburg rule – re-creating the empire of Charles V. This prospect particularly worried the British, weakening support for Charles within the anti-Bourbon alliance, and both sides agreed to seek peace. The resulting Treaties of Utrecht in 1713 ended the wider European conflict, but the Catalans still resisted the Bourbon inheritance until 1715, when Philip's forces recaptured Barcelona, uniting all of Spain under the new Bourbon dynasty.

The Treaties of Utrecht confirmed Philip's right to rule Spain and its overseas possessions, but he renounced any claim to the French throne. He also yielded the Spanish Netherlands (Belgium) and his possessions in Italy. Belgium, Naples, Milan, and Sardinia went to Austria, Sicily to the Duke of Savoy, and Spain ceded Gibraltar and Minorca to Great Britain. Spain also recognized Portugal's right to the Colônia do Sacramento in the Río de la Plata, providing a valuable entrepôt for contraband trading to Spanish South America. Finally, the Utrecht settlement conceded to the British the *asiento* (monopoly contract) to market slaves in the Spanish colonies and the additional right to send one 500-ton ship annually to the trade fairs held at Veracruz and Portobelo. Nonetheless, with the exception of Gibraltar, Spain remained intact, and most importantly, the new Bourbon king retained his rich American empire.

When Philip V surveyed his exhausted patrimony at the end of the War of the Spanish Succession, however, the pressing need for the reform and renovation of Spain and her empire seemed obvious.[2] Parts of the Iberian Peninsula had suffered the depredations of war, the armada had practically disappeared, and commerce had declined as contrabandists plied trade routes in the Caribbean, the South Atlantic, and the Pacific with impunity. To keep his dominions supplied during the war, King Philip had made trade concessions to the French in the Pacific, allowing them to enter colonial ports, and they continued this commerce illegally after the cessation of hostilities. Moreover, the Dutch and the British (along with exploiting the concessions of the Utrecht Treaties) aggressively expanded their inroads into the

---

[2] Philip abdicated the throne in 1724 in favor of his eldest son, Louis, who died later that year from smallpox; Philip then resumed the throne until his death in 1746. See Kamen, *Philip V of Spain*. According to Kamen, the Iberian peninsula did not experience as much economic dislocation as other historians have averred. Henry Kamen, *The War of the Succession in Spain, 1700–1715* (Bloomington: Indiana University Press, 1969), passim.

Caribbean, marketing contraband goods in undersupplied Spanish colonies. As a result of this adversity, royal revenues declined alarmingly just as the crown faced the prospect of repaying heavy debts accumulated during its years at war. To deal with these disturbing trends, the crown looked to the resources of the Indies to resuscitate the beleaguered metropolis.

THE BOURBON REFORMS

Under Philip and his son and successor Ferdinand VI (1746–1759), Spanish reformers attempted to curb smuggling, curtail the power of the Church, modernize state finances, establish firmer political control within the empire, end the sale of bureaucratic appointments, and fill the depleted royal coffers. Behind many of these crown initiatives was the drive to reverse the damaging effect of trade concessions awarded to Great Britain at Utrecht and to limit both contraband and the influence of foreign merchants supplying goods for the legal trade through Seville and, later, Cádiz. Elsewhere, Madrid modernized its system for garrisoning its far-flung colonial defenses on land and registered important gains in rebuilding its armada. At the same time, however, attempts by Philip V to advance his family's dynastic claims to lands in Italy embroiled Spain in complicated entanglements and in additional wars, which heightened the debt and too often distracted the crown from its reformist objectives. Moreover, the ill health of both King Philip V and – toward the end of his reign – King Ferdinand VI further inhibited creative initiatives.

The first reforms began under Abad (later Cardinal) Julio Alberoni, Philip's influential court favorite. Alberoni attempted to undo trade concessions made to other European powers both at Utrecht and before, particularly those regarding the Indies trade, and he asserted control over key Spanish seaports to curtail foreign penetration. His reformist initiatives for the Indies included the transfer of the *Casa de la Contratación* (Board of Trade) and the *Consulado de Cargadores* (merchant guild) from Seville to Cádiz, the creation of the Viceroyalty of New Granada, the establishment of a tobacco monopoly in Cuba to supply the royal factory in Seville, and the reorganization of Havana's fixed garrison into a modern battalion. This agenda, although implemented piecemeal, addressed key areas of what would become the Bourbon reformist program for the secular realm. Much of it depended upon the vision and audacity of one man, however, and it would stall without him.

Alberoni fell from power in 1719 after his attempts to challenge foreign domination of the commercial system, as well as to seize Italian possessions for the king's children, provoked the disastrous War of the Quadruple Alliance with Great Britain, France, Austria, and Savoy. Reform began anew in 1726 with the rise to power of the cardinal's protégé, José Patiño (1726–1736). As virtual prime minister, Patiño, who controlled the Ministry of Marine and the Indies directly, redoubled efforts to curtail contraband trade and to rebuild the armada. Moreover, he effectively resurrected the cardinal's reform initiatives, which conservative politicians had suppressed after his downfall. Nonetheless, the crown's dynastic ambitions in Europe again complicated and at times impeded ongoing efforts to modernize the colonial commercial system and to undo the concessions granted to foreign powers.

The second wave of reform began in 1737, just two years before the War of Jenkins' Ear, as the crown subordinated the powerful, arrogant *Consulado* of Cádiz by breaking the grip of the self-recruiting *sevillano* elite, finally completing the transfer to Cádiz begun in 1717. Associated with the ideas of Spain's most influential eighteenth-century political thinker, José de Campillo y Cossío, this critical breakthrough advanced piecemeal, but it accelerated greatly in the later 1740s. It also marked the real beginning of commercial reform, and it laid the foundation upon which subsequent magistrates could build. On another level, wartime exigencies provoked an expansion of the Cuban system of fixed battalions across the Caribbean. Over the years, the resuscitated armed forces were destined to consume the lion's share of royal finance and to pose an increasingly worrisome challenge to the Royal Treasury.

The advances of the second phase's early years were extended substantially by the successful commercial and ecclesiastical initiatives coming under the aegis of King Ferdinand VI's two chief ministers, the Marqués de la Ensenada and José de Carvajal y Lancaster. After the conclusion of the War of Jenkins' Ear (which began in 1739 and then merged into the War of the Austrian Succession lasting from 1740 to 1748), the regime turned its full attention to reform within the empire. As one prominent historian of Bourbon Spain, John Lynch, has noted: "The new regime accepted that Spain's interest resided not in European battlefields but in the Atlantic and beyond."[3] Thus, while the two ministers sustained an ambitious domestic program, they also innovated meaningfully in the Indies. Building upon the work of their predecessors, they promoted the use of licensed register ships in the American trade, replacing the increasingly cumbersome and obsolete Portobelo fairs. They also ended the systematic sale of colonial bureaucratic appointments by 1750.[4] A further success was the Concordat of 1753, which dramatically increased the king's patronage power over church appointments throughout the empire. Perhaps the most significant clerical reform in the Indies, however, was the decision made between 1749 and 1753 to divest the religious orders of their rural indigenous parishes (*doctrinas de indios*), greatly curtailing their wealth and

[3] John Lynch, *Bourbon Spain, 1700–1808* (Oxford: Basil Blackwell, 1989), p. 156.
[4] Mark A. Burkholder and D. S. Chandler, *From Impotence to Authority: The Spanish Crown and the American Audiencias, 1687–1808* (Columbia: University of Missouri Press, 1977), p. 89.

power. In the end, however, this creative period ended prematurely after Carvajal's death in 1754, when the reactionary elite at court and their powerful foreign allies – aided by King Ferdinand's wife, Queen Barbara of Braganza – combined to topple Ensenada from power and thereby dull the reforming impulse. With the death of his wife in 1758, King Ferdinand slowly lapsed into depression and then madness, before his own passing the following year. In the period between the fall of Ensenada and the monarch's death, reform in the Spanish Atlantic stalled once again.

During the reign of Ferdinand's half-brother and successor, Charles III (1759–1788), the reformist agenda regained momentum, and entered into its third and most ambitious phase. Impelled in part by the shocking loss of Havana to English invaders in 1762, King Charles and his advisors in Madrid strengthened defenses in the Indies and, in the politics at court, opened the door to the resumption of Ensenada's reformist program. The expenses incurred via higher military outlays prompted the crown to tighten administrative controls and raise taxes throughout the empire. It also required a more systematic effort to curtail contraband commerce and the penetration of foreign merchants into the legal trade and, more fundamentally, to advance the cause of commercial reform. Moreover, Charles continued to reign in the influence of the religious orders when he expelled the wealthy and powerful Society of Jesus from Spain and the empire, gaining control of the Jesuits' lucrative assets. In short, the crown sponsored a major effort to rethink the nexus of political, fiscal, economic, social, and religious relationships within the Spanish Atlantic system and to initiate policies aimed at enhancing Madrid's authority and its capacity to wage war effectively.

Charles III and his ministers highlighted the third and most aggressive phase of the reform process by dispatching royal inspectors (*visitadores*) to various parts of the Indies to gain information and to initiate administrative, fiscal, military, and commercial changes. After ending the sale of appointments to high-ranking colonial offices by 1750, the crown had begun replacing creole officeholders with younger, well-trained, peninsular-born bureaucrats theoretically more loyal to the crown, and this process quickened under Charles. Crown officials in Madrid also created new, high-powered administrative units in formerly peripheral regions of South America, which had evolved into centers of contraband trade. Madrid had already reestablished the Viceroyalty of New Granada (present-day Ecuador, Colombia, Panama, and Venezuela) during the reign of Philip V, and in 1776 the government of Charles III created the Viceroyalty of the Río de la Plata (present-day Argentina, Bolivia, Paraguay, and Uruguay) followed the next year by the Captaincy General of Caracas (roughly equivalent to modern-day Venezuela). The crown also sent out a series of intendants, who were responsible for provincial administration, including finance, justice, and defense. The intendants linked regional authority with audiencias in the major provincial capitals. Overall, these initiatives enlarged the local bureaucracy, which worked to decrease the inflow of contraband goods and the illicit outflow of silver through the Caribbean and South Atlantic.

The defeat at Havana in 1762 led Charles to elevate military imperatives to the top of his reformist agenda for America. Madrid enhanced local defenses by strengthening the regular army and, in strategic localities, by forming a disciplined militia comprised largely of local subjects. At the same time, it expanded the fleet aggressively. To fund these costly undertakings, royal officials raised new taxes, collected existing levies more effectively, and created royal monopolies for the sale and distribution of coveted commodities such as tobacco. These fiscal policies led to a dramatic increase in royal revenues from colonial treasuries, particularly in New Spain, where modernized mining techniques also contributed to the surge. It was a time of sweeping imperial innovations, which persisted even after Spain's triumph in the War of the American Revolution, as Charles's military ambitions grew. This reformist momentum would survive his death and continue under Charles IV (1788–1808). In possession of a well-armed, highly productive empire and the second largest navy in the world, Spain appeared a power of the first order as it entered the 1790s. War and reform had evolved into the central themes in the eighteenth-century Spanish Atlantic world.

Within this context, critical innovations in commercial policy responded to military imperatives. Madrid justified the first regulation of "free trade," for the Caribbean islands in 1765, as an attempt to develop Cuba's economy and thus bolster Caribbean defenses, while the sweeping liberalization capped by the Regulation of 1778 came on the eve of Spain's intervention in the War of the American Revolution. In addition, the extension of that deregulation to include Mexico and Caracas in 1789 occurred against the backdrop of Madrid's frantic naval buildup and the Royal Treasury's consequent, ever pressing need for increased revenues. Finally, the last wave of commercial reform, a radical multiplication of American merchant guilds during the mid-1790s, clearly expressed the crown's ongoing commitment to developing the empire's militarily exposed peripheries.

Yet Spain's military status was surprisingly fragile because too much depended on commerce and the reliable remissions of American revenues. War with Great Britain in 1796 led to a blockade that first interrupted and then cut commercial ties between Spain and the Indies. Predictably, the crown yielded to the fiscal imperatives needed to wage this bitter and ultimately unsuccessful conflict, which consumed the lion's share of New World resources husbanded by a century of reform, but they were not enough to stave off defeat.

ENLIGHTENED REFORM IN THE SPANISH ATLANTIC WORLD

The eighteenth-century Bourbon reforms were strongly influenced by intellectual currents in Europe associated with the Enlightenment, which began in

Northern Europe and spread throughout the Euro-Atlantic world. The fundamental ideas of the era stressed reason and observation, a greater sense of tolerance and justice, and the need to compile empirical information to solve the scientific, political, economic, and social issues of the day, rather than looking to tradition and faith. Enlightened ideas led to crown-sponsored scientific expeditions to catalog the flora and fauna of the Indies in an effort to understand the natural world and reform education, incorporating new subjects at all levels of the curriculum. Moreover, in Spain and the Indies, the Enlightenment spread out from the universities through the creation of new magazines and pamphlets, and the visits of educated foreign travelers to the empire added to the mix.[5] When renovating the Spanish Atlantic system, reformers attempted to use "enlightened," scientific, rationalist thought to devise specific proposals for the empire and to promote progress.

Influenced by enlightened ideas, the Spanish crown gradually took a more active role in championing "public happiness" (*felicidad pública*), which involved expanding the powers of the state to secure political centralization and to advance economic growth.[6] Before the Bourbon accession, Spain and its overseas empire had formed a "composite monarchy," comprised of distinct provinces or kingdoms united only by a common monarch.[7] Composite monarchies held together because of a compact between the monarch and the ruling classes of the different provinces, most often in partnership with the powerful Roman Catholic Church. By the eighteenth century, reformist ministers of the Bourbon monarchs (known as regalists) sought to accrue political power in a strong centralized state, to curtail the powers of the church, and to promote economic growth as a means of attaining the full realization of public well-being and national strength.[8] Bourbon regalists were not explicitly anticlerical, but they did seek to limit the power of the papacy over the church in Spain, and to curtail the church's control over national resources, which they believed impeded economic development and national prosperity. Reformers also viewed promoting commerce with the Indies as a principal vehicle to stimulate economic and

---

[5] John Tate Lanning, *Academic Culture in the Spanish Colonies* (Oxford: Oxford University Press, 1940); Dorothy Tank Estrada, *La Educación Illustrada, (1776–1836)* (México: El Colegio de México, 1977).

[6] Gabriel B. Paquette, *Enlightenment, Governance, and Reform in Spain and its Empire, 1759–1808* (Surry: Palgrave-MacMillan, 2008), pp. 57–67.

[7] This view of the political organization of early modern European monarchies is presented in two path-breaking articles: J. H. Elliott, "A Europe of Composite Monarchies," *Past and Present*, 137 (November, 1992), pp. 48–71; and H. G. Koenigsberger, "Dominium Regale or Dominium Politicum et Regale," in H. G. Koenigsberger, ed., *Politicians and Virtuosi: Essays in Early Modern History* (London: Hambledon Press, 1986), pp. 1–25.

[8] Paquette argues that regalism's "core principal was the state's pre-eminence and supremacy in relation to the Church, accompanied by its protection and support of the Church." Paquette, *Enlightenment, Governance and Reform*, p. 6.

demographic growth in Spain. In this way, the Bourbon reforms can profitably be understood from an Atlantic vantage point: Commerce and revenues from the Indies would be important vehicles for attaining renovation in the metropolis and the military strength to resist Spain's competitors. Reform, public happiness, and the political and economic subordination of the Indies were thus all integrally interconnected in the minds of Bourbon regalists. These reformers wanted to replace the composite monarchy of the Habsburgs with a more centralized, efficient, and militarily powerful state, capable of revitalizing Spain and its Atlantic empire. Thus, military, commercial, administrative, clerical, and revenue reforms formed core objectives of the crown's eighteenth-century regalist ministers.

Attempts to reform the Spanish Atlantic empire led to a heightened demand for information and the means to compile, summarize, and analyze it before making appropriate political decisions.[9] Crown officials throughout the empire began to create information systems to organize and manage the data needed to conduct the king's affairs and to promote public happiness. This involved drawing reliable maps of different regions, compiling more accurate enumerations of the population (not just notoriously inaccurate lists of taxpayers), writing reports on economic activities – such as business conditions, prices, trade data, or local national resources – and collecting information needed by the military to conduct the defense of the crown's far-flung possessions. This not only involved collecting data more systematically, but also devising appropriate ways to manage and to summarize it. Indeed, the various provincial and colonial capitals of the Spanish Atlantic became regional clearing houses for information sent to the king's ministers in Madrid.

Even Enlightenment science could serve concrete political ends. When the Spanish crown authorized a French scientific expedition – accompanied by two young Spanish naval officers, Jorge Juan and Antonio de Ulloa – to measure a degree of latitude on the equator, it was not just to settle a theoretical scientific debate about whether the earth bulged at the equator or flattened at the poles. Such information was needed to make accurate measurements of meridians of longitude, crucial to drawing precise, accurate maps.[10] When Jean-Baptiste Colbert commissioned the Academy of Sciences to complete an accurate map of France, for example, the final calculations in 1682 demonstrated that the west coast was farther east and the Mediterranean coast was farther north than previously thought, meaning that the territory of France was actually several hundred square miles smaller

---

[9] For a discussion of the general move toward gathering and using information in Europe, see Daniel R. Headrick, *When Information Came of Age: Technologies of Knowledge in the Age of Reason and Revolution* (New York: Oxford University Press, 2002).

[10] For a discussion of the Condamine expedition, see Neil Safier, *Measuring the New World: Enlightenment Science in South America* (Chicago: University of Chicago Press, 2008).

than previous maps had shown. Such data had profound fiscal, political, and military implications.[11]

In another even more directly relevant example, the Count-Duke of Olivares's assessment to the Catalans for their share of the Unión de Armas in the 1630s – an effort to have each kingdom pay for the maintenance of a common army for Spain – seriously overestimated the population and resources of the principality. Anger over such a dramatic new tax hike was a major cause of the principality's revolt in 1640.[12] Moreover, while involved in the French expedition, Juan and Ulloa made a series of scientific observations about the geography, resources, and fauna and flora of the king's Andean provinces.[13] At the behest of the Marqués de la Ensenada, however, they also subsequently compiled a secret report on the political ills of the kingdom, notoriously known as the *Noticias secretas de América*, which pointed to widespread political and clerical corruption and bad government throughout the region.[14]

Over the course of the eighteenth century, colonial officials also collected, summarized, and communicated large amounts of fiscal data more effectively than ever before. Although crown treasury officials had compiled detailed accounts of income and expenditures throughout the Indies from the sixteenth century, such accounts were assembled more consistently and became more detailed over the course of the eighteenth century, particularly with the application of double-entry bookkeeping in the 1780s.[15] Reorganization of the fiscal bureaucracy in the Spanish Atlantic also allowed the crown to understand and process fiscal data accumulated from the royal kingdoms more efficiently, leading to major increases in royal revenues. In the later eighteenth century, royal reports also began summarizing large quantities of fiscal data in tables, which allowed royal officials to make sense out of the masses of financial information that previously might have been overlooked or lost.

The crown established an effective royal mail service, which greatly improved and regularized communication throughout the Spanish Atlantic empire. Regalists recognized that state power depended on reliable systems of

---

[11] Headrick, *When Information Came of Age*, p. 99.

[12] J. H. Elliott, *The Count-Duke of Olivares: The Statesman in an Age of Decline* (New Haven: Yale University Press, 1986), pp. 257–58.

[13] José P. Merino Navarro and Miguel M. Rodríguez Vicente eds., *Relación histórica del viaje al América meridional de Jorge Juan y Antonio de Ulloa* (Madrid: Fundación Universitaria Española, [1748] 1978).

[14] The best historical study and critical edition of this memorial is Luis J. Ramos Gómez, *Las Noticias secretas de América de Jorge Juan y Antonio de Ulloa (1735–1745)*, 2 Vols. (Madrid: Consejo Superior de Investigaciones Científicas, 1985).

[15] On the history of double-entry bookkeeping, see Edward Peragallo, *Origin and Evolution of Double Entry Bookkeeping: A Study of Italian Practice from the Fourteenth Century* (New York: American Institute of Publishing Company, 1938).

communication, and merchants required up-to-date information about markets in the Indies to ply their trade successfully. The *Consulado* of Cádiz had operated the mail system through its packet ships (*navíos de aviso*), but the failure of this system was manifest with the loss of Havana and the British capture of the official mail outside of Cádiz in 1762.[16] The crown established a modernized royal mail system by royal decree on August 24, 1764.[17] Small ships would leave La Coruña for Havana each month and fan out across the empire to deliver and collect the mail. To defray the costs of the voyage, the mail ships could carry European goods for sale in the Indies and on the return trip bring colonial products to Spain. All such innovations allowed crown ministers to make more informed decisions and more effectively monitor the activities of the thousands of crown servants throughout the Spanish Atlantic world.

Another important, more traditional source of information for crown ministers came from memorials (*memoriales*) and petitions from citizens and corporate groups. Every subject in the empire had the right to petition the crown to voice opinions, state grievances, and call for specific policy changes. These petitions, and the usually more detailed memorials, could represent a window into public opinion in the crown's far-flung provinces. It was also a privilege that exempted the writers from secrecy norms, which often prohibited or at least discouraged public discussion of many political issues.[18] The *Noticias secretas* of Jorge Juan and Antonio de Ulloa is only one of many such documents that circulated in governing circles in Madrid. At the same time, creoles, crown bureaucrats, Spanish travelers to America, and elite indigenous intellectuals all developed their own proposals for changing the Spanish Atlantic system.[19] During the eighteenth century, Madrid was a cosmopolitan capital city, where ideas from Europe and the Indies continuously intersected. In 1749, for example, a mestizo member of the Franciscan order, Fray Calixto de San José Túpac Inka, wrote a famous memorial to the king complaining about abuses of the colonial government in Peru.[20] As remedies, he called for the end of forced labor drafts (*mita*), demanded that

---

[16] We would like to thank G. Douglas Inglis for providing this information.

[17] *Reglamento provisional que manda S. M. observar para el establecimiento del Nuevo Correo mensual que ha salir de España a las Indias Occidentales*, San Ildefonso, August 24, 1764, Archivo General de Indias (hereinafter AGI), Correos, leg. 484.

[18] For a study of how petitions and memorials influenced the creation of a public sphere in early modern England, see David Zaret, *Origins of Democratic Culture: Printing, Petitions, and the Public Sphere in Early-Modern England* (Princeton: Princeton University Press, 2000).

[19] For a detailed discussion of the principal *memoriales* from the Andes by indigenous authors, see Alcira Dueñas, *Indians and Mestizos in the 'Lettered City:' Reshaping Justice, Social Hierarchy, and Political Culture in Colonial Peru* (Boulder: University of Colorado Press, 2010).

[20] Impatient to give his manuscript to the king and lacking the proper recommendation from the Council of the Indies needed to deliver it, Fray Calixto and his Franciscan traveling companion, Fray Isidoro de Cala y Ortega, waited for the royal carriage to return from the king's hunting trip and thrust the document through the window. Fray Calixto de San José

Andeans obtain appointments as *corregidores* and be eligible for the priesthood, receive access to schooling, and serve in a new tribunal (composed of Spanish, *mestizo*, and Andean leaders that would be independent of the viceroy and the audiencias) to set policy for the viceroyalty.[21] Although the crown decided not to act on these recommendations, later reformist magistrates under Charles III, such as the Marqués de Esquilache, the Conde de Floridablanca, Pedro Rodríguez Campomanes, and José de Gálvez pulled together ideas from throughout Europe, but also from the Indies, to fashion concrete proposals for keeping Spain's Atlantic empire more firmly under metropolitan control.[22]

Despite the circulation of ideas, written matter, and data within the eighteenth-century Spanish Atlantic, a full-blown public sphere that allowed popular opinion to mediate between the state and civil society emerged only slowly.[23] Crown officials and the Inquisition still censored written materials, often denying the publication of even major works on politics, literature, and religion that ran afoul of official crown or church policies. Moreover, literacy levels varied dramatically within the empire; in Mexico City perhaps 50 percent of the population possessed at least basic reading skills, while in less cosmopolitan regions, such as Santa Fe de Bogotá in New Granada, only 1 to 3 percent of the citizenry had any schooling at all.[24] Print materials were seldom readily available for most people, and the first major newspaper in South America, Lima's *Mercurio Peruano*, did not appear until 1791.[25] Nonetheless, Sociedades de los Amigos del País (literary and scientific groups or societies) discussed economic issues, and the growth of salons by the late eighteenth century allowed for literate political, social, and intellectual exchanges that would change the course of public discourse by the late colonial period.[26] All of these trends stimulated a greater circulation of knowledge, which increasingly politicized debates over reform in the Spanish Atlantic world.

Tupac Inca to Mui Ilustre Cabildo de la Ciudad de Lima, Madrid, November 14, 1750, AGI, Lima, leg. 988.

[21] Francisco A. Loayza, ed., *Fray Calixto Túpak Inka: Documentos originales y, en su mayoría, totalmente desconocidos, auténticos, de este apóstol indio, valiente defensor de su raza, desde el año 1746 a 1760* (Lima: Bibliografía particular indígena, 1948), pp. 85–94.

[22] For an example of how these ideas intersected and influenced the thinking of reformers, see Kenneth J. Andrien, "The *Noticias Secretas de América* and the Construction of a Governing Ideology for the Empire," *Colonial Latin American Review*, 7:2 (December 1998), pp. 175–92.

[23] Rebecca Earle, "Information and Disinformation in Late Colonial New Granada," *The Americas*, 54 (October 1997), pp. 167–84.

[24] Ibid., pp. 168–69.

[25] Victor M. Uribe-Uran, "The Birth of a Public Sphere in Latin America during the Age of Revolution," *Comparative Studies in Society and History*, 42 (April 2000), p. 440.

[26] Ibid., pp. 425–57.

In order to reform the composite monarchy inherited by King Philip V in 1700, Spain's eighteenth-century regalists advanced the power of the Bourbon state over the church and both colonial and peninsular interest groups. This process often led to friction, dissent, and even political unrest in response to new initiatives. We believe that the many competing viewpoints about the reform and renovation of the eighteenth-century Spanish empire led to inevitable political contestation on both sides of the Atlantic. The infighting among key interest groups – with different ideas about the wisdom of various undertakings – frequently determined the success or failure of specific Bourbon policies. These battles over royal policy usually involved a broad array of social groups in Spain and the Indies, who mobilized to influence the political process and to advance their own particular goals.[27] The outcome of such conflicts in the political arena, whether they involved elites or a broad coalition of social groups, provided the essential context for understanding social, cultural, and economic change in the Spanish Atlantic. The exact configuration of political groups varied considerably within each area of the diverse Spanish Atlantic world. As a result, the frequent give and take in the unstable, contested political arenas in Spain and the Indies helps to explain why no single, cohesive plan for reform ever emerged during the eighteenth century.

HISTORIOGRAPHY OF BOURBON REFORMS

For decades, historians of the Bourbon reforms have debated the coherence and effectiveness of crown policies, focusing largely on the reign of Charles III. According to an important early synthesis by John Lynch, Caroline reformers framed policies that curtailed colonial political and economic freedoms, and collectively the reforms represented nothing less than a "second conquest of America."[28] The crown ceased selling public offices, renovated

---

[27] On the rebellions resulting from changes brought about by the Bourbon reforms, see Felipe Castro Gutiérrez, *Nueva ley y Nuevo rey: Reformas borbónicas y rebelión popular en Nueva España* (Zamora: Colegio de Michoacán, 1996); John Leddy Phelan, *The People and the King: The Comunero Revolution in Colombia, 1781* (Madison: University of Wisconsin Press, 1978); Ward Stavig, *The World of Túpac Amaru: Conflict, Community, and Identity in Colonial Peru* (Lincoln: University of Nebraska Press, 1999); Sinclair Thomson, *We Alone Shall Rule: Native Andean Politics in the Age of Insurgency* (Madison: University of Wisconsin Press, 2002); Sergio Serulnikov, *Subverting Colonial Authority: Challenges to Spanish Rule in Eighteenth-Century Southern Andes* (Durham: Duke University Press, 2003); and Scarlett O'Phelan Godoy, *Rebellions and Revolts in Eighteenth-Century Peru and Upper Peru* (Cologne: Böhlau, 1985).

[28] John Lynch, *The Spanish American Revolutions, 1808–1826* (New York, 1973), pp. 1–37. This viewpoint has also been presented very forcefully in D. A. Brading, *Miners and Merchants in Bourbon Mexico* (Cambridge: Cambridge University Press, 1971), 33–92; and idem, "Bourbon Spain and Its American Empire," in Leslie Bethell, ed., *Colonial Spanish America*, vol. I (Cambridge: Cambridge University Press, 1987), pp. 112–62.

military establishments in the Indies, liberalized the commercial system, reformulated administrative boundaries, increased taxes, and limited the church's power. D. A. Brading has contended that such policies led to colonial opposition and "the permanent alienation of the creole elite."[29] Other scholars, however, have argued that Bourbon policies lacked such ideological coherence, emphasizing instead the diverse and often contradictory aims of Madrid policy makers, who struggled haltingly and inconsistently to balance the crown's various fiscal, commercial, administrative, and military objectives. This position was stated most clearly by John R. Fisher:

One wonders occasionally . . . if the Bourbon Reforms tend to bewitch all who study them. Did they really comprise the smooth, coherent, masterly program of imperial change and revival that generations of commentators, from the very imperial policy-makers of eighteenth-century Spain to the researchers of today, have identified? Might they not be more realistically depicted in terms of a halting, uncertain, inconsistent desire for imperial modernization and centralization, characterized more by delay, contradiction, and obstruction than by decisiveness?[30]

In line with Fisher's reasoning, Allan J. Kuethe has demonstrated that Spanish reformers sometimes promoted markedly different kinds of policies for provinces in its diverse Atlantic empire. Kuethe documents that Madrid, attempting to promote growth in the vulnerable periphery, loosened trade regulations for Havana's tropical produce, while sustaining monopoly controls over the well-developed Mexican trade. Indeed, the crown even redirected large sums from Mexico's treasuries to support Cuba as a strategic Caribbean military outpost following the Seven Years' War.[31] Kuethe's findings have also been supported by Jacques Barbier, who examines how political and military events in Europe forced the Madrid government of Charles III to engage in extensive borrowing to finance its wars. European conflicts forced his son and successor, Charles IV, to lurch from one policy to another by the mid-1790s, in a desperate search for resources needed to meet the exigencies of war, even resorting to arranging for neutral vessels and later contracting with enemy

[29] D. A. Brading, "Bourbon Spain and its American Empire," p. 438. For the intellectual foundations of this opposition, see idem, *The First America: The Spanish Monarchy, Creole Patriots, and the Liberal State, 1492–1867* (Cambridge: Cambridge University Press, 1991), pp. 467–91.

[30] John Fisher, "Soldiers, Society, and Politics in Spanish America, 1750–1821," *Latin American Research Review*, 17: 1 (1982), p. 217.

[31] Allan J. Kuethe, *Cuba, 1753–1815: Crown, Military, and Society* (Knoxville: University of Tennessee Press, 1986), and idem, "La desregulación comercial y la reforma imperial en la época de Carlos III: los casos de Nueva España y Cuba," *Historia Mexicana*, XLI (October–December 1991), pp. 265–92. See also, Allan J. Kuethe and G. Douglas Inglis, "Absolutism and Enlightened Reform: Charles III, the Establishment of the *Alcabala*, and Commercial Reorganization in Cuba," *Past and Present: A Journal of Historical Studies* 109 (November 1985), pp. 118–43.

British merchant houses to supply the Indies with European goods in exchange for colonial silver and other exports.[32]

More recently, Stanley J. and Barbara H. Stein have contributed to scholarly discussions about the Bourbon reforms with their three-volume study of the complex and tangled web of interest groups struggling to shape crown policies.[33] In their first book, *Silver, Trade, and War: Spain and America in the Making of Early Modern Europe*, the Steins argue that Spain's long-term economic weaknesses allowed French, Dutch, and particularly British merchants to gain access to enormous amounts of colonial silver from contraband commerce and provided merchandise and capital to lower-Andalusian merchants trading legally through Cádiz.[34] Spanish reformers, inspired by *proyectistas*, attempted to curb contraband commerce, regain control over American trade, modernize state finances, and promote bureaucratic controls. Opposition from corrupt members of the bureaucracy, the entrenched merchant community (centered in the Cádiz *Consulado*), and their powerful foreign merchant allies combined to thwart this first phase of reform. In their second volume, *Apogee of Empire: Spain and New Spain in the Age of Charles III, 1759–1789*, the Steins explain how King Charles III and his ministers favored raising revenues, broadening the tax base, and liberalizing trade after losing Havana in 1762 during the Seven Years' War.[35] Reform

---

[32] Jacques A. Barbier, "The Culmination of the Bourbon Reforms, 1787–1792," *Hispanic American Historical Review* (hereinafter *HAHR*), 57:1 (February 1977), pp. 51–68; idem, "Peninsular Finance and Colonial Trade: The Dilemma of Charles IV's Spain," *Journal of Latin American Studies*, 12:1 (May 1980), pp. 21–37; idem, "Venezuelan Libranzas, 1788–1807: From Economic Nostrum to Fiscal Imperative," *The Americas*, 37:4 (April 1981), pp. 457–78; Jacques Barbier and Herbert S. Klein, "Revolutionary Wars and Public Finances: The Madrid Treasury, 1784–1807," *Journal of Economic History* 41:2 (June 1981), pp. 315–37; Jacques Barbier, "Indies Revenues and Naval Spending: The Cost of Colonialism for the Spanish Bourbons, 1763–1805," *Jahrbuch für Geschichte von Staat, Wirtschaft und Gesellschaft Lateinamerikas*, 21 (1984), pp. 171–88; idem, "Imperial Policy Toward the Port of Veracruz, 1788–1808: The Struggle Between Madrid, Cádiz, and Havana Interests," in Nils Jacobsen and Hans-Jürgen Puhle, eds., *The Economies of Mexico and Peru During the Late Colonial Period, 1760–1810* (Berlin: Colloquium Verlag, 1986), pp. 240–51; idem, "Comercio Neutral in Bolivarian America: La Guaira, Cartagena, Callao, and Buenos Aires," in Reinhard Liehr, ed., *América Latina en la época de Simón Bolívar* (Berlin: Colloquium Verlag, 1989), pp. 363–77; and idem, "Comercio secreto: The Economic and Political Significance of a Fiscal Expedient, 1800–1808," (unpublished paper presented at the International Congress of Americanists, Amsterdam, 1987).

[33] The three books provide empirical evidence supporting a thesis that the authors promulgated in *The Colonial Heritage of Latin America: Essays in Economic Dependence in Perspective* (Oxford: Oxford University Press, 1970), where they argue that from 1492 onward Spain and Portugal were dependent on northern Europe's more developed economic powers.

[34] Stanley J. Stein and Barbara H. Stein, *Silver, Trade, and War: Spain and America in the Making of Early Modern Europe* (Baltimore and London: Johns Hopkins University Press, 2003).

[35] Stanley J. Stein and Barbara H. Stein, *Apogee of Empire: Spain and New Spain in the Age of Charles III, 1759–1789* (Baltimore and London: Johns Hopkins University Press, 2003).

culminated with the extension of free trade (*comercio libre*), first to Spain's Caribbean islands in 1765 and to the entire empire in 1778, except for New Spain and Venezuela (which were included only in 1789).[36] Nonetheless, the Steins argue that these Caroline reformers never intended any large-scale structural reforms; they sought only "calibrated adjustment" designed to "shore up the Gothic edifice" of Spain's Atlantic empire.[37] The third volume examines the efforts of Spanish politicians to preserve commercial linkages between the metropolis and Spain's wealthiest Atlantic colony, New Spain, as the empire became swept up in the international conflicts resulting from the French Revolution and the rise of Napoleon Bonaparte. As a result of these conflicts, reform failed, and Spain ultimately lost its rich Atlantic empire, remaining little more than an underdeveloped nation incapable of supplying or even maintaining its control over the Indies.[38] The Steins conclude that American silver ironically both shaped the decline of Spain and fueled the rise of Northern European capitalism.

Within the past decade, scholars of the eighteenth century have broadened and deepened discussions about the Bourbon reforms. These studies have focused on a range of topics such as the intellectual origins of reform, the spread of scientific knowledge, the Atlantic context for reform, efforts to curtail church power, Bourbon social engineering – such as reform of marriage, the treatment of slaves, and colonial poverty – and the success or failure of crown polices in different parts of the empire.[39] Some scholars have even

---

[36] See Kuethe and Inglis, "Absolutism and Enlightened Reform," pp. 118–143.

[37] Stein and Stein, *Apogee of Empire*, p. 27. The view that the reforms represented little more than "shoring up the Gothic edifice" of empire was expressed in Stein and Stein, *The Colonial Heritage of Latin America*, p. 104.

[38] Barbara H. Stein and Stanley J. Stein, *Edge of Crisis: War and Trade in the Spanish Atlantic, 1789–1808* (Baltimore: Johns Hopkins University Press, 2009).

[39] The recent scholarly literature on the Bourbon reforms is voluminous, but some of the most influential book-length studies include: Jeremy Adelman, *Sovereignty and Revolution in the Iberian Atlantic* (Princeton: Princeton University Press, 2006); J. H. Elliott, *Empires of the Atlantic World: Britain and Spain in America, 1492–1830* (New Haven: Yale University Press, 2006), pp. 292–324; Agustín Guimerá, *El reformismo borbónico: Una visión interdisciplinaria* (Madrid: Alianza, 1996); Francisco Sánchez Blanco, *El absolutismo y las luces en el Reinado de Carlos III* (Madrid: Marcial Pons, 2002); Jorge Cañizares Esguerra, *How to Write the History of the New World: Historiographies, Epistemologies, and Identities in the Eighteenth-Century Atlantic World* (Stanford: Stanford University Press, 2001); Jordana Dym and Christophe Belaubre, *Politics, Economy, and Society in Bourbon Central America, 1759–1821* (Boulder: University of Colorado Press, 2007); Safier, *Measuring the New World*; Paquette, *Enlightenment, Governance, and Reform*; Daniela Bleichmar et al., eds., *Science in the Spanish and Portuguese Empires, 1500–1800* (Stanford: Stanford University Press, 2009); Cynthia E. Milton, *The Many Meanings of Poverty: Colonialism, Social Compacts, and Assistance in Eighteenth-Century Ecuador* (Stanford: Stanford University Press, 2007); Ann Twinam, *Public Lives, Private Secrets: Gender, Honor, Sexuality, and Illegitimacy in Colonial Spanish America* (Stanford: Stanford University Press, 1999); and Patricia H. Marks, *Deconstructing Legitimacy: Viceroys, Merchants,*

questioned the traditional emphasis on the reign of Charles III, examining how important crown policies during the first half of the eighteenth century contributed to reform in Spain's overseas empire.[40] Moreover, influential studies of imperial centers, such as Mexico and Peru, have argued that Bourbon policies had lasting and sometimes very detrimental long-term consequences.[41] Carlos Marichal, for example, demonstrates the profound impact of the reforms on the fiscal organization and evolution of the colonial Mexican state, arguing that New Spain became the financial sub-metropolis of the Caribbean, exporting silver subsidies (*situados*) to important centers of imperial defense, such as Cuba. These subsidies allowed Spain to defend its empire in an era of successive international conflicts, until the fiscal pressures of war outstripped the Mexican tax base, leading to the defeat and bankruptcy of the monarchy.[42] Other scholars, however, such as Anthony McFarlane and Jacques Barbier, have written studies contending that the reforms had only limited impact in New Granada and Chile.[43] Moreover, one new study even argues that Bourbon policies, such as the establishment of new merchant guilds and economic-aid societies, were embraced by elites in imperial peripheries, such as Cartagena, Havana, and Buenos Aires.[44] As a result, despite all the new research on the eighteenth century Spanish Atlantic

and the Military in Late Colonial Peru (University Park: Pennsylvania State University Press, 2007).

[40] For examples of this viewpoint, see Adrian Pearce, *Early Bourbon Government in the Viceroyalty of Peru, 1700–1759* (Unpublished Ph.D. diss., University of Liverpool, 1998); Kenneth J. Andrien, "The Coming of Enlightened Reform in Bourbon Peru: Secularization of the *Doctrinas de indios*, 1746–1773," in Gabriel B. Paquette, *Enlightenment, Governance, and Reform in Spain and its Empire, 1759–1808* (Surry: Palgrave-MacMillan, 2008), pp. 183–202; Allan J. Kuethe, "The Colonial Commercial Policy of Philip V and the Atlantic World," in Renate Pieper and Peer Schmidt, eds., *Latin America and the Atlantic World (1500–1850)* (Cologne: Böhlau-Verlag, 2005), pp. 319–33; idem, "Proyectismo et reform commercial à l'époque de Philippe V," in Nejma Kermele and Bernard Lavallé, *L'Amérique en projet: Utopies, controverses et réformes dans l'empire espagnol (XVI-XVIII siècle)* (Paris: L'Harmattan, 2008), pp. 243–51. Two important studies that argue that the Bourbon reforms really began later, particularly with the reign of Charles III, are Elliott, *Empires of the Atlantic World*, pp. 294–301; and J. R. Fisher, *Bourbon Peru, 1750–1824* (Liverpool: Liverpool University Press), pp. 3–4.

[41] See especially Carlos Marichal, *Bankruptcy of Empire: Mexican Silver and the Wars Between Spain, Britain, and France, 1760–1810* (Cambridge: Cambridge University Press, 2007), pp. 1–80; and Marks, *Deconstructing Legitimacy*, pp. 55–106.

[42] Marichal, *Bankruptcy of Empire*, passim; and Carlos Marichal and Matilde Souto Mantecón, "Silver and Situados: New Spain and the Financing of the Spanish Empire in the Caribbean in the Eighteenth Century," *HAHR*, 74:4 (November 1994), pp. 587–613.

[43] Jacques A. Barbier, *Reform and Politics in Bourbon Chile, 1755–1796* (Ottawa: University of Ottawa Press, 1980); and Anthony McFarlane, *Colombia Before Independence: Economy, society, and politics under Bourbon Rule* (Cambridge: Cambridge University Press, 1993).

[44] Gabriel Paquette, "State-Civil Society Cooperation and Conflict in the Spanish Empire: The Intellectual and Political Activities of the Ultramarine *Consulados* and Economic Societies, c. 1780–1810," *Journal of Latin American Studies* 39:2 (May 2007), pp. 263–98.

world, historians remain divided about the overall impact and effectiveness of the Bourbon reforms.[45]

These divisions are clearly visible in an ongoing debate among economic historians over the impact of imperial free trade on the economic evolution of Spain and the Indies. The pioneering work by Josep Fontana and Antonio García-Baquero argued that the *Reglamento para el comercio libre* of October 12, 1778, had only a limited impact on the evolution of Catalan industry.[46] By contrast, John Fisher's examination of 6,824 ship registries of individual merchant vessels trading between Spain and the Indies from 1778 to 1796 found that Spanish imports from the Americas grew fifteen fold during the period. He also found that Spanish exports to the empire were 400 percent higher (between 1782 and 1796) than they were in 1778.[47] García-Baquero revised Fisher's figures downward by arguing that 1778, a war year, was a poor choice to measure the increased volume of trade, and he contended that Fisher's data undercounted the number of ships sailing within the Spanish empire. Nonetheless, García-Baquero did find a substantial increase in imperial trade during the period, although at levels lower than Fisher had indicated.[48] A number of other economic historians, however, followed with studies arguing that imperial free trade had little impact in promoting economic growth in local regions within Spain.[49]

---

[45] Paquette, *Enlightenment, Governance, and Reform,* pp. 20–22.

[46] Josep Fontana Lázaro, *La economía española al final del Antiguo Regimen,* Vol. III *Comercio y colonias* (Madrid: Alianza, 1982), pp. xxii–xxiii; Antonio García-Baquero,"Comercio colonial y producción industrial en Cataluña a fines del siglo XVIII," *Actas del Coloquio de Historia Económica de España* (Barcelona: Editorial Ariel, 1975), pp. 268–94.

[47] John Fisher, "Imperial 'Free Trade' and the Hispanic Economy, 1778–1796," *Journal of Latin American Studies* 13:1 (May 1981), pp. 21–56; idem, "The Imperial Response to 'Free Trade": Spanish Imports from Spanish America, 1778–1796," *Journal of Latin American Studies,* 17:1 (May 1985), pp. 35–78. Both articles were published in book form as John Fisher, *Commercial Relations Between Spain and Spanish America in the Era of Free Trade, 1778–1796,* Manchester: Manchester Free Press, 1985).

[48] Antonio García-Baquero, "Los resultados de libre comercio y "el punto de vista": Una revision desde la estadística," *Manuscrits* 15 (1997), pp. 303–22.

[49] J. M. Delgado Ribas, *El comerç entre Cataluña i Amèrica (segles XVII I XIX)* (Barcelona: L'Avenç, 1986); idem, "Libre comercio: mito y realidad," in T. Martínez Vera, ed., *Mercado y desarrollo económico en la España contemporánea* (Madrid: Siglo XXI de España, 1986), pp. 69–83; idem, "El impacto de la reforma del "comercio libre" sobre el comercio colonial," in J. Casas Pardo, ed., *Economic effects of European expansion, 1492–1824* (Stuttgart: F. Steiner, 1992), pp. 387–434; Josep Fontana Lázaro and Antono Miguel Bernal, eds., *El "comercio libre" entre España y América (1765–1824)* (Madrid: Fundación Banco Exterior, 1987); Leandro Prados de la Escosura, *De imperio a nación. Crecimiento y atraso económico en España (1780–1930)* (Madrid: Alianza Editorial, 1988); P. Tedde de Lorca, "Política financiera y política comercial en el reinado de Carlos III," *Actas del Congreso Internacional sobre 'Carlos III y la Ilustración,'* 3 vols. (Madrid: Ministerio de Cultura), II, pp. 139–217.

Historians have also debated the benefits for the monarchy of drawing increased sums through taxation and larger remittances of revenue from the Americas after 1778. In two important articles assessing the income and expenditures of the Royal Treasury in Madrid during the late eighteenth century, Jacques A. Barbier and Herbert S. Klein argue that the rigidity of crown tax income forced the monarchy to borrow heavily to finance its foreign wars. Indeed, these authors argue that wars impeded the Madrid government's ability to foster fiscal, economic, and social reform in Spain, leaving the country virtually bankrupt by the time Charles III died in 1789.[50] At the same time, an article by Carlos Marichal finds that revenues from the Indies (bolstered largely by heavy remittances from New Spain) rose dramatically from the late eighteenth century, becoming a larger percentage of the crown's total income, particularly after the French invasion in 1808.[51] Javier Cuenca Esteban has argued that at the height of *comercio libre* (1784–1792) Spain's treasury and private commercial interests drew larger financial returns from the Indies than their British enemies could manage from their far-flung colonial and commercial enterprises.[52] Most recently, Rafael Torres Sánchez has written a comprehensive study of the institutional and fiscal evolution of the General Treasury in Madrid, citing the efforts of Ensenada in 1753 to establish the treasury as the central repository for all the king's revenues (except for the armada). These reforms ensured the government of Charles III a sound fiscal system that could provide a stable flow of revenues to pay for his reform of the Spanish Atlantic world.[53]

Despite these significant scholarly advances, ongoing disagreements among historians of the eighteenth century demonstrate clearly the complexity of Bourbon reform policies and the difficulty of measuring their impact on the economic development of the Spanish Atlantic world. In their recent revisionist articles on Spanish imperial finances, for example, economic historians Alejandra Irigoin and Regina Grafe contend that the Bourbon reforms had little real impact on the evolution of the eighteenth-century Spanish Atlantic empire. They first take issue with Nobel laureate Douglas North's

---

[50] Jacques A. Barbier and Herbert S. Klein, "Las prioridades de un monarca ilustrado: El gasto publico bajo el reinado de Carlos III," *Revista de historia económica*, III:3 (Fall 1985), pp. 473–95. Indeed, Barbier and Klein even contend that Charles III's reputation as an enlightened reformer must be seriously reconsidered, given his expenditures on warfare over reformist policies. See also Barbier and Klein, "Revolutionary Wars and Public Finances," passim.

[51] Carlos Marichal, "Beneficios y costes fiscales del colonialismo: Las remesas Americanas a España, 1760–1814," *Revista de historia económica*, XV:3 (Otoño-Invierno 1997), pp. 475–505.

[52] Javier Cuenca-Esteban, "Statistics of Spain's Colonial Trade, 1747–1820: New Estimates and Comparisons with Great Britain," *Revista de historia económica*, XXVI:3 (Otoño-Invierno 2008), pp. 323–354.

[53] Rafael Torres Sánchez, *La llave de todos los tesoros: La Tesorería General de Carlos III* (Madrid: Sílex ediciones, 2012).

criticisms of fiscal overcentralization within the Spanish empire, which North argues stifled entrepreneurship and impeded economic development.[54] Irigoin and Grafe contend instead that the Bourbon state in Spain and the Indies was weak, decentralized, and largely served to redistribute income from central zones, such as Mexico, to colonial peripheries. They argue that the Bourbon reforms had little impact on strengthening this weak Spanish fiscal apparatus, which functioned primarily by negotiation and establishing consensus with wealthy, powerful colonial elites – a phenomenon the authors term "bargained absolutism." In the end, Irigoin and Grafe assert that this fiscal redistribution of wealth provided capital and an economic stimulus to poorer peripheral regions of the empire. These redistributions of wealth ended with independence, however, contributing to economic decline and political instability in nineteenth-century Spanish America.[55]

While Irigoin and Grafe minimize the impact of the Bourbon reforms, a synthetic book by James Mahoney argues that the reforms had a profound impact on the socioeconomic trajectory of Spanish America even after independence.[56] Mahoney identifies two types of colonialism in Spanish America. The earlier mercantilist phase (1492–1700) was characterized by an emphasis on extracting gold and silver, exploitation of indigenous labor in mines and on large landed estates, imposition of a colonial bureaucracy, and monopoly control over trade dominated by urban centers in the colonial core zones – Mexico, Peru, and Bolivia. Areas outside of the core zones, such as Argentina, Chile, Venezuela, and Central America remained peripheral to the empire, and they never developed the powerful mercantilist elites and oppressive ethnic and social hierarchies found in the core.

Mahoney identifies the era of the Bourbon reforms as the "liberal" phase of Spanish colonialism (1700–1808). He argues that the reforms attempted to implant "a new class of commercial actors with greater political autonomy and an orientation toward generating wealth from exchanges in open markets."[57] Rising peripheries, particularly Argentina, Uruguay, and Venezuela gained liberal institutions, and new entrepreneurial elites emerged, largely

---

[54] Douglas C. North, "Institutions and Economic Growth: An Historical Introduction," *World Development*, 17:9 (1989), p. 1328.

[55] Regina Grafe and María Alejandra Irigoin, "The Spanish Empire and its legacy: fiscal redistribution and political conflict in colonial and post-colonial Spanish America," *Journal of Global History* 1:2 (2006), pp. 241–267; Alejandra Irigoin and Regina Grafe, "Bargaining for Absolutism: A Spanish Path to Nation-State and Empire Building," *HAHR* 88:2 (May 2008), pp. 173–209. These controversial views are discussed in a forum in the journal; see Carlos Marichal, "Rethinking Negotiation and Coercion in an Imperial State," Ibid., pp. 211–18; William R. Summerhill, "Fiscal Bargains, Political Institutions, and Economic Performance," Ibid., pp. 210–33; and Alejandra Irigoin and Regina Grafe, "Response to Carlos Marichal and William Summerhill," Ibid., pp. 235–45.

[56] James Mahoney, *Colonialism and Postcolonial Development: Spanish Colonialism in Comparative Perspective* (Cambridge: Cambridge University Press, 2010).

[57] Ibid., p. 120.

because these regions had no strong mercantilist past. Argentina eventually evolved into a core zone, while Uruguay and Venezuela became semi-peripheries. In older core regions, well-entrenched mercantilist elites opposed market-oriented forces. The result was that although Mexico remained a core zone, it retained a mixed liberal-mercantilist colonial heritage, which impeded its economic development after independence. These same internal struggles between liberal and mercantilist values produced decline in Peru and Bolivia from core to semi-peripheral status. Some peripheries, such as most of Central America remained largely untouched by both phases of Spanish colonialism and remained backwaters. In the end, these differing colonial heritages played a major role in the fate of these regions after independence, with the strong liberal zones enjoying greater economic dynamism and social well-being, while regions with strong mercantilist institutions and social hierarchies stagnated.

THE BOURBON REFORMS AND AN ATLANTIC PERSPECTIVE

Some of the most innovative recent perspectives on the Bourbon reforms have come from scholars attempting to place those policies within the context of the wider Atlantic world. Although works examining the Spanish Atlantic emerged relatively recently, there were a number of important precursors of this effort to place the history of Spain and the Indies within a single analytic framework. After Herbert Eugene Bolton's call for a common history of the Americas in 1933, succeeding generations of scholars have advanced numerous approaches for studying the Spanish Atlantic. This trend accelerated after World War II, when the establishment of the North Atlantic Treaty Organization (NATO) brought the notion of a common Atlantic heritage to wide public attention.[58] Clarence Haring's important work, for example, defined the institutional structure of Spain's overseas empire.[59] This was followed by the massive compilation of Spain's transatlantic trade statistics by *Annales* historians Pierre and Huguette Chaunu, which defined the Spanish Atlantic as commercial "space," and in 1966, J. H. Parry emphasized the maritime dimensions of the Spanish empire in his classic *The Spanish Seaborne Empire*.[60] Scholars such as John Robert McNeil, Peggy Liss,

---

[58] See Herbert Bolton, "The Epic of Greater America," *American Historical Review*, 38:3 (April, 1933), pp. 448–74; Bernard Bailyn, *Atlantic History: Concepts and Contours* (Cambridge: Harvard University Press, 2005), pp. 6–12.

[59] C. H. Haring, *The Spanish Empire in America* (New York: Harcourt, Brace, and World, Inc., 1947).

[60] John H. Parry, *The Spanish Seaborne Empire* (New York: Knopf, 1966); Huguette and Pierre Chaunu, *Seville et l'Atlantique, 1504–1650*, 8 vols., (Paris: Colin, 1955–1959). A number of Spanish scholars have explored the commercial reach of the Spanish Atlantic system. A few of the most prominent examples are: Antonio García Baquero González, *Cádiz y el Atlántico, 1717–1778. El comercio colonial español bajo el monopolio gaditano*,

Anthony Pagden, and Patricia Seed have also written more recent path-breaking comparative studies.[61]

Since the late 1960s, much of the historical debate has revolved around problems of colonialism, imperialism, and underdevelopment, and the neo-Marxist dependency paradigm (*dependencia*) influenced most of this literature.[62] Dependency advocates (*dependentistas*) argued that the spread of capitalist commercial transactions led to widespread underdevelopment and layers of subordination of peripheral regions, such as the Spanish Indies, to the economic core nations in Northern Europe – the Netherlands, France, and finally England.[63] Despite its seductive explanatory power of linking Europe to the Indies in a single system, most historians are now quite critical of or even ignore the dependency paradigm. Many have focused on a central paradox of *dependencia*: It is not a theory to be proven, but a paradigm that cannot be verified by the sort of empirical research that underpins most academic histories.[64] As a result, the long-term influence of *dependencia* on studies of the Spanish Atlantic is negligible today.[65]

Despite the eclipse of the dependency paradigm, Atlantic history has emerged as a full-blown, recognized subfield in a number of different disciplines, leading to an impressive list of scholarly publications during the last decade. The most ambitious of the works using an Atlantic perspective is the magisterial synthesis by J. H. Elliott, *Empires of the Atlantic World: Britain and Spain in the Americas, 1492–1830*, which compares the evolution of the British and Spanish Atlantic empires, including the reforms of the eighteenth century.[66] Another important addition to this growing scholarly literature on

---

2 vols., (Sevilla: Escuela de Estudios Hispano-Americanos, 1976); Enriqueta Vila Vilar, *Los Corzo y los Mañara: Tipos y arquetipos del mercader con América* (Sevilla: Escuela de Estudios Hispano-Americano, 1991); Antonio-Miguel Bernal, *La financiación de la carrera de Indias (1492–1824) Dinero y crédito en el comercio colonial español con América* (Sevilla: Fundación el Monte, 1992); Lutgardo García Fuentes, *El comercio español con América, 1650–1700* (Sevilla: Diputación Provincial de Sevila, 1980); Pablo Emilio Pérez-Mallaina Bueno, *Los hombres del océano. Vida cotidiana de los tripulantes de las flotas de India, Siglo XVI* (Sevilla: Diputación de Sevilla, 1992).

[61] John Robert McNeil, *Atlantic Empires of France and Spain: Louisbourg and Havana, 1700–1763* (Baltimore: Johns Hopkins University Press, 1985); Peggy K. Liss, *Atlantic Empires: The Network of Trade and Revolution* (Baltimore: Johns Hopkins University Press, 1983); Patricia Seed, *Ceremonies of Possession in Europe's Conquest of the New World* (Cambridge: Cambridge University Press, 1995); idem, *American Pentimento: The Invention of Indians and the Pursuit of Riches* (Minneapolis: University of Minnesota Press, 2001).

[62] For a summary of the dependency literature and the closely related world system's paradigm, see Kenneth J. Andrien, *The Kingdom of Quito, 1690–1830: The state and regional development* (Cambridge: Cambridge University Press, 1995), pp. 4–7.

[63] Stein and Stein, *Colonial Heritage of Latin America*, passim.

[64] Andrien, *The Kingdom of Quito*, p. 6.

[65] The recent works of Stanley J. and Barbara H. Stein are three of the most obvious examples of empirical work directly influenced by the dependency paradigm. See Stein and Stein, *Silver, Trade, and War; Apogee of Empire;* and *The Edge of Crisis.*

[66] Elliott, *Empires of the Atlantic World.*

the Atlantic world is Thomas Benjamin's encyclopedic study, *The Atlantic World: Europeans, Africans, Indians and their Shared History, 1400–1900*.[67] Studies of migration across the Atlantic space, ecological change, and the spread of diseases have also made substantial contributions to understanding the Spanish Atlantic in the age of reform.[68] Historians of the slave trade, such as Philip Curtain and Herbert Klein and Ben Vinson, have examined the role of Africa and slavery in the Spanish Atlantic system.[69] Another major contribution placing the Bourbon reforms within an Atlantic context is Jeremy Adelman's *Sovereignty and Revolution in the Iberian Atlantic*, which examines how notions of sovereignty became uncertain, contested, and unstable in response to European imperial crises in the eighteenth century, leading finally to the dissolution of the Iberian colonial regimes by 1825.[70] A recent study of Spanish trade from Bilbao and Cádiz to the Indies by Xabier Lamikiz, argues that Spanish merchants limited the inherent risks of the transatlantic trade by relying on trusted agents, partners, or clients (most often kinsmen), which allowed them to overcome the problems of distance and gain higher-quality information on colonial markets.[71] Although it does not explicitly take an Atlantic perspective, a book that gives important new information on commerce in the Atlantic and Caribbean is Adrian J. Pearce's *British Trade with Spanish America, 1763–1808*.[72]

---

[67] Thomas Benjamin, *The Atlantic World: Europeans, Africans, Indians, and Their Shared History* (Cambridge: Cambridge University Press, 2009).

[68] Peter Boyd-Bowman, *Índice geobiográfico de cuarenta mil pobladores españoles de América en el siglo XVI*, 2 vols. (Bogotá: Instituto Caro y Cuervo, 1964); Ida Altman, *Transatlantic Ties in the Spanish Empire: Brihuega Spain and Puebla Mexico, 1560–1620* (Stanford: Stanford University Press, 2000); idem, *Emigrants and Society: Extremadura and America in the Sixteenth Century* (Berkeley and Los Angeles: University of California Press, 1989); Alfred Crosby, *Ecological Imperialism: The Biological Expansion of Europe, 900–1900* (Cambridge: Cambridge University Press, 1986); Noble David Cook, *Born to Die: Disease and the New World Conquest, 1492–1650* (Cambridge: Cambridge University Press, 1998), and J. R. McNeill, *Mosquito Empires: Ecology and War in the Greater Caribbean, 1620–1914* (Cambridge: Cambridge University Press, 2010).

[69] Philip Curtain, *The Atlantic Slave Trade: A Census* (Madison: University of Wisconsin Press, 1969) and Herbert S. Klein and Ben Vinson, *African Slavery in Latin America and the Caribbean* (Oxford and New York: Oxford University Press, 1977) are important contributions, but the literature on the Atlantic slave trade is immense. Apart from Klein and Vinson, two overviews are David Eltis, *The Rise of Atlantic Slavery in the Americas* (Cambridge: Cambridge University Press, 2000) and Herbert S. Klein, *The Atlantic Slave Trade* (Cambridge: Cambridge University Press, 2010).

[70] Adelman, *Sovereignty and Revolution*, passim.

[71] Xabier Lamikiz, *Trade and Trust in the Eighteenth-Century Atlantic World: Spanish Merchants and Their Overseas Networks* (Suffolk and Rochester: Royal Historical Society and the Boydell Press, 2010).

[72] Adrian J. Pearce, *British Trade with Spanish America, 1763–1808* (Liverpool: Liverpool University Press, 2007).

Intellectual and cultural approaches to the Spanish Atlantic have also appeared, first with D. A. Brading's ambitious book, *The First America: The Spanish Monarchy, Creole Patriots and the Liberal State, 1492–1867*.[73] Another influential contribution to intellectual history came with Jorge Cañizares Esguerra's *How to Write a History of the New World: Histories, Epistemologies, and Identities in the Eighteenth-Century Atlantic World*.[74] Stuart B. Schwartz has also published a recent prize-winning study of popular religious beliefs in the Iberian Atlantic world.[75] Two important overviews are presented in edited volumes: Horst Pietschmann's *Atlantic History: History of the Atlantic System, 1580–1830* and recently, Gabriel Paquette's *Enlightened Reform in Southern Europe and its Atlantic Colonies, c. 1750–1830*.[76] Nonetheless, much remains to be done; studies of the Spanish Atlantic world are just now defining a coherent set of methodological perspectives that will give direction to the field.

An Atlantic perspective allows scholars to examine the interconnections among global, regional, and local processes linking the four continents – Europe, North and South America, and Africa – surrounding the Atlantic basin. Such a perspective also permits historians to examine important historical changes without regard to modern political borders, and it encourages comparisons among the European overseas empires. This viewpoint highlights differences between densely populated central regions and the more sparsely settled frontier zones within empires – where European rule was more insecure as various indigenous groups challenged their control, along with rival colonial powers. Studying frontier zones such as Florida or New Mexico has led to renewed scholarly interchanges among specialists of Spanish, Portuguese, Dutch, French, and English America. Moreover, an Atlantic perspective emphasizes the world of merchants and maritime commercial exchanges, including marginal people – sailors, pirates, innkeepers, and prostitutes – who played a role in this trade, particularly in the Caribbean. The Atlantic basin was also the site of gendered relationships, where men and women of very different cultures interacted, often leading to generations of mixed-race children. Wars also connected European overseas possessions as conflicts in Europe spread to America and beyond, while the commerce in slaves sometimes prompted wars among African polities. An Atlantic perspective places renewed emphasis on movement, particularly the migration of humans, ideas, and commerce back and forth across oceans. To accomplish this goal, Atlantic histories may benefit from perspectives drawn

---

[73] Brading, *The First America*.
[74] Jorge Cañizares Esguerra, *How to Write a History of the New World*.
[75] Stuart B. Schwartz, *All Can Be Saved: Religious Tolerance and Salvation in the Iberian Atlantic World* (New Haven: Yale University Press, 2008).
[76] Pietschmann, *Atlantic History: History of the Atlantic System, 1580–1830*; Paquette, *Enlightened Reform in Southern Europe* .

from other disciplines, such as literary studies, anthropology and archaeology, and gender studies. Methods drawn from ethnohistory and cultural studies, for example, have been particularly influential in allowing scholars to examine how contact between Europeans and native peoples shaped new societies with different political, cultural, economic, and social trajectories. Works that cross disciplinary lines are useful for studying the complex human interactions, and the political, economic, social, and cultural exchanges in the Atlantic world. In short, Atlantic history encourages scholars to explore a wide range of topics and to see old problems from different perspectives.

As historians have utilized the Atlantic as an "arena of analysis," their works have fallen into three basic typologies identified by historian David Armitage.[77] Circum-Atlantic histories provide a transnational view of the region, seeing the Atlantic world as a unified zone of exchange, circulation, and transmission of people, ideas, goods, or warfare. The emphasis here is on the whole Atlantic region, rather than specific imperial national, regional, or local histories.[78] An excellent example of circum-Atlantic history is Joseph C. Miller's *Way of Death: Merchant Capitalism and the Angolan Slave Trade, 1730–1830*.[79] The second approach to Atlantic history, which Armitage calls trans-Atlantic, involves international comparisons across the ocean and the continents that face it.[80] A recent example of trans-Atlantic history is J. H. Elliott's *Empires of the Atlantic World*.[81] The third type identified by Armitage is cis-Atlantic history, which examines particular places, regions, empires, or even institutions within a wider Atlantic context, focusing on the interplay between local events and a wider web of connections or comparisons.[82] It is this third framework of analysis that will serve as the basis for the present study of the whole century-long project to reform and renovate Spain and its Atlantic empire. We believe that the Bourbon reforms can be understood best within such an Atlantic framework, whereby events in the metropolis and the colony had a constant and enduring impact on each other. The Indies and Spain were linked not just by a common legal system, ideology of empire, and bureaucratic ties, but by facing the same challenges of dynastic ambitions, warfare, commerce, and the migrations of people and ideas across the vast Atlantic basin. Efforts to revive the imperial tie also produced vigorous military responses from Spain's rivals in Europe and the Americas. Events in Spain and the Indies were thus inextricably joined to each

---

[77] David Armitage, "Three Concepts of Atlantic History," in David Armitage and Michael J. Braddick, eds., *The British Atlantic World, 1500–1800* (Surry: Palgrave-MacMillan, 2002), p. 27.

[78] Ibid., pp. 15–18.

[79] Joseph C. Miller, *Way of Death: Merchant Capitalism and the Angolan Slave Trade, 1730–1830* (Madison: University of Wisconsin Press, 1988).

[80] Armitage, "Three Concepts of Atlantic History," pp. 18–21.

[81] Elliott, *Empires of the Atlantic World*.

[82] Ibid., pp. 21–25.

other and to the political, social, and economic currents present throughout the rest of the Atlantic world.

This book studies the deep political divisions that emerged over the Bourbon reforms on both sides of the Atlantic. We do not present the reforms as a "second conquest" of America, nor do we see them as conflicts between mercantile and liberal colonialism. Instead, we see them as emerging from a series of political conflicts within Spain and the Indies, which shaped the outcome of crown polices in different regions of the empire. In Spain, reformers bickered with each other over colonial policy, and they also collided with entrenched interest groups, such as the monopolists of the *Consulado* of Cádiz. Dynastic ambitions of the Bourbon monarchs or power politics in Europe also intervened to stall, derail, and sometimes even impel the reform process, as Spain's ministers sponsored innovations to prepare for war. At the same time, bureaucrats in the Indies, churchmen, and colonial middling and subaltern groups all attempted to shape the reform process to their own ends. The configuration of these conflicting interest groups varied over time in each region of the empire. The result was not the bargained absolutism of Irigoin and Grafe or the calibrated adjustments that the Steins argue were designed to "shore up the Gothic edifice" of Spain's Atlantic empire.[83] Rather, reform engendered bitter political clashes on both sides of the Atlantic, which largely determined the long-term outcome of these policies in each district of the Spanish empire. As Spain's regalists attempted to transform a composite monarchy into a more absolutist state, serious political squabbles developed, sometimes even erupting into armed conflict.

We present the evolution of reform in Spain and give different case studies of the political conflicts that shaped the course of royal policy there and in different areas of the Indies over the eighteenth century. Such debates over the course of reform within this empire could only be resolved in volatile and unpredictable political arenas on both sides of the Atlantic. We will argue that the success or failure of Bourbon initiatives in Spain's Atlantic empire resulted from just such political struggles over the period from 1713 to 1796. In Spain, regalists and powerful political opponents clashed over reform and how to prepare for the next stage of conflicts with Spain's rivals. The *Consulado* in Seville and later Cádiz, for example, played a major role in controversies ranging from moving the House of Trade from Seville to Cádiz to the implementation of imperial free trade beginning in 1765. Opposition also formed in the Indies as colonial interest groups clashed over crown innovations; in addition, some colonial officials imposed crown reform policies as written, while others moved more slowly and haltingly to initiate potentially disruptive changes. This largely explains why the reforms generated abundant revenue in Mexico, while they had a lesser impact in New Granada,

---

[83] Stein and Stein, *Colonial Heritage of Latin America*, p. 104.

where the Comunero Rebellion convinced authorities to proceed more slowly in implementing crown policy. Even the crown could shape policies differently for different regions, favoring Cuba with commercial liberalization to develop the local sugar economy while waiting until 1789 to extend imperial free trade to New Spain. Moreover, conflicts with Spain's European rivals over dynastic ambitions or colonial practices also periodically disrupted the reform process in various areas of the empire. On other occasions, the threat of war and past defeats could be used as justifications to advance reforms in the Spanish Atlantic world. Indeed, it was the outcome of this symbiosis between political contestation and the threat of war that shaped the implementation of Bourbon reform policies, giving them distinctive outcomes in different regions of the empire.

While political conflicts over the colonial reorganization reached their apex during the reign of King Charles III, we also argue that reform started much earlier, shortly after the accession of the Bourbon dynasty. A major reason why previous studies have ignored or downplayed these earlier reforms has been the relative lack of documentation in Spanish archives about the reign of Philip V, since much of these materials burned in the fire at Madrid's Royal Alcázar in 1734. We have relied largely on rich French diplomatic documentation to reconstruct these early Bourbon reforms, in order to analyze the different outcomes produced by the early crown policies. Our study begins with the first series of colonial policy changes under Cardinal Julio Alberoni and later under José Patiño, and then it examines the second era of reformist policies under first José de Campillo and later the Marqués de la Ensenada. Each of these stages of reform prepared the way for the next. The innovations of Alberoni and Patiño, for example, allowed Spain to exert greater control over her port cities and the contraband trade in the Spanish Main, and paved the way for greater commercial liberalization later in the century. Finally, we focus on the high watermark of reform under Charles III. His expulsion of the Jesuits can now be seen as an extension of policies under Ensenada to curb the power of the religious orders by removing them from administering their lucrative indigenous parishes. We conclude the book in 1796, when war with Great Britain effectively ended ambitious innovations in colonial policy as the British navy cut Spain off from its empire, forcing the Spanish monarchy and its ministers to devote all of their energies to finding fiscal expedients needed to support the increasingly unsuccessful war effort. European conflicts had stalled and ultimately ended the Spanish reforming impulse by 1796.

ORGANIZATION OF THE BOOK

The book is divided into three chronological sections. Part I, "Alberoni, Patiño, and the Beginnings of Atlantic Reform, 1713–1736" examines the opening Bourbon reforms in the Spanish Atlantic from 1713 to 1736.

Chapter 1 addresses the initiatives of Cardinal Alberoni, the influential Italian who guided policy decisions for Philip V and his wife, Elizabeth Farnese, from 1715 to 1719. It focuses especially on his efforts to assert control over key Spanish seaports and to expunge foreign interests from Spanish commerce, particularly trade with the Indies. Chapter 2 treats Alberoni's chief reforms in the Indies: the transfer of the *Casa de la Contratación* and the *Consulado* from Seville to Cádiz in 1717, the foundation of the Viceroyalty of New Granada, the establishment of the tobacco monopoly in Cuba, and the reorganization of strategic Havana's military in 1719. Chapter 3 examines the slow course of reform under the decade-long guidance of José Patiño, who brought new strength to the ministry governing the Indies, resuscitated the Alberoni agenda, rebuilt the armada, and sought to curtail the foreign contrabandists operating in the Indies. The principal problems faced by reformers were the European dynastic designs of King Philip and his wife, who sought Italian kingdoms for their children, leading to European conflicts that distracted Madrid from the task of reorganizing the relations between Spain and its overseas possessions in the Indies.

Part II deals with the next phase of the Bourbon reorganization, which was highlighted by the initiatives of the Marqués de la Ensenada, José de Carvajal y Lancaster, and the king's confessor Francisco de Rávago (known collectively as the Jesuit Party for their strong support for that order). Chapter 4 shows how the crown curtailed the autonomy of the *Consulado* of Cádiz, and how it opened the door to the widespread use of register ships during the War of Jenkins' Ear, while concurrently advancing administrative and military reform. The peace treaties that ended the war revoked the commercial concessions that the South Sea Company had enjoyed since Utrecht, finally freeing Madrid's hand to modernize its colonial commercial system. Chapter 5 explores the agenda of Ensenada and his allies – now unencumbered by diplomatic constraints and dynastic wars – as they promoted ambitious commercial, administrative, and ecclesiastical reforms. Chapter 6 addresses the downfall of the powerful Ensenada, which dulled the reformist impulse during the remaining years of Ferdinand VI.

Coming during the reign of Charles III, the apex of reform is the subject of the Part III "Pinnacle of the Bourbon Reforms, 1759–1796." Chapter 7 deals with the early years of the new king's reign after his arrival from Naples, when he found himself beset by the crisis arising from the British conquest of Havana in 1762. This chapter covers the sweeping military reform in Cuba, the ambitious initiatives in colonial administration and finance that supported it, the legalization of imperial free trade for Cuba and the other Spanish Caribbean islands – the capstone that broke the historic Andalusian monopoly, and the subsequent extension of this reform package to New Spain and beyond. Parallel developments involved the modernization of the colonial mail system and an aggressive expansion of the armada. Chapter 7 also explores the expulsion of the powerful Society of Jesus from the Spanish Atlantic world, an action that effectively subordinated the religious orders to the crown. Chapter 8 studies the wide-ranging reform agenda associated with the ministry of José de Gálvez, highlighted by the expansion of imperial free trade between 1776 and 1778, and the tightening of administrative controls through the establishment of the Viceroyalty of the Río de la Plata, but also including further military reorganizations and aggressive revenue and provincial administrative reform. Each of these innovations provoked the ire of interest groups in the colonies, sometimes leading to armed insurrections, particularly in Mexico, the Andes, and New Granada. Chapter 9 addresses the consolidation and refinement of the reform policies in the Spanish Atlantic world until the wars of the French Revolution embroiled Spain once again in European conflict. Although the armada had reached impressive dimensions, the traditional alliance with France eventually led Spain into a disastrous war with Great Britain in 1796, which allowed the British navy to cut the sea lanes between Spain and its colonies, leading to the slow strangulation of the eighteenth-century reforming impulse. The Conclusion discusses the whole century-long process of reform in the Spanish Atlantic world.

I

ALBERONI, PATIÑO, AND THE BEGINNINGS OF ATLANTIC REFORM, 1713–1736

I

Alberoni and the First Stirrings of Reform, 1713–1721

Although the Utrecht Treaties confirmed his Spanish inheritance, Philip V entered the postwar years of his reign a troubled monarch, ruling a divided and exhausted nation. The settlement denied him his rights to Spanish possessions in the Netherlands and Italy, and it recognized the British conquests of Gibraltar and Menorca. While his claim to the American empire was affirmed, Spain had to concede to the British demand for legal entry into colonial commerce through the slave trade monopoly, with damaging attendant codicils. And in February 1714, Philip lost his beloved Savoyard queen, Marie Louise, to tuberculosis. While he soon found solace in an Italian bride, Elizabeth Farnese, the king was plagued by chronic emotional instability, leading him to rely heavily on his wives.

Abad Julio Alberoni, the favorite of the new queen, emerged as the unlikely strong man of Madrid, although he held no public office and relied solely on his connections to the monarchs to maintain power. Neither contemporaries nor later historians have been kind to Alberoni, regarding him as a political neophyte who dazzled both young Italian queens with his mastery of their country's cooking, a welcome alternative to the uninspiring Spanish fare served at court previously. Although in his portrait, shown in Figure 1.1, the cardinal strikes a very dignified pose, Alberoni was actually a diminutive and rotund man, perhaps too fond of his own cooking. One contemporary observer dismissively described Alberoni as a mere "pygmy whom fortune made a colossus."[1] His protégé, José Patiño, was probably closer to understanding the Italian cardinal when he remarked that Alberoni "turned impossibilities into mere difficulties."[2] Alberoni recognized that

---

[1] Quoted in John Lynch, *Bourbon Spain, 1700–1808* (Oxford: Basil Blackwell, 1989), p. 76; and taken from William Coxe, *Memoirs of the Kings of Spain of the House of Bourbon, from the Accession of Philip V to the Death of Charles III, 1700–1788* (London: Longman, Hurst, Rees, Orme, and Brown, 1813), II, p. 108.

[2] Quoted in Lynch, *Bourbon Spain*, p. 78.

FIGURE 1.1 Julio Alberoni (1664–1751) by Rafael Tegeo in the Museo Naval. This is a copy painted by Tegeo in 1828 from an original painted by an unknown artist. (See plate section for color version)

that the keys to reviving Spain and restoring it to greatness were improving royal finances, rebuilding the navy, and reviving trade with the Indies. Although his economic policies resembled those of Colbert and his financial innovations drew some inspiration from Jean Orry, Alberoni was essentially a political pragmatist, not an intellectual. Despite the adversity confronting Spain, in the postwar years, the Italian would oversee a time of impressive innovation in the administration of Spain and the American empire, although accomplishments arrived piecemeal, unevenly, and often painfully.

Commerce with the Indies was a key to the renovation of Spain, but Atlantic commercial reforms faced a web of interrelated problems involving opposition groups in Spain, the Indies, and the monarchy's major foreign rivals – Britain, France, and the Netherlands. The principal problem was rampant contraband trading throughout the Spanish Atlantic world, which flourished during the War of Succession when Spain could not supply its overseas possessions. In this period, French traders captured colonial markets in the Pacific while British, Dutch, and French contrabandists used the preoccupation of Spain to operate with impunity in the Caribbean and South Atlantic. Moreover, foreign merchant houses in Seville and Cádiz supplied most of the manufactured goods shipped through the legal trading system to the Indies. The colonial bureaucracy in the Indies was riddled with corruption, as venal officeholders at the very highest levels of government facilitated the incursions of French, English, and Dutch contrabandists, taking a cut from the illegal commerce rather than trying to stop it. Such illicit trade undermined any hope of reviving the system of *Flotas y Galeones*, which also led to a serious decline in crown revenues from taxes on the transatlantic trade. Finally, the Utrecht settlement imposed impediments to the modernization of the colonial commercial system, as did the privileged position of the *Consulado de Cargadores a Indias de Sevilla* (Merchant Guild of Seville). Reform in the Spanish Atlantic was a complicated process. While shades of the coming Enlightenment and its rationalization were already seeping into the mentality at court, the early reformist agenda would be essentially pragmatic, arising from the long recognized need to shore up damaged segments of the imperial system.

Alberoni and other reformers needed a decade of peace to modernize the commercial system, but attempts to curtail contraband and regain control over colonial markets threatened the interests of Spain's commercial rivals and those profiting from illicit trade in the Indies. In addition, Alberoni's political future depended entirely on his relationship with the king and queen, and their dynastic aspirations in Europe also threatened war. In the end, Alberoni's reckless attempts to gain Italian possessions for the royal children led to disastrous military adventurism in Italy, and a resounding defeat. European affairs impeded any ongoing efforts to root out corruption and revive the transatlantic trade. Nonetheless, the process of reforming the Spanish Atlantic system had begun, and Alberoni's efforts would be taken up by future generations of Spanish and colonial politicians.

CONTRABAND, CORRUPTION, AND TRADE CONCESSIONS

By the end of the War of Succession, the remittance of public revenues from the Indies had declined steadily to alarming levels. Income levels of the Mexican treasuries remained stable throughout the seventeenth and early eighteenth centuries, and the remittances of tax revenues fluctuated between a high of nearly 8 million pesos between 1711 and 1719 and a low of fewer than 5 million pesos (1701–1709).[3] The situation was much more dire in the Viceroyalty of Peru, where income levels had fallen since the 1660s, and remittances of revenue had declined from a seventeenth-century high of nearly 15 million pesos (1631–1640) to more than 1 million pesos by the period from 1681 to 1690.[4] This trend only worsened in the early eighteenth century as remittances fell to a low of 77,411 pesos from 1711 to 1719. As a percentage of total expenditures, these shipments of revenue from Peru fell from a high of 51 percent in the years from 1607 to 1610 to just 1 percent in its lowest point in the period from 1711 to 1719.[5] For most of the remainder of the century, the Peruvian viceroyalty shipped only small amounts to the metropolis, retaining the bulk of its revenues to meet local administrative and military needs. In large part, this fall in remittances stemmed from declines in the mining economy, particularly at the formerly dominant mining center of Potosí, where legally registered silver fell from a high of 887,448 marks in 1592 to fewer than 200,000 marks by the early eighteenth century.[6]

The near collapse of income flowing into the central treasury office in Lima demonstrates the serious fiscal crisis in the Viceroyalty of Peru by the early eighteenth century. The Lima treasury (*caja*) was the clearinghouse for all royal income; each of the subordinate treasuries of the viceroyalty sent their surplus income (all revenues remaining after paying administrative expenses) to Lima, so that office's receipts reflected the flow of royal income throughout the Peruvian viceroyalty. As Figure 1.2 indicates, income levels in Lima continued to decline after the mid-seventeenth century, falling from a modest high of 3,503,217 pesos in 1706 to a dismal low of 258,645 in 1714, before rallying to 2,321,810 in 1719. Although the mining decline at Potosí was the major cause of this slide, contemporaries also pointed to the flood of French contraband goods in viceregal markets, largely paid for with unregistered and untaxed silver, smuggled from the highland mines.

During the War of Succession, the French lobbied hard to gain trade concessions in the Spanish Indies. After failing to secure approval for direct trade after the war's end, French traders turned their attention to supplying goods illegally to South American markets in return for bullion from Peruvian mines. During the war, beleaguered Spain could not supply European wares to South America, and King Philip was forced to give licensed French merchantmen the right to trade periodically in American markets. The French

[3] John J. TePaske, "New World Silver, Castile, and the Far East (1590–1750)" in John F. Richards, ed., *Precious Metals in the Later Medieval and Early Modern Worlds* (Durham: Duke University Press, 1983), tables 1, 2.

[4] Kenneth J. Andrien, *Crisis and Decline: The Viceroyalty of Peru in the Seventeenth Century* (Albuquerque: University of New Mexico Press, 1985), p. 67.

[5] TePaske, "New World Silver," tables 1, 2.

[6] Peter J. Bakewell, "Registered Silver Production in the Potosí District, 1550–1735," *Jahrbuch für Geschichte von Staat, Wirtschaft, und Gesellschaft Lateinamerikas*, 12 (1975): pp. 94–97.

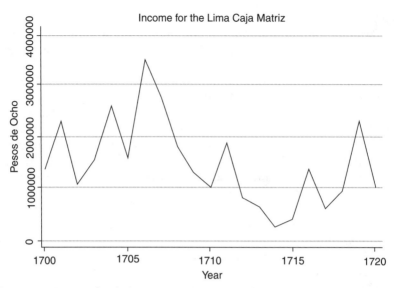

FIGURE 1.2 Income for the Lima Caja Matriz

even formed the Compagnie de la Mer Pacifique to allow merchants from St. Malo to deal in South America.[7] The French turned particular attention to this illicit trade when they lost their contract to supply slaves legally to the British in the Spanish Indies under the terms of the Utrecht accord. One-hundred and seventy-eight merchant vessels from France returned with 54,602,791 Spanish pesos between 1701 and 1725. This largely illicit trade reached its peak in 1714, when French merchant vessels returned with nearly 8.5 million pesos.[8] During the height of this trade, contemporaries estimated that over 65 percent of the goods sold in Peruvian markets were French contraband.

French smuggling only continued with the connivance of colonial officials, at one point even involving the viceroy of Peru, Don Manuel de Oms y Santa Pau Olim de Sentmenat y de Lanuza, the first Conde de Castelldosríus (1707–1710). The viceroy was a Catalan aristocrat, an accomplished literary figure, and a diplomat with experience in the courts of Portugal and France, where he developed a close relationship with King Louis XIV. As a Catalan loyal to the Bourbon claimant to the throne, Philip of Anjou, Castelldosríus had his family assets confiscated when Cataluña supported the Habsburg claimant, Charles of Austria. By the time he arrived in Lima in May of 1707, Castelldosríus was

[7] Geoffrey J. Walker, *Spanish Politics and Imperial Trade, 1700–1789* (Bloomington: Indiana University Press, 1979), pp. 22–28.
[8] Carlos Daniel Malamud Rikles, *Cádiz y Saint Malo en el Comercio Colonial Peruano (1698–1725)* (Cádiz: Diputación de Cádiz, 1986), p. 67.

deeply in debt.[9] With brutal celerity, the viceroy took control of the contraband trade in the Pacific by placing friends and cronies in key positions (such as Pisco and Ica on the coast) and making alliances with those already serving in other strategic ports, such as Arica, Callao, Concepción de Chile, Guayaquil, and Trujillo. The viceroy formed a partnership with his son Don Ramon Tamarit (whom he named head of the viceregal guard) and another fellow Catalan, Don Antonio Martí Ginovés, who had long-standing mercantile connections in Lima. French merchant vessels were allowed to unload goods, particularly at Pisco, where informal trade fairs took place, supervised by Tamarit's viceregal guard. The viceroy and his cronies then allegedly extracted a 25 percent tax on this illegal French merchandise sold to Peruvian merchants, some of whom were members of the Lima *Consulado.*[10]

While Castelldosríus reaped large profits from the contraband trade, he also shamelessly bullied Lima's merchant community into participating in the Portobelo Fair of 1707. The *limeño* merchants balked, complaining that contraband goods had saturated Peruvian markets, making it fruitless to buy higher-priced European wares at Portobelo. The viceroy scraped together a mixture of forced loans and what remained in the Lima treasury to remit nearly 1.7 million pesos to relieve the financial distress of the crown, demonstrating his loyalty and efficiency. He then pressured the *Consulado* to set sail for Panama with 7 million pesos (including the public monies amassed by the viceroy). Castelldosríus convinced the Lima *Consulado* to launch the Pacific armada by promising to curtail the contraband activities of his company and others involved in the French trade to ensure a market for goods purchased at the fair. For their part, the merchants agreed to divert some of the 350,000 pesos owed in trade taxes (*avería*) to help repay the viceroy's debts.[11]

After the commander of the galleons forced the Peruvians to pay the full *avería*, depriving Castelldosríus of his debt relief, the *limeños* set sail for Callao. During their return voyage, however, they were attacked by English pirates and lost much of their cargo. When the beleaguered Peruvians finally returned to Lima by 1709, they found that Castelldosríus had betrayed them; French contraband goods had continued to stream into viceregal markets, making it virtually impossible for them to profit from the sale of merchandise obtained in Portobelo. It is no small wonder that the viceroy's enemies denounced him, leading to his suspension by the Council of the Indies in

---

[9] Núria Sala i Vila, "Una corona bien vale un virreinato: El Marqués de Castelldosríus, Primer Virrey Borbónico del Perú," en Alfredo Moreno Cebrián y Núria Sala i Vila, eds., El *"premio"* de ser virrey: Los intereses públicos y privados del gobierno virreinal en el Perú de Felipe V (Madrid: Consejo Superior de Investigaciónes Científicas, 2004), pp. 19–34, 47–50.

[10] Walker, *Spanish Politics and Imperial Trade,* pp. 38–42; Sala i Vila, "Una corona bien vale un virreinato," p. 54.

[11] Walker, *Spanish Politics and Imperial Trade,* pp. 41–46; Sala i Vila, "Una corona bien vale un virreinato," pp. 42–50.

1710.[12] His untimely death that same year spared Castelldosríus the disgrace of prosecution, but an inventory of his estate revealed that he had amassed an illegal personal fortune of 1,294,060 pesos during his three-year reign.[13] The whole sordid affair reflected the deep-seated political culture of corruption that had permeated Spain's colonial bureaucracy by the early eighteenth century. These politics of corruption and deceit were not just confined to the southern viceroyalty. The Viceroy of New Spain, the Duke of Albuquerque, was accused of similar trafficking in contraband merchandise and only escaped prosecution by paying a 700,000-peso indemnity to the Royal Treasury.[14]

Quite apart from the crown's fiscal penury and problems with contraband, commercial concessions made in the Treaty of Utrecht inhibited a through-going reform in the Spanish Atlantic. Major obstacles arose from the British right to operate the American slave trade, secured under the settlement. Lacking factories on the African coast as a consequence of the Treaty of Tordesillas, Spain historically depended on middlemen to manage the traffic in human beings.[15] Versailles had used its position as protector of the new dynasty to extract the privilege of operating the slave trade through the Royal Guinea Company in 1701, but now this prize served to compensate the British for acceding to the Bourbon succession. Under provision of the treaty, the British South Sea Company – a joint stock company founded in 1711 to consolidate and reduce the costs of Britain's national debt – would be allowed to provide America with 4,800 *piezas* of either sex and of any age annually for a period of thirty years beginning May 1713. These imports would thus potentially entail at least 144,000 slaves; but during the first twenty-five years more bondsmen might be introduced if the demand existed in the Indies.[16]

---

[12] The suspension was later overturned because the deceased viceroy's daughter, Catalina, used her influence at court to reopen the case and clear her father's name. He was exonerated posthumously at his residencia, despite the overwhelming evidence against him. *Spanish Politics and Imperial Trade*, pp. 47–49; Sala i Vila, "Una corona bien vale un virreinato," pp. 50–78.

[13] Sala i Vila, "Una corona bien vale un virreinato," p. 111.

[14] Christoph Rosenmüller, *Patrons, Partisans, and Palace Intrigues: The Court Society of Colonial Mexico* (Calgary: University of Calgary Press, 2008), chap. 8; Sala i Vila, "Una corona bien vale un virreinato," pp. 56–57.

[15] For an overview of the earlier operation of the slave trade, see Enriqueta Vila Vilar, *Hispanoamérica y el comercio de esclavos* (Seville: Escuela de Estudios Hispano-Americanos, 1977).

[16] "Artículos del asiento de Negros," article 6, with French commentary, Archives des Affaires Étrangères: Correspóndance Politique, Espagne (hereinafter AAE:CPE), vol. 241. fols. 155–67. The South Sea Company made substantial loans to the government and took over large amounts of government debt in return for having the holders of existing debt exchange their securities for stock at par in the company. The South Sea Company also received monopoly trading rights in the South Seas through the concessions made to Britain by Spain in the

The South Sea Company was also permitted to send one 500-ton ship during each of the slave contract's thirty years to trade at the fairs in Portobelo or Veracruz, giving the British a coveted legal foothold in the American marketplace.[17] Perhaps more damaging was the provision imposed in the preliminary treaty of March 27, 1713, which committed the monarchy to reestablish its colonial commercial system in conformity with the fundamental laws of the Indies and with Spain's historic treaties. Spain also promised to refrain from conceding to any other foreign power the legal right to trade with its colonies.[18] This codicil effectively preserved the traditional convoy system, which gave meaning to the 500-ton "ships of permission" as the Spanish called them, and it restricted Spain's freedom to modernize the basic structures of the colonial commercial system. Indeed, not until the Treaty of Madrid in 1750 would Spain enjoy the diplomatic latitude it needed to effect basic reform. Further undermined by political corruption, contraband trading in the Caribbean and the Pacific, and political squabbles in Spain, the fleet system never approached the profits gained in the previous century.

To ameliorate the burdens imposed on the monarchy by the *asiento* the agreement contained provisions to provide some benefits to the Spanish monarchy. The treaty entitled the Royal Treasury to receive a fee of 33 1/3 pesos for each of the first 4,000 authorized slave imports, payable regardless of the actual traffic, and a beginning loan of 200,000 pesos.[19] The king was entitled to 25 percent of the profits from the ships of permission, and he could levy a tax of 5 percent on the remainder.[20] In view of the acrimony that accompanied the *asiento* and the hostility between the Spanish crown and the South Sea Company, however, the actual rewards reaching the Royal Treasury over the years really amounted to very little. Finally, the goods arriving via the ships of permission enjoyed an exemption from regular import levies, which

---

Treaties of Utrecht. See Dorothy Marshall, *Eighteenth Century England* (New York and London: David McKay Company, Inc., 1962), pp. 118–25.

[17] "Articulos del asiento de Negros," article 42.

[18] AAE:CPE, vol. 221, fols. 145–73. Clause 13 of the preliminary peace treaty provided that "His Catholic Majesty promises that in the future he will not concede licenses or any other permissions to any foreign nations, without exception, for any reason or pretext, to trade in the Spanish Indies, and His Majesty will restore the aforementioned commerce in conformity to and on the basis of the historic treaties and the fundamental laws of Spain relating to the Indies." Part of this provision was quoted in Pablo Emilio Pérez-Mallaina Bueno, *La política española en el Atlántico, 1700–1715* (Seville: Escuela de Estudios Hispano-Americanos, 1982), p. 271, and Allan J. Kuethe and Lowell Blaisdell, "French Influence and the Origins of the Bourbon Colonial Reorganization," *HAHR*, 71 (August 1991): p. 583.

[19] *The Assiento or Contract for . . . Importing Negroes into the Spanish America* (London 1713), articles 2–3.

[20] "Convention pour l'assiento des negres," 1716, in Saint Aignan to Versailles, June 12, 1716, AAE:CPE, vol. 251, fols. 61–76.

gave the British dealers an advantage of some 25 to 30 percent in colonial markets over goods sent from Spain to the fairs in Veracruz and Portobelo.[21]

While the Seville *Consulado* deplored the intrusion of foreign smugglers into the American colonies, it benefited from treaty provisions mandating the preservation of the historic system of *Flotas y Galeones*. For more than 150 years, the guild had operated a monopoly out of the port of Seville under the supervision of the *Casa de la Contratación*.[22] The single port and monopoly guild system simplified administration and control, while the *Consulado* provided a vital service to the crown – furnishing loans, donations, and on certain occasions, special fees (*servicios*). This arrangement could entail considerable sums of money. During the period between 1687 and 1705, for example, *Consulado* loans totaled 4,174,000 pesos, 970,000 escudos, and 16,000 doblones; its donations amounted to 1,325,000 pesos, 870,000 escudos, and 5,000 doblones; and its fees were 90,000 pesos, 200,000 escudos, and 200,000 ducados.[23] In the absence of a modern banking system (something that Spain would not develop until 1782), these loans and donations proved indispensable for emergency finance. As one member of an ad hoc junta investigating alleged improprieties by the *Consulado* asserted in 1709, it was necessary "to promote commerce ... otherwise it could not have the funds to serve H. M. with donations and loans when urgencies arise."[24] The reciprocity of this arrangement was well understood and stated openly. Recognizing a *servicio* that had been rendered in 1690, His Majesty expressed his "acceptance and gratitude" and went on to promise that "I will remember it and look out for you and favor you in all that concerns your comfort and preservation."[25]

The guild wielded powerful political influence in Madrid. The *Consulado* constantly outmaneuvered the French when they attempted to gain permanent, direct access to American markets during the War of Succession, a time when Versailles enjoyed maximum influence. Emboldened by their seemingly omnipotent position as Philip's principal ally, the French hoped to manipulate Spanish colonial commercial policy, aiming to modernize and reform it in

---

[21] Walker, *Spanish Politics and Imperial Trade*, pp. 73–74, 81.

[22] For an excellent perspective on the creation of the *Consulado* in 1543, see Enriqueta Vila Vilar, "Algunas consideraciones sobre la creación del *Consulado* de Sevilla," en *Congreso de Historia del Descubrimiento* (Madrid: Real Academia de la Historia,Confederación Española de Cajas de Ahorros, 1992), IV, 53–65. For the *Casa de la Contratación*, see Antonio Acosta Rodríguez, Adolfo González Rodríguez, coordinators, *La Casa de la Contratación y la navegación entre España y las Indias* (Sevilla: Universidad de Sevilla, 2003).

[23] "Servicios hechos al estado y a algunos cuerpos particulares de la Nación por el Comercio de Cádiz, 1555–1803," Archivo General de Indias Consulados, leg. 15.

[24] Quoted in Pérez-Mallaina, *La política española*, pp. 222–23.

[25] "Servicios hechos al estado y a algunos cuerpos particulares de la Nación por el Comercio de Cádiz, 1555–1803." AGI, Consulados, leg. 15, quoted in Allan J. Kuethe, "El fin del monopolio: Los Borbones y el Consulado andaluz," in Enriqueta Vila Vilar y Allan J. Kuethe (eds.), *Relaciones de poder y comercio colonial: Nuevas perspectivas* (Madrid: Consejo Superior de Investigaciones Científicas, 1999), pp. 37–38.

ways favorable to their own interests. In 1705, following the formation of the Junta de Restablecimiento del Comercio, two influential French members – agents Nicolás Mesnager and Ambrosio Daubenton – attempted unsuccessfully to replace the convoys with individual ships. The following year, Mesnager offered a plan to have colonial commerce officially leave from Cádiz, not Seville, replacing the *sevillano Consulado* with a guild located in the new port of departure. Allies would have the right to trade in America, but Spanish ships would carry all merchandise. The crown rejected this plan, like the one before it, largely because of the *Consulado* of Seville's important financial support to the war effort, the guild's vehement opposition and political lobbying, and delays in the Council of the Indies. The French had to settle for the privilege of providing a third of the cargoes on six frigates sent out from Cádiz for Veracruz in 1708.[26] No permanent French access to colonial markets resulted, as Versailles's influence declined during the political tensions that divided the two courts in 1709, permitting Seville to recover lost ground.[27]

THE YEARS OF FRENCH INFLUENCE

Given the limitations on colonial policy imposed by treaty obligations and uncontrolled contraband, administrative reform focused on the European side of the Atlantic, under the watchful eyes of the king's French allies. Innovations in colonial policy were also connected to the fortunes of the royal family, particularly the mental instability of the king. During the War of Succession, Philip showed impressive signs of kingly leadership, but over time his unstable mental condition, marked by increasingly long and deep bouts of depression, weakened him noticeably.[28] Philip's vulnerability led to his extreme reliance on his young wife, Marie Louise of Savoy, and Anne Marie de la Trémoille-Noir Moutier, the Princess Ursins, who was the widow of a Spanish grandee and a close associate of Louis XIV's consort, Madame de Maintenon.[29] In anticipation of Philip's marriage, Versailles had dispatched

---

[26] Pérez-Mallaina, *La política española*, pp. 234–64.

[27] Ibid., pp. 97–102.

[28] Recent histories addressing Philip's mental difficulties include Carlos Martínez Shaw and Marina Alfonso Mola, *Felipe V* (Madrid: Arlanza Ediciones, 2001); Ricardo García Cárcel, *Felipe V y los Españoles: Una visión periférica del problema de España* (Barcelona: Plaza y Janés, 2002); María Angeles Pérez Samper, *Isabel de Farnesio* (Barcelona: Plaza y Janés, 2003); and Juan Luis Castellano, *Gobierno y poder en la España del siglo XVIII* (Granada: Editorial Universidad de Granada, 2006). For Philip's wartime heroics and leadership, see Henry Kamen, *Philip V of Spain: The King who Reigned Twice* (New Haven: Yale University Press, 2001), chaps. 2–3.

[29] Many authorities attribute this dependency to an overactive sexual drive, coupled with a religious piety that did not permit him the kingly luxury of extramarital companionship. A recent example is Philippe Erlanger, *Felipe V, esclavo de sus mujeres*, translated by Robert Sánchez (Barcelona: Ariel, 2003). A different perspective can be found in Kamen, *Philip V*. While acknowledging Philip's dependence on his queens, Kamen argues that his strengths should not be underrated.

PLATE 1 Julio Alberoni (1664–1751) by Rafael Tegeo in the Museo Naval. This is a copy painted by Tegeo in 1828 from an original painted by an unknown artist.

PLATE 2 *José Patiño (1666–1736)* by Rafael Tegeo in the Museo Naval. This is a copy painted by Tegeo in 1828 from an original painted by an unknown artist.

PLATE 3 *The Family of Philip V* by Louis Michael van Loo, in 1743 in the Museo del Prado. Left to right in an imaginary assemblage: María Ana Victoria, infanta and future queen of Portugal; Barbara de Braganza, wife of Ferdinand; Ferdinand, Prince of Asturias and future king of Spain; King Philip V; Louis, infante-cardinal; Queen Elizabeth Farnese; Philip, duke of Parma; Louise Elizabeth of Bourbon (France), Philip's wife; María Teresa, infanta and future wife of Dauphine Louis; María Antonia, infanta and future queen of Piedmont-Sardinia; María Amalia of Saxony, wife of Charles; and Charles, king of Naples and future king of Spain. In the foreground are the infant children of the duke of Parma and the king of Naples.

PLATE 4 Zenón de Somodevilla, Marqués de la Ensenada (1702–1781) in the Museo del Prado, shown wearing the Toisón de Oro of the Order of San Jenaro, painted by Jacopo Amigoni sometime after 1750, the year that the Marqués received the Toisón.

PLATE 5 King Charles III (1716–1788, reigned 1759–1788) in armor, painted by Antón Rafael Mengs in 1761 in the Museo del Prado.

PLATE 6 José Moñino, Conde de Floridablanca (1728–1808) in the Museo del Prado, wearing the insignia of the Order of Charles III, apparently painted by Francisco de Goya y Lucientes, although some authorities claim it was done by (a) student(s) in his studio.

El Exmo. Sr. Br. F. D. Antonio Valdes Fernandez Bazan Gran Cruz, y Comendador del Orden de S. Juan, del Consejo de Estado, Gefe de Esquadra, y Secretario de Estado, y del Despacho Unibersal de Marina Obtubo este Empleo en 2 de Marzo de 1783 habiendo seguido todos los grados de su carrera Militar desde 26 de Octubre de 1752 e q. sentó plaza de Guardia Marina. Mandó varios buques y Divisiones de la Armada fue Sub Inspector de Arsenales Insp.or Gr.l de Marina. desempeñó importantes Comis.es del R. Servicio, y entre ellas la de restablecer en el año de 1782 la fundicion de Artilleria de hierro de las fabricas de la Cavada Nacio en Burgos á 25 de Marzo de 1744

PLATE 7 Fray Antonio Valdés y Bazán (1744–1816) in the Museo Naval, painted by Rafael Tegeo in 1828 from an original painted by an unknown artist.

Ursins, who was in her late fifties, as *camarera mayor* (head of the queen's household) to escort his thirteen-year-old bride to Madrid and oversee her development as a proper queen.[30] In this role, Ursins quickly began to counsel the royal family in affairs of state, and she assumed a privileged position at court, nurturing a close relationship with Marie Louise, Special Financial Advisor Jean Orry, and French Ambassador Michel-Jean Amelot (1705–1709).[31] After the unexpected death of the queen in February 1714, Princess Ursins consolidated her hegemony, becoming a de facto regent.[32] The king took his meals with her, and she controlled his daily agenda. Few besides his closest ministers had ready access to him.[33]

One of the King's most influential ministers, Jean Orry, was a relatively obscure figure when Louis XIV dispatched him to Spain to advise his grandson during the periods from 1702 to 1704 and 1705 to 1706. A mousy character with an abrasive personality, Orry proved a shrewd, energetic minister, and he advanced a plethora of plans to improve Spanish finance and to reorganize the government.[34] Philip thought so highly of Orry that he summoned the Frenchman to Spain once again in 1713, and Orry repaid the King's confidence with unswerving loyalty, which often upset French officials, who thought the minister should be little more than an instrument of the French government.[35] The Marquis de Brancas, who was ambassador to Spain in 1714 (and the brother-in-law of Minister of State Jean Baptiste Colbert, the Marquis de Torcy) disapproved of Orry's overreaching meddling and clearly disliked him personally.[36] Both men arrived in Madrid in 1713, and Brancas, like Orry, had extensive knowledge of the *madrileño* scene.[37] Brancas lamented his countryman's independence of mind, remarking that

---

[30] For a succinct biographical treatment of Ursins, see Kendall W. Brown, "Marie-Anne de la Tremouille," in Anne Commire and Deborah Klezmer (eds), *Women in World History: A Biographical Encyclopedia*, 16 vols (Waterford, CT: Yorkin Publications, 1999–2002), 10, pp. 358–62.

[31] There are many descriptions of the role of the Princess Ursins and of the emotional problems of Philip V. In addition to Erlanger's *Felipe V, esclavo*, see Lynch, *Bourbon Spain*, pp. 31, 46–52, 62, 73–74.

[32] Erlanger, *Felipe V, esclavo*, p. 227.

[33] Brancas to Torcy, Madrid, February 19, 1714, AAE:CPE, vol. 228, fols. 159–61.

[34] Alfred Baudrillart, *Phillippe V et La Cour de France*, I (Paris: Fermin-Didot et cie, 1890), pp. 73–74, 575–76; Lynch, *Bourbon Spain*, pp. 31, 47, 62, 73–74.

[35] Philip's letter to his grandfather is instructive: "As I am currently attempting to put my finances in order and Mr. Orry, who being well informed, is accordingly vital to me, I fervently hope that he might come here quickly [and] therefore I beg Your Majesty to grant to him permission to do so, something that would please me very much." Philip V to Louis XIV, Madrid, March 13, 1713, AAE:CPE, vol. 221, fol. 27.

[36] The ambassador's correspondence with Colbert, the Marquis de Torcy, during early 1714 contains repeated criticisms. See, for example, his reports of January 8 and 16, February 17, and March 23, AAE:CPE, vol. 228, fols. 37–42, 54–62, 153–58, and vol. 229, fols. 67–69.

[37] Ambassadorial appointment, Brancas, Versailles, June 15, 1713, and "Extrait," anonymous letter, Bayonne, April 15, 1713, AAE:CPE, vol. 221, fols. 164, 221.

"all the harm that Orry does in Spain reflects upon France," and he even suspected Orry of opening his correspondence with Versailles.[38] Philip depended on the financial wizard for money, and Orry wisely maintained close ties with the powerful Princess Ursins. Indeed, on one occasion, the princess, who may well herself have seen copies of Brancas's dispatches to Versailles, felt compelled to reproach the ambassador for criticizing Orry.[39]

The dominant Spaniard in Philip's government was José Grimaldo, one of the very few close confidants of the king. A Basque of comparatively humble origins, Grimaldo was an early example of the new kind of administrator whose merits found an astonishing degree of social mobility during the Bourbon century.[40] A pleasing, tactful, cautious individual, Grimaldo was portly, and he liked to place his hands upon his ample stomach while speaking.[41] His strengths were integrity and the ability to manage capably multiple tasks, sustain harmony and equilibrium, and avoid making enemies.[42] During this period, he also cultivated excellent relations with the Princess Ursins.[43] Grimaldo was not a great reformer, and his instincts were quite conservative with little inclination toward innovative thinking.[44]

During his time in Spain, Jean Orry radically changed the administration of the empire by installing a system of four ministries – State, War, Justice and Government (*Justicia y Gobierno Político*), and Marine and the Indies – on November 30, 1714. Finance was placed under the management of an intendant general. This reorganization had long been a priority for Orry, who worked in collaboration with the Spaniard Melchor de Macanaz.[45]

---

[38] Brancas to Torcy, Madrid, February 17, 1714, and March 19, 1714, AAE:CPE, vol. 228, fol. 153–58, and vol. 229, fols. 58–61.

[39] Brancas to Torcy, Madrid, January 16, 1714, and memoire, Madrid, May 3, 1714, AAE:CPE, vol. 228, fols. 54–62 and vol. 229, fols. 130–35; Lynch, *Bourbon Spain*, pp. 52, 73. Brancas returned to Paris in April 1714; curiously, he would again serve as ambassador in the late 1720s. The Princess Ursins to Torcy, Madrid, April 29, 1714, and *memoire pour servir d'instruccion au Marquis de Brancas*, April 26, 1728, AAE:CPE, vol. 229, fol. 141 and vol. 354, fols. 277–98.

[40] For a prosopographic study of the eighteenth-century leadership at court, see Teresa Nava Rodríguez, "Problemas y perpectivas (sic) de una historia social de la administración: Los secretarios del Despacho en la España del siglo XVIII," *Mélanges de la Casa de Vélazquez*, 30 (1994), pp. 151–56.

[41] José Antonio Escudero, *Los orígenes del Consejo de Ministros en España* (Madrid: Editora Nacional, 1979), pp. 41–42; Lynch, *Bourbon Spain*, pp. 73, 80; Erlanger, *Felipe V, esclavo*, p. 287.

[42] A French perspective can be found in the Instruction for Special Envoye Marquis de Maulevrier, Versailles, July 9, 1720, and Maulevrier to Versailles, Madrid, October 21, 1720, AAE:CPE, vol. 295, fols. 217–36, and vol. 298, fols. 188–96.

[43] Escudero, *Los orígenes*, pp. 45, 49.

[44] For Grimaldo's background and role during the War of the Spanish Succession, see Concepción de Castro, *A la sombra de Felipe V: José Grimaldo, ministro responsable (1703–1726)* (Madrid: Marcial Pons, 2004).

[45] Royal order, November 30, 1714, AGI, Indiferente General (hereinafter IG), leg. 472. See also Lynch, *Bourbon Spain*, 73–74. In a message to Versailles, a gratified Orry reported that the

Under the Hapsburgs, the crown had functioned through a series of councils led by the Council of Castile, with colonial affairs assigned to the Council of the Indies. This institution, like any committee, depended on the quality of its members for results, but in functioning collectively it tended to be deliberative and slow, more reactive than proactive. As Europe entered the eighteenth century, several European states were already developing ministerial systems featuring individual accountability.[46] This included France, and Spain followed.

The new ministry for the colonies and the navy officially carried the complicated designation Secretary of State and of the Universal Office of Marine and the Indies (*Secretario de Estado y del Despacho Universal de Marina e Indias*). Organically, the ministerial system grew out of the Secretariat of the Universal Office for the Council of State (*Secretaría del Despacho Universal*), the highest ranking council within the Hapsburg system of administration. Owing to this connection, ministers called themselves secretaries of the Universal Office. In 1705, the Universal Office had been transformed with the establishment of two secretariats, one for War and Treasury in the hands of José Grimaldo, the other for everything else (*todo lo demás de cualquier material que sea*), but essentially justice and ecclesiastical matters.[47]

When the Universal Office was reorganized into four secretariats in 1714, those appointed were Miguel Fernández Durán (War), Manuel Vadillo (Justice and Government), and Bernardo Tinajero de la Escalera (Marine and the Indies).[48] José Grimaldo, who had become a marqués, assumed State.[49] Because Orry retained his superior oversight of finance, that critical function was set apart from the ministerial structure.[50] The Secretariat of Marine and the Indies would retain its dual personality until 1754, when Ferdinand VI separated the two branches. Over its early years, Marine and the Indies would commonly find itself administered by an individual controlling one or more other portfolios, which brought about a kind of ad hoc interministerial coordination within the royal cabinet.

---

reorganization had come "*enfin.*" Orry to Versailles, Madrid, December 3, 1714, AAE:CPE, vol. 234, fol. 12.

[46] See, for example, Leo Gershoy, *From Despotism to Revolution, 1763–1789* (New York: Harper and Row, 1944).

[47] Escudero, *Los orígenes*, pp. 12, 26–28, 41–42. An excellent analysis of the early struggle to evolve from the Hapsburg system can be found in Castellano, *Gobierno y poder*, chap. 2.

[48] Escudero, *Los orígenes*, pp. 52–53. Durán described his position as "Secretary of State and of the Universal Office of War in His [Majesty's] cabinet." Durán to Torcy, Madrid, December 4, 1714, AAE:CPE, vol. 234, fol. 42.

[49] Grimaldo to Torcy, Madrid, November 19, 1714, AAE:CPE, vol. 233, fol. 99.

[50] Chargé d'Affaires Jean Baptiste Pachau to Versailles, Madrid, November 10, 1714, AAE:CPE, vol. 233, fols. 67–69. Finance was placed under an "*intendente universal de la veeduría general.*" Royal order, December 1, 1714, AGI, IG, leg. 472.

Matters designated for ministerial competence were assigned to what was called the *vía reservada*. In the case of Marine and the Indies, these included matters of day-to-day administration:

The correspondence with the viceroys, provincial governors, and individuals. Their given names, last names, social status and birthplaces. All jurisdiction over wages, the number of troops that ought to comprise the garrisons, their salaries and assignments. The archbishops, bishops, chapters, abbots, priors, convents of both sexes, parishes, number and names of the ecclesiastics and the religious [and] provinces and places where each derives its income and what it is. That of all the encomiendas, their locations, incomes, and who possesses them.... The tribunals, *corregimientos*, *alcaldías* and other jurisdictions, accountants, their salaries and functions. The mints, officials, wages, and where they are located. The tax administrators [and] farmers, the name of each one, his production, liabilities and what they produced since the year 1640. With respect to having formed a Junta for Finance of the Indies and of troop maintenance, this secretary and that for War will attend. All that involves the navy, the purchase and construction of ships [and] their funds in order that H. M. may allot them.[51]

Although the Council of the Indies survived the reorganization, it would play a secondary albeit important role. Under the new arrangement, the council's responsibilities concerned legal appeals as well as the processing of appointments involving judicial and ecclesiastical matters. It also acted as a consultative body for issues requiring study and deliberation. The conventional venue for His Majesty's governance would become the royal order issued in the king's name through the Ministry. The royal *cédula*, the historic legal instrument of the Council, would also be employed by the Ministry for matters requiring formal legislation or for appointments originating under its purview.[52]

The first secretary of the Office for Marine and the Indies was Bernardo Tinajero, a man of impressive drive and ability. Tinajero rose through his attachment to French Ambassador Michel Jean Amelot, de facto prime minister from 1705–1709, and to the French clique that dominated the early court of Philip V.[53] A disaffected member of the *Consulado* of Seville, he was one of 129 members who in 1697 protested how the guild leadership assigned individual assessments for loans conceded to the Royal Treasury. Unable to gain satisfaction, he appealed to the *Casa de la Contratación* in 1705, where he failed and found himself banished from future general assemblies of the *Consulado* (*juntas generales de comercio*). Tinajero's fortune

---

[51] Quoted in Escudero, *Los orígenes*, p. 53.

[52] Mark A. Burkholder, "The Council of the Indies in the Late Eighteenth Century: A New Perspective," *HAHR*, 56 (August 1976), p. 405; José Joaquín Real Díaz, *Estudio diplomático del documento indiano*, 2nd printing (Madrid: Dirección de Archivos Estatales, 1991), pp. 70, 179–81, 200–201.

[53] Brancas reporting to Torcy, Madrid, January 16, 1714, expressed admiration for Tinajero, describing him as a "man of spirit ... very able" AAE:CPE, vol. 228, fol. 54–62.

changed abruptly when his appeal to the Council of the Indies came to the attention of Amelot, who was in the process of establishing the Junta de Restablecimiento del Comercio. One of the principal goals of this committee was to break the power of the *Consulado* and to allow more direct French commerce with America. While these initiatives failed, they allowed the disaffected faction of the merchant guild to exact revenge. Amelot found its complaints a handy instrument to further his designs, and when a royal decree of 15 December 15, 1705, established the Junta de Cuentas to review *Consulado* finances, he had Tinajero named *fiscal*. Tinajero quickly acted to settle old scores, and he had the *Consulado* leaders from the years 1689 to 1705 imprisoned and their goods embargoed. In 1707, Tinajero also secured the right to nominate candidates for the posts of prior and consul, with the final selection resting with the general assembly of the *Consulado*. In this way, he had a direct hand in fashioning the new elite for the merchant guild while destroying the old.[54]

Tinajero used his connections to secure the position of secretary of the Council of the Indies in 1706, and thereafter he remained a prominent figure at court. He emerged as a resolute advocate of the Andalusian commercial monopoly, despite his close connections to the French.[55] In 1712, his expertise in maritime affairs led to his appointment to a special commission, formed under the Duke of Veragua, studying how to revitalize the Royal Armada. During the War of Succession, Spain bought warships when it could, but generally relied on renting costly French escorts for its treasure fleets.[56] To correct this situation, Tinajero personally authored a master plan that called for the construction of ten ships of the line and two coast guard vessels at the Havana shipyards. Havana possessed all the characteristics needed for this undertaking: a magnificent deep water bay where a shipyard suited to both constructing and servicing ships could be fashioned, a strategic location along the major colonial shipping lanes, and a broad hinterland with ample timber resources, including a durable variety of cedar (particularly in tropical waters) which splintered less than Iberian oak when struck by cannon fire. Tinajero's proposal underpinned his belief that Atlantic concerns must by necessity take priority over Mediterranean concerns.[57] Manuel López Pintado, a prominent admiral, who had successfully commanded the 1710 *Azogues* (mercury ships) expedition to Veracruz, would

---

[54] Kuethe, "El fin del monopolio," pp. 39–40.

[55] Pérez-Mallaina, *Política naval*, pp. 87, 261.

[56] Ibid., pp. 139, 142–51.

[57] G. Douglas Inglis, "The Spanish Naval Shipyard at Havana in the Eighteenth Century," in *New Aspects of Naval History: Selected Papers from the 5th Naval History Symposium* (Baltimore: Nautical and Aviation Publishers, 1985), pp. 47–48. For the properties of Cuban timber, see John Robert McNeill, *Atlantic Empires of France and Spain: Louisbourg and Havana, 1700–1763* (Chapel Hill: University of North Carolina Press, 1985), pp. 133, 174.

manage the construction of the new vessels, providing both the materials and the craftsmen for the enterprise.[58]

With the return in 1713 of Jean Orry, who preferred to purchase ships rather than construct them, Tinajero's plan was placed on hold. Moreover, López Pintado's expedition in Cádiz to secure naval stores and artisans for Havana was first diverted to the siege of Barcelona and then subsumed into the commercial convoy eventually dispatched to New Spain in 1715.[59] Tinajero harshly criticized the Orry strategy, but to no avail.[60] Nonetheless, Tinajero secured his appointment as secretary of the Office for Marine and the Indies, surely the pinnacle of his career.

The transition to the system of secretariats or ministries constituted a highly significant innovation. The replacement of collective with individual responsibility furnished an administrative mechanism that encouraged and facilitated the emergence of talent in ways that the councils did not. This is not to discount the significance of outstanding statesmen, such as Lerma or Olivares, but the eighteenth century would allow a steady stream of talent to emerge. Even when the king had personal failings, such as in the case of Philip V – who, as John Lynch has perceptively remarked, "was probably no better a king than Charles II" – the monarchy remained sound despite the king's periodic lapses into debilitating bouts of depression.[61] Over the century, supremely talented ministers such as Patiño, Ensenada, Esquilache, Floridablanca, and Aranda would rule, but they were often supported by a host of other able men, such as Grimaldo, who played important roles in shaping royal policy and administering it. Collectively, it would be these individuals, later backed by able monarchs such as Ferdinand VI and Charles III, who would guide the resurgence of eighteenth-century Spain and its empire.

ALBERONI AND REFORM, 1715–1719

A challenge to French influence soon appeared with the astonishing rise of Abad (abbot) Julio Alberoni of Plasencia. He had arrived in 1710 with the Marshal Duke of Vendôme, when the general transferred to Spain to assume command of the Bourbon forces. The orphan son of a gardener, the quick-witted Alberoni had secured the protection of the Parmesan clergy, gained a Jesuit education, and taken minor orders.[62] His skills attracted Vendôme's

---

[58] Perez-Mallaina, *Política naval*, pp. 10–13.

[59] Inglis, "The Spanish Naval Shipyard," p. 48; Allan J. Kuethe and José Manuel Serrano, "El astillero de la Habana y Trafalgar," *Revista de Indias*, 67 (September–December 2007), p. 766.

[60] Brancas to Torcy, Madrid, January 16, 1714, AAE:CPE, vol. 228, fol. 54–62.

[61] Lynch, *Bourbon Spain*, p. 115.

[62] Lucien Bély, *Espions et Ambassadeurs au Temps de Louis XIV* (Paris: Fayard, 1990), p. 326.

attention when the duke commanded the Franco-Spanish forces in northern Italy; Alberoni soon became his right-hand man, procuring supplies for the army in Spain. Known for his fabulous skills as a cook as well as his personal grace and charm, the suave Alberoni gained the confidence of Queen Marie Louise, who granted him Spanish citizenship and a pension. Alberoni remained in Madrid after the duke's death in 1712.[63] His fortune improved further when he secured appointment as envoy for the Duke of Parma.[64]

After the death of the queen, Alberoni proposed to Ursins and the king that Philip marry the twenty-one-year-old niece and stepdaughter of the Duke of Parma, Elizabeth Farnese, a match that entailed diplomatic advantages for Spanish aspirations in Italy.[65] Among Elizabeth's purported qualities were her kind and religious nature, her devotion to embroidery and music, and a character innocent of intrigue.[66] After Philip and Elizabeth were married by proxy in September, she began her lengthy journey to Madrid. Discouraged by an encounter with bad weather aboard ship that forced her to take refuge in Genoa, Elizabeth resolved to proceed at a leisurely pace by land. The young queen did not reach Spain until December, entering through Navarre. Abad Alberoni, as Parma's envoy, met her in Pamplona. An impatient Philip set out to receive her at Guadalajara. The Princess Ursins, however, quite irritated with Elizabeth's independent behavior, went beyond Guadalajara to Jadraque to prepare the young queen for her encounter with the king.

The meeting of the two women at Jadraque on December 23 changed the course of Philip's reign. While the details are unknown, Elizabeth clearly did not feel obliged to suffer the dominance of an older woman as she assumed her throne. She sent the princess packing to Versailles in the middle of that very same bitterly cold winter night, eventually followed by the entourage of French advisors and hangers-on that had cluttered the court in Madrid.[67] Orry departed the following February. The man of the hour was Abad Alberoni, soon to be the new power at court. When Elizabeth wrote Louis XIV to complain about Ursins's "*incredible … audacia*" and "*discorsi insolenti*," she wrote to the French monarch in Italian.[68] As time would prove, the Italian attachments of the new queen would have direct implications for reform in America.

[63] Manuel Ríos Mazcarelle, *Reinas de España* (Madrid: Alderabán 1999), p. 35.

[64] Erlanger, *Felipe V, esclavo*, p. 225.

[65] Martínez Shaw, *Felipe V*, pp. 95–96; Pérez Samper, *Isabel de Farnesio*, pp. 14–16. As her uncle had no sons, Elizabeth was heir to Parma and Plasencia and apparently would also have a claim to Tuscany, where an unmarried uncle reigned.

[66] Erlanger, *Felipe V, esclavo*, pp. 228–30.

[67] A succinct account of this transition can be found in Kamen, *Philip V*, pp. 97–98; see also Ríos, *Reinas*, pp. 51–52.

[68] Elizabeth Farnese to Louis XIV, Madrid, s.d. in Grimaldo to Torcy, Madrid, December 29, 1714, AAE:CPE, vol. 234, fols. 143–45, 148.

Repercussions from the dramatic events at Jadraque had a direct impact on the Ministry of Marine and the Indies. Alberoni quickly established his grip on the palace as de facto prime minister without portfolio, overshadowing all the secretaries of the Office. In April 1715, Alberoni relieved the Francophile Tinajero, whose priority was the Atlantic.[69] Alberoni then suppressed his secretariat, dividing its duties among the three remaining ministries.[70] Marine and the Indies would remain submerged until 1721, when it was reestablished in a new political environment. Nonetheless, Tinajero's blueprint for rebuilding the navy would survive in the long run, and over the century many of Spain's finest seagoing vessels would emerge from Havana's shipyards.[71] Rumors at court during this same period had it that the three remaining ministries would be reduced to two.[72] Although this never happened, Alberoni delivered a clear political message when he assigned the three secretaries of the Office to a single room, useable through daily rotations – the Italian would be the real source of political power.[73] Moreover, he personally monitored the correspondence arriving from the Indies.[74]

Alberoni would also tolerate no interference from the Council of the Indies, the historic instrument of the conservative aristocratic elite, in formulating his policies of Atlantic reform. The royal decree of January 20, 1717, clarified any doubts that might have arisen concerning the Council's prerogatives in the aftermath of the Ministry's partition, stating:

... everything that according to my previous resolutions came under it [the Council] institutionally, arising from contentious actions and other cases of simple justice, it shall not touch hereafter ... because all that is of that nature and quality and ... that relates to the governmental, economical, and providential, I reserve in me personally to order enacted through the vía reservada.[75]

After Alberoni had departed the scene and the Secretariat of State for Marine and the Indies was reestablished, this prescription remained, although weighty matters would be referred to the Council in *consulta* for a studied opinion.

With the downfall of Bernardo Tinajero, the French faction at court was replaced by a new clique of outsiders from Italy.[76] These included three

---

[69] Grimaldo to Tinajero, Buen Retiro, April 28, 1715, Archivo Histórico Nacional (hereinafter AHN), Estado, leg. 2933.

[70] Royal decree, Palace, April 3, 1717, Archivo General de la Marina Alvaro de Bazán (hereinafter AGMAB), leg. 5021. The decree assigned War and Navy for the Indies to War and the rest to Justice and Government (*gobierno político*). Finance lost its autonomy and was attached to Justice and Government.

[71] Inglis, "The Spanish Naval Shipyard," pp. 52–56.

[72] Saint Aignan to His Majesty, the Escorial, June 14, 1717, AAE:CPE, vol. 258, fols. 81–83.

[73] Saint Aignan to His Majesty, the Escorial, June 28, 1717, AAE:CPE, vol. 258, fols. 96–97.

[74] Saint Aignan to Huxelles, Madrid, October 12, 1716, AAE:CPE, vol. 253, fols. 37–41.

[75] Quoted in Real Díaz, *Estudio diplomático*, p. 179.

[76] Revealingly, Saint Aignan reported to his king in mid-July that "[t]he enemies of Mr. Tinajero continue the persecution .... His situation is really very sad; none of his remaining friends dare act on his behalf, because the brick wall that is against him is too powerful." Saint Aignan

influential military officers: the Duke of Popoli, a grandee and confidant of the queen, whom the French rated as particularly worrisome; the Marqués de San Felipe, who compiled an insightful account of the reign of Philip; and the Príncipe Pío of Savoy, perhaps the top field commander, who first acted as governor of Madrid and later Barcelona.[77] Antonio de Judice, the Prince of Cellamare and nephew of the highly influential Cardinal Judice, became the Spanish ambassador to Versailles. His flagrant conspiracy against the regency, however, would eventually earn him expulsion.[78] Annibale Scotti was a confidant of the queen from Plasencia, who, among other things, oversaw the construction of the luxurious Coliseo de los Caños theatre for Madrid. He would remain at her side even during the dark years following Philip's death.[79] Finally, Alberoni relied on two Spaniards of Italian descent, José Patiño, who served as intendant of Marine, and became Alberoni's right-hand man, and his elder brother, the Marqués de Castelar, who served as Minister of War. Needless to say, the French deplored this Italian influence, which they believed rightfully should have been their own.

The immediate challenge confronting Alberoni concerned gaining control over the ports of Spain, which had serious implications for trade with America. This problem essentially involved treaty privileges granted in the seventeenth century to the British, French, and Dutch. Britain initially had not reacted with hostility to the succession of Philip V, but it eventually joined the war to arrest French domination and to protect the lucrative legal and illicit commercial inroads that it had developed into the Spanish Indies.[80] Based on a long-standing accumulation of treaty rights, the English presence in Cádiz depended on complex, vague, and often deceptive treaty privileges, which

sustained a personal friendship with Tinajero, commenting in late 1716 that, "I often consult him." Saint Aignan to Louis XIV and Huxelles, Madrid, July 15, 1715, AAE:CPE, Madrid, December 22, 1716, vol. 241., fols. 150–54, and vol. 253, fols. 272–78. The grateful French provided him a 2,000-escudo annual pension in 1717, hoping that he might someday regain influence, but he never did. Huxelles to Saint Aignan, Versailles, January 2, 1717, AAE:CPE, vol. 257, fols. 27–32.

[77] Kamen, *Philip V*, pp. 22, 95, 124–25. The instruction to Extraordinary Envoy Marquis de Maulevrier, Versailles, July 9, 1720, AAE:CPE, vol. 295, fols. 217–36 contains revealing information on the French concerns about Popoli. For San Felipe, see José Antonio Armillas Vicente, "La política exterior de los primeros Borbones," *Historia general de España y América: La España de las reformas hasta el final del reino de Carlos IV*, X-2, coordinated by Carlos E. Corona and José Antonio Armillas Vicente (Madrid: Rialp, 1984), p. 276 and San Felipe's *Comentarios de la guerra de España e historia de su rey Felipe V, el animoso*. This work was republished in the *Biblioteca de Autores Españoles* (Madrid: Editorial Atlas, 1957), with a preliminary study by Carlos Seco Serrano. An impressive number of Italian officers penetrated the lower ranks as well. See Juan Marchena Fernández, "Italianos al servicio del rey de España en el ejército de América, 1740–1815," in *Italiani al servizio straniero in etá moderna: Annali di storia militare europea* (Milan 2008), pp. 135–77.

[78] Castro, *A la sombra de Felipe V*, pp. 321, 328.

[79] Pérez Samper, *Isabel de Farnesio*, pp. 64, 331–32, 385, 397, 416, 424, 427–28.

[80] Jean O. McLachlan, *Trade and Peace with Old Spain, 1667–1750* (Cambridge: University Press, 1940), chap. 2.

allowed them access to the colonial trade. Defined in the commercial treaty of 1667, these rights – with antecedents dating back to three *cédulas* issued in 1645 – mirrored privileges that the Hanseatic League had gained under the Treaty of Munster in 1648, but they had precedents going back to at least 1609. The British received broad immunities from intrusive customs inspections both of ships at anchor in Spanish ports and of English warehouses. These protections were upheld by a special judge conservator (*juez conservador*) nominated by the British and technically confirmed by Madrid, who adjudicated any cases involving British traders. A resident British consul in Cádiz complemented the powers of the judge conservator, giving British citizens what amounted to extra-territoriality and thus investing them with broad immunities from Spanish justice. The most favored nation status conceded in 1667 also assured the British the same tariff rates as their competitors, the Dutch and the French.[81] Article 10 of the 1667 treaty, protecting English traders from threatening inspections, was incorporated virtually word for word into the later Utrecht settlement.[82]

Some two and a half years after the preliminary commercial settlement with Britain at Utrecht, the Treaty of Madrid (December 14, 1715) clarified those points left muddled in 1713. Often known for George Bubb-Dodington, the young envoy who negotiated it, this agreement confirmed the tariff rates established in 1667, granting English residents most favored nation status. The treaty also specified that the duties paid by the English would not exceed those for the Spanish; and it confirmed that English exports would pay the *palmeo*, a tax assessed by volume. The document further affirmed the English right to select a judge conservator. It also conceded them the right to mine salt at the small island of Tortuga off the Venezuelan coast, which provided a strategic foothold along the Spanish Main for contraband traders.[83] These concessions were the price Alberoni paid for London's diplomatic support for Spanish aspirations in Italy, which now intensified

[81] Memoires, privileges of English and Dutch consuls in Spanish ports, Madrid, December 1714, Huxelles, Versailles, 1716, and complaints in Spanish ports, Madrid, August 7, 1720, AAE: CPE, vol. 234, fols. 181–85, vol. 253, fols. 321–24 and vol. 298, fols. 217–37; Stanley J. and Barbara H. Stein, *Silver, Trade, and War: Spain and America in the Making of Early Modern Europe* (Baltimore: Johns Hopkins University Press, 2000), pp. 58–67.

[82] Copy, treaty articles, Spain and England, May 25, 1667, AAE:CPE, vol. 253, fols. 326–27; Concepción Menéndez Vives and Carmen Torroja Menéndez, *Tratados Internacionales suscritos por España ... (siglos XII al XVII)* (Madrid: Dirección de Archivos Estatales, 1991), pp. 67–71, 84–85.

[83] A copy of this treaty, signed in Madrid by Bubb and the Marqués de Bedmar, can be found in the AAE:CPE, vol. 243, fols. 157–60, and in Charles Jenkinson (comp.), *A Collection of all the Treaties of Peace, Alliance, and Commerce, between Great Britain and other Powers from the Treaty Signed at Munster in 1648, to the Treaties Signed at Paris in 1783 ...*, II (London, J. DeBrett, 1785). The Spanish rates were 5 percent upon leaving Andalusia, 2 percent upon arrival in America, 5 percent when departing America, and 2 percent upon reaching Spain. Royal *cédula*, August 14, 1714, AAE:CPE, vol. 230, fols. 190–93.

with the new queen's first pregnancy.[84] Alberoni would eventually sacrifice Spanish commercial priorities in America to such dynastic objectives, and this interplay between reform and dynastic claims would become a recurrent theme throughout the remaining years of the partnership between Philip V and Elizabeth.[85]

A second Anglo-Spanish treaty followed on May 26, 1716. No *Galeones* or *Flotas* had sailed in 1714, and the two ships of permission dispatched in 1715 had earned disappointing profits. The flota commanded by López Pintado arrived in Mexico in November, but port authorities levied taxes on the privileged cargo of the South Sea Company in apparent contravention of the promised exemptions. Meanwhile in Cartagena, where a mini-fair was held in January 1716, Spanish officials found that excess tonnage had arrived in the English permission ship and so embargoed its entire cargo, causing a serious dispute with the South Sea Company that would last for decades.[86] The incident also demonstrated that Spanish officials would use any opportunity to harass British merchants seeking to trade with the Indies and to deny them rights granted in the Utrecht and Bubb treaties.

Under the additional refinements in a second Bubb Treaty, Madrid affirmed its commitment to mount fleets annually to Veracruz and Portobelo. If the Spanish vessels did not arrive on schedule, the ships of permission could begin sales without them after waiting four months.[87] And to compensate for the 1,500-ton deficit for the years 1714–1716, each such ship to sail between 1717 and 1726 was allowed to carry an extra 150 tons. The Bubb treaties represented yet another triumph for the artful British, albeit a temporary one.[88] Alberoni had hoped through these concessions to cultivate a rapprochement with the British, possibly resulting in an alliance. Bubb proposed just such a step, but Foreign Minister James Stanhope rejected the idea. Unknown to Alberoni, London was playing a duplicitous game. In Vienna, days before the second Bubb Treaty, Britain had secretly reestablished its alliance with the emperor, pledging to support his territorial claims in Italy rather than Spain's.[89]

[84] McLachlan, *Trade and Peace*, pp. 21–22, 67–70. The queen's ambitions are discussed in Saint Aignan to His Majesty, Aranjuez, June 24, 1715, AAE:CPE, vol. 241, fols. 84–85. Charles was born on January 20, 1716.

[85] Lucio Mijares, "Política exterior: La diplomacia," *Historia general de España y América: América en el siglo XVIII, los primeros borbones*, XI-1, coordinated by Luis Navarro García (Madrid: Rialp, 1983), pp. 82–83.

[86] Walker, *Spanish Politics and Imperial Trade*, pp. 81–87. Subsequent intelligence indicated that British losses at Cartagena were vastly exaggerated. Vera Lee Brown, "The South Sea Company and Contraband Trade," *The American Historical Review*, 31 (July 1926), p. 668.

[87] A copy can be found in AAE:CPE, vol. 251, fols. 54–64.

[88] McLachlan, *Trade and Peace*, pp. 24, 73.

[89] Mijares, "Política exterior," p. 83.

French ships entering Spanish ports had enjoyed broad immunities dating back to the Treaty of the Pyrenees of 1659. A seminal agreement for Paris, this accord made French commercial rights equal to the privileges enjoyed by the English and by the Hanseatic League. In 1670, following its agreement with London three years previously, Spain renewed these French guarantees.[90] Minister of State Grimaldo reaffirmed them once again in March 1713.[91] As for the Dutch, they had also long enjoyed a privileged status in Andalusia, having secured status equal to the north Germans under treaty arrangements defined in 1651.[92]

During this period, the British interest in Cádiz waned, owing to the lucrative contraband opportunities developing for them in the Caribbean and elsewhere. The same was true of the Dutch, who held island bases on the Spanish Main. The French penetration of the Spanish American trade, however, came largely through the *gaditano* marketplace, where they remained the dominant outside commercial force.[93] Although Spanish law prohibited direct foreign entry into the American trade, the French circumvented this prohibition. As Roman Catholics, they gained acceptance more easily than the English or the Dutch. Frenchmen procured locals to act on their behalf, frequently even marrying *gaditanas*, begetting Spanish-born children.[94] The War of Succession had afforded a golden opportunity to strengthen these ties.

Exploiting their position as ally, the French had effectively taken control of the Peruvian trade, but Alberoni sought to end their commercial penetration in the Pacific trading zone. Under pressure from Madrid, Versailles had forbidden further sailings to the Spanish Pacific with the threat of severe penalties. Alberoni capped his struggle to regain control of the Peruvian

---

[90] Memoire, Huxelles, 1716, and abstract, article 22, Treaty of Spain and the Hanseatic League, 1648; articles 3, 6, 10, 14, and 15, Treaty of the Pyrenees, 1659; article 10, Anglo-Spanish Commercial Treaty, 1667, AAE:CPE, vol. 253, fols. 321–28.

[91] Memoire, documenting the vexatious treatment of French commerce, Spain, August 7, 1720, AAE:CPE, vol. 298, fols. 217–37.

[92] Memoire, privileges and prerogatives of the English and Dutch consuls in the ports of Spain, December 1714, AAE:CPE, vol. 234, fols. 181–85. See also Ana Crespo Solana, *Entre Cádiz y los Países Bajos: Una comunidad mercantil en la ciudad de la ilustración* (Cádiz: Ayuntamiento de Cádiz, 2001), pp. 38–41. For published descriptions of foreign dominance in Cádiz, see Antonio Domínguez Ortiz, *Los extranjeros en la vida española durante el siglo XVII y otros artículos* (Seville: Diputación de Sevilla, 1996), pp. 43–46 and José María Oliva Melgar, "La Metrópoli sin territorio. ¿Crisis del comercio de Indias en el siglo XVII o pérdida del control del monopolio?," in Carlos Martínez Shaw and Oliva Melgar (eds.), *El sistema atlántico español (siglos XVII-XIX)* (Madrid: Marcial Pons, 2005), pp. 19–73.

[93] Malamud Rikles, *Cádiz y Saint Malo*, p. 78.

[94] Manuel Bustos Rodríguez, *Cádiz en el sistema atlántico: La ciudad, sus comerciantes y la actividad mercantil (1650–1830)* (Cádiz: Universidad de Cádiz, 2005), pp. 54, 140–44, 166–69; Margarita García-Mauriño Mundi, *La pugna entre el Consulado y los jenízaros por las exportaciones a Indias (1720–1765)*, (Sevilla: Universidad de Sevilla, 1999) pp. 43–53.

trade by dispatching to Lima an Italian confidant, the Prince of San Bueno (Carmine Nicolás Carácciolo), as viceroy in 1716, followed by the deployment of a squadron of four ships that promptly began clearing the Peruvian coast of French merchantmen.[95]

While still keeping watchful eye on the Dutch, the French now complained endlessly about the British abusing their "excessive" privileges, but this apparent concern for their Spanish cousins was little more than thinly disguised jealousy against their Anglo rivals.[96] Saint Aignan understood quite clearly what was at stake when he remarked that "should the accord [asiento] flourish over the treaty's thirty-year duration ... England has very much assured itself the necessary means for the aggrandizement of its power in the Indies."[97] Meanwhile, the death of Louis XIV on September 1, 1715, led to the succession of Philip's nephew, the child king Louis XV, and to the regency of his personal enemy, the Duke of Orleans. Their animosity dated back to differences that developed while the duke served in Spain during the War of Succession, and they were now aggravated by Philip's ill-disguised longing to gain the French throne.[98]

The French and Dutch had expected their commercial houses in Cádiz to resume business as usual in the aftermath of Utrecht, but such hopes quickly faded as Alberoni attempted to secure control over Spain's Atlantic ports from foreign penetration. While he aimed to nurture close collaboration with the British, as reflected in the two Bubb treaties, Alberoni showed no such inclination toward Versailles. As early as March 1716, a series of commercial incidents flared along the Mediterranean coast involving the French consulates in Barcelona, Valencia, and Alicante.[99] By royal order issued in February, foreign consuls became simple advocates.[100] Moreover, in contravention of

[95] John R. Fisher, *Bourbon Peru, 1750–1824* (Liverpool: Liverpool University Press, 2003), pp. 15–17; Mijares, "Política exterior," pp. 81–82; Malamud Rikles, *Cádiz y Saint Malo*, pp. 62–67, 78, 161–67, 242–44, 249.

[96] "Reflecions sur les prejudices qui resulteront a l'Espagne...," in Saint Aignan to Versailles, Madrid, August 1715, and Saint Aignan to His Majesty, Madrid, December 14, 1715, AAE: CPE, vol. 242, fols. 31–45, and vol. 243, fols. 164–82. A revealing summary of French frustration and objectives appears in Memoire, consul for commerce, Madrid, 1720, AAE: CPE, vol. 295, fols. 65–79. "Les Anglois aruont en vain extorque le Traite de Madrid du 1 Decembre 1715." "It would be a profound injustice to attempt to uphold its enforcement to our exclusion and the total ruin of our commerce ... to render us outsiders in the commerce of Spain, while the English are treated like children of the home." This jealousy and feigned concern for Spanish rights lingered. Excellent examples can be found in the Memoire, commercial treaty arrangements, 1720, AAE:CPE, vol. 295, fols. 122 ff.

[97] Saint Aignan to His Majesty, Madrid, June 12, 1716, AAE:CPE, vol. 251, fols. 61–76.

[98] Kamen, *Philip V*, pp. 61–62

[99] Saint Aignan to His Majesty, Madrid, March 2, 1716, the Escorial, March 16, 1716, Aranjuez, May 11, 1716, AAE:CPE, vol. 250, fols. 4–11, 34–42, 205–12. One issue concerned the consulates' right to fly the royal coat of arms. See also, intelligence reports, np., 1716, AAE:CPE, vol. 251, fols. 176–78, 208–209.

[100] McLachlan, *Trade and Peace*, p. 76.

historic treaty guarantees, customs officials boarded and searched ships aggressively at anchor in Spanish harbors; in Valencia they even entered a French warehouse.[101] To make matters worse, a French merchantman was seized in San Juan, Puerto Rico.[102] In all cases, Spanish authorities presented legal justifications for their actions, but to Versailles, accustomed to enjoying broad liberties, it appeared that dangerous new policies now undermined its commercial relations with Spain. The French quite correctly associated this change to the emergence of Alberoni and to his pro-British inclinations.[103] These new Spanish initiatives represented Alberoni's first attempt to assert control over Spanish ports and, hence, over the larger Spanish Atlantic commercial system.

Differences over how to resolve outstanding commercial disputes festered as the summer wore on, and communications between Saint Aignan and Alberoni broke down.[104] Also uneasy over the second Bubb Treaty, Regent Orleans and Minister of State Marquis de Huxelles sensed an opportunity to regain lost ground when the Spanish court announced the festivities to be held in connection with the baptism of the infante Philip.[105] To be held on August 25, the feast day of St. Louis, the French hoped that this event might become a Bourbon moment. Equipped with a diamond-studded cross to adorn the child, as well as a portrait of his cousin, King Louis, Versailles dispatched the Marquis de Louville as envoy extraordinary to Madrid during late July. A confidant of Orleans, Louville also bore personal letters from the regent to Elizabeth and Philip, requesting that they receive his envoy and discuss the issues dividing the two courts. Louville was instructed to bypass Alberoni, delivering the messages directly upon his introduction to the royal family.[106] As for his rivals, Orleans aimed to promote a "[c]oup against Italians and once and for all destroy Alberoni himself."[107]

Recent events raised hopes for the Marquis de Louville's success. Word had reached Madrid in late June of the British-Austrian alliance, leading the French

---

[101] Memoires, violence in Valencia, Paris, March 31, 1716, Huxelles, Versailles, 1716, AAE: CPE, vol. 250, fols. 98–99, vol. 253, fols. 321–34.

[102] Crown to Saint Aignan, Paris, March 31, 1716, AAE:CPE, vol. 250, fols. 61–66.

[103] Saint Aignan to the crown, Madrid, March 2, 16, and 24, 1716, Segovia, March 29, and Aranjuez, April 19, and to Huxelles, Segovia, March 29, 1716, AAE:CPE, vol. 250, fols. 12–17, 26–33, 34–42, 88–97, 133–39.

[104] In the words of Saint Aignan, "He told me that I came to set traps, that he did not want to see me again, and that he did not care about either me or my overtures." Saint Aignan to His Majesty, Aranjuez, May 3, 1716, AAE:CPE, vol. 250, fols. 182–91. The exchange was especially remarkable in that Alberoni was a mere abbot and Saint Aignan a duke. See also Huxelles to Saint Aignan, Paris, August 4, 1716, and Saint Aignan to the crown, Madrid, September 7, 1716, AAE:CPE, vol. 252, fols. 5, 237–42.

[105] Philip, son of Marie Louise, was born June 7, 1712. He died in December 1719.

[106] Secret instructions, Louville, Versailles, June 24, 1716, with letters for Elizabeth and Philip, AAE:CPE, vol. 251, fols. 141–49.

[107] Ibid.; Huxelles to Saint Aignan, Versailles, August 18, 1716, AAE:CPE, vol. 252, fols. 113–14.

to believe that the Spanish monarchs might be more receptive to their overtures. Orleans's letter to Philip envisioned great prosperity for both powers arising from close commercial cooperation. In addition, Ambassador Saint Aignan had detected increasing anti-Alberoni sentiment in Madrid. During a recent public procession held in veneration of the Blessed Sacrament, where he had ridden close to the person of the king, the ambassador had clearly heard shouts of "long live Felipe V, death to the traitor."[108]

Anticipating Orleans's designs, the wily Alberoni simply denied Louville entrance to Court on the implausible grounds that he was in disgrace back home. Versailles reacted with disbelief and fury.[109] To make matters worse, the French also learned of the confiscation of two French ships in Barcelona, which reinforced their worst fears about a fundamental change in Spanish commercial policy. Regarding these changes, Huxelles gave a pointed directive on the matter to Saint Aignan: "It appears to His Highness the Regent that not only the commerce of the King's subjects is at stake but the honor of the French flag as well."[110] In short, with the dynasty's honor offended, grounds for war now existed. Orleans soon thereafter issued secret instructions to the ambassador to work behind the scenes at court to rid Spain of the Italian intruder.[111] Louville departed Madrid on August 24, the day before the baptism, and although Saint Aignan delivered the presents, relations remained frigid.[112]

Once news of the Austrian alliance exposed British duplicity, they received treatment similar to the French in Spanish ports. Alberoni's conciliatory policies were meant to produce opportunities on the continent, and when it became clear that British priorities differed from his own, they too confronted stubborn intransigence at court regarding their mounting complaints about violations of treaty rights. And to make matters worse, the Royal Treasury demanded donations from British merchants, in a manner similar to the services expected of the *Consulado*. As the British consul in Alicante put it, "they do with us what they will."[113]

British and French protests grew ever more strident as Alberoni's intention to ignore their commercial privileges and restrict foreign influences at Spanish ports became clear.[114] Discussions then began in earnest among

---

[108] Saint Aignan to the crown, Madrid, June 17 and 29, 1716, and July 20, 1716, AAE:CPE, vol. 251, fols. 98–127, 168–70, and vol. 252, fols. 2–4.

[109] Reports, Saint Aignan, July 30, 1716, and Louville, Madrid, July 30, 1716, AAE:CPE, vol. 252, fols. 43–44, 51–68, 69–77, 86–92.

[110] Huxelles to Saint Aignan, Paris, August 4, 1716, AAE:CPE, vol. 252, fol. 5.

[111] Secret memoire, Duke of Orleans to Saint Aignan, Versailles, August, 1716, AAE:CPE, vol. 252, fols. 225–27.

[112] Saint Aignan to Huxelles, Madrid, August 24 and 30, 1716, AAE:CPE, vol. 252, fols. 202, 216–18.

[113] Quoted in McLachlan, *Trade and Peace*, p. 76.

[114] Memoire, new provocations in Spain, Paris, August, 1716, and Saint Aignan to the crown, Madrid, September 7, 1716, AAE:CPE, vol. 252, fols. 117–18, 237–42.

Versailles, London, and the Hague concerning joint action to uphold their historic prerogatives. These negotiations, significantly, occurred well before fears arose concerning possible Spanish adventurism in Italy. By late August 1716, the preliminaries for a Triple Alliance had been drafted, but the signatories withheld final approval and kept the proceedings secret.[115] No relaxation of Spanish policy occurred, however, and that fall a royal decree blocked the entrance into Spain of chocolate and sugar from the French colonies in order to protect Spanish American interests in Caracas and Havana.[116] On November 28, 1716, London and Paris formalized a Dual Alliance committed specifically to uphold the Utrecht Treaties.

Alberoni remained unintimidated by these diplomatic deals, and he boldly challenged his rivals with his decree of December 23, commanding all customs authorities to enact a systematized, rigorous inspection of ships entering the ports of Spain. Treaty arrangements had provided that only one customs official might board such ships and then only after three days at anchor and after proper arrangements had been made with the resident consul. Alberoni's decree tripled the number of the officials assigned to board ships and ignored the traditional restraints placed upon them.[117] The rigorous implementation of the decree in Cádiz raised serious concerns in Versailles, and news that a French ship offered resistance and fled Barcelona further inflamed emotions.[118] Meanwhile, the Netherlands, which nurtured complaints similar to the French and the British, formally joined the anti-Alberoni pact on January 4, 1717.[119] Meanwhile, the Italian established the Marine Intendancy in Cádiz under José Patiño on January 28, unifying the Caribbean and Mediterranean fleets under a single command. This move explicitly entailed the controversial transfer of the *Casa de la Contratación* and the *Consulado* from Seville to Cádiz.

Most historians have argued that the Triple Alliance arose over fears that the new regime in Spain threatened dynastic arrangements sanctioned by

---

[115] A copy of the preliminary treaty of August 24, 1716, can be found in AAE; Traites, Grande Bretagne, TR 103. By September, Saint Aignan was aware of "*la negociation de l'alliance que Votre Majesté* [Regent Orleans] *se propose de conclure*," but he was under instructions to keep the matter confidential. Saint Aignan to the crown, Madrid, September 28, 1716, and Huxelles to Saint Aignan, Versailles, October 27, 1716, AAE:CPE, vol. 252, fols. 280–86 and vol. 253, fols. 83–87.

[116] Memoire, commercial treaty arrangements, 1720, AAE:CPE, vol. 295, fols. 122–41.

[117] Royal decree, Madrid, December 23, 1716, and memoire on customs visitations in Spanish ports, Paris, April 26, 1717, AAE:CPE, vol. 253, fols. 293–96, and vol. 261, fols. 82–85.

[118] Statement, Spanish Ambassador Prince of Cellamare, Paris, January 28, 1717; memoire (the visitation of French ships in Spanish ports), Paris, April 26, 1717, AAE:CPE, vol. 261, fols. 12–18, 82–85.

[119] Alberoni reacted coolly. St Aignan to Huxelles, Madrid, January 25, 1717, AAE:CPE, vol. 257, fols. 54–57.

Utrecht. This dimension was a less important part of the mix.[120] Philip's yearning to return to France was ill-disguised and raised concerns at Versailles, where a sickly youth reigned. Moreover, Madrid's sympathy for the Jacobite pretender irritated London. These, however, were distant threats and hardly immediate causes for a general war. In addition, the Dutch also had no dynastic claims to preserve. Instead, the commercial issues raised in Spanish ports clearly fueled the initial fires of war. The Triple Alliance aimed to uphold the Utrecht settlement in the broadest sense, being committed to "defending all of the kingdoms, provinces, states, *rights, immunities, and advantages*, which each of the said allies respectively shall really be possessed of, at the time of the signing of this alliance."[121] Even so, a declaration of war would not follow for another year, and by then the crisis would also involve directly the dynastic, territorial designs of Elizabeth and Philip in Italy, drawing Spain into armed hostilities.

WAR, DEFEAT, AND THE DOWNFALL OF ALBERONI

Alberoni's Italian designs arose from the maternal ambitions of Elizabeth Farnese, shared by the king, which eventually overwhelmed efforts to reform the Spanish Atlantic commercial system. With the birth of their son, Charles (who had three surviving older half-brothers ahead of him to inherit the Spanish throne) in 1716, Elizabeth and Philip turned their territorial ambitions toward Italy. Her family ties to the Farnese and Medicis afforded her claims to the northern Italian duchies of Parma and Plasencia and of Tuscany, and she had ambitions to gain territories there for Charles and future offspring. Elizabeth also hoped that securing Italian lands would ensure a stable future for herself after Philip's demise, when she might find herself reduced to a dowager in Spain.[122] These ambitions multiplied when Philip was born in 1720, although his older half-brother, also named Philip, had died the previous year.[123] As for the king, he displayed highly bellicose inclinations

---

[120] In the literature on Spanish America, this interpretation dates back at least to Herbert Ingram Priestley, *José de Gálvez: Visitor-General of New Spain (1765–1771)* (Berkeley: University of California Press, 1916), pp. 14–15. See also Mijares, "Política exterior," p. 83.

[121] Italics by the authors. A Treaty of Alliance between … France … Great Britain, and … the United Provinces … January 4, 1717, art. V, in Jenkinson, *A Collection of all the Treaties*, II, p. 192. A contemporary manuscript account, assembled by one Monsieur Montuela, "Analyse historique et raisonnée des negotiations relatives au traité de la Quadruple Alliance et autres depuis la paix d'Utrech jusqu'à celle conclue en 1739 entre la France et l'Autriche," can be found in AAE: Memoirs et Documents Fonds Divers (hereinafter MDFD), vol. 87, fols. 178–380.

[122] Antonio Béthencourt massieu, *Patiño en la política internacional de Fellipe V*, with introduction by Vicente Palacio Atard (Valladolid: Universidad de Valladolid, 1954), p. 33.

[123] The infante Philip was born on March 15, 1720, three and one-half months after his half-brother's death. The king and queen elected to give him the same name as the son they had tragically lost. Grimaldo to Abad Dubois, Madrid, January 1, 1720, and Philip V to Louis

throughout his reign, and the very thought of armed conflict momentarily restored him to lucidity.[124]

While Alberoni eventually hoped to advance Elizabeth's dynastic claims in the north, as already shown during his negotiation of the Bubb treaties, the Italian territories that Spain had ceded under the Utrecht treaties commanded greater urgency following the birth of Charles. These included Sardinia and Naples, which had gone to the emperor, and Sicily, which went to the king of Savoy. The reassertion of Madrid's control over its ports preceded, and then paralleled, its plans to retake both islands. The whole process began when a naval force first assembled in Barcelona by Marine Intendant José Patiño seized Sardinia in August 1717.[125] At the same time, Spanish authorities continued to harass allied commerce in Cádiz. The British consul reported that "the ministers [Spanish] interpret the Articles of Peace and observe them or not observe them as they please, and it's their conveniency and in conclusion we are in all respects on a worse foot than the trade was before the late war." He went on to lament that "from the prospect I have of affairs I fear it will be everyday worse."[126]

In Madrid, local anger against Alberoni ran deep, which became evident in the spring of 1717 when the monarchs left the capital. Tragedy had struck the royal family in April when the month-old infante Francisco died during convulsions brought on by erysipelas.[127] In early May, Philip and Elizabeth, accompanied by the king's Jesuit confessor Fr. Guillermo Daubenton, Alberoni, and the three secretaries of the Office, visited San Lorenzo del Escorial, where the child's remains had been interred. The following day, they continued on to Segovia and a change of scene.[128] Disturbing reports soon arrived, however, that vitriolic anti-government sentiment had appeared in Madrid, in part aroused by the exile of several nobles suspected of loyalty to the Austrian Hapsburgs. Much hostility was aimed directly at Alberoni. The Italian's office was swamped with anonymous

XV, Madrid, March 15, 1720, AAE:CPE, vol. 294, fols. 2, 233–34. As discussed later, their second son, Francisco, died a month after he was born in 1717.

[124] For Philip's role in shaping policy and his militant inclinations, see Kamen, *Philip V*, pp. 72, 105–11, 119–20, 195. In the end, Kamen describes Spain's repeated adventures in Italy as the "wars of Elizabeth Farnese," p. 237.

[125] Alberoni had initially misled the allies about his intentions through assurances that the fleet aimed to help protect Christian Italy from the Turks. Saint Aignan to His Majesty, Aranjuez, May 3, 1716, and Madrid, March 1, 1717, AAE:CPE, vol. 250, fols. 182–91 and vol. 257, fols. 119–22.

[126] Quoted in McLachlan, *Trade and Peace*, p. 74.

[127] Born on March 21, Francisco died on April 21. Philip V to Louis XV, Madrid, March 21, 1717, and Saint Aignan to Huxelles, April 21, 1717, AAE:CPE, vol. 257, fols. 175, 241–43.

[128] Saint Aignan to His Majesty, Madrid, May 3, 1717, AAE:CPE, vol. 258, fols 3–5. As the ambassador commented the following month, "It cannot be doubted also that he (Alberoni) cannot find any support from the Spanish and that, on the contrary, they bear with difficulty his administration and the absolute power that he wields." Saint Aignan to His Majesty, Madrid, June 18, 1717, AAE:CPE, vol. 258, fol. 47.

hate messages, while pasquinades appeared on his door.[129] Although origi-nally planning to participate in Madrid's Corpus Christi procession, the monarchs prudently elected instead to spend the month of June at the Escorial before moving on for the remainder of the summer at El Pardo on the capital's outskirts.[130]

When word arrived in July that Alberoni, backed by the royal family, had been made a cardinal, the elevation both irritated his critics and enhanced his prestige. Nonetheless, his hold on power remained tenuous.[131] When Spain successfully seized Sardinia the following month, the operation helped to muffle his critics further.[132] As a contemporary chronicler, Vicente Bacallar, commented, "Spain never tolerated a more inflexible government than his ... with the coveted purple snatched from the Pontiff's hands, he unleashed his schemes, all calculated to win glory."[133]

Yet French Ambassador Saint Aignan perceptively understood the fragility of the Italian's position: "The Abbot Alberoni will never find support among the Spanish, [while] at the same time I do not doubt that those who nurture hopes of making themselves masters of the government would happily sacri-fice him."[134] The ambassador later put it more succinctly: "The principal objective ... is the reestablishment of the Spanish government and the banish-ment of the Italians."[135] Later that summer, the king incurred a severe siege of mental instability that afflicted him well into the autumn.[136]

Once Alberoni's military objectives in Italy became evident, alarm spread through the courts of Europe, and members of the Triple Alliance prepared for military action to counter Spanish aggression. Matters worsened when the cardinal raised the stakes and struck again, occupying Sicily in June 1718. The emperor then joined the coalition, thus making it the Quadruple Alliance. Armed conflict erupted when the British under Admiral George Byng

---

[129] Saint Aignan to His Majesty, Segovia, May 10, 1717, AAE:CPE, vol. 258, fols. 17–21. See also Saint Aignan to His Majesty, Segovia, May 17, El Escorial, June 7 and 14, 1717, and Saint Aignan to Huxelles, Segovia, May 17, 1717, and El Escorial, June 21, 1717, AAE:CPE, vol. 258, fols 33–40, 66–69, 81–83 and vol. 261, fols. 171–73.

[130] Saint Aignan to His Majesty, Madrid, May 3 and 24, 1717, AAE:CPE, vol. 258, fols. 3–5, 40–43.

[131] San Aignan to Huxelles, Madrid, July 25, 1717, AAE:CPE, vol. 259, fols. 61–64. The queen had written personally to the pope. Saint Aignan to His Majesty, Madrid, May 31, 1717, AAE:CPE, vol. 258, fols. 51–53.

[132] Broadsides had continued to appear on into mid-July. Saint Aignan to Huxelles, Madrid, July 19, 1717, AAE:CPE, vol. 259, fols. 58–59.

[133] Quoted in García, *Felipe V*, p. 152.

[134] Saint Aignan to His Majesty, the Escorial, June 21, 1717, AAE:CPE, vol. 258, fols. 90–92.

[135] "Memoire sur la situation presente de la Cour d'Espagne" in Saint Aignan to Huxelles, Madrid, November 26, 1717, AAE:CPE, vol. 260, fols. 304–308.

[136] Saint Aignan to Huxelles, Madrid, September 6 and 29, October 19 and 26, and November 9, 1717; Saint Aignan to His Majesty, Madrid, October 25–26, November 8 and 22, and December 6, 13, and 20, 1717, AAE:CPE, vol. 260, fols. 6–8, 110–11, 168–71, 173–78, 262–67, 272–73, 293–94, 327–28, 362–64, 391–93.

destroyed a large Spanish naval force off Cape Passaro near Sicily on August 11, 1718, even before a declaration of war. The Netherlands, preferring to defend its commercial interests separately and without war, withdrew from the alliance, not returning until the following year.[137] Meanwhile, the king of Savoy, who saw his claim to Sicily under attack, joined in November.[138]

The declaration of war did not follow immediately, as both London and Versailles persisted in their attempts to resolve the crisis diplomatically.[139] Rather than soften his policy regarding Spanish commerce, however, Alberoni broadened his initiatives. When the *Flota* under the command of Antonio Serrano arrived in Cádiz on August 16, 1718, some 800,000 pesos belonging to French traders were seized on grounds of improper registry.[140] This challenge to foreign penetration of the American trade deepened in October when *gaditano* customs officials, backed by armed guards, dared violate the immunities accorded to French warehouses, seizing alleged contraband and business records.[141]

The British raised similar grievances about searches and seizures during the summer and fall of 1718, and they also complained about suffering losses to Spanish privateers in Caribbean waters.[142] In response to Madrid's angry inquiry into the meaning of Byng's ambush of the Spain Mediterranean fleet, Foreign Minister Craggs delivered what amounted to an ultimatum to the Spanish ambassador. Although first deploring Spain's transgressions in Italy, and then accusing the Spanish navy of "starting the hostilities" at Cape Passaro, Craggs detailed four areas of Spanish misconduct affecting trade that required correction. He charged that Madrid had violated its commitments by arbitrarily imposing tariffs on British merchandise. It had excluded from its ports products permitted by treaty. Spain had refused the South Sea Company *cédulas* for its annual ships.[143] Finally, it had forcefully embargoed

---

[137] Kamen, *Philip V*, pp. 122–24; Crespo, *Entre Cádiz y los Países Bajas*, pp. 68–69. The emperor joined on July 18, 1718.

[138] Armillas Vicente, "La política exterior," p. 278

[139] Derek McKay, *Allies of Convenience: Diplomatic Relations between Great Britain and Austria* (New York: Garland Publishers, 1986), pp. 203–207.

[140] Instructions, Marquis de Maulevrier, Paris, September, 1720, AAE:CPE, vol. 296, fols. 103–07; Antonio García-Baquero González, *Cádiz y el Atlántico (1717–1778)*, I (Sevilla: Escuela de Estudios Hispano-Americanos, 1976), pp. 280–81. The French listed this sum as "piastras," which was the equivalent of Spanish "pesos." Malamud Rikles, *Cádiz y Saint Malo*, p. 44.

[141] Memoire on bad treatment and provocations, Cádiz, August 7, 1720, AAE:CPE, vol. 298, fols. 217–37. As early as May 1717, ships arriving via the Barbary Coast had simply been denied entrance into Cádiz.

[142] Stanhope to Grimaldo, Madrid, September 18, 1718, AHN, Estado, leg. 2819; McKay, *Diplomatic Relations*, p. 207.

[143] "The South Sea Company has been denied the cédulas for the annual ships in violation of what the treaty stipulates, without giving a better reason than the Court in Madrid does not find it convenient to issue them." Craggs to Ambassador Marqués de Monteleón, London, n.d., AHN, Estado, leg. 2819.

British vessels in all the ports of Spain, even making them unload their cargoes. Moreover, some individuals daring to resist these impositions had their ears cropped! Craggs declared that Britain had no intention of foregoing its privileges within the Spanish commercial system.[144] London declared war on December 17, and Versailles followed on January 9.[145] By this time, the Spanish had expelled French Ambassador Saint Aignan.[146] The French had ousted Spanish Ambassador Cellamare in December and used his alleged conspiracy against the regency to justify the decision to begin hostilities.[147]

Spain suffered rapid, humiliating, and decisive defeats in the war. French forces quickly occupied the Basque provinces of Álava, Guipúzcoa, and Vizcaya, burning the shipyard at Pasajes. They later invaded Catalonia, while in America an expedition advanced from New Orleans to seize Pensacola, and a small French detachment harassed the Spanish mission at Los Adaes in east Texas.[148] The British, who had destroyed most of the Spanish navy at Cape Passaro, shelled shipyards along the Basque and Cantabrian coasts and later invaded Galicia. And Austrian forces, transported by the British navy, landed in Sicily. The Principe Pío, summoned from Barcelona, led the resistance but to no avail.[149]

On December 5, 1719, Philip directed Miguel Durán to deliver a decree written with the royal hand, notifying Alberoni of his dismissal. He was given eight days to abandon Madrid, three weeks to be out of Spain, and commanded never to appear at court or any other place where he might encounter the monarchs.[150] By a *cédula* of January 26, 1720, Philip reluctantly surrendered by adhering to the demands of the Quadruple Alliance. Spain signed a formal armistice on February 16–17.[151] The man of the hour was Grimaldo, who must have taken immense personal satisfaction from the demise of Alberoni. He had been the only one of the old ruling clique to survive the fall of the Princess Ursins, and now he had survived Alberoni as well. Although overshadowed by the cardinal, the Minister of State had remained

---

[144] Ibid.

[145] Declaration of War, Paris, January 9, 1719, AHN, Estado, leg. 2819. It will be recalled that the emperor had technically remained at war with Philip since the disputed succession.

[146] Royal decree, El Pardo, December 10, 1718, AHN, Estado, leg. 2819.

[147] Royal flier, Cellamare expulsion, Paris, December, 1718, AHN, Estado, leg. 2819. See also Kamen, *Philip V*, pp. 123–24; Armillas, "La política exterior," p. 278.

[148] Giraud, Marcel, *Histoire de la Louisiane Francaise*, III, *L'Époque de John Law* (1717–1720) (Paris: Presses Universitaires de France, 1966), pp. 299–303 ; Donald E. Chipman, *Spanish Texas, 1519–1821* (Austin: University of Texas Press, 1992), p. 118.

[149] Kamen, *Philip V*, pp. 124–27.

[150] Castellano, *Gobierno y poder*, p. 83.

[151] Royal *cédulas*, Madrid, January 26, March 8, and April 4, and San Lorenzo, August 30, 1720, AAE:CPE, vol. 295, fols. 13–15 and vol. 298, fols. 38–39, 101–102, 250–53; "Tratado de la Cuádruple Alianza," The Hague, February 17, 1721, *Colección de los tratados de paz, alianza, comercio, etc. ajustados por la corona de España ... de orden del Rey*, II (Madrid 1800), pp. 3–46.

close to the king, had commanded Alberoni's respect, and in recent years had served as the personal secretary of the queen.[152] Tinajero, the other dominant figure from the years before the Alberoni ascendancy, had died in August 1717.[153]

DEFEAT AND THE PROJECT OF 1720

Spain's defeat forced the monarchy to uphold all its pledges under the Treaty of Utrecht, including its commercial concessions. During 1720, the French Foreign Ministry reviewed at length the historic rights that Versailles expected Madrid to honor in the ports of Spain.[154] The consul for trade assigned to Madrid put it concisely in his report: "Today, as work advances toward definite treaties, and stable peace and commerce among all the powers that were engaged in the last war, the commerce of the Indies will undoubtedly be one of the principal points that will be addressed." The expectation from Philip was "a decree declaring that his intention always was and still is adherence to the historic treaties, that the subjects of the King [of France] enjoy in Spain the same privileges, and that the exemptions existing beforehand are or will be accorded to the most favored nation."[155] The documentation concerning the validation of Spain's historic commercial commitments also included tracts on the evacuation of occupied territories, but it contained nothing about dynastic considerations in France or Britain, which seems to have served more as pretext for war than as a truly substantive issue.[156]

The well-known Project of 1720, which constituted official American trade policy until the reformist regulations of "free trade" in 1765 and 1778, should be understood within the context of Spain's military humiliation at the hands of the Quadruple Alliance. Promulgated on April 5, 1720, the *Proyecto para Galeones y Flotas del Perú y Nueva-España, y para navios*

---

[152] Lynch, *Bourbon Spain*, p. 60; "*Inventaire des Pieces qui concernent la comision donnée a M. le Chevalier de Marieu pour accompagner M. le Cardinal Alberoni a son Passage en France,*" 1720, AAE:CPE, vol. 294, fols. 86–95.

[153] Saint Aignan to His Majesty, Madrid, August 16, 1717, AAE:CPE, vol. 259. fols. 117–26. The French ambassador remarked that Tinajero was a "good servant to the king of Spain, who could have served him usefully in the premier positions of the monarchy if the animosity of his enemies had not imposed insurmountable obstacles over a long time."

[154] Memoires, Versailles, n.d., 1720 (three), April 1720, and September 1720 and Cádiz, August 7, 1720, AAE:CPE, vol. 295, fols. 47–53, 84–89, 122–41, vol. 296, fols. 103–107, and vol. 298, fols. 217–37.

[155] Memoire, French consul for trade, Madrid, 1720, AAE:CPE, vol. 295, fols. 69–79, 84–87. Quoted in Allan J. Kuethe, "The Colonial Commercial Policy of Philip V and the Atlantic World," in Renate Pieper and Peer Schmidt (eds.), *Latin America and the Atlantic World* (Cologne and Vienna: Böhlau, 2005), pp. 330–31.

[156] In general, vol. 295 of AAE:CPE and especially Grimaldo to Secretary of State Abbot Guillaume Dubois, Madrid, April 2, 1720, fols. 2–5 and royal *cédulas* (two), Madrid, April 4, fols. 7–15, and extract of Spanish affairs, 1720, fols. 47–53.

de registro, y avisos, que navegaren a ambos reynos dutifully adhered to the mandates of the Utrecht settlement and the Bubb treaties.[157] It came only months after Philip's capitulation on January 26, in which he agreed to affirm the principles of the Quadruple Alliance and Spain's historic commitments. Based closely on the royal projects that had governed the fleets of 1711, 1715, and 1717, the regulation was obviously a hurried, unfinished effort, as additional provisions amended and completed the regulation over the following months, including a *cédula* defining local port fees and a new policy detailing the operation of the *avisos* or mail ships. The *avisos*, which had historically been connected to the fleet system, actually appeared in the title of the Project of 1720, but received only vague references in its original articles, an oversight surely resulting from the haste with which the regulation was assembled.

The establishment of the mail system came in a royal decree of May 31, 1720, issued from the desk of Minister of War Fernández Durán. The mail between Spain and America had operated through the *Consulado* under the nominal supervision of the *Casa de la Contratación*, but during the War of Succession and its aftermath, the service had been contracted to individuals.[158] The decree of July 29, 1718, affirmed the principle of eight annual mail ships. Given its dependence on the *Consulado* in the aftermath of recent defeats, the crown allowed the guild to operate a mail system with eight *avisos* per year, four "to each kingdom" – Peru and New Spain, and New Granada – to carry royal and private mail and to report on market conditions.[159] Marine Intendant Francisco Varas y Valdés negotiated the new agreement with the *Consulado*. The mail ships would be small, between sixty and one hundred tons, and would sail at intervals determined by weather patterns: at the beginning of January, at the end of March or early April, in mid-June, and at the beginning of November. The guild declined to transport agricultural products on the outgoing vessels, and it refused to carry gold, silver, and produce on the returns, citing the need to depart unencumbered and to sail with speed. In the name of economy, however, the guild attempted to reduce the number of sailings to two or three annually per viceroyalty, but Madrid held fast to its objective of four each. To finance the mail service, the *Consulado* agreed to collect an appropriate fee from its members. This would take the form of a 1 percent levy on commerce (*puro*

---

[157] A copy can be found in AGI, Consulados, leg. 33.

[158] Antonia Heredia Herrera, "Asiento con el Consulado de Cádiz, en 1720, para el despacho de avisos," *Instituto de Estudios Gaditanos, Diputación Provincial* (Cádiz: Diputación de Cádiz, 1975), p. 165.

[159] *Aprobación de la escritura en que el Consulado, y el Comercio de Cádiz, se encarga del despacho annual de ocho avisos*... 1720, AGI, IG, 2324. The regulation did not explain how the *Consulado* might use eight annual *aviso* ships to serve three kingdoms with four ships each. Apparently, the recently established Viceroyalty of New Granada had not yet fully entered the royal mind.

comercio), which the guild would administer.[160] In practice, the *Consulado* would satisfy its obligations quite irregularly over the ensuing years.

The provisions of the Project of 1720 calling for annual fleets to Portobelo and Veracruz, the *Galeones* and the *Flotas*, fulfilled Spain's obligation under Article 13 of the preliminary treaty of March 27, 1713. This required Spain to maintain its historic commercial system, a commitment that the second Bubb treaty had reaffirmed with specificity. As Grimaldo tersely observed: "His Majesty is again finding himself obliged to honor this provision."[161] The language opening chapter 3 of the Project echoed the spirit of this imposition: "In the vessels that comprise the *Flotas*, or *Galeones* ... all the commercial produce and merchandise must be loaded *in the manner practiced up to now, without any changes.*"[162]

The preservation of the traditional system of annual fleets must be understood then as an act of capitulation, not as an authentic response to commercial objectives, and historians should not be surprised that during subsequent years Cádiz made little effort to live up to its standards.[163] The provision served the British ambition to send an "annual" ship to America. In 1720, Spain's potential sales in the American marketplace simply did not justify the volume of trade that mounting annual convoys would entail.

Another curious aspect of the Project of 1720 was the assessment of export duties by volume – not by value – through a tax called the *palmeo*. Replacing the *almojarifazgo* that had been administered by tax farmers, this seemingly irrational provision has long puzzled historians, who have frequently interpreted it as an attempt to simplify port procedures.[164] The *palmeo*, however, should also be associated with the highly important provision in chapter 5 protecting sealed boxes from searches:

---

[160] Ibid. The *Aprobación* contained a summary of the steps taken to reach agreement. The confirming *cédula* was dated May 31.

[161] Grimaldo to L'Abbé Dubois, Madrid, March 8, 1720, AHN, Estado, leg. 3388.

[162] Italics added by authors.

[163] At least since the days of Clarence Haring, historians have taken these regulations as genuine royal policy – as a prescription to which the royal administration aspired, albeit without much success. That interpretation is flawed. Although the provisions of the Project concerning schedules for individual convoys seem to have represented actual targets to which at least superficial lip service would be given, the objective of mounting annual fleets to South and North America had no basis in reality. To believe that veteran administrators of the Andalusian colonial trade such as Pez, Patiño, Varas y Valdés, López Pintado, or, in Madrid, José Grimaldo, or anyone else connected to it actually took this objective seriously is beyond credulity. The provision was for show, a kind of diplomatic capitulation formalized through written colonial policy. Clarence Haring, *The Spanish Empire in America* (New York: Harcourt, Brace and World, 1947). A more recent example is Antonio García-Baquero González, *Cádiz y el Atlántico*, 2 vols. (Sevilla, Escuela de Estudios Hispano-Americanos, 1976), especially, I, pp. 152–58.

[164] García-Baquero, *Cádiz y el Atlántico*, pp. 197–99. See also, for example, Walker, *Spanish Politics and Imperial Trade*, pp. 110–11 and García-Mauriño, *La pugna*, p. 114.

When the time comes to load the produce or merchandise ... five and one half reales will be paid per each cubic *palmeo*, and regarding the assessment which each parcel, bale, box, pack, package, or barrel of merchandise accrues ... *they are not to be opened, nor what is inside examined.*[165]

These provisions were particularly important to victorious France, whose merchants penetrated the American trade by using agents tied to local families in Seville and Cádiz to supply manufactures to the convoys.[166] Sealed boxes could disguise merchandise that had entered Spain without paying the proper duties and could go out posing as national goods. To give substance to this capitulation, taxes on boxed exports had to be assessed by volume, meaning that a bolt of sackcloth for slaves would pay the same rate as fine silks. Like the provision for annual convoys, the *palmeo* should be interpreted as another major capitulation to the French mercantile interests.

To provide greater flexibility in trading with the Indies, the Project made provision for register (*registro*) ships, which might sail independently of the convoys. These had existed previously to serve the areas bypassed by the convoys, but their role would mushroom during the following decades. Apart from Veracruz, Cartagena, and Portobelo, the regulation specifically identified destinations including Buenos Aires, Honduras, Santa Marta, and Caracas; and it alluded in general to other ports of Tierra Firme, Cuba, and the Windward Islands. The same system of taxation levied on the *Flotas y Galeones* applied. Freight charges differed, of course, according to destination and cargo.[167]

Owing to Austrian reluctance to participate, the Allies failed to assemble at Cambrai to negotiate a general peace treaty as originally planned. Given that the French supplied the American marketplace largely through agents in Cádiz, they negotiated a separate peace affirming their historic rights in the ports of Spain. Special Envoy Langeron Maulevirier negotiated such an agreement with Grimaldo in Madrid in the form of a defensive alliance dated March 27, 1721. Article VI contained the key provision wherein Philip promised to honor:

all the advantages and all the privileges conceded to the French Nation by his predecessor Kings, as in the Treaty of the Pyrenees, confirmed by those of Nimwegan and Ryswick, as well as through individual cédulas for that Nation ... to the effect that French merchants ... always enjoy in Spain the same rights, prerogatives, advantages, and privileges for their people and for their commerce ... that they have enjoyed or should enjoy by virtue of said Treaties or Cédulas and all of those that have been or will be conceded by Spain to the most favored Nation.[168]

---

[165] Italics added by authors.
[166] Bustos Rodríguez, *Cádiz en el sistema atlántico*, pp. 144–45.
[167] *Proyecto para Galeones y Flotas*, chaps. V–VIII.
[168] Armillas, "La política exterior," p. 279. The Treaty of Madrid can be found in *Colección de los tratados*, pp. 78–90.

The British secured a similar affirmation of their rights in Spain and Spanish America with a treaty of friendship the following June.[169]

The Spanish had little choice. Nevertheless, Elizabeth secured a French promise to defend the prerogatives of the Duke of Parma; she claimed those rights of inheritance for her family, which could and eventually did pass to her heirs. Given his own aspirations for Parma, however, the emperor refused to recognize this claim.[170] Throughout his reign, it should be remembered, Philip always displayed a willingness to sacrifice Spain's national interests in America to advance dynastic claims in Italy. The 1721 settlements essentially brought Spain back to where it had found itself in 1713 on reforming the American trade.

CONCLUSION

After disastrous defeats in the War of the Quadruple Alliance, Spain was shackled with severe restrictions in shaping its commercial policy, which left the door wide open to massive foreign penetration of the Spanish American trade. The British abuse of the ships of permission and of the opportunities provided through the slave trade monopoly, as well as the exploitation of Caribbean bases strategically located in Jamaica and Barbados for contraband trading are legendary. The French also found their way into the American marketplace through Cádiz and exploited their own flourishing Caribbean holdings to introduce contraband goods into the Indies. Meanwhile, the Dutch dominated the southern Caribbean. Saddled with the archaic commercial policy reimposed at Utrecht and reaffirmed through the War of the Quadruple Alliance, the Spanish monarchy found its options severely limited. It continued to sustain a monopoly port system, which now featured Cádiz, and it continued to mount inefficient, economically unviable convoys to Cartagena and Portobelo, and to Veracruz.[171] In the future, able ministers such as Patiño (1726–1736), José de la Quintana (1739–1741), José del Campillo y Cossío (1741–1743), and the Marqués de la Ensenada (1743–1754) would do what they could by relying more and more on register ships (dispatched individually) to provide a measure of marketing flexibility, establishing commercial companies for Caracas and Havana, strengthening the colonial coast guard, and even resorting to privateers. The lion's share of Spanish American trade nevertheless remained in foreign hands and that reality constituted a primary characteristic of the Atlantic economy. Not until the Treaty of Madrid extinguished the *asiento* in

---

[169] "Tratado particular de Paz y Amistad ..." Madrid, June 13, 1721, in *Colección de los tratados*, pp. 92–105.

[170] "Tratado de Alianza defensiva ..." Madrid, March 27, 1721, in *Colección de los tratados*, art. V.

[171] Walker, *Spanish Politics and Imperial Trade*, chaps. 6–10.

1750 would Spain be able to reassess and reform its commercial system in any fundamental ways and to reclaim its rightful share of the fruits of colonialism.[172] Events in Europe shaped the prospects of ministers seeking to reform transatlantic trade, and the desire of Spain's European rivals to penetrate markets in the Spanish Indies helped to determine alliances, wartime coalitions, and policies in capital cities such as London, Paris, and the Hague. European and American concerns became intertwined, defining the essential context for reform in the Spanish Atlantic system.

---

[172] Allan J. Kuethe, "El fin del monopolio," pp. 35–66; John Fisher, *Commercial relations between Spain and Spanish America in the Era of Free Trade, 1778–1796* (Liverpool 1985).

2

Alberoni and Colonial Innovation

While Alberoni's ambitious attempts to regain control over Spain's ports contributed to the outbreak of the disastrous War of the Quadruple Alliance (1718–1720), he also promoted other serious reforms within the Spanish Atlantic world. The Italian knew that Spain controlled an Atlantic empire, and any attempts to renovate the metropolis and restore Spanish prestige and power in Europe must rely on tax revenues and trade from the Indies. Interest groups in Spain and the Americas, however, stood ready to oppose changes that might undermine their own partisan interests. The wealth of the Indies also drew the attention of Spain's rivals, who wanted unrestricted access to American markets, and they were even prepared to go to war to control the wealth of the Spanish Indies. A serious reform of Spain's transatlantic trade would have consequences felt throughout the Atlantic world. Fraud, unregistered cargoes, and corrupt local officials in the Indies had always plagued Spain's transatlantic trade to some degree, but in the years following the War of Succession, contraband trade controlled by English, French, and Dutch traders escalated to alarming levels. This illicit commerce led to disappointing commercial profits for Spanish and colonial merchants and to diminished tax returns on trade fairs in Veracruz and Portobelo. Moreover, from their foreign bases in the Caribbean, Spain's enemies preyed on the *Flotas* and *Galeones* returning to Spain. Within this context, the concessions at Utrecht to the British – Europe's emerging commercial leader in the early eighteenth century – were potentially even more damaging. In short, widespread contraband in the Pacific and the Caribbean threatened the very commercial lifeline of the monarchy. It is no small wonder that the ambitious Alberoni made reform on both sides of the Atlantic a major priority.

Alberoni promoted ambitious innovations that spanned the four principal areas of reformist activity in the Spanish Atlantic empire during the eighteenth century: commercial, military, administrative, and fiscal policy.[1] Although historians have traditionally understood comprehensive reform initiatives as beginning much later, the innovations undertaken by Alberoni represented fundamental breakthroughs in crucial areas of colonial policy.[2] While they arrived piecemeal, so too would most of the initiatives attempted under Spain's premier "enlightened" reformer, Charles III. Alberoni's reputation as a reformer of the Spanish Atlantic system suffers largely because he was long gone by the time most of his program bore appreciable fruit, and his protégé José Patiño has received most of the credit for the successful implementation of these policies. Yet Alboroni's agenda shows that Madrid was committed to implementing fundamental changes in the colonial sphere during the early reign of Philip V.

Although the transfer of the *Casa de la Contratación* and the *Consulado de Cargadores a Indias* from Seville to Cádiz in 1717 (the first of the Alberoni reforms) focused on Europe, it involved the colonial system and bore deep implications for the American trade. Two other important initiatives in 1717 included the establishment of the Viceroyalty of New Granada and the installation of the tobacco monopoly in Cuba. The reorganization of Havana´s fixed garrison into a modern battalion followed in 1719. The distinguishing characteristic of all these measures was their tempo and tone. They were introduced without the expected, customary process of studied bureaucratic consideration and preparation, or meaningful consultation with the affected parties. Consequently, they provoked heated controversy and entailed serious political risks. The struggles in Spain and the Indies that emerged from these early reformist initiatives elucidate the many vested interest groups opposed to reform in the early eighteenth-century Spanish Atlantic world.

Despite the risks of moving ahead quickly with reform, Alberoni was a man in a hurry. He had promised the monarchs that he could return Spain to the status of a world power within five years, provided he could have peace. Given Spain's frustrations at Utrecht and the commitment of her rivals to penetrating markets in the Spanish Indies, Alberoni knew that peace was unlikely.[3] A rank outsider without personal or familial connections to the Spanish elite, the ambitious Italian had the unconditional backing of Elizabeth and Philip, so he felt free to act swiftly and decisively in Andalusia, New Granada, and Cuba. But Alberoni's method was also his

---

[1] The ensuing analysis is built on Allan J. Kuethe, "Cardinal Alberoni and Reform in the American Empire." in Francisco Eissa-Barroso and Ainara Vázquez, eds., *Early Bourbon Spanish America: Politics and Society in a Forgotten Era* (Leiden: Konionklijke Brill, 2003).

[2] For an historian identifying a significant shift in imperial policy before Charles III, who cites initiatives during Patiño's ministry, see John R. Fisher, *Bourbon Peru, 1750–1824* (Liverpool: Liverpool University Press, 2003), p. 4.

[3] Manuel Ríos Mazcarelle, *Reinas de España* (Madrid: Alderabán, 1999), p. 57.

weakness, for his initiatives, no matter how meritorious, rested on shaky political foundations. They depended on his own strong will and the support of the monarchs, not legitimate administrative processes. Moreover, these measures were not connected to any broadly articulated reformist program or package. They appeared then and now as pragmatic, ad hoc steps designed to address specific problems or to increase royal revenues, which would allow the monarchy to wage war more effectively.

THE CORROSIVE INFLUENCE OF CONTRABAND IN THE SPANISH ATLANTIC

Among the most daunting challenges facing reformers in the Spanish Atlantic empire was the penetration of foreign merchants into the legal transatlantic trading system. The problem stemmed from the failure of Spanish manufacturers to produce enough high-quality goods to meet demand in the Indies. Although the crown prohibited all foreign participation in transatlantic commerce, from the early seventeenth century French, English, Dutch, and Genoese merchants moved to Seville and became naturalized citizens, or they married Spanish women, making their offspring citizens (called *jenízaros*) and eligible to engage in commerce with the Indies.[4] Foreign merchant houses also sold goods to Spanish front men (called *prestanombres*), who shipped these products in their own names in return for a commission.[5] These foreigners profited from a series of unequal treaties, giving them the right to establish consuls to protect their rights and granting extraterritoriality or virtual immunity from prosecution under Spanish law.[6] As a result, by the late seventeenth century foreigners supplied the bulk of the goods sent from Seville to the Indies. In 1682, for example, the convoy returned from fairs at Veracruz and Portobelo with 22,808,977 pesos, and over 56 percent of the bullion left the country to repay to foreign suppliers – 2.5 million pesos to France; 2.5 million to England; 3.5 million to Holland; and 4.5 million to Genoa. Much of what remained went to foreign suppliers resident in Spain. By this period, contemporaries estimated that 94 percent of all manufactured goods shipped from Seville consisted of foreign products, a clear testimony to the failure of Spanish industry to supply the Indies.[7]

---

[4] Adrian Pearce, *British Trade with Spanish America, 1763–1808* (Liverpool: Liverpool University Press, 2007, p. 4; Margarita García-Mauriño Mundi, *La pugna entre el Consulado de Cádiz y los jenízaros por las exportaciones a Indias (1720–1765)* (Sevilla: Universidad de Sevilla, 1999).

[5] Stanley J. Stein and Barbara H. Stein, *Silver, Trade, and War: Spain and America in the Making of Early Modern Europe* (Baltimore: Johns Hopkins University Press, 2000), pp. 15–16. Pearce, *British Trade with Spanish America*, pp. 4–5.

[6] Stein and Stein, *Silver, Trade, and War*, pp. 58–65.

[7] Carlos Daniel Malamud Rikles, *Cádiz y Saint Malo en el comercio colonial Peruano (1698–1725)* (Cádiz: Diputación provincial de Cádiz, 1986), p. 97.

Apart from the hemorrhaging of colonial silver to foreign merchant suppliers, extensive contraband plagued the legal Spanish trading system, as goods leaving Seville and the licensed ports in the Indies went unregistered and untaxed. Although this untaxed merchandise allowed merchants to exchange European goods for colonial silver at lower prices, it undoubtedly cost the crown millions of pesos in tax revenues. It is impossible to know the precise extent of such contraband, but during the heyday of the fleet system in the seventeenth century, some contemporaries estimated that the amounts of unregistered merchandise leaving Spain for the Indies fluctuated between 50 and 90 percent.[8] While such figures are probably exaggerations, they do point to the upward trend in the amounts of unregistered merchandise in the *Flotas* and *Galeones* over the course of the century. Merchants from Mexico and Peru also brought large quantities of unregistered colonial goods and silver to trade at their respective fairs, which facilitated their clandestine purchase of European wares.

Contraband trading on such a large scale required the connivance of officials in Seville, the active participation of *Consulados* in Seville and the Indies, and local colonial authorities overseeing the fairs. After the Portobelo Fair of 1624, for example, a treasury officer in Panama, Cristóbal de Balbas, lodged a legal complaint about fraud, and in the ensuing investigation officials determined that over 75 percent of the goods shipped to Lima had escaped paying taxes.[9] Given such high levels of contraband, the crown may well have been justified in confiscating private funds or demanding loans or forced donations from the *Consulados* of Seville (and later Cádiz), Lima, and Mexico City in times of fiscal exigency. Despite high levels of contraband, however, the legal trading system still provided the crown with substantial tax revenues and allowed merchants to make impressive profits during the seventeenth century.

The gravest threat to the Spanish Atlantic trading system came from European contrabandists, operating from bases in the Caribbean and the Atlantic. In 1494, the papacy had divided the non-European world between Spain and Portugal, awarding Asia, Africa, and Brazil to Portugal and the bulk of America to Spain. As a result of this donation, the Spanish and Portuguese claimed complete sovereignty over the lands and sea lanes outside of Europe. Other European powers challenged these claims, first by licensing privateers to prey on Spanish shipping, and later the Dutch and English even licensed joint stock companies to advance their commercial interests and found overseas enterprises in the Americas. The Dutch took Curaçao in 1634; the English captured Jamaica in 1655; and the French established footholds by mid-century in Saint Dominique, Guadalupe, and Martinique.

---

[8] Enriqueta Vila Vilar, "Las ferias de Portobelo: Apariencia y realidad del comercio con Indias," *Anuario de estudios americanos*, 39 (1982), p. 309.
[9] Ibid., p. 323.

By the late seventeenth century, these colonies supplied large numbers of slaves, European manufactured goods, iron, and other products to the Spanish Indies in return for bullion, dyes, and cacao. By the 1690s, England received 440,000 pesos annually from its illicit trade with Spanish America (mostly through Jamaica), and an additional 1.2 million pesos from supplying manufactured goods through Seville for legal trade to America. This provided enough silver to finance all commercial activities in Asia.[10] Moreover, French contraband traders in the Pacific and in the South Atlantic drained large amounts silver (much of it unregistered and untaxed) from the Viceroyalty of Peru to pay for European wares, mostly textiles from St. Malo. Along with the inflow of illicit Oriental goods from the Manila galleon at Acapulco, the English, Dutch, and French contrabandists provided ample supplies of trade goods to colonial markets, undermining the demand for goods at the legal trade fairs. This also led to an outflow of bullion that could have paid for goods sold by Spanish merchants, leading to a decline in taxes levied on the transatlantic trade. As contraband grew by the early eighteenth century, prospects for reviving legal commerce at the trade fairs appeared dim.

Given rising levels of foreign contraband goods circulating in the Indies, concessions made in the Treaty of Utrecht to the South Sea Company threatened to destroy Spain's legal trading system altogether. The British company received the unprecedented "legal" right both to supply slaves to the Spanish Indies and to send a ship of 500 tons (later raised to 650 tons in 1716) to the trade fairs at Veracruz and Portobelo. This allowed the company to introduce cheaper manufactured goods and undermine the sales of Spanish merchants. Moreover, the British permission ships often carried cargoes well in excess of the legal limit, and these contraband articles sold even more cheaply to colonial merchants. Apart from the legal and illicit goods carried on the permission ships, the Company set up bases in the Caribbean and South Atlantic to introduce contraband merchandise into the Indies.[11] While local Spanish officials might receive generous bribes from abetting contrabandists, much of the South Sea Company's trade was authorized by the crown, leaving less opportunity to gain normal bribes and kickbacks. It also aroused the ire of the *Consulado* of Seville, making the whole arrangement fraught with controversy. Moreover, the South Sea Company's arrangement also competed with the contraband activities of French, Dutch, and other British merchants operating independently of the company. Nonetheless, the British company's business activities posed a serious threat to Spain's transatlantic commerce and complicated efforts to revive the legal trading system, already weakened by contraband commerce.

Regaining control over trade with the Indies required solving daunting commercial, administrative, military, and fiscal challenges. Alberoni, Patiño,

---

[10] Pearce, *British Trade with Spanish America*, p. 18.
[11] Ibid., 18–32; Stein and Stein, *Silver, Trade, and War*, pp. 106–44.

and other reformers had to devise ways to end the political culture of corruption in the Indies, curtail the flow of contraband and unregistered goods in the Carrera de Indias, and collect crown revenues more effectively. The early trade fairs at Veracruz in 1706, 1708, 1711, and 1715 and the disastrous 1707–1708 fair at Portobelo (see Chapter 1) had produced only small remittances of public and private funds to Spain, and the convoys lost several ships at sea or to foreign attacks.[12] This dismal record has led generations of historians to argue that the fleet system was antiquated, inefficient, and doomed. Despite its many defects, however, the system was not the real problem, a fact not lost on reformers in Spain. No trading system could revive legitimate commerce in the Spanish Atlantic in the face of widespread contraband, corrupt Spanish bureaucrats, and the broad concessions given the British South Sea Company in 1713. Moreover, Alberoni and others committed to reform had to solve these problems quickly, without somehow provoking the ire and opposition of powerful foreign and domestic interest groups in Spain and the Americas. Alberoni also had to balance reform with the dynastic ambitious of the monarchy in Europe. It was a situation fraught with danger, and so Alberoni moved forward in a piecemeal way to tackle the difficulties facing the empire, taking practical steps to confront recognized deficiencies. It should come as no surprise that he failed to make radical improvements in solving such difficult problems by the time of his dismissal in 1719.

THE TRANSFER OF THE COLONIAL TRADE APPARATUS FROM SEVILLE TO CÁDIZ

In a pivotal reform of the Spanish Atlantic commercial system, a royal decree of May 8, 1717, transferred the historic *Casa de la Contratación* and the *Consulado de Cargadores a Indias* from Seville to Cádiz. For an event of this magnitude, affecting so many people and involving so many vested interests, the order arrived without extensive institutional deliberation and preparation. Although transferring the *Casa* and the *Consulado* to Cádiz had profound consequences for colonial commerce and for the economic and demographic future of Andalusia, the legislation was motivated primarily by Spanish objectives in the Mediterranean.[13] To support Spain's ambitions in Italy, Alberoni had to consolidate its naval forces and to rationalize naval administration, including the transfer of the *Consulado* and the *Casa* to Cádiz.

To prepare for these new policies, Alberoni made several important administrative changes, beginning in 1715 with the purge of Bernardo Tinajero. Then, in January 1717, the *gaditano* admiral Andrés de Pez was named

[12] Malamud, *Cádiz y Saint Malo*, pp. 48, 112; Geoffrey J. Walker, *Spanish Politics and Imperial Trade, 1700–1789* (Bloomington: Indiana University Press, 1979), pp. 34–67.

[13] Antonio Bétencourt, "Las aventuras italianas de Felipe V" in *España y el mar en el siglo de Carlos III*, coordinated by Vicente Palacio Atard (Madrid 1989), p. 323.

governor of the Council of the Indies.[14] Soon after, Alberoni selected his confidant José Patiño to serve as intendant general of Marine, superintendant of the Kingdom of Sevilla, and president of the *Casa de la Contratación*.[15] Both Pez and Patiño had extensive experience, and they enjoyed the full trust of Queen Elizabeth Farnese. Pez had managed and largely funded the naval phase of her journey to Spain; Patiño, as intendant of Barcelona, had facilitated the process.[16] The venerable admiral had successfully commanded the Franco-Spanish convoy to Veracruz of 1708–1710, returning safely, and he was known as a great promoter of Cádiz.[17] Patiño, the son of a *gallego* military officer and an Italian noblewoman, had been born in Milan and educated by Jesuits. Married to an Italian, Beatriz Rosales Fancini, he never lost his predilection for things Italian.[18] Patiño was recalled to Spain in 1702 with the entourage of Philip V, and he rose steadily within the Spanish administrative system, becoming superintendant of Extremadura in 1711. Philip assigned him the difficult task of governing recently subdued Catalonia in 1713, where he installed the New Plan (*Nueva Planta*) of government, which abolished the traditional Catalan *fueros* (legal privileges).[19] Some form of marine intendancy had existed since 1715, when the crown named Francisco Varas (an *oidor* of the audiencia of the *Casa de la Contratación*) to the position with broad powers over naval finance.[20] The appointment of Patiño as president of the *Casa* and intendant of Marine, however, gave him the authority to unify under a single command the naval forces of the Mediterranean and the Atlantic in Cádiz.[21]

---

[14] Ailing President Conde de Frigiliana had reached an advanced age and was retired with full salary and honors to make way for Pez. Saint Aignan to the king, Madrid, February 1, 1717, AAE:CPE vol. 257, fols. 70–74, 80.

[15] Saint Aignan to the king, Madrid, January 11, 1717, AAE:CPE, vol. 257, fols. 23–26.

[16] Adolfo de Castro, *Vida del Almirante D. Andrés de Pes, ministro de marina* (Cádiz: Imp. de la Revista Médica de Federico Joly, 1879), pp. 25–28.

[17] Pablo Emilio Pérez-Mallaina Bueno, *La política española en el Atlántico, 1700–1715* (Sevilla: Escuela de Estudios Hispano-Americanos, 1982), p. 11.

[18] Antonio Béthencourt Massieu, *Patiño en la política internacional de Felipe V*, with introduction by Vicente Palacio Atard (Valladolid: Universidad de Valladolid, 1954), p. 13

[19] Antonio Rodríguez Villa, *Patiño y Campillo: Reseña histórico-biográfica de estos dos ministros de Felipe V* (Madrid: Establecimiento tipográfico de los sucesores de Rivadeneyra, 1882), pp. 12–14.

[20] Pérez-Mallaina, *Política naval*, pp. 345–46.

[21] As the royal *cédula* stated: "I have resolved to select and name you intendant general of my Spanish marine, placing under your charge ... all that involves the economy and policy and operation of my navy ... [and therefore] it is necessary that all the supervision and care should be focused in the port of Cádiz, where the *Flotas, Galeones*, and squadrons should be readied and dispatched as appropriate for my royal service; I have resolved that you go to reside and exercise your employment in that city of Cádiz, and that the superintendancy of the Kingdom of Seville also fall under your responsibility ... and that you preside over the Tribunal of *Contratación* ... as also you should supervise Commerce ... to which end the deputies of the *Consulado* should also go to reside in Cádiz, so that it, like the tribunal of *Contratación*, might

The royal decree of May 8 simply formalized the transfer. Since Alberoni did not head a ministry, the decree arrived from the desk of Fernández Durán, secretary of the Office for War, who had controlled naval affairs since the suppression of Marine and the Indies in 1715.[22] Under normal circumstances, an innovation of this magnitude should have involved extensive study and surely consultation with the Council of the Indies. Instead, Pez simply signed Alberoni's instructions, issued through the Council.[23]

The transfer of the *Consulado* and *Casa* from Seville to Cádiz provided real advantages for American commerce. Cádiz boasted superior port facilities, possessing a large bay opening directly out onto the ocean, while Seville, a river port, lay eighty kilometers upstream. The *cabecera* for the convoys had moved to Cádiz in 1680, but the administrative offices remained in Seville, which offered a more sophisticated, comfortable environment and was the home to most of the shippers.[24] Conducting the American trade from a port open to the ocean naturally made it more accessible to contrabandists and more difficult to defend from foreign navies than Seville. At the time of the transfer, rumors flourished (and persisted for decades) that Alberoni had extracted large bribes from mysterious foreign interests (hoping to profit from contraband commerce with the Indies through Cádiz) for the expedition to Italy.[25] It is also noteworthy that during the second half of the seventeenth century, Cádiz had regularly contributed to the Royal Treasury.[26] Most of these contributions originated from the multitude of foreign operators who lived and worked within the permissive setting of the *gaditano* port. The *Consulado* habitually lent or donated money to the crown, but the generosity of the Cádiz merchant community implied that foreigners were using their money to influence royal policy.

The transfer to Cádiz occurred when the city of Seville suffered from internal divisions, economic setbacks, and disease. The traditional home of the *Consulado* had been a house divided since Bernardo Tinajero's triumph as *fiscal* in 1705, when he managed to imprison the old leadership and seize its properties. To make matters worse for the old establishment, the crown

more expeditiously attend to ... the measures ... that their dependants should pursue before their court. Royal *cédula*, Madrid, January 28, 1717, reproducido en Cesáreo Fernández Duro, *Armada española desde la unión de los Reinos de Castilla y de Aragón*, VI (Madrid: Museo Naval, 1972–1973), pp. 222–23.

[22] Saint Aignan to Huxelles, the Escorial, June 21, 1717, AAE:CPE, vol. 258, fols. 93–94.

[23] Royal decree, Segovia, May 8, 1717 and royal *cédula*, Segovia, May 12, 1717, AGI, IG, leg. 2039.

[24] Lutgardo García Fuentes, *El comercio español en América, 1650–1700* (Sevilla: Escuela de Estudios Hispano-Americanos, 1980), pp. 63–65.

[25] *Consulta*, Consejo de Indias, 1777, AGI, IG, leg. 2409; Albert Girard, *La rivalité commerciale et maritime entre Séville et Cadix jusqu'a la fin du XVIII siècle* (Paris and Bordeaux : E. de Boccard, 1932), pp. 80–82.

[26] Manuel Bustos Rodríguez, "Prólogo," in Ana Crespo Solana, *La Casa de Contratación y la Intendencia General de la Marina en Cádiz* (Cádiz: Universidad de Cádiz, 1996), pp. 5–6.

suspended payment in 1706 on the loans it had contracted from the guild, including 2.5 million pesos seized from the treasure salvaged from the fleet of Manuel Velasco in 1702.[27] Pursued by the British as they returned from New Spain at the outbreak of war, sixteen ships of Velasco's fleet had taken refuge at Vigo in the northwest of Spain, but the British broke into the bay, destroying the convoy. Although over 10 million pesos had been salvaged before the ships burned, this achievement still left Seville at risk of having the money confiscated for the strapped Royal Treasury, which lay much closer to Galicia than Seville. Desperate for silver to fund the war, the crown seized 6.5 million of the rescued funds, confiscating 4 million as the property of enemy powers and declaring the remainder a loan. The so-called *valimiento de Vigo* would remain a matter of controversy throughout the century and beyond.[28]

In 1709, the Royal Treasury, working through the Junta de Prorrateo, with Tinajero acting as *fiscal*, assumed responsibility for debts to the *Consulado*, but the money went only to those members designated as "legitimate creditors," all of whom were part of Tinajero's clique.[29] That same year an epidemic ravaged the city, costing a great loss of life.[30] In 1708, moreover, the English trapped the *Galeones* of José Fernández de Santillán in Cartagena Bay; the fleet was laden with Peruvian silver secured at the Portobelo fair, which was eventually lost. Following that disaster, in 1715 the *Flota* of Juan de Ubilla – in the company of four ships under Antonio Echevers from Cartagena – went down in a hurricane in the Bahama Channel.[31] So severe were the financial problems of the *Consulado* that its officers could not claim their salaries in 1713 or 1714.[32] But Seville was still far from finished.

Alberoni's political vulnerability undermined the smooth transfer from Seville to Cádiz. The crushing defeat of the Spanish navy at Cape Passaro, and Spain's subsequent humiliation at the hands of the Quadruple Alliance opened the door for nativist, anti-reformist groups determined to undo the program that the Italian had so arbitrarily imposed. Alberoni fell from power on December 19, 1719, and went into exile.[33] Peace negotiations brought Spain's adherence to the principles of the Quadruple Alliance on January 26 of the following year.[34] A chastised Spain would respect the delicate balance

---

[27] Pérez-Mallaina, *Política naval*, p. 80.

[28] Report on "los 10,182,039 pesos escudos de plata que ... se salvaron de la flota de ... Vigo," AGI, Consulados, libro 271.

[29] Pérez-Mallaina, *Política naval*, pp. 209, 220.

[30] Ana Gloria Márquez Redondo, *Sevilla "ciudad y corte" (1729–1733)* (Sevilla 1994), p. 27.

[31] Pérez-Mallaina, *Política naval*, pp. 14, 18–19, 36–39, 48–49.

[32] The prior to José Grimaldo, Seville, August 6, 1715, AGI, Consulados, leg. 282, and the *Consulado* to Diego de Morales de Velazco, Seville, August 25, 1716, AGI, IG, leg. 2042.

[33] Exile was a common fate for reformers. Other exiles included the Marqueses de la Ensenada, Esquilache, Grimaldi, and the Conde de Floridablanca.

[34] Real *cédula*, Grimaldo, Madrid, January 26, 1720, and Grimaldo to Abad Dubois, Madrid, January 26, 1718, AAE:CPE, vol. 294, fols. 109–11, 121–23.

established at Utrecht. For America, this affirmation found expression in the promulgation of the *Proyecto para Galeones y Flotas* of April 1720.[35] In Europe, Elizabeth and Philip would search for other means to satisfy their ambitions in Italy.

The collapse of the Alberoni government, accompanied by the demotions of Pez and Patiño, signaled a shift at the top, which opened the door to lobbying from Seville.[36] During this period, Elizabeth's power at court also declined, while Philip momentarily regained his health.[37] The queen exerted her influence indirectly through the person of the king and court favorites, so the downfall of Alberoni and the recovery of Philip naturally reduced her day-to-day political power.[38] Elizabeth knew that she enjoyed little love from the Spanish people, and in return, she cared little for them.[39] She dared not assert power in her own right. While she almost always accompanied the king during his audiences and did most of the talking, Elizabeth invariably insisted that she was faithfully expressing Philip's will, not her own. It was a subtle but critically important deception that legitimized her role.[40] She was not the mother of the Prince of Asturias, the heir to the throne, which itself imposed very real limits on her political clout. When the king's life suddenly seemed fragile during his medical crisis in the fall of 1717, for example, the astute French Ambassador Duc de Saint Aignan, observed that "custom does not allow a Queen, who is not the mother of the presumptive heir to the throne, to act as regent."[41]

After the downfall of Alberoni, the crown revived the system of ministries. In December 1720, Finance (under the Marqués del Campoflorido) finally acquired ministerial status, although Marine and the Indies still remained attached to War except for ecclesiastical matters, which came under the purview of Justice and Government.[42] The fall of Fernández Durán at the beginning of the new year led to the division of his responsibilities and

---

[35] A copy can be found in AGI, Consulados, leg. 33.

[36] Castro, *Vida del almirante D. Andrés de Pez*, p. 45.

[37] Henry Kamen, *Philip V of Spain: The King who Reigned Twice* (New Haven: Yale University Press, 2001), pp. 132–37.

[38] John Lynch, *Bourbon Spain, 1700–1808* (Oxford: Basil Blackwell, 1989), p. 89, comments "that not all Spanish ministers were cyphers, that an element of politics survived, and that the queen had to work to impose her will."

[39] Ibid., p. 76.

[40] Elizabeth habitually wrote personal notes on the back side of Philip's official correspondence. The AAE:CPE has letters from Philip and Elizabeth so configured in nearly every volume for this period. Ambassadors repeatedly commented on her omnipresence during their meetings with the throne. For a persuasive commentary on the role of Elizabeth, see María Ángeles Pérez Samper, *Isabel de Farnesio* (Barcelona: Plaza y Janés, 2003).

[41] *Memoire sur la situation presente de la Cour d'Espagne* in Saint Aignan to Huxelles, Madrid, November 26, 1717, AAE:CPE, vol. 260, fols 304–08.

[42] The Marqués de Campoflorido had been governor of the Council of Hacienda since January 1717. Saint Aignan to the crown, Madrid, January 25, 1717, AAE:CPE, vol. 257, fols. 52–53, 58–60.

reestablishment of the fifth ministry.[43] This opened the way for the rehabilitation of Pez, who acceded to secretary of the Office for Marine and the Indies while concurrently regaining the governorship of the Council.[44] Baltasar, the elder Patiño, assumed War, and the irrepressible José returned to the Marine Intendancy.[45] Neither Pez nor Patiño, however, had the broad powers that they had enjoyed under Alberoni.

Having extricated Spain from the War of the Quadruple Alliance, Grimaldo became the dominant political figure in Madrid.[46] At his side was Juan Bautista de Orendain, his understudy and a fellow Basque, who had risen to *oficial mayor* in the Secretariat of the Office for State. A big talker but a man of only mediocre talent, Orendain can be characterized, generously, as flexible in the political game at court.[47] Meanwhile, the melancholic king and his ambitious wife took refuge more and more in the north at Valsaín, near the construction site of the new palace of La Granja de San Ildefonso, where they communicated very little with the outside world.[48]

Partisan interests in Seville took advantage of the fluid political environment in Madrid to protest its loss of the *Casa de la Contratación* the *Consulado*. A profound and widespread anti-Alberoni sentiment pervaded at court and throughout Spain after the exile of the authoritarian outsider, providing the Seville interests with an opportunity to stage a counter coup.[49] In response to the clamor of Seville, and to resolve the controversy arising from the abrupt transfers, in July 1722, Grimaldo instructed Luis Miraval y Espínola, governor of the Council of Castile, to form an investigative committee. Miraval came from a prominent family in Jerez de la Frontera; his brother, Martín José, had served on the Council of the Indies as fiscal and as *ministro togado*.[50] A talented, able individual "endowed with good sense,

[43] Juan Luis Castellano, *Gobierno y poder en la España del siglo XVIII* (Granada: Editorial Universidad de Granada, 2006), p. 85.

[44] Castro, *Vida del almirante*, p. 51. Fernández Durán was transferred to the Council of the Indies. Teresa Nava Rodríguez, "Problemas y perpectivas (sic) de una historia social de la administración: los secretarios del Despacho en la España del siglo XVIII," *Mélanges de la Casa de Velázquez*, 30 (1994), p. 164.

[45] José Antonio Escudero, *Los orígenes del Consejo de Ministros en España*, I (Madrid: Editora Nacional, 1979), pp. 58–61.

[46] Grimaldo was the only minister who held the prestigious albeit largely honorific title of Councilor of State. Castellano, *Gobierno y poder*, p. 85.

[47] Ricardo García Cárcel, *Felipe V y los españoles: Una visión periférica del problema de España* (Barcelona: Plaza y Janés, 2002), p. 122; Lynch, *Bourbon Spain*, pp. 82, 87; Escudero, *Los orígenes*, p. 65.

[48] Lynch, *Bourbon Spain*, pp. 80–81. Work had begun on the palace in 1721. See also Kamen, *Philip V*, pp. 143–45.

[49] The Marquis de Maulevrier to Versailles, Madrid, October 21, 1720, AAE:CPE, vol. 296, fols. 188–96.

[50] Mark A. Burkholder, *Biographical Dictionary of Councilors of the Indies, 1717–1808* (New York: Greenwood Press, 1986), p. 80.

experience, and ... a strong work ethic," he was an ally of Grimaldo in Madrid politics.[51] In 1709, during the struggle to reshape the *Consulado*, Miraval had served on the Junta de Prorrateo that had ruled in favor of the claims by Tinajero's friends against the Royal Treasury.[52] The *Consulado* could not have hoped for a more sympathetic choice.

Miraval selected a committee comprised of magistrates from the five major councils, including Castille, the Indies, the Supreme Inquisition, Orders, and Finance. The councils historically served as bastions of the aristocracy and conservatism. Also named were Pez as Minister of Marine and the Indies (and governor of the Council); Patiño as Marine intendant; and Francisco Varas y Valdés as an official of the *Casa* and a veteran political insider at the *Consulado*, as well as one deputy each from Seville and Cádiz.[53] Grimaldo appointed Miraval to chair the committee. To represent Seville, he named the Marqués de Thous, a highly influential man of immense fortune, who over the years had benefited from his connections with Tinajero. He had served as rector of the *Consulado* in 1711, 1713, and 1715–1717.[54] Thous personally covered the expenses and salaries of the guild during the difficult years of 1713–1714.[55] He had personal access to Orendain and Miraval and, more importantly, he was a friend of the Minister of State.[56] In the background stood the Council of the Indies, another conservative voice with strong connections to Seville's partisan interests.

Aware beforehand that the committee would likely rule against the transfer of the *Consulado* and *Casa*, both Pez and Patiño attempted to excuse themselves from serving, but without success. Grimaldo needed both men for appearances. The junta produced its preliminary findings in November 1722, recommending that His Majesty return the *Casa* as well as the *Consulado* to Seville.[57] With the downfall of Alberoni and the influence of the Italian queen apparently reduced, conservative vested interests had returned to power and dominated politics in Madrid. The disillusioned Admiral Pez died three and one-half months after the junta issued its preliminary report, certain that his beloved Cádiz would never host the *Casa de la Contratación* and the

---

[51] The description is from William Coxe, *España bajo el reinado de la casa de Borbón...*, II (Madrid 1846), cited by Escudero in *Los orígenes*, p. 69. See also Saint Aignan, *memoire*, October 12, 1717, AAE:CPE, vol. 253, fols. 42–44.

[52] Pérez Mallaina, *Políítica naval*, p. 220.

[53] Miraval to Grimaldi, Madrid, July 12, 1722, AHN, Estado, leg. 2093.

[54] Antonia Heredia Herrera, *Sevilla y los hombres del comercio (1700–1800)* (Sevilla: Editoriales Andaluzes Unidas, 1989), pp. 153–54, 166–69.

[55] Allan J. Kuethe. "Traslado del Consulado de Sevilla a Cádiz: Nuevas perspectivas." in *Relaciones de poder y comercio colonial: nuevas perspectivas*, redactado por Enriqueta Vila Vilar y Allan J. Kuethe (Sevilla: Escuela de Estudios Hispano-Americanos, 1999), p. 71.

[56] Ibid.; Crespo, *La Casa*, p. 105.

[57] Kuethe, "Traslado del Consulado," pp. 74–76.

Consulado de Cargadores a Indias.[58] For Cádiz, the death of its champion and its voice within the circles at court represented a devastating loss.

Before effecting the transfer, officials had to assure that the Guadalquivir River was navigable and to make several administrative changes involving the fleet. Interests in Seville wanted one final test of the San Lúcar Channel, to be conducted during the summer by favorably disposed Manuel López Pintado. The admiral concluded his report on September 6.[59] At the same time, the separation of the *Casa* from the intendancy required the resolution of certain appointments in the Sala de Gobierno. Policy matters involving the fleet had been attached directly to the intendancy in 1717, but the new circumstances required their restoration to the *Casa*.[60]

Meanwhile, the instability of the king worsened. In January 1724, he shocked Spain by announcing his abdication, retreating to La Granja with Elizabeth.[61] His son and successor, Louis, a youth of sixteen years, soon fell under the influence of the powerful conservative voices at court. Moreover, to ensure continuity during the transition, Philip brought Grimaldo with him. Orendain, now elevated to State, remained in Madrid. Mirabal headed a special advisory council that Philip established to guide the young king.[62] All appeared ready for the return of the *Casa de la Contratación* and the *Consulado* to Seville.

Chance intervened, however, as small pox claimed the life of the young king after a reign of less than eight months. Louis had favored the decision to return the *Casa* and the *Consulado* to Seville, but redefining institutional arrangements and naming candidates to fill the positions delayed the royal decree and the instruction ordering a return to Seville. The Council was still considering aspirants when the news arrived of the young king's death, leaving the process suspended until the restoration of Philip V and a return to normalcy. There seemed no compelling reason to rush the return. The royal decree restoring the *Casa* and the *Consulado* arrived in Seville on September 21, 1725.[63] Having prepared an opulent celebration, the *sevillanos* hung *luminarias* around the Casa de Lonja, and for three nights the city celebrated its apparent triumph.[64] Only the paperwork connected to the appointments – in many cases reappointments – of the personnel remained to restore the *Casa*.[65]

---

[58] Castro, *Vida del almirante*, pp. 92–93.

[59] Kuethe, "Traslado del Consulado," p. 76

[60] An excellent discussion of the institutional changes involved in the transfer can be found in Crespo, *La Casa*, p. 49. The *Casa de la Contratación* retained the *Sala de Justicia* after its move to Cádiz.

[61] Construction on the palace had advanced to the point where the monarchs could take up residence in it.

[62] Castellano, *Gobierno y poder*, pp. 92–94; Lynch, *Bourbon Spain*, pp. 82–83.

[63] AGI, IG, leg. 2039.

[64] Kuethe, "Traslado del Consulado," pp. 77–78

[65] Crespo, *La Casa*, p. 52.

The return of Elizabeth Farnese to the throne, however, sealed the fates of those favoring a return of the *Casa de la Contratación* and the *Consulado* to Seville. The queen clearly disliked her exile from Madrid politics, and she had pushed her husband to favor the interests of Cádiz over Seville. She clearly had the upper hand during Philip's second reign. In this new political environment, the influential Miraval was replaced at the Council of Castille by the Bishop of Sigüenza, who was hostile to the Seville partisans.[66]

The instrument of political change would again be an outsider, the Duke of Riperdá, a Dutchman and another creature of the queen. A figure of fleeting power at court, he nevertheless had sufficient time to play a central role in frustrating the aspirations of Seville. Adventurer par excellence, Riperdá had arrived as a diplomat in Madrid, where he soon attached himself to Alberoni. He later gained an appointment as superintendant of the royal textile factory at Guadalajara and eventually over all royal factories. He also ingratiated himself with Elizabeth, and during the late autumn of 1725, he found himself on a fateful mission to Vienna.

Riperdá played a central role in a major crisis gripping Spain during 1725, which facilitated his rise to power. In an effort to restore familial harmony in the aftermath of the War of the Quadruple Alliance, the Bourbon dynasties had entered into a defensive entente on March 27, 1721. Under the terms of the alliance, France returned Pensacola, and the two powers attempted to cement their friendship through contracting dual marriages.[67] Louise Elizabeth of the House of Orleans became the bride of Louis, who was then the Prince of Asturias, while Philip and Elizabeth sent their three-year-old daughter, María Ana Victoria, to Versailles to wed Louis XV when she reached a suitable age. The French were delighted when Louise Elizabeth became queen, but the agreement ceased to serve their interests when she became a dowager. French worries about Louis XV's health added urgency to the need for a wife capable of begetting a dauphine, rather than waiting for the maturity of the young Spanish princess. The French outraged the Spanish court by arranging the marriage Louis to a physically mature Polish princess and returning the child María Ana Victoria to Spain. The Spanish retaliated by sending Louise Elizabeth back to France and dispatching Riperdá to Vienna to explore the possibility of an alliance with the emperor.[68]

Riperdá and his partner, the irrepressible new Minister of Finance, Juan Bautista Orendain, negotiated a treaty of friendship in Vienna that secured

---

[66] Castellano, *Gobierno y poder*, p. 95.

[67] José Antonio Armillas Vicente, "La política exterior de los primeros Borbones," *Historia general de España y América: La España de las reformas hasta el final del reino de Carlos IV*, X-2, coordinated by Carlos E. Corona and José Antonio Armillas Vicente (Madrid: Rialp, 1984), p. 279.

[68] Philippe Erlanger, *Felipe V, esclavo de sus mujeres*, translated by Robert Sánchez (Barcelona: Editorial Ariel, 2003), pp. 283–99.

the emperor's recognition of the Bourbon succession. The Spanish envoys also secured a promise for the engagement of Archduchess Maria Theresa to the infante Charles.[69] This arrangement gave every indication of having monumental importance for Spain as well as Europe, shifting the balance of power against France. When Riperdá returned to Madrid in triumph in late December, Spain and France were on the brink of war. As Ambassador Marcillac reported, "To me, things here appear [to have become] very sour following the arrival of Mr. Riperdá. If the credibility of Mr. Riperdá prevails over that of the other ministers of the King of Spain, we will have war after the arrival of the galleons."[70] Both countries braced for conflict.

Although the alliance ultimately failed and the marriage never took place, Riperdá was the temporary political sensation at court, while Orendain became the Marqués de la Paz. Soon the new favorite of the queen made himself secretary for the Offices of War and Marine and the Indies, as well as the de facto Minister of State, displacing the Marqués de Castelar and Antonio de Sopeña.[71] On New Year's Eve of 1725, Riperdá simply decreed that "until further orders, the execution of those that were to be issued returning the Tribunal of the *Casa de la Contratación* and the *Consulado* from Cádiz to Seville is suspended."[72] The new favorite took this action arbitrarily, without convoking another junta, conducting new tests of the San Lúcar Channel, or even consulting with the Council of the Indies.

Although the decision came in part because the crown wanted to retain unified authority of the Marine Intendancy when war seemed imminent, a mysterious, unsigned letter urged Riperdá to put an end to the *sevillano* monopoly.[73]

Duke, your return has certainly been opportune regarding the suspension of the [return of] Commerce (*Consulado*) and tribunal (*Casa de la Contratación*) to Seville, because the ministers who ruled on that were all cronies (*pan y aguados*) of Miraval and against wind and tide .... Seville procured it (the return) by the means that you know, and Orendain was also an agent in return for various gifts, and the deputy of Seville (Thous) arranged the decree, and the most deplorable are the despicable ministers whom Varas nominated for his own ends, and thus I tell you that it is never desirable that he be president of Contratación but [kept] far away because through him Commerce has enriched itself .... [I]n no other city of Spain do they

---

[69] Orendain had also ingratiated himself with the queen. During the reign of Louis I, when Grimaldo accompanied the king to la Granja, Orendain had secured appointment as minister of State. To his displeasure, however, he had to settle for Finance when Grimaldo reclaimed the more prestigious ministry upon the restoration of Philip V. Escudero, *Los orígenes*, p. 79.

[70] Marcillac to Minister of State Compte de Morville, Madrid, December 17, 1725, AAE:CPE, vol. 342, fols. 387–88.

[71] Escudero, *Los orígenes*, p. 84; Lynch, *Bourbon Spain*, pp. 86–87.

[72] Royal order, Madrid, December 31, 1725, AGI, IG, leg. 2039.

[73] AHN, Estado, leg. 2933. Quoted in original Spanish text in Kuethe "Traslado del Consulado," pp. 79–80.

defraud the king as much as in Seville .... [L]ook at it all with wisdom and impose a solution .... God keep you and give you the skills, Duke, to heal the monarchy. Likewise, I caution you, Duke, regarding the elections of the Consulado .... [E]very-thing is done at the pleasure of Thous, the deputy of Seville, who having been master of the consuls of Commerce since the time of Tinajero, has enriched himself .... [A]nd thus, Duke, fix it all ... what until now has all been a mess.

This message likely came from Queen Elizabeth herself, who was deeply involved in the affairs of government during this period. In addressing the duke, the familiar form was employed, something very few other people at court would have dared to use, and no one else would have directed him so boldly on a matter of such importance and delicacy. In the end, whether or not the letter originated from Elizabeth or one of her close courtiers, the queen's influence over politics in Madrid foiled the aspirations of Seville and brought victory to Cádiz. Once again the instrument for change was an outsider, backed by the queen, who defeated vested interests at court.

Riperdá's power collapsed in May 1726, leading to the rise of José Patiño, a strong advocate for Cádiz.[74] Riperdá had plotted to banish his rival to Flanders, hoping to remove him far from Madrid, but Patiño, aware of the Dutchman's vulnerability, delayed his departure. He then succeeded Riperdá in the Secretariat of the Office of Marine and the Indies and soon thereafter added Finance.[75] Patiño, a confidant of the queen and the man who had effected the transfers in 1717, had no interest in reversing the royal order of December 31. The *Casa de la Contratación* and the Marine Intendancy remained united in Cádiz and the *Consulado* stayed there too.[76] As for the aging and infirm Grimaldo, the queen persuaded Philip to relieve his old friend of his responsibilities at State in September 1726.[77] Orendain, the Marqués de la Paz, realized his dreams by succeeding his old protector.

While the *Casa de la Contratación* moved to Cádiz, the *Consulado* did not share the same fate. Although its administrative apparatus stayed in Cádiz, the greater portion of the *Consulado*'s membership remained in Seville.

---

[74] Orendain communicated to his old collaborator, Riperdá, the news of his dismissal at 11:00 in the evening. Interestingly, this termination did not include exile, but rather a generous pension. French ambassador to Versailles, Madrid, May 20, 1726, AAE:CPE, vol. 343, fols. 343–345. When the Dutchman got cold feet, however, and sought refuge in the British embassy, the Council of Castille proclaimed him an enemy, had him arrested, and imprisoned him at Segovia. Castellano, *Gobierno y poder*, 100–01.

[75] El Pardo, February 27, 1726, AGI, IG, leg 2039; Escudero, *Los orígenes*, pp. 84–87.

[76] A final decree, issued in 1727, confirmed the permanence of the institutions in Cádiz. Ana Gloria Márquez Redondo, *Sevilla <Ciudad y corte> (1729–1733)* (Sevilla: Ayuntamiento de Sevilla, 1994), p. 35. The Presidency of the *Casa* and the Intendancy of Marine did not separate until 1754. Luis Navarro García, *La Casa de la Contratación en Cádiz* (Cádiz: Instituto de estudios gaditanos, 1975), p. 49.

[77] Lynch, *Bourbon Spain*, p. 89. The frail Grimaldo managed to live until 1734, the year of Ordendain's death. Concepción de Castro, *A la sombra de Felipe V: José de Grimaldo, ministro responsable (1703–1726)* (Madrid: Marcial Pons, 2004), p. 379.

According to the arrangement that Patiño worked out (confirmed in 1726) twenty of the electors would come from Seville, ten from Cádiz, and the prior and the first consul would always be *sevillanos*.[78] Under this compromise, control of the *Consulado* remained in Seville, although the seat of the institution had departed. Full dominance would not pass to Cádiz until reforms in 1744 would finally marginalize Seville.[79] What had initially seemed a decisive innovation had instead become a long political struggle.

THE CREATION OF THE VICEROYALTY OF NEW GRANADA

The most ambitious innovation in the New World was the attempt to establish a viceroyalty in New Granada, but it too became a drawn out process that took even longer to resolve than the transfer of the *Casa de la Contratación* and *Consulado* to Cádiz. New Granada´s status as a captaincy general with an audiencia in Santa Fe dated back to the sixteenth century, but by the time of Alberoni, compelling administrative reasons existed to convert the northern region of South America into a separate viceroyalty. New Granada's distance from Lima invited chronic neglect and abuse. A *visita general* of the captaincy general, commissioned in 1685 and conducted by Carlos Alcedo y Sotomayor, unmasked a disturbing disregard for royal authority. Instead of acting on the findings of Alcedo, the *visita* ended abruptly when the governor of Cartagena arrested Alcedo and shipped him off to Havana. A shocking incident occurring in 1715 reaffirmed the instability of royal governance in Santa Fe, when three *oidores* of the audiencia overthrew their president and captain general and imprisoned him in Cartagena. The Council of the Indies commissioned incoming Oidor Antonio Cobían Valdés to investigate, but Alberoni's decision to establish the viceroyalty superseded his commission.[80]

By the early eighteenth century, the presence of foreign rivals in the Caribbean also made manifest the need to strengthen the administrative apparatus of the region. With the British secure in Jamaica and Barbados and the Dutch in Curacao, smuggling abounded all along the Spanish Main.[81] Moreover, the concession extracted by the British at Utrecht to operate the slave trade monopoly – affording them legal entrance onto the mainland – further highlighted the compelling need to tighten administrative controls over the Caribbean coast of South America. The French siege, conquest, and occupation of Cartagena in 1697 during the War of the League of Augsburg

---

[78] Heredia, *Sevilla y los hombres de comercio*, p. 127–33

[79] Kuethe has treated the circumstances that resulted in the reforms of 1744 in "El fin del monopolio: Los Borbones y el Consulado andaluz," in *Relaciones de poder*, pp. 43–47.

[80] Anthony McFarlane, *Colombia before Independence: Economy, Society, and Politics under Bourbon Rule* (Cambridge: Cambridge University Press, 1993), pp. 24–26, 188–89.

[81] See, for example, Gregorio de Robles, ed., *América fines del siglo XVII: Noticia de los lugares de contrabando* (Valladolid: Casa-Museo de Colón y Seminario Americanista de la Universidad, 1980), pp. 29–38, 79–82, 87–95.

forcefully exposed Spain's military vulnerability at its key strongpoint in South America.[82] The failed attempt by Scots to colonize Darién at the end of the seventeenth century demonstrated both foreign ambitions to penetrate the Spanish empire and the weakness of its defenses.[83] In 1717, as he prepared to seize Sardinia and ran the risk of war in Europe, Alberoni envisaged the immediate need to strengthen a strategic, exposed zone of the empire.

The enabling legislation came by royal decree on April 29, followed by the royal *cédula* of May 27.[84] The first viceroyalty to be established since Peru in 1544 would stretch from Guayana in the northeast to Quito in the southwest, with an administrative center at Santa Fe de Bogotá and its principal port and military strongpoint located at Cartagena de Indias. The jurisdiction of Caracas and surrounding provinces, which had been subject to the Audiencia of Santo Domingo, would now also become attached to the tribunal in Santa Fe. Panama would remain subject to Lima.[85] Treasury officials from Quito and Caracas had to render accounts at the tribunal in the viceregal capital.

Establishing a new viceroyalty required careful planning of financial and military affairs, jurisdictional boundaries, and the status of the subordinate audiencias. Crown officials also had to anticipate potential problems arising from the intrusion of royal authority into a habitually neglected portion of the colonial domain. Such preparations did not occur.[86] Instead, the royal *cédula* simply commissioned Antonio de la Pedrosa y Guerrero, a minister of the Council of the Indies, to travel to New Granada. Once on the scene, he was instructed to establish the viceroyalty, laying the groundwork for the viceroy named to follow him.

---

[82] Juan Marchena Fernández, *La institución militar en Cartagena de Indias, 1700–1810* (Sevilla: Escuela de Estudios Hispano-Americanos, 1982), pp. 67–81.

[83] Dennis R. Hidalgo, "To Get Rich for Our Homeland: The Company of Scotland and the Colonization of the Isthmus of Darien," *The Colonial Latin American Historical Review*, 10 (Summer 2001), pp. 331–36. The commander of the Spanish squadron that expelled the Scots was Antonio Gaztañeta, who was destined to revolutionize the design of Spanish warships. John D. Harbron, *Spanish Navy*, p. 19.

[84] AGI, Santa Fe, leg. 542.

[85] For a monographic account of this affair, María Teresa Garrido Conde, *La primera creación del Virreinato de Nueva Granada(1717–1723)* (Sevilla: Escuela de Estudios Hispano-Americanos, 1965), pp. 20–22.

[86] Informal discussions concerning the establishment of a second viceroyalty in South America had occurred from time to time prior to Alberoni's initiative. One such plan found its way to France. Although unfortunately unsigned and undated, textual referents indicate that it came after the French invasion and before the experiment of 1717. Interestingly, the author argued that to include Quito in the new jurisdiction would challenge geographic realities and that the presidency should remain attached to Lima despite its responsibility for funding Cartagena's *situado*. Under this plan, the viceroy would reside at Cartagena by reason of military priorities, despite the impediments imposed by climate, and further, the Audiencia of Santa Fe would be transferred to that same port city. To reduce costs, the Audiencia of Panama, less needed with a tribunal now available on the Caribbean coast, would be suppressed. AAE:MDFD, vol. 262, fols. 309–13.

Despite these vague instructions, royal priorities were clear. The crown gave the new viceroy the powers of governor, captain general, and president, and commanded him to introduce order into the colonial administration and its treasury. Above all, the *cédula* insisted, he should be ready: "to proceed promptly to the *plaza* or *plazas* that enemies of my crown intend to invade."[87] The *situados* (monetary support transfers) for the Caribbean coastal defenses would remain assigned to Quito and Santa Fe.[88] Pedrosa's *cédula* of appointment dated July 1, 1717, granted him virtually all the powers of a viceroy. This document and the other enabling legislation came through the *vía reservada*, from the desk of Fernández Durán.[89]

The crown instructed Pedrosa to abolish the Audiencias of Quito and Panama. These cuts entailed substantial savings, which would defray the costs of establishing a viceregal court in Santa Fe.[90] The radical step of abolishing the two audiencias was part of a general purge of the American courts, which attempted to undo the damage caused by the widespread sale of judicial appointments during the War of the League of Augsburg and the War of the Spanish Succession. When the Panamanian audiencia was extinguished in 1718, for example, all five of its ministers initially faced criminal charges, and one of them was ordered to Spain. The scandals in the Audiencia of Santa Fe revolved around the attempt by three justices to overthrow President Meneses in 1716. The crown recalled all three of them (Arambuzo, Yepes, and Zapata) to Spain as prisoners, with their goods embargoed. President Meneses was simply admonished to return to Madrid at the first opportunity.[91]

The judges of Quito's high court were also an eccentric and fractious group, who became enmeshed in a bitter dispute involving the alleged contraband activities of the court's president, Juan de Sosaya. Sosaya was a prominent Lima merchant, who had purchased his position in 1706 for 20,000 pesos, which he allegedly attempted to recoup with illicit trade activities. According to his enemies, Sosaya had earned nearly 900,000 pesos by selling contraband cacao, French cloth, and oriental goods through Guayaquil, where his close friend Juan de Meléndez served as *corregidor*. When word of these denunciations reached the Council of the Indies, the councilors named a justice on the Lima court, Juan Bautista de Orueta e Irusta (serving as temporary governor of

---

[87] A pronounced Bourbon tendency to employ high-ranking military officers as colonial viceroys would soon become evident. Francisco A. Eissa-Barroso, "'Of Experience, Zeal, and Selflessness': Military Officers as Viceroys in Early Eighteenth-Century Spanish America," *The Americas*, 68 (January 2012), pp. 317–45.

[88] For a comprehensive study of defense funding for New Granada, see José Manuel Serrano, *Ejército y fiscalidad en Cartagena de Indias: Auge y declive en la segunda mitad del siglo XVIII* (Bogotá: El Áncora Editores, 2006).

[89] AGI, SF, leg. 542.

[90] Report, state of the Viceroyalty of New Granada, Francisco Silvestre, Santa Fe, December 3, 1789, AGI, SF, leg. 552.

[91] Royal decree, San Lorenzo, October 31, 1718, AGI, SF, leg. 542.

Panama) to head a special investigation (*pesquisa*) into the matter in 1711. The investigation provoked bitterness and deep divisions among members of the audiencia and local elites, however, as partisan groups formed to support either Sosaya or Orueta. Despite the political infighting in Quito, Orueta presented a case before the Council based on the testimony of forty-four witnesses in Quito and thirty-one in Guayaquil roundly condemning Sosaya. In the end, however, the Council found the evidence insufficient to convict the president in 1713, and they reversed Orueta's suspension of those justices supporting Sosaya, instead fining his accusers. Despite the outcome, tensions and partisan divisions persisted in Quito for decades. Such factionalism and discord undoubtedly factored in the crown's decision to suppress the Audiencia of Quito in 1717.[92]

The crown named the first viceroy, Jorge Villalonga, by royal decree of October 31, 1718.[93] By mid-1719, when Villalonga arrived in Santa Fe, Antonio de la Pedrosa had restored a measure of order to Santa Fe's chaotic and chronically depleted finances, even managing to put together a small surplus for shipment to Spain. The new viceroy undid these gains, however, by spending lavishly on his entry into Bogotá, ostensibly to establish the prestige of his new office.[94] Moreover, on his visit to Cartagena from December 1719 to May 1720 to prepare for the arrival of the *Galeones*, the viceroy allegedly trafficked in contraband merchandise in the port city. He also purportedly allowed French traders to unload contraband merchandise, which saturated local markets in advance of the *Galeones'* arrival.[95] In Spain, the downfall of Alberoni enabled conservative forces to use Villalonga's shortcomings as a pretense to attack the administrative reforms creating the Viceroyalty of New Granada. The residencia of Villalonga, which focused principally on alleged smuggling activities in Cartagena and abuses of power, produced no less than eight legajos of documentation, but in the end, he was exonerated on all thirty-three counts raised against him.[96]

After deliberations in the Council of the Indies, the abolition of the viceroyalty came in a royal *cédula* of November 5, 1723. The *cédula* restored New Granada's former administrative apparatus, including the Audiencias of Panama and Quito.[97] The *cédula* justified this action by the:

little if any redress secured by the creation of a Viceroy: without an increase in revenues, nor having been able to prevent fraud and the other disorders that have

[92] Andrien, *The Kingdom of Quito*, pp. 166-73.
[93] AGI, SF leg. 542.
[94] McFarlane, *Colombia before Independence*, pp. 189–92.
[95] For the intimate interplay between the contraband trade and governance in New Granada during the first two-thirds of the Bourbon century, see Lance Grahn, *The Political Economy of Smuggling: Regional Informal Economies in Early Bourbon New Granada* (Boulder: Westview Press, 1997), especially pp. 111–14 for Villalonga.
[96] Garrido Conde, *La primera creación*, p. 104.
[97] AGI, SF, leg. 542

arisen; the benefits that have followed the establishment of the Viceroy being very limited; and to be more attuned to and in harmony with the principles of a sound economy, to extinguish this office to avert the disbursement of the many resources that sustaining a viceroy necessarily entails.[98]

Despite the corruption and jurisdictional conflicts that accompanied the creation of the viceroyalty, the complex political environment following the downfall and exile of Cardinal Alberoni largely explain the decision.[99] It is highly unlikely that charges of corruption astonished a savvy, experienced politician such as José Grimaldo. Indeed, Madrid even restored to office magistrates of the Audiencia of Panama, who five years earlier had all been removed for corruption![100] In addition, the finances were surely no worse in 1723 than six years before when the viceroyalty was established, and jurisdictional conflicts had always formed part of the empire's political culture. The move was simply part of the conservative backlash that followed the fall of Alberoni. In nearly every case, conservative politicians in Madrid undid his daring innovations, which he had often imposed arbitrarily. The abolition of the viceroyalty paralleled chronologically the nullification of the transfer to Cádiz of the *Casa de la Contratación* and the *Consulado*. And within Spain itself, the suppression of the intendant system that Alberoni had imposed in 1718 followed quickly upon his fall and exile.[101] The period just before and during the reign of Louis I thus represented the high point of the reaction against the perceived abuses of Alberoni. Moreover, with the end of the crisis posed by defeat in the War of the Quadruple Alliance, the positive strategic gains of creating the viceroyalty surely seemed less compelling.

The only major residual of the first viceroyalty was the system of military districts or commandancies general. This office accorded military authority to the governors of Cartagena, Panama, and Caracas, who exercised supervision over adjoining provinces. In the case of Cartagena, these included Santa Marta and Riohacha; for Panama, Portobelo, Darién, Veragua, and Guayaquil; and for Caracas, Maracaibo, Cumaná, the Orinoco River,

---

[98] Ibid.

[99] Garrido Conde was highly skeptical of the reasoning and the factual assertions that justified the reduction of the viceroyalty, especially regarding the alleged failure to improve finances, which she disputed, and the sudden concern over costs, which she believed to be a manageable problem. *La primera creación*, pp. 97–102.

[100] Burkholder and Chandler, *From Impotence to Authority*, p. 41.

[101] The initial step came in 1721, followed by a second in 1724. Henry Kamen, 'El establecimiento de los intendentes en la administración Española, *Hispania*, no. 95, Madrid, 1964, pp. 368–95; Horst Pietschmann, *Las reformas borbónicas y el sistema de intendencias en Nueva España: Un estudio político administrativo*, trans. by Rolf Roland Meyer Misteli (Mexico City: Fondo de Cultura Económica, 1996), pp. 51–55; Luis Navarro García, *Las reformas borbónicas en América: El plan de intendencias y su aplicación* (Seville: Universidad de Sevilla, 1995), pp. 24–25.

Trinidad, and Margarita.[102] In later years, the president of Quito was made commandant general over Popayán, Cuenca, and Guayaquil, which was detached from Panama, while in 1777 Caracas would become an autonomous captaincy general.[103]

THE ROYAL TOBACCO MONOPOLY AND MILITARY REFORM IN CUBA

The idea of establishing a royal tobacco monopoly in Cuba had circulated at court at least since the days of Jean Orry. The monopoly in Spain dated back to 1636, and Havana – compensated by silver transfers from the Royal Treasury in Mexico – had become a coveted supplier for the royal factory in Seville. Too much leaf, however, escaped through contraband trading to foreign markets.[104] Alberoni, desperate to strengthen royal finances as Spain prepared for war, ordered the establishment of a royal tobacco monopoly in Cuba with the royal instruction of April 11, 1717:

In view of the serious damage that results from the extraction of tobacco that the island of Cuba produces to foreign Kingdoms, leaving the Spanish peninsula without that needed to supply it [and] compelling purchases from other Kingdoms to the detriment of my treasury and vassals . . . I have resolved to prohibit the liberality that its nationals have enjoyed up to now with those tobaccos, monopolizing them in the form that their producers and owners may not sell them to any other person than to . . . the superintendent general.[105]

The royal administration calculated Cuba's annual production at 7.3 million pounds of leaf, and it assigned 5 million to Spain; 500,000 to the Canary Islands; 300,000 to Lima, Chile, and Buenos Aires; and 1.5 million to foreign kingdoms. Most production would come from Havana's hinterland, but the monopoly would also establish factors in Santiago de Cuba, Bayamo, Trinidad, and Sancti Spíritus.

This was the first such experiment in America and a daring colonial fiscal reform. Ten months before establishing the tobacco monopoly, using methods

---

[102] Report, current state of the Viceroyalty of New Granada, Francisco Silvestre, Santa Fe, December 3, 1789, AGI, SF, leg. 552. This subject is discussed in Garrido Conde, *La primera creación*, p. 22.

[103] Allan J. Kuethe, *Military Reform and Society in New Granada, 1773–1808* (Gainesville: University Presses of Florida, 1978), p. 11.

[104] An excellent account of the establishment of the tobacco monopoly in Cuba can be found in Leví Marrero, *Cuba: Economía y sociedad*, VII (San Juan: Editorial San Juan, 1978), pp. 41–56. See also, John Robert McNeill, *Atlantic Empires of France and Spain: Louisbourg and Havana, 1700–1763* (Chapel Hill: University of North Carolina Press, 1985), pp. 117–18. A comprehensive, recent treatment is Santiago de Luxán Meléndez, Montsserrat Gárate Ojanguren and José Manuel Gordillo, *Cuba-Canarias-Sevilla: El estanco español del Tabaco y Las Antillas, 1717–1817* (Las Palmas de Gran Canaria: Ediciones del Cabildo de Gran Canaria, 2012).

[105] Quoted in Marrero, *Cuba*, VII, p. 46.

employed in New Granada, Governor and Brigadier General Vicente Raja arrived in Havana, accompanied by four aides bearing instructions to investigate the procedures for establishing a monopoly. The instructions to proceed with the monopoly followed a report from two of Raja's aides, Manuel de León y Navarro and Diego Danza, who had toured the island assessing its productive capacity. The two officers apparently consulted with Cuban growers only in vague terms about the process, because local producers understood only that a new tax was under consideration.[106]

Alberoni's initiative reached Havana and its hinterland in a *bando* of July 27, which also announced the appointment of Salvador Olivares as director. Olivares was the intendant of tobacco in Spain, and one of the experts who had accompanied Raja. The initial Cuban reaction was bewilderment, which quickly turned to anger. The monopolists showed themselves ill-prepared to execute their enterprise, since they brought only 100,000 pesos worth of goods, which they hoped to exchange for an annual tobacco production worth over seven times that amount. The ayuntamiento voted to send a delegate to seek relief from the government in Spain, while the ecclesiastical authorities in Havana urged Madrid to withhold action until local producers could voice their concerns. Governing an empire clearly entailed much more than simply firing off decrees, no matter how long overdue and well intentioned. Raja found himself in an impossible situation given his instructions, but he resolved to proceed with the implementation of the monopoly despite opposition in Cuba. The result was the first major anti-reformist violent uprising during Bourbon rule in Spanish America.[107]

The response of the tobacco growers (*vegueros*) was direct and astonishingly audacious. Four to five hundred men, armed with machetes and some firearms, congregated on August 21 at Jesús del Monte in the eastern hinterland of Havana, and they quickly mobilized to seize control of the countryside and block entrances into the capital. Attempts at mediation by the ayuntamiento and Bishop Gerónimo Valdés failed. When Havana's ill-prepared garrison did not respond to the royal administration's call to arms, the insurgents entered the city, occupying the Plaza de San Francisco. The insurgents' refrain would become familiar over the eighteenth century: "Long live the king and death to bad government." Governor Raja prudently took refuge in the Castle of La Fuerza Vieja, and when the opportunity arose, he escaped to a warship in the harbor along with Olivares, Danza, and León, who all returned to Spain. The ayuntamiento recognized Gómez Marauver – the acting lieutenant governor who enjoyed considerable popularity – as interim governor. The *vegueros* of the Havana hinterland had easily succeeded in overthrowing the royal governor.

---

[106] Ibid., pp. 45–47. Alberoni did submit this question to discussion in Spain, under his direct supervision. Rodríguez Villa, *Patiño y Campillo*, p. 23.

[107] For the first *veguero* uprising, see Marrero, *Cuba*, VII, pp. 47–51.

In 1718, Alberoni responded with neither negotiations nor a compromise, instead ordering 1,000 troops to Havana under Brigadier General Gregorio Gauzo Calderón to crush the rebellion. It took four warships to transport the troops. The Italian's program included a general pardon but also the arrest of the rebel leaders and alleged collaborators within the ayuntamiento. He clearly held local elites responsible for the rebellious citizenry. Finally, Alberoni improved the financial arrangements to support the monopoly. The cardinal's strategy of combining bayonets with a general pardon – after identifying suspected ringleaders – established a model employed in later rebellions during the century, which repeatedly tested the mettle of Madrid's reformers.[108]

Entering Havana in June 1718, Gauzo issued the general pardon for the mass of the insurgents, and he arrested five members of the ayuntamiento, shipping them off to Madrid to face Alberoni. A sixth escaped. Backed by bayonets, the governor personally assumed control over what was left of the monopoly in January 1919. Factors went out to Santiago de Cuba, Bayamo, Trinidad, and Sancti Spíritus. New funding included a 300,000-peso transfer from Mexico, and monopoly officials established standards for financial support. In October of that same year, Madrid returned to Havana the five captive regidores, now properly chastised.

After suppressing the *vegueros*, Secretary of the Office for War Miguel Fernández Durán took advantage of Alberoni's deployment of troops to Havana to order a major military reform in the colony. Based on the model developed in France, the battalion, along with the regiment, had replaced the tercio as the standard tactical unit in the peninsula during the War of Succession, and Durán now introduced that system into Cuba.[109] Although he displayed political flexibility during this period by subordinating his own ambitions to those of the de facto prime minister, Durán (now the Marqués de Tolosa) was no mere creature of Alberoni.[110] Before his assignment to War in 1714, Durán had enjoyed a distinguished career in military administration, serving on the Councils of War and Military Orders and, after 1706, as an official in the Secretariat of War and Treasury under Grimaldo.[111]

Fernández Durán codified policy for the military in the Havana garrison, including its general staff and fortification commanders, in the *Reglamento para la guarnición de La Habana ... 1719*, a comprehensive code with eighty

---

[108] A recent treatment of this point can be found in Derek Williams, "'Who induced the Indian communities?' The Los Pastos Uprising and the Politics of Ethnicity and Gender in Late-Colonial New Granada," *Colonial Latin American Historical Review*, 10 (Summer 2001), pp. 278, 292–94.

[109] Henry Kamen, *The War of Succession in Spain, 1700–1713* (Bloomington: Indiana University Press, 1969), pp. 62–63.

[110] A description of Durán can be found in the instructions for Special Envoy the Marquis de Maulevrier, Versailles, July 9 and 20, 1720, AAE:CPE, vol. 295, fols. 217–36, 266–68.

[111] Nava, "Problemas y perspectivas," p. 164.

articles.[112] He based this policy on recommendations drafted by Ignacio Francisco de Barrutia, commander of Havana's cavalry company. Barrutia knew the local scene in Cuba intimately, and he returned to Madrid to report on the events of 1718.[113] The new policy combined the seven individual companies, which previously had been contracted out to individuals, with the Spanish reinforcements to form a fixed battalion. This new battalion included six 100-man infantry companies, a seventh of newly introduced grenadiers, and an upgraded, modernized officer corps. Separate companies continued for the artillery and the cavalry, now set at 100 and 30 men respectively. The new regulation barred Cubans from serving as officers and set the percentage of locals that might enlist at 20 percent, demonstrating Madrid's belief that Spanish control of the military was essential to sustain the empire. Crown officials only tolerated Cuban enlistments to ease recruitment difficulties and to curtail transportation costs. Only natives over twenty could serve, while Spaniards qualified at sixteen.[114]

Alberoni's program did not respond to Cuban concerns over the crown-imposed monopoly on the purchase of Cuban tobacco. As a result, in June 1720 a second anti-monopoly uprising erupted when some 200 armed horsemen attacked the farms of monopoly collaborators in the districts of Santiago de las Vegas and Guanabacoa to the east of Havana, uprooting plantings and burning buildings.[115] Again, the conspirators congregated at Jesús del Monte to plot strategy. This time, the rebels not only interrupted the food supply into Havana but also took control of the aqueduct supplying water to the city, and the rebel numbers grew daily. Gauzo threatened to use force, but instead he reacted moderately in accord with the changing political mood in Madrid after the fall of Alberoni. He delayed action while enabling José Bayona y Chacón, a highly influential magnate, and Pedro Agustín Morell de Santa Cruz, the diocesan vicar, to mediate a cessation of hostilities, but this turned out to be only a temporary lull in the crisis.

The conservative government in Madrid now pursued a more moderate, conciliatory policy. Despite the military forces now available to crush the rebellion, the Grimaldo government, acting through Fernández Durán, issued a general pardon in October and November 1720. Officials in Spain also attempted to mollify Cuban producers by revising monopoly policy to permit the sale of tobacco surpluses on the free market, allowing exports to other Spanish colonies.[116] Cubans quickly exploited this opportunity by selling

---

[112] *Reglamento para la guarnición de La Habana … 1719* (His Majesty to Fernández Durán), Buen Retiro, April 11, 1719, AGI, Santo Domingo (herinafter SD), 2104-A

[113] Report, Ignacio Francisco Barrutia, Parral, May 28, 1728, AGI, Guadalajara, leg.110.

[114] For Cubans, the regulation specified "that they not hold any offices."

[115] For the second *veguero* uprising, see Marrero, *Cuba*, VII, pp. 51–52.

[116] Royal decrees, Valsaín, October 25, 1720, and San Lorenzo, November 17, 1720, AGI, SD, leg. 325.

their leaf in Portobelo, Cartagena, Trinidad de Barlovento, Cumaná, and La Guaira.[117]

The truce lasted two years, as the Spanish monopolists and some Cuban producers attempted to make the new system work. Nonetheless, a satisfactory political settlement still eluded authorities. Madrid's moderate posture did not gain the support of everyone in Havana, and apprehension arose about the monopoly's manipulative purchasing practices and from the amount of space assigned independent purchasers on the *Galeones* of Baltasar de Quebara, then in port. Fear spread that the hated restrictions of the recent past might return. In February 1723, proclaiming a moratorium on new plantings while negotiations about a satisfactory price structure proceeded, several hundred radicals threatened to uproot all the tobacco plants owned by monopoly collaborators. Attacks on the properties of producers in the San Miguel del Padrón, Guanabacoa, and Jesús del Monte districts demonstrated the seriousness of the threat, and militants also menaced Santiago de las Vegas and San Felipe y Santiago.

Attempting to protect loyal producers, Governor Guazo called out his troops. Matters quickly turned violent when elements of the fixed garrison confronted some 500 to 600 insurgents near Santiago de las Vegas. Before the day was done, a firefight had erupted and both sides suffered light casualties. Two days later, with his troops deployed at Jesús del Monte, the center of rebel territory, Guazo panicked at rumors of rebel plans to rescue eleven prisoners taken earlier by his men. Tragically, he ordered the prisoners immediately shot at the historic rebel gathering place. He then ordered the bodies displayed from trees along the Royal Highway, where they remained for forty hours, before he allowed burial. Guazo followed the executions with a royal pardon.[118]

The governor's brutal actions in executing the rebels without a trial horrified authorities in Madrid. As a royal *cédula* of June 17 stated:

And to my displeasure [has been] the great haste with which the punishment was administered upon those prisoners, without having provided the time, albeit brief, for justice to hear them and to find out, through their statements, who had been the primary instigators of the uprising, so that the appropriate penalty might be imposed for the crime that had been committed.[119]

Moreover, the pardon permitted culpable leaders to escape royal justice. On the recommendation of the Council of the Indies, the crown severely reprimanded

---

[117] Marrero, *Cuba*, VII, p. 52.

[118] Resumen para que se vea en el Consejo la carta adjunta de Gregorio Guazo Calderón, Madrid, August 6, 1723, AGI, SD, leg. 484. Of the executed, three each were from the rebel districts of Jesús del Monte, San Miguel, and Guanabacoa. One hailed from Havana, the other was a drifter. Guazo claimed that two Jesuits heard the men's confessions. For a general overview of the third *veguero* uprising, see Marrero, *Cuba*, VII, pp. 52–56.

[119] Royal *cédula*, Madrid, June 17, 1724, AGI, SD, leg. 484.

Guazo. A royal *cédula*, issued under Louis I on June 17, 1724, resolved the crisis by reaffirming free trade in tobacco, abolishing the monopoly.[120] Another Alberoni initiative thus came undone, as the opponents of reform won the political battle at court. Plans for a tobacco monopoly in Cuba and a viceroyalty in New Granada would lie dormant while conservative politicians controlled the government.

Even Alberoni's military reforms drew criticism from conservatives in Madrid, particularly from the venerable Admiral Andrés de Pez. On October 15, 1719 – two months before the Italian's exile – Pez criticized the new regulation for the Havana garrison. Firstly, he doubted that bayonets could assure the fidelity of Spain's American subjects. Secondly, as a naval officer, Pez deplored the predicted escalating army costs of the program. The changes, he argued,

only serve [to increase] costs ... for under the previous arrangements the *situado* came to 114,000 pesos [annually], while today it exceeds 160,000 according to the regulation, and it is not wise to introduce innovations, nor new ordinances for the Indies, but rather to focus all attention on what was observed in the past, and consequently H.M. [should] order the [regulation] for Havana recalled as prejudicial to the royal service, as much for the increase in salaries as for their being superfluous.[121]

Perhaps his advanced age led him to favor the old ways, but the admiral nevertheless identified what over the long haul would become the Achilles heel of Bourbon reformism: the considerable costs involved.

Despite its critics, military reform in Cuba was the only major initiative in America to outlast Alberoni. This can partly be explained by the survival in office of Fernández Durán, who defended the Cuban regulation as a modernization of the army, not merely as an instrument of colonial pacification.[122] The army's ability to keep the rebels out of Havana during the second *veguero* uprising in the summer of 1720 also vindicated those supporting the new establishment. Fernández Durán's fall in January 1721, and his replacement by Baltasar Patiño and Pez occurred just as news of the insurgency reached Madrid.[123] The admiral died in March 1723, before he could undo the reform. The Fixed Battalion of Havana thus remained in place to become the core of the future Cuban army, essentially financed by the Mexican *situado*.

Yet, even in early military reform, the reaction against Alberoni and his policies took its toll. Fernández Durán had intended to extend the Havana regulation throughout the American empire, but this did not occur immediately.

[120] *Consulta*, Council of the Indies, Madrid, October 23, 1723, and royal *cédula*, Madrid, June 17, 1724, AGI, SD, leg. 484.

[121] Summary, debate "sobre el reglamento militar de La Habana," s.d., AGI, SD, leg. 2104A.

[122] Durán, who remained in Madrid while Grimaldo traveled with the monarchs, had to channel his work through the Minister of State. Maulevrier to Versailles, October 21, 1720, AAE: CPE, vol. 296, fols. 188–96.

[123] Nava, "Problemas y perspectivas," p. 164.

The new policy would lie dormant outside of Cuba until Patiño resurrected it (see Chapter 3). The lessons arising from the events of 1717–1723 in Cuba would long be remembered in Madrid. The cadre of reformers sent to Havana under Charles III came prepared to consult and to compromise with the local community, not to act arbitrarily (see Chapter 7).

CONCLUSION

Alberoni left a mixed legacy. After the defeats in the War of the Quadruple Alliance, conservatives reversed most of his heavy-handed initiatives affecting colonial policy. His weakness arose from his inability or his unwillingness to build consensus. Without consulting Patiño, he had even initiated action in 1719 to replace Portobelo with Buenos Aires as the terminus for the South American fleet. Apparently, the Marine intendant's threat to resign delayed Alberoni's initiative, and his regime's collapse later that year put an end to the plan.[124] At the same time, he framed policies designed to attack the principal issues impeding a revival of colonial commerce, which was the lifeblood of the Atlantic empire. Widespread contraband and foreign penetration of the legal trade had undermined commerce, a problem begun in the seventeenth century, which worsened with Spanish weakness in the War of Succession. Gaining control of Spain's ports and moving the *Consulado* and *Casa de la Contratación* from Seville to Cádiz were important policies designed to gain more authority over the legal trade in the Spanish Atlantic. Foreign mercantile interests were undoubtedly necessary to supply the Indies, but they had grown too influential economically and politically. Likewise, the imposition of the tobacco monopoly in Cuba had the potential to provide a stimulus to the tobacco industry in Spain and a bonanza in royal revenues. It also promised to curtail the contraband trade in Cuban leaf in the Caribbean. The establishment of the Viceroyalty of New Granada was another important first step in curtailing the escalating contraband trade in the Caribbean, a situation made even more serious by the concessions granted to the British at Utrecht. Without curtailing contraband, the transatlantic convoy system could never work profitably, which threatened the whole Spanish Atlantic commercial order. As a practical reformer, Alberoni knew instinctively that problems on both sides of the Atlantic were intertwined, and only by enacting reforms in both Spain and the Indies could he achieve any success. Such reforms also had international implications, involving Spain's principal rivals in the Atlantic – Britain, France, and the Netherlands.

As he traveled across southern France en route to Italy during early 1720 in the company of an escort, the Chevalier de Marcieu, the cardinal reflected upon

---

[124] Rodríguez Villa, *Patiño y Campillo*, p. 45.

the royal administration that he had dominated for five years. He declared it weak, and he saw little prospect for its future. As for the people around the king and queen, he liked Daubenton personally and respected Grimaldo, but he found little to praise in the many others at court.[125] Although Alberoni was a rank outsider, this condition was also his strength. No Spaniard would have dared to innovate as audaciously and as broadly as he attempted to do. Nonetheless, Alberoni, like Orry before him, was a "loose cannon," who depended solely on his relationship with the royal family to maintain power. As a result, he was forced into the dynastic adventures in Italy that led to his downfall. Although his agenda suffered defeat after defeat following his fall from power, it would ultimately triumph through efforts of the brilliant Galician-Italian José Patiño, who had flourished under his protection. His ideas would become the foundation for the reformist agenda of the eighteenth-century empire, as subsequent governments would seek to modernize commercial structures, improve colonial administration, enhance royal income, and bolster the armed forces.

As the early reforms under Alberoni demonstrate, the process of Atlantic reform led to political upheavals involving a wide range of interest groups in Spain and the Indies. They also involved the interests of Spain's rivals, Britain, France, and the Netherlands. Alberoni's attempts to control Spain's ports, for example, produced bitter antagonisms with all three of the monarchy's foreign competitors, and it was a major provocation leading to the disastrous War of the Quadruple Alliance. The attempt to move the principal institutions of colonial commerce from Seville to Cádiz also set off political conflicts with the *Consulado* in Seville, and foreign interests deeply involved in supplying European wares for legal trade with the Indies. Indeed, only the unexpected death of King Louis I, the temporary triumph of Riperdá in Vienna, and the apparent secret intervention of Queen Elizabeth salvaged the plan to move the commercial port of call for the Indies to Cádiz. Other reforms championed by Alberoni, such as the establishment of the tobacco monopoly and the creation of the new Viceroyalty of New Granada, did not survive his downfall. Moreover, efforts to establish the tobacco monopoly led to a popular coalition of tobacco growers and workers opposed to the innovation, leading to the first rebellion against the Bourbon dynasty in the eighteenth century. Even the military reforms in Cuba barely outlasted the efforts of conservatives like Admiral Pez to reverse them. Only the long-standing fears of yet another new rebellion in Cuba salvaged the modernized system. In short, Alberoni's first

---

[125] His criticism could be harsh, as for example when assessing the Duke of Veraguas, whom he found "a big talker, a big coward, and of a sordid miserliness, capable of doing anything for money . . . [and] of a superficial spirit incapable of following through on anything that he says and that he proposes." Invantaire des Pieces concernent la comisión donnée a M. le Chevalier de Marcieu. . .1720, AAE:CPE, vol. 294, fols. 86–95.

efforts to transform the Spain's empire from a composite monarchy to a more centralized, absolutist state produced serious political disputes and even led to armed revolts in Cuba. Such political conflicts, along with the dynastic ambitions of Philip and Elizabeth, largely shaped the course of early eighteenth century reform, leading to its frustration in the short run.

3

José Patiño and the Revival of Reform, 1726–1736

Following the collapse of Alberoni's attempt to recapture control of Spanish ports and the colonial trade, his successors worked to revive transatlantic commerce through the legal system of fleets, but this effort faced enormous obstacles and would enjoy only limited success. Spain's ministers had to hinder the South Sea Company's commercial activities – legal and illegal – while also limiting the smuggling of Dutch, French, and British traders working independently of the South Sea Company. Foreign traders, particularly in Britain, had long sought direct trade with the Spanish empire, and they viewed the Spanish crown's attempts to regulate commerce with the Indies as an unfair restriction of free trade.[1] The Spanish regarded commerce in the Spanish Atlantic as a closed metropolitan monopoly, and they wanted to shut out all foreign intruders. This involved gaining control of sea lanes in the Caribbean, the Pacific, and the South Atlantic without provoking war with foreign rivals, particularly Great Britain, the premier naval power in the world. It also meant mediating among colonial and Spanish interest groups opposed to change, while dramatically curtailing the culture of political corruption in colonial bureaucracies in New Spain and Peru. It was a daunting task that fell to one of Spain's most experienced ministers of the period, José Patiño. In his portrait (shown in Figure 3.1), Patiño appears every bit the proud, self-confident public servant, and his decade in power would be a time of real accomplishment.

Patiño's ten years in power (1726–1736) saw none of the tumultuous political divisions in Spain and violent conflicts in the Indies that helped to discredit Alberoni's reforms after the disastrous War of the Quadruple Alliance. The great minister's background combined both Spanish and Italian credentials, allowing him to sustain a stable relationship with the royal family, especially the queen. Coming from a Galician family, he also

---

[1] For the British perspective on penetration of Spanish Atlantic markets, see Dorothy Marshall, *Eighteenth Century England*, (London: Longman Group Limited, 1962), pp. 176–77.

FIGURE 3.1 *José Patiño (1666–1736)* by Rafael Tegeo in the Museo Naval. This is a copy painted by Tegeo in 1828 from an original painted by an unknown artist. (See plate section for color version)

reassured political elites and the mass of Spaniards who much preferred to be governed by one of their own. His stable, confident method of governance also contrasted with the volatile character of the leadership that preceded him, from Orry to Alberoni to Riperdá.

For America, this decade witnessed both consolidation and transition as Patiño picked up the unfinished work of his former protector and advanced it, focusing on naval affairs and colonial reform. This period saw no sweeping institutional innovations, however, leading one prominent scholar to remark: "Patiño was not an original thinker, or even a reformer. He was a conservative, pragmatic and indefatigable official who possessed superior administrative talents and wide experience."[2] Nonetheless, his colonial policies focused on the central problems plaguing the Spanish Atlantic – contraband, corruption, and foreign incursions into the Spanish Main. He pursued a dogged struggle for control of the American trade, while obstructing whenever possible the restrictive conditions imposed at Utrecht and reaffirmed by Spain's humiliation in the War of the Quadruple Alliance. Given his limited options, Patiño established a close collaboration with the *Consulado* of Cádiz, which allowed him the means to make substantial advances toward reclaiming Spain's colonial trade.

THE MINISTRY OF STATE FOR MARINE AND THE INDIES

Patiño's power derived from his dual position as secretary of the Office for Marine and the Indies and secretary of the Office for Finance, and on his special relationship with the queen. His older brother, Baltasar, the Marqués de Castelar, had headed the Ministry of War since 1721, while the aging Orendain, the Marqués de la Paz, remained at State. In 1730, when a diplomatic crisis led to the deployment of Baltasar Patiño in Versailles as ambassador extraordinaire, José also assumed his portfolio for War. Meanwhile, Orendain's declining health reduced his effectiveness as early as the late 1720s. Patiño again filled the gap, but he did not officially assume State until the minister's death in 1734.[3] With Patiño controlling the key ministerial portfolios, a level of administrative coordination reigned that would not be duplicated until the Junta de Ministros appeared during the early years of Charles III. Although his reforms had an impact on both sides of Spain's Atlantic empire, Patiño avoided the political clashes with vested interest groups that had undermined Alberoni's policies. Nonetheless, Patiño depended on the queen to remain in power, and to retain her loyalty the minister periodically had to subordinate his own policies for reviving American trade and the navy to pursue the dynastic interests of the royal family. As Elizabeth's family grew to three sons and three daughters, her challenge must have seemed almost impossible. A painting of the royal family by Louis Michael van Loo in 1743 shows the king's son by his first marriage, Ferdinand, who was in line to gain the Spanish throne before the queen's eldest child, Charles. As a result Elizabeth Farnese had to find thrones for her own children in Italy. As future events demonstrated, however, the determined queen would enjoy remarkable success in placing her children (see Figure 3.2).

Resurrected in 1721 following the collapse of the Alberoni regime, the Secretariat of State for Marine and the Indies served as the principal policy-making body for reform in the Spanish Atlantic during Patiño's decade in

---

[2] John Lynch, *Bourbon Spain, 1700–1808* (Oxford: Basil Blackwell, 1989), p. 91.
[3] Antonio Béthencourt Massieu, *Patiño en la política internacional de Felipe V*, introduced by Vicente Palacio Atard (Valladolid: Universidad de Valladolid, 1954), pp. 14–15.

FIGURE 3.2 *The Family of Philip V* by Louis Michael van Loo, in 1743 in the Museo del Prado. Left to right in an imaginary assemblage: María Ana Victoria, infanta and future queen of Portugal; Barbara de Braganza, wife of Ferdinand; Ferdinand, Prince of Asturias and future king of Spain; King Philip V; Louis, infante-cardinal; Queen Elizabeth Farnese; Philip, duke of Parma; Louise Elizabeth of Bourbon (France), Philip's wife; María Teresa, infanta and future wife of Dauphine Louis; María Antonia, infanta and future queen of Piedmont-Sardinia; María Amalia of Saxony, wife of Charles; and Charles, king of Naples and future king of Spain. In the foreground are the infant children of the duke of Parma and the king of Naples. (See plate section for color version)

power. The secretariat subdivided into five desks – Mexico, Guatemala, Peru, New Granada, and the Navy. The four Indies desks each had between seven and nine departments. Mexico, for example, included departments for the viceroy, the Audiencia of Mexico, the tribunal of Guadalajara, the Philippines, the Armada de Barlovento, the *Flotas*, and for Mexican register ships and *avisos*, *consultas* (administrative proceedings) and decrees, and appointments.[4] The desk for Guatemala also managed miscellaneous matters such as the Almadén mines, the Factoría de Indias, the *Casa de la Contratación*, the *Consulado*, and the Audiencia of Santo Domingo. New

---

[4] The Council of the Indies considered various issues and made recommendations to the king in the form of a *consulta*, and made a recommendation for action on the matter. For a more detailed discussion of the *consulta*, see Kenneth J. Andrien, "Legal and Administrative Documents," in Joanne Pillsbury et al., *Guide to Documentary Sources for Andean Studies, 1530–1900*, vol. I (Norman: University of Oklahoma Press, 2008), p. 109.

Granada included Panama, even though that jurisdiction pertained to Peru.[5] This administrative structure filtered the enormous inflow of colonial correspondence so that the minister would see only matters his subordinates judged important. To guarantee access to a higher level in the office, colonial officials could label items *muy* (very) *reservada*, and some transmissions might be designated for the minister's eyes only. Ordinarily, the men who served at the several desks of the Secretariat did not rise further in the system; their skills were primarily bureaucratic, not political.[6]

As Patiño broadened his administrative control through the Ministry for Marine and the Indies, the power of the Council of the Indies continued to wane comparatively. Despite the reduction of its duties, the Council remained the traditional mouthpiece of the aristocratic elite, and Patiño still consulted it on major policy initiatives. In addition to its judicial prerogatives, the Council's audit tribunal (*contaduría*) oversaw *Consulado* finances relating to taxes on colonial trade. Patiño was no more inclined than Alberoni, however, to brook interference with his agenda.[7] When Council President Baltasar Zuñiga died in 1727, Patiño left the office vacant for the rest of his ministry, rendering the Council virtually powerless to act independently in colonial matters.[8]

During this period, King Philip governed during his healthy moments, and on occasion he experienced bursts of hyperactivity, but these episodes were inevitably followed by long periods of depression, withdrawal, and inactivity. He became so incapacitated in late 1726 that he signed a decree formally making Elizabeth governor, a step repeated the following summer. Thereafter, Elizabeth frequently assumed direct responsibility for decision-making.[9] As the queen represented the crown de facto, she struggled to protect both her vulnerable spouse and her dynastic interests. Nonetheless, Patiño provided the political and administrative continuity that stabilized the government. In 1735, the Venetian ambassador observed:

---

[5] Guatemala also included its audiencia, that of Santo Domingo, Florida, the Canaries, the *Seminario*, and the Council of the Indies, and as well as for Mexico, *consultas* and decrees, appointments, and register and *aviso* ships. Peru encompassed the viceroy, its audiencia, those for Charcas and Chile, the Armada del Sur, and registers and *avisos, consultas* and decrees, and appointments. New Granada entailed the viceroy, its audiencia, those for Panama and Quito (which were about to be abolished), registers and *avisos, consultas* and decrees, appointments, and individual registers *(registros de partes)*. Pez to Campoflorido, Madrid, April 27, 1721, AGI, IG, leg. 918.

[6] Juan Luis Castellano, *Gobierno y poder en la España del siglo XVIII* (Granada: Editorial Universidad de Granada, 2006), pp. 88–91.

[7] In general, the councils lost standing under Patiño. See Castellano, *Gobierno y poder*, pp. 109–12.

[8] Gildas Bernard, *Le Secrétariat D'État et le Conseil Espagnol des Indes (1700–1808)* (Geneva: Droz, 1972), pp. 79, 211.

[9] Henry Kamen, *Philip V of Spain: The King who Reigned Twice* (New Haven: Yale University Press, 2001), pp. 159–62, 184–85.

Patiño is the man who has rendered himself necessary to the queen, to the aggrandizement of her sons and to the kingdom. He is clear-sighted, ready in resource, untiring in labour, and disinterested. He may fitly be called first minister, though he has not been formally appointed, for he gives orders and forms decisions in every class of business, with full authority, and only communicates to the queen what he thinks most necessary.[10]

Although Philip never developed the close personal ties with Patiño that he had with Grimaldo, the king still had to work with him.[11]

Philip's mental problems took a severe turn for the worse in 1728, culminating in an attempted second abdication in June.[12] His escape from the palace was frustrated, however, when a guard alerted the queen.[13] In an effort to divert the king from his mental problems, the royal family journeyed in January 1729 to a bridge especially constructed over the Caya River near Badajoz, where the infanta María Ana Victoria ("Marianina") was exchanged again, this time for Barbara of Braganza, who was engaged to marry the Prince of Asturias, Ferdinand. Marianina was betrothed to John, the future king of Portugal.[14] Instead of returning to Madrid, however, the court continued on to Seville, where it remained for an extended stay.

Sevillanos greeted the royal family enthusiastically and expectantly, hoping to cultivate royal favor and retrieve the *Casa de la Contratación*. Philip showed an initial burst of energy and of good behavior, but he soon vanished behind the walls of the Alcázar. The royal family would not return to Castile until May 1733, when Spain found itself entangled in an international crisis arising from the death of August II of Poland in February, leading to the outbreak of a general European war.

THE LEGACIES OF UTRECHT AND THE ASIENTO

Patiño and his political allies viewed commercial concessions imposed by the Treaty of Utrecht as the principal impediment to any serious reform of Spain's transatlantic trading system. The slave monopoly and the annual ships of permission gave the British a coveted legal opening to market goods in Spanish America and served as an instrument for smuggling. The shrewd and ruthless Henry St. John, who was the Viscount Bolingbroke and the British foreign minister at the time of Utrecht, had been quite open in his

---

[10] Quoted in ibid., p. 203.

[11] Ibid., p. 205.

[12] The French Foreign Ministry viewed the situation as so delicate that it returned Lieutenant General Marquis de Brancas to Madrid as special ambassador. Brancas, it will be recalled, had served in Spain in 1714. Memoire, instructions for Brancas, Versailles, April 26, 1728, AAE: CPE, vol. 354, fols. 277–98.

[13] Elizabeth had been ill at the time with a badly inflamed throat. The incident left her so out of sorts that her physician felt compelled to bleed her.

[14] María Ángeles Pérez Samper, *Isabel de Farnesio* (Barcelona: Plaza y Janés, 2003), pp. 233–39.

assessment that the chief value of the slave trade monopoly would be as a cover for illicit commerce, and he was undoubtedly correct.[15]

Jamaica served as a major center of this illicit trade, and the volume of goods shipped from England far exceeded the demand offered in the English American colonies.[16] Contrabandists on their way to the Spanish Caribbean would commonly make stopovers in Jamaica to load up enough captives to pass as slavers operating under the *asiento*.[17] Even British warships, ostensibly providing "protection" from pirates, served as transporters of contraband. In the South Atlantic, slavers smuggled contraband, sometimes supplied from other ships plying the same waters.[18] According to the treaty, the British "may import and vend the said Negroes in all the Ports of the North Sea, and that of Buenos Aires at their choice."[19] Contraband also entered through slave-trade factories, which had the legal right to rent buildings for storing imported supplies and land to produce foodstuffs for the sustenance of those slaves awaiting sale.[20]

In Panama, the South Sea Company used Panama City or other points on the Pacific coast as bases for supplying slaves and contraband to Peru, employing craft in the range of 400 tons. In Buenos Aires, the British constructed a factory to supply the Río de la Plata with 800 slaves annually, with another 400 destined for Chile.[21] Company ships laden with European wares could even store goods in the Buenos Aires factory, according to the terms of the second Bubb Treaty (see Chapter 1).[22] These ships then returned with Peruvian bullion gained through the sale of slaves and also illicit produce in Spanish American markets.[23] Such facilities were privileged areas, exempt from routine inspections.[24] Moreover, well-placed bribes usually sufficed to induce the cooperation of local Spanish officials.[25]

[15] Jean O. McLachlan, *Trade and Peace with Old Spain, 1667–1750* (Cambridge: University Press, 1940), p. 61.

[16] Memoire, abuses of the Royal Assiento Company, Spain, April 30, 1725, AAE:CPE, vol. 343, fols. 143–46.

[17] Report, Spain, s.d., AAE:CPE, vol. 295, fols. 122 ff.

[18] Memoire, abuses of the Royal Assiento Company, Spain, April 30, 1725, AAE:CPE, vol.343, fols. 143–46; Arthur S. Aiton, "The Asiento Treaty as Reflected in the Papers of Lord Shelburne," HAHR, 8 (May 1928), p. 175.

[19] *The Assiento; or Contract for Allowing to the Subjects of Great Britain the Liberty of Importing Negroes into the Spanish America* (Madrid, March 26, 1713), art. 8. A copy can be found in Charles Jenkinson, comp., *A Collection of all the Treaties of ... Great Britain and Other Powers ...* (London 1785), vol. 1, pp. 375–99.

[20] Ibid., arts. 22, 34–35.

[21] Ibid., art. 9.

[22] "Convention pour l'assiento des negres," clause V, in Saint Aignan to Versailles, Madrid, June 12, 1716, AAE:CPE, vol. 251, fols. 61–76.

[23] Ibid., art. 10.

[24] *The Assiento*, arts. 14–15; French commentary, AAE:CPE, vol. 241, fols.155–67.

[25] Vera Lee Brown, "The South Sea Company and Contraband Trade," *The American Historical Review*, 31 (July 1926): pp. 662–78.

The treaties permitted ships returning to Britain to carry only payments in coin or goods received directly from the sale of slaves, but this provision was seldom honored. Shippers regularly transported unregistered silver back to Europe, allowing miners and merchants to avoid paying the royal fifth on new production.[26] They also sent agricultural products such as cacao, sugar, dyes, vicuña wool, tallow, and hides.[27] Tobacco was a favorite of smugglers returning from Havana.[28] Cuba's leaf had already acquired a coveted reputation in Europe, and it attracted buyers to the island in abundance.[29] In 1734, for example, a slave ship from the South Sea Company sailed fearlessly into Havana's harbor to exchange its cargo of twelve slaves and a large quantity of smuggled European wares for Cuban tobacco. The new governor, Juan Francisco Güemes de Horcasitas stunned the smugglers when he ordered a detachment of troops to take control of the ship and seize whatever contraband they found. The bemused French consul observed that "the English have not run into anything like this here in the past eighteen years."[30] One more smuggler fell into Horcasitas's net before the news circulated that an unusual administrator (who would make a stellar administrative career as the Conde de Revillagigedo) had come to govern in Havana. Smugglers had to find other means to extract Cuban tobacco, but the young governor was not typical of the corrupt Spanish officials that enterprising British traders might expect to encounter.[31] Alberoni had established the royal monopoly on Cuban tobacco precisely to stop this illicit trade in Cuban leaf.

British legal ships of permission also inflicted significant damage to the Spanish trade fairs at Portobelo and Veracruz. The *Royal George* arrived at the Portobelo Fair of 1722 with 1,000 tons of high-quality, reasonably priced merchandise. These goods came with legal tax exemptions providing an advantage of 25 to 30 percent over the price of *Consulado* goods.[32] By offering enticing credit terms, the British easily won the competitive battle, and some twenty other merchantmen lurked in nearby waters, ready to unload contraband merchandise under cover of the *Royal George*.[33] As a

---

[26] Ibid., p. 669.

[27] George H. Nelson, "Contraband Trade Under the Assiento," *The American Historical Review*, 51 (October 1945), p. 62.

[28] At least some of the Cuban tobacco went to Hamburg. See also Leví Marrero, *Cuba: Economía y sociedad* , VI (San Juan: Editorial San Juan, 1978), pp. 20–22.

[29] John Robert McNeill, *Atlantic Empires of France and Spain: Louisbourg and Havana, 1700–1763* (Chapel Hill: University of North Carolina Press, 1985), pp. 154–56.

[30] Beloquine to Maurepas, Havana, April 30,1734, Archives Nacionales de France, Correspondance Consulaire (hereinafter cited as ANF:CC), B1, vol. 616.

[31] Beloquine to Maurepas, Havana, October 24, 1734, ANF:CC, B1, vol. 616.

[32] Geoffrey J. Walker, *Spanish Politics and Imperial Trade, 1700–1789* (Bloomington: Indiana University Press, 1979), p. 145. A 500-ton ship could carry a cargo well in excess of its weight (at least double). Malamud Rikles, *Cádiz y Saint Malo*, p. 67.

[33] Fisher, *Bourbon Peru, 1750–1824* (Liverpool 2003), pp. 18.

result, much of the Spanish cargo shipped from Cádiz remained unsold for years.

British permission ships also undermined the fairs at Veracruz. In 1717 and 1718, the *Royal Prince*, which sailed with the fleet of Antonio Serrano, captured the Mexican market, introducing a large quantity of merchandise at better prices than *Consulado* merchants could offer. The War of the Quadruple Alliance interrupted all maritime traffic (legal and illegal) for the period between 1718 and 1720, and no fleet could sail soon after Serrano's. However, Mexican markets remained glutted with foreign goods when merchants arriving under Fernando Chacón Medina y Salazar opened their fair at Jalapa in February of 1721.[34] *Consulado* agents also faced stiff competition from another ship of permission at that fair, a pattern that undermined their sales during subsequent Mexican fairs in 1723, 1725, and 1732–1733. Only in 1729 and in 1736–1737, when no British ships participated, did things go relatively smoothly for monopoly merchants from Andalusia.[35]

The overall results of the fleet system proved disappointing and frustrating. Between 1721 and the outbreak of war in 1739, only six *Flotas* departed for Veracruz, and the *Galeones* for Cartagena and Portobelo sailed only four times. Merchants from Cádiz delayed sailing for the American fairs until they could anticipate an advantageous market, to avoid finding themselves shunned or manipulated by local monopolists well stocked with British goods from the permission ships and contraband merchandise. As a result, merchandise delivered by Spanish traders to the fairs sold poorly, and dealers very often remained in the Indies for several years to market their wares. Merchants from the Lima and Mexico City merchant guilds were normally reluctant to venture out with their silver to Portobelo and Veracruz – or, later, Jalapa – where they came under administrative pressure to purchase goods that they could not readily sell. As a consequence, viceroys very frequently had to negotiate or compel their participation. A final complication for merchants in New Spain was the competition provided by the Manila Galleon, which regularly introduced into Mexico attractively priced Asian cloth, which frequently found its way south to Peru.[36]

Gaining the *asiento* and long years of experience in the contraband trade allowed some British merchants to secure accurate market information and to establish commercial networks. British factors positioned at key points such as Havana, Veracruz, Panama, Cartagena, Maracaibo, and Buenos Aires enjoyed the liberty to travel inland and appraise the need for slaves, but

---

[34] Walker, *Spanish Politics and Imperial Trade*, pp. 90–92, 114–16.

[35] Ibid., pp. 115–19, 128–36, 173–77, 188–92. For the Mexican side of these difficult years, see Iván Escamilla González, *Los intereses malentendidos: El Consulado de Comerciantes de México y la monarquía española, 1700–1739* (Mexico City: Universidad Nacional Autónoma de México, 2011).

[36] Escamilla González, *Los intereses malentendidos*, chaps. 5–10

they used this privilege to assess local demand and to penetrate forbidden colonial marketplaces.[37] Even after the crown limited direct French smuggling into the Pacific trading zone, contraband persisted across the long and arduous but still profitable overland routes originating both in Río de la Plata and in New Granada's Magdalena and Cauca Rivers.[38] Legal residence in the Spanish colonies enabled British agents to approach Spanish officials and gain their tacit cooperation for contraband commerce. Returning slaves ships also transported Spanish-American dealers and their goods back to England.[39] Finally, by spending long periods of residence in the Indies, British merchants could gain entry into local society, making invaluable social and economic connections to colonial elites.

An excellent example of a British agent who worked the system effectively was Ricardo O'Farrill y O'Daly, the first factor of the South Sea Company in Havana, who used his position to amass an impressive personal fortune, which in turn allowed him to become a prominent figure in *habanero* society.[40] Born in Monserrate to an Irish family, O'Farrill quickly ingratiated himself with his employer and the Spanish royal administration by denouncing the illegal trading of a local factor of the French Guinea Company, after which Havana's governor confiscated 586 slaves. This provided a lucrative windfall for the crown and for the South Sea Company, which managed their sale.[41] O'Farrill then began operating as intermediary between Jamaica and Cuba; he developed investments on both ends of the slave trade. That commerce, however, formed part of a much larger private operation. In 1718, for example, in the midst of war between England and Spain, O'Farrill obtained authorization to introduce 698 barrels of flour at considerable gain in return for Cuban tobacco.[42] O'Farrill also allied himself with Councilman (Regidor) Sebastián Calvo de la Puerta, one of Cuba's most vocal advocates for an aggressive development of the sugar industry. Calvo was one of the five councilmen deported to Madrid by Gazo Calderón after the suppression of resistance to the tobacco monopoly, but the impressive *habanero* used his time at court to win friends and escape punishment.[43] In 1723, in conjunction

---

[37] *The Assiento*, art. 11.

[38] Anthony McFarlane, *Colombia before Independence: Economy, Society, and Politics under Bourbon Rule* (Cambridge: Cambridge University Press, 1993), pp. 194–96; Walker, *Spanish Politics and Imperial Trade*, p. 181.

[39] Memoire, abuses of the Royal Assiento Company, Spain, April 30, 1725, AAE:CPE, vol. 343, fols 143–46.

[40] For an overview of the O'Farrill family in the eighteenth century, see José Manuel Serrano Álvarez and Allan J. Kuethe, "La familia O'Farrill y la élite habanera," in *Élites urbanas en Hispanoamérica*, edited by Luis Navarro García (Sevilla: Universidad de Sevilla, 2005), pp. 203–12.

[41] Leví Marrero, *Cuba: Economía y sociedad*, VII (San Juan: Editorial San Juan, 1978), VI, pp. 18–19.

[42] Ibid., p. 174.

[43] Ibid., p. 149.

with Calvo, O'Farrill successfully solicited the right to establish his own sugar plantation located in the Sabanilla district southeast of Havana, which eventually became one of the four largest sugar plantations in Cuba.[44]

By 1720, O'Farrill had amassed enough wealth to resign from the South Sea Company, and later that year, he married prominent *habanera*, María Josefa de Arriola y García de Londoño. Her father, Bartolomé de Arriola, was chief accountant (*contador mayor*) of the Real Tribunal de Cuentas for Cuba and the man who had established the royal shipyard of Havana in 1713. Following his marriage, O'Farrill obtained naturalization as a subject of the Spanish crown. Over the years, he parlayed his knowledge of the Havana marketplace into a large personal fortune. Until his death in 1730, O'Farrill obtained special concessions from the government to operate a slave trade between Jamaica and Cuba, serving as a medium for English penetration into Havana.[45]

O'Farrill's children also became major figures in local society. His daughter Catalina married the son of Sebastián Calvo de la Puerta, Pedro José, in 1746, cementing the alliance between the O'Farrill and Calvo families.[46] In due course, Pedro became the first Conde de Buena Vista. Juan O'Farrill, Ricardo's only son, would later become a prominent member of the disciplined militia's officer corps. Married to Luisa María Herrera y Chacón, the daughter of the fourth Marqués de Villalta, Juan secured the office of lieutenant colonel in the newly formed Volunteer Cavalry Regiment in 1763, established with the military reforms of Field Marshal Alejandro O'Reilly after the fall of Havana in the Seven Years' War. Owner of one of the largest plantations in the Havana district, Juan served on the ayuntamiento as *alcalde ordinario*, and he diversified his economic interests by providing lumber for the royal shipyard.[47] In short, Ricardo O'Farrill used his position as factor for British business interests to amass a fortune and to secure entry for himself and his offspring into the colonial elite, but his was hardly a unique story in the American empire.

Despite the success of individuals such as Ricardo O'Farrill, the slave *asiento* and ships of permission proved disappointing to South Sea Company investors. The Company rarely sold more than half of its annual allotment of slaves. Its agents often concerned themselves more with their own contraband activities than with promoting company business ventures, and profits from these private dealings seldom accrued to the Company's shareholders.[48] Despite some successes at particular trade fairs, the ships of

---

[44] Ibid., VII, pp. 2, 12, 19–22.

[45] Ibid., VI, p. 9.

[46] Ibid.

[47] Ibid., VIII, pp. 19, 167.

[48] The trade produced little if any profit for the company. Richard Pares, *War and Trade in the West Indies, 1739–1763* (Oxford: The Clarendon Press, 1936), pp. 19, 53; Adrian J. Pearce, *British Trade with Spanish America, 1763–1808* (Liverpool: Liverpool University Press, 2007), p. 20.

permission also failed to meet expectations. Over the years, sailings were frequently interrupted by war, difficulties in securing the necessary *cédulas* of authorization, the obstructionism of hostile Spanish officials, or the chronic delays between convoys, which impeded the South Sea Company's efforts to develop a reliable market relationship with customers in Veracruz or Portobelo.[49] Ironically, the South Sea Company's profits depended on the continuation of the fleet system, but its own sales and contraband activities undermined the legal trading apparatus. By the mid-1730s, frustrated South Sea Company investors voted to recommend to the crown that it liquidate the *asiento* entirely. The directors and the British government, however, opposed the idea and nothing came of it.[50] Spanish obstacles, delays, and bothersome taxes ultimately undermined the trade even during periods of peace, and in time of war the company's profits declined further.

DIPLOMACY AND DYNASTIC DISTRACTIONS

The Patiño government inherited a complex set of foreign policy objectives, influenced by the need to balance the monarchs' dynastic objectives in Italy with the need to regain control over American trade. Elizabeth's eyes remained fixed on Italy and the Duchies of Tuscany and of Parma and Piacenza, where she claimed rights of inheritance for her children.[51] At the same time, the struggle to recapture the American trade remained Patiño's top priority.[52] Friction over the system established at Utrecht continued straining relations between Spain and Britain. The British retention of Gibraltar and Menorca imposed other, festering sores. Grimaldo had signed a treaty of friendship and peace as well as a defensive alliance with Minister of State James Stanhope in Madrid on June 13, 1721, but only three years later the Spanish became so disgusted with the British that they withdrew from the Quadruple Alliance.[53] A naval war erupted briefly in 1727, which included an unsuccessful five-month Spanish siege of Gibraltar. In America, British Admiral Francis Hosier took up a position off Portobelo to bully the Spanish, disrupt the fair that was underway, and protect British dealers.[54] An attempt

---

[49] Béthencourt, *Patiño*, p. 55; McLachlan, *Trade & Peace*, p. 24.
[50] Walker, *Spanish Politics and Imperial Trade*, p. 201.
[51] Béthencourt, *Patiño*, pp. 7–8.
[52] A handy account of Spanish diplomacy during the Patiño era can be found in Béthencourt, *Patiño*. For American issues, see especially pp. vii, 5–6, 17.
[53] José Antonio Armillas Vicente, "La política exterior de los primeros Borbones," *Historia general de España y América: La España de las reformas hasta el final del reino de Carlos IV*, X-2, coordinated by Carlos E. Corona and José Antonio Armillas Vicente (Madrid: Rialp, 1984), pp. 278–79. A breakdown in French relations came almost concurrently. See Chapter 1.
[54] Walker, *Spanish Politics and Imperial Trade*, pp. 155–56.

to resolve Anglo-Spanish differences at the Congress of Soissons during the summer of 1728 failed miserably.

At this point, dynastic concerns took priority as the monarchs pressed claims on behalf of Prince Charles in northern Italy. To secure London's support, Spain grudgingly confirmed British rights and privileges within its commercial system in the Treaty of Seville, signed on November 9, 1729. Under the terms of this treaty, the British maintained control over Gibraltar while recognizing the claims of Elizabeth Farnese and her family to the Duchy of Parma. This accord seemingly brought an end to antagonisms that had lingered since the War of the Quadruple Alliance. When the British failed to uphold their end of the bargain, however, an undeclared naval war erupted again in American waters. After the Duke of Parma died in January 1731, the Spanish monarchs saw an opening to secure the Duchy of Parma and Plasencia. Anglo-Spanish hostilities receded with a joint declaration that reconfirmed the commitments made at Seville, ratified in a second declaration of February 8, 1732.[55] Meanwhile, the Austrians, under intense international pressure, withdrew their troops from Parma and Plasencia. Escorted by the British navy, Spanish vessels landed troops at Leghorn, Italy, in October 1731, followed by the infante Charles, who took possession of the duchy as his mother's inheritance.[56] Even this newfound harmony proved only momentary, however. By 1734, friction arising from Spain's impatience over British smuggling in the Indies led to another cycle of deteriorating diplomatic relations.[57]

Relations with France remained more cordial after Paris pledged its support for Spanish claims in Italy at the Treaty of Seville. This introduced an uneasy collaboration within the Bourbon family lasting until the French Revolution. Apart from the lingering antagonisms that had separated the two kingdoms since the War of the Quadruple Alliance, personal animosity between Philip and the Duke of Orleans, the regent for Louis XV, soured relations between the two powers. The death of Orleans in December 1723 did not significantly improve relations, and the two powers came close to war when the French returned Marianina. After the more conciliatory Cardinal André-Hercule de Fluery's rise to power in June 1726, relations began to mend.[58] Indeed, to induce Versailles to support Elizabeth's claims in Italy, Philip offered to reduce the penalty on French contraband "discovered" on

---

[55] Béthencourt, *Patiño*, pp. 31–51.

[56] Anthony H. Hull, *Charles III and the Revival of Spain* (Washington: University Press of America, 1981) pp. 21–25. Diplomatic provision was made with Austria by treaty on July 22, 1731. Antonio de Béthencourt Massieu, *Relaciones de España bajo Felipe V* (Valladolid: Universidad de Valladolid, 1998), pp. 125–28.

[57] Lucio Mijares, "Política exterior: la diplomacia," en *Historia general de España y América*, **XI**-1 (Madrid 1983), pp. 93–94.

[58] Kamen, *Philip V*, pp. 61–62, 110, 123–26, 153, 160–61.

the *Galeones* (imposed after the return of Marianina) from 55 to 15 percent in 1718.[59]

During the War of the Polish Succession (1733–1738) Spain allied with the French against the Austrians under the first of three Bourbon family compacts. France gained Spain's support for its favored pretender to the Polish throne (the father of its queen) while they pledged to uphold the claims of Elizabeth and Philip's children in Italy. For its part, Spain promised France coveted most favored nation status on the same terms as Great Britain.[60] This alliance of November 7, 1733, did not signal a deep rapprochement between the Bourbon rivals; both powers entered the war on their own terms and each was quite willing to seek peace separately. The Spanish government found the independent French peace agreement with the Austrians in October 1735 particularly galling because it surrendered Bourbon claims to Parma and Plasencia and to Tuscany. As French designs on Poland faded, so too did Versailles's enthusiasm for the aims of the Spanish monarchs.[61]

Despite lukewarm French support, Isabel and Philip realized important dynastic gains from the war. Spain attacked Austrian holdings in southern Italy and Sardinia with success.[62] At the head of an impressive army that had invaded Italy from Barcelona, the infante Charles rode into Naples in 1734 with General José Carrillo de Albornoz, the Conde de Montemar. Charles was proclaimed king, and the following January he entered Palermo in Sicily. These triumphs resolved half the preoccupation of Elizabeth and Philip V, but the infante Philip's need for a kingdom to rule remained unattended. Montemar was redeployed to northern Italy to pursue opportunities for the infante there, but Spain could not prevail alone. Many Spanish politicians, however, worried about the huge investments of treasure and manpower in Italy merely to pursue the royal family's dynastic ambitions.[63] At the same time, problems within the royal family emerged as Ferdinand now felt jealous when his younger half-brother became a king before him.[64]

PATIÑO'S STRATEGIES FOR AMERICAN REFORM

Over the years, Patiño struggled to find ways to make the system of *Flotas* and *Galeones* work, but without achieving any startling breakthroughs. During

[59] Béthencourt, *Patiño*, p. 32.
[60] Ibid., pp. 58–62. As Lucio Mijares has perceptively remarked, "From the moment that Philip V ascended the throne, Spain was almost inevitably condemned to cooperate with France." Mijares, "Política exterior," pp. 94–95.
[61] Béthencourt, *Patiño*, pp. 68–75.
[62] Armillas, "Política exterior," p. 278.
[63] Kamen, *Philip V*, pp. 195–96.
[64] This petty jealousy worried Elizabeth and she warned Charles about it. San Ildefonso, August 7, 1734, Archivo General de Simancas (hereinafter AGS), Estado, leg. 5927. The authors wish to thank Alexandra Gitterman of the University of Hamburg for sharing this document.

the two-year period from 1726 to 1728, he conducted a series of meetings with experts including Francisco Varas y Valdés (who had succeeded him as Marine intendant), López Pintado, and representatives from the *Consulado* and the Council of the Indies, which resulted in the decision to move the Mexican fair inland to Jalapa, away from disease-ridden Veracruz. Beginning in 1734, another consultation involving an array of experts, including a representative from the *Consulado* of Lima, recommended ways to make the convoy system more workable, but in the end it achieved little. The resulting royal *cédula* of January 21, 1735, temporarily suspended the *Galeones* and trimmed the size of the *Flota* to eight ships of 3,000 tons. The great minister undoubtedly longed for 1744, when the *asiento* and its attendant codicils would expire.[65]

Restricted by provisions of the Utrecht Treaty and the operations of contrabandists plying the Caribbean, South Atlantic, and Pacific, Patiño based his American commercial policy on four interlinked strategies. One was to rebuild the navy as rapidly as possible. The second was to strengthen the colonial coast guards and to enlist privateers to supplement them. Thirdly, he sought to curtail the role of French agents in Cádiz. Finally, he attempted to place loyal, capable men in key bureaucratic posts (instead of merely selling them to the highest bidder) in the Indies to curtail the corrupt practices that sustained the contraband trade. In all four instances, he would enjoy some important successes, often in cooperation with the *Consulado* of Cádiz.

Patiño managed to extract periodic donations from the *Consulado* of Cádiz for the crown, but he also favored the guild by not enforcing existing regulations too carefully. Under his rule, the guild was treated as a partner in solving Spain's commercial problems, not as an obstacle to reform. Patiño recognized that contraband was the principal threat to the Atlantic trade, and it served the interests of the crown and the *Consulado* to curtail illicit commerce. Moreover, he had served over eight years in Cádiz as Marine intendant, where he had supervised the transfer of the *Casa de la Contratación* and the *Consulado* and played a key role in fashioning the Royal Project of 1717, which laid the basis for the subsequent codifications of 1720. He knew the *Consulado* well and obviously felt comfortable working with its members. This did not preclude differences with the guild over specific issues, since Patiño served the interests of the crown and this sometimes led to conflicts.[66]

The collaboration between Patiño and merchant guild sometimes approached cronyism. When fleets returned safely to Cádiz, the crown customarily assessed donations, amounting to 1,783,767 pesos in 1727;

---

[65] Walker, *Spanish Politics and Imperial Trade*, pp. 162–63, 195–200.
[66] Ibid., pp. 89–90, 96, 166–67, 200.

2,930,170 in 1731; 100,000 in 1733; and 80,000 in 1734.[67] On the other hand, Patiño displayed a permissive attitude toward supervising the guild's accounts, which listed loans or financial commitments the guild had made with the crown. These included the *lonja* and *infantes* taxes, which covered royal debts, and the 1 percent levied to finance the *avisos* and satisfy claims arising from the *valimiento de Vigo* (see Chapter 2). During the period before 1726, these funds had been laxly audited under the supervision of Patiño when he had served as president of the *Casa*. While this caused great consternation in the *contaduría* of the Council of the Indies when it tried to audit the accounts, the councilors could do little.[68] The Council remained weak, particularly after the death of its president, Baltazar Zúñiga, in 1727, whom Patiño had failed to replace.[69]

In a landmark decree of September 23, 1729, the Patiño government made a major concession to the *Consulado*, permitting it to define its own membership. This concession greatly strengthened the guild in its ongoing struggles with foreign interests. The legislation provided that the:

commercial community be composed of all the present carriers in the *Carrera de Indias*, of the *Flotas* and of the *Galeones* as well as the register ships for Buenos Aires and the others that navigate to my American kingdoms, and that, registered by the *Consulado* and consuls, they continue selecting from among themselves all those who satisfy the said *Consulado* and the current commercial community [and] to it I concede the power to deny any person admission to its membership.[70]

This concession formed part of Patiño's strategy to circumvent treaty concessions that helped foreigners penetrate the American trade through Cádiz. On the one hand, this regulation cemented Patiño's commitment to work with the *Consulado* and its *sevillano* leadership to control who took part in the Indies trade. The *Consulado* could hold *competencias* to judge suitability for membership, and to exclude foreigners and the naturalized offspring of foreign merchants (*jenízaros*).[71] The guild's established families had confronted *jenízaros* since 1722, attempting to limit their participation in the Indies trade. The *jenízaros* frequently maintained ties with relatives running merchant houses in their native lands, and they exploited these relationships

---

[67] "Servicios hechos al estado y a algunos cuerpos particulares de la nación por el comercio de Cádiz, 1555–1803," AGI, Consulados, leg. 15.

[68] Secretary of the Office for Marine and the Indies José de la Quintana to Secretary of State Marqués de Villarías, Buen Retiro, June 26, 1741, AGI, IG, leg. 2303.

[69] Bernard, *Le Secrétariat D'État*, pp. 79, 211.

[70] Quoted in Julián B. Ruiz Rivera, *El Consulado de Cádiz: matrícula de comerciantes, 1730–1823* (Cádiz: Diputacion Provincial de Cádiz, 1988), p. 20, and Antonia Heredia Herrera, *Sevilla y los hombres del comercio (1700–1800)* (Sevilla: Editoriales Andaluzas Unidas, 1989), pp. 128–29.

[71] *Expediente*, reestablishment of the commerce of the Indies, 1729, AGI, IG, leg. 2301. An example of how this exclusionary process worked can be found in the case of José del Duque and Francisco Novoa, 1732, AGI, IG, leg. 2300.

to funnel foreign wares into the Indies trade, limiting the profits of guild members.[72] With the legislation of February 23, Patiño made the *Consulado* a self-recruiting corporation, run by a legally entrenched elite exercising broad privileges over the American trade.[73]

The strategy of Patiño produced mixed results. Candidates for membership in the guild had to be residents of Seville, Cádiz, Puerto de Santa María, or San Lúcar, but the law also stipulated that they be "native Spaniards without foreign origins."[74] This gave the *Consulado* the ability to police its membership and regain powers lost during Alberoni's assault on its privileges. On the other hand, the guild could deny membership not only to foreigners and *jenízaros*, but also to worthy Spaniards or enterprising Americans who might wish to enter the colonial trade. This was no small price for Patiño to pay. Nonetheless, not a single foreign name would appear in the guild's registry over the next thirteen years.[75] The number of French commercial establishments in Cádiz, however, declined only marginally after 1729.[76] Foreign interests still found ways to participate in the legal trading system by using Spanish front men, the notorious *prestanombres*, but Patiño, in partnership with the *Consulado*, had made great strides in keeping Cádiz from falling completely under foreign control. Unlike Alberoni, whose efforts to control Spain's ports and regain domination over the Atlantic trade led to war, Patiño managed to restrict the power of foreign merchants and *jenízaros* without provoking armed conflict with foreign rivals.

The success of the Spanish commercial system depended on reducing all forms of foreign contraband in the Caribbean, South Atlantic, and Pacific. Madrid had intimate knowledge of the various ruses that British smugglers employed to penetrate the American marketplace, thanks to the defection at the Congress of Soissons of two well-placed agents of the South Sea Company.[77] As the problem of contraband threatened to overwhelm the legal trading system, Patiño urged the *Consulado*, now secure in its privileges, to assume responsibility for financing the work of an expanded Royal Coast Guard in America. On March 28, 1732, the guild acceded to this request,

---

[72] Margarita García-Mauriño Mundi, *La pugna entre el Consulado de Cádiz y los jenízaros por las exportaciones a Indias (1720–1765)* (Sevilla: Universidad de Sevilla, 1999), pp. 73–109.

[73] "Respuesta que dan algunos hijos de españoles antiguos Seville, 1722, AGI, Consulados, leg. 35. During this period, a broad tendency emerged within European institutions whereby privileged, constituted bodies gained control over entry mechanisms to become self-recruiting elites. R.R. Palmer, *The Age of Democratic Revolutions: A Political History of Europe and America, 1760–1800* (Princeton: Princeton University Press, 1959), pp. 74–86.

[74] Royal decree, San Lorenzo, September 23, 1729, reproduced in Ruiz Rivera, El *Consulado* de Cádiz, p. 20.

[75] Ruiz Rivera, *El Consulado de Cádiz*, pp. 21, 111–30.

[76] Malamud Rikles, *Cádiz y Saint Malo*, pp. 104–05.

[77] Brown, "The South Sea Company," pp. 662–78, and "Contraband Trade: A Factor in the Decline of Spain's Empire in America," HAHR, 8 (May 1928), p. 180.

offering an import levy of 4 percent on silver, gold, and *grana fina* to pay for the coast guard in the form of a donation.[78] The levy remained unaltered until 1739, when the percentage imposed on gold was reduced to 2 percent. The *Consulado* shouldered this obligation willingly, because it financed an offensive against British, French, and Dutch smuggling. Between mid-1739 and 1761, this levy produced 16,661,861 pesos, 5 *reales*.[79]

The navy inherited by Philip V was in shambles, and the British had destroyed the force assembled by Alberoni and Patiño at Cape Passaro. To make matters worse, the English coastal raids of 1719 ruined the shipyards at Pasajes, with six new ships of the line on the stocks, and at Santoña, with three other ships under construction.[80] In the aftermath of these disasters, Patiño accorded the highest priority to reestablishing the navy, first as Marine intendant, then as Minister of Marine and the Indies. In Europe, he initially had to make do with the aging facilities on the Basque and Catalonian coasts, but in 1722 he established a modern, defensible shipyard at Guarnizo near Santander, later followed by facilities at El Ferrol, Cádiz, and Cartagena de Levante. In addition, he resurrected Tinajero's unfulfilled plan of 1713 to exploit the advantages of a shipyard in Havana.[81] Finally, in 1717 Patiño established in Cádiz Spain's first naval academy, the Real Compañía de Guardias Marinas.[82]

The Spanish had no realistic hope of matching British sea power in the Atlantic. Freed from the need to maintain a large army on the Continent and blessed with Europe's most advanced banking system, the British could always spend more. An improved Spanish navy would, nevertheless, provide indispensable protection for colonial treasure ships moving across the Atlantic, and it could transport troops to colonial strongpoints, providing tactical support during sieges. Patiño accepted the concepts of naval architect and Admiral Antonio Gaztañeta, which featured slender, longer, and faster vessels of sixty guns, designed to provide escort service. Spanish strategy avoided challenging the British in open battle for control of the seas. When a warship found itself engaged militarily, it was imperative to extract itself as expeditiously as possible. Only when the treasure ships themselves were imperiled might the navy be expected to fight pitched sea

---

[78] Royal *cédula*, Seville, June 8, 1732, AGI, Consulados, leg. 32.

[79] These were the only years with reliable figures. Report, *Contador Mayor* of the *Casa de la Contratación* Carlos Valenciano, Cádiz, May 29, 1762, AGI, Consulados, leg. 62.

[80] John D. Harbron, *Trafalgar and the Spanish Navy* (London: Conway Maritime Press, 1988), p. 173.

[81] G. Douglas Inglis, "The Spanish Naval Shipyard at Havana in the Eighteenth Century," in *New Aspects of Naval History: Selected Papers from the 5th Naval History Symposium* (Baltimore: Nautical and Aviation Publishers, 1985), p. 49.

[82] Vicente Rodríguez Casado, "El ejército y la marina en el reinado de Carlos III," *Boletín del Instituto Riva Agüero*, 3 (1956–1957), pp. 151–52.

battles.[83] Indeed, during the course of the eighteenth century, the Spanish navy lost fewer ships of the line to the British than to weather.[84]

The Havana shipyard, the empire's largest facility, produced thirty-six warships ranging from fifty-two to seventy guns and seven frigates during the Patiño period. Over the century, it would surpass all other facilities, producing 198 warships, among them 74 ships of the line – some of Spain's largest vessels.[85] Although located in distant America, Havana's prominence stemmed from the quality of its facilities, its sturdier hardwood lumber, and its lower costs.[86] Juan de Acosta became master shipwright and administrator of the shipyard in 1730. Lorenzo Montalvo, who later served as a key figure in Havana and in the Spanish navy, became commissary in 1734. He oversaw the construction of the new shipyard, finished during the late 1730s.[87]

Funding these costly undertakings was an impossible task for Havana, so the crown assigned increased fiscal transfers (*situados*) from the Mexican treasuries, which had first begun in the sixteenth century. As the data presented in Figure 3.3 indicate, Mexico sent remittances both to Spain and to the Caribbean. The Caribbean *situados* paid for local defenses and special projects, such as the construction of the Havana shipyards. The Mexican treasuries sent similar *situados* to the Philippines to maintain the royal government and support local defenses in the Pacific. Remittances to Spain fluctuated from year to year, and in 1725, 1727, 1729, and 1738 the Mexican treasury sent no funds at all to Castile. This was never the case with the Caribbean *situados*, which certainly fluctuated from one year to the next, but followed a clear upward trajectory during the period (see Figure 3.3). During the crucial years of the shipyard's construction in the 1730s, the *situado* from Mexico generally ranged from 700,000 to 1.1 million pesos. The only year the *situado* fell below this range was 1734, when Mexico shipped just under 309,000 pesos.[88] The crown clearly assigned a higher priority to supporting Caribbean defenses and its shipyard in Havana than to shipments of silver from Mexico to the metropolis.

The Royal Treasury in New Spain could support the burden of supplying funds to the Caribbean colonies, Spain, and the Philippines because its economy began a century-long period of growth beginning in the late 1690s. Demographic increases and mining fueled the first phase of this economic expansion. The indigenous population had recovered from the

---

[83] McNeill, *Atlantic Empires of France and Spain*, pp. 57–58, 77–78, 174; Inglis, "The Spanish Naval Shipyard," p. 48.

[84] Harbron, *Trafalgar*, p. 20.

[85] Ibid., pp. 15–17, 33.

[86] McNeill, *Atlantic Empires*, 174–76.

[87] Inglis, "The Spanish Naval Shipyard," pp. 49–51.

[88] Carlos Marichal and Matilde Souto Mantecón, "Silver and Situados: New Spain and the Financing of the Spanish Empire in America," *HAHR*, 74 (November 1994), pp. 594, 612–613.

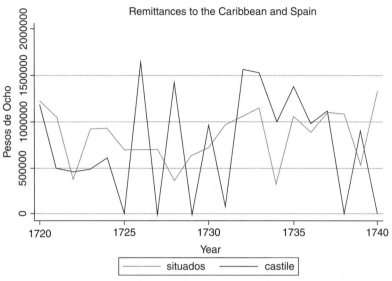

FIGURE 3.3 Remittances to the Caribbean and Spain

epidemics of the previous century, stimulating demand for a range of goods and foodstuffs and also providing a cheap labor supply. This in turn encouraged a mining resurgence, particularly between 1695 and 1725.[89] The internal growth of the economy laid the groundwork for an even more impressive mining boom and an overall economic expansion in the second half of the century. Economic growth also led to an increasing inflow of tax revenues into the Mexican treasuries. As Figure 3.4 – showing the average annual income from Mexico's treasuries – indicates, the funds flowing each year during the first forty years of the Bourbon period grew steadily, particularly after 1720.[90] This increase in revenues enabled the crown to shift income from Mexico to bolster Caribbean defenses, and when feasible to send sizeable sums to Spain (see Figure 3.3).

Spanish achievements in building the navy predictably attracted foreign suspicions, particularly among British observers. As early as 1728, British Ambassador Keene remarked:

Ever since I returned to this county, I observed with the greatest concern the progress Patiño was making towards a powerful marine. That idea is so strong in him that

[89] Alan Knight, *Mexico: The Colonial Era* (Cambridge: Cambridge University Press, 2002), pp. 202–203.
[90] Herbert S. Klein, *The American Finances of the Spanish Empire: Royal Income and Expenditures in Colonial Mexico, Peru, and Bolivia, 1690–1809* (Albuquerque: University of New Mexico Press, 1998), p. 58.

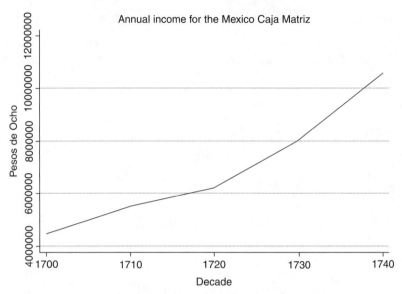

FIGURE 3.4 Annual Income for the Mexican Caja Matriz

neither the subsidies paid to the emperor nor the misery of the Spanish troops nor the poverty of the household nor tribunals can divert him from it.[91]

By Patiño's death, Spain possessed fifty ships of the line, a formidable fighting and convoy force. Most of these vessels were of the 60-gun model designed by Antonio Gaztañeta, but the navy also began adding larger ships, including, for example, the *Real Felipe*, a triple decker boasting 114 guns, which was launched at Guarnizo in 1732.[92]

Private enterprise provided an important means to combat British, Dutch, and French intrusions into Spanish commercial space, as the Madrid government sponsored privateers to harass contrabandists. Piracy was a game that all could play, and the Spanish learned well from their tormentors.[93] Based in Puerto Rico, Miguel Enríquez became a powerful agent of Spain's aggressive naval strategy, and its most visibly successful corsair.[94] Effective too were privateers operating out of Santiago de Cuba and Portobelo.[95] The official

[91] Quoted in Kamen, *Philip V*, p. 173.

[92] Harbron, *Trafalgar*, pp. 24, 33–34.

[93] Pablo Emilio Pérez-Mallaina Bueno, *La política española en el Atlántico, 1700–1715* (Sevilla: Escuela de Estudios Hispano-Americanos, 1982), pp. 59–61; Manuel Lucena Salmoral, *Piratas, corsarios, bucaneros, y filibusteros* (Madrid: Editorial Mapfre, 2005), pp. 294–99; Béthencourt, *Patiño*, pp. 40–41.

[94] Angel López Canto, *Miguel Enríquez* (San Juan: Ediciones Puerto, 1998), especially pp. 345–50.

[95] Pares, *War and Trade*, pp. 14–18, 22–24; John McNeill, *Atlantic Empires*, pp. 89–90, 98–99.

coast guard ships also proved a nuisance to foreign contrabandists, and the rising seizures of contraband cargoes provoked the ire of the British parliament, which saw Spanish privateers as impeding free commerce in the Caribbean. During the naval war of 1727, corsairs raided British shipping and confiscated the properties of the South Sea Company at every opportunity. After the war, Patiño continued enlisting corsairs to collaborate with the Royal Armada and the coast guard to combat smuggling. The unrestrained attacks of Spanish corsairs, like the shady contraband business that it sought to combat, functioned without clear boundaries and rules, and illicit and legitimate commerce alike suffered serious losses in the Caribbean.

Under the terms of the Treaty of Seville, Britain and Spain agreed to send commissioners to mediate commercial differences, but Patiño was loath to reign in Spanish corsairs. By 1730, the level of conflict had reached such intensity that the British crown ordered its naval forces to escort commercial traffic under the British flag and demanded the return of prizes taken unjustly, even threatening reprisals. The Declaration of Seville the following year reaffirmed British commercial rights and privileges, but Patiño remained committed to combating British smuggling, particularly in the Caribbean.[96]

After the combined British-Spanish fleet had delivered the infante Charles to Italian soil, Patiño and British Ambassador Keene signed yet another declaration on February 8, 1732. It reaffirmed established commitments and established a fund, supported by fees paid by corsairs receiving patents to work for each crown, which would provide for paying damages on cargoes seized illegitimately. The following year while Anglo-Spanish cooperation flourished in Europe, the seizures of British merchantmen in American waters declined appreciably.[97] In that same year, however, Patiño convinced the *Consulado* to impose the 4 percent levy to finance a more vigorous coast guard. The newly formed coast guard could substitute for the more controversial program of encouraging Spanish corsairs. Royal policy still focused on curtailing contraband by whatever means, as long as it did not provoke a needless war with Great Britain.

Despite numerous agreements, Spain's commitment to cooperate with Britain remained fragile, and in the end, attempts of commissioners from both countries to negotiate and resolve outstanding commercial differences failed completely. Conferences began in Seville in February 1732 and ended in Madrid in December 1734, over two and one-half years later, without resolving any concrete issues. While it was possible to agree theoretically on general principles in treaties and bilateral declarations, negotiations about their practical application floundered. The differences between the two powers were simply too great, whether the issue was the British cutting of dyewood in Campeche, their advance into Georgia, or Spanish fishing rights on the

---

[96] Béthencourt, *Patiño*, 40–41, 44.
[97] Ibid., pp. 50–51.

Newfoundland Bank. Patiño simply refused to order an end to seizures of British merchantmen, whether engaged in smuggling or merely suspected of contraband.[98]

A variety of factors – coast guard interceptions, the actions of privateers, rooting out corruption in the bureaucracy, and even Dutch competition – posed serious difficulties for British smugglers by the latter half of the 1730s, reducing their trade by two-thirds or more.[99] Finally, the lingering diplomatic tensions between Britain and Spain indicate that Patiño's program enjoyed a measure of success. Seizures by the coast guards and privateers produced a steady stream of protests from London, but the Spanish government remained intransigent.[100] Renewed conflict might lead to the abrogation or even reconsideration of the Utrecht settlement, a prospect which Patiño found an alluring possibility. Anglo-Spanish naval confrontations in American waters would ultimately erupt into a general conflict – the War of Jenkins' Ear in 1739 – three years after Patiño's death.

Another major policy change, begun even before Patiño, was the attempt to name more honest, loyal officeholders to key bureaucratic posts in the Indies instead of merely selling the offices. When Patiño rose to power in 1726, he initiated deliberations about reorganizing the *Galeon* trade with the Viceroyalty of Peru. His committee's discussions undoubtedly benefitted from a lengthy report on the problem by dogged and imperious reforming Viceroy José de Armendáriz y Perurena, the Marqués de Castelfuerte (1723–1736). Given his authoritarian personality, Castelfuerte recommended harsh measures to ensure the loyal participation of the Lima *Consulado* in the Portobelo fairs. Firstly, he argued that the viceroy should set a firm date for the departure of the *Armada del Sur*, and guild members should begin immediate preparations for the trip. The *Consulado* could request only two postponements, but the viceroy had the final say in the matter. If guild merchants delayed further, they would either have to pay the full expenses of the *Galeones* and the *Armada del Sur*, or its ships would be sent to Panama empty and return with the Spanish merchants, who could then sell their goods freely in Lima. Patiño and his committee wisely rejected these harsh terms, but Castelfuerte's plan indicates his seriousness of purpose in reviving the trade with Panama.[101]

Castelfuerte demonstrated his dedication to stamping out contraband and reestablishing the legal trading system from his arrival in Lima in 1724. He quickly reissued a royal *cédula* of December 31, 1720, prohibiting smuggling under pain of death, and even demanded that capital punishment be meted out to any government officials complicit in smuggling. He also outfitted

---

[98] For a British perspective, see Pares, *War and Trade*, pp. 14–19.
[99] Nelson, "Contraband Trade," pp. 62–64.
[100] Pares, *War and Trade*, chap. 2.
[101] Walker, *Spanish Politics and Imperial Trade*, pp. 164–66.

coast guard vessels to ward off foreign smugglers. Within the year, the contraband activities of French traders – so widespread under the viceregency of the Marqués de Castelldosríus – had declined precipitously. The viceroy then began prodding the Lima *Consulado* to prepare for the upcoming Portobelo trade fair. Members of the merchant guild complained that Lima's markets remained saturated with contraband merchandise, making trade goods procured at Portobelo unsalable. The viceroy tried cajoling, threatening, and bullying the Lima merchants, even requiring that they provide a loan of 200,000 pesos to cover the costs of the *Galeones* waiting in Cartagena. Despite Castelfuerte's angry admonitions, the *Armada del Sur* did not leave Callao until January 14, 1726. Competition from English traders on the permission ship undermined the sale of merchandise from Spain, however, and the arrival of the British fleet of Admiral Hosier allowed a horde of contraband traders to descend on Portobelo, ruining the prospects for a successful exchange. Nonetheless, the stubborn Castelfuerte had finally gotten the Lima merchants to leave Callao, and his frustrations in dealing with them prompted his angry report to Patiño and his committee in Madrid.[102]

Despite his reputation for honor, integrity, and loyalty to the crown, the Marqués de Castelfuerte was not above using his office for personal gain. The viceroy's enthusiasm for dispatching coast guard vessels to capture contrabandists stemmed in part from his custom of skimming a share of the proceeds when the cargoes of captured vessels were sold at public auction. The viceroy also turned a tidy profit from authorizing friends to operate gambling houses, which allowed every sort of game of chance. Indeed, his passion for gambling allegedly led to confrontations with his predecessor as viceroy, the Archbishop of Lima Diego Morcillo Rubio de Auñón. Castelfuerte also received kickbacks from men he named to lucrative rural magistracies (*corregimientos de indios*). Although the crown had the final say in naming *corregidores*, viceroys customarily appointed interim magistrates later confirmed by Madrid. During Castelfuerte's decade in power, 237 magistracies became vacant, and the viceroy named 118 – appointing friends, family, and political allies. Since the positions were customarily sold and *corregidores* could make small fortunes while in office supplying indigenous communities with European wares through the infamous *repartimiento de comercio*, the opportunities for kickbacks, bribes, and other forms of skullduggery were enormous.[103] When he left office in 1736, Castelfuerte had amassed a personal fortune of nearly 790,000 pesos *de ocho* (apart from his legal salary) by

---

[102] Ibid., pp.152–56.
[103] Alfredo Moreno Cebrián, "Acumulación y blanqueo de capitales del Marqués de Castelfuerte (1723–1763)" in Alfredo Moreno Cebrián y Núria Sala i Vila, *El "premio" de ser virrey: Los intereses públicos y privados del gobierno virreinal en el Perú de Felipe V*, (Madrid: Consejo Superior de Investigaciones Científicas, 2004), pp. 233–63.

various nefarious schemes.[104] This hardly compares to the nearly 1.3 million pesos amassed by the Marqués de Castelldosríus in a mere three-year term, but it does indicate that the political culture of corruption endured even in the administration of a viceroy who prided himself on his personal probity and loyalty to the crown. Making money on the side was a perquisite of office in the Spanish empire.

THE RETURN TO ALBERONI'S REFORM AGENDA

In conjunction with Patiño's campaign to shield the American trade from outside intrusions and curtail corruption, the minister resurrected some reform initiatives from the American agenda of his former patron Cardinal Alberoni. In 1727, for example, Patiño restored the tobacco monopoly in Cuba, but on a more flexible basis that was palatable to local tobacco growers. In 1730, the crown extended the model established for Havana's fixed garrison to Cartagena. Work also began in 1734 to reestablish the Viceroyalty of New Granada and reassert royal control over the old Spanish Main. The enlarged bureaucracy could more effectively oversee the dispatch of coast guard vessels and army patrols to obstruct smugglers. Patiño's fourth ambitious innovation involved the establishment of the Real Compañía Guipuzcuoana de Caracas in 1728 to combat the lucrative contraband cacao trade. This ambitious four-part reformist program aimed to revolutionize commerce in the southern Caribbean.

The resurrection in 1727 of Alberoni's initiative to establish a government-sponsored tobacco monopoly in Cuba attempted to direct the island's production to supply Spanish Royal Tobacco Factory in Seville and to furnish much-needed income for the Royal Treasury. Following Madrid's capitulation in 1724 and the return to deregulated sales, the crown purchased leaf on the free market, but in 1727 Patiño reestablished the monopoly under the title of the General Tobacco Intendancy. A private contractor or *asentista*, José Tallapiedra, replaced the intendancy in 1734, operating until 1738 when the Marqués de Casa Madrid took control. The new monopoly functioned in a more flexible, moderate way than Alberoni's scheme. Tobacco producers could sell surpluses on the open market after meeting the annual quotas set by the monopoly.[105] Patiño had learned from Alberoni's mistakes and avoided repeating the same authoritarian policies that had provoked Cuban opposition. This time the monopoly would endure until 1817.

Military reform returned piecemeal to the empire, but the first step came from a local initiative, not on any orders from Madrid. In 1728, Ignacio Francisco Barrutia, who had drafted the 1719 regulation for Havana, imposed the same reforms as governor of New Vizcaya (in northern New Spain) to the

---

[104] Ibid., p. 269.
[105] McNeill, *Atlantic Empires*, pp. 118–19, 154–55.

infantry companies in the eight presidios under his jurisdiction. He responded to the findings of Pedro de Rivera, who had reviewed the defenses of New Spain's northern frontier between 1724 and 1728.[106] Rivera had identified problems concerning the presidios of Texas, which had been rapidly established following the French advance to the Red River during the fall of 1713 and their founding of Natchitoches. That outpost threatened east Texas during the War of the Quadruple Alliance, serving as the base to menace Los Adais. During the relative calm that followed this war, however, the Texas presidios required adjustments in the scope of their activities to the west and in their maintenance costs.[107] Barrutia's initiative would appear later in a more general form as the *Reglamento para todos los presidios de las provincias internas . . .* of 1729.[108]

The model established for the Havana garrison was also extended to Cartagena de Indias in 1736.[109] In June 1730, Patiño sent a copy of the Havana policy to Governor Antonio Salas with instructions to consider how to implement the reforms in that Caribbean strongpoint and to submit his recommendations to Madrid for approval. After receiving the order on August 23, Salas complied quickly, sending a comprehensive draft in October, recommending the adaptations that he judged appropriate for his jurisdiction.[110] Madrid, however, would not promulgate the formal codification of those recommendations for another six years.

The reasons for this hiatus reveal the sometimes ponderous nature of the Spanish bureaucracy. Communication difficulties delayed the initial implementation of the reform. The mail system was notoriously slow and inefficient, and delays of a year or more in getting an official a response from Madrid to the Indies was not uncommon.[111] To complicate matters, the court had relocated to Seville, which separated Patiño from his secretariats and their administrative archives. Over a year and a half after sending his proposed regulations to Spain, Governor Salas became aware that the court still had not received his report. Again he responded quickly, dispatching a second

---

[106] Report, Ignacio Francisco de Barrutia, Parral, May 28, 1728, AGI, Guadalajara, leg. 110.

[107] The Rivera *misión* has been treated in Jack Jaskson, ed. and intro., *Imaginary Kingdom: Texas as Seen by the Rivera and Rubí Military Expeditions, 1727 and 1767* (Austin: University of Texas Press, 1995). Jackson attributes the authorship of the regulation to Rivera himself, p. 60. See also José Manuel Serrano Álvarez and Allan J. Kuethe, "La Texas colonial entre Pedro de Rivera y el marqués de Rubí, 1729–1772: aportaciones económicas al sistema presidial," *Colonial Latin American Historical Review*, 14 (Summer 2005), pp. 281–311.

[108] A copy can be found in AGI, Guadalajara, leg. 144.

[109] For an overview, see Juan Marchena Fernández, *La institución militar en Cartagena de Indias, 1700–1810* (Seville: Escuela de Estudios Hispano-Americanos, 1982), pp. 98–101.

[110] Letter, Antonio Salas, Cartagena, October 12, 1730, AGI, SF, leg. 938.

[111] For example, Salas to Patiño, Cartagena, August 16, 1730, and royal order, Seville, November 16, 1731, AGI, SF, leg. 938.

draft in July 1732.[112] When the desk of the Secretariat for the Office of Marine and the Indies received this response in late 1732 or early 1733, the functionaries within the ministry searched for the lost file rather than preparing a prompt summary for Patiño.[113]

The ministry's staff eventually located the missing document, but with the confusion accompanying the transfer of the court from Seville back to Madrid in the summer of 1733, the matter was apparently forgotten. There matters stood when the royal palace of Madrid, the Alcázar, burned to the ground on Christmas Eve 1734, taking with it a large share of the royal archives. At this point, military reform coincided with plans to resuscitate the viceroyalty, which gave the matter greater urgency. In September 1735, asserting that the palace fire had destroyed the governor's proposal, Patiño asked for a fresh report on the garrison, the militia, and the physical defenses of Cartagena.[114] This time Salas sent a report in duplicate with such detail that it was an imposing file well over one inch thick and not easily misplaced or overlooked.[115] The regulation was promulgated November 13, 1736, ten days after the untimely death of Patiño. It is no small wonder that the first reform Charles III would address was the royal mail system.

Along with the new regulation to viceregal authorities in New Granada, the crown included instructions to Governor Dionisio Martínez de la Vega of Panama ordering him to prepare a report on the applicability of Cartagena's regulations to Panama.[116] The governor recommended only modest changes; he broadened local participation from 20 to 30 percent, given the impossibility of attracting a sufficient number of Spanish-born volunteers in that sparsely populated region. Promulgated in 1738, full implementation of the Panamanian regulation awaited the arrival of recruits from Spain.[117]

Patiño next revived Alberoni's plan to establish the Viceroyalty of New Granada to gain greater control of sea lanes in the Caribbean and curtail contraband commerce. The need for tightening administrative controls in the area was even more pressing than in 1717, particularly after the establishment of an expanded coast guard and with plans to found the Caracas Company.

[112] Royal order, Seville, November 30, 1731, and Salas to Patiño, Cartagena, July 28, 1732, AGI, SF, leg. 938.

[113] "If one searches for it among the processed papers or those about to be processed, it undoubtedly will turn up; and for that reason, do not send a summary of the duplicate that arrived with this card because it does not seem right to use time on worthless work." Intra-ministerial note slip, sd., sp., AGI, SF, leg. 938.

[114] Royal order, San Ildefonso, September 20, 1735, AGI, SF, leg. 938. Ironically, the original draft and attendant documentation still exist in the ministry records! Most likely, they had not yet made the transfer back to Madrid.

[115] Salas to Patiño, Cartagena, April 9, 1736, AGI, SF, leg. 938. Salas went to the extreme of listing the name of every man enlisted in the militia.

[116] Royal order, San Lorenzo, November 30, 1736, AGI, SF, leg. 938.

[117] AGI, Panama, leg. 355, SF, leg. 938. As shown in Chapter 4, the authorized creole participation was also broadened somewhat in Cartagena.

In April 1734, Patiño summoned the Marqués de Torreblanca, a prominent naval officer who had served in the Pacific, to confer about the means to revitalize the commerce with Peru. In August of that year, Patiño received a proposal by Bartolomé Tienda de Cuervo (a treasury official during the first viceroyalty) to reestablish the Viceroyalty of New Granada.[118] The Minister of the Indies responded by convoking a special junta of ministers, including Torreblanca, to advise him on the matter. Members of the junta could find no good reason why the viceroyalty had indeed been extinguished. As their report stated:

> in said junta the documents and a secret vote that Don Antonio de la Pedraza conducted were examined and nowhere did substantive material appear that could explain why the viceroyalty was extinguished . . . . [T]his junta thus infers that the ministers who conducted the *consulta* and Don Antonio de la Pedraza himself were confused . . . in overturning an undertaking of such weight and importance.[119]

Having moved beyond the backlash against Alberoni, politics in Madrid now permitted the creation of a viceroyalty on its own merits.

Patiño now had all the relevant political forces in Madrid squarely behind the revival of the Viceroyalty of New Granada. His special junta and a *consulta* of the Council of the Indies all focused on asserting control over the Caribbean coastline of New Granada. In addition, authorities in Madrid touted the potential riches in gold from mines in the Chocó and Antioquia and also the pearl fishery off Riohacha. Advancing efforts to curtail contraband involved subjugating the Guajiro Indians of Riohacha and the Cunas of Darién, situated on the eastern zone of the Isthmus of Panama. The independence of both peoples opened huge strategic gaps along the coast that invited foreign contraband activity.[120] Government officials said very little about strengthening defenses in the region to protect it against foreign military incursions. The royal order to reestablish the viceroyalty came on February 25, 1739, just as the Spanish and the English attempted to diffuse the mounting crisis over the seizure of shipping in the Caribbean. That diplomacy would fail, however, and the actual establishment of the viceroyalty occurred on the eve of renewed hostilities in the War of Jenkins' Ear. In the end, the military leadership of Viceroy Sebastián de Eslava and Blas de Lezo during the British siege of Cartagena in 1741 would pay great dividends, but the crown never did fully meet its objectives in curtailing smuggling in New Granada. Moreover, while the Chocó would be an important producer of gold, the viceroyalty never contributed substantially to the flow

---

[118] Antonio Salas to Patiño, Cartagena, July 28, 1732, AGI, SF, leg. 938.

[119] Marqués de Torreblanca to Secretary of the Office for Marine and the Indies Marqués de Torrenueva, Madrid, December 20, 1737, AGI, SF, leg. 385.

[120] *Expediente*, the reestablishment of the Viceroyalty of New Granada, 1734–1739, AGI, SF, leg. 385.

of precious metal to Iberia. In many regards, New Granada would consistently fail to meet the expectations of the strategic planners in Madrid.[121]

The founding of the joint-stock Caracas Company clearly ended the historical monopoly of the *Consulado* of Cádiz in the transatlantic trade. Operating from San Sebastián in the Province of Guipuzcoa, Basque shareholders – not Andalusian merchants – dominated the Caracas Company, and the king and queen also gave their blessing by investing in the enterprise. The crown authorized the company to trade directly with La Guaira (the satellite port for Caracas) and Puerto Cabello. The Caracas Company also accepted the responsibility to patrol the coast with armed vessels to suppress foreign interlopers, particularly the Dutch in Curacao, who had dominated commerce in the region for many years.[122] Founding the Caracas Company also demonstrated Madrid's growing determination to exploit the agricultural potential of its empire, using a modern trading company to implement its mercantilist agenda. Further, the establishment of the company signaled flexibility in dealing with the weaknesses in the convoy system, which simply could not service the needs of perishable products, such as cacao produced in the Caracas district.[123]

The *Consulado* of Cádiz predictably reacted with surprise and consternation at news that the crown might impinge on its monopoly by licensing a joint-stock company. Moreover, Patiño failed even to consult its membership in the deliberations, which culminated in the royal *cédula* of September 28, 1728, chartering the company.[124] Through friends at court, word had reached the *Consulado* weeks before of plans to found a company, not from information given to the guild's *apoderado*, Marcos Antonio de Veróstegui. As the monopoly operating the American trade, members of the *Consulado* waited patiently for formal consultation by crown authorities in Madrid. The guild naturally planned to protest vigorously and to obstruct any intrusion into its privileged sphere in the transatlantic trade, even though the cacao trade from Caracas had never been a major commercial priority for the *Consulado*. Preserving its monopoly trading rights was sacrosanct for guild members.

---

[121] Allan J. Kuethe, "The Early Reforms of Charles III in the Viceroyalty of New Granada, 1759–1776," in John R. Fisher and Allan J. Kuethe, eds., *Reform and Insurrection in Bourbon New Granada and Peru* (Baton Rouge: Louisiana State University Press, 1990), pp. 19–23.

[122] Montserrate Gárate Ojanguren, *La Real Compañía Guipuzcoana de Caracas* (San Sebastián: Grupo Doctor Camino de Historia Donostiarra : Sociedad Guipuzcoana de Ediciones y Publicaciones 1990), chap. 5; Roland Dennis Hussey, *The Caracas Company, 1728–1784* (Cambridge, MA: Harvard University Press, 1934), chap. 2.

[123] *Consulado* to Verótegui, Cádiz, July 31 and November 2, 1728, and Veróstegui to the *Consulado*, Madrid, August 10, November 9, and November 16, 1728, AGI, Consulados, libro 66 and leg. 53.

[124] A copy can be found in AGI, Caracas, leg. 724.

Patiño had other ideas about guild prerogatives in the transatlantic trading system. While he was perfectly prepared to coddle and nurture the *Consulado* when it served the crown's purposes, he viewed the guild as little more than a trading company. Enlightened reformers at court would not tolerate interference from private parties such as the *Consulado* in any matters relating to royal revenues or to the defense of the realm. Consultation and compromise occurred, but in this case only with "relevant" parties – the Basque businessmen whose interests coincided with the crown's needs.[125] Under these circumstances, the *Consulado* received its copy of the *cédula* after the fact.[126] In later years, the chartering of the Caracas Company provided a precedent that clearly undermined the *Consulado* of Cádiz's monopoly claims over trade with the Indies.[127]

José Patiño died after a brief illness on November 3, 1736 at age seventy. Taken together, his innovations in America touched all four areas central to what was becoming the Bourbon reformist agenda: commercial, fiscal, administrative, and military reform. For the *Consulado*, the Patiño decade stood as a golden age of privilege and special arrangement. Although the guild resented the breaches in its monopoly granted at Utrecht and to the Caracas Company, it could only applaud the provisions mandating a return to historic commercial practices, which confirmed its place at the center of operations. That situation would soon change.

CONCLUSION: THE FIRST AGE OF REFORM, 1713–1736

Although historians have typically downplayed the contributions of Alberoni and even Patiño to the Bourbon reforms in the eighteenth century, their efforts yielded some impressive and enduring results. Alberoni's innovations certainly floundered initially after humiliating defeats in the War of the Quadruple Alliance, and conservatives in Madrid did their best to reverse all of his efforts except the military reform in Havana. When Patiño came to power in 1726 after the fall of Riperdá, he slowly consolidated power in the renewed Ministry for Marine and the Indies, placing younger, more dedicated public officials in key positions in Spain and the Indies. Men like the Marqués de Castelfuerte, despite his personal financial shenanigans, made serious efforts to reform government in Peru, curtail the French contraband trade in the Pacific, and force the *Consulado* of Lima to participate in the Portobelo fairs. Likewise, in Spain a generation of young politicians committed to reform in the Spanish Atlantic world got their start in politics working for

---

[125] Gárate, *La Real Compañía*, pp. 19–40.

[126] AGI, Consulados, leg. 53, containing Veróstegui's correspondence with the *Consulado*, holds a handwritten copy.

[127] Patiño quickly followed the Caracas experiment with another for the Philippines, but it would enjoy less success. Royal *cédula*, Seville, March 29, 1733, AGI, Consulados, leg. 35.

Patiño – José de Campillo y Cossío, Zenón de Somodevilla (later Marqués de la Ensenada), Sebastián de Eslava, and others. These new politicians played important roles in the reformist agenda of Patiño between 1726 and 1736.

Patiño and his fellow reformers also learned well from the mistakes of Alberoni. The Italian's years in power had stirred up vigorous opposition in Spain and the Indies, but Patiño's considerable experience allowed him to identify potential opponents and deal with them more effectively. In some cases the minister simply outmaneuvered his potential adversaries, as he did with the *Consulado* of Cádiz in chartering the Caracas Company. Patiño had given the guild broad powers to control its own membership and exclude the *jenízaros* of Cádiz, but he tolerated no interference in regulating the cacao trade from Caracas. In other cases, he simply made compromises that defused opposition. Tobacco growers in Cuba, for example, found the terms of the new tobacco monopoly much more palatable in 1727 than they had just a few years earlier. In other cases, Patiño outlasted potential opponents. By the time he began the process of reestablishing the Viceroyalty of New Granada in 1736, opposition to the measure had largely dissipated.

Patiño managed to push through an impressive array of reforms in his decade in power. Some originated under Alberoni, but others emerged ad hoc as Patiño grappled with the pressing problems facing Spain's Atlantic empire. To revive the transatlantic trading system and secure the defenses of the sea lanes, he rebuilt the navy, which was devastated with the defeat at Cape Passaro. He also began promoting military reforms in Cartagena and Panama. Patiño recognized the serious threat posed by foreign contraband trade in the Caribbean, the South Atlantic, and the Pacific, and he took concrete steps to curtail its corrosive effects on the legal fleet system. He established an effective coast guard in the Caribbean to harass foreign contrabandists, founded the Caracas Company to divert the cacao trade into legal channels, resurrected the tobacco monopoly (without the popular uprisings that plagued Alberoni's first efforts), and reestablished the Viceroyalty of New Granada, a project that would only come to fruition in 1739, three years after the minister's death. While dynastic wars diverted Patiño periodically from his principal goals in reforming the transatlantic trading system, they never led to the devastating defeats that had undermined his first protector Cardinal Alberoni. Moreover, his steady leadership and mastery of bureaucratic politics in Madrid avoided many of the tumultuous struggles that accompanied Alberoni's innovations a decade earlier. Ultimately, only his efforts to curtail contraband commerce would provoke a conflict in the Americas, with the War of Jenkins' Ear in 1739, but that would not break out until after the minister's death.

One important measure of the importance and impact of the first stirrings of the Bourbon reforms is the rising levels of income remitted from the Indies to the *Depositaría de Indias*, the treasury of the *Casa de la Contratación*. The *Casa* regulated transatlantic commerce in the Spanish Atlantic, but the

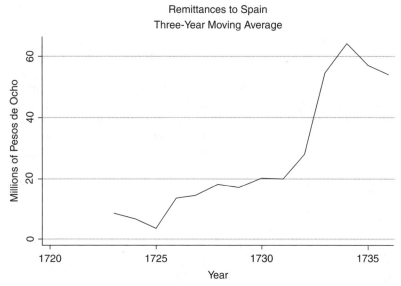

Remittances to Spain
Three-Year Moving Average

FIGURE 3.5 Remittances to Spain, Three-Year Moving Average

Depositaría fell under the jurisdiction of the Ministry of Marine and the Indies after 1721, an office held by José Patiño from 1726 until his death a decade later. The *Contaduría* (comptroller's office) of the Council of the Indies had the responsibility for auditing the accounts of the *Depositaría*.[128] As a result, the accounts of the *Depositaría* provide the best indicator of income flows from American treasuries to Spain during the early Bourbon reform period. Figure 3.5 (a three-year moving average of income from the Indies flowing into the *Depositaría de Indias*) indicates that income levels remained sluggish in the aftermath of the War of Succession, ranging from 224,346 *reales de vellón* in 1727 to a high of 10,682,864 *reales de vellón* in 1724. After 1727, however, income from the American treasuries rose steadily throughout the Patiño years, annually reaching peaks ranging from 40 million to more than 60 million *reales de vellón*.[129] This steady rise represented an annual average increase of 4.8 percent, which demonstrates a recovery from the disastrous tax yields in the late seventeenth and early eighteenth centuries from the American treasuries. Given the rising income levels of the Mexican treasuries (see Figure 3.4), it also demonstrates the growing importance of New Spain as a revenue producer for the crown,

---

[128] This analysis relies on a path-breaking article by Jacques A. Barbier, "Towards a New Chronology for Bourbon Colonialism: The "Depositaría de Indias" of Cádiz, 1722–1789," *Ibero-Amerikanisches Archiv*, 6:4 (1980): pp. 335–39.

[129] Ibid., pp. 352–53.

supporting high levels of remittances to the Caribbean and to Spain (see Figure 3.3). In short, the reforms of Alberoni and Patiño may not have produced revolutionary changes in the empire, but they did have a discernable impact on remittances from the Indies to Spain, despite repeated problems with reestablishing the transatlantic fleet system in the early eighteenth century. These early reform initiatives also reversed the long decline in public revenues collected in America and remitted to Spain. In the end, the early Bourbon reforms laid the framework for the administrative, commercial, military, and fiscal reforms of the mid-eighteenth century and ultimately for later reforms under Charles III and Charles IV.

II

THE SECOND WAVE OF REFORM, 1736–1763

4

War and Reform, 1736–1749

Following Patiño's decade in power, the outbreak of war with Great Britain and new attitudes about imperial reform in Madrid opened the door to fundamental changes in the Spanish Atlantic empire. The customary harmony between royal administration and the *Consulado* of Cádiz abruptly collapsed, leading to reform initiatives that reduced the privileged position of the Andalusian elite. Most of this tumultuous period found Spain engulfed in the War of Jenkins' Ear (1739–1748), a dangerous struggle in the American theater where Spanish arms competed successfully with the aggressive and powerful forces of an expansionist British foe. This first war fought exclusively over colonial issues later merged with dynastic conflicts in Europe producing the War of the Austrian Succession (1740–1748). The pressures imposed on the transatlantic trade during this international conflict led the Madrid government to abandon temporarily the traditional system of *Flotas* and *Galeones* in favor of using individual register ships, a transformation bearing profound implications for the future.

Strong ministerial leaders pushed forward these important changes, particularly with the emergence of José del Campillo y Cossío, who championed a wide range of reforms, most notably free trade within the empire. Campillo's ideas about imperial reform marked a major change from the more narrowly pragmatic policies of Alberoni and Patiño, which emphasized gaining control over Spain's port cities, attacking foreign contraband commerce in the Caribbean, South Atlantic, and Pacific, and reestablishing a strong convoy system in the transatlantic trade. After Campillo's premature death, power passed to Zenón de Somodevilla, the Marqués de la Ensenada, one of the Bourbon century's most impressive and successful leaders. During this second era of reform, however, Ensenada would advance well beyond the pragmatism of Alberoni and Patiño, ending the sale of bureaucratic appointments, modernizing state finances, liberalizing trade with South America, and curtailing the power of the church. The death of Philip V in 1746 and the succession of his son, Ferdinand VI, also removed Elizabeth Farnese from the court, and an Atlantic agenda quickly replaced her narrowly focused Italian dynastic priorities, which had so often led to conflict in the past. After the war ended in 1748, a new era of reform and renovation produced profound changes in the Spanish Atlantic world and laid the foundation for many others.

The fundamental transformations emerging within the empire led to bitter political conflicts among reformers and traditional interest groups against innovation. The *Consulados* of Cádiz, Lima, and Mexico City opposed the continued use of individual register ships when it extended into the postwar period. Likewise, discontent with the low prices and commercial quotas imposed by the Caracas Company, along with the end of slave imports from the South Sea Company during the war and its aftermath, threatened to end the cacao boom in the Governorship of Venezuela, leading to armed rebellion. Royal troops from Santo Domingo and later Spain ultimately overwhelmed the rebels and punished the leaders of the uprising, but the reforms implemented a decade earlier by Patiño had prompted this major challenge to Bourbon rule in Venezuela.

THE RISE OF JOSÉ DEL CAMPILLO Y COSSÍO

The death of José Patiño left four secretariats vacant, leading to a difficult period of transition in royal administration.[1] Sebastián de la Cuadra, a native of Vizcaya and a disciple of Patiño, established himself as the leading minister in the new administration. De la Cuadra had served as *oficial mayor* in the Secretariat for State, where he had extensive experience, and he acquired that ministry on November 6, three days after Patiño's death.[2] De la Cuadra enjoyed the full confidence of the monarchs, and he was the only official permitted to meet with them on a regular basis. Moreover, he became the personal secretary (*mayordomo mayor*) for Elizabeth, a position that had remained vacant since the death of Orendain in 1734. He also supervised the Secretariat of War, pending a permanent appointment. In the interim, De la Cuadra placed its day-by-day administration in the hands of Casimiro de Ustáriz, an arrangement that would endure until 1741.[3] José Rodrigo remained at Justice.[4]

---

[1] Antonio Béthencourt, *Patiño en la política internacional de Felipe V* (Valladolid: Universidad de Valladolid, 1954), pp. 4, 15.

[2] De la Cuadra entered State under Grimaldo in 1705. Teresa Nava Rodríguez, "Problemas y perpectivas (sic) de una historia social de la administración: Los secretarios del Despacho en la España del siglo XVIII," *Mélanges de la casa de Velázquz*, 30 (1994), p. 161.

[3] French Ambassador Compte de Vaulgrenant to Minister of State Chauvelin, San Lorenzo, November 12, 1736, and Madrid, January 7, 1737, and to Minister of State Amelot, Madrid, April 1, 1737, AAE:CPE, vol. 437, fols. 282–87 and vol. 444, fols. 7–9, 49–50.

[4] José Antonio Escudero, *Los orígenes del Consejo de Ministros en España* (Madrid: Editora Nacional, 1979), I, pp. 58, 101.

De la Cuadra's chief rival was the Duque de Montemar, who expected to receive the War ministry. At the time of Patiño's death, the general served as the commander of the Spanish forces deployed in northern Italy. Clearly the preeminent army officer of his time, his lasting accomplishments included the establishment of the reformed militia system in the provinces of Castille in 1734. He was, however, unable to reach an agreement with the monarchs concerning his possible service as minister. The general wanted direct access to the throne, but he proved unable to break the grip that de la Cuadra held over the king and queen. He eventually left court without securing the ministry.[5] Without his leadership, the royal cabinet lacked the prestige and power enjoyed by Patiño.

Historians have generally viewed de la Cuadra as a hard worker, much preoccupied by administrative procedure and routine, but as weak, indecisive, and totally submissive to the queen.[6] This impression can be traced back to British Ambassador Benjamin Keene's assessment, which called him "more dull and stubborn than I could well conceive."[7] On the other hand, the Compte de Vaulgrenant, the French ambassador, observed that "every day since he became minister, one discovers in him qualities and talents that were unknown until he became an administrative head."[8] While de la Cuadra was no Patiño or even a Montemar, he was clearly a magistrate of substance. His submissiveness to the queen simply reflected his good sense. So too might his prudent inclination to work collectively rather than attempting to accrue the personal power held by Patiño.[9] After all, de la Cuadra survived in his difficult office for ten years, which shows impressive durability in a troubled wartime

---

[5] Vaulgrenant to Chauvelin, San Lorenzo, November 12, 1736, and to Amelot, Aranjuez, April 1, 1737, May 13, 22, and June 10, 17, 1737, and Valsaín, July 29, August 19, 26, and September 9, 23, 1737, AAE:CPE, vol. 437, fols. 282–87, and vol. 444, fols. 49–50, 74–76, 79, 97–99, 111–13, 137, 152–53, 156, 161–64, and 171–72; Johann Hellwege, *Die Spanischen Provinzialmilizen im 18.Jahrhundert* (Boppard am Rheim: Holdt, 1969), chaps. 1–2; Anthony H. Hull, *Charles III and the Revival of Spain* (Washington, D.C.: University Press of America, 1981) pp. 28–33; Béthencourt, *Patiño*, pp. 85–87

[6] Escudero, *Los orígenes*, p. 99; Béthencourt, *Patiño*, p. 26.

[7] Keene predicted that "La Quadra will place his utmost merit entirely on his resignation to their [Majesties'] orders, without prompting them to any party, or making himself responsible for the least imaginable accident. His fear of speaking more than he should will keep him from talking as much as he ought .... [H]e passes for a very honest man .... He will be slow in his operations, and will demand information and reports upon any trivial matter of commerce, in the same manner as the marquis de la Paz, and as was constantly practiced here till Patiño broke through those tedious formalities." In William Coxe, *Memoirs of the Kings of Spain of the House of Bourbon from the Accession of Philip V to the Death of Charles III, 1700 to 1788. Drawn from the Original and Unpublished Documents*, 2nd ed., III (London: Longman, Hurst, Rees, Orme,and Brown, 1815), pp. 293–94.

[8] Vaulgrenant to Chauvelin, Madrid, January 7, 1737, AAE:CPE, vol. 444, fols. 7–9.

[9] Béthencourt, *Patiño*, p. 26, notes de la Cuadra's preference to interact with juntas and councils.

period. In 1739, Philip honored him with the title Marqués de Villarías, and in 1741 the king added the portfolio for Grace and Justice to his duties.[10]

The Marqués de Torrenueva, secretary of the Office for Treasury, was second in the new hierarchy, and he was also a man of ability. He also held Marine and the Indies on an interim basis, but Torrenueva retained that secretariat until 1739, when he abandoned his ministerial duties for a less taxing position with equal salary, as minister of *capa y espada* on the Council of the Indies.[11] Yet while he held Marine and the Indies, Torrenueva initiated reforms later advanced by his successors, José de la Quintana and José del Campillo y Cossío. The Conde de Montijo was named president of the Council of the Indies in June 1737, ending the ten-year period of neglect that Patiño had allowed to develop. Montijo, previously Madrid's ambassador to London, was recalled to accept the appointment to which renewed prestige and a salary of 3,000 pesos were attached.[12] Half Italian by birthright, he became part of Her Majesty's inner circle, serving as her first equerry.[13]

Torrenueva was succeeded in his dual appointment by Juan Bautista de Iturralde at Finance and Quintana at Marine and the Indies on March 7, 1739. Quintana, another *vizcaino*, came over from the Council of the Indies.[14] Like Torrenueva, Quintana was a relatively obscure figure in Spanish administrative history, but he would play a significant role in laying the foundation for the commercial reforms that his more famous successor, Campillo, would begin to push forward.[15]

José del Campillo y Cossío was born in Asturias of modest hidalgo origins, but he was already both an experienced bureaucrat and a well-regarded intellectual when he was given the Ministry of Finance in 1741, followed later by the portfolios of War and Marine and the Indies. The Enlightenment made its first clear appearance in the upper administration through Campillo, a magistrate known for his well-informed, liberating search for modernizing alternatives. Campillo wrote a number of important reformist tracts, but his most famous work dealing with colonial matters was the *Nuevo sistema de*

---

[10] Nava, "Problemas y perpectivas," p. 161.

[11] Escudero, *Los orígenes*, pp. 99–103.

[12] Vaulgrenant to Amelot, Aranjuez, June 17, 1737, AAE:CPE, vol. 444, fols. 111–13. The revitalization of the Council of the Indies reflected De la Cuadra's preference to work collectively.

[13] Mark A. Burkholder, *A Biographical Dictionary of Councilors of the Indies, 1717–1808* (Westport, CT: Greenwood Press 1986), pp. 99–100.

[14] Ambassador Extraordinary Compte de la Marck to Versailles, Madrid, March 9, 1739, AAE: CPE, vol. 452, fols. 189–91.

[15] Béthencourt, *Patiño*, p. 26, describes him as a "colorless man with long preparation, well versed in American problems and commerce, he would end up making himself, with his advice (*dictámenes*), the true minister of foreign affairs. He would become the authentic continuity from Patiño up to Campillo and Ensenada."

gobierno económico para la América, which appeared in 1743.[16] The *Nuevo sistema* was a position paper, most certainly drafted by a ghostwriter on behalf of the ambitious minister. Nonetheless, it undoubtedly reflected Campillo's own thoughts and those of a growing number of regalists in Madrid, men of reason who embraced royal authority as a means to progress.[17] Addressing a wide variety of topics and advancing a far-reaching, ambitious agenda, the document showed where reformist thought stood at the time. At the core was a modernized mercantilist vision of how the colonies might reach greater levels of productivity and how Spain might harness this prosperity to enrich itself.

The *Nuevo sistema* asserted confidently that Spain could improve the benefits it reaped from the American empire through the liberalization of its economic structures, beginning with maritime commerce. The Cádiz monopoly should be broken, with ships authorized to depart from any Spanish port, essentially promoting free trade within the empire. While those coming back to the Mediterranean should pass through Cádiz, where duties would be assessed, those from the north could return through La Coruña or Santander. Moreover, he advocated abolishing export taxation by weight and volume (the *tonelada* and the *palmeo*) and lowering levies on Spanish goods sent to the Indies.[18] Such innovations were unthinkable in the time of Patiño, but by now Madrid had renounced the *asiento* and the related treaties it had negotiated after the War of the Spanish Succession.

Citing the successes of the British and French, the *Nuevo sistema* encouraged the production of agricultural products in the Indies such as tobacco, sugar, cacao, coffee, indigo, flax, cotton, and hemp and other exotic plants.[19] It also emphasized the centrality of mining to Spain's mercantilist aspirations and advocated both lowering the tax on precious metals and a modernization of mining practices through adopting Saxon and Swedish techniques.[20] Campillo proposed holding regional trade fairs in the Indies to stimulate commerce and curtail the sale of contraband merchandise. He also called for the formation of commercial companies in Spain and the Indies to promote trade and economic development. Moreover, a modernized mail system operating out of La Coruña or Cádiz would tighten colonial administration and furnish market information for Spanish traders. Spanish officials in the Indies would also send current data about economic activities to Spain, where they would be published on a regular basis in a national gazette.[21]

---

[16] José del Campillo y Cossío, *Nuevo sistema económico para América*, ed. by Manuel Ballesteros Gaibrois (Oviedo: Grupo Editorial Asturiano, 1993), passim.

[17] On the question of authorship, see Luis Navarro García, "Campillo y el *nuevo* sistema: Una atribución dudosa," *Temas americanistas*, 2 (Seville 1983), pp. 22–29.

[18] Campillo y Cossío, *Nuevo sistema económico*, pp. 203–16.

[19] Ibid., pp. 171–80.

[20] Ibid., pp. 191–202.

[21] Ibid., pp. 253–66 .

Campillo, who had spent four years in America, envisioned sweeping reforms to accompany the revitalization of the mercantilist system.[22] A series of high-powered *visitas* would set the stage for an administrative regeneration, including the transfer of the intendant system to the colonies. This administrative modernization would put an end to the political culture of corruption in the Indies.[23] The most startling policy of the *Nuevo sistema* stressed the need to convert an underproductive Amerindian population into something resembling Spanish peasants by giving them an education, teaching them Castilian, and having them wear Spanish dress. Campillo further called for distributing land to the Amerindians. This new hispanicized Amerindian population would be productive producers and consumers in the New World, instead of remaining an inert, impoverished, and oppressed caste.[24] As long as it did not compete with Spanish export objectives, the colonial administration should also promote industry and permit intercolonial trade.[25] Campillo believed that royal monopolies over tobacco and aguardiente in the colonies would produce lucrative returns. He also encouraged foreign immigration from Roman Catholic regions of Europe to populate the Indies and promote economic development.[26] In the end, the *Nuevo sistema* offered the crown a comprehensive reformist agenda designed to forge a strong, unified, and prosperous imperial system largely freed from foreign economic penetration.

The appearance of this tract in the ministry of the secretary of the Office for Marine and the Indies placed the question of commercial deregulation squarely before the crown. Campillo anticipated deep-seated opposition to the liberalization of commerce from vested interests and other conservatives who might oppose innovations. He was quite correct.[27] Once the crown freed itself from the treaty impositions at Utrecht, it would face fierce internal opposition to trade liberalization. The issue of commercial reform remained a burning issue, but it would not be addressed by Campillo, who suffered a fatal seizure in April, when the ink had barely dried on his innovative tract.

[22] This service occurred in Cuba and Mexico. Iván Escamilla González, *Los intereses malentendidos: El Consulado de Comerciantes de México y la monarquía española, 1700–1739* (Mexico City: Universidad Nacional Autónoma de México, 2011), pp. 171–75.

[23] Campillo y Cossío, *Nuevo sistema económico*, pp. 79–88.

[24] Ibid. pp. 171–80.

[25] For a succinct overview of Campillo and his thought, see José Martínez Cardos, "Don José del Campillo y Cossío," *Revista de Indias*, nos. 119–22 (1970), pp. 501–42.

[26] Campillo, *Nuevo sistema económico*, pp. 283–92.

[27] "I do not doubt that some, whether because of their personal ambitions or because they do not understand clearly the issues, will oppose the full liberty that the new system concedes to commerce between Spain and the Indies." Ibid., p. 166.

THE CONSULADO OF CÁDIZ AND THE ROAD TO WAR

Tensions between Spain and Great Britain encouraged commercial reform in the Spanish Atlantic. Patiño oversaw the transfer to Cádiz of the *Casa de la Contratación* and the headquarters of the *Consulado*, as well as the establishment of the Caracas Company. The changes that arrived in the post-Patiño years would go to the heart of the system, involving the role of the merchant guild itself. An impatient crown would rein in the *Consulado* and curb its traditional autonomy and power in order to break the control of *sevillano* elites over colonial commerce. These changes began in 1737 under the Marqués de Torrenueva, continued under José de Quintana and the brief but brilliant ministry of José del Campillo y Cossío and concluded through advances imposed by the Marqués de la Ensenada (1743–1754).[28] The War of Jenkins' Ear hastened the first steps in a long struggle to curb the power, privileges, and special arrangements that the *Consulado de Cargadores a Indias* had enjoyed since the sixteenth century.

The *Consulado*'s privileged position first came under scrutiny when Torrenueva requested a donation of 15 percent of the specie, produce, and goods arriving with the *Flota*, and the mercury transports (*Azogues*) returning from New Spain under the command of Manuel López Pintado in 1738. This percentage encompassed the fees customarily exacted on silver, including the 5 percent levy defined by the Project of 1720, 4 percent for the coast guards, and 1.5 percent for freight on royal warships, leaving an increase, or "donation," of 6 percent for most of the cargo, a relatively modest amount. The Jalapa fair had been unusually profitable, owing to the absence of a British ship of permission, and López Pintado transported 17 million registered pesos to Cádiz. Torrenueva expected the donated funds to secure relief for the hard-pressed Royal Treasury just as war with Britain loomed.[29]

The *Consulado* refused to acquiesce to Torrenueva's demands. Earlier that year, the crown had devalued the copper *real* used in the peninsula by 6.25 percent against the silver peso (from 16:1 to 20:1). By insisting on a donation of 6 percent, the crown intended to skim most of the gain that the *Consulado* would have reaped from the increased valuation of silver. Similar devaluations of copper in 1726 and 1728 had passed without incident, bringing appropriate donations from the guild.[30] The situation in 1737 differed because the crown had converted the accounts of the *Depositaría de Indias*

---

[28] Significantly, Quintana, Campillo, and Ensenada had all risen under the protection of Patiño. Béthencourt, *Patiño*, p. 15.

[29] Allan J. Kuethe and Lowell Blaisdell, "French Influence and the Origins of the Bourbon Colonial Reorganization," HAHR, 71 (August 1991), pp. 585–86.

[30] Torrenueva to Villarías, Madrid, October 1737 in *consulta*, Junta de Ministros, AGI, IG, 2300; services, *Consulado* of Cádiz, 1555–1805, AGI, Consulados, leg. 15.

to the devalued copper.[31] Protesting in alarm, the *Consulado* claimed that the devaluation harmed it financially because of the increase in taxes it was now obliged to pay and because it had based its contracts on the earlier valuation.[32] The guild's counter offer to Torrenueva was a paltry 250,000 pesos.

Dickering of this sort about "donations" was hardly unusual, but the royal accounts languished in a precarious condition even before the outbreak of war with Britain. Patiño's ship-building program had been incredibly costly, absorbing everything he could squeeze out of the treasury. Moreover, outfitting the fleet for war involved additional costs, since it took four times as much to maintain ships at sea as in port.[33] In addition, merely four years before, Rodrigo de Torres had lost his treasure fleet – carrying cargo worth at least 12.5 million pesos – during a hurricane in the Florida Straits.[34] In addition, the royal palaces had become a demanding burden. Maintenance and refinements of the palaces at Buen Retiro in Madrid, San Lorenzo del Escorial, and La Granja de San Ildefonso absorbed large sums, and in 1727 Philip began building a new residence for spring at Aranjuez, on the Tagus River south of Madrid. Then too, the tragic fire on Christmas Eve of 1734 destroyed the Alcázar.[35] Clearing the ruins was a burden and replacing it with the massive, sumptuous Oriente Palace added enormous costs.[36] All together, the royal households consumed some 11 to 12 percent of the annual royal income.[37]

[31] Jacques A. Barbier, "Towards a New Chronology for Bourbon Colonialism: The "Depositaría de Indias" of Cádiz; 1722–1789" *Iber-Amerikanisches Archiv*, 6 (1980), pp. 339–40. For the revaluation of 1728, see Geoffrey Walker, *Spanish Politics and Imperial Trade, 1700–1789* (Bloomington: Indiana University Press, 1979), p. 160.

[32] In 1686, the valuation assigned to the American silver peso, *plata antigua*, had been 128 *cuartos*, a *cuarto* being worth four copper maravedís. In 1726, the peso was revalued to 152 *cuartos*, in 1728 to 160, and on May 16, 1737, to 170. Barbier, "Towards a New Chronology," pp. 339–40.

[33] John Robert McNeill, *Atlantic Empires of France and Spain: Louisbourg and Havana, 1700–1763* (Chapel Hill: University of North Carolina Press, 1985), p. 73.

[34] John D. Harbron, *Trafalgar and the Spanish Navy* (London: Conway Maritime Press, 1988), pp. 65–67.

[35] Tragically, the fire destroyed volumes of documentation on the early decades of Philip's reign.

[36] As the royal order of September 18, 1737, explained, "the magnificence that should grace . . . a residence worthy of a monarch such as ours makes the lofty sums that are required understandable as well as those solicited to defray all the costs needed to finish it, and thus preclude that the Kings and all the royal family [suffer] the lamentable need to reside in those [palaces] in the country for lack of their own house at court, enduring the discomforts occasioned by their constrictions, with the vassals of other nations looking on (although without justification) and seeing them without the serenity and decorum that the splendor of a proper royal palace provides for grandeur and for sovereignty." Madrid, AGI, IG, leg. 2300. Cited in Allan J. Kuethe, "El fin del monopolio: Los Borbones y el consulado andaluz," in Enriqueta Vila Vilar and Allan J. Kuethe, eds., *Relaciones de poder y comercio colonial* (Seville 1999), p. 43.

[37] Henry Kamen, *Philip V of Spain: The King who Reigned Twice* (New Haven: Yale University Press, 2001), p. 243.

The very real danger of war with Britain complicated this difficult financial situation, and so Torrenueva responded to the *Consulado* with uncommon severity. When haggling with the guild failed, he alleged massive fraud and named a select junta of four ministers and three theologians to meet with him at his residence to evaluate the *Consulado*'s conduct and recommend appropriate penalties.[38] The junta found that the *Consulado* had defrauded the crown of some 4 million pesos in unregistered goods and specie. The non-negotiable sentence imposed on the guild (in return for a pardon) was 20 percent of the specie, including the standing levies but excluding produce and goods.[39] The royal conscience was assuaged by the knowledge that the vast majority of the silver and gold belonged to foreign merchants anyway.[40]

With war at hand and the *asiento* soon to be renounced in 1739, the crown saw an opportunity to break the monopolistic grip of the *sevillano* elite. Torrenueva's successor, José de Quintana, ordered the ships at anchor in Cádiz measured, which proved that the *Consulado*'s dealers habitually understated the sizes of their ships. Given that taxes were levied by volume, hidden cargoes could go unnoticed, allowing guild members to evade crown levies.[41] Next, Quintana launched an investigation of the *Consulado*'s accounts, which exposed chronic fraud and shoddy administrative practices. An audit found accounts going back to 1729 in a deplorable state, largely beyond reconstruction. A *cédula* of November 13, 1741, from the desk of Campillo y Cossío, who had replaced Quintana by that time, demanded strict regulation of the guild's salaries and expenses. It also called for tight auditing standards to be enforced by the comptroller of the *Casa de la Contratación*, under the supervision of the Council of the Indies. Finally, in September 1742, Campillo ordered all ships carrying cargoes to America (including those from the armada) be measured (*se arqueen*).[42] These policies replaced the benign neglect that had characterized the Patiño decade, establishing a new level of royal control over the embarrassed and increasingly discredited guild.[43]

Despite the hefty fines levied on the *Consulado*, King Philip suspended payments on crown debts in 1739, just as war seemed inevitable.[44] After

---

[38] The ministers included Andrés González de Barcia, José Ventura Guell, Antonio Álvarez de Abreu, and Pedro de Ontalba y Arce; the theologians Pedro de Ocaña, Agustín Sánchez, and Martín Sarmiento. Findings, Junta de Ministros, Madrid, October 25, 1737, AGI, IG, leg. 2300.

[39] File, pardon (*indulto*), Consulado de Cádiz, 1737, AGI, IG, leg. 2300.

[40] Resolution, Juna de Ministros, Madrid, October 25, 1737, AGI, IG, leg. 2300

[41] Antonio García-Baquero González, *Cádiz y el Atlántico (1717–1778)*, I (Seville: Escuela de Estudios Hispano-Americanos, 1976), pp. 217–19.

[42] Royal order, San Ildefonso, September 19, 1742, AGS, Marine, leg. 767.

[43] Quintana to Villarías, Buen Retiro, June 26, 1741, and September 12, 1741, and royal *cédula*, November 13, 1741, AGI, IG, leg. 2303. See also Kuethe, "Los Borbones y el consulado," pp. 43–48.

[44] Pablo Fernández Albaladejo, "El decreto de suspensión de pagos de 1739: Análisis e implicaciones," *Moneda y crédito* (Madrid), no. 142 (1977), pp. 51–85.

enormous difficulty securing the necessary funding, two warships carrying Viceroy Sebastián de Eslava and 600 infantrymen – to form the Fixed Battalion of Panama and to reinforce Cartagena – departed El Ferrol for New Granada in mid-October. They did not arrive in time to save Portobelo, which fell to a surprise British attack in November.[45] In the end, the *Consulado* conceded loans to the crown of 1.4 million pesos between 1740 and 1741 for emergency war expenses. The newly formed Caracas Company advanced over 6 million copper *reales* (worth 300,000 pesos) for the fleet at El Ferrol, and it provided five ships to transport 1,000 reinforcements from the Regiments of Portugal and Almanza to the Caribbean.[46] The *Consulado*'s prestige diminished as that of the Caracas Company rose. Indeed, a grateful crown elevated the rights of the *Real Compañía Guipuzcoana* to those of a monopoly in 1741, and it extended them to include Maracaibo.[47] Over the anguished protests of Cádiz, it also established the Royal Havana Company on December 18, 1740, half of whose shares were held by Cubans.[48]

Campillo y Cossío inflicted another major blow to the monopoly rights of the *Consulado* by opening membership in the Andalusian guild to worthy outsiders, undoing the special arrangement that it had secured from Patiño. The *cédula* of April 20, 1742, sought to remedy the previous error of having agreed

to remove the supervision of this affair from my Council of the Indies and the tribunal of the Casa de la Contratación, reserving only for my royal decision the doubts and actions that might arise ... without the Consulado having to explain to neither one nor the other whatever reason there might have been for their exclusion.[49]

This reform essentially cracked the grip that the Marqués de Thous and the *sevillano* elite had held on the guild since at least 1729.

The opening of the *Consulado*'s membership allowed the descendants of foreign merchants living in Cádiz, the *jenízaros*, to participate actively in the transatlantic trade once again. Although the *jenízaros* never accounted for

[45] Quintana to Villarías, Buen Retiro, July 11, 1739; Eslava to Quintana, El Ferrol, October 4, 1739, and aboard the warship *Galicia*, October 18, 1739, AGI, Panama, leg. 355 and SF, leg. 572.

[46] Files, Caracas Company loans of 6 million *reales*, 1740–1741 and of five ships, 1741–43, AGI, SF, leg. 939.

[47] Montserrat Gárate Ojanguren, *La Real Compañía Guipuzcoana de Caracas* (San Sebastián: Grupo Doctor Camino de Historia Donostiarra : Sociedad Guipuzcoana de Ediciones y Publicaciones, 1990), chap. 2.

[48] Royal *cédula*, Buen Retiro, December 18, 1740, AGI, Ultramar, leg. 882; Leví Marrero, Cuba: Economía y sociedad, VII (San Juan: Editorial San Juan, 1978), pp. 110–17.

[49] The royal *cédula* has been reproduced in Julián Ruiz Rivera, *El Consulado de Cádiz: Matrícula de Comerciantes (1730–1823)*, (Cádiz: Diputación Provincial de Cádiz, 1988), p. 21.

more than 25 percent of the trade conducted in the *Flotas* to New Spain, the *Galeones* to Portobelo, or the later register ships, their participation increased significantly after the edict of 1742. During the years when Patiño gave the *Consulado* control over its membership, the *jenízaros* accounted for between 9 and 2.75 percent of the goods carried in the *Flotas*, but that number increased to more than 20 percent by 1765.[50] The majority of the merchandise provided by *jenízaros* for the New World consisted of manufactured goods, mostly cloth from foreign producers.[51] As a result, they served as middlemen for foreign interests, much like Spanish merchants in the *Consulado*. The *jenízaros* never constituted a majority group in the *Consulado*, however, which remained dominated by Spanish-born *gaditano* merchants.

Campillo y Cossío's, successor was Zenón de Somodevilla, the Marqués de la Ensenada. Born in Logroño of poor but honorable hidalgo parentage, he had risen rapidly through the military and later the Ministry of Marine.[52] Somodevilla had served in Montemar's expedition to Oran, where he met and befriended three young officers who would later advance his reformist goals serving in the Indies – Sebastián de Eslava (as viceroy of New Granada), Juan Francisco de Güemes y Horcasitas (as captain general of Cuba and later viceroy of New Spain), and José Manso de Velasco (as viceroy of Peru).[53] Somodevilla's breakthrough came when Patiño entrusted him with organizing the successful expedition that escorted Charles to assume his throne in Naples. That achievement won him his title as Marqués de la Ensenada in 1736.[54] Ensenada would aggressively sustain and expand the reformist agenda that Campillo had championed. While his predecessors Alberoni and Patiño saw themselves as heavily burdened but serene magistrates, Ensenada liked to be portrayed (as in Figure 4.1) with a cheerful, optimistic confidence expressed in the ubiquitous "smile of reason" so common to the sages of the eighteenth-century Enlightenment (see Figures 1.1, 3.1, and 4.1).

Well before Ensenada succeeded Campillo in the Secretariat for Marine and the Indies, he enjoyed a prominent position at court. The monarchs established the Almirantazgo on March 14, 1737, to keep the restless Prince

---

[50] Margarita García-Mauriño Mundi, *La pugna entre el Consulado de Cádiz y los jenízaros por las exportaciones a Indias (1720–1765)* (Sevilla: Universidad de Sevilla, 1999), pp. 236–40.

[51] Ibid., pp. 240–42.

[52] José Luis Gómez Urdáñez and Pedro Luis Lorenzo Cadarso, *Castilla en la edad moderna*, second part, *Historia de Castilla de Atapuerca a Fuensaldaña*, ed.by Juan José García González, Julio Aróstegui Sánchez, Juan Andrés Blanco Rodríguez. (Madrid: La Esfera de los Libros, 2008), pp. 509–10.

[53] Víctor Peralta Ruiz, *Patrones, clients y amigos. El poder burocrático indiano en la España del siglo XVIII* (Madrid: Consejo Superior de Investigaciones Científicas, 2006), p. 117.

[54] Francisco Cánovas Sánchez, and José Antonio Escudero, José María García Marín, et al., *La época de los primeros Borbones*, vol. I, *La nueva monarquía y su posición en Europa (1700–1759)* in *Historia de general de España*, dir. by José María Jover Zamora, vol. XXIX (Madrid 1985), p. 462.

FIGURE 4.1 Zenón de Somodevilla, Marqués de la Ensenada (1702–1781) in the Museo del Prado, shown wearing the Toisón de Oro of the Order of San Jenaro, painted by Jacopo Amigoni sometime after 1750, the year that the marqués received the Toisón. (See plate section for color version)

Philip occupied, naming him admiral general of State and of all naval forces. In a *cédula* of June 21, 1737, the monarchs formed a Junta de Marina, composed of the admiral general and three marine lieutenants general, and Ensenada became secretary of both the Almirantazgo and the junta. Soon thereafter he assumed the title of Marine intendant. When Philip left in 1741 to claim his inheritance in Italy, Campillo acted as the prince's stand-in (*lugarteniente)* as admiral general, a responsibility that Ensenada also assumed after Campillo's death.[55]

---

[55] Ana María Vigón, *Guía del Archivo Museo "D. Alvaro de Bazán"* (Viso de Marqués 1985), pp. 19–21.

Ensenada's reformist agenda appeared quickly as he forcefully completed the break with Seville. He charged the priors and consuls for the years 1728 to 1743 with fraud and confiscated and sold their property in a purge reminiscent of Tinajero's actions early in the century.[56] In that case, the effect was to transfer power from one clique to another; now not only factions but cities were at play. In December 1743, Ensenada imposed a new system for the apportionment of electors, which finally completed the transfer of power in the *Consulado* from Seville to Cádiz begun by Alberoni in 1717. The new system reduced Seville's number of delegates from twenty to ten, equal to the representation of Cádiz, while the other ten would come from the *gaditano* satellites of Puerto de Santa María (four), Jerez de la Frontera (three) and San Lúcar de Barrameda (three).[57] Meeting in San Lúcar, the electors would choose one new consul annually, alternating between Cádiz, Seville, and the satellites. The consul with seniority became the prior.

The Marqués de Thous was among those charged with fraud, and he fought this persecution mightily, but the days of the *sevillano* elite had passed.[58] In succeeding years, a growing number of members would relocate to Cádiz and Seville's grandeur gradually faded.[59] Significantly, the reformed guild was far less autonomous and became much more a tool of the monarchy. Meanwhile, Ensenada periodically continued demanding donations from the guild after commercial successes occurred.[60]

The establishment of the Royal Havana Company broke important new ground. The company secured a legal monopoly over the island's agricultural exports and its European imports. This arrangement entailed canceling the Marqués de Madrid's contract to supply tobacco to the Royal Factory of Seville. The crown continued expecting the monopoly to provide some 3.5 million pounds of high-quality leaf annually. While the bulk of this production would come from the Havana district, 400,000 pounds were purchased in the central and eastern portions of the island. The policy aimed to secure quality tobacco for Spain while concurrently suppressing contraband. This enterprise exercised a powerful impact on royal finances in Spain, producing profits ranging from 7 to 10 million pesos each year.[61] While securing these large tobacco profits was the primary goal, the crown also granted both

---

[56] He assigned the proceeds to cover the shortfalls in the *lonja* and *infants* funds.

[57] This reform came via the royal order of December 17, 1743, and was confirmed by royal *cédula* the following February 1, both found in AGI, IG, leg. 2302.

[58] Kuethe, "El fin del monopolio," p. 47.

[59] Antonia Heredia Herrera, *Sevilla y los hombres de comercio (1700–1800)* (Sevilla: Editoriales Andaluzas Unidas 1989), pp. 127–40. For the flourishing of Cádiz, see Manuel Bustos Rodríguez, *Cádiz en el sistema atlántico: La ciudad, sus comerciantes y la actividad mercantil (1650–1830)* (Cádiz: Universidad de Cádiz, 2005), especially pp. 90–106.

[60] Report, *Consulado* contributions since 1717, December 1760, AGI, IG, leg. 2308. See also AGI, Consulados, leg. 36.

[61] McNeill, *Atlantic Empires*, pp. 119–22, 159.

Cuban sugar and hides tariff-free entry into Cádiz. This step clearly represented a concession to influential *habanero* interests, but it also formed part of a broad policy of stimulating economic development in imperial peripheries producing agricultural export crops.[62] In the long run, the sugar industry would come to dominate Cuba and constitute a major force for economic growth in the empire.

In return for these privileges, the company incurred costly obligations, particularly subsidizing the construction of a determined number of warships and financing the Havana shipyard. The yard launched the first two ships of the line in 1744, with each bearing seventy guns. Four more of equal size appeared by 1748, along with another of sixty-four guns. Finally, the company also accepted the responsibility to transport military supplies to Havana at its own cost.[63]

THE WAR OF JENKINS' EAR

Tensions between Britain and Spain arising from disputes over Spanish efforts to eliminate contrabandists in the Caribbean and from mounting British pressure against Spanish territories in Florida and Central America grew, and by mid-1738 the two powers were on the verge of war. The antagonists attempted through the Conventions of London in November 1738, and El Pardo in January 1739 to resolve the explosive issue of prizes (*presas*) taken at sea by Spanish coast guard vessels, without achieving success. In the end, Spain accepted a net liability of 95,000 pounds to compensate Britain, but before rendering payment insisted that the 68,000 pounds that the South Sea Company owed Philip V for his percentage of its proceeds be deducted first. When the South Sea Company, which was virtually bankrupt, refused to accept these conditions, Spain countered by withholding further *cédulas* for ships of permission. When the company persisted in opposing the Spanish terms, Madrid unilaterally terminated the *asiento*, while affirming its liability for the 95,000 pounds.[64]

The British ministry, led by Sir Robert Walpole, attempted to resolve the dispute with Spain, but opposition members clamored for war. Walpole believed that British merchants prospered most in times of peace, not war, and so wished to avoid hostilities. When West India merchants petitioned

---

[62] Royal *cédula*, Buen Retiro, December 18, 1740, art. 34, AGI, Ultramar, leg. 882.

[63] G Douglas Inglis, "The Spanish Naval Shipyard at Havana in the Eighteenth Century," in *Selected Papers from the 5th Naval History Symposium*, ed. by the U.S. Naval Academy (Baltimore: Nautical and Aviation Publishers, 1985), pp. 51–52.

[64] Lucio Mijares, "Política exterior: La diplomacia," in *Historia general de España y América*, XI-1 (Madrid: Rialp, 1983), p. 95. Indications are that the South Sea Company hoped to provoke war through its intransigence. See also Richard Pares, *War and Trade in the West Indies, 1739–1763* (Oxford: The Clarendon Press, 1936), chap. 2, and Walker, *Spanish Politics and Imperial Trade*, pp. 205–07.

Parliament on March 3, 1738, to seek compensation for cargoes confiscated by Spanish coast guard ships in the Caribbean, Walpole tried to block its consideration. Opposition leaders then brought up the complaints of an English captain, Robert Jenkins, who claimed that the Spanish coast guard had seized his ship illegally in 1732 and that the Spanish officer inspecting the vessel had cut off his ear.[65] Claims that English sailors languished in Spanish prisons only gave credence to Jenkins's story, leading the mercurial William Pitt to call for an end to Spanish depredations in the Caribbean. Members of the opposition and the patriotic essays in the popular press demanded war, and even King George II wanted an end to all Spanish searches and seizures of British vessels.[66] Conflicts over Spanish claims to Georgia and British efforts to protect their right to cut logwood off the coast of Honduras added to the rising diplomatic problems between the two nations. The drift toward war was inevitable, and Walpole could do little to stop it.

The lure of gaining control over markets in the Spanish Indies prompted a flurry of articles in the popular press that expressed widespread beliefs about British war aims. Anonymous authors argued naively that British soldiers would be welcomed as liberators by creoles anxious to escape the yoke of Spain. They contended that Spanish Americans would ask nothing more than to share the "rights" of Englishmen, and after their liberation from Spanish tyranny, they would prosper from increased trade with Great Britain.[67] Several "anonymous advisors of the government" even argued that Britain should retain the Spanish system of *Flotas* and *Galeones*, with trade fleets sailing from London (not Cádiz) stocked with English manufactured goods. They claimed that this would secure the loyalty of great merchant houses in Lima and Mexico City, who would benefit from having direct access to British goods without having to compete in colonial markets with contraband wares. Although the convoy system would be reformed of its abuses – delays, irregular sailings, and high taxes – buyers and sellers in both Great Britain and the Indies would profit.[68] As a result, the War of Jenkins' Ear promised to end Spanish dominance in the Americas, allowing Britain its long-awaited direct access to the rich markets of the Indies.

After failing to intercept the mercury ships returning from Veracruz, the British issued a formal declaration of war on November 3, 1739.[69] By then, a fleet had already been dispatched to the Caribbean under Vice Admiral Edward Vernon, a member of the war party in Parliament, to catch the Spanish possessions in the Caribbean by surprise. Vernon's capture of

---

[65] Dorothy Marshall, *Eighteenth Century England*, (London: Longman, 1962), pp. 176–83.
[66] Ibid.
[67] Pares, *War and Trade*, p. 71.
[68] Ibid., p. 73.
[69] Béthencourt, *Patiño*, pp. viii, 102. The mercury ships were usually two or three small craft escorted by a frigate.

Portobelo crushed one of the most annoying corsair bases in the Caribbean, but the grander hope of catching the *Galeones* in port failed to materialize. The assault on Portobelo was also the first step in the British plan to seize first Panama and then open the gate to the South Sea and Peru. By later capturing Cartagena de Indias, the British also hoped to consolidate safely their control over the isthmus and foment rebellion in Peru and New Spain. A fleet under Commodore George Anson sailed for the Pacific in September 1740, seeking the opportunity to collaborate in an eventual assault on Panama City, which might serve as a base for controlling the Pacific and the sea lanes to Peru.[70]

Sixteen months after his conquest of Portobelo, Vice Admiral Vernon appeared off Cartagena with a massive force – twenty-nine ships of the line, a host of smaller craft, and a landing force of 12,000 under the command of Major General Thomas Wentworth. In 1740, Vernon had probed the city's external defenses several times. He launched his assault on March 15, 1741, and it concluded six weeks later with the humiliated British survivors withdrawing in defeat. A British victory opening the way to the riches of Peru could well have diverted London's interest away from the North American continent and dulled the attraction for those lands being occupied by the French to the west of the Appalachian Mountains, with incalculable consequences for the later history of North America.

The defensive strategy of the Spanish rested on several premises. The enemy would likely enjoy great numerical superiority. While Spain had to spread its human and financial resources out over a vast area, the enemy could choose the point of attack and concentrate forces. Small veteran garrisons, largely of peninsulars, could hold out by fighting behind well-placed fortifications. Disease would arrive eventually, taking hold in the enemy army and destroying it. An essential element of land defense then was the tactic of delay. The enemy must be met on the beach and his advance slowed at every opportunity. The more water he drew from local wells and the more local fruits and vegetables he consumed the better. Dysentery would quickly take hold and, eventually, so would the black vomit – yellow fever.[71]

Cartagena's long, deep harbor was protected by fixed fortifications at its southern entrance, called Boca Chica, and at the point where it narrowed in the north, forming an interior bay called the Surgidero near the city. Cartagena itself was cut off from an approach by land on the ocean side by swamps to the north and by a second entrance into the bay, Boca Grande, to

---

[70] Antonio de Béthencourt, "La Guerra de la Oreja: El corso marítimo," in Vicente Palacio Atard, ed., *España y el mar en el siglo de Carlos III* (Madrid: Marinvest, 1989), p. 341.

[71] The Spanish had no idea where yellow fever originated, but having long coped with the tropics they grasped very clearly its itinerary. For a recent account of the battle placing the role of ecology and disease into a clear perspective, see J. R. McNeill, *Mosquito Empires: Ecology and War in the Greater Caribbean, 1620–1914* (Cambridge: Cambridge University Press, 2010), pp. 155–64.

the south. Boca Grande was too shallow for large ships but deep enough to cut off the Island of Tierra Bomba that extended southward to Boca Chica. Cartagena itself was heavily fortified with a massive wall. The fortress San Felipe de Barajas blocked potential land routes into the city. Rough seas in the afternoons made entry into the harbor a necessity for an invader, but the land along the inland, eastern side of the bay was pitted with bogs and swamps.

Cartagena was defended by the fixed battalion of nine infantry companies and one artillery that had been established in 1736. It had an authorized strength of 700 men, but Governor Pedro Fidalgo had found only 166 soldiers remaining from the separate companies that predated military reform.[72] He recruited local troops to make up the deficit, and consequently the battalion was populated by soldiers who were, as one officer observed, a "confusion of colors" of the sort that inhabited the coast.[73] By 1737, the unit had 500 men, and it sustained that level into 1741.[74] Reinforcements arrived with Viceroy Eslava in April 1740, but of the 600 who left El Ferrol, only 450 survived the crossing.[75] Of these, Eslava sent 300 men, all from the second battalion of the Regiment of Granada, to Panama when he was able to do so in late 1740 and early 1741.[76] The squadron of Rodrigo de Torres delivered troops from the second battalions of the Regiments of Spain and Aragon in late 1740. Despite its limitations, the practice of reinforcing the American fixed garrisons with Spanish battalions and regiments would become the standard. All together, the fixed garrison and the two Spanish units mustered some 1,100 infantrymen and a company of artillerymen to face Vernon's invaders.[77] The local militia of 500 men supplemented the veteran forces, but the reformed system had not yet been extended to the Indies and the volunteers could provide little more than support services once the battle began.[78]

Lieutenant General Blas de Lezo, who had risen under Patiño, commanded six warships, the product of Patiño's labors to rebuild the fleet.[79] Lezo had

---

[72] Fidalgo to Torrenueva, Cartagena, May 8, 1737, AGI, SF, leg. 938.

[73] Captain Antonio de Salas to Minister of the Indies José de Gálvez, Panama, October 24, 1776, AGI, SF, leg. 948.

[74] Fidalgo to Torrenueva, Cartagena, April 5 and May 8, 1737, AGI, SF, leg. 938.

[75] Eslava to Quintana, Cartagena, May 22, 1740, AGI, SF, leg. 939. Of these 600 men, 400 were earmarked for Panama, 200 for Cartagena.

[76] Eslava to Quintana, Cartagena, December 24, 1740, and March 4, 1741, and Governor Dionisio Martínez de la Vega to Campillo, Panama, December 23, 1741, AGI, SF, leg. 572 and Panama, leg. 356.

[77] Eslava to Villarías, Cartagena, March 31, 1741, AGI, SF, leg. 572; Allan J. Kuethe, "La batalla de Cartagena de 1741: Nuevas perspectivas," Historiografía y bibliografía americanistas, 18 (1974), p. 27.

[78] Juan Marchena Fernández, *La institución militar en Cartagena de Indias, 1700–1810* (Sevilla: Escuela de Estudios Hispano-Americanos. 1982), p. 125.

[79] Lezo had been an *hombre de confianza* of Patiño. Bibiano Torres Ramírez, *La Armada del Mar del Sur* (Sevilla: Escuela de Estudios Hispano-Americanos, 1987), p. 241.

arrived with the *Galeones* of 1737, and as the highest ranking officer, he assumed command of the naval forces. A battle-scarred veteran, lacking one arm and one leg, he understood that the 600 sailors and 400 marines who manned his ships would likely need to reinforce the landed resistance.

Vernon began the assault against Boca Chica on March 20. Wentworth landed his forces on Tierra Bomba to assist directly from the land, but his delay in testing the defenses proved costly because it afforded the Spanish time to organize their resistance. It took Vernon seventeen long days to batter Boca Chica into submission and penetrate the harbor. Once inside, a British rush toward the city might have produced a victory, with the defenders in disarray. Wentworth, however, was confident of victory, and he delayed the advance until he had completed the proper preparations for an assault. This pause enabled the Spanish to regroup and to plot how to impede the British advance.[80]

On the water, Blas de Lezo had positioned four ships at Boca Chica to back the fortifications. When those positions fell, he hastily abandoned his ships, ordering them scuttled, and he retreated to where the harbor narrowed to form the Surgidero or inner bay. There, he scuttled the two remaining warships beside some merchantmen. His intent was to block a direct advance by British naval forces to the city's edge, although the same effect might have been achieved with the ships remaining above water firing their guns. Indeed, the British managed to pull one of the scuttled vessels far enough aside to allow smaller craft to enter the Surgidero and shell the city. While sitting aboard his flagship at Boca Chica, Lezo took a splinter in the arm that eventually cost him his life.

Landing on the mainland edge of the bay, the British army attempted to slog its way through swampy ground toward the formidable San Felipe de Barajas and behind it, the city. Here the invaders encountered delaying tactics from the Spanish infantry and the fixed battalion.[81] By the time Wentworth was prepared to assault San Felipe de Barajas on April 20, a month had passed since his men first came ashore. Exposed to the blistering heat, drawing water from local wells, and taking extra nourishment where it could be found, they were soon ravaged by disease. A desperate attempt to storm the fortress failed miserably and at high cost. With his forces disappearing before his very eyes,

---

[80] Various witnesses within the Spanish resistance affirmed that for several days the defense had fallen into total disarray and confusion. Charles E. Nowell, "The Defense of Cartagena," *HAHR*, 42 (November 1962), pp. 492–98.

[81] Many of the new recruits were not up to the challenge. As one officer later recalled, "in Cartagena de Indias, during the siege of the year forty-one, [it was necessary] to wedge the battalion of the plaza between two files, that of my Regiment of Aragon and that of [the Regiment of] Spain, with the lieutenants [positioned] to the rear, with orders to run a sword through the chests of those who broke ranks, and with such intense urgency (upon which depended the defense of the plaza) it [victory] was won." Quoted in Kuethe, "La batalla de Cartagena," pp. 22–23.

Vice Admiral Vernon had no choice but to withdraw to Jamaica, beginning on April 28. He did not pause to bury the thousands of British dead. The Spanish strategy had worked.

But Vernon was not finished. In July of that same year, he threw the remnants of his forces against Santiago de Cuba, deploying a landing force of some 4,400 men carried on forty-one transports escorted by twenty-one warships. Santiago was a major base for Spanish corsairs, and it could provide a strategic position on the Windward Passage.[82] Under the leadership of Governor Francisco Cagigal de la Vega, the strongpoint possessed a garrison of only five undermanned companies, but it had been reinforced by four more from Spain. Santiago's formidable harbor fortifications convinced the vice admiral to land to the east at Guantánamo Bay and attack by land, but Guantánamo was separated from Santiago by fifty miles of difficult terrain. The veteran troops offered stubborn resistance while the militia, employing guerilla tactics, harassed the invading columns at every opportunity. After an offensive of seventeen days failed to achieve appreciable results, the British withdrew to Guantánamo. There Vernon remained for three more months trying to establish a permanent enclave, but reinforcements from Havana arrived at Santiago, disease set in, and the admiral once again found himself compelled to abandon an ambitious campaign. He completed his withdrawal in early December.[83] The events at Guantánamo also seemed to validate Spanish defense planning.

In April 1742, the persistent Vice Admiral Vernon, reinforced by several thousand men from England, planned to cross the isthmus and seize Panama City. After departing from Jamaica on March 16, he squandered precious time searching in vain for Spanish reinforcements that he suspected might be sailing to Cartagena. He seized Portobelo harbor but discovered that its garrison, which had been reinforced by Eslava, had deployed inland to block both the highway crossing the isthmus and the water route via the Chagres River.[84] Moreover, local intelligence suggested that the viceroy had sent troops to Panama City from Peru. As the admiral had learned at Santiago, sieges conducted over long distances and rough terrain and against entrenched opposition offered little chance of success. In addition, the rainy season would begin in May, rendering the Chagres River impassable. This time caution prevailed, and Vernon cancelled the invasion. In October, he returned to London, where he managed to heap all the blame on the hapless Wentworth and resume his career in politics.[85]

---

[82] McNeill, *Atlantic Empires*, pp. 89–91, 98–99.
[83] Olga Portuondo Zúñiga, *Una derrota británica en Cuba* (Santiago: Editorial Oriente, 2000), chaps. 4–5.
[84] Martínez de la Vega to Campillo y Cossío, Panama, December 23, 1742, AGI, Panama, leg. 356.
[85] J.C.M. Ogelsby, "The British and Panama – 1742," *Caribbean Studies*, 3 (July 1963), pp. 71–79.

In celebrating their victories, the Spanish failed to recognize how close they had come to defeat in the great battle at Cartagena. The British challenged the city with an attack force of over 12,000 men, which was an unprecedented number up to that point in the Caribbean. Then too, both at Boca Chica and in the advance on San Felipe de Barajas, Wentworth delayed while the Spanish forces turned disarray into order. Although the reformed system of fixed battalions reinforced by emergency troops from Spain had triumphed, the British did as much to lose the battle as the Spanish did to win it. Moreover, good fortune lent Spain a hand when yellow fever arrived right on time. These realities might have given cause for reflection in Madrid. They did not. Instead, the successful commanders from the war were all promoted to positions of greater influence, believing in their strategy. Eslava became the Marqués de la Real Defensa. Ensenada named him captain general of Andalusia and summoned him to serve on various special royal commissions. He would rise to secretary of the Office for War in 1754. The Conde de Revillagigedo, captain general of Havana, became the viceroy of New Spain in 1746. Francisco Cagigal de la Vega was elevated to Havana.[86] Finally, in another kind of promotion, Lezo, who lingered until September 7, became immortalized as a heroic martyr to military glory.[87]

In the end, Patiño's successors gradually extended the regulation formulated for Havana to other garrisons of the Caribbean. Panama's defenders converted to the modern footing when Eslava reinforced the old separate companies with the troops he had brought from Spain.[88] In 1738, Madrid ordered the establishment of a fixed battalion in Santo Domingo, but permitted the percentage of creoles to rise to 50 percent. When the reform reached San Juan in 1741, that percentage was obtained there too. Moreover, policy in San Juan, constructed during wartime, reduced the minimum age for local recruits to eighteen years.[89]

On the seas, the Spanish enjoyed additional successes. The effective number of ships of the line stood at an impressive forty-six in 1740, aided by the recent purchase of nine vessels from France and Genoa.[90] The Havana

---

[86] Allan J. Kuethe, *Cuba, 1753–1815: Crown, Military, and Society* (Knoxville: University of Tennessee Press, 1986), p. 12.

[87] Royal order, Madrid, October 21, 1741, AGI, SF, leg. 572.

[88] Nevertheless, keeping troops healthy and units up to strength was so difficult in Portobelo and Panama that the authorities subsequently reduced the battalion from 10 companies with 100 men each to 7 of 53, and that level also proved impossible to sustain. Governor Manuel Montiano to Ensenada, Panama, May 16, 1750, AGI, Panama, leg. 356.

[89] The regulations for Santo Domingo and San Juan can be found in AGI, IG, leg. 1885.

[90] Harbron, *Trafalgar*, p. 15. The shortage of skilled seamen quickly emerged as a serious problem. Indeed, Eslava was compelled to assign 500 men from his veteran garrison to serve aboard the ships of Rodrigo de Torres when it departed for Havana, which helps explain why Cartagena's defenses were so badly undermanned when Vernon attacked. Eslava, troop report, Cartagena, December 24, 1740, AGI, SF, leg. 572.

squadron, reinforced by a French naval force – although technically at peace with Britain – kept Vernon confined in Jamaica for a good part of 1740.[91] The essential mission of the Spanish Armada was defensive, reflecting both the need to conserve scarce resources and the fear that Spanish ships could not prevail in a pitched naval battle with the British. Typical was the indecisive confrontation between Spanish and British forces off Havana in 1748, when the Spanish fought only long enough to permit the treasure ships to escape. That was the third convoy to cross successfully during the war.[92] In 1744, near Toulon at Cape Sicié, the Spanish and French fought an English fleet to a draw. The Spanish commander, Juan José Navarro, was exalted as Marqués de la Victoria, while the English commander faced a court martial and was dismissed from service.[93] Meanwhile, in the Caribbean, privateers enjoyed impressive successes in snatching British merchantmen.[94]

THE FLOTAS AND GALEONES AND REGISTER SHIPS

During the war, it proved unfeasible to sustain the system of *Flotas* and *Galeones*. The convoys were an enticing target for the British navy, which controlled the sea lanes in the Caribbean and Atlantic. Nonetheless, in 1737, on the eve of the conflict, Spain mounted one last attempt to dispatch the *Galeones* to Cartagena with a small escort under the command of Blas de Lezo. These ships were trapped when war broke out and ultimately became involved in the historic battle. Plans to follow up on the successes of López Pintado with another *Flota* for Mexico were simply cancelled.[95]

The outbreak of war made the normal operation of the trade fair at Portobelo impossible; the British fleet under Vice Admiral Vernon had taken the city and the Spanish merchants remained bottled up in Cartagena, while the Lima merchants remained exposed in Panama. Before the Lima merchants could return home, they sought refuge with their silver inland at Quito, a city that suffered from habitual political instability. The president, José de Araujo y Río, was an irascible venal officeholder from Lima who had a long history of conflict with Lima's *Consulado*. After taking office, Araujo began feuding with the guild's representatives in Quito, Lorenzo Nates and Simón Alvarez Monteserín, who had denounced him for introducing

---

[91] Marchena, *La institución militar*, pp. 142–44; Béthencourt, *Patiño*, p. viii.

[92] J.C.M. Oglesby, "Spain's Havana Squadron and the Preservation of the Balance of Power in the Caribbean, 1740–1748," *HAHR*, 49 (August 1969), pp. 473–88; McNeill, *Atlantic Empires*, p. 98.

[93] Harbron, *Trafalgar*, pp. 79, 94. For biographical information on Navarro, see Hugo O'Donnell, *El primer marqués de la Victoria, personaje silenciado en la reforma dieciochesca de La Armada* (Madrid: Real Academia de Historia, 2004).

[94] According to Béthencourt, *Patiño*, p. 104, privateering was so lucrative that the "marine of every country solicited the issuance of patents by Philip V."

[95] Walker, *Spanish Politics and Imperial Trade*, pp. 204–09.

contraband merchandise into the city. According to Nates, this illicit merchandise had flooded local markets, lowered prices, and ruined many traders on the eve of the 1739 fair.[96] Soon after the Peruvian merchants took refuge in Quito, squabbles arose with the president. When the guild members agreed to band together to trade with the Spaniards in Cartagena as a group, Araujo undermined them by granting licenses for select allies to trade as individuals at the Caribbean port. While these independent merchants made considerable sums selling goods obtained in Cartagena, loyal guild members and their silver languished in Quito. One guild member, Manuel Labeano, wrote Madrid charging that Araujo had demanded bribes, allowed locals to charge the *limeños* exorbitant prices for moving their specie upland to Quito, and had extorted over 100,000 pesos from the guild to provision Cartagena after the British attack in 1741.[97] In the end, Araujo defended himself against these attacks, but it was clear that he relished having the power to punish his enemies in the Lima *Consulado*. The Lima merchants finally returned to the capital, but the *Galeones* of 1737 and the aborted trade fair had failed miserably.

To conduct commerce with the Indies during the war, the crown suspended the *Flotas* and *Galeones* and resorted to individual register ships. The register ships offered less of a target than convoys, although these ships might band together when facing an enemy threat. These departures responded primarily to strategic considerations of the moment, but they also served as an experiment in providing the marketing flexibility offered by individual sailings. The *Consulado* viewed them as dangerous precedents, while surely resenting the popularity of the Caracas Company and the presence of Havana in court circles. Moreover, Ensenada initiated the practice of licensing the register ships directly through the *vía reservada* in Madrid rather than through the *Casa de la Contratación* as was customary, a dangerous innovation that caused deep concern in Cádiz, especially in view of the piecemeal reforms that the crown had imposed on it in the aftermath of 1737. Those licenses normally came at a price to the individual shipper, often the forgiveness of long-standing claims held against the Royal Treasury arising from loans or seizures of an earlier time.[98] Such concerns rightfully deepened when Ensenada maintained these practices in the postwar period (see Chapter 6). They in effect represented a major step in the reformist transition from the Project of 1720 to the deregulation that would be effected under Charles III.

During the war years (1739–1748), 120 register ships sailed to New Spain and the Indies. They kept the American markets open, and the flow of goods

---

[96] Kenneth J. Andrien, *The Kingdom of Quito, 1690–1830: The State and Regional Development* (Cambridge: Cambridge University Press, 1995), pp. 175–76.

[97] Ibid., p. 178.

[98] Kuethe, "El fin del monopolio," pp. 48–49.

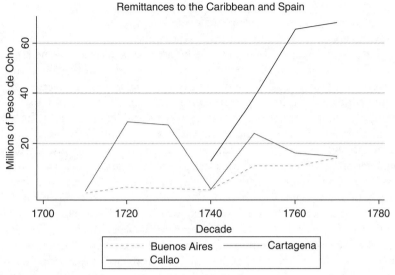

FIGURE 4.2 Register Ship Cargoes to Spain

across the Atlantic continued despite the war. As Figure 4.2 indicates, the amount of legal specie and merchandise flowing from the three principal ports of South America to Spain grew steadily during the war and the years following the peace in 1748. Ships leaving Lima carried approximately 13 million pesos worth of specie, cacao, and cascarilla between 1740 and 1750, while that number jumped to 68 million pesos between 1760 and 1770 (see Figure 4.2). The exports of specie and hides from Buenos Aires also rose from 2 million pesos during the war years to nearly 15 million pesos between 1760 and 1770 (see Figure 4.2). The numbers for Cartagena are less dramatic, but the amounts of specie, cacao, and cascarilla also rose impressively during the same time period (see Figure 4.2). Moreover, the range of goods moving across the Atlantic to Spain increased dramatically, particularly perishable or bulk commodities. During the twenty years of the restored *Galeones*, for example, Buenos Aires exported only 61,497 pesos in hides to Spain but in the years from 1770 to 1778, that figure increased to 1.5 million pesos worth of hides. Even the export of precious metals rose dramatically. Silver shipped to Spain rose from an annual average of 2 million pesos between 1720 and 1739 to over 4 million pesos annually during the operation of the register ships.[99] In short, the register ships were a tremendous boon to commerce in the Spanish Atlantic world.

[99] These figures are taken from George Robertson Dilg, "The Collapse of the Portobelo Fairs: A Study in Spanish Commercial Reform, 1720–1740" (Unpublished Ph.D. dissertation, Indiana University, 1975), pp. 275–76; the material for Figure 4.2 was taken from Appendix L. These are figures taken from summaries drawn from ship registries and as a result, they represent

Despite the successes of the register ships in exchanging goods across the Atlantic during wartime, once peace came in 1748 the *Consulados* of Lima and Mexico City lobbied for a return to the convoy system. The register ships supplying New Spain allowed Spanish merchants to market their goods throughout the viceroyalty without always relying on the *Consulado* of Mexico to act as a middle man. Some Spanish merchants even took up permanent or at least long-term residence in Mexico City to sell goods from the register ships, and by 1755 there were sixty Spanish agents in New Spain.[100] The Peruvian *Consulado* had similar problems in the unpredictable arrival of register ships sailing around Cape Horn. *Consulado* merchants could choose to purchase the whole cargo, but this entailed the risk of having to sell goods at low prices if the Peruvian markets were saturated. Like their Mexican counterparts, members of the *Consulado* faced competition from Spanish merchants seeking to sell their wares directly to markets in Peru. Moreover, the Peruvians also faced competition from Buenos Aires, which became a favored destination for register ships seeking to sell European wares for Upper Peruvian silver during the war. Since transport costs for goods from Buenos Aires were lower than hauling products overland from Lima to Upper Peru, merchants operating out of the River Plate could undercut their counterparts from the viceregal capital.[101] As a result, merchants in both Lima and Mexico City began lobbying in Madrid to restore the more predictable system of *Flotas* and *Galeones*, which gave them greater control over the transatlantic trade.

Merchants in Cádiz also perceived that their long-run interests were better served by reestablishing the traditional convoy system. Although Spanish merchants gained greater leverage over colonial markets transporting goods via register ships, the licenses for many of those ventures now came from Madrid, entailing a loss of local control. Also alarming was the news that several ships departed from ports other than Cádiz, perhaps calling into the question the permanency of its monopoly.[102] Moreover, the fleet system allowed the Spaniards to transport large quantities of goods securely, which would take the register ships several years to accomplish. The Spaniards also had to spend long years in the Indies marketing their goods piecemeal, and the uneven arrival of the individual ships made gauging colonial demand difficult. If they arrived too often, markets could become glutted, cutting profits. As a result, the *Consulado* of Cádiz joined the guilds of Lima and Mexico City in recommending the return to the more predictable system of *Flotas* and *Galeones*.[103] The successes of commercial reforms undertaken of necessity

general trends. Such summaries often contain errors, and the most accurate way to compile the data is to reconstruct the totals from the individual registry entries, not the summaries.

[100] Walker, *Spanish Politics and Imperial Trade*, pp. 211–12.
[101] Ibid., pp. 212–15.
[102] Kuethe, "El fin del monopolio," pp. 48–49.
[103] Ibid., pp. 215–16.

during wartime did not serve the long-term interests of merchants, who had traditionally dominated trade in the Spanish Atlantic since the sixteenth century.

THE WAR OF THE AUSTRIAN SUCCESSION AND ACCESSION OF FERDINAND VI

As the conflict with Great Britain continued, Spain sought to strengthen the alliance with France. During the early years, France had remained aloof, although its fleet cooperated with the Spaniards in American waters. The French became more interested in developing ties with Spain, however, with the controversial succession of Maria Theresa to the Austrian throne, which threatened to upset the European balance of power. The new Austrian queen held Parma and Plasencia, still coveted by Elizabeth, as well as Milan, which Philip had lost under the Utrecht settlement. Frederick the Great's seizure of Silesia in December 1740 triggered the War of the Austrian Succession in Europe, which pitted Britain, Austria, and the Dutch Republic against Prussia, France and Spain. This European conflict merged with the existing Anglo-Spanish War of Jenkins' Ear. Given the Spanish victories in America and colonial reforms that Madrid had undertaken, Paris wanted to use an alliance with Spain to ensure its access to American markets, particularly through supplying the Cádiz monopoly. In April 1743, representatives from the mercantile community urged the French Foreign Ministry to seek from the Spanish a "solemn treaty [promising] not to innovate with the commerce of the Indies or with the established regulations."[104]

The Bourbon powers signed the Second Family Compact at Fontainebleau on October 25, 1743.[105] Madrid promised not to renew the *asiento* with the British, while Versailles pledged to support Spain's territorial ambitions in Italy, the restoration of Gibraltar and Minorca, and the destruction of the small British colony in Georgia. As part of the "perpetual alliance," Madrid extracted an explicit commitment from the French to refrain from separate

---

[104] The deputies of commerce to Amelot, Paris, April 8, 1743, AAE:CPE, vol. 474, fol. 29.

[105] A measure of the resentment that Madrid harbored for Versailles can be gauged by its message conveying a "good will" concession to the French: "The king finds himself with reliable information and authentic proof concerning the generality and license with which all ships under the French flag, that have gone to the ports of the Indies chartered by Spaniards, have committed innumerable frauds practiced with malice and arrogance, causing great harm to the Royal Treasury and to the commerce of those kingdoms and to the charterers themselves ..... [To perpetuate] all those frauds and the insolent means of committing them, the French established in Cádiz have given orders and instructions ... violating the laws of the Indies ... [but] by an act of pure commiseration he [the king] has condescended to pardon all the excesses and the frauds thus committed." Ensenada to Rennes, San Lorenzo, October 23, 1743, AAE:CPE, vol. 474, fols. 365–69. A copy of the Second Family Compact, October 25, 1743, can be found in AAE:CPE, vol. 474, fols. 375–81.

diplomatic negotiations. A year later, the bickering allies once again strength-ened their compact through marriage, as Philip and Elizabeth's youngest daughter, María Teresa, and the dauphine, Louis, wed in December 1744.[106] What this might have meant for Bourbon relations and subsequent European history is incalculable, because the infanta died giving birth in 1746, soon after her father's passing.

Neither ally fully lived up to its commitments. The ink was barely dry on the compact when Madrid imposed a prohibition on cotton textiles, which the French viewed as inconsistent with Spain's promises, contributing to deep misgivings.[107] In America, Versailles expressed shock and outrage when the colonial authorities denied its traders entrance into Cartagena de Indias, where they had hoped to supply foodstuffs, while the English, repulsed in a bloody battle for that city just two and one-half years beforehand, received emergency trading privileges from Viceroy Eslava. Apparently, the English offer was better. By 1744, the now famous Eslava had detailed French misconduct and, under the circumstances, the crown saw fit to support its war hero, agreeing that Spain would "suffer less harm dealing with the enemy than with friends."[108]

Despite France's obligations, French Foreign Minister Renato D'Argenson soon hedged its commitments in the torturous – indeed treacherous – politics of the Italian theater. Lest Spain gain too much dominance, Versailles entered into separate, secret negotiations in late 1745 with Piedmont-Sardinia, Spain's immediate rival on the peninsula. When revealed in Madrid, the French duplicity stunned the royal family.[109] Philip sent the prestigious Duke of Huéscar to Paris to intervene, but he arrived too late to prevent a separate accord.[110] Madrid's relations with Versailles would not soon recover. Dominated by mutual distrust, military collaboration proved inef-fective and led to disappointing results.

In the Two Sicilies, King Charles VII suffered humiliation as a British fleet blockaded Naples in 1742 and threatened to level the city if he did not withdraw the 10,000 troops he had positioned in central Italy in support of

[106] María Angeles Pérez Samper, *Isabel de Farnesio* (Barcelona: Plaza y Janés, 2003), pp. 305–08. The marriage took place on December 20, 1744.

[107] Controller-General Philibert Orry to Rennes, Versailles, December 2, 1743, AAE:CPE, vol. 474, fols. 417–18.

[108] Villarías showed neither sympathy nor guilt in his response to the protest that he received from Ambassador Bishop of Rennes. He reminded him that "the complaints that [His Majesty] frequently receives from the governors of America [are] that the French, under the pretext of carrying food, introduce into those domains all sorts of merchandise and that the courtesy passes that are sometimes granted out of good will . . . only serve to encourage abuse and more disorder." Villarías to Rennes, San Ildefonso, July 23, 1744, AAE:CPE, vol. 474, fols. 180–82.

[109] Pérez Samper, *Isabel de Farnesio*, pp. 293–304.

[110] Juan Molina Cortón, *Reformismo y neutralidad: José de Carvajal y la diplomacia de la España ilustrada* (Mérida: Regional de Estremadura, 2003), p. 105.

the Spanish army of Montemar. With his capital in a state of panic and without the means to resist, the young king had no choice but to accede.[111] It was a blow to his honor and pride that Charles would never forget, even after he gained the Spanish throne in 1759.

The death of King Philip V came suddenly, and it undoubtedly shocked the court. The brief seizure that ended Philip's life at age sixty-two struck on July 9, 1746. His eldest son, Ferdinand VI, inherited the throne, and the principal questions were what would become of his stepmother Elizabeth, and how would the reign of a new monarch affect Spanish policy? Elizabeth departed the royal palace on August 5 in a poignant moment captured by the French ambassador:

Thus it is that Elizabeth Farnese has left the royal palace, where she reigned for over thirty years. I have seen funeral pomp but never before have I seen anything that has made such a strong impression on me. It appeared to me as if she were going to her own funeral.[112]

She moved into a nearby palace formed from mansions provided by the Principe Pío, the Italian general and former governor of Madrid, and the Duque de Osuna, a prominent grandee, renaming it "The Palace of the Dowager Queen."[113] Philip had left La Granja de San Ildefonso to Elizabeth in his will and in July of the following year, with encouragement from the new king, she transferred there.[114] Without her dogged pursuit of

---

[111] Reed Browning, *The War of the Austrian Succession* (New York: St. Martins Press, 1993), pp. 118–19.

[112] Rennes to D'Argenson, Madrid, August 6, 1746, AAE:CPE, vol. 490, fols. 317–24.

[113] Rennes to D'Argenson, Madrid, July 17, AAE:CPE, vol. 490, fols. 193–94. The ambassador coldly observed that "after Philip's death, the people let out harangues and songs against his widow; [but] the imprisonment of some thirty people deadened the satire [and] measures were taken to prevent indecencies along the road of the dowager queen, who in effect arrived at her residence without insults. Word has it that Mr. Montijo distributed some coins to some people to shout 'viva' when she passed. And in effect, during the visit that I made to her the next day, she said to me, 'I have received *vivas* just like the others.' [What a] strange glimpse into the misery and the human vanity of a person, who, after having made all the world tremble for thirty years, took comfort in shouts coming from the street." Montijo had been named personal secretary to Elizabeth in 1745. Didier Ozanam, *La diplomacia de Fernando VI: Correspondencia entre Carvajal y Huéscar, 1746–1749* (Madrid: Consejo Superior de Investigaciones Científicas, 1975), p. 83.

[114] Rennes to D'Argenson, Madrid, July 11, 1756, AAE:CPE, vol. 490, fols. 166–74. French ambassador Rennes had predicted this move, citing Elizabeth's desire to escape the demands and the "bourgeoisie" society of Madrid in favor of the hunt and the quiet of the mountains. Rennes to D'Argenson, Madrid, August 6, 1746, AAE:CPE, vol. 490, fols. 317–24. Yet she complained endlessly about her life at La Granja, as she obviously missed presiding on center stage at court. Ferdinand had to nudge her out of Madrid because she insisted on intriguing and meddling and simply made a nuisance of herself. She presumably would have preferred to join Charles in the Two Sicilies, but she had inescapable familial responsibilities in Spain with two infantes to look after, Louis and María Antonia. María Antonia married Victor Amadeus of the House of Savoy in 1750, heir to the throne of Piedmont-Sardinia. Louis

dynastic claims in Italy, the new monarch was free to pursue policies focused on the Atlantic.

Ferdinand inherited the throne at a difficult time. Although the war went well in America, the Franco-Spanish forces advancing the infante Philip's dynastic claims in northern Italy had been crushed by the Austrian army at Plasencia in June 1746.[115] Finances were exhausted and the court was febrile with intrigue.[116] Despite affirming his determination to sustain continuity in Spanish foreign policy, Ferdinand was unwilling to commit the same level of national resources that his father had expended to support the claims of his half-brother.[117] Scant political support existed among the Spanish for continuing the struggle.[118] And the French, who had gained little from trade concessions in the American colonies and whose ambitions in Europe had narrowed, saw little advantage for themselves in supporting Spanish causes in Italy.[119] During the time of Elizabeth and Philip, right up to the end of their reign, American commercial interests had been repeatedly sacrificed to dynastic objectives.[120]

Ferdinand, although habitually indecisive and of only mediocre ability, brought a fresh approach that emphasized national priorities over dynastic ones.[121] D'Argenson shrewdly observed, "The government in Spain was French during the time of Louis XIV and Italian during the rest of Philip's

became a cardinal. Meanwhile, María Ana Victoria became queen of Portugal in 1750. Pérez Samper, *Isabel de Farnesio*, pp. 415–24.

[115] Ozanam, *La diplomacia*, p. 6.

[116] As the French Foreign Minister observed, "King Ferdinand takes the reigns of government at the most difficult time to come along in quite a while. The military forces in Italy, their position critical, the finances exhausted, the navy inactive, discord at court, and the absence of acumen in the choice of subjects to fill places of confidence." D'Argenson to Rennes, Versailles, July 17, 1746, AAE:CPE, vol. 490, fols. 183–85.

[117] Ferdinand VI to Louis XV, Buen Retiro, July 29, 1746, AAE:CPE vol. 490, fols. 277–78. His intention was "to find peace by means of war, ensure the Kingdom of Naples, establish the infante Don Philip, my brother, and give total priority to maintaining the most perfect harmony with Your Majesty." But, as Villarías reflected, "His Majesty ... does not hide [his view] that establishing the *infante* is not a direct interest of his crown." Quoted in Ozanam, *La diplomacia*, p. 25.

[118] Rennes to D'Argenson, Madrid, July 11, 1746, AAE:CPE, vol. 490, fols. 166–74.

[119] Ibid.; D'Argenson to Rennes, Versailles, July 26, 1746, AAE:CPE, vol. 490, fol., 236. By this time, D'Argenson described the Family Compact as "passé ... [and] unworkable and onerous for the king." Quoted in Cánovas Sánchez, *La época*, p. 639, n. 106.

[120] Indeed, days before his death, Philip had confided to French Special Envoy Marshal Noailles, "if they [the English] wish to contribute to the establishment of the infante in Italy, Spain will grant them commercial advantages more or less in proportion to the grandeur of the position that they manage to secure for him." Memoire, Marshal Noailles, Madrid, July 8, 1746, AAE:CPE, vol. 490. fols. 14–43.

[121] D'Argenson to Rennes, Versailles, September 2, 1746, AAE:CPE, vol. 491, fols. 14–21. The French ally expected a shift in Spanish policy but did not believe that Ferdinand would totally abandon Italy, and he did not.

reign; today it will become Castilian and National."[122] The month following Philip's death, the Prince of Campoflorido, an Italian disciple of Elizabeth, was replaced as ambassador to Versailles by the Duke of Huéscar and reassigned to the Kingdom of the Two Sicilies.[123] Throughout his reign, moreover, Ferdinand would nurture the hope that peace might best serve Spain's interests.[124]

Ensenada still held the ministries of War, Finance, and Marine and the Indies. The dismissal of Sebastián de la Cuadra, the Marqués de Villarías, from State came in December, but as a measure of respect, Ferdinand permitted him to retain Grace and Justice for another year.[125] Villarías's replacement at State was José Carvajal y Lancaster, an *extremeño* from Cáceres. Carvajal was cautiously pro-British in orientation and would effect a reorientation of Spanish diplomacy with profound implications for colonial policy. A jurist educated at Salamanca, Carvajal's first appointment came as *oidor* of the Audiencia of Valladolid followed by a position on the Council of the Indies in 1740. He rose to interim governor of the Council just two years later, assuming the duties of the ailing, then traveling, Conde de Montijo. He continued to hold that position after his appointment as secretary of the Office for State, acquiring proprietary authority in January 1748 when Montijo joined Villarías in retirement.[126] Meanwhile, he also assumed the presidency of the Junta General de Comercio y Moneda.[127]

In the end, in October 1748, the Peace of at Aix-la-Chapelle rescued some but far from all of the inheritance of the infante Philip. He received Parma and Plasencia through his mother's rights by inheritance and, in addition, the small Duchy of Guastalla, but not Milan or Tuscany.[128] Spanish claims to the restoration of Gibraltar and Minorca remained unfulfilled. The disgust in

---

[122] D'Argenson to Rennes, Versailles, July 17, 1746, AAE:CPE, vol. 490, fols. 183–85.

[123] Ferdinand VI to Louis XV, Buen Retiro, August 9, 1746, and Campoflorido to the infante Philip, Paris, August 29, 1746, AAE:CPE, vol. 490, fols. 337, 445–46. Ozanam, *La diplomacia*, p. 11.

[124] José Luis Gómez Urdañez, *Fernando VI* (Madrid: Arlanza Ediciones, 2001), pp. 145–46.

[125] The transition was dignified. Villarías continued to manage the ministry until Carvajal could take charge. Rennes to D'Argenson, Madrid, December 6 and 10, 1746, AAE:CPE, vol. 492, fols. 222–34. His retirement came with the salary and honors of councilor of State. He died in 1766. Nava, "Problemas y perpectivas," p. 161.

[126] Curiously, the Conde de Montijo retained his position as president. This led to the unique arrangement whereby the Council had at the same time both a president and a governor, a situation that endured until Montijo's retirement in 1748. Gildas Bernard, *Le Secrétariat d'État et le Conseil Espagnol des Indes (1700–1808)* (Geneva: Droz, 1972), pp. 77–78, 211–12. For the French commentary on this rising talent, see Rennes to D'Argenson, Madrid, August 6, 1746, AAE:CPE, vol. 490, fols. 317–24.

[127] José Miguel Delgado Barrado, *El Proyecto político de Carvajal: Pensamiento y reforma en tiempos de Fernando VI* (Madrid: Consejo Superior de Investigaciones Científicas, 2001), pp. 14–15.

[128] Needless to say, Elizabeth was outraged. Pérez Samper, *Isabel de Farnesio*, p. 421.

Madrid over what seemed to be double-dealing by the French and over Versailles's overbearing tendency to treat the Spanish like a junior partner, all too often pretending to speak for them, as well as the void left in family ties as a practical consequence of the tragic death of María Teresa on July 22, 1746, prompted opportunities for British diplomacy to split the Bourbon alliance.[129] This opened the way for a rapprochement between Great Britain and Spain, and in 1750 the Treaty of Madrid would terminate diplomatically the *asiento* and its attendant treaties, providing an opportunity to advance the reformist agenda for colonial commerce.

LEÓN'S REBELLION AND THE CARACAS COMPANY

The end of the War of Jenkins' Ear and the termination of the South Sea Company's *asiento* undoubtedly produced relief to governing circles in Madrid, but it led to serious unrest in the Governorship of Venezuela. The region had experienced a cacao boom during the first half of the eighteenth century, and the Patiño government had chartered the *Compañia Guipuzcoana de Caracas* in 1728 to direct this profitable export commodity though legal commercial channels. Venezuela had not been well served by the system of *Flotas* and *Galeones*, so the company was given the right to export cacao to Spain and New Spain, patrol the coast to prevent contraband, and promote an increase in royal revenues in the province. Exporters could still send some cacao exports directly to New Spain, after having met the company's quotas. The South Sea Company supplied the provinces with slaves under the terms of its *asiento*, paid for with cacao, which the British company then exported at great profit to New Spain. The end of the *asiento* and the resulting shortage of slaves hurt cacao production, particularly on the newer plantations on the Tuy River frontier. Moreover, without competition from the British, the Caracas Company set very low prices for local cacao, which fell from a high of 18 pesos/fanega in 1735 to only 5 pesos in 1749.[130] The government and the company also colluded to hinder efforts by local producers to ship cacao directly to Veracruz, by having company ships loaded first (called the *alternativa*) before private ships could load their product, further ensuring low prices and disruptions in trading to Veracruz.[131]

While the labor needs of more established cacao producing areas were not serious, in the newer haciendas of the Tuy frontier, the shortage of slaves by 1748 produced an economic crisis. Many Tuy settlers had emigrated from the

---

[129] For an overview of the maneuverings leading to the treaty, see Molina Cortón, *Reformismo y neutralidad*, pp. 183–222.

[130] Robert J. Ferry, *The Colonial Elite of Early Caracas: Formation and Crisis, 1567–1767* (Berkeley: University of California Press, 1989), p. 138. This discussion of the Leon rebellion is drawn from this excellent monograph of Robert Ferry.

[131] Ibid., pp. 155, 157, 181–82.

Canary Islands, and these *isleños* resented the Basque managers of the Caracas Company. The settlers also mistrusted the local bureaucracy, particularly the Basque governor in Caracas, Gabriel José de Zuloaga (1737–1747), whom they rightly suspected of having strong sympathies with the Caracas Company.[132] The situation was made worse by the government prohibition from 1735 on shipping cacao by sea to La Guaira, forcing hacendados in Tuy to ship their beans overland to Caracas. Given the higher cost of sending their beans overland, Tuy hacendados could not make a profit on the sale of their produce in the capital. Royal authorities had imposed the ban on shipping by sea to curtail contraband, but in practice low prices and high transport costs to Caracas forced more Tuy farmers to sell to smugglers, particularly Dutch traders operating out of Curacao.[133]

The leader of the protest in Tuy over the practices of the Caracas Company was the *isleño* Juan Francisco de León, the local magistrate in the region, who owned his own cacao hacienda. On April 19, 1749, León led a ragtag group of isleños, free blacks, and a few slaves and Amerindians to Caracas to protest the unfair company practices with Governor Luis Castellanos. The governor had planned to flee to La Guaira, but León and his men arrived in Caracas first on April 21. At their meeting, Castellanos agreed to remain in the capital, and he issued a pardon for León and his followers. The next day León and his supporters called an open meeting of the city cabildo, which denounced the company and its restrictive control over the commerce in cacao. Support from the cabildo and many of the elite in Caracas only added to the gravity of the protest. Castellanos, who had previously signed a document repudiating any agreements he might make under coercion, ignored his promises to León, and on May 3 he fled (disguised a priest) to La Guaira. With the governor's flight from Caracas, León's protest against the company could be interpreted now as a treasonous rebellion against crown authority. León understood that the governor's flight had likely turned him into a rebel, and he blocked the road to the port city and planned an attack on La Guaira, set for August 1.[134] Armed hostilities were only averted when Governor Castellanos forced personnel of the Caracas Company to leave the province, and he pardoned León and his men once again.

Authorities in Spain and the Indies reacted with alarm at this rebellion against royal authority, apparently abetted by the Caracas elite. They responded swiftly and sternly. The captain general of Santo Domingo sent three ships with troops to pacify the rebellion, and in late October the Marqués de la Ensenada dispatched two additional warships and 1,200 men from Cádiz under the command of his protégé, the newly appointed Governor of Caracas, *Bailío* Julián de Arriaga. Fray Arriaga was a knight of

---

[132] Ibid., p. 144.
[133] Ibid., pp. 144–45.
[134] Ibid., pp. 145–52.

the order of St. John of Jerusalem and an experienced naval officer, who had served as rear admiral in the Royal Armada.[135] Once he arrived in La Guaira on November 28, Arriaga made his way with a small escort to Caracas, where he met with Juan Francisco de León, who had mustered his supporters to move on the capital again. Arriaga quickly took stock of the situation and used a display of military force to intimidate León's supporters, forcing them to back down. Once in control of events, Arriaga offered a pardon to León and his men (although he forced León to kneel in the plaza before him for two hours before a public reading of the document).[136]

Arriaga's reports to Ensenada in January 1750 indicated the he found no proof that the elite had participated in the protest, and he further underscored that the rebels had challenged the Caracas Company, not crown authority. Finally, Arriaga acknowledged that the company had abused its monopoly privileges by setting artificially low prices for cacao and disrupted trade by insisting on the *alternativa* in loading ships in La Guaira.[137] Although Venezuela remained subdued, the activities of the Caracas Company were suspended in the province. Arriaga also entertained petitions from the Caracas cabildo, local elites, and Tuy hacendados protesting its harmful policies.

The situation in Caracas still posed daunting challenges from the perspective of the Marqués de la Ensenada in Madrid. Evidence indicated that in the absence of the Caracas Company, contraband trade in cacao through Dutch Curacao had risen alarmingly. Moreover, Ensenada and his fellow ministers were in the midst of a thorough review of commercial policies in the Spanish Atlantic following the War of Jenkins' Ear. As a result, they favored a reinstatement of the company's monopoly in Venezuela in order to curtail the contraband trade in cacao and channel commerce through approved legal channels. Ensenada decided to send General Felipe Ricardos (son-in-law of the Duke of Montemar), along with 600 veterans of the Italian wars to Caracas to put an end to León's rebellion once and for all. Ricardos had precise instructions to capture León and any other rebel leaders by force and to punish any members of the Caracas elite complicit in the insurrection.[138] After arriving in the capital in May 1751, Ricardos ordered the arrest of key members of the local elite, shipping some back to Spain, and he revoked any pardons issued by former governors. His soldiers then hunted down Juan Francisco de León and his son for six months, until they both surrendered

---

[135] The term *bailío* indicates a special honor or encomienda reserved for distinguished members of the order of Saint John. See María Baudot Monroy, "Orígenes familiares y carrera profesional de Julián de Arriaga, Secretario de Estado de Marina e Indias (1700–1776)," *Espacio, Tiempo y Forma, Serie IV, Historia Moderna*, vol. XVII, pp. 163–85.

[136] Ferry, *The Colonial Elite of Early Caracas*, pp. 152–54.

[137] Ibid., pp. 155–57.

[138] Ibid., pp. 157–64.

voluntarily in January 1752. Both were sent to Spain for trial. A dozen men associated with the rebellion received the death sentence.[139]

Once Ricardos had punished the most prominent rebels, he allowed the Caracas Company to resume operations in Venezuela in accord with the terms of its original charter. This effectively ended the loathsome *alternativa*, and both company and private ships could now load cacao simultaneously in La Guaira. Moreover, cacao planters regained the right to send their cacao to Veracruz or Spain on private ships. The only limit to free trade with New Spain was the proviso that cacao planters in Venezuela meet a quota on the beans sent to Spain, to satisfy demand in the metropolis. Ricardos resolved the thorny issue of the price paid for cacao by the company by arranging for a committee, consisting of the governor, the regidor of the cabildo, and the Caracas Company's factor to determine the official price for local cacao each year.[140] In the end, this reform settled the outstanding issues leading to the outbreak of the León rebellion.

CONCLUSION

In the years following the death of Patiño, a new generation of reformers emerged who began advancing imaginative solutions to solve the problems of the Spanish Atlantic world. During the crisis that preceded the War of Jenkins' Ear, officials in Madrid forcefully curbed the power and the independence of the *Consulado* of Cádiz and its *sevillano* elite, a process that culminated during the early years of the conflict. Once at war, reformers replaced the traditional system of *Flotas* and *Galeones* with individual register ships, and they founded new monopoly trading companies such as the Royal Havana Company to exploit emerging resources in the colonial peripheries.

The seminal work for this new breed of politicians was José de Campillo y Cossío's *Nuevo sistema*, which provided a blueprint for a thorough overhaul of Spain's imperial relationships. Campillo called for an end to the Cádiz monopoly, and he encouraged commerce in a wide range of export commodities, from silver to more exotic tropical produce such as cacao, indigo, tobacco, sugar, coffee, and hemp. The traditional convoy system, with its unpredictable sailings and limited carrying capacity, could not meet the more demanding delivery needs of such perishable bulk products, and so Campillo advanced the quite radical notion of sponsoring free trade within the empire. He also called for a modern, efficient mail service, regional trade fairs, an overhaul of government to curtail the culture of political corruption, and the integration of Amerindians in the Indies as producers and consumers in the market economy. Although Campillo would never live to see the

[139] Ibid., pp. 164–69.
[140] Ibid., p. 161.

implementation of his policies, the ideas embodied in the *Nuevo sistema* influenced the decisions of his successors, and they changed the political debate over reform.

Campillo knew that innovation would provoke opposition, and so it did. As reform emerged in contested, volatile political areas, interest groups (foreign and domestic) on both sides of the Atlantic struggled to shape or cope with policies of the Spanish crown. Efforts to curtail the power of the *Consulado* of Cádiz and to replace the *Flotas* and *Galeones* during wartime with individual register ships led to a steady flow of goods across the Atlantic, despite British control over the sea lanes. It also promoted a diversification of products sent from the Indies to Spain, as tropical produce and other perishable products could now be conveyed efficiently across the Atlantic. Nonetheless, the register ships incited opposition in the *Consulados* of Cádiz, Lima, and Mexico City, who saw their traditional monopoly rights compromised by the new system, however well it functioned. Discontent with unfair practices of the Caracas Company in Venezuela and the royal effort to control the contraband trade in cacao (particularly after the end of the South Sea Company's *asiento*, which had supplied slaves to the governorship) contributed to the outbreak of León's rebellion. While officials in Madrid had tried to sabotage the British *asiento* and the contraband commerce that it facilitated even before the ink was dry on the Utrecht Treaty, the agreement with the South Sea Company had provided slaves needed to fuel and sustain the cacao boom in Venezuela.

As Spain approached the mid-century, these multiple, complex struggles gave the reform process its halting, unpredictable, and contradictory quality. Nevertheless, while Spain's defeats in earlier wars had led to the disgrace and downfall of reformers such as Alberoni, victories in the War of Jenkins' Ear, particularly in the American theater, allowed Ensenada and Carvajal y Lancaster to emerge with enhanced prestige and power. Moreover, when King Philip died, the new king removed his stepmother, Elizabeth Farnese, from the court. The Madrid government could finally ignore her dynastic claims in Italy and turn its attention to reform and renovation in the Atlantic world.

5

Clerical Reform and the Secularization
of the *Doctrinas de Indios*

Following the War of Jenkins' Ear in 1748, the new Bourbon monarch, Ferdinand VI (1746–1759) presided over a full-fledged reforming impulse to strengthen the state apparatus, to build a stronger military (particularly the navy), to control political and commercial ties with the empire, and to curb the power of Rome over the Spanish church. While earlier Bourbon efforts to reform the imperial system focused largely on the transatlantic trade, these new initiatives would involve a fundamental reexamination of the role of important interest groups within the empire, including the traditionally close relationship between church and state in the Spanish Atlantic world. The power of the more independent religious orders – such as the Franciscans, Augustinians, Dominicans, Mercedarians, and Jesuits – came under particularly close scrutiny. Indeed, clerical reforms begun by King Ferdinand's regalist ministers set the agenda for relations between church and state, which his successor, Charles III (1759–1788), later advanced with the expulsion of the Jesuits in 1767.[1] These Bourbon reforms of the church merged Enlightenment ideas from Europe with a variety of discourses of reform from the Indies about local political, social, and economic ills. Regalist policy makers in Madrid drew on all this information to fashion pragmatic imperial reforms using the most up-to-date ideas available to them. At the same time, Bourbon clerical reforms emerged in a highly contested political arena with many competing ideological agendas, which shaped its contours over the course of the eighteenth century.[2]

One of the least examined yet most influential of the Bourbon clerical reforms in the middle years of the century began on October 4, 1749, when

---

[1] For a fine examination of the ecclesiastical policies of Ferdinand VI and his ministers, see Rafael Olaechea, "Política eclesiástica del gobierno de Fernando VI," *Cátedra Feijóo, La época de Fernando VI* (Oviedo: Cátedra Feijóo, Universidad de Oviedo, 1981), p. 141.

[2] Gabriel Paquette, *Enlightenment, Governance, and Reform in Spain and its Empire, 1759–1808* (Surry: Palgrave MacMillan, 2008), pp. 152–53.

the crown issued royal *cédulas* ordering that all *doctrinas* (parishes) administered by the religious orders in the Archdioceses of Lima, Mexico City, and Santa Fe de Bogotá be transferred to the secular clergy.[3] This attempt to limit the wealth and social prestige of the religious orders was triggered by a series of letters written in 1746 by Viceroy José Manso de Velasco (1745–1761) decrying the overabundance of regular clergy in Peru and calling for removing the orders from parish work.[4] After determining that the process was advancing without any strong popular protests in support of the orders, the crown issued a further edict on February 1, 1753, extending the process of secularization to *doctrinas* in all dioceses of Spanish America. With these landmark edicts, the Bourbon dynasty began the process of stripping the religious orders of parishes that they had administered, in some cases, since the "spiritual conquest" in the sixteenth century. Moreover, these measures limited not only the orders' wealth but also their social prestige in the Indies. In the end, separating the orders from their parishes had immense financial consequences, leading to the shrinking wealth and numbers of the regular clergy by the end of the century.[5] This attack on the power of the regular clergy altered significantly the traditional partnership between church and state in the Spanish Atlantic empire. The edicts of 1749 and 1753 signaled an important step toward imposing the power of the renewed Bourbon state over the Catholic Church, reflecting the advance of "regalism" over the decentralized composite monarchy ruled by the Hapsburgs.

CRITICISM OF THE REGULAR CLERGY IN EARLY BOURBON PERU

Criticism of the corruption and immorality of the clergy abounded in the eighteenth century, but one of the strongest early condemnations of clerical abuse appeared in a report sent to the pope in 1722, ostensibly written by the archbishop of Lima, Antonio de Saloaga. In reality, the author of the text was an Italian secular clergyman, José María Barberí, who came to Peru as an advisor to his fellow countryman, Cármine Nicolás Caraccioli, the Príncipe de Santo Bono and Viceroy of Peru (1716–1722).[6] According to the report, the regular clergy had all but abandoned most of their missionary enterprises

---

[3] Royal *Cédula* to Virrey del Perú, Buen Retiro, October 4, 1749, AGI, Lima, leg.1596; and a second edict sent to the Archbishop of Lima: Royal *Cédula* to Arzobispo de Lima, Buen Retiro, October 4, 1749, AGI, Lima, leg. 1596.

[4] Manso de Velasco to crown, Lima, October 12, 1746, AGI, Lima, leg. 415.

[5] By 1800 "most Lima Franciscans were living by their wits and no longer maintained their *convento*." Antonine S. Tibesar, "The Suppression of the Religious Orders in Peru, 1826–1830 or the King Versus the Peruvian Friars: The King Won," *The Americas: A Quarterly Review of Inter-American Cultural History*, 29:2 (October 1982), p. 217.

[6] Alfredo Moreno Cebrián, "El regalismo borbónico frente al poder Vaticano: Acerca del estado de la iglesia en el Perú durante el primer tercio del siglo XVIII," *Revista de Indias*, 63:227 (2003): 223–74.

on the frontiers of the viceroyalty in favor of living in the cities or administering lucrative rural parishes. Barberí alleged that friars living in urban areas traveled about the cities without wearing their habits, sponsored parties with women of loose morals, and fell into illicit sexual relationships or even outright concubinage. The frequent and bitter disputes surrounding the election of provincials of the regular orders or a visitation of local religious houses frequently degenerated into scandalous public spectacles. Despite these ills, Barberí argued that administering 1,000 rural Amerindian parishes was the most corrupting influence on the religious orders, whose members often lived outside their religious houses in *doctrinas* dispersed throughout the countryside.[7] Barberí contended that these *doctrinas* enriched the regular clergy, yet also led to moral laxity since the friars could not be supervised and forced to adhere to the rules of their orders. Moreover, these friars ruthlessly exploited indigenous parishioners, levying excessive fees for performing sacraments such as weddings or funerals. They even forced their charges to buy European wares at fixed prices (a practice that mirrored the notorious *repartimiento de comercio* practiced by the *corregidores de indios*). Control over the parishes became yet another source of disorder within the religious houses, as the friars squabbled continuously over who would get the choicest parishes. In short, Barberí recommended a thorough reform of the religious orders, removing them from the rural parishes and replacing them with secular clergymen.[8]

Many of these same charges appeared in a highly influential and much more detailed report written in 1749 by two well-connected young naval officers: Jorge Juan and Antonio de Ulloa. Both men had travelled to the Indies in 1735 to assist an officially sanctioned French scientific expedition to the viceroyalty, intending to measure a degree on the equator. After the return of Juan and Ulloa in 1746, the Marqués de la Ensenada, commissioned them to write a secret account of problems in the empire, which later became known as the *Noticias secretas de América*.[9] The exposé circulated in governing circles, and its recommendations and viewpoints anticipated some of the very ideas presented in the edicts of secularization in 1749 and 1753.

---

[7] According to Moreno Cebrián, the report emerged from a long struggle for political and religious power that pitted the viceroy of Peru, the Príncipe de Santo Bono (1714–1720) and the archbishop of Lima, Antonio de Soloaga, against the former viceroy and bishop of Quito, Diego Ladrón de Guevara (viceroy from 1710–1716). Ladrón de Guevara was supported in this struggle by Diego Morcillo Rubio de Auñón, the archbishop of Lima from 1723 to 1730, who later served as Santo Bono's successor as viceroy from 1720 to 1724. Ibid., 230–32.

[8] Ibid.

[9] The Marqués de la Ensenada held the positions of secretary of War, Finance, and Marine and the Indies, and he was arguably the most powerful politician in Spain. See John Lynch, *Bourbon Spain, 1700–1808* (Oxford: Basil Blackwell, Ltd,1989), pp. 157–95; Stanley J. Stein and Barbara H. Stein, *Silver, Trade, and War: Spain and America in the Making of Early Modern Europe* (Baltimore: Johns Hopkins University Press, 2000), pp. 231–59.

In the *Noticias secretas*, Jorge Juan and Antonio de Ulloa wrote a scathing indictment of clerical malfeasance, corruption, and licentiousness in the Andean provinces. Juan and Ulloa mounted their initial attack against the clergy by condemning their scandalous behavior in the indigenous *doctrinas* of the Andes. As they remarked:

> The Indians suffer at the hands of their priests, who should be their spiritual fathers and defenders against the extortions of the corregidores. The clergy emulate and rival the corregidores in extracting wealth from the blood and sweat of a people who are so miserable and so wretched that even though they have no food for sustenance, they labor for the enrichment of others.[10]

Although Juan and Ulloa condemned the malfeasance, corruption, and moral laxity of all churchmen, they heaped particular abuse on all of the religious orders except the Jesuits. The young officers maintained that throughout the realm regular clergymen kept concubines publicly, even fathering several children, whom they often acknowledged by giving the illegitimate offspring their family names. Apart from the Jesuits, too many among the religious orders lived outside of their religious houses, where policing their immoral lifestyles proved difficult.

According to Juan and Ulloa, the provincial of the Franciscan and Dominican orders controlled massive annual incomes of 300,000 to 400,000 pesos.[11] This great wealth – in urban and rural properties, liens and loans, donations, and parish fees – meant that the provincials and their political allies often fought bitterly with rival factions in their religious houses, even leading to violent confrontations. Although the secular clergy committed similar abuses, lack of supervision and training among the regulars made them even more subject to vice and moral laxity. Only the Jesuits – who lived in *conventos* (religious houses) and rigorously policed their members – escaped the condemnation of the young naval officers.

Juan and Ulloa then turned their attention to the shameful state of frontier missions run by the regular clergy. The regular orders usually failed to send adequate numbers of missionaries to the frontier zones. Even when missionaries did enter these frontier regions, the regular clergy and local Spanish citizens too often mistreated new converts. These exploited people occasionally rose up against the missions, making the whole frontier evangelization effort a risky enterprise. In one notable case, a rebellion led by Juan Santos Atahualpa broke out in the tropical forestlands east of Jauja and Tarma in the

---

[10] Jorge Juan and Antonio de Ulloa, *Discourse and Political Reflections on the Kingdoms of Peru. Their Government, Special Regimen of Their Inhabitants and Abuses Which Have Been Introduced into One and Another, with Special Information on Why They Grew Up and Some Means to Avoid Them.* Edited and with an introduction by John J. TePaske and translated by John J. TePaske and Besse A. Clement (Norman: University of Oklahoma Press, 1978), p. 102.

[11] Ibid., p. 300.

Cerro de la Sal and the Gran Pajonal in 1742, and the rebels killed or expelled the local Franciscan missionaries, effectively ending the friars' evangelization efforts in the region for decades. Juan and Ulloa argued that only the Jesuits among the regular orders enjoyed a high level of success in evangelizing along the frontier, maintaining large, well-funded missions.[12] This exposé – written some three years after Juan and Ulloa's return to Madrid – surely reflected what both men had observed in South America, but the tract followed too perfectly a preordained reformist agenda at court to be taken entirely at face value. With five copies circulating in court circles, it represented a working paper, which Ensenada hoped to use in advancing his reforms.

Juan and Ulloa proposed several measures for reforming clerical behavior, which clearly reflected views expressed in reform policies soon to be sponsored by the crown. Firstly, they urged the crown to remove the regular clergy from parish duty, particularly in the indigenous *doctrinas*, because the religious orders were harder to control and more subject to corrupt practices than secular clergy. Secondly, they urged the crown to limit the number of young men allowed into the religious orders. This would shrink the size of the orders and encourage more men to live productive lives as laymen, marrying and adding wealth to the kingdom instead of becoming lascivious, nonproductive friars. Finally, to promote evangelization in frontier provinces, they urged the crown to allow only the Jesuits to maintain missions.[13]

The material presented in both Barberí's memorial and the *Noticias secretas* reflected the complex political and intellectual crosscurrents of the mid-eighteenth century Spanish Atlantic empire. By the 1740s, numerous political tracts by reformers in Spain and Peru circulated in Madrid – from *proyectistas*, Jansenists, bureaucratic reformers in America, and hispanicized indigenous elites – and each presented its own intellectual and political agenda. Juan and Ulloa used their own observations, other eye-witness accounts, and many stories of clerical abuses, particularly those perpetrated by the religious orders, to fashion their statement. The two young naval lieutenants brought these discourses of protest together into a powerful exposé of Spanish misrule, designed to reform the colonial regime and reinvigorate the state's power. Whether or not the Marqués de la Ensenada and other key officials in Madrid used the views presented in the *Noticias secretas*, these ideas about the renovation of the empire formed part of a public debate about reform in governing circles.[14]

---

[12] Ibid., pp. 154–88.

[13] Ibid.

[14] For a discussion of how these diverse groups influenced Juan and Ulloa and their ideas expressed in the *Noticias secretas*, see Kenneth J. Andrien, "The *Noticias Secretas de América* and the Construction of a Governing Ideology for the Spanish American Empire," *Colonial Latin American Review*, 7:2 (1998): 175–92.

THE EARTHQUAKE OF 1746 AND REFORM
IN THE VICEROYALTY OF PERU

The impulse to reform the clergy targeted religious orders for legislative action beginning in the early eighteenth century. Royal *cédulas* in 1705 and 1717 established prohibitions on the foundation of new *conventos* and hospitals without prior approval from Madrid. In 1703, an edict ordered that *conventillos* (small religious houses) in rural areas had to contain at least eight permanent friars in residence or face closure. This measure was aimed at the regulars' practice of assigning friars to these *conventillos*. Parish priests, even members of the regular clergy were legally subject to the local bishop, but assigning them to a *conventillo* made them legally subject to the head of the order. The orders frequently counted the holders of these parishes (*doctrineros*) as members of these small communities, whether or not they actually lived there, in order to swell the numbers officially listed in the *conventillos*. The repeated reissuing of the edict (in 1708, 1727, 1731, and 1739) likely indicates that it was not well enforced, at least until the crown removed the regular orders from their rural parishes in 1749 and 1753.[15]

The severe earthquake that struck Lima on October 28, 1746 – followed by a tidal wave that inundated and destroyed the port city of Callao – brought concerns about reforming the religious orders to the point of crisis. Over 6,000 people perished – of a population of approximately 50,000 – while most of the major buildings of the city were destroyed or damaged, many beyond repair.[16] Virtually all of the main religious houses in the city and the port suffered serious structural damage, forcing hundreds of nuns and male religious onto the streets of the city. Although Lima's numbers of religious for its total population were similar to the numbers in most Spanish cities, the destruction of the *conventos* made the regular clergymen and nuns more visible than ever. Having large numbers of regular clergy living in makeshift dwellings or private residences meant that religious discipline was impossible to monitor. The earthquake also damaged many estates of the regular clergy, and their income from interest payments on liens and loans (*censos*) held against private urban and rural properties diminished markedly. This situation worsened when Viceroy José Manso de Velasco cut the principal on all *censos* by 50 percent and lowered their interest rate from 5 percent to either 2 or 1 percent (depending on the type) and granted a two-year moratorium on payments.[17] The viceroy imposed these changes to ease the burdens on property owners and to aid recovery in the city and its hinterland.

---

[15] Adrian J. Pierce, *"Early Bourbon Government in the Viceroyalty of Peru, 1700–1759"* (Ph.D. diss., University of Liverpool, 1998), p. 190.

[16] Ibid., p. 60.

[17] Pablo Emilio Pérez-Mallaina Bueno, *Retrato de una ciudad en crisis: La sociedad limeña ante el movimiento sísmico de 1746* (Sevilla: Escuela de Estudios Hispano-Americanos, 2001),

The man entrusted with governing Peru in this time of crisis, José Manso de Velasco, was a self-confident, energetic military officer from modest *hidalgo* origins in La Rioja, who had served eight successful years as captain general in Chile before his promotion to Viceroy of Peru in 1745. Like his counterpart in New Spain (Juan Francisco de Güemes y Horcasitas, the first Count of Revillagigedo), Manso de Velasco was a protégé and close associate of the powerful Marqués de la Ensenada (a fellow *riojano*), and all three men had become friends while serving under Montemar in the successful siege of Oran in 1732. Ensenada gave the new viceroy extensive fiscal powers by naming him *superintendente de real hacienda*. Although Manso de Velasco ran afoul of Lima's upper classes by trying to promote safer construction methods and modernize the city's street design, he was chiefly remembered for getting food and water to survivors of the quake. He also received much credit for rebuilding the city (especially its cathedral) and for constructing the Real Felipe fortress and the new port city of Bellavista to replace Callao.[18] In fact, the crown rewarded him in 1748 with the title Conde de Superunda (on the crest of the wave), and his portrait still hangs in Lima's cathedral against the backdrop of the city cathedral in the midst of its reconstruction.[19]

Viceroy Manso de Velasco used the problem of homeless clergy in Lima to propose a major reform of the orders in two strong letters to his friend and patron, the Marqués de la Ensenada. The viceroy called for reducing the numbers of religious to levels that could be supported from the orders' income, and he also recommended secularization of the *doctrinas* of the regular clergy. He averred that without the income from their parishes, the orders would have to curtail their numbers to a level appropriate to their other rents.[20] The viceroy wanted to curb the power of the church, and particularly the religious orders, giving them a diminished, less visible role as he planned the reconstruction of Lima and its economy. Armed with the recent report that Juan and Ulloa had provided and the letters of Manso de Velasco, Ensenada launched a thorough investigation into the role of the regular clergy in the Spanish Indies.

---

pp. 309–11. The rate was cut to 2% on *censos* that were limited in time (and could be redeemed) and 1% on permanent liens or loans.

[18] Ibid., passim. See also Charles F. Walker, "The Upper Classes and Their Upper Stories: Architecture and the Aftermath of the Lima Earthquake of 1746," *HAHR*, 83:1 (February 2003), pp. 53–82.

[19] A copy of the original portrait (painted by Cristóbal Lozano), composed by Lozano's student José Joaquín Bermejo, shows the Conde de Superunda against the backdrop of the Bay of Callao. See Joseph Rishel and Suzanne Straton-Pruitt, *The Arts in Latin America, 1492–1820*, (Philadelphia: Philadelphia Museum of Art, 2006), p. 462.

[20] Pearce, "Early Bourbon Government," p. 196; Conde de Superunda to crown, Lima, December 18, 1748, AGI, Lima, leg. 643.

CONFLICTS AND CONSPIRACIES IN PERU

The viceroy's attitudes about the orders produced simmering tensions with the religious orders (particularly the Franciscans), which only worsened following the earthquake of 1746. Ever since Juan Santos Atahualpa had expelled the Franciscan missionaries from the lowland forests below Tarma and Jauja, members of the order had complained about the government's inadequate efforts to defeat the insurrection and restore the missions.[21] This mistrust turned to anger when Manso de Velasco threatened to cut the government's annual subsidy of 6,000 pesos for the missionary effort in half, reasoning that the order did not need the full amount when the missions were not operating.[22] Coupled with the viceroy's lowering of the interest rates on *censos*, this was yet another unwelcome economic setback for the order. For his part, the head of the Franciscan missions Joseph de San Antonio wrote a detailed memorial to the crown in 1750 arguing for more, not less, government support for the Franciscan missions – in the Cerro de la Sal, the Gran Pajonal, and their newer missions in Cajamarquilla and Manoa in the tropical lowland frontier north and east of Huánuco.[23]

Such tensions hardened into mistrust and ill will when two Franciscan missionaries from Peru appeared unexpectedly in Madrid to give King Ferdinand VI a detailed exposé on the exploitation of the Amerindians in the viceroyalty. The two friars, a mestizo Franciscan lay brother (*donado*), Fray Calixto de San José Tupak Inka and his colleague, Fray Isidoro de Cala y Ortega, lingered outside the king's hunting resort and delivered their manuscript to the surprised King Ferdinand VI through the open window of his moving carriage during an evening ride.[24] This text provided a bitter denunciation of Spanish rule in the Andes, modeled after the Old Testament lamentations of the prophet Jeremiah. The document repudiated Juan Santos Atahualpa's revolt, but it also argued that the corruption of Spanish authorities and their blatant exploitation of the Andean peoples had forced many indigenous people to support such radical solutions. Casting blame on the abuses of viceregal officials for causing the rebellion also removed any

---

[21] The affront of having their Christianized charges so quickly go over to the rebellion was only worsened when the viceroy sent a small group of Jesuits to meet with Juan Santos Atahualpa to try and end the conflict. José Amich, *Historia de las misiones del convento de Santa Rosa de Ocopa*, edited with an introduction by Fr. Julián Heras (Iquitos: IIAP-CETA, 1988, 1771), p. 176.

[22] Conde de Superunda to crown, Lima, September 1, 1753, AGI, Lima, leg. 418.

[23] *Consulta* del Consejo de Indias, Madrid, November 5, 1750 AGI, Lima, leg. 366.

[24] Fray Calixto de San José Tupac Inca to Mui Ilustre Cabildo de la Ciudad de Lima, Madrid, November 14, 1750, AGI, Lima, leg. 988. The two friars traveled illegally from Cusco to Buenos Aires through the Portuguese port of Colonia de Sacramento to Rio de Janeiro. From Rio they took a ship to Lisbon, where they traveled overland to Madrid, arriving on August 22, 1750. They delivered the manuscript to the surprised King Ferdinand VI the next day.

responsibility from the Franciscans for the collapse of their missions in the area. To ameliorate these abuses of the Amerindians, the "Representación verdadera" called for the suppression of the *corregimientos de indios*, ending the *mita*, and establishing a special tribunal just to hear Amerindian cases. Moreover, it recommended that indigenous people be granted access to the religious orders as full brothers (*legos*) and be given access to political offices heretofore reserved only for Spaniards.[25] His fellow Franciscan, Isidoro de Cala y Ortega wrote a text in Latin sent to the pope in Rome, which made very similar accusations and suggestions for reform.[26] Given the recent report of Juan and Ulloa on misrule in the Andes, the memorials of the two Franciscans aroused the interest of the king and his key ministers.

The exposés of Fray Calixto and Isidoro de Cala provoked controversy and consternation in Peru. The Franciscans were experienced missionaries, who claimed first-hand knowledge of the abuses presented in their memorials, and King Ferdinand's concern over the treatment of his Amerindian subjects was well known. Although the friars had failed to get legal permission to publish these works or even to travel from Peru to Spain, viceregal officials became alarmed when the king ordered the Council of the Indies to explore the allegations of the Franciscan friars. Moreover, when the friars later met with the councilors, Fray Calixto explained that the "Representación verdadera" had been written over a year earlier in 1748, circulated among noble Indians in Lima and Cusco, and edited to reflect their common views about the abuses of Spanish rule.[27] Thus, the memorial represented the collective experience of the Franciscan missionaries and the indigenous elites of the viceroyalty. The whole affair stirred controversy and debate in Peru, and it also embarrassed the viceregal government, particularly the Conde de Superunda.

[25] The text was entitled "Representación verdadera y exclamación y lamentable que toda la nación Indiana hace a la majestad del señor rey de las Españas y emperador de las Indias, el señor don Fernando VI, pidiendo los atienda y remedie sacandolos del afrentosos vituperio y oprobio en que estan mas de doscientos años. Exclamación de los indios americanos, usando para ella de la misma que hizo el profeta Jeremías a Dios en el capítulo 5 y último de sus lamentaciones," in Fernando A. Loayza, ed., *Fray Calixto Tupak Inka: Documentos originales y, en su mayoría, totalmente desconocidos, auténticos, de este apóstol indio, valiente defensor de su raza, desde el año 1746 a 1760* (Lima: Los Pequeños Grandes Libros de Historia Americana, 1948), pp. 5–61. The original may be found in AGI, Lima, leg. 988.

[26] The text ostensibly written in Latin by Fray Isidoro Cala was entitled "Planctus indorum christianorum en america peruntina," In *Una denuncia profética desde el Perú a mediados del siglo XVIII: el Planctus indorum christianorum en America peruntina*, ed. José María Navarro (Lima: Pontífica Universidad Católica del Perú, 2001), pp. 141–471. For an analysis of the text of Fray Calixto, see Alcira Dueñas, *Indians and Mestizos in the "Lettered City": Reshaping Justice, Social Hierarchy, and Political Culture in Colonial Peru* (Boulder: University of Colorado Press, 2010), passim.

[27] Fray Calixto de San José Tupac Inca to Mui Ilustre Cabildo de la Ciudad de Lima, Madrid, November 14, 1750, AGI, Lima, leg. 988.

As officials in Spain considered the reforms proposed by the two Franciscans, the "Representación verdadera" and Fray Calixto himself were implicated in two serious indigenous uprisings in the Viceroyalty of Peru in 1750. While still recovering from the earthquake, news reached the viceroy of a planned indigenous rebellion in Lima. The Lima conspirators allegedly planned to take over the viceregal palace and its armory, murder the city's Spanish population, recruit the urban slave and freedmen populations, and then unite with the rebels of Juan Santos Atahualpa.[28] If successful, their plans threatened to produce a bloodbath that could end Spanish rule in the Andes.[29] The authorities rounded up and later executed the key conspirators in Lima. Nevertheless, one leader, Francisco García Jiménez escaped to Huarochirí, a highland province that connected Lima and the coast to the mountains. While there, he led a bloody but unsuccessful uprising, which resulted in the deaths of dozens of Spaniards and creoles. In clear reference to the two Franciscans, the Conde de Superunda alleged that the rebels were inspired by "manifestos written by two priests of little talent."[30] Once news of the unsuccessful uprisings in Lima and Huarochirí reached Madrid, crown authorities immediately recognized the explosive nature of the memorials. Officials in Madrid suppressed the manifestos of Fray Calixto and Fray Isidoro de Cala, detaining both men in Spanish monasteries.

While Fray Isidoro de Cala remained under virtual house arrest in Cádiz, the crown permitted Fray Calixto to return to Lima in 1753, and he quickly ran afoul of the viceregal government. The Franciscan raised the suspicions of local authorities by holding clandestine meetings with local Amerindian leaders in the city, including those suspected of involvement in the Lima conspiracy. The friar even complained vociferously about the brutal punishments meted out to the leaders of the aborted uprising of 1750. Viceregal authorities exerted pressure on the Franciscans to search Fray Calixto's cell in Lima, where they claimed to find a series of incriminating papers, linking the friar directly to the uprisings of 1750.[31] These documents allegedly proved that the Franciscan had met many times with the conspirators, even allowing

---

[28] The rebels intended to recruit black and Amerindian groups throughout Peru and also to link up with Juan Santos and his rebels. Some among the rebels wanted to offer the crown of a restored Inca empire, while others envisaged an interim government led by indigenous nobles until they could decide on a ruler. The most complete summary of the uprisings is Karen Spalding, *Huarochirí: An Andean Society Under Inca and Spanish Rule* (Stanford, CA: Stanford University Press, 1984), 271–89. Another analysis of the indigenous people of Lima in this period, which also examines the failed rebellion of 1750 is Lyn Brandon Lowry, "*Forging and Indian Nation: Urban Indians under Spanish colonial control (Lima, Peru, 1535–1765)*" (Unpublished Ph.D. diss., University of California at Berkeley, 1991).

[29] Loayza, *Fray Calixto Tupak Inka*, pp. 84–92; and Conde de Superunda to crown, Lima, September 24, 1750, AGI, Lima, leg. 417.

[30] Charles F. Walker, *Shaky Colonialism: The 1746 Earthquake-Tsunami in Peru and its Long Aftermath* (Durham, NC: Duke University Press, 2008), p. 174.

[31] Loayza, *Fray Calixto Tupak Inka*, pp. 84–92.

them to hatch their planned rebellion in his cell. Crown authorities immediately sent the friar back to Spain in 1760, and secluded him in a Franciscan house in the most remote region of Granada, far from the sea.[32] The crown also kept Fray Isidoro de Cala in Cádiz under virtual house arrest in a Franciscan *convento*. Although his superiors in Cusco petitioned for de Cala's return to missionary activity, he remained in custody until his sentence was commuted in 1768 through the efforts of his brother, Casimiro, a prominent Franciscan and a member of the Inquisition.[33] In the end, the entire affair tainted the reputation of the Franciscan order in Peru, tying their accusations of misrule and the actions of the two friars with a dangerous, bloody rebellion.

REFORM AND THE SECULARIZATION OF THE DOCTRINAS DE INDIOS

The decision in 1749 to move against the religious orders by secularizing their rural parishes formed part of a broad, sweeping reform program in the Spanish Atlantic empire promulgated by the crown's ministers, particularly the Marqués de la Ensenada. In the metropolis, the restless and energetic Ensenada and his allies used the end of the War of Jenkins' Ear in 1748 to promote a major tax reform. After commissioning a census (*catastro*) of the realm in 1750, his government proposed a single tax, graduated according to income, replacing the burdensome *rentas provinciales* – the *alcabalas, cientos,* and *millones*.[34] Even before imposing this single tax on income, Ensenada recommended taking over direct royal administration of the *rentas provinciales*, ending tax farming. In 1749, his government also extended the intendancy system throughout Spain. And it renewed the ambitious, expensive naval shipbuilding program.

In the Indies, Ensenada and his fellow reformers curbed the independence of the *Consulado* of Cádiz (Chapter 4), broke the grip of the *sevillano* elite, and promoted the use of licensed register ships to trade with authorized American ports and in the process replaced the increasingly cumbersome *Galeones*. The crown also ended the systematic sale of colonial appointments in 1750 to stamp out the pervasive political culture of corruption in the colonial bureaucracy. One of the crown's greatest successes, however, was the Concordat of 1753, which dramatically increased the king's patronage power over church appointments throughout the empire.[35] This treaty surely

---

[32] Ibid., pp. 92–94.

[33] Victor Peralta Ruiz, "Las razones de la fé: La iglesia y la ilustración en el Perú, 1750–1800," in Scarlett O'Phelan Godoy, ed., *Perú en el siglo XVIII: La era borbónica* (Lima: Pontífica Universidad Católica del Perú, 2003), p. 201.

[34] The single tax was ultimately never implemented, but the *rentas provinciales* were collected by state officials, not tax farmers from 1750 onward. Lynch, *Bourbon Spain*, p. 169.

[35] Ibid., pp. 160–195. Negotiating the concordat was left largely to the king's confessor, Francisco de Rávago.

expressed the growing force of enlightened, regalist principles in the royal administration.

But much more was involved in the politics at court. The triumvirate that ruled on behalf of Ferdinand VI during the postwar period nurtured an ambitious pro-Jesuit agenda. In addition to Ensenada with his multiple ministries and Carvajal at State, the king's confessor, Francisco de Rávago, exercised great influence. Rávago, like all the confessors of Bourbon monarchs who preceded him, was a Jesuit, and together the trio was known in the politics of Madrid as the "Jesuit party."[36] Hence, while a new regalism cast in enlightened terms would burst onto the scene mid-century, an intriguing subtheme would be the exoneration, indeed elevation, of the Society of Jesus, which stood to gain as its rivals contended with the weight of selective ecclesiastical reform.

To deal with the reforms proposed by Manso de Velasco in his letters, the Marqués de la Ensenada persuaded King Ferdinand VI to appoint a special ad hoc committee, the Junta Particular de Ministros, in November 1748, headed by Minister of State José de Carvajal y Lancaster and comprised of Father Rávago; the archbishops-elect of Lima, Mexico City, and Santa Fe; four members of the Council of Castile; and three members of the Council of the Indies.[37] After deliberations in Carvajal's country estate outside of Madrid, the Junta Particular issued its recommendations, calling for limits on the numbers admitted to the regular orders and banning the orders from establishing any *conventos* in the newly constructed port city of Bellavista.[38] The most significant recommendation, however, was the decision to remove all regular clergy from administering *doctrinas* of the Archbishoprics of Lima, Mexico City, and Santa Fe de Bogotá whenever they fell vacant, replacing them with secular clergy.

In response to this report, the king issued royal *cédulas* on October 4, 1749, ordering the secularization of rural parishes controlled by regular orders in the Archdioceses of Lima, Mexico City, and Santa Fe de Bogotá as vacancies arose.

---

[36] Even their strong endorsement of the Jesuits reflected views commonly held in Madrid. The Society had provided the personal confessors of all the Bourbon monarchs, and the Marqués de la Ensenada, José de Cárvajal y Lancaster, and Francisco de Rávago (the confessor of Ferdinand VI) were the three most powerful ministers, and collectively, they were known as the Jesuit Party. Pierce, "Early Bourbon Government," p. 14.

[37] Carvajal y Lancaster also held the titles of governor of the Council of the Indies and president of the Junta del Comercio. Ibid., p. 190; Pérez-Mallaina Buenos, *Retrato de una ciudad en crisis*, pp. 320–21; Brading, *Church and State in Bourbon Mexico*, p. 63. See also, Ismael Sánchez Bella, *Iglesia y estado en la América Española* (Pamplona: Ediciones Universidad de Navarra, 1990), pp. 124–39; and Lynch, *Bourbon Spain*, p. 189. The original document is in the Biblioteca del Palacio Real, II 1601E. We are very grateful to Professor Charles Walker for kindly providing us with a photocopy of the original.

[38] Alfredo Moreno, ed., *Relación y documentos de gobierno del virrey del Perú, José Manso de Velasco, Conde de Superunda (1745–1761)* (Madrid: Consejo Superior de Investigaciones Científicas, Instituto Gonzalo de Oviedo, 1983), p. 270.

The crown argued that numerous reports had complained of regulars living in *doctrinas* and private residences away from their *conventos*. Furthermore, too often the regular clergymen apparently left the mundane duties of administering their parishes to assistants. The crown concluded that the only way to reform the orders and end abuses in the parishes was to place the *doctrinas* in the hands of secular clergy. The king ordered the courts not to hear complaints about this new policy, leaving it to the viceroys and the archbishops to enforce the law. The crown commanded that these officials keep the *cédula* itself confidential, instead of publishing its contents throughout the realm.[39] The king wanted to avoid the prejudice and endless legal wrangling that would follow if the law's specific provisions were divulged to the orders.

Manso de Velasco waited to implement the royal edict of secularization until September 1, 1751, approximately two months after the arrival the new archbishop of Lima, Pedro Antonio de Barroeta y Ángel. The *cédulas* had little effect on the Jesuits, who had only one parish in the archdiocese, the indigenous district of Santiago del Cercado, Lima; but other regular orders – the Franciscans, Dominicans, and Mercedarians – depended heavily on the tithes (*diezmos*) and salaries (*sínodos*) from *doctrinas* to support their religious houses and missions, particularly given the devastation wrought by the earthquake on their urban and rural holdings in the archdiocese.[40] Nonetheless, the viceroy and the archbishop commanded that any parishes of the orders pass to the secular clergy as vacancies arose.[41]

THE MENDICANT ORDERS STRIKE BACK, 1751–1756

The orders reacted to the edict of secularization with a mixture of surprise and indignation. The heads of the three key orders, Fernando Dávila (prior of Santo Domingo), Pedro Mangarino (provincial of San Francisco), and Joseph Martínez de Ayala (provincial of La Merced) wrote a joint memorial to the crown protesting the edict of secularization on the very same day that they received notice of the *cédulas*. After defending their long years of service in evangelizing the Amerindians, the orders' leaders demanded to see the original royal edict, which the viceroy and Archbishop Barroeta had refused to provide.[42] The three leaders contended that they were entitled to inspect any royal edict, even those marked confidential. They wanted to ensure that the law gave the viceroy those broad powers that he claimed and also to see that the edict was issued legally through the Council of the Indies.[43] The leaders also

---

[39] Royal *cédula* to Virrey del Perú, Buen Retiro, October 4, 1749, AGI, Lima, leg. 1596, and Royal *cédula* to Arzobispo de Lima, Buen Retiro, October 4, 1749, AGI, Lima, leg. 1596.

[40] Conde de Superunda to crown, Lima, November 1, 1751, AGI, Lima, leg.1596.

[41] Archivo de San Francisco de Lima (hereinafter ASF), Registro II, No. 2:24, fol. 236.

[42] Ibid., ff. 438–430 *vuelto*.

[43] As provided for in the *Recopilación de leyes de los reynos de los Indias*, (Madrid: Ediciones Cultura Hispánica, 1973 edition), Volume 13, Title 1, law 23.

demanded an audience with the viceroy to discuss the measure, arguing that any law harming an innocent third party must be publicized and discussed openly. Finally, they claimed that whenever the crown issued an unjust, prejudicial law, the orders had a duty to exercise their *arbitrio judicial* – to obey without complying.[44]

On October 23, 1751, the provincial of the Franciscans wrote a longer and much fuller defense of his order's continued control of *doctrinas*.[45] He stated that the Franciscans had possessed parishes from the earliest days of the conquest, and the mendicants had carried out their duties in the parishes at the cost of their own sweat and blood. The right to evangelize and care for new converts derived from a "tacit" agreement with the kings of Castile, beginning with Ferdinand and Isabel. These grants were meant to be permanent, not temporary nor subject to revocation without cause. The provincial vehemently denied that the viceroy had any right to end this tacit contract with the king, particularly without approval from both the head of the order in Rome and the pope. The viceroy's only legal justification for removing the order from its parishes was if the friars had managed them carelessly or had abused the laity, which they denied. In short, the Franciscans demanded that the crown rescind the order of 1749.[46]

The memorial then attacked the scandalous and malicious arguments advanced to justify depriving the Franciscans of their *doctrinas*. Firstly, the provincial argued that the Franciscans had received these parishes not because of any shortage of secular priests, but because of the secular clergy's "defects." The mendicants simply did a better job of converting and ministering to the indigenous peoples, and replacing their beloved friars with mere secular priests would compromise the spiritual welfare of neophytes in the parishes. Secondly, there were not enough qualified secular clergy to serve in the *doctrinas de indios*, since so few priests had adequate training in indigenous languages. Thirdly, the unexpected edict to replace the orders with secular clergy had caused untold mischief in Lima, particularly among common folk. Rumors circulated that friars had robbed poor Indians to enrich themselves, engaged in immoral and licentious behavior, and routinely disobeyed crown laws. These "scandalous lies" were compounded by the viceroy's refusal to publish the royal edict on secularization and to give the heads of each order a public audience to discuss the issues.[47] This unfortunate situation led to the "unjust infamy" heaped on the orders by rumor mongers in Lima, leaving the mendicants isolated and disgraced throughout the archdiocese.[48] Finally, the conflict over the parishes had also

---

[44] Ibid., ff. 441–443.
[45] Fr. Juan Gutiérrez de la Sal to crown, n.d., AGI, Lima, leg. 1596.
[46] ASF, Registro II, No. 2:24, ff. 445–45 *vuelto*.
[47] Ibid., ff. 458–60.
[48] Ibid.

inflamed traditional tensions between regular and secular clergy, unnecessarily undermining peace in the kingdom.[49]

The Franciscan provincial then argued that his order would suffer serious financial losses by forfeiting its parishes, particularly after the earthquake and tsunami of 1746. The mendicants all depended on tithes and missionary stipends (*sínodos*) from parishes to support a variety of projects – hospitals, missions in frontier provinces, and even food for friars in the *conventos*. The earthquake had damaged buildings on their rural estates and rendered the land sterile, while epidemics had taken the lives of workers and slaves. Income from loans and liens on rural estates and urban real estate also had plummeted, particularly when the viceroy cut the principal and interest rates on all *censos*. Moreover, bequests for pious works (*obras pías*), for religious confraternities (*cofradías*) sponsored by the friars, and alms had declined markedly. Under these circumstances, the memorial argued that provincials would not have the funds to visit *conventos* under their jurisdiction, to support missionary activities, or even to transport friars to and from Spain. In short, the devastation of the 1746 earthquake coupled with losing their parishes had undermined the religious mission of the mendicant order.[50]

In truth, the religious orders risked suffering huge financial losses by forfeiting rural parishes. According to a study commissioned by Manso de Velasco in 1748, the viceregal treasury paid out 442,587 pesos annually in salaries to regular clergymen working in parishes throughout the realm.[51] Moreover, members of the orders customarily charged fees (*obvenciones*) for performing duties, such as baptisms, marriages, or burials. According to the viceroy, some parish priests made 4,000 to 8,000 pesos annually in salaries and fees.[52] The religious orders only allowed their members to keep a portion of these benefits, with the remainder going to the order to support its various religious houses, missions, and charitable activities. It is no small wonder that the provincials of the Franciscan and Mercedarian orders went to Madrid in a futile effort to convince the king himself to rescind the edict of secularization.[53]

The strong opposition of the orders made it difficult for Manso de Velasco to implement the edict of secularization. In a letter of November 1, 1751, the viceroy lamented that the regulars considered themselves the "absolute owners" of the *doctrinas*, and that they felt free to use *sínodos* and tithes from these parishes for routine expenses at the *conventos* or to reinvest the money

---

[49] Ibid., ff. 494.

[50] Ibid., ff. 485–99.

[51] "Resumen general de las pensiones consignados en las reales cajas y provincias del distrito del tribunal y audiencia rl de quentas de este reyno, con separación de sus repectivas aplicaciónes," Lima, June 30, 1748, AGI, Lima, leg. 1596.

[52] Marqués de Regalia to Marqués de la Ensenada, Madrid, July 20, 1751, AGI, Lima, leg.1596; Junta Particular de Ministros, Madrid, July 20, 1751, AGI, Lima, leg. 1596.

[53] Marqués de Regalia to Marqués de la Ensenada, Madrid, July 20, 1751, AGI, Lima, leg. 1596.

in rural estates. The Franciscans proved particularly recalcitrant in handing over parishes when a vacancy arose. Instead, the provincial named an interim friar, calling him a "guardian" of the parish. By making such interim appointments, the Franciscans managed to keep control over lucrative parishes, delaying the time when the order would cede them to secular clergyman.[54] Manso de Velasco also complained of the orders' insistence on seeing the text of the edict of October 4, 1749, which he had denied them in accordance with the king's wishes.

Despite opposition from the orders, the viceroy assured the monarch that he would continue to enforce the law, which represented the long-term best interests of the crown, the Amerindian parishioners, and even the orders themselves. Losing their parishes would force the orders to trim their excessive numbers and keep them living in *conventos*, where it would be easier for the leadership to enforce the "rules" of each order.[55] The only regular order exempted from the edict was the Jesuits, who had only one small parish in Santiago del Cercado in Lima, where they maintained a school for the children of indigenous leaders (*caciques*). The viceroy argued that depriving the Society of this small parish might force them to close an important school unnecessarily.[56]

Within a few weeks, the archbishop of Lima wrote his own letter about the problems resulting from secularization and offered some possible grounds for a compromise to end the political imbroglio in Lima. Archbishop Barroeta explained that the regulars saw the parishes as a reward for service in the spiritual conquest of Peru, ceded by the Catholic kings and verified by succeeding monarchs. The regular orders viewed the viceroy's actions as illegal and arbitrary. Orders controlled sixty-one *doctrinas* in 1751 (while the secular clergy held ninety), and they provided a great deal of wealth to the regular clergy amidst the economic problems following the earthquake of 1746. To ease these rising tensions, the archbishop suggested allowing the orders to keep a few parishes, to enjoy a temporary exemption from tithes on their rural properties where the land had been rendered sterile by the earthquake, and to extend the time that they could enjoy the benefits of their parishes. Nonetheless, Archbishop Barroeta believed that the orders should be removed from parishes over time. He also argued that they should not reconstruct all of their *conventos*, and the prelate suggested an inspection (*visita*) to determine how to curb the excessive numbers of regular clergy in the city. In short, the archbishop wanted to limit the size of the orders, curtail their freedom in the city, and ensure that they adhered strictly to the disciplinary rules of their orders over the long term.[57]

---

[54] Conde de Superunda to crown, Lima, November 1, 1751, AGI, Lima, leg. 1596.
[55] Ibid.
[56] Conde de Superunda to crown, Lima, November 20, 1751, AGI, Lima, leg. 1596.
[57] Pedro Antonio Arzobispo de Lima to crown, November 26, 1751, AGI, Lima, leg. 1596.

On November 17, 1752, reformer Pope Benedict XIV dealt a serious blow to the regular orders of Peru when he issued a bull supporting Ferdinand VI and his edicts of 1749 ordering secularization of the parishes. According to Pope Benedict, his predecessor, Pius V, had granted regulars the right to administer *doctrinas* in the Indies on March 24, 1567, but this concession was a temporary measure to deal with shortages of qualified secular priests. The pope made clear that the *Real Patronato* granted King Ferdinand the power to reverse this concession, particularly given the numbers of secular clergy capable of administering parishes. Finally, Pope Benedict stated that in all pastoral matters (such as administering *doctrinas*) regular clergymen were under the jurisdiction of the bishops and archbishops.[58]

After receiving confirmation of its powers from the papacy, the crown issued a new *cédula* on February 1, 1753, extending the policy of replacing regular clergy with secular priests to every bishopric in the Indies. According to the crown, the original law of 1749, which applied only to the large archbishoprics of Lima, Mexico City, and Santa Fe de Bogotá, was extremely successful and universally approved, even by the religious orders themselves. The crown extended the power of bishops to reform the regulars and end unrest and upheavals, which had disrupted *conventos* in the Indies for many years.[59]

Accompanying this new royal edict was a letter from the Marqués de la Ensenada to his friend and protégé Manso de Velasco, which reiterated the king's strong desire to have this new policy rigorously enforced. Ensenada did not want to compromise with the orders, which he argued should not be given: "a pension nor a division of the profits" from the parishes.[60] The long memorial from the Franciscan provincial had no effect on changing the royal will, and the crown would not consider extending any benefits to the regular orders to compensate for losing *doctrinas*. Ensenada reminded the viceroy that his counterpart in Mexico, the Conde de Revillagigedo "admitted no resistance to enforcing the royal order." As he made clear: "the express and absolute resolution of the King is the complete divestment of the regulars from the parishes."[61]

When Manso de Velasco conducted a survey of the *doctrinas* throughout the Viceroyalty of Peru in 1754, he found that regular clergymen still held most of their original parishes, even in the archbishopric of Lima. According to Table 5.1, the orders controlled 59 parishes in the archbishopric: the Dominicans with 30, the Franciscans with 13, the Mercedarians with 15, and the Jesuits with their lone parish in Santiago del Cercado in Lima. This

---

[58] Papal Bull of Benedict XIV, Rome, November 17, 1752, AGI, Lima, leg. 1596.
[59] Royal *cédula*, Buen Retiro, February 1, 1753, AGI, Lima, leg. 1596.
[60] Marqués de la Ensenada to Conde de Superunda, Madrid, February 1, 1753, AGI, Lima, leg. 1596.
[61] Ibid.

TABLE 5.1 Doctrinas *in the Viceroyalty of Peru, June 22, 1754*

Bishopric	Dominicans	Franciscans	Augustinians	Mercedarians	Jesuits	Seculars
Lima	30	13	0	15	1	102
Chuquisaca	7	0	6	6	0	116
Misque	0	2	0	0	8	6
Cusco	7	1	7	9	0	107
La Paz	3	2	3	2	4	68
Arequipa	9	1	0	1	0	47
Huamanga	11	0	0	1	0	68
Trujillo	3	17	12	9	0	50
Total	70	36	28	43	13	564

Source: Alfredo Moreno, ed., *Relación y documentos de gobierno del virrey del Perú, José A. Manso de Velasco, Conde de Superunda (1745–1761)* (Madrid: Consejo Superior de Investigaciones Científicas, Instituto Gonzalo de Oviedo, 1983), pp. 241–46.

was only two less than the regular orders had controlled in 1749.[62] As the viceroy and the archbishop had predicted, the process of secularizing parishes in the Archdiocese of Lima would be a long, steady process, particularly with the recalcitrant Franciscans. In the other bishoprics, however, the presence of the regular orders was much less pronounced, except in the frontier region of Misque, where Jesuit missionaries outnumbered secular clergymen, and in Trujillo where the Franciscans, Augustinians, and Mercedarians still held a total of thirty-eight parishes, compared to fifty by the secular clergy (see Table 5.1). In most other districts, however, moving toward secular control was less controversial than in the archbishopric of Lima. In fact, a survey of the *doctrinas* of Lima in 1756 indicated that over the subsequent two-year period, the regular orders had been reduced from fifty-nine to forty-five parishes – the Dominicans still held twenty-three (down from thirty), the Franciscans nine (down from thirteen), the Mercedarians thirteen (down from fifteen), and the Jesuits one.[63]

THE WAR OF ATTRITION OVER THE DOCTRINAS IN PERU

Given the ongoing controversy over secularization in Peru, the crown issued a Royal *cédula* on June 23, 1757, designed to placate the religious orders by allowing them to retain a few of their richest parishes. By this time, Carvajal had died and both Ensenada and Rávago had fallen from power. In the severe

[62] This was approximately the same number of *doctrinas* that the regular clergy held in Lima in the mid-seventeenth century. See, Kenneth Mills, *Idolatry and its Enemies: Colonial Andean Religion and Extirpation, 1640–1750* (Princeton: Princeton University Press, 1997), p. 9. According to Mills's figures, the regulars held 67 parishes and the secular priests 108.

[63] Joseph de Barbadillo y Frías to crown, Lima, February 21, 1756, AGI, Lima, leg. 1596.

reaction that followed the exile of Ensenada (see Chapter 6), both the new Minister of the Indies, Julián de Arriaga, and the new royal confessor, Manuel Quintano Bonifaz, were prepared to take a more conciliatory stand with the orders.[64] The new edict of 1757 provided that each order could retain one or two of the choicest (*más pingües*) parishes in each "district" where they had *conventillos*, but these religious houses had to be officially licensed by the crown and have at least eight friars in permanent, continual residence.[65] Instead of pacifying the orders, however, this new edict prompted nearly two decades of acrimonious disputes between viceregal authorities and the orders over what constituted a district. The orders thought that a district was a civil unit (such as a *corregimiento*), while the viceroy and bishops contended that a district meant a province of the orders, which roughly corresponded to a bishopric. These conflicting interpretations of the 1757 edict made a considerable difference in the number of parishes in dispute by both sides.

The viceroy wrote the crown on August 12, 1760, about his slow but steady progress in transferring parishes to secular control. Manso de Velasco explained that the 1753 edict of secularization had called for implementing the order with "the utmost gentleness," so he worked to ease tensions in the viceroyalty. He ordered that parishes be transferred to secular clergymen only after a vacancy occurred, naming a suitable candidate with language skills to administer each *doctrina*. If no qualified secular priest could be found, then the authorities appointed a suitable member of the religious orders. Moreover, according to the edict of 1757, Manso de Velasco and Archbishop Barroeta had designated one or two of the choicest *doctrinas* in each bishopric for the regular orders to support missionary activities in the viceroyalty. The viceroy pointed out, however, that the Dominicans and Mercedarians had no ongoing missions, the Augustinians maintained only a few remote outposts, and the Franciscans had been driven from their largest missions along the Tarma-Jauja frontier over a decade earlier by the rebel Juan Santos Atahualpa. Although the orders still resisted losing their parishes, the viceroy assured authorities in Madrid that secularization continued apace.[66]

By 1760 each of the prelates in the viceroyalty presented a report to the crown about the process of secularization, indicating which parishes in their districts the orders would retain, according to the provisions of the *cédula* of 1757. Archbishop Barroeta began his memorial by vigorously denying rumors spread by the orders that their members had been deprived of parishes before a vacancy had occurred, leaving groups of unemployed vagabond friars to roam the countryside. He further argued that no legitimate rural

---

[64] D. A. Brading, *Church and State in Bourbon Mexico: The Diocese of Michoacán, 1749–1818* (Cambridge, Eng., 1994), p. 67.

[65] Conde de Superunda to crown, Lima, August 12, 1760, AGI, Lima, leg. 1596; ASF, registro 2:23, f. 500.

[66] Conde de Superunda to crown, Lima, August 2, 1760, AGI, Lima, leg. 1596.

conventillos existed in the archbishopric, denying Franciscan claims that many of their parishes were annexed to missions.[67] The bishop of La Paz reported that regular clergymen still held thirteen parishes, but all would eventually be secularized, except four Jesuit parishes supporting their missions in Juli.[68] The bishops of Arequipa and Huamanga reported no parishes tied to missions or to rural *conventillos* (with at least eight resident friars).[69] The bishop of Trujillo wrote that he had not been in his district long enough to give a thorough report, but he listed only seven parishes linked to rural *conventillos*.[70] Finally, the bishop of Cusco reported no parishes tied to *conventillos*, while the bishop of La Plata listed seventeen parishes under the control of the orders, but he acknowledged that none were tied to formal *conventillos*, making all subject to secularization as vacancies occurred.[71]

The process of secularization continued its slow inexorable path as vacant parishes controlled by regular orders went to secular clergymen. According to Manso de Velasco's successor, Manuel de Amat y Junient, the religious orders continued to lobby for parishes in each civil district, forcing the crown to resolve once and for all the ambiguous language in the edict of 1757. In a Royal *cédula* issued from Aranjuez on July 3, 1766, the crown commanded that one or two choice parishes be reserved for each "religious" province of the orders, not for each *corregimiento* as the orders had demanded.[72] This edict effectively deprived the religious orders of any legal grounds for resisting the overall process of secularization in the Viceroyalty of Peru.

SECULARIZATION OF THE DOCRTINAS DE INDIOS IN NEW SPAIN

The responsibility for overseeing the secularization of the *doctrinas de indios* in New Spain fell to two well-connected, experienced officials, Viceroy Juan Francisco de Güemes y Horcasitas (first Count of Revillagigedo) and Archbishop Manuel Rubio de Salinas.[73] The Count of Revillagigedo had

---

[67] Pedro Antonio Arzobispo de Lima to crown, Lima, January 2, 1760, AGI, Lima, leg. 1596.

[68] Diego Antonio Obispo de La Paz to crown, La Paz, April 15, 1759, AGI, Lima, leg. 1596.

[69] Jacinto Obispo de Arequipa to crown, Arequipa, March 13, 1759 AGI, Lima, leg. 1596; Phelipe Obispo de Guamanga to crown, Guamanga, March 14, 1759, AGI, Lima, leg. 1596.

[70] Francisco Xavier Obispo de Trujillo to crown, Trujillo, December 5, 1759, AGI, Lima, leg. 1596.

[71] Juan Obispo de Cusco to crown, Cusco, February 16, 1760, AGI, Lima, leg. 1596; Cayetano Obispo de La Plata to crown, La Plata, February 15, 1760, AGI, Lima, leg. 1596.

[72] Vicente Rodríguez Casado and Florentino Pérez Embid, eds., *Manuel de Amat y Junient, Virrey del Perú, 1761–1776: Memoria de gobierno* (Sevilla: Escuela de Estudios Hispano-Americanos, 1947), p. 57.

[73] The process of secularization in New Spain has been studied by D. A. Brading, *Church and State in Bourbon Mexico*, pp. 62–81; D. A. Brading, "Tridentine Catholicism and Enlightened Despotism in Bourbon Mexico," *Journal of Latin American Studies*, 15:1 (May 1983), pp. 1–22; William B. Taylor, *Magistrates of the Sacred: Priests and Parishioners in Eighteenth-Century Mexico* (Stanford, CA: Stanford University Press, 1996), pp. 83–86,

served as a lieutenant general in the army during the sieges of Gibraltar and Oran, where he developed a close personal and professional relationship with the Marqués de la Ensenada. As captain general of Havana, he presided over the reform of the local military establishment, and under his leadership the garrison repulsed British attacks on the island during the War of Jenkins' Ear. Revillagigedo also had a well-deserved reputation for curtailing the rampant contraband trade from the British and Dutch possessions in the Caribbean. His successes in Cuba led to his elevation to viceroy in New Spain in 1746, where he also continued efforts to reform the treasury and curtail contraband commerce through Veracruz.[74]

His counterpart, Archbishop Rubio de Salinas had studied at Alcalá de Henares, where his academic successes and piety led him to the priesthood. Shortly after his ordination, Rubio de Salinas was named chaplain to King Philip V. While serving in that role, he became a protégé of the king's powerful confessor, the Jesuit Francisco de Rávago. Rubio de Salinas had also participated in the Junta Particular de Ministros in the country home of José de Carvajal in 1748. The committee recommended the secularization of the *doctrinas de indios*, and when the archbishop arrived in Mexico City in 1749, both he and Revillagigedo worked together to implement the policy.[75]

Despite the enthusiastic support of the viceroy and the archbishop of Mexico, the process of secularization took the same contested, torturous path as in Peru. The colonial authorities enraged the mendicant orders by taking away not only their *doctrinas de indios* but also by expropriating convent churches and priories, arguing that these buildings had been constructed without securing royal licenses. The process itself was usually a two-day process. On the first day, the friar handed over the keys to the local church, followed by a ceremony that involved exposing the host and a procession around the entire church. On the second day, the secular priest took possession of the parish record books, inventories, and the account books of the religious brotherhoods (*confradías*). The secular clergyman

---

506–10; Dorothy Tanck de Estrada, *Pueblos de Indios y educación en el México colonial, 1750–1821* (México: Colegio de México, 1999), pp. 161–69; Brian Belanger, "*Secularization and the Laity in Colonial Mexico: Querétaro, 1598–1821*," (Unpublished Ph.D. diss., Tulane University, 1990); Francisco Morales, "Secularización de doctrinas: fin de un modelo evangelizador en la Nueva España?" *Archivo Ibero-Americano: Revista Franciscana e estudios históricos*, 52: 205–208 (1992): pp. 465–495; Ernest Sánchez Santiró, "El Nuevo orden parroquial de la ciudad de México: población, etnia, y territorio (1768–1777), *Estudios de Historia novohispana*, 30 (enero-junio, 2004): pp. 63–92; For a study of the earlier seventeenth-century effort to secularize doctrinas in Puebla, Mexico, see Virve Piho, *La secularización de las parroquias en la Nueva España y su repercusión en San Andrés Calpan* (México: Instituto Nacional de Antropología e Historia, 1981), passim.

74 Antonio del Valle Menéndez, *Juan Francisco de Güemes y Horcasitas, Primer Conde de Revillagigedo, Virrey de México: La Historia de un Soldado (1681–1766)* (Santander: Ediciones de Librería Estudio, 1998), pp. 55–61; 128–35; 326–35.

75 Sánchez Bella, *Iglesia y estado*, pp. 121–35.

received "the parish church and doctrina, with all its visitas, goods, furnishings, incomes, ornaments, jewels, vessels, convents, and houses."[76] On some occasions, the viceroy even dispatched soldiers to occupy the priories without notice, forcing the friars to leave immediately with only their personal possessions. Since this involved expelling 101 friars from the 189 parishes in the Archdiocese of Mexico, the numbers of mendicants involved in the 1749 secularization edict alone was considerable. When the decree was extended to include all of New Spain in 1753, the numbers of friars removed from their *doctrinas* rose much higher.[77]

The vigorous protests of the Franciscan, Augustinian, and Dominican leaders in both Spain and New Spain mirrored those lodged by their counterparts in the Viceroyalty of Peru. The mendicants complained that the crown treated its loyal, long-suffering servants like criminals, not even extending the courtesies granted to the Moors and Jews when they were expelled from the kingdoms of Spain long ago. Apart from the insult to the orders' honor, the edicts of secularization also ignored the pioneering role the mendicants had played in the evangelization of the indigenous peoples and the sufferings of their many martyrs who had died over the years in the frontier missions of New Spain. Without the support of their rural parishes, the orders argued that they would be reduced to penury and misery, without the means to support and house the many friars removed from their parishes. Moreover, the secular clergy lacked the language skills to minister to the Amerindians. Even the cabildo of Mexico City sent a long memorial to the crown attesting to the many harmful effects of secularization.[78]

Despite this opposition, the viceroy and the archbishop remained steadfast in their plans to implement secularization. The Conde de Revillagigedo argued that the orders had broken the law by establishing priories and churches without appropriate crown licenses and that too many were simply *conventillos*, with less than the requisite eight permanent residents. The superiors of the orders also moved friars from one district to another without even gaining proper canonical appointments.[79] He further argued that the rights of appointment rested with the prelates of New Spain, not the orders:

It is their responsibility to judge the need or utility of removing the friars, without waiting until the priests die or resign, with no other action required of the viceroy other than to facilitate their measures or determinations, and I have acted accordingly, issuing my decrees in the terms that they asked of me.[80]

[76] Belanger, *Secularization and the Laity in Colonial Mexico*, pp. 87, 89–90.
[77] Brading, *Church and State in Bourbon Mexico*, p. 71.
[78] Ibid., pp. 64–65.
[79] Ibid., p. 65.
[80] Valle Menéndez, *Juan Francisco de Güemes y Horcasitas*, p. 627.

For his part, Archbishop Rubio y Salinas also wrote a long letter to the crown defending secularization. He denied that secular clergy lacked the language skills to minister to the indigenous people, arguing that over 174 candidates for parishes had competency in Nahuatl, and he had taken the precaution of establishing a chair of Mexican language in his diocesan seminary. Moreover, he agreed with the viceroy that the orders had built priories without obtaining proper licenses. Rubio y Salinas explained that he replaced friars with secular clergy in the parishes only after the death or retirement of the incumbent, unless they did not have a proper canonical appointment.[81] In short, both the viceroy and the archbishop believed that secularization served the interests of the church hierarchy, the crown, and the indigenous parishioners.

Secularization in settled, urban areas proved complicated, since local parishes often supported a major religious house. The Franciscan *convento* at Querétaro, for example, was attached to the parish of Santiago, which provided much of the financial support for the order in the region. As a result, crown authorities allowed the Franciscans to retain the parish and the large church attached to the *convento*. In 1758, however, the viceroy ordered the secularization of Santiago, although all *cofradías* and pious funds founded specifically to help sustain the *convento* in Querétaro remained attached to the order, while any others transferred to the newly secularized parish.[82] Prior to secularization, the Franciscans had three large priories at Querétaro, Valladolid, and Celaya that supported 326 friars. By 1772, secularization had deprived the order of most of its parishes, and the numbers of friars in the region had fallen to 239, including novices and lay brothers.[83]

The process of secularization had a severe impact on the orders in Michoacán, where the Franciscans administered 35 and the Augustinians 29 of the 114 parishes in the diocese.[84] Although both orders resisted secularization, the Augustinians fought a particularly long, bitter struggle to retain their richest parishes along with the large haciendas that together supported the order in the region. In 1754, Viceroy Revillagigedo ordered the secularization of all the parishes administered by the Augustinians, ordering the immediate occupation of all churches and priories situated on Amerindian lands. The order argued that its five *doctrinas* of San Sebastián and Santa Cruz de México and those of Capuluac, Actopan and Tianguistenco were actually tied to *conventos* of the order and should not be turned over to secular clergy.[85] In addition, the order refused to hand over its large hacienda of San Nicolás within the limits of the *doctrina* of Yuririapúndaro, which was valued at 500,000 pesos. The adjacent priory

[81] Brading, *Church and State in Bourbon Mexico*, pp. 66–67.
[82] Belanger, *Secularization and the Laity in Colonial Mexico*, pp. 86–90.
[83] Brading, *Church and State in Bourbon Mexico*, pp. 76–77.
[84] Ibid., p. 71.
[85] Valle Menéndez, *Juan Francisco de Güemes y Horcasitas*, pp. 620–22.

of Yuriria also served as the residence of the Augustinian provincial. The order took the matter to the audiencia in Mexico City and initially received a favorable verdict. The local bishop, Anselmo Sánchez del Tagle, appealed the case to the Council of the Indies, however, denouncing the viceroy and the justices of the high court for upholding the Augustinian claims to the priory and hacienda. Ultimately, in 1781 the Council supported the bishop's case and the priory and the estate reverted to the secular clergy.[86]

The response of Amerindian parishioners to secularization varied widely, depending on the historic relations between the friars and the laity and on any local political conflicts. In the parish of Cuanacalcingo in Morelos, for example, the indigenous parishioners petitioned to have their newly imposed secular priest, José Eusebio de Ortega, removed and replaced by three Franciscans who had worked "wholeheartedly for the good of our souls."[87] Some parishioners found the secular clergy too remote, unlike their more gentle Franciscan "fathers." In other cases, long-standing disputes between the friars and the indigenous parishioners over clerical fees and perquisites had led to friction. In 1730, for example, indigenous parishioners from Tetecala in Morelos had refused to pay the clerical fees charged by the Franciscan *doctrinero*, and they charged him with imposing illegal forced labor demands, operating a private jail, and extorting fees above the legal rate.[88] Sometimes, these disputes even carried over when the secular priests took over the *doctrina*, as parishioners used the transition to balk at paying clerical fees and debts to the priest, arguing that their formal agreements had been with the friars, who were no longer in charge. In the town of Zacualpan de las Amilpas, Amerindian parishioners refused to pay fees and to attend Mass, and they even began to reassert their pre-Christian religious practices.[89] In short, the relations between clerical authorities and the indigenous parishioners were often contentious, regardless of whether the friars or the secular clergy administered the *doctrina*.

The process of secularization in New Spain was tied to efforts at expanding the number of schools in the *doctrinas* that taught the Amerindians in Castilian. In Peru, clerical authorities went to great pains to find secular priests fluent in local indigenous tongues, but in New Spain large numbers of Amerindians already knew Castilian. In the Archdiocese of Mexico, for example, over 287 schools teaching in Castilian operated in the 281 towns of the district by 1754.[90] Indeed, Archbishop Rubio y Salinas chided the mendicants for employing native languages in the Mass and other Catholic rituals, arguing that it was a chief cause of native cultural backwardness. Although

---

[86] Ibid., pp. 72–75.
[87] Taylor, *Magistrates of the Sacred*, pp. 506–07.
[88] Ibid., p. 507.
[89] Ibid.
[90] Tanck de Estrada, *Pueblos de indios y educación*, p. 160.

the archbishop countered mendicant claims that too few secular clergymen knew native languages by establishing a Chair in Nahuatl in his diocesan seminary, he argued strongly that schools should teach indigenous parishioners to learn Castilian.[91] This policy echoed the earlier recommendations of Campillo in his *Nuevo sistema* that the indigenous peoples should be taught to read and write in Castilian and that they should wear Spanish clothes.[92] As Rubio y Salinas wrote to King Ferdinand VI: "with punishments appropriate for their ages, the children of both sexes are required to speak Castilian correctly [in order to] achieve the [objective] of finally banishing the barbaric languages from this archdiocese."[93] Clearly, the policy in Peru was to preach in native tongues, while in Mexico clerical authorities attempted to use the school system to have secular priests advance the spread of Castilian among native parishioners.

The edicts of secularization severely undermined the prestige and material well-being of the mendicants in New Spain, just as they had in Peru. Once the process had begun, bishops sent periodic pastoral visitations to parishes still under mendicant control to target abuses, and as soon as vacancies occurred, they turned the parishes over to secular priests. Although the 1757 *cédula* allowed the orders to retain two of the choicest parishes in each bishopric, the mendicants still lost the bulk of their lucrative parishes over the subsequent decades. Without their parishes, the orders could not support as many friars, leading to a marked decline in their membership. The province of Santo Evangelio in central Mexico, for example, reported 787 members in 1764 but only 577 in 1776.[94] The Junta Particular de Ministros in 1748 had recommended secularization and reducing the numbers in the regular orders, and despite resistance from the orders, crown policy had certainly attained both of these goals in both the Viceroyalties of New Spain and Peru by the end of the eighteenth century.

CONCLUSION

Secularization of the rural parishes constituted a forceful, direct attack on the considerable wealth and power of the regular clergy in the eighteenth century. By 1754, the orders in the Viceroyalty of Peru controlled 190 parishes and received nearly 450,000 pesos annually in *sínodos* from the Peruvian treasuries. The situation in New Spain was similar. Moreover, the imposing religious houses of the orders dominated the urban landscape in Lima and Mexico City, and they played a central role in religious, political, and social life in both capital cities. The secularization policy undermined the

[91] Brading, *Church and State in Bourbon Mexico*, p. 66.
[92] Tanck de Estrada, *Pueblos de indios y educación*, pp. 164–65.
[93] Ibid., p.164.
[94] Taylor, *Magistrates of the Sacred*, p. 85.

entrenched regular orders, particularly the Dominicans, Franciscans, Augustinians, and Mercedarians, who slowly lost their lucrative parishes over the course of several decades. These orders were vulnerable because of reports about their corruption, moral laxity, and abuse of Amerindian parishioners in Peru. The devastating earthquake of 1746 in Lima provided the spark to begin consideration to reform the orders and limit their wealth and power throughout the Spanish Indies. The missionary activities of the regular orders, which had long been used to justify their administration of the *doctrinas*, had also diminished considerably by the eighteenth century, particularly in Peru after the Franciscans were expelled from the Tarma-Jauja frontier in 1742. Losing their *doctrinas* led to a gradual decline in income for the orders, and their poverty and lack of political influence made it relatively easy for the new republican governments to expel the regulars from Peru and Mexico after independence in the nineteenth century.[95]

The edicts of secularization succeeded over time because they had divided the church, leaving the regular orders exposed on one side, while the secular clergy gained control over rich parishes formerly held by regular clergymen. The Jesuits were the one religious order less directly affected by the edicts of secularization, since they administered few parishes outside of missionary areas, largely exempting them from the edicts of 1749 and 1753. Moreover, the Jesuits were protected from these crown policies by the three most powerful ministers during King Ferdinand's rule, José de Carvajal y Lancaster, the Marqués de la Ensenada, and Francisco de Rávago, who were known collectively as the "Jesuit Party" because of their well-known support for the Society of Jesus.[96] The Jesuits would only later fall victim to the advance of regalism when King Charles III and a new group of "enlightened" ministers expelled them from Spain and the empire in 1767. The real winner in the struggle over the *doctrinas*, however, was the crown, which dramatically extended its power over the church by replacing the more independent regular orders with secular clergy, over whom the crown had considerably more control. By depriving the regular clergy of their parishes, reformers in Spain, New Spain, and Peru extended the state's power over the orders, fundamentally altering the traditional partnership between church and state in Spain's Atlantic empire.

As the political struggles over secularization in Bourbon Peru and New Spain indicate, enlightened reform emerged after a long, complicated political process in which the crown, colonial interest groups, and the church contested for power. Although the Enlightenment provided the broad intellectual context for reform, these ideas fused with a variety of reformist proposals sent from the Indies by Juan and Ulloa and others, all addressing the supposed

[95] Tibesar, "The Suppression of the Religious Orders in Peru," 220–34.
[96] Pérez-Mallaina Bueno, *Retrato de una ciudad en crisis*, p. 322; Pierce, "Early Bourbon Government," p. 14.

political, social, and economic ills of the empire. Many of these concerns went back to the Habsburg era, including efforts to remove the regular orders from parish work, which crown authorities, reformers (*arbitristas*), and some churchmen had discussed during the seventeenth century. Bishop Juan de Palafox y Mendoza, for example, expelled the regulars from parishes in his diocese in Puebla, Mexico, although the effort ultimately ended when the crown recalled him in 1649.[97] Even though Palafox was a favorite of King Philip IV and the Conde-Duque de Olivares, the Madrid government ultimately proved unable to mount a consistent challenge to the entrenched power of the religious orders in the Indies during this earlier period.[98] By the reign of Ferdinand VI, however, reformers, crown ministers, and the progressive Pope Benedict XIV, remained committed to removing the regulars from parish work in the Indies, marking a clear and permanent shift in crown policy toward the church.[99] Moreover, the astute political maneuvering of the viceroys – José Manso de Velasco in Peru and Juan Francisco de Güemes y Horcasitas in New Spain – allowed them to accumulate the political clout needed to separate the religious orders from their parishes and outwit political rivals.

---

[97] Cayetana Alvarez de Toledo, *Politics and Reform in Spain and Viceregal Mexico: The Life and Thought of Juan de Palafox, 1600–1659* (Oxford: Clarendon Press, 2004); J. I. Israel, *Race, Class, and Politics in Colonial Mexico, 1610–1670* (Oxford, Oxford University Press, 1975), pp. 199–247; and Piho, *La secularización de las parroquias en la Nueva España*, pp. 117–92.

[98] J. H. Elliott, *The Count-Duke of Olivares: The Statesman in an Age of Decline* (New Haven: Yale University Press, 1986), p. 489.

[99] Sánchez Bella, *Iglesia y estado*, pp. 132–33.

6

The Downfall of Ensenada and the
Pause, 1750–1763

The Treaty of Madrid in 1750 finally liberated Spain from all the constraints imposed at Utrecht, which allowed reformers to seize the opportunity for a long-awaited modernization of the commercial system and for undermining powerful vested interests opposed to reform. The secularization of the *doctrinas de indios* attacked the economic power and social prestige of the religious orders, and the use of register ships undercut the historic privileges of the powerful *Consulados* of Cádiz, Mexico City, and Lima. These bold policy changes went well beyond the earlier initiatives in defense, finance, and administration undertaken by Alberoni and sustained by Patiño. Madrid's priorities had clearly become imperial, not just national or dynastic, and the government's focus had shifted decisively from the Mediterranean to the Atlantic. With the end of war in Europe and the Indies, revenues from America rose to unprecedented levels as Ensenada's men in the New World – the Conde de Revillagigedo, the Conde de Superunda, and Sebastián de Eslava – clamped down on contraband, bureaucratic corruption, and government inefficiencies. The Marqués de la Ensenada could now use these revenues to replace losses sustained by the armada during the war and expand the number of warships in the fleet. It was a time of widespread change and innovation throughout the Spanish Atlantic system.

Such fundamental shifts in royal policy would not come easily. Powerful interests vehemently opposed commercial modernization, and tradition-bound forces within the royal administration and without sought to impede change. Although the Marqués de la Ensenada had dominated the political arena in Spain for over a decade, his policies always had powerful opponents, who contributed to his fall from power in 1754. The departure of Rávago from Madrid followed the exile of Ensenada by months. The conservative backlash was reminiscent of the events following the destitution of Alberoni. Political drift at the top reached its nadir with the mental breakdown of King Ferdinand VI followed by his untimely death. The new king, Charles III appeared to energize Madrid when he acceded to the throne, but when English invaders appeared off

Havana in 1762, the strongpoint of the American empire fell after a two-month siege. After the loss of Havana, the consequences of the failed colonial policy of neutrality and the opportunities lost became alarmingly apparent.

THE TREATY OF MADRID

Signed at Buen Retiro on October 5, 1750, the Treaty of Madrid was the handiwork of José de Carvajal y Lancaster as secretary of the Office for State. Despite its historic importance, this agreement was a relatively simple document of only ten articles. In return for a cash settlement, the British surrendered the four remaining years of the *asiento*, which opened the way at last for Madrid to reform its commercial system. The accord confirmed essential elements of the first Bubb Treaty (see Chapter 1), guaranteeing Britain most favored nation status in Spanish ports and the tariff rates existing during the reign of Charles II. Although the settlement provided modest benefits for Spain, the British gained important commercial concessions while giving up little, and the settlement laid the groundwork for separating Madrid from Versailles diplomatically.[1] Ambassador Ricardo Wall, born in France but of Irish ancestry, had worked in London to bring the two powers closer together.[2]

Carvajal was guardedly inclined toward the British. While he warned the king that "the English are its [Spain's] natural enemies," he had been profoundly antagonized by the French behavior during the final years of the war and the peace negotiations.[3] As he wrote to the Duke of Huéscar, "The wound will be incurable," and "If I have no means to avenge myself, I will die disconsolate."[4] Moreover, Carvajal's Portuguese ancestry undoubtedly disposed him toward an indulgence of the British, Portugal's staunch ally since its successful rebellion against Spain in 1640.[5] In January 1750, Carvajal had negotiated a separate Treaty of Madrid with Lisbon, temporarily settling the nagging issue of colonial boundaries.[6] By 1753 he had come to nurture the hope that Spain would somehow play the role of a neutral arbiter in European affairs.[7]

---

[1] A succinct summary can be found in José Miguel Delgado Barrado, *El proyecto político de Carvajal: Pensamiento y reforma en tiempos de Fernando VI* (Madrid: Consejo Superior de Investigaciones Científicas, 2001), pp. 96–97. A copy of the treaty is in AAE: MFDE, vol. 345, fols. 99–101.

[2] For a recent study of Wall and his career, see Diego Téllez Alarcia *El ministerio Wall: La <España discreta> del <ministro olvidado>* (Madrid: Marcial Pons, 2012). See also Didier Ozanam, *La diplomacia de Fernando VI: Correspondencia entre Carvajal y Huéscar, 1746–1749* (Madrid: Consejo Superior de Investigaciones Científicas, 1975), pp. 33–34, 118.

[3] Quoted in Ozanam, *La diplomacia de Fernando VI*, p. 47.

[4] Ibid., p. 39.

[5] Delgado Barrado, *El proyecto político*, p. 15.

[6] Ibid., pp. 92–94.

[7] Ibid., pp. 29, 37.

The royal family also leaned toward reconciliation with Great Britain. Ferdinand had been angered by his cousin the French king's arrogant behavior during the war.[8] Moreover, he felt humiliated and embittered when France refused to accept his youngest half-sister, María Antonia, to replace the recently deceased María Teresa as the dauphine's second wife.[9] Queen Barbara reinforced Ferdinand's inclinations. The new Portuguese queen was deeply attached to her Austrian mother and quite sympathetic to London.[10] While Barbara was a much more restrained woman than Elizabeth, her views carried weight with her husband, who often invited her to join him in the office. The queen had assumed a traditional role at first; when at official administrative functions, she spoke only when asked by Ferdinand.[11] As time passed, however, her interest in the affairs of state grew, and so too did her influence at court.[12] When María Ana Victoria, Ferdinand's half-sister, became queen of Portugal upon the succession of John II on July 31, 1750, the royal family's inclination toward Britain only increased.[13]

Although Ensenada was not pleased with the Treaty of Madrid, his resentment against the French led him to favor neutrality. A forceful, ambitious personality who frequently intruded beyond the limits of his ministries, Ensenada had seen the Madrid agreement negotiated without his participation.[14] He not only felt slighted personally, but he believed that Carvajal had fallen short in upholding Spain's best interests. London gave up very little in return for Spain's reaffirmation of the Bubb Treaties. A general settlement, presumably, should have brought Spain much more.[15] Nonetheless, Ensenada had shared the sense of betrayal that had so angered the Madrid government in the years leading up to Aix-la-Chapelle, and he clearly aimed to see Spain

---

[8] As he stated at the time: "There was no reason whatever why the minister of Your Majesty should hasten to sign without my knowledge, there being so many good reasons not to do so and so many concerns that were not of mutual interest ... but mine alone." Ozanam, *La diplomacia de Fernando VI* , p. 39.

[9] María eventually served to normalize Spain's position in Italy through her marriage in 1750 to the Prince of Piedmont, the heir to the throne of Sardinia. Delgado, *El proyecto político*, pp. 82, 98–99.

[10] The French were quite correctly concerned from the start about Barbara's attachments, but they failed to grasp fully the dangerous implications of their own behavior at the end of the war. Versailles, July 20, 1746, AAE:CPE, vol. 490, fols. 203–05. Louis XV instructed his ambassador to determine "with exactitude and precision the character or the inclination of that princess." Louis XV to Ambassador Bishop of Rennes, ibid., fols. 224–25.

[11] Rennes to Minister of State Renato Luis d'Argenson, Madrid, July 26, 1746, AAE:CPE, vol. 490, fols. 238–47.

[12] Ozanam, *La diplomacia de Fernando VI* , pp. 17, 23.

[13] María Ángeles Pérez Samper, *Isabel de Farnesio* (Barcelona: Plaza y Janés, 2003), p. 423.

[14] His meddling in foreign affairs left Carvajal flabbergasted. Ozanam, *La diplomacia de Fernando VI* , p. 52.

[15] Ambassador Duke of Duras to Versailles, Madrid, March 8, 1753, with "Traduction des observations ... sur le traité ... de 5 octobre du 1750 par le partie du ministre espagnol qui est opposé a ce traité," AAE:CPE, vol. 513, fols. 159–68.

distance itself from Versailles.[16] For these reasons, the *riojano* believed that Madrid must tread cautiously with the French. On the other hand, he never lost sight of the reality that the monarchy's principal rival was Great Britain, whose interests in America were incompatible over the long term with those of Spain.[17] As he commented to French Ambassador Duke of Duras in 1753 : "within two or three years, I won't fear them any more; with your help ... I will always be a good Frenchman."[18] In this way, Ensenada pursued a policy of armed vigilance, while Spain's foreign policy drifted into what has come to be known as *neutralidad fernandista*. Meanwhile, in June 1752 at Aranjuez, Carvajal completed his third landmark treaty, settling Spain's differences with Austria and Piedmont-Sardinia through a defensive alliance that finally brought stability to Italy.[19] Two years before, Ferdinand's half-sister, María Antonia, who had been rejected by the French, had married Victor Amadeus, the heir to the Sardinian throne.[20]

ENSENADA AND THE REFORMING IMPULSE

For Ensenada, strengthening the armada was a top priority to secure the sea lanes defending Spain's Atlantic empire. At he explained to Ferdinand VI in 1747, "There is no power in the world that needs naval forces more than Spain, for it is a peninsula and has to protect the vast American dominions that belong to it."[21] A year later, he asserted that "Without a navy, the Spanish monarchy cannot command respect, maintain dominion over her vast holdings, nor this peninsula flourish, the center and heart of everything."[22] Between 1739 and

---

[16] As he stated to the king in 1746, "France will feign desires for union and even war with the enthusiasm of the moment, but it will be to advance the success of its objectives at our expense." Regarding America, he observed that "With regard to issues concerning the Indies, France maintains a deep silence, because what it has there it usurped from us [and] never legitimized it by any agreement or pact, like Holland and England," in "Idea de lo que parece preciso en el día para la dirección de lo que corresponde á Estado y se halla pendiente," in Antonio Rodríguez Villa, *Don Cenón de Somodevilla, Marqués de la Ensenada* ... (Madrid: Librería M. Murillo, 1878), pp. 33, 41.

[17] As he informed the king, "it is necessary to understand that these two powers cannot be united, and that it is in the interest of both to work against the other, to which can be added that, observing that Spain, half armed and with the funds to sustain war, will be respected and not vulnerable to suffer, as up to now, the law that they [the British] wish to impose ... " Ensenada to Ferdinand VI, "Plano que se forma para fixar ... las obligaciones ordinarias ...," Aranjuez, May 18, 1752, in Rodríguez Villa, *Don Cenón de Somodevilla*, p. 96.

[18] Duras to Minister of State Saint Contest, Aranjuez, May 16, 1753, AAE:CPE, vol. 513, fols. 390–98.

[19] Charles in Italy did not approve. Delgado, *El proyecto político*, pp. 98–99.

[20] Pérez Samper, *Isabel de Farnesio*, pp. 422–23.

[21] Ensenada to Fernando VI, "Representación dirigida ... sobre el estado del Real Erario," Aranjuez, June 18, 1747, in Rodríguez Villa, *Don Cenón de Somodevilla*, p. 62.

[22] Quoted in Francisco Cánovas, José Antonio Escudero, José María García Marín, et al., *La época de los primeros borbones*, vol. I, *La nueva monarquía y su posición en Europa*

1748, Spain had sustained losses from combat, accidents, and deterioration that had returned the armada to the level where Patiño had left it in 1736.[23] To replace these vessels and strengthen the fleet, Ensenada planned to construct fifty ships of the line within eight years at a cost of 1 million pesos annually.[24] As he explained, "it is easy indeed for Your Majesty to have a sufficient number of vessels that, united with those of France ... might deny the English the dominion that they have acquired at sea."[25] Construction proceeded at a furious pace in the three Spanish arsenals and in Havana, supervised by the Royal Havana Company. Meanwhile, Ferdinand had suppressed the *almirantazgo* in 1748, which Ensenada replaced with a director general of the armada.[26] This post was occupied for one year by the Conde de Bena (1749–1750) and then by the Marqués de la Victoria, hero of the Battle of Cape Sicié, who served until his death in 1772.[27] To plan for future shipbuilding, Ensenada had some 2 million oak trees planted.[28]

Carvajal assigned top priority to colonial affairs, and he appreciated the need to foster the armada. He agreed with Ensenada that Spain should build fifty new ships of the line to bring her naval forces up to strength.[29] But he also emphasized the need for moderation: "Our navy should increase, but proportionately and quietly, for now we are upsetting the world with that."[30] The wise and ever careful Carvajal wanted to protect the Spanish empire but without provoking another war or straining the Royal Treasury. He knew too well that the reforms that he and Ensenada favored would require peace and money from the Indies.

Even when the government had sufficient money to fund ambitious ship construction, finding enough sailors to man the ships was nearly an insurmountable obstacle. Because of the comparative weakness of Spain's merchant marine (in comparison to England's) there were never enough Spaniards with seafaring skills. Ensenada saw no easy answer:

(1700–1759) in *Historia de España*, vol. **XXIX**, dir. by José María Jover Zamora (Madrid: Espasa-Calpe, 1985), p. 465.

[23] Cánovas, *La época de los primeros Borbones*, I, p. 464

[24] It cost 143,000 pesos to build the eighty-gun *Rayo* in 1749. John D. Harbron, *Trafalgar and the Spanish Navy* (London: Conway Maritime Press, 1988), p. 41.

[25] Ensenada to Ferdinand VI, "Representación dirigida ... sobre el estado del Real Erario," Aranjuez, June 18, 1747, in Rodríguez Villa, *Don Cenón de Somodevilla*, pp. 62–63.

[26] Royal decree, San Lorenzo, October 30, 1748, AGS, Marine, leg. 768.

[27] Cánovas, *La época de los primeros Borbones*, I, pp. 477–78. For the first six years, the appointment was interim, but in 1756 he was promoted to captain and governor general of the armada, a position that he held until his death in 1772.

[28] Harbron, *Trafalgar*, p. 41.

[29] Delgado, *El proyecto político*, pp. 29, 110–12.

[30] Quoted in Ozanam, *La diplomacia de Fernando VI* , p. 46. The armada had, he lamented, "consumed millions endlessly." Ibid., pp. 46, 76. Carvajal had a pronounced tendency to see both sides of an issue.

The means to have a navy today are to pay it punctually, something not done up to now; welcome the foreigner [but] favor the native; by laws and ordinances, permit all the ships and craft that wish to go to America to leave from any port of Spain, and foment fishing; [and] concede exemptions to provide relief for those who are employed in navigation and commerce.[31]

To compensate for the lack of trained men, the *Matrícula de Mar*, a seamen's registry or a kind of naval militia, had been established in 1737, which promised some help if Spanish commercial shipping increased.[32]

Ensenada brought enlightened thought to new heights, laying the foundation intellectually and institutionally for the future achievements of Charles III and his ministers. A dedicated regalist, he envisaged a new centralized, bureaucratic state to replace the traditional view of the monarchy presiding over a judicial governmental apparatus. Building upon Campillo y Cossío, he sought to formalize, standardize, and codify the policies governing the ministries and the corporations under his purview.[33] The period between 1748 and 1754 was a golden age of enlightened absolutism, which made its mark in Spain through a series of reformist laws. This included ordinances promulgated for the armada during 1748, a regulation for the *Matrícula de Mar* in 1751, and an ordinance and instruction, dated October 13, 1749, for reestablishment of intendants in Castile.[34] Of particular interest for the empire, the great minister sponsored an instruction, promulgated in 1753, which codified the procedures governing the accounts of the *Depositaría de Indias*, the treasury of the *Casa de la Contratación*.[35] But as José Luis Gómez Urdáñez has perceptively observed, Ensenada aimed

to reform in order to preserve the immutable of the Old Regime, "to modernize" the system to eliminate the deficiencies that certain occurrences exposed, but without threatening the underlying pillars ... to govern accepting enlightened ideas, which were still less "philosophical" than technical and pragmatic.[36]

During the years following the Treaty of Madrid, Ensenada expanded the system of fixed battalions that had been extended to much of the Caribbean

---

[31] Ensenada to Fernando VI, "Representación dirigida ... sobre el estado del Real Erario," Aranjuez, June 18, 1747, in Rodríguez Villa, *Don Cenón de Somodevilla*, pp. 63–64.

[32] Harbron, *Trafalgar*, pp. 86–88.

[33] Juan Luis Castellano, *Gobierno y poder en la España del siglo XVIII* (Granada: Editorial Universidad de Granada, 2006), p. 162.

[34] José Luis Gómez Urdáñez and Pedro Luis Lorenzo Cadarso, *Castilla en la edad moderna*, second part, *Historia de Castilla de Atapuerca a Fuensaldaña*, ed. by Juan José García González, Julio Aróstegui Sánchez, Juan Andrés Blanco Rodríguez, et al. (Madrid: La Esfera de los Libros, 2008), pp. 503, 507; Luis Navarro García, *Las reformas borbónicas en América: El plan de intendencias y su aplicación* (Sevilla: Universidad de Sevilla, 1995), p. 25.

[35] Jacques A. Barbier, "Towards a New Chronology for Bourbon Colonialism: The 'Depositaría de Indias' of Cádiz; 1722–1789" *Iber-Amerikanisches Archiv*, 6 (1980), pp. 337–38.

[36] José Luis *Gómez Urdañez, Fernando VI* (Madrid: Arlanza Ediciones, 2001), p. 148.

during the War of Jenkins' Ear. This early expression of military reform had, after all, seemingly worked during the war, most apparently at Cartagena. The crown promulgated new regulations for Veracruz in 1749 and Yucatán in 1754, both vaguely based on the Cuban model, but with the social prescriptions favoring Spaniards loosened. The original limit on the number of Americans was ignored completely, although the policy for Yucatán explicitly barred *castas* and foreigners. When Valdivia established its fixed battalion in 1753, it actually included one company for *pardos* out of its seven. The new regulation promulgated for Callao that same year maintained silence altogether on social restrictions, but it broke new ground by offering a ten-peso reward for each recruit.[37] Soldiers were hard to find, and local authorities had to adjust to the realities encountered, no matter what sort of norms the magistrates in Madrid might concoct for them.[38]

These army reforms continued the more cautious innovations on the land begun by Alberoni and Patiño. Campillo y Cossío had advocated extending Castile's militia system to the colonies, but Ensenada never favored this innovation in his many reports written to the king about defending Spain and its empire.[39] To defend a seaborne empire, he thought primarily about the armada. In addition, the Duke of Montemar, father of the provincial militia in Spain, had departed the political scene. Relieved of his command in 1742 by impatient monarchs who had expected a rapid advance into Milan, he had returned to court, dying, in June 1747.[40] The man of the hour was Sebastián de Eslava, the victor at Cartagena. Upon his return from New Granada, Ensenada named Eslava captain general of Andalusia and frequently summoned him to Madrid for advice. Eslava remained wedded to what had worked at Cartagena, including a traditional emphasis on fixed fortifications.[41] During subsequent years, when Eslava served as Minister of War, the fast-rising and innovative Conde de

---

[37] Copies of the various *reglamentos* are located in AGI, IG, legs. 1317 and 1885.

[38] Yet policy in Cuba retained its original standard limiting Americans to 20%. From 1748 to 1753, Ensenada had worked through the Conde de Revillagigedo, now viceroy of Mexico, to expand Havana's fixed garrison to provide detachments for both Santiago and St. Augustine, Florida. The result was a regiment of four battalions with six companies each, totaling 2,080 men, complemented by a commensurate increase in the companies of dragoons and of artillery. If the local population of Spaniards be found lacking, recruitment should be undertaken in the Canary Islands as well as in Mexico City and Puebla, where vagrant *peninsulares* might usefully be rounded up. Obviously, the crown had higher expectations for Cuba than for Yucatán. *Allan J. Kuethe, Cuba, 1753–1815: Crown, Military, and Society* (Knoxville: University of Tennessee Press, 1986), pp.12–13.

[39] Many of Ensenada's essays can be found in Rodríguez Villa, *Don Cenón de Somodevilla.*

[40] Julio Albi de la Cuesta, Leopoldo Stampa Piñero, and Juan Silvela y Miláns de Bosch, *La caballería española: Un eco de clarines* (Madrid: Tabapress, 1992).

[41] Lucio Mijares Pérez, "Programa político para América del Marqués de la Ensenada," *Revista de historia de América*, no. 81 (Jan.–June 1976) pp. 82–103.

Aranda clashed repeatedly with him over his reluctance to modernize the army.[42]

The other great influence at court was Francisco de Rávago, the Jesuit confessor of Ferdinand. While the men who occupied this key position had very frequently assumed prominent roles in palace politics under Philip V, Rávago was exceptional in his skill and influence (see Chapter 5). He replaced the Frenchman Jacques-Antoine Fèvre in April 1747, as part of the purge arising from Versailles's duplicitous diplomatic maneuvers.[43] Born in Cantabria, the confessor was a close personal friend of Carvajal, and he enjoyed the respect of Ensenada, who held the Society of Jesus in high esteem and developed close ties with Rávago over time.

During this same period, the Madrid government focused on defending the Texas frontier. Given the deep mistrust of Versailles shared by Carvajal and Ensenada, and the aggressive westward posture assumed by the French from Louisiana, the weak Texas frontier protecting the northern flank of New Spain's mines demanded attention.[44] Ensenada mounted two separate expeditions to consolidate Spanish positions north of the Mexican silver mines. One, under Colonel José de Escandón y Helguera, established New Santander on the rim of the Gulf of Mexico just below the Río Grande. The effort, largely funded by local entrepreneurs between 1748 and 1755, sponsored an extensive colonization program transferring hundreds of families from neighboring areas under military protection. Paralleling the decline in the influence of the regular orders, the program reflected a fundamental emphasis on secular solutions in strategic areas, and it clearly deemphasized the mission as an instrument to advance and to protect the frontier.[45]

To block French penetration into Texas, the crown sponsored three Franciscan missions located on the San Gabriel River well above San Antonio, established between 1746 and 1751. Under the command of Captain Felipe de Rávago, the nephew of the king's confessor, a presidio backed these

[42] Antonio Álvarez de Morales, "Los proyectos de reforma del ejército del conde de Aranda," in Javier Alvarado Planas and Regina María Pérez Marcos, eds., *Estudios sobre ejército, política y derecho en España (siglos XII-XX)* (Madrid: Ediciones Polifemo, 1996), pp. 154–60.

[43] Castellano, *Gobierno y poder*, pp. 147–49.

[44] As Ensenada counseled Ferdinand, "Although it may be advantageous to negotiate a treaty with her [France] ... prudence dictates that one proceed with care, taking precautions for all that might develop .... Add to this placing all the frontier strongpoints on their best defensive footing." Ensenada, "representación dirigida ... sobre el estado del Real Erario, y sistema y método para el futuro," Aranjuez, June 18, 1747, in Rodríguez Villa, *Don Cenón de Somodevilla*, p. 61.

[45] David J. Weber, *Indios Bárbaros: Spaniards and Their Savages in the Age of Enlightenment* (New Haven: Yale University Press, 2005), pp. 105–07; Patricia Osante, "Colonization and Control: The Case of Nuevo Santander," in Jesús F. de la Teja and Ross Frank (eds), *Choice, Persuasion, and Coercion: Social Control on Spain's North American Frontiers* (Albuquerque: University of New Mexico Press, 2005), pp. 231–35, and Patricia Osante, *Orígenes del Nuevo Santander (1748–1772)* (Mexico City: Universidad Nacional Autónoma de México, 1997), chaps. 3–4.

missions, bearing the name of a famed Jesuit, San Francisco Xavier.[46] A plan subsequently devised by Felipe's uncle Pedro later transferred the presidio to a more advantageous location farther west, on the San Sabá River. Accompanied by a mission established to minister to the Apaches, this strongpoint, San Luis de las Amarillas, would be the farthest penetration north in west central Texas.[47] While in an earlier time missionaries bore the principal thrust of frontier expansion, in an increasingly secular age where military concerns were involved, missionaries now followed soldiers, playing a secondary role.[48]

This initiative paralleled developments in northern South America, where the Spanish, under orders from Carvajal, aimed to close off expansion of the French in Guayana and the Dutch in Surinam, both centers of contraband into Venezuela. Indeed, during the uprising of Francisco León, the rebels received arms from the Dutch. Consequently, the Minister of State planned Spanish settlements to block further foreign penetration, a program that eventually bore fruit after his death.[49]

After war's end, the central question confronting Spain's ministers concerned the commercial deregulation of the historic system of *Flotas* and *Galeons*, and both Ensenada and Carvajal inclined toward greater trade liberalization. Urgencies of war had permitted Ensenada to abandon the convoy system in favor of using individual register ships in the transatlantic trade, and the Treaty of Madrid, which ended the British ships of permission, also opened the door diplomatically to greater commercial deregulation. During the period after the peace settlements, the ministers continued relying on register ships rather than reestablishing the fleet system. Facilitating greater marketing flexibility, this tactic represented a substantial step toward dismantling the constraints imposed under the Project of 1720. Moreover, the opening of the Cape Horn route to the Pacific region of South America, which paralleled the suspension of the *Galeones*, opened up great commercial opportunities.[50]

---

[46] Felipe hailed from the same *montañés* village as Francisco. Donald E. Chipman, "New Light on Felipe de Rábago y Terán, *The Southwestern Historical Quarterly*, 111 (Oct. 2007), pp. 161–63.

[47] Robert S. Weddle, *The San Sabá Mission: Spanish Pivot in Texas* (Austin: University of Texas Press, 1964), pp. 30–60. Pedro Rábago died before implementing the plan, and was replaced by Colonel Diego Ortiz Parrilla. Felipe's career had been derailed by criminal charges brought against him by the Franciscan missionaries. Details on the presidio can be found in Bennett R. Kimbell, "El Baluarte del Sur: Archeological and Historical Investigations of the Southeast Bastion at Presidio San Sabá ..." *Bulletin of the Texas Archeological Society*, 81 (2010), pp. 1–102.

[48] José Manuel Serrano Álvarez and Allan J. Kuethe, "La Texas colonial entre Pedro de Rivera y el marqués de Rubí: Aportaciones económicas al sistema presidial," *Colonial Latin American Historical Review*, 14 (2008), pp. 281–311.

[49] Delgado, *El proyecto político*, p. 95; Manuel Lucena Giraldo, *Laboratorio tropical: La expedición de límites al Orinoco, 1750–1767* (Madrid: Consejo Superior de Investigaciones Científicas, 1993), pp. 87–92, 188–96.

[50] Antonio García-Baquero González, *Cádiz y el Atlántico (1717–1778)*, I (Sevilla: Escuela de Estudios Hispano-Americanos, 1976), p. 268.

As Ensenada described his strategy: "I sought to destroy the monopolistic attitude produced by the restrictions on commerce with America, establishing the ships called registers, that arrived there independently from the *Flotas* and *Galeones.*"[51] Carvajal agreed on the need to adjust colonial commercial policy, but he was inclined to favor an ambitious expansion of the number and role of privileged trading companies.[52] Regardless of the tactic employed, the ministers favored curtailing the monopoly privileges of the *Consulado* of Cádiz encoded in the Project of 1720.

Although this reliance on register ships led to a quickening of commercial activity, particularly following the ending of hostilities (see Figure 4.1), the *Consulados* of Cádiz, Mexico City, and Lima had lobbied hard for the restoration of the fleet system.[53] Guild members argued that the reliance on register ships had caused great damage to the proper conduct of colonial trade.[54] While the interests of the American guilds commonly differed from those of Cádiz, they remained united on preserving their monopoly rights within a restored convoy system.[55] The *Consulado* of Cádiz had produced a 300,000-peso "donation" in 1749, which members evidently believed entitled them to leverage with the Madrid government, but Ensenada coldly instructed the guild that its position was not "to discuss nor propose policy for navigation and the manner to supply the dominions of America [but to] facilitate the means to make the commerce of these and those kingdoms flourish."[56]

The Marqués de la Ensenada faced great political risks in attempting to break the historic monopoly of the *Consulado* of Cádiz, and he proceeded carefully. He first transferred the responsibility for licensing register ships to the *vía reservada* in Madrid, a prerogative that had belonged to the *Casa de la Contratación* in Cádiz. Those licenses represented a dangerous diminution of the port city's role in the transatlantic trade and of the guild's ability to influence the choice of who conducted this commerce. In addition, during the war several ships departed from ports other than Cádiz, calling into question the permanency of its monopoly.[57] Against strong opposition

---

[51] Ensenada, "Estado de las cosas . . . .," San Lorenzo, November 15, 1749, in Rodríguez Villa, *Don Cenón de Somodevilla*, pp. 77–79.

[52] Delgado, *El proyecto político*, pp. 163, 167–69, 176–87; Josep M. Delgado, "La paz de los siete años (1750–1757) y el inicio de la reforma del comercio colonial español," *1802: España entre dos siglos de ciencia y economía* (Madrid: Sociedad Estatal de Conmemoraciones Culturales, 2003), p. 323–24.

[53] García-Baquero, *Cádiz y el Atlántico*, I, p. 546.

[54] File, protests of Cádiz and Mexico, 1750–1754, AGI, Mexico, leg. 2980.

[55] Geoffrey J. Walker, *Spanish Politics and Imperial Trade, 1700–1789* (Bloomington: Indiana University Press, 1979), pp. 205–207.

[56] Royal order, Madrid, June 22, 1749, AGI, IG, leg. 2304. Quoted in Allan J. Kuethe, "El fin del monopolio: Los Borbones y el consulado andaluz," in Enriqueta Vila Vilar and Kuethe, eds., *Relaciones de poder y comercio colonial* (Sevilla: Consejo Superior de Investigaciones Científicas, 1999) p. 49.

[57] Kuethe, "El fin del monopolio," pp. 48–49.

from Cádiz, the crown issued a royal order on June 20, 1749, giving American merchants the right to send funds to Spain to purchase commodities directly.[58] This allowed commercial interests in Callao and Buenos Aires, in particular, to bypass the *Consulado* and develop close ties with mercantile houses in Spain, making them less wedded to restoring the *Galeones*.

While these changes slowly undermined the monopoly privileges of Cádiz, Ensenada was prepared to go much further. In his report to Ferdinand on the state of the affairs under his jurisdiction, dated November 15, 1749, he made his preferences clear once again, recommending that "licenses be issued to all who request them to go with Spanish ships."[59] This assertion clearly indicates Ensenada's thinking about the direction of commercial reform.

Despite the prevalence of reformist tracts at court, the thinking of Ensenada and other influential ministers does not appear to be overly influenced by the works of *proyectistas* from this period. Descendants of the *arbitristas* of the preceding century, they flooded the court with "projects" or essays promoting innovations of one sort or another, many advancing formulas to resolve the dilemma of colonial commerce.[60] Although these random essays drifting into court may have reinforced the ideas of men such as Ensenada or Carvajal on the issues of the day and how to address them, they had little direct influence over government policies. *Proyectistas* were usually self-promoters, often seeking appointments or personal improvements as the result of their Panglossian expositions. Most pieces contained little that was truly original or even innovative.[61] The Conde de Fernán-Núñez, an insider at court who had little respect for these operators, described them as

people, who ordinarily are called *proyectistas* and who scrutinize the disposition of the ministers, only seek[ing] the means to adapt to their ideas in order to make their fortunes, without concern for the means nor the public harm that their ventures might occasion.[62]

The Spanish minister in Rome, Cardinal Joaquín-María Portocarrero, for example, forwarded to Ensenada a project concocted by an influential nobleman advocating a system of floating batteries to defend Spain's *plazas fuertes*. He asked for Ensenada's comments as a personal favor; but he hastened to explain, with some embarrassment, "I know very well what *proyectos* are and that they are worth little or nothing."[63]

---

[58] Walker, *Spanish Politics and Imperial Trade*, p. 218.

[59] Ensenada, "Estado de las cosas . . . .," San Lorenzo, November 15, 1749, in Rodríguez Villa, *Don Cenón de Somodevilla*, p. 79.

[60] The *proyecto* replaced the *árbitro*. For a useful analysis of this transition, see Delgado, *El proyecto político*, pp. 43–52.

[61] Delgado, *El proyecto político*, p. 45.

[62] Quoted in Escudero, *Los orígenes*, p. 291.

[63] Cardinal Portocarrero to Ensenada, Rome, May 7, 1750, AGS, Marine, leg. 712. The project did not impress Ensenada.

Not all such projects were dismissed or necessarily doomed to failure. A decade later José de Gálvez, then a young lawyer in Madrid, engaged in *proyectismo* with a tract outlining a reformist agenda for the colonies, which seems to have been of some use to him in securing the appointment as visitor general to New Spain (see Chapter 7).[64] Such works usually carried little weight, however, in the day-to-day evolution of Spanish commercial policy at court.

At the same time, even some government ministers served as *proyectistas* from time to time, writing ministerial position papers addressing the pressing issues of the day. In an age when the regalist, bureaucratic state was establishing its imperatives, both Ensenada and Carvajal penned lengthy, detailed, and almost formulaic tracts concerning a wide variety of topics.[65] Even the famous *Nuevo sistema* of Campillo y Cossío should be seen within this context. Unlike the pessimism of the previous century, however, these *proyectos* conveyed an underlying sense of optimism, an enlightened faith in progress through reason. These tracts were intended for a small audience, certainly not the public, and they were calculated to sway the royal cabinet and His Majesty himself.

In May 1750, Ensenada summoned six leaders from the *Consulado* of Cádiz to study and propose to His Majesty "all the means conducive to make it (commerce) flourish, to secure its growth, and to ensure its utility to the Royal Service and the common good of his vassals and the individuals of commerce both in Spain and America."[66] These men were selected from a list of names provided in a confidential report by José Banfi y Parrilla, acting on instructions he received from Ensenada through the president of the *Casa de la Contratación*, Francisco Varas y Valdés. Banfi reported that the wealthy families in the *Consulado* numbered some forty or fifty and that an irreconcilable hatred arising from a conflict of interest over foreign commissions divided the members from Cádiz into two groups, *españoles antiguos* and *jenízaros*. Most of the *jenízaros* were of French descent and had entered the guild after the membership reform imposed by Campillo y Cossío in 1742.[67] Ensenada invited four representatives from Cádiz, only one of them a *jenízaro*, and he added another from Seville and one from Jerez de la

---

[64] Luis Navarro García, "El primer proyecto reformista de José de Gálvez," in *Homenaje al Dr. José Antonio Calderón Quijano* (Seville: Escuela de Estudios Hispano-Americanos, 1997), pp. 387–402. A copy can be found in the Biblioteca del Palacio, Miscelánea de Ayala, vol. 1.

[65] For Ensenada, Rodríguez Villa, *Don Cenón de Somodevilla* contains an excellent sample. José Miguel Delgado has treated the writings of Carvajal in *El proyecto político* and in *José de Carvajal y Lancáster: Testamento político o idea de un gobierno católico (1745)* (Córdoba: Universidad de Córdoba, 1999).

[66] Royal order, Buen Retiro, September 14, 1750, AGI, IG, leg. 2304.

[67] For a detailed exploration of this rivalry, see Margarita García-Mauriño Mundi, *La pugna entre el Consulado de Cádiz y los jenízaros por las exportaciones a Indias (1720–1765)* (Sevilla: Universidad de Sevilla, 1999).

Frontera. This distribution reflected the relative weight economically and politically of the three divisions of the *Consulado's* leadership.

The intransigence of the mercantile elite quickly became evident, as most of the *Consulado* members of the committee tried to avoid serving on the junta. All but two found justifications to beg exemptions because of advanced age, fragile health, and in one case (the sole *jenízaro*) wedding plans, while one of the other two men died. While it is impossible to know the actual condition of those pleading physical incapacity, Varas y Váldes surely thought they could all make the trip. Ensenada refused to excuse two of the four, but when he sought replacements for the other two, at least four others attempted to avoid the call.[68] In the end, the impatient Ensenada could not assemble the merchant junta until September.

Ensenada's instructions to the gathering made his intentions clear: "His Majesty's will is that the freedom to conduct this commerce not be limited nor inhibited under the label of monopoly nor any other, as he wishes that it be equal for all of his vassals who have the means to handle it."[69] Not surprisingly, leaving their internal squabbles aside, the six *andaluces* closed ranks against the reformist threat to their historic privileges. While differing in details, all of the opinions urged the restoration of the fleet system and the suppression of register ships.[70] The group resolved that the *Flota* to New Spain should resume in 1753, and some time thereafter the *Galeones* should be restored. Only Alonso García of Cádiz dissented, favoring the abolition of both the *Galeones* and the *tercio*, the privilege that afforded local Andalusian producers one-third of the shipping space on the fleets for agricultural produce, which he considered an onerous obligation for the shippers.[71]

The crown also called a series of special juntas to assess the means to impede British intrusions into Central America to procure dyewood, curtail Dutch smuggling along the Spanish Main, and combat contraband in the Indies, including the prescription of a proper policy for the Spanish coastguard.[72] The committee dealing with contraband and the coastguard met in the residence of Sebastián de Eslava, where it deliberated over several meetings in 1753. On April 19, 1754, the group issued an ordinance to govern the activities of Spanish corsairs. In its findings, the junta made plain its conviction that the basic problem was the outmoded fleet system operating the colonial trade. In a separate *dictamen*, Armada Captain José de Iturriaga y Aguirre went further,

---

[68] File, nominations for the junta of experts, May–September, 1750, AGI, IG, leg. 2304.
[69] Royal order, Buen Retiro, September 14, 1750, AGI, IG, leg. 2304. The members included Nicolás Macé (*jenízaro*), Alonso García, Andrés de Loyo, Nicolás Basto, Manuel Clemente Rodríguez Raquejo (Seville), and Jacinto Barrios (Puerto de Santa María). Barrios replaced the nominee from Jerez, who had managed to elude the call.
[70] File, junta of the six individuals from Cádiz, Madrid, 1750, AGI, Mexico, leg. 2980.
[71] Opinion, Alonso García, ibid.
[72] Reports, select juntas, Madrid, May 24 and July 4, 1752, AGS, GM, leg. 6799.

calling directly for an end to the Cádiz monopoly as well as the reduction of tax rates and a rationalization of inspection procedures and paperwork.[73]

Iturriaga's opinion carried great weight. An officer who held his own with the best, he had served as the first director of the Caracas Company and was no friend of Cádiz. A confidant of Ensenada, he held a commanding presence in the several juntas assembled by the great minister. Moreover, his expertise on Venezuela would lead Carvajal to name him to the triumvirate leading the boundary commission he had established to collaborate with the Portuguese in defining the limits between the two powers in the Orinoco basin.[74] This was the recommendation that Ensenada had long awaited; the stage had now been set for important commercial reforms.

While Ensenada advanced his agenda for commercial reorganization, he made limited but important advances in administrative and revenue reform. In 1749, he reestablished the system of provincial intendants in Spain. As early as 1746, Ensenada had asked the viceroys of New Spain and Peru for opinions on introducing the intendant system into their kingdoms. Revillagigedo cautioned that "I believe that the establishment of intendants would be very damaging here, much more so than what is beneficial for these kingdoms."[75] Although this advice apparently occasioned second thoughts, a Royal *cédula* of June 30, 1751 established a superintendancy in New Spain.[76]

During this same period, a profound but subtle transformation began when the crown ceased selling appointments to high judicial offices in the American bureaucracy. Concurrently, the crown phased out the systematic sale of special exemptions, such as the right to marry locally. The perennially strapped monarchy had begun selling treasury offices in 1633, followed by *corregimientos* in 1678, and even appointments to the colonial high courts, the audiencias of the Indies in 1687.[77] Despite the obvious loss of royal authority over these venal office holders, the urgencies of war finance inevitably frustrated efforts to

---

[73] File, junta celebrated in the residence of Sebastián Eslava, AGS, Guerra Moderna, leg. 6799. See also Lucio Mijares Pérez, "Programa político para América del marqués de la Ensenada," *Revista de historia de América*, no. 81 (Madrid January-June 1976), pp. 87–93, 101–17. Iturriaga held the appointment of rear admiral. Other members included Councilor of the Indies Marqués de la Regalía and Fiscal Manuel Pablo Salcedo; Vice Admiral Joaquín de Aguirre, who had recently completed two volumes of ordinances for the armada and was finishing a third; and Lieutenant General Benito Antonio de Spínola.

[74] Lucena Giraldo, *Laboratorio tropical, pp. 105–106*; Montserrat Gárate Ojanguren, *La Real Compañía Guipuzcoana de Caracas* (San Sebastián: Grupo Doctor Camino de Historia Donostiarra : Sociedad Guipuzcoana de Ediciones y Publicaciones, 1990), pp. 56–57.

[75] Navarro García, *Las reformas borbónicas*, pp. 33, 55.

[76] Horst Pietschmann, *Las reformas borbónicas y el sistema de intendencias en Nueva España: Un estudio político administrativo* (México: Fondo de Cultura Económica, 1996), p. 135. German edition 1972.

[77] Mark A. Burkholder and D. S. Chandler, *From Impotence to Authority: The Spanish Crown and the American Audiencias, 1687–1808* (Columbia: University of Missouri Press, 1977), esp. pp. 15–18, 83–98; Kenneth J. Andrien, "The Sale of Fiscal Offices and the Decline of

end the controversial practice. Now, with the prospects of a new era of neutrality and peace, the crown could cease selling colonial judicial appointments, a policy that had concerned reformers and conservatives alike since the previous century. This step, however, raised alarms in America where elite society had become accustomed to placing its sons on the courts, or marrying its daughters to Spanish judges, and it would remain a sore point between Madrid and America throughout the second half of the century.

In the area of revenue reform, an important step came with the extension of the Royal Tobacco Monopoly to Peru in 1752, Chile in 1753, and Upper Peru and Buenos Aires in 1755. Formalized by ordinance in 1759, this appearance of the monopoly differed from Cuba because it was oriented toward local consumption rather than export to the factory in Seville. Although profits were small initially, the enterprise held great promise for the future.[78] Viceroy Conde de Revillagigedo blocked a similar initiative for Mexico, however, arguing as he had for intendancies, that such a step would entail too many risks politically.[79]

The Madrid government sponsored another fiscal reform in 1751, legalizing the notorious forced distributions of goods by Spanish rural magistrates to the indigenous communities in Peru and New Spain, the *repartimiento de comercio* (or *repartimiento de mercancías* or *reparto*). In Peru the local *corregidores de indios* worked with merchant suppliers to provide mules and European merchandise to indigenous communities, who were forced to purchase the animals or goods at prices set by the magistrates.[80] In the *Noticias secretas*, Juan and Ulloa wrote that the system was fraught with abuses, as the *corregidores* forced the Andeans to consume inferior merchandise at highly inflated prices.[81] In New Spain, local *alcaldes mayores* sometimes distributed goods to indigenous communities, but in southern New Spain (from Oaxaca and Yucatán to

Royal Authority in the Viceroyalty of Peru, 1633–1700," HAHR, 62 (February 1982), pp. 49–71; Alberto Yalí Román, "Sobre alcaldías mayores y corregimientos en Indias," *Jahrbuch für Geschichte von Staat, Wirtschaft, und Geselschaft Lateinamerikas*, 9 (1974), pp. 1–39.

78 John R. Fisher, "El estanco del tabaco en el Perú borbónico," in Agustín González Enciso and Rafael Torres Sánchez (eds.), *Tabaco y economía en el siglo XVIII* (Pamplona: Ediciones Universidad de Navarra, 1999), pp. 42–45; Guillermo Céspedes del Castillo, "La renta del tabaco en el virreinato del Perú," *Revista histórica*, no. 21 (1954), pp. 7–10.

79 Susan Deans-Smith, *Bureaucrats, Planters, and Workers: The Making of the Tobacco Monopoly in Bourbon Mexico* (Austin: University of Texas Press, 1992), pp. 9–10.

80 Alfredo Moreno Cebrián, *El Corregidor de indios y la economía peruana en el siglo XVIII* (Madrid: Consejo Superior de Investigaciones Científicas, 1977), passim; idem "Fiscalidad, connivencia, corrupción y adecuacción al mercado: La regulación del comercio provincial en México y Peru," in Enriqueta Vila Vilar and Allan J. Kuethe, *Relaciones de poder y comercio colonial* (Sevilla: Escuela de Estudios Hispano-Americanos, 1999), pp. 227–75.

81 Jorge Juan and Antonio de Ulloa, *Discourse and Political Reflections on the Kindoms of Peru, Their Government, Special Regimen of Their Inhabitants and Abuses Which have Been Introduced into One and Another, with Special Information on Why They Grew Up and Some Means to Avoid Them*, ed. with intro. by John J. TePaske and trans. by John J. TePaske and Besse A. Clement (Norman: University of Oklahoma Press, 1978), pp. 77–86.

Nicaragua) the magistrates advanced money and credit to indigenous communities for local produce (most famously for cochineal dye).[82] The cochineal
was later sold to cloth producers in New Spain or to merchants who shipped
the dye to Europe.[83] Although the situation was apparently less exploitative in
New Spain than Peru, the whole system was unregulated and the magistrates
paid no sales tax (*alcabala*) on the transactions.

When he arrived in Peru, the Conde de Superunda wrote Madrid asking
for the legalization of the *repartimientos* and for the formation of lists
(*aranceles*) of approved goods and prices to govern the actions of local
corregidores. The Council of the Indies opposed the move, arguing that
the practice was illegal and should be suppressed. For his part, Superunda
contended that the *repartimiento* was impossible to suppress; it would be
best to legalize, tax, and regulate the practice.[84] The crown finally relented
and ordered the formation of *juntas de aranceles* in both Peru and New
Spain on March 9, 1751. The Peruvian committee completed its work and
sent its *arancel* for the *repartimiento* in 1754, but the Mexican committee
never finished the task.[85] Making an *arancel* that set fixed interest rates for
credit advanced to induce the production of cochineal was simply not
necessary to avoid corruption, so while the *repartimiento* remained legal,
it remained virtually unregulated and untaxed. In the case of Peru, it also
proved difficult to regulate and tax the *repartimiento*, and so abuses persisted until the practice was abolished in 1781 in the wake of the Tupac
Amaru revolt.

THE DOWNFALL OF ENSENADA

The fall of Ensenada came abruptly on July 20, 1754. Given the power that he
had once wielded, and his seemingly omnipotent, indeed overbearing presence in the royal cabinet, his demise came with surprising ease. The dismissal
notice, signed by Ricardo Wall, stated that "The King has resolved to relieve
you of the positions and responsibilities that he has placed in your care, and
he orders you to proceed to the city of Granada, where you should remain

---

[82] Robert W. Patch, *Maya and Spaniard in Yucatán, 1648–1812* (Stanford: Stanford University Press, 1993), pp. 30–32.

[83] Jeremy Baskes, *Indians, Merchants, and Markets: A Reinterpretation of the Repartimiento and Spanish-Indian Economic Relations in Colonial Oaxaca, 1750–1821* (Stanford: Stanford University Press, 2000), pp. 39–61; idem, "Coerced or Voluntary? The Repartimiento and Market Participation of Peasants in Late Colonial Oaxaca," *Journal of Latin American Studies*, 28 (1996), 707–733; idem, "Colonial Institutions and Cross-Cultural Trade: Repartimiento, Credit, and Indigenous Production of Cochineal in Eighteenth-Century Oaxaca, Mexico," *Journal of Economic History*, 65:1 (March 2005), pp. 186–210.

[84] Moreno Cebrián, "Comercio provincial en México y Perú," pp. 235–36.

[85] Ibid., pp. 244–246; Baskes, *Indians, Merchants, and Markets*, pp. 42–44.

pending further instructions from His majesty."[86] Unlike the solicitous treatment accorded some previous ministers, Ensenada was taken from his home in the middle of the night, deposited in a waiting in coach, and escorted to his place of exile by the *alcalde de corte* and an officer of the palace guard, a procedure that suggests some degree of apprehension by Ferdinand VI and those who organized the coup.[87] The cursory dismissal of the once powerful Ensenada signaled the crown's rejection of his reform policies, designed to transform key aspects of the Spanish Atlantic empire.

Ensenada's position had begun to erode when he failed to determine the replacement for Carvajal y Lancaster, who had died suddenly on April 8. Afflicted by a frail disposition and apparently exhausted from chronic overwork, the Minister of State succumbed to an inflammation at age fifty-six.[88] Ensenada's nemeses were the British Ambassador Keene, who quite correctly saw the great minister and his reform policies as a threat to Britain's strategic and commercial interests in the Atlantic, and the Duke of Huéscar, formerly protected by Ensenada, who had become his personal enemy.[89] Born in Austria and embittered by the French during his stint at Versailles in the controversial final years of the war, the duke was determined to block any rapprochement between the Bourbon monarchs.[90] As heir to the Duke of Alba, Huéscar occupied a preeminent position at court that gave him direct access to the king. Governor of the royal household and first gentleman-in-waiting, he was also dean of the Council of State and grand chancellor of the Council of the Indies. Moreover, he was the leader of the grandees, who found Ensenada's reformist agenda offensive and threatening.[91]

An indolent but ambitious man, the duke had blocked Ensenada's hope to secure State either for one of his allies or for himself by persuading Ferdinand to grant him the interim appointment. Unlike his friend Carvajal, the duke would not condescend to accept a proprietary appointment. But with his access to the king, he was in a position to work his designs and plan the coup against Ensenada.[92]

[86] Wall to Ensenada, Buen Retiro, July 20, 1754, reproduced in Rodríguez Villa, *Don Cenón de Somodevilla*, pp. 196–97.

[87] José Antonio Escudero, *Los orígenes del Consejo de Ministros en España* (Madrid: Editoria Nacional, 1979), I, p. 219.

[88] He very frequently worked until two o'clock in the morning. José Miguel Delgado Barrado, *José de Carvajal y Lancáster: testamento político o idea de un gobierno católico* (Córdoba: Universidad de Córdoba, 1999), p. xxvi.

[89] For Ensenada's support of Huéscar as a young diplomat, see Ozanam, *La diplomacia de Fernando VI*, pp. 9–10.

[90] Escudero, *Los orígenes*, pp. 208–11.

[91] Gildas Bernard, *Le Secretariat d'État et le Conseil Espagnol des Indies (1700–1808)* (Geneva: Droz 1972), p. 212.

[92] Huéscar and Carvajal had maintained a lengthy correspondence. Ozaman, *La diplomacia de Fernando VI*.

Huéscar and Keene secured the active support of Ricardo Wall, who returned from London to assume the permanent appointment at State on May 15. To promote his own ambitions, Wall betrayed Ensenada, who had once befriended and protected him.[93] Among other things, Wall harbored personal resentment over the criticism that Ensenada had leveled at the treaty he had negotiated with London.[94] Over the years, the queen had shown high esteem for Ensenada, but when her choice came down to England or France she withdrew her long-time support for Ensenada. To make matters worse for Ensenada and Rávago, a complication intervened with the resistance of the Guaraní mission Indians in Paraguay over the transfer of seven Jesuit reductions to Portugal as the 1750 boundary settlement had stipulated. That resistance fired sentiment against the order and its supporters at court, and the controversy alienated Queen Barbara.[95] Wall was known for his antipathy toward the Jesuits.[96]

The final issue that enabled the coup to proceed came with allegations from London that Ensenada, on his own authority, had ordered military action against the British dyewood outposts along the Mosquito Coast and in Honduras. As Keene, who had supplied London with the "information," stood in the shadows, Huéscar and Wall eagerly showed the charges to the monarchs. "We are at war without knowing it," exclaimed an exasperated Ferdinand.[97]

With Wall as preeminent minister in the cabinet, Ferdinand replaced Ensenada with three different people. Juan de Gaona y Portocarrero, who was the Conde de Valparaíso, the secretary and first equerry of the queen, and a leader of the grandees, received Finance. Sebastián de Eslava, captain general of the army, took the Ministry of War, while Julián de Arriaga, rear admiral of the Royal Armada, received Marine. The king divided the Secretariat of Marine and the Indies, which had grown too large to be administered as a single unit. As an extension of that action, the presidency of the *Casa de la Contratación* and the Marine Intendancy, united since 1717, were separated institutionally.[98] Wall took the Indies and snatched control of Marine's finances.[99] He later relinquished the Secretariat for the Indies, and

[93] Rodríguez Villa, *Don Cenón de Somodevilla*, pp. 185–87. Orendain, it will be recalled, betrayed Grimaldo. See Chapter 2.

[94] Duras to Saint Contest, Aranjuez, May 16, 1753, AAE:CPE, vol. 513, fols. 390–98.

[95] José Luis Gómez Urdáñez, *El proyecto reformista de Ensenada* (Lérida: Milenio,1996), pp. 129–30. For a succinct description of this incident, see John Lynch, *Bourbon Spain, 1700–1808* (Oxford: Basil Blackwell, 1989), pp. 179–82.

[96] Téllez Alarcia, *El ministerio Wall*, pp. 34–35.

[97] Gómez Urdáñez, *El proyecto reformista*, pp. 126–47.

[98] Gildas Bernard, "La Casa de la Contratación de Sevilla, luego de Cádiz en el siglo XVIII," *Anuario de Estudios Americanos*, 12 (1959), pp. 4–5.

[99] María Baudot Monroy, *"Julián de Arriaga y Rivera: Una vida al servicio de la Marina"* (Ph.D. diss., Universidad Nacional de Educación a Distancia, 2010), pp. 483–87.

Ferdinand added that office to Arriaga's duties. Nevertheless, the Indies and Marine remained distinct entities administratively. Finally, Alonso Muñiz remained at Grace and Justice.[100]

Completing the palace revolution, Rávago departed Madrid in the fall. While his close ties to Ensenada had obviously compromised the Jesuit's position, his customary political role could not have conformed to the new system, which consisted of six ministries divided among five equals.[101] It was surely no coincidence that the crown removed two *montañés* allies of the Jesuit confessor operating in northern New Spain. His nephew Captain Felipe de Rávago – at the presidio San Francisco Xavier in Texas – found himself deposed unceremoniously, while Colonel José de Escandón y Helguera, the commander of the expedition to New Santander, found himself subject to a lengthy investigation, eventually leading to his destitution.[102]

A knight of the Order of St. John of Jerusalem and a gentleman-in-waiting with access to the monarchs, Julián de Arriaga had risen through service in the armada. His prudent work during the period from 1749 to 1751 in suppressing the León revolt in Venezuela sealed his status within the administrative elite. In November, after his return from Caracas, Ensenada named him president of the *Casa de la Contratación* and intendant of marine, replacing the aged Francisco Varas y Valdés.[103] Despite his long friendship with Ensenada, the *bailío* was not an original thinker nor committed to reform, but he commanded universal respect for his personal rectitude.[104]

The English were undoubtedly the big winners in the palace revolution. Indeed, Ferdinand was so pleased with Ambassador Keene that, when London awarded him the Order of the Bath, he personally presented the award. Meanwhile, the ambassador triumphantly gloated to London, now "they will build no more ships in Spain."[105] The French, finding themselves isolated in the face of a mounting British threat in the Americas, sullenly realized the full extent of their losses, although it is not at all clear that Versailles ever realized its own responsibility for the downfall of Ensenada.[106] Queen Barbara promoted moderation so that Spain would not lean too heavily toward London.[107] Wall maintained Carvajal's policy of neutrality, just as clashes between the British and French forces west of the Appalachians erupted.

[100] Escudero, *Los orígenes*, pp. 227–35.
[101] Castellano, *Gobierno y poder*, pp. 156–57.
[102] Weddle, *The San Sabá Mission*, p. 34; Osante, *Orígenes*, pp. 251–55.
[103] Royal *cedula*, Buen Retiro, November 23, 1751, AGI, IG, leg. 545.
[104] For Arriaga's background, see María Baudot Monroy, "Orígenes familiares y carrera profesional de Julián de Arriaga, Secretario de Estado de Marina e Indias (1700–1776)," in *Espacio, tiempo, y forma, IV Series, Historia moderna*, 17 (2004), pp. 163–85.
[105] Gómez Urdáñez *El proyecto reformista.*, p. 128 and *Ferdinand VI*, pp. 111–12.
[106] *Memoire*, after the disgrace of Ensenada, July 1754, to September 1755, AAE: MDFDE, vol. 346, fols. 2–189.
[107] Escudero, *Los orígenes*, pp. 237–38.

THE END OF ATLANTIC REFORM

Not since the backlash against Alberoni had colonial policy changed course so abruptly, particularly regarding commercial modernization. Here the reaction against Ensenada was devastating for the reformist agenda. In 1752, when, as president of the Casa, Arriaga reflected on the future of the commercial system, he made plain his preferences:

All the evidence compels me to believe that it is a very opportune [time] to close the door on separate registers, and that the kingdom [New Spain] be supplied every two years with the number of tons of clothing and wares that are deemed necessary . . . . For, although it is held that in excessive abundance all lose, and that no one is obliged to trade in that which is unprofitable, it is most appropriate that the King, as father of all, prescribe rules that assuage this problem. [108]

On October 11, 1754, Arriaga responded to the clamoring from his friends in Cádiz and to the pleadings of the *Consulado* of Mexico by reestablishing the *Flota* to Veracruz. As the royal order stated: "His Majesty has resolved to suspend the system of individual registers and that in the future that kingdom [New Spain] should be supplied by means of *Flotas* departing on the first of June of 1756, without any [ships] leaving in the meantime, or afterwards, except the mercury ships."[109] The latter, however, only might carry agricultural products, not textiles. The last fleet had sailed before the War of Jenkins' Ear. Now Cádiz was authorized to send one every two years.[110] Although the first post-war *Flota* did not depart until 1758, a second followed after the prescribed two-year interlude.[111]

While the reestablishment of the convoy system to Veracruz represented a major gain, the *Consulado* lamented the crown's failure to restore the *Galeones* to serve South America. Ensenada actually began rebuilding Portobelo's fortifications in 1753, but for strategic reasons; he had no intention of resurrecting the *Galeones*.[112] In fact, the *Galeones* were simply beyond redemption. The Portobelo Fair of 1732 and the aborted fair of 1739 had failed miserably. Meanwhile, the stunning successes of the register ships rounding Cape Horn made it virtually impossible to consider reinstating the fleet system to South America (see Figure 4.1). Exports of silver, cacao, and cascarilla (a tree bark rich in quinine) to Spain increased markedly in the postwar years, as register ships exchanged Spanish wares for these Peruvian

---

[108] AGI, Mexico, leg. 2980. Quoted in Kuethe, "El fin del monopolio," p. 52.

[109] Royal order, San Lorenzo, October 11, 1754, AGI, Mexico, leg. 2980.

[110] File, protests of Cádiz and Mexico, 1750–1754, AGI, Mexico, leg. 2980

[111] José Joaquín Real Díaz, *Las ferias de Jalapa* (Sevilla: Escuela de Estudios Hispano-Americanos, 1959), pp. 96–97.

[112] Alfredo Castillero Calvo, "La fortificaciones," in *Historia general de Panamá*, I-2, ed. by Castillero Calvo (Panama City: Editorial Planeta de Agostini, 2004), pp. 45–48.

products.[113] Likewise, rising exports of silver, hides, and gold from Buenos Aires flowed to Spain in the period from 1749 to 1760, proving the utility of replacing the outmoded *Galeones* with individual licensed ship sailings.[114] Although competition from contraband traders in the Caribbean undercut the legal traffic in register ships to and from Cartagena, exports of silver, gold, and cacao remained at impressive levels in the post-war era.[115] Any return to the *Galeones* was simply impractical, given the successes of the register ships.

While Madrid retreated from commercial innovation following the downfall of Ensenada in 1754, creole merchants, finding flexibility on their own, embraced contraband trade, sailing directly to Jamaica or to the lesser islands to exchange specie for slaves and manufactured goods. This new smuggling pattern responded to a lessening of tensions following the Treaty of Madrid, as peaceful co-existence replaced suspicion and hostility. Over time, creoles took over from English merchants in Caribbean waters as the primary agents for illegal trade.[116] In 1766, London would attempt to exploit this turn of events by establishing a system of free ports in Jamaica and Dominica to lure customers from neighboring Spanish colonies. In other respects, continuity reigned during the 1750s. British dealers, protected under the privileges reaffirmed in the Treaty of Madrid, resumed their penetration of Cádiz, supplying a large portion of the merchandise carried on register ships, rivaling even the long-entrenched French.[117]

Wall's policy of neutrality attempted to limit the risk of war, lessening the need for aggressive military reforms. The establishment of the Fixed Battalion of Callao in 1753 marked the end of expansion in the regular army.[118] Despite his experience in Caratagena, Sebastián de Eslava pursued only a half-hearted approach to shoring up military fortifications in Havana and elsewhere in the Indies. In the area of shipbuilding, the frantic efforts of Ensenada to rebuild the armada slowed down, and a reversal in policy set in, well beyond the moderation that Carvajal had advocated. While work already underway continued, little new construction began. Wall controlled the navy budget, and he skimped on expenditures to hoard a handy surplus for the crown. The output of ships of the line dropped from fifteen in 1754 to thirteen in 1755, eight in 1756, three in 1757 and 1758, and two in 1759.[119]

---

[113] George Robertson Dilg, *"The Collapse of the Portobelo Fairs: A Study in Spanish Commercial Reform, 1720–1740"* (Unpublished Ph.D. diss., Indiana University, 1975), Appendix L.

[114] Ibid.

[115] Ibid.

[116] Adrian J. Pearce, *British Trade with Spanish America, 1763–1808* (Liverpool: Liverpool University Press, 2007), pp. 9–10, 29–30.

[117] Ibid., pp. 8–9.

[118] Álvarez de Morales, "Los proyectos de reforma," pp. 155.

[119] Cánovas, *La época de los primeros Borbones*, p. 466.

This policy reversal occurred against the ominous backdrop of a general war that would soon threaten the entire Spanish Atlantic world.[120]

While the reformist energy built by Ensenada dissipated in the 1750s, innovation did not halt completely. In 1755, the crown established the Barcelona Company to supply the islands of Santo Domingo, Puerto Rico, and Margarita, as well as Honduras and Guatemala on the mainland, and eventually it would also include Cumaná. Although Carvajal had long favored the establishment of such privileged trading companies, it was Eslava who championed the idea to ensure adequate supplies for the Caribbean peripheries and their defenses.[121]

Despite these modest innovations, the post-Ensenada government clearly lacked the quality of leadership exercised in the previous decade. With the secretaries of the ministries functioning autonomously, and State occupied by Wall, an outsider of questionable vision and ability, strong leadership failed to emerge.[122] In September 1757, a frustrated Wall even attempted to resign, but an apprehensive Ferdinand urged him to stay. Eslava became increasingly irascible and short-tempered with age, which only aggravated the climate at court.[123] This situation demanded strong leadership from the king, but the gentle, hesitant Ferdinand grew increasingly weak, especially when Barbara showed signs of deteriorating health. As a result, as hostilities escalated between the French and the British, Madrid was adrift politically, and neutrality was its only option.

On August 10, 1759, the reign ended tragically when Ferdinand VI died after a lengthy bout with depression that had lapsed into madness. Barbara, stricken by uterine cancer, had preceded him on August 27 of the previous year at Aranjuez, which touched off the king's mental and physical decline. After her death, Ferdinand retreated to Villaviciosa west of Madrid, refusing to leave or to see anyone except his physicians, and occasionally Wall. Despite abundant medication and regular bleedings, or perhaps because of them, he continued to deteriorate, and by February his case had become hopeless.[124] The king's reign, which had begun with such promise and with a flurry of

---

[120] At the same time, the senior officer corps in the navy was aging. In 1760, the Marqués de la Victoria, still the highest ranking Spanish naval officer, observed that "when seniority elevates them to rear admiral and from there to vice admiral, they are already at such an advanced age, with such fragile health or with a debilitating imbecility that they are best suited for a restful retirement than for service at sea, whose never fully appreciated functions justifiably demand men who are healthy, strong, robust and in the age of virility." Quoted in ibid., p. 479.

[121] José María Oliva Melgar, *Cataluña y el comercio privilegiado con América: La Real Compañía de Comercio de Barcelona a Indias* (Barcelona: Universitat de Barcelona, 1987), pp. 34–60; Mijares, "Programa político para América," pp. 121–22.

[122] For a moderately favorable assessments of Wall, see Delgado Rivas, "La paz de los siete años" and Téllez Alarcia, *El ministerio Wall.*

[123] Escudero, *Los orígenes,* pp. 240–42.

[124] Ibid., p. 243.

important imperial innovations ended with a conservative faction in power, which was uninterested in reform.

THE ACCESSION OF CHARLES III

Once it became evident that Ferdinand could not recover and that political opportunists threatened to take advantage of the vacuum at the top, on February 13, 1759, Charles empowered his mother to rule as regent in the event of his half-brother's death.[125] A reanimated Elizabeth prepared to govern Spain, a role that she had exercised on so many occasions during her husband's illnesses. This was her moment. Over the years, her faithful correspondence with Charles had consistently conveyed the hope that he might return to rule Spain and that she might herself regain prominence.[126] As she poignantly reminded Charles, "in the end, my son, I console myself in that, with God enabling me to see you, all will be clarified and be calmed; because you cannot cease being my son, nor I your mother."[127]

Elizabeth remained in reasonably good health, although her eyesight had faded, which she blamed on the mountain snow.[128] Waiting discreetly but impatiently at La Granja de San Ildefonso, she expressed deep concern to Charles as Ferdinand's illness lingered and court politics festered. Too make matters worse, Eslava died in June, while the Seven Years' War raged in Europe and America.[129] With Elizabeth's approval, Wall assumed responsibility for War on an interim basis.[130] Two days after Ferdinand's death, the dowager queen, now regent, issued a decree notifying all appropriate authorities of her empowerment, and she managed the monarchy until Charles arrived.[131] Nevertheless, the affairs of the Indies drifted aimlessly for some time. While Arriaga administered the ministry's routine affairs competently, he had no inclination to innovate during a critical interlude in colonial history.

With his wife, María Amalia of Saxony at his side, Charles arrived in Barcelona from Naples in October 1759 to claim his Spanish inheritance. Six children, including Carlos, the Prince of Asturias, accompanied him. He left two sons in Naples: his successor, Ferdinand IV, and the eldest, Felipe Pascual,

---

[125] Royal *pragmática* Caserta, February 13, 1759, AHN, Estado, leg. 2850.

[126] Anthony H. Hull, *Charles III and the Revival of Spain* (Washington, D.C.: University Press of America, 1981), pp. 85–86, 89–92. Elizabeth to Charles, February 5 and 26, 1759, AHN, Estado, leg. 2548.

[127] February 19, 1759, AHN, Estado, leg. 2548.

[128] Duras to Saint Contest, Aranjuez, May 16, 1753, AAE:CPE, vol. 513, vols. 390–98. The French ambassador had sought out a personal interview with the dowager queen.

[129] Elizabeth to Charles, San Ildefonso, April 30, May 7, June 27, July 9, and July 16, 1759, AHN, Estado, leg. 2548.

[130] Escudero, *Los orígenes*, p. 247.

[131] Wall to Arriaga, Buen Retiro, Buen Retiro August 13, 1759, with royal decree, San Ildefonso, August 12, 1759, AGI, IG, leg. 545.

who was incapacitated.[132] Charles brought with him a favorite advisor from Italy, Leopoldo di Grigorio, the Marqués de Esquilache, who had served him as Minister of Finance, War, and the Navy in Naples.[133] An unusual part of the entourage that transferred from Naples to Madrid was the Marquis d'Ossun, the French ambassador to the Two Sicilies. Charles had developed a close friendship with D'Ossun, and Versailles happily acceded to his request that it assign the diplomat to Madrid.[134]

When he reached court in December, Charles largely maintained the administration that he had inherited during the regency. He assigned Finance to Esquilache and removed Valparaíso from Madrid, naming him ambassador to Poland. He did not tamper with the rest of the cabinet.[135] Indeed, the new monarch expanded Wall's powers by making his appointment at War permanent. Although the minister did not share Charles's anti-British orientation, he had been active in preparing for his return to Spain, even before the gravely ill Ferdinand died. Moreover, Wall had served Elizabeth competently during her rule as regent.[136]

A native of Messina, Esquilache had humble origins, but he possessed a strong work ethic and held an intense loyalty for Charles. As a foreigner, he remained an unpopular figure who made few close friends at court. Spaniards thought his behavior coarse, and many believed that he thought and behaved more like an accountant than a courtier; indeed, the Sicilian lacked the conversational graces appropriate for fashionable chit-chat with the good-timers at court. Moreover, the Conde de Valparaíso, whom he had replaced, was a leader of the grandees along with Huéscar. The count's sudden death in February, before he could depart Madrid, led to even more bitterness against the Sicilian who had displaced him.[137]

The most tantalizing and controversial personnel development in the transition was the return of Ensenada. Charles lifted his exile and recalled him to court, where he arrived in May 1760.[138] In June, the king elevated Ensenada to counselor of State and placed him on a special junta monitoring the implementation of the Single Tax.[139] Ensenada's rehabilitation sent a strong signal that the new monarch had sympathy for a reformist agenda, and his return undoubtedly encouraged the beleaguered French. The return of

---

[132] Five daughters died in childhood. Pérez Samper, *Isabel de Farnesio*, pp. 470–71.
[133] The minister spelled his name "Squilache," but the Spanish insisted on adding the vowel.
[134] Hull, *Charles III*, p. 94.
[135] The illness of an infanta in Saragossa delayed the king's arrival. Escudero, *Los orígenes*, I, p. 269.
[136] Pérez Samper, *Isabel de Farnesio*, pp. 451–55.
[137] Escudero, *Los orígenes*, p. 277, 295, 304.
[138] Rodríguez Villa, *Don Cenón de Somodevilla*, pp. 206–209. Ferdinand had transferred the banished magistrate to Puerto de Santa María for reasons of health in 1757.
[139] Rodríguez Villa, *Don Cenón de Somodevila*, pp. 284–85; D'Ossun to Minister of State Duke of Choiseul, Madrid, June 23, 1760, AAE:CPE, vol. 528, fols. 385–87.

Ensenada also heartened loyalists seeking to advance their careers, and he had the support of a powerful insider, the Duke of Losada.[140] Naturally, those who had engineered his downfall, or who had benefitted from it were filled with apprehension.[141] Rumors first had it that Charles, who was much indebted to Ensenada personally for past services, would place him in the Secretariat for the Indies; then gossip had it to be State, and, finally, Marine.[142] This situation led the cabinet to close ranks in the face of a common threat, and Arriaga thereafter allied himself closely with Wall.[143] Charles wisely held Ensenada in reserve in case his services were required.[144] Once having been the "secretary of everything," as his friend Father José Francisco de Isla had described him, Ensenada would surely have had difficulty limiting his ambitions once inside Madrid's governing circle.[145]

Charles lost his beloved wife, María Amalia, during his first year in Spain, and Elizabeth then resumed her role as the dominant female at court. As she did so, Elizabeth could take great satisfaction in having placed her children in positions of influence. Against great odds, Charles was now king of Spain, while her grandson, Ferdinand IV, reigned as king in Naples. Philip ruled the Duchies of Parma and Plasencia and of Guastalla. María Ana Victoria was queen of Portugal and the youngest daughter, María Antonia, was positioned to become queen of Piedmont-Sardinia. Only the status of Louis, who now lingered at his brother's court, remained a problem.[146] Ill-suited for the cardinal's hat that Elizabeth had fitted for him, he had renounced the archbishoprics of Toledo and Seville in 1754, joining her at La Granja. He would remain a problem for years to come.[147] The new king held his mother in high esteem, and she remained an important source of counsel and support.[148]

Charles III placed commercial reform at the top of his personal agenda. He spoke of deregulation within a year of his arrival in Madrid, and the subject

---

[140] Escudero, *Los orígenes*, p. 274, 295–96.

[141] D'Ossun to Choiseul, Aranjuez, April 28, May 19, May 26, June 2, and June 9, 1760, AAE: CPE, vol. 528, fols. 199–204, 250–54, 290–94, 308–14, 340–50,

[142] D'Ossun to Choiseul, Aranjuez, June 5, and Madrid, June 23 and September 28, 1760, AAE: CPE, vol. 528, fols. 322–25, 385–87, and 529, fols. 295–300.

[143] Escudero, *Los orígenes*, I, pp. 274–75; D'Ossun to Choiseul, San Ildefonso, August 25, 1763, AAE, CPE, vol. 539, fols. 157–58.

[144] D'Ossun to Choiseul, Aranjuez, June 5, 1760, Madrid, June 23, 1760, AAE:CPE, vol. 528, fols. 322–25, 385–87.

[145] Quoted in Gómez Urdáñez, *El proyecto reformista*, p. 55.

[146] Pérez Samper, *Isabel de Farnesio*, pp. 420–25. Victor Amadeus would become king of Sardinia in 1773.

[147] Pérez Samper, *Isabel de Farnesio*, pp. 420–25. Over the years, he had served Elizabeth as a spy at court, and he had unsuccessfully attempted to visit Ferdinand during his fatal illness. For the attempted visit, see Escudero, *Los orígenes*, p. 243.

[148] D'Ossun to Choiseul, Madrid, September 18 and 28, 1760, AAE:CPE, vol. 529, fols. 265–72, 295–300.

remained very much on his mind into 1761.[149] As D'Ossun reported to Choiseul, "The King of Spain, sir, appears to me strongly inclined to facilitate the navigation of his subjects to the Indies and to shape a new system for that important matter, which has not been addressed for over 200 years."[150] The extent that Ensenada influenced Charles about commercial deregulation is unclear, although the king did consult him about colonial policy, and it is inconceivable that the subject did not arise. Soon, however, more pressing problems intervened as Spain became swept up into the Seven Years' War.

SPAIN AND THE SEVEN YEAR'S WAR

In America, the British war machine relentlessly rolled up victory after victory against France, which found itself isolated diplomatically. Louisbourg fell in 1758, and in September 1759, while Charles was still en route to Spain, James Wolfe scored his decisive victory at Quebec. The following year, the British occupied Montreal and subsequently extended their position in the west out to the Mississippi River. In the Caribbean, Guadeloupe had fallen easily to the British navy, while Martinique and St. Lucia would fall in early 1762. Such military calamities exposed the folly of favoring neutrality over collaboration with the French, and these defeats confronted Madrid with the unwelcome prospect of facing a bellicose and hegemonic Great Britain on its own.

Charles had few diplomatic alternatives. Acting through the increasingly discredited Ricardo Wall, the king sought to restore equilibrium through Spanish mediation, but London held the upper hand and was in no mood to be conciliatory.[151] Fearing that he would be left to face the British alone, Charles found himself drawn closer to Versailles.[152] These diplomatic and military priorities intervened to obstruct the new monarch's reformist agenda, as negotiations with France advanced through the spring and summer of 1761. Charles's mother also favored close ties with the French. Elizabeth had despised Carvajal, and she did not attempt to separate this animosity from his pro-British policies.[153]

On August 15, 1761, Charles took the fateful step of entering into the Third Family Compact, an offensive and defensive alliance. The Marqués de

[149] AAE:CPE, vol. 530. Madrid, January 12, 1761, AAE:CPE, vol. 531, fols. 25–41. Sources also cited in Allan Christelow, "French Interest in the Spanish Empire during the Ministry of the Duc de Choiseul, 1759–1771," *HAHR*, 21 (1941), pp. 394–406.

[150] D'Ossun to Choiseul, Aranjuez, June 5, and June 23, 1760, AAE:CPE, vol. 528, fols. 322–25, 385–87.

[151] For a French perspective on the Spanish position, see D'Ossun to Choiseul, Aranjuez, January 21, February 11, and June 9, 1760, AAE:CPE, vol. 527, fols. 91–101, 190–94, and vol. 528, fols. 340–50. For Wall's gradual awakening to reality and his disillusionment with British behavior, see Téllez Alarcia, *El ministerio Wall*, pp. 79–124.

[152] D'Ossun to Choiseul, Madrid, February 22, 1761, AAE:CPE, vol. 531, fols. 276–87.

[153] Duras to Saint Contest, Aranjuez, May 16, 1753, AAE:CPE, vol. 513, fols. 390–98.

Grimaldi, the Spanish ambassador to France, negotiated the pact.[154] Apart from the "perpetual" alliance proclaimed in the document, a secret agreement accompanied the compact. Its prologue and justification summarized eloquently the motives behind Spain's abandonment of the formerly promising strategy of neutrality:

All Europe should now recognize the danger to which maritime equilibrium is exposed in view of the ambitious operations of the British court and the despotism that it seeks to impose upon all the seas. The English Nation clearly shows through its behavior in this respect, especially over the past ten years, that it intends to make itself the absolute Master of [all] navigation and not permit others but a passive and dependent commerce. With this objective it began and sustains the present war with France, and likewise its Ministry has refused to restore the usurpations that the English have inflected upon the Spanish dominions in America, and by appropriating the exclusive privilege to fish cod, with other rights based only on a temporary tolerance. The Most Christian King sustains and will sustain the war, and the Catholic Monarch is resolved to fight in just opposition to these prideful pretenses if the British court does not accept the peace that the Most Christian King offers it on reasonable terms, and if the well founded grievances of the Catholic Monarch are not satisfied properly. And in order to coordinate their respective peace negotiations, or if upon confronting irreconcilable differences with the English [they must] unite their forces against them, it has become advisable to establish a specific Convention [and] at the same time, girded by present realities, to establish a perpetual Family Compact.

The allies promised to cooperate militarily and diplomatically and to refrain from seeking a separate peace. Should the British not have acceded to French peace initiatives by May 1, 1762, Spain pledged to declare war. If the British declared war on Spain before May 1, the same treaty agreements would apply.[155]

Apart from its concern about the shifting balance of power in America, Madrid harbored specific grievances that had developed during the 1750s despite its efforts to maintain neutrality. The British had contested Spain's historic fishing rights on the Newfoundland Banks, and they had continued their wood cutting incursions into Central America. Moreover, during the present war, they had all too frequently found pretexts to seize Spanish shipping. Charles was also determined to strike a blow against British contrabandists trading with his possessions in the Indies. The French solemnly promised to support Madrid's claims on all these issues.[156]

The king had hoped that Spanish support for France might induce the British to negotiate an acceptable settlement. It did not. Instead, the Spanish

---

[154] Charles III to Louis XV, El Pardo, January 14, 1761, AAE:CPE, vol. 531, fol. 54. Grimaldi had risen in the diplomatic corps under Ensenada. See Chapter 7.

[155] Secret Convention, August 15, 1761, AAE:CPE, vol. 533, fols. 290–301.

[156] These issues arose repeatedly in the discussions between Madrid and Versailles in 1761. See, for example, D'Ossun to Choiseul, Madrid, January 26 and February 14, 1761, AAE:CPE, vol. 531, fols. 87–95 and 242–47 and Pearce, *British Trade with Spanish America*, p. 30.

empire provided fresh, inviting targets for renewed British expansion. Spain was prepared to fight another War of Jenkins' Ear, but the military balance of power in 1761 had shifted greatly in favor of Great Britain. While the British had become much stronger, Spanish rearmament in America had not made comparable strides. The garrisons of the colonial *plazas fuertes* were too few to resist the power of Britain's war machine. The armada had stagnated following the exile of Ensenada. When Charles took the throne, he found only fifty-eight ships of the line in the fleet, and only forty-nine of them were serviceable. That was not enough.[157] By this time, the French fleet had suffered losses, and the combined Franco-Spanish fleet could not resist British sea power. Moreover, Americans were not yet meaningfully involved in the challenge of defense. Fearful of the implications of a French collapse in America, Charles exposed his empire to severe risk, and he paid the price.

The British declaration of war came on January 4, 1762. Within six months, a massive British force of 200 warships and transports carrying an invasion army of 14,000 men appeared off Havana. In the autumn of 1760, Charles had dispatched Brigadier General Juan de Prado Portocarrero and the French engineer Colonel Francisco Ricaud to Havana. He had personally consulted with both men to impress upon them the urgency of their assignments – the installation of fortifications upon the Cabaña heights overlooking the Morro Castle, which defended the entrance to the harbor along with the Punta, an artillery battery on the western side. The Cabaña had long been identified as a weak spot in Havana's defenses, but at this late date little could be done. Labor was in short supply and, to make matters worse, yellow fever stuck during the summer of 1761, claiming Ricaud among its victims.[158] Arriaga and Wall sent reinforcement battalions from the regiments of Spain and Aragon, the same units that had fought at Cartagena a generation earlier, but the epidemic severely weakened their numbers along with those of the fixed garrison. When the invasion came, Havana possessed only some 2,330 troops.[159] On the water, the defenders had twelve ships of the line and six frigates, a force that amounted to nearly one-third of the entire Spanish Armada.[160]

Although Governor Prado initially dismissed the approaching British force as the Jamaican sugar fleet sailing for England, the Red Coats began landing at Cojímar to the east of Havana on June 7. The invaders easily occupied the exposed Cabaña heights the following day. The battle that followed lasted for two long, brutal months before Governor Prado capitulated. The key episode

---

[157] William Coxe, *Memoirs of the Kings of Spain of the House of Bourbon, from the Accession of Philip the Fifth to the Death of Charles the Third: 1700 to 1788*, III (London: Longman, Hurst, Rees, Orme, and Brown, 1813), pp. 244–45.

[158] Celia María Parcero Torre, *La pérdida de La Habana y las reformas borbónicas en Cuba (1760–1773)* (Valladolid: Junta de Castilla y Leon, 1998), pp. 39–45.

[159] Kuethe, *Cuba, 1753–1815*, pp. 16–17.

[160] Gustavo Placer Cervera, *Inglaterra y La Habana: 1762* (Havana: Editorial de Ciencias Sociales, 2007), pp. 102–103.

of the siege was the fall of the Morro Castle on July 31 after a merciless battering from the Cabaña and well-placed mines blew a passage through its wall. In an equally decisive encounter, the British seized and diverted the canal (*zanja*) that supplied the city with its water from its western side.[161]

As in the battle at Cartagena a generation before, the badly outnumbered defenders depended heavily on Spanish naval forces in the harbor. Indeed, Captain Luis Vicente Velasco, who led the defense of the Morro, has gone down as one of Spain's great military heroes.[162] The militia again played little role in the battle itself, although irregulars did manage to control the roads outside of Havana.[163] Reminiscent of the tactics of Blas de Lezo at Cartagena, Governor Prado scuttled three warships to block the entrance to the harbor. This tactic, however, eliminated the opportunity for the substantial Spanish naval force to counterattack. As a result, the British were free to bring in reinforcements and fresh supplies from Jamaica and North America and to divide their forces and open a second front to the west. The Spanish did deploy several vessels to reinforce the Morro from within the bay, while others helped block enemy advances southward that aimed to encircle the defenses. The armada was also free to contribute sailors to battle on land, but they were not enough. Juan de Prado, who failed to evacuate the royal treasure before surrendering, served subsequently as a handy scapegoat at court, along with the former viceroy of Peru, the Conde de Superunda, who was in Havana awaiting transport to Spain when the invasion took place.[164]

Under the terms of the Treaty of Paris signed on February 10, 1763, Spain regained Havana in return for giving up Florida. The British kept Canada and the lands west to the Mississippi River, while returning Martinique, St. Lucia, and Guadeloupe to the French. To induce Madrid to accept peace, France ceded Louisiana to Spain, a step that completed its expulsion from the North American continent.[165] The final settlement legitimized the English logwood settlements in Honduras as long as London refrained from fortifying its positions. Moreover, Spain obtained no recognition of its historic claims to fishing rights along the Newfoundland Banks. The treaty exposed the folly of

---

[161] For detailed accounts of the battle from a military perspective, see Placer Cervera, *Inglaterra y La Habana* and Parcero Torre, *La pérdida*, chaps. 4–5.

[162] An anonymous epic poem penned during the months after the surrender immortalized Velasco in Cuban literature. Lourdes Ramos-Kuethe (ed. with intro), *Romance anónimo sobre el sitio y la toma de La Habana por los ingleses en 1762* (Prague: Karolinum, 2011).

[163] Kuethe, *Cuba, 1753–1815*, pp. 19–20; Pablo J. Hernández González, "*La otra guerra del inglés: La resistencia a la presencia británica en Cuba (1762–1763)*," 2 vols. (Ph.D. diss., University of Seville 2001).

[164] Kuethe, *Cuba, 1753–1815*, p. 22.

[165] Versailles had dangled Louisiana before Madrid during 1761 and 1762 as it attempted unsuccessfully to lure Spain in an earlier entrance into the war and to secure a loan to bolster its failing finances. Arthur S. Aiton, "The Diplomacy of the Louisiana Cession," *The American Historical Review*, 36 (July 1931), pp. 701–20.

Ferdinand's dream of Spanish neutrality, and the defeat at Havana created new opportunities for the reformist elements at court wishing to challenge the established order.

CONCLUSION: THE EBB AND FLOW OF REFORM, 1736–1762

Despite real accomplishments by Campillo, Ensenada, and Carvajal, many historians have argued that the Bourbon reforms in the Spanish Atlantic did not begin until the reign of Charles III (1759–1788).[166] According to an influential synthesis by John Lynch, for example, "Campillo and Ensenada were excellent civil servants .... Once promoted to minister, however, they became captives of the crown, tied to their brief, which was to provide the resources for war."[167] While it is true that all royal ministers served the interests of the crown, after the end of the War of Jenkins' Ear the priorities of the Madrid government moved from dynastic concerns to an Atlantic focus. Ensenada, Carvajal, and Rávago formed a powerful triumvirate in Madrid to oversee a significant overhaul of government, commerce, and society in the Spanish empire during the reign of Ferdinand VI. The ministers often relied on the *Nuevo sistema* of José de Campillo y Cossío, which provided many ideas about reform for the generations that followed Patiño.

These enlightened ministers planned important domestic reforms, such as the single tax, but for the Indies they attacked the power of the *Consulados* of Cádiz, Lima, and Mexico City by limiting their privileges, and continued to promote monopoly companies developing imperial peripheries in the Caribbean. They also broadened the use of licensed register ships to trade with the Indies by 1740. These ships kept commercial ties open with the Indies during wartime, and after the peace they greatly expanded commercial exchanges, particularly with South America. Reformers also advanced the power of the Bourbon state over the Roman Catholic Church. The Concordat of 1753 greatly enhanced the king's patronage power over the church, and the secularization of the *doctrinas de indios* undermined the economic power and

---

[166] See, for example, Lyle N. McAlister, *The "Fuero Militar" in New Spain, 1764–1800* (Gainesville: University Presses of Florida, 1957) and Lynch, *Bourbon Spain*. The most significant and influential overview of this view that the Bourbon reforms really began in earnest during the reign of Charles III is D. A. Brading, "Bourbon Spain and its American empire," vol. 1, *The Cambridge History of Latin America* (Cambridge: Cambridge University Press, 1984), pp. 389–439, but the view has even influenced a major synthesis of the British and Spanish Atlantic worlds. See J. H. Elliott, *Empires of the Atlantic World: Britain and Spain in America, 1492–1830* (New Haven: Yale University Press, 2006). For an extensive list of titles that take this position, see the introduction to this book, and for a full annotated bibliography on the Bourbon reforms, see "The Bourbon Reforms." In *Oxford Bibliographies in Latin American Studies*. Ed. Ben Vinson.New York: Oxford University Press, 2012.

[167] Lynch, *Bourbon Spain*, p. 98.

FIGURE 6.1 Remittances to Spain, Three-Year Moving Average

social prestige of the previously more independent religious orders in the Indies. Reformers also enhanced the strength of the navy, promoted a reform of the army, and phased out the insidious practice of selling high bureaucratic appointments in the Indies. Moreover, Ensenada dispatched a new generation of public servants in the New World, such as Sebastián de Eslava, the Conde de Superunda, and the Conde de Revillagigedo, who shared his regalist vision of centralizing power in a strong, efficient state apparatus, loyal to the monarchy rather than to powerful vested interests or even the church. These colonial officials curtailed contraband commerce, bureaucratic corruption, and the power of venal colonial officeholders in the New World.[168]

One index of the successes of this phase of reform was the significant increase in royal income derived from the empire. The *Depositaría de Indies*, which served as the treasury of the *Casa de la Contratación*, registered both fiscal remittances from the colonies and taxes levied on American commerce. As Figure 6.1 (a three-year moving average of revenues entering the *Depositaría*

---

[168] Despite his reformist credentials and his many accomplishments in the Indies, the Conde de Superunda also used his office to gain considerable wealth, using much the same formula as the Conde de Castillar a decade before him, sending 490,500 pesos back to Spain, a sum which far exceeded his legal salary as viceroy. Even reformers could use the powers of their office for personal gain. See Pilar Latasa, "Negociar en red: familia, amistad, y paisanaje. El virrey Superunda y sus agentes en Lima y Cádiz (1745–1761)," *Anuario de Estudios Americanos* 60 (2003), pp. 463–92.

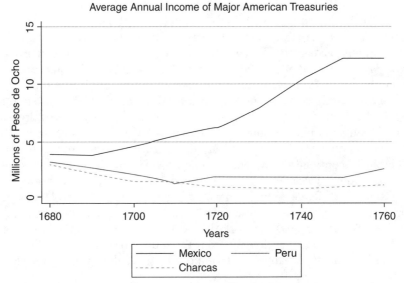

FIGURE 6.2 Annual Income of Major American Treasuries

de Indias) indicates, crown income flowing into the treasury from America more than doubled from the levels reached during the government of Patiño. Remittances from the Indies into the *Depositaría* fell during the War of Jenkins' Ear, when the British navy disrupted commerce in the Spanish Atlantic world, but after the Peace of Aix-la-Chapelle, income rose quickly to attain unprecedented levels, exceeding 1 million *reales de vellón*.[169] Revenues only dipped below 90 million *reales de vellón* after the downfall of Ensenada, when the pace of reform had slowed appreciably. Revenues dropped off yet again with the outbreak of war with Britain in 1762, which also disrupted Spain's transatlantic commerce. The salutary influence of using register ships in peacetime is also clearly evident in the rising levels of remittances and commercial taxes flowing into the *Depositaría de Indias*. This steady rise in income between 1748 and 1753 from America represented an annual average increase of 14 percent, demonstrating the enhanced ability to draw income from the Indies during this mid-eighteenth century reform period.

A major reason for the increased inflow of revenue from the Indies was the concurrent rising income levels of the New World treasuries, particularly New Spain. Figure 6.2 (of average annual income flowing into the treasuries)

---

[169] These figures from the D*epositaría de Indias* are taken from Jacques A. Barbier, "Towards a New Chronology for Bourbon Colonialism: The 'Depositaria de Indias' of Cádiz, 1722–1789," *Ibero-Amerikanisches Archiv*, 6:4 (1980), pp. 342–43.

demonstrates clearly that income levels rose dramatically in New Spain, Peru, and Charcas by mid-century.[170] Despite these overall gains, however, New Spain's production of tax revenue dwarfed the amounts generated in Peru and Charcas. In large part, this stemmed from a mining boom that began around 1700 and continued unabated until 1750. Since surplus income (income minus expenses) from New Spain not only went to Spain but also paid for the defenses of the Caribbean, the Havana shipyard, and Cuban tobacco to supply the royal monopoly, the surge in tax revenues in that viceroyalty was crucial for maintaining the integrity of the entire Spanish Atlantic system. The reform initiatives of Ensenada built on the early reforms of Patiño and Alberoni to continue the rise in revenue flowing into American treasuries well beyond the levels attained in the 1730s. At the same time, reforms in transatlantic trade, curtailing contraband, and keeping the sea lanes open with register ships allowed these American treasuries to remit larger sums to the *Depositaría de Indias*. In short, the second phase of reform led to significant increases in income flowing from the Indies to Spain, which laid the foundation for later changes that would take place during the pinnacle of reform under Charles III.

Although the reforming triumvirate of Ensenada, Carvajal, and Rávago dominated the political arena in Spain, their policies always had powerful opponents. The British Ambassador Keene, conservative politicians such as the Duke of Huéscar and Ricardo Wall, and vested interest groups opposed to reform and led by the *Consulado* of Cádiz contributed to Ensenada's precipitous fall from power in 1754, shortly after the death of Carvajal. With the downfall of Ensenada, followed by the removal of Rávago from court and the mental breakdown of King Ferdinand VI, Enlightened reform lost momentum until the reign of Charles III. Arriaga and Wall reinstated the *Flota* to New Spain and allowed the buildup of the armada and the reform of the army to languish. Growing income levels at the *Depositaría de Indias* also began to slow down from the heights reached in the early 1750s. While the prospects of reform seemed bright after the end of the War of Jenkins' Ear, foreign enemies and conservative forces at court eventually blunted the reformist initiatives of the Marqués de la Ensenada, leaving the empire much as Ferdinand VI had found it.

In the end, the events at mid-century showed that leadership at the top mattered. Able ministers had been able to advance meaningful change under the weak and often disabled Philip V and that continued during the early years of the more capable Ferdinand VI. But the stagnation that followed the banishment of Ensenada and the vulnerability occasioned by the naïve hope

[170] These figures are taken from Herbert S. Klein, *The American Finances of the Spanish Empire: Royal Income and Expenditures in Colonial Mexico, Peru, and Bolivia, 1680–1809* (Albuquerque: University of New Mexico Press, 1998), pp. 38–41; 58, 75.

that accommodation might somehow change the behavior of the British lion must be laid at Ferdinand's own feet. In the aftermath of Spain's humiliation at Havana, King Charles III, whose Enlightened reformist vision and energy far exceeded that of his father and his half-brother, would lead his government to new levels of achievement and reestablish Spain as a power of the first order.

III

PINNACLE OF THE BOURBON REFORMS, 1763–1796

7

The First Phase of Reform under Charles III, 1763–1767

After acceding to the throne in 1759, King Charles III indicated his intention to revive and extend reforms in the Spanish Atlantic world begun by his half-brother Ferdinand and the Marqués de la Ensenada. While king of Naples (1734–1759), Charles had worked closely with his chief minister, Bernardo Tanucci, to make a series of ecclesiastical, fiscal, administrative, and economic reforms designed to centralize state power, and he was inclined to pursue a similar regalist agenda in his new kingdoms. Soon after taking the Spanish throne, Charles recalled Ensenada from exile and made him a councilor of State, indicating that he intended to shake Madrid from the political somnolence of the last years of Ferdinand's reign.[1] Although Charles and his ministers began planning key reforms, the Seven Years' War intervened, leading to defeat and humiliation at the hands of Great Britain. The loss of Havana posed a great danger to the empire, since that Caribbean fortress protected the sea lanes to New Spain, the wealthiest Spanish possession in the Indies. Although Spain regained the key Caribbean stronghold in the Treaty of Paris ending the war, the king and his ministers recognized the need to shore up defenses in the Indies. Building on the achievements of Ensenada, they also planned a wide range of fiscal, administrative, commercial, and religious innovations aimed at strengthening Spain's control over its Atlantic empire. The *visita general* of José de Gálvez to New Spain (1764–1772) implemented important new fiscal and administrative initiatives, but the first phase of reform under Charles III culminated with the extension of imperial free trade to Spain's Caribbean Islands (1765) and the expulsion of the Jesuits (1767). Past wartime defeats had interrupted or reversed reform, but the threat of Britain's unrivaled power spurred the king and his ministers to support widespread modernization throughout the Spanish Atlantic world.

---

[1] The men had a relationship extending back to when Ensenada fought in the military campaigns that won Charles his kingdom in Naples, and for his part, Charles had prevailed upon his half-brother to grant Somodevilla a noble title.

During the reign of Charles III, a new generation of enlightened regalist magistrates emerged who would implement the king's reformist agenda. Although Charles ended the baroque extravagance at court promoted by King Ferdinand and Queen Barbara, he remained a patron of learning and the arts. The Madrid of Charles III was a cosmopolitan city where ideas from Europe and Spain's far-flung empire converged, and enlightened men and women (*ilustrados* or *luces*) engaged in philosophical and political discussions in private salons and at court about the salient issues of the day. This lively intellectual atmosphere gave rise to a diverse group of politicians, most steeped in the Enlightenment, who were capable of advancing the king's policies.[2] Some were Italians, such as the Marqués de Esquilache, who had accompanied Charles from Naples. A very few were Spanish grandees, principally Pedro Pablo Abarca de Bolea, the Conde de Aranda, a military man who served as president of the Council of Castille (1766–1773). Many of the king's new ministers, however, came from the lower nobility or the rising middle classes. Pedro Rodríguez Campomanes and José de Moñino (later Conde de Floridablanca), for example, served as attorneys (*fiscales*) on the Council of Castille, while José de Gálvez made his reputation in New Spain and later as Minister of the Indies. These men from very different backgrounds were nonetheless all energetic, resourceful, and competent administrators who shared a commitment to the reform and renovation of the Spanish Atlantic world.

Like previous generations of reformers, the ministers of Charles III faced powerful enemies both foreign and domestic who opposed the king's innovations. Foreign rivals such as Great Britain would use contraband, diplomacy, and even military force to gain access to the wealth of the Spanish Indies. A host of conservative politicians in Spain and the still powerful *Consulado* of Cádiz opposed many of the king's reformist projects, particularly any effort at commercial deregulation. Finally, an array of different interest groups in the Indies stood to lose power and influence as Charles and his ministers attempted to alter traditional political, commercial, and social relationships. These included members of the conservative clergy in Spain and the Indies who opposed regalist efforts to curtail the traditional role of the church.

One of these clerical groups opposing many of the king's polices was the independent-minded Society of Jesus. The Jesuits were a rich and powerful international order, and they had acquired a well-deserved reputation as a bastion of anti-regalist sentiment. The Society maintained its primary allegiance to the papacy, resisting the crown's efforts to subordinate the Spanish

---

[2] On the court of Charles III, see Charles Noel, "In the House of Reform: The Bourbon Court of Eighteenth-Century Spain," in Gabriel Paquette, ed., *Enlightened Reform in Southern Europe and its Atlantic Colonies, c. 1750–1830* (Surry: Ashgate Publishing Limited, 2009), pp. 145–66.

Church to royal authority. The Jesuits also opposed many reformist elements within the church, particularly the Jansenists, who frequently allied with the king's enlightened ministers. King Charles himself had long mistrusted the Society, and when he took the throne in Spain, he broke with the Bourbon tradition of having a Jesuit as his confessor and named instead an anti-Jesuit Franciscan, Fray Joaquín Eleta. Although the secularization of the *doctrinas de indios* had curtailed the economic power and social prestige of most regular orders in the Indies, it had little effect on the Jesuits. The Society maintained few indigenous *doctrinas* in the New World, except those parishes supporting their large missionary efforts, and these were exempt from the edicts of secularization. Moreover, Ensenada and Francisco de Rávago, King Ferdinand's influential Jesuit confessor, had protected the order until their downfalls in 1754. When popular riots against the crown broke out in Madrid in 1766, however, followed by unrest in other Spanish cities, the king's regalist ministers found the Jesuits a convenient scapegoat, and the king expelled the order from the Spanish empire beginning on April 2, 1767. The expulsion of the Jesuits then served as a platform to sweeping political, commercial, and social reforms during the remainder of the reign of Charles III.

CHARLES III AND HIS MINISTERS

Charles believed in absolute monarchy, and accordingly he promoted a modern bureaucratic state.[3] At the same time, he governed through his ministers, and after setting the basic policy parameters, the king expected his subordinates to work out the details. Charles had a gift for selecting able ministers and councilors. He expected and received unswerving loyalty from these magistrates, and they received the same from him.[4] Charles seldom changed ministers and then only with the greatest reluctance.[5] Spain's defeat in the Seven Years' War opened the way for the ambitions of the Marqués de Esquilache. Spain's losses reflected the military's lack of preparedness, and Ricardo Wall, the secretary of the Office for War and State, bore the greatest responsibility for those defeats.[6] Given his advanced age, Wall submitted his resignation in August 1763, which enabled Charles to add War to Esquilache's powers, while appointing the Marqués de Grimaldi, Spain's ambassador to France and the architect of the Third Family Compact, as Minister of State. Charles held Esquilache in high regard, and the king viewed

---

[3] Juan Luis Castellano, *Gobierno y poder en la España del siglo XVIII* (Granada: Editorial Universidad de Granada, 2006), pp. 175–81.

[4] This behavior was seen earlier in Italy. Anthony H. Hull, *Charles III and the Bourbon Revival In Spain* (Washington, D. C.: University Press of America,1981), p. 50.

[5] Vicente Rodríguez Casado, *La política y los políticos en el reinado de Carlos III* (Madrid: Ediciones Rialp, 1962).

[6] French Ambassador D'Ossun to Minister of State Choiseul, San Ildefonso, July 18 and August 8, 1763, AAE:CPE, vol. 539, fols. 54, 92.

joining War and Finance under a single minister as sound strategy given the fiscal and military challenges that Spain faced.[7]

The dowager queen proved an important force in this ministerial reorganization, and Charles conferred with his mother before making most appointments.[8] Elizabeth used her influence to give staunch support to her fellow Italian, Esquilache. Upon the resignation of Wall, Elizabeth backed the Sicilian's efforts to advance the cause of Grimaldi, as he competed for State against Agustín de Llano, a disciple of Wall and the favorite of the conservative faction at court. Grimaldi also enjoyed strong support from the French government, which undoubtedly helped him, but the influence of Esquilache and the queen mother was decisive.[9] In contrast to the customary treatment of a magistrate with long service to the crown, Wall received no departing honors, although he did retain his position on the Council of State.[10]

Bailío Julián de Arriaga remained at Marine and the Indies, even though he bore much responsibility (along with Wall) for the defeat at Havana. Suffering from fading eyesight, Fray Arriaga found himself increasingly isolated from the intrigue at court.[11] Widely admired for his honesty, dignity, and American experience, Arriaga nevertheless lacked imagination and seemed incapable of large-scale planning and vision.[12] Charles might have encouraged him to follow Wall into retirement, and speculation lingered at court that Ensenada would replace him.[13] Demonstrating his traditional loyalty to his subordinates, however, Charles preferred to work around Arriaga's limitations rather than dismiss and humiliate him. Moreover, the venerable Minister of the Indies provided a respectable, conservative, native balance in the royal cabinet, offsetting the controversial presence of foreign reformers. At the same time, the king allowed Esquilache to take control of

---

[7] José Antonio Escudero, *Los orígenes del Consejo de Ministros en España* (Madrid: Editoria Nacional, 1979), I, p. 289.

[8] D'Ossun to Choiseul, San Ildefonso, August 25, 1763, AAE:CPE, vol. 539, fols. 157–58. The queen mother worked to undermine Wall's position. For Llano's connection to Wall, see Diego Téllez Alarcia, *El ministerio Wall: La España discreta del <ministro olvidado>* (Madrid: Marcial Pons, 2012), p. 30 and Escudero, *Los orígenes*, p. 274.

[9] D'Ossun to Choiseul, San Ildefonso, August 29, 1763, AAE:CPE, vol. 539, fol. 163. This subject has been treated more fully in Allan J. Kuethe and Lowell Blaisdell, "The Esquilache Government and the Reforms of Charles III in Cuba," *Jarhbuch für Geschichte von Staat, Wirtschaft und Gesellschaft Lateinamerikas*, 19 (1982), pp. 117–36.

[10] Téllez Alarcia, *El ministerio Wall*, p. 61; José Luis Gómez Urdáñez and Pedro Luis Lorenzo Cadarso, *Castilla en la edad moderna, second part, Historia de Castilla de Atapuerca a Fuensaldaña*, ed. by Juan José García González, Julio Aróstegui Sánchez, and Juan Andrés Blanco Rodríguez, et al. (Madrid: La Esfera de los libros, 2008), p. 540.

[11] Arriaga to Ricla, San Lorenzo, November 16, 1764, AGI, IG, leg. 1630.

[12] D'Ossun to Choiseul, Madrid, March 8, 1764, AAE:CPE, vol. 540, fols. 182–86. Frances P. Renaut, *Pacte de Famille et l'Amerique : La Politique Coloniale Franco-Espagnole de 1760 à 1792* (Paris: Lerroux, 1922) pp. 99–100.

[13] D'Ossun to Choiseul, Madrid, May 19 and 26, 1760, and Choiseul to D'Ossun, Versailles, June 10, 1760, AAE:CPE, vol. 528, fols. 250–54, 290–94, 353–54.

priority reforms for the Indies. In early 1764, for example, Arriaga discretely complained that the king had appointed three officials to his ministry without consulting him. Charles bluntly reminded the old gentleman that given his blunders during the war, he ought to be thankful that he had not been dismissed.[14] When the king named Esquilache and Grimaldi councilors of State, he ignored the *bailío*, reminding the old minister of his secondary status in the cabinet.[15]

As a consequence of these personal relationships at court, the king created the Junta de Ministros when the new secretary of the Office for State arrived from France in October 1763. Consisting of Arriaga, Esquilache, and Grimaldi, the junta met weekly to formulate policies to strengthen the colonies, increase American revenues, and restore and expand the fleet.[16] In this manner, Arriaga was consulted and proper decorum maintained, while at the same time Esquilache had an adequate institutional basis for intruding into affairs of the Indies. The creation of the junta also represented a step toward integrating policy for Spain and the Indies. In the days of a Patiño or an Ensenada, this coordination came through the offices of a single minister holding multiple portfolios. Now this integration assumed an ad hoc institutional dimension, which Charles would advance and formalize toward the end of his reign.

The retention of Arriaga as Minister of the Indies created the illusion that the *bailío* actually made policy.[17] Although Esquilache signed some major orders, most bore Arriaga's signature, as did nearly all routine correspondence. This illusion of Arriaga's power has made it difficult to account for the discontinuity between the years of bold experimentation and new initiatives after the war (1763–1766) and the later years (1766–1776) when ministerial actions appeared comparatively listless and unimaginative. Esquilache authored most of the major reforms of 1763 to 1766, personally won Charles's approval, and then sent the documents on to Arriaga for his signature. With the fall and exile of the Italian in March 1766, this process came to an end, and the reforming impulse weakened markedly.

From the beginning, Charles worked to free the royal administration from its financial dependence on the *Consulado*. Soon after his arrival in Madrid, by decree of February 22, 1760, he committed 10 million copper *reales* per year to pay off his father's debt, with an immediate infusion of 50

---

[14] D'Ossun to Choiseul, Madrid, March 8, 1764, AAE:CPE, vol. 540, fols. 182–86.

[15] Escudero, *Los orígenes*, I, p. 297.

[16] The minutes of these meetings, if they were kept, have not been found. Fortunately, the French ambassador, D'Ossun, monitored them through his close friend Grimaldi and reported to Choiseul. See AAE:CPE, vols. 539–40. The Junta is sometimes also called the Committee of Imperial Defense or the Junta Interministerial.

[17] With Lowell Blaisdell, Kuethe corrected this misconception in "The Esquilache Government," pp. 117–36 and "French Influence and the Origins of the Bourbon Colonial Reorganization," *HAHR*, 71 (May 1991), pp. 579–607.

million.[18] King Charles did not borrow from the guild during his intervention in the Seven Years' War, and following the Treaty of Paris he continued liquidating any inherited debts, working through *contaduría* of the Council of the Indies. The king summoned the *Consulado*'s prior, Francisco Montes to court in 1768 to hasten the process. The authorities reached a settlement with the *Consulado* in 1771, which defined the lingering royal debt at a meager 1,095,792 pesos. This would be liquidated by applying surpluses arising from the 1 percent fund established to finance the *avisos*, soon to be replaced by a royal mail service.[19] The final settlement reflected the crown's desire to end its financial dependence on Cádiz, freeing it to pursue new commercial policies independent of the old monopoly system. At the same time, the wily Montes acquired appointments to the Council of the Royal Treasury and as senior treasurer, implying that the link between the crown and the *Consulado* was not yet completely severed.[20]

DEFEAT, HUMILIATION, AND THE RENEWAL OF REFORM

The loss of Havana undoubtedly inflicted a profound shock at court, but the defeat was hardly the enormous humiliation that Charles and his inner circle pretended. The defenders had held out for two months, which should have been long enough for disease to devastate the British army as it had at Cartagena. In fact, an epidemic in their ranks had begun even as they marched into Havana.[21] Moreover, Havana was not Cuba. The occupying force controlled only the *plaza fuerte* and Matanzas harbor to the east, not the whole island. The invaders had essentially found themselves bottled up in the city and its immediate environs. Cuban irregular forces controlled the surrounding roadways, and the governor of Santiago de Cuba had dispatched a column to relieve Havana.[22] Slowed by disease, however, his army failed to arrive in time to be of immediate use, and it redeployed to the Bay of Jagua southeast of the city.[23] In reality, the British forces held little more than Havana, and they were surrounded by the enemy while disease ravished their ranks.

[18] Royal decree (to Esquilache), Buen Retiro, February 22, 1760, AGS, Marine, leg. 770.
[19] File, debt settlement with *Consulado*, 1761–1771, AGI, Consulados, leg. 705.
[20] File, report of Francisco Montes, n.d., AGI, IG, leg. 2325; Escudero, *Los orígenes*, I, pp. 410, 414.
[21] John Robert McNeill, *Atlantic Empires of France and Spain: Louisbourg and Havana, 1700–1763* (Chapel Hill: University of North Carolina Press, 1985), 103.
[22] Gustavo Placer Cervera, *Inglaterra y La Habana: 1762* (Havana: Editorial de Ciencias Sociales, 2007), pp. 172–81, 187–91.
[23] Pablo J. Hernández González, "La otra guerra del inglés: La resistencia a la presencia británica en Cuba *(1762–1763)*," 2 vols. (Ph.D. diss., University of Seville, 2001); Sherry Johnson, "Revisiting the British Capture of Havana in 1762," paper presented at the Conference on Latin American History, American Historical Association Meeting, 2005.

London's exchange of strategic Havana for marginal Florida in the Treaty of Paris appeared an unequal trade. It is clear that the jealous Jamaican planter class in Parliament lobbied aggressively to return Cuba, whose rich sugar plantations would have competed with the British Caribbean Islands, but much more was involved.[24] As peace negotiations advanced during the autumn and winter of 1762 and 1763, the British military position in the Caribbean had deteriorated. As a result, the advantages of a secure Atlantic seaboard anchored by Florida offered London an excellent bargain.

The king and his ministers used the crisis mentality at court following the loss of Havana to advance their reformist agenda with great political skill. *Urgencias de guerra* (military imperatives) now justified everything, and entrenched vested interests dared not oppose the security of the empire. The army required reorganization and expansion, fortifications needed to be rebuilt and expanded, and the means found to finance those innovations. Adding urgency to the military preparations, both Charles and his French ally viewed the Treaty of Paris as little more than a truce. Humiliated by the British in Naples in 1742 and now once more, Charles thirsted for revenge at the first opportunity.[25] Military reform would lead the way, followed by the means to support it. Commercial deregulation, which remained a key dimension of the reformers, briefly moved into the background. Enlightened though he may have been, Charles saw himself first and foremost as a military leader, a posture perceptively captured by Mengs, who painted the genial-looking, smiling king in armor, a sword fastened to his side (see Figure 7.1).

Even before the war ended, Charles accepted a plan authored by the Conde de Ricla to reorganize the armed forces in Cuba by strengthening the regular army and establishing a reformed militia along lines already developed in Spain.[26] An expansion of the regular garrisons distributed throughout America was prohibitively expensive, especially given Spain's military obligations in Europe and the additional costs that the navy imposed. As a result, Ricla proposed the revolutionary step of arming systematically American subjects, a step with profound long-range implications, but he viewed this measure as indispensable given the threat of British power in America.[27]

---

[24] Hugh Thomas, *Cuba: The Pursuit of Freedom* (New York: Harper and Rowe, 1971), pp. 55–56.

[25] Herbert Ingram Priestley, *José de Gálvez: Visitor-General of New Spain (1765–1771)* (Berkeley: University of California Press, 1916), p. 4; A. S. Aiton, "Spanish Colonial Reorganization under the Family Compact," *HAHR*, 12 (August 1932), pp. 269–80.

[26] "Discurso general," Conde de Ricla, January 20, 1763, AGI, SD, leg. 2116.

[27] As Ricla stated, "in order to hold that domain [Cuba] . . . I envision only these means: one, very costly and almost impossible, is to maintain a [sufficient] army there, [but] there is not enough funding for that nor even [the] people; another [is] to reinforce it with auxiliary troops [but] this is risky, because even when enough [men] for its defense are sent, they may not arrive on time for their mission and the effort would be worthless; the third is the one in which I have the most confidence, and it comes down to the establishment of a local militia in proportion to that

FIGURE 7.1 King Charles III (1716–1788, reigned 1759–1788) in armor, painted by Antón Rafael Mengs in 1761 in the Museo del Prado. (See plate section for color version)

Ricla, the cousin of the powerful Conde de Aranda who led the Aragonese faction at court, obviously represented more than himself. A lieutenant general of the army and a grandee, Aranda had long championed military

which is deemed sufficient in order to command respect from the enemy, over all the island. Beyond not being very costly to the treasury, [this would not be] a burden to the land either, because armed service fundamentally does not keep those people from their farm labors and employments . . ." ibid.

modernization, and in the 1750s, he had clashed with Sebastián de Eslava when the hero of Cartagena hesitated to innovate. Aranda preferred using regular troops rather than provincial militia in the peninsula.[28] In the American theater, however, Aranda saw the need to create an armed colonial militia. Given Britain's naval supremacy, the enemy could always choose the point of attack, and trained colonial units could advantageously supplement limited regular forces.

The risks of arming the crown's American subjects entailed a dangerous transfer of political power to the colonies. Mindful of that concern, Ricla insisted that,

> There are also some misgivings about whether or not it be wise to arm the inhabitants of the island, but the precautions envisioned for storing the weaponry addresses that concern . . . and in case some sort of disorders arise, I believe the strength of the Spanish veteran troops is adequate to counter the insults of the natives.

Moreover, he continued, armaments would remain in the custody of veterans: "Only for training days, or when mobilized for royal service, will volunteers have weapons in their possession, returning them afterwards to the arsenals or designated buildings where the king's troops should assume custody of them."[29] Such limitations on the use of weaponry in the colonial militia, however, would prove impossible to enforce in practice.

Lacking realistic alternatives, Charles accepted Ricla's proposal on March 16, 1763, naming him governor and captain general of Cuba.[30] In late April 1763, the new governor departed to take possession of Havana and implement a reform program capable of securing the island's defense. Accompanying Ricla were his close friend, fast-rising Field Marshal Alejandro O'Reilly, and some 600 officers and enlisted men designated to act as advisors for the new militia.[31] A descendant of Irish nobility, O'Reilly had immigrated to Spain as a child and, like so many other Irishmen, joined the Spanish military to fulfill his ambitions.[32] While maintaining a routine correspondence with the Ministry of the Indies, the reformers in Cuba also

---

[28] Antonio Álvarez de Morales, "Los proyectos de reforma del ejército del conde de Aranda," in Javier Alvarado Planas and Regina María Pérez Marcos, eds., *Estudios sobre ejército, política y derecho en España (siglos XII-XX)* (Madrid: Ediciones Polifemo, 1996), pp. 154–60.

[29] "Discurso general," Conde de Ricla, January 20, 1763, AGI, SD, leg. 2116.

[30] Royal order, Buen Retiro, March 16, 1763, AGI, SD, leg. 1211.

[31] For a more detailed analysis of the Cuban military reform, see Allan J. Kuethe, "The Development of the Cuban Military as a Socio-Political Elite, 1763–1783," *HAHR*, 61 (Nov. 1981), pp. 695–704.

[32] Bibiano Torres Ramírez, *Alejandro O'Reilly en las Indias* (Seville 1969), pp. 5–8. For the Irish in the Spanish American military, see Juan Marchena Fernández, "Los oficiales militares irlandeses en el ejército de América. 1750–1815" in Enrique García Hernán y Oscar Recio Morales (coords.), *Extranjeros en el ejército. Essays on the Irish Military Presence in Early Modern Spain. 1580–1818* (Madrid: Ministerio de Defensa, Secretaría General Técnica, 2007), pp. 317–53.

sustained a separate line of communication with Esquilache, who coordinated work in Spain to shape a coherent reform program.[33] Ricla tended to administrative priorities in Havana, including preparing the way for fiscal, administrative, and commercial reform, delegating to O'Reilly the military reorganization. Before Ricla departed Spain, Esquilache instructed him to seek the financial means to support the new, enlarged military establishment in consultation with the Havana elite.[34]

O'Reilly reestablished the fixed garrison and increased its strength to two battalions, supported by a Spanish regiment. He recruited a modernized militia (on the model of Spanish provincial units) consisting of eight infantry battalions and individual regiments of cavalry and dragoons, totaling 7,500 men.[35] These he termed "disciplined" to distinguish them from earlier militia units. O'Reilly provided the new disciplined units with standardized tables of organization, firearms, and uniforms. He integrated veteran soldiers and corporals into the companies at the higher ranks of corporals and sergeants, and he appointed veteran sergeants to act as lieutenants and to guide the volunteer captains. An army captain would act as *sargento mayor*, the planning and training officer, who would advise the battalion colonel, a volunteer. In this way, the Irishman skillfully balanced community leadership with trained personnel.

O'Reilly selected the colonels and captains from local elites, which in Havana made them almost all members of the emerging sugar planter class. Such leadership, with strong ties to the political establishment, was essential to guarantee that enlisted men would appear for weekly company drills, which usually occurred after Sunday Mass in their local neighborhoods, and for the yearly assemblies to complete the ranks and undertake large-scale unit maneuvers. The municipalities funded the uniforms, but the weapons normally came from Spain. Militiamen customarily drilled with aged weapons, but during firing practice they employed newer muskets held in reserve.

The Cuban militia included two battalions of free *pardos* (mulattoes) and one of free *morenos* (blacks). The use of black militiamen dated back to the sixteenth century and responded to the demographic realities typical of Caribbean society, where freedmen comprised a significant portion of the population.[36] Moreover, men recruited from the *libre* estate of society

[33] See, for example, AGI, SD, legs. 2118, 2077, 2078, and AGS, Hacienda, leg. 2342.

[34] For a treatment of the reform mission to Cuba, see Allan J. Kuethe and G. Douglas Inglis, "Absolutism and Enlightened reform: Charles III, the Establishment of the *Alcabala*, and Commercial Reorganization in Cuba," *Past & Present: A Journal of Historical Studies*, no. 109 (November 1985), pp. 118–43.

[35] Allan J. Kuethe, *Cuba, 1753–1815: Crown, Military, and Society* (Knoxville: University of Tennessee Press, 1986), pp. 37–45.

[36] Herbert S. Klein, "The Colored Militia of Cuba, 1568–1868," *Caribbean Studies*, 4 (July 1966), pp. 17–27.

typically responded more aggressively to the prestige of the uniform and to military privilege than did whites.[37] To ensure proper instruction, O'Reilly attached segregated white *planas mayores* to the three battalions. In October 1764, Esquilache personally ordered the Cuban policy codified and published, which occurred the following year.[38]

A final issue concerned military judicial privileges. Ricla believed military privilege indispensable to motivate Cuba's volunteers, including *pardos* and *morenos*, and he quickly granted them the *fuero militar*, which allowed militiamen to be tried in military courts for both civil and criminal offences.[39] As he put it,

I knew since my arrival in this colony that it would not be possible to achieve the advantageous level of discipline that His Majesty desires and that is so essential for the defense of this important island without conceding to all militiamen the benefit of the *fuero militar*.[40]

By contrast, the *fuero* of the enlisted men in Spain's provincial militia extended only to criminal causes.[41] After careful consideration, moreover, the Cuban privilege was refined to define that of sergeants and officers as "active," encompassing cases where the individual was the plaintiff. This construction of the *fuero* was rare in military law, since only a few corps such as the king's guard were so privileged. Bestowing such a broad definition of the *fuero militar* also ran counter to the enlightened impulse to weaken privilege and special arrangements, and it bore serious long-term institutional implications for civil-military relations in Spanish America; but pressing defense needs prevailed. In the absence of the financial means to reward the expanded army, corporate privileges offered the only realistic alternative. *Preminencias*, including exemptions from an array of municipal fees and levies as well as the quartering of troops, rounded out the militiaman's rights.[42]

While O'Reilly reshaped the army, Ricla addressed the challenges of royal finance, administration, and commercial policy as he sought to identify and tap funding sources to support the military reorganization. At all stages of the reform process in Cuba, the royal administration consulted openly with the Havana elite. The crown had learned from the mistakes of Alberoni, but

---

[37] *Libres* functioned under a separate set of laws that imposed greater limitations on their behavior and harsher punishments.

[38] Esquilache to Ricla, San Lorenzo, October 24, 1764, in *Reglamento para las milicias de infantería, y caballería de la Isla de Cuba* (Havana, 1765). A copy can be found in AGI, SD, leg. 2120.

[39] Ricla to Arriaga, Havana, April 1, 1764, AGI, SD, leg. 2118.

[40] Quoted in Kuethe, *Cuba, 1753–1815*, p. 45.

[41] Lyle N. McAlister, *The "Fuero Militar" in New Spain, 1764–1800* (Gainesville: University Presses of Florida, 1957), pp. 8–9.

[42] This subject has been treated in greater detail in Kuethe, *Cuba, 1753–1815*, pp. 45–49.

under present circumstances, reform policy in Cuba involved much broader implications. When Charles and Esquilache instructed the new governor to solicit *habanero* input, they knew that local elites wanted a flexible commercial system to accommodate the island's growing sugar output. That desire fit nicely with their reformist agenda to deregulate Spanish commerce with the Indies, not just Cuba. At the same time, crown officials hoped to secure elite acquiescence to higher taxes and to tighter administration, which were essential to finance the expanded military establishment in the Caribbean.

Ricla sponsored two meetings with the heads of the most influential families of Havana, thirty on the first occasion, which occurred during the fall, and forty-seven on the second a year later. He initially operated through a Jesuit intermediary, Ignacio Tomás Butler, who secured tacit Cuban acceptance for higher taxation, with the expectation of commercial concessions that would help generate those monies.[43] Meanwhile, O'Reilly named many members of those same families as captains or colonels when he organized the disciplined militia on the island. This more consultative, conciliatory policy served both Ricla and the elites very well.[44]

Ricla's report, addressed directly to Esquilache, listed a wide variety of possible sources of additional income identified by José Antonio Gelabert, the chief auditor of the local treasury.[45] To sift through these recommendations and formulate policy, Esquilache worked through the Junta de Ministros. The result was Charles's first attempt at revenue reform in the colonies. The royal order of April 25, 1764, raised the Cuban *alcabala* from 2 to 4 percent and established new taxes on aguardiente and a local liquor, *sambumbia*.[46]

The crown established an intendancy in Havana to streamline the collection and disbursement of royal revenues. This *intendente de ejército* was empowered to act independently of the governor to improve financial management.[47] Although the order to establish the intendancy went out under Arriaga's signature, Esquilache formulated the proposal and the regulation, obtained Charles's approval, and then apprised Arriaga of the plan so that it might be dispatched through the Ministry of the Indies.[48] Arriaga was not

---

[43] The details of these meetings are in Kuethe and Inglis, "Absolutism and Enlightened Reform," pp. 127, 133.

[44] Kuethe, *Cuba, 1753–1815*, pp. 56–60.

[45] Ricla to Esquilache, Havana, December 14, 1763, AGS, Hacienda, leg. 2342.

[46] "*Acuerdo de la Junta de Señores Ministros*," El Pardo, March 15, 1764, and royal order, April 25, 1764, AGS, Hacienda, leg. 2342.

[47] For a description of the Cuban intendancy, see William Whatley Pierson, Jr., "The Establishment and Early Functioning of the 'Intendencia' of Cuba," in *Studies in Hispanic American History*, James Sprunt Historical Studies, *19* (Chapel Hill: University of North Carolina Press, 1927), pp. 113–33.

[48] Royal order (Esquilache to Arriaga), San Ildefonso, October 13, 1764, AGS, Hacienda, leg. 2342. The Italian also sent Arriaga a list of officials to appoint for the new institution, including Miguel de Altarriva for intendant. Royal order (Esquilache to Arriaga), San Ildefonso, October 23, 1764, ibid.

enthused about these policy developments, and he warned Ricla that the regulation contained a number of "excusable" provisions though it bore his signature.[49]

Faced with new taxes, an intendant system, and only vague assurances of concessions in Cuba's trade with Spain, the Havana ayuntamiento pressed for the second meeting with Ricla's representative to make more explicit its needs and hopes. At this gathering on October 24, 1764, Gelabert, representing the crown, went so far as to offer opening the treasury books to justify revenue reform. For their part, the Cubans petitioned forcefully for direct access to all Spanish ports, even in their own ships, the right to procure slaves from any available source, and a modernization of the levies placed on commerce.

The process that produced actual commercial reform advanced along an involved, complex route. In conjunction with his duties in raising the disciplined militia, Ricla had commissioned O'Reilly to conduct a *visita* of the island, seeking the means to curtail contraband, stimulate the economy, and generate additional revenues. In an expansive report, O'Reilly urged the opening of Cuba to direct commerce with the several ports of Spain, the unrestricted importation of slaves to stimulate agriculture, and a tightening of administrative controls.[50] Ricla hurried this petition to Madrid with his strong, personal endorsement.[51] Except for his recommendation about the slave trade, where a separate agreement was already being negotiated in Spain, the report could have been written before O'Reilly left Madrid, since it reflected perfectly the reformist agenda formulated by Campillo and his successors.[52]

While Ricla and O'Reilly worked in Cuba, Esquilache established a special commission to review commercial policy for the entire Spanish Atlantic. In 1764, he named five experts for the task, at least three of whom had previously submitted projects calling for greater deregulation of the commercial system. Especially noteworthy of these were the Marqués de Los Llanos, who was the nephew of the Marqués de Villarías and who had long been an outspoken exponent of extinguishing the fleet and the monopoly port systems, and Tomás Ortiz de Landázuri. Both would play a long-term role in shaping reform policy.[53] The committee had at its disposal O'Reilly's statement championing the deregulation of Cuban trade, an *habanero* petition that

---

[49] Arriaga to Ricla, San Lorenzo, November 16, 1764, AGI, IG, leg. 1630.

[50] File, *Visita general* of the island of Cuba, AGI, Santo Domingo, leg. 1509. For a more detailed account of the economic reforms in Cuba, see Kuethe, "Alejandro O'Reilly y las reformas económicas de Carlos III en Cuba," *Memoria del Cuarto Congreso Venezolano de Historia*, 3 vols. (Caracas: Academia Nacional de Historia, 1982), II, pp. 117–34.

[51] Ricla to Arriaga, Havana, October 30, 1764, AGI, SD, leg. 2188.

[52] Bibiano Torres Ramírez, *La Compañía Gaditana de Negros* (Seville: Escuela de Esudios Hispano-Americanos, 1973), pp. 31–41.

[53] The other who had already authored reformist tracts was Pedro Goosens. Simón de Aragorri, and Francisco Craywinkle completed the committee. Goosens to Wall, Bilbao, January 31 and

had arrived later that year, and a host of other documents. To no one's surprise, the exhaustive report produced by Esquilache's commission on February 14, 1765 advocated the replacement of the Cádiz monopoly with imperial free trade.[54] A year earlier, the Junta de Ministros had already recommended the same changes. Now it had informed opinion to support it.[55] The report also advocated replacing the *palmeo*, which had lingered since the Project of 1720, with taxes based on value.

The first real breakthrough to reform came when Charles reorganized the colonial mail system. Royal absolutism depended on sound communications, while good information permitted merchants to ply their trade more effectively. Charles placed the responsibility for this innovation with Grimaldi as the secretary of State, where the *vía reservada* customarily had assigned such matters, but the shrewd monarch undoubtedly knew that the capable Grimaldi would handle the matter efficiently.[56] The *Consulado* of Cádiz, which operated the system of *Avisos*, expected to be consulted about any modification of the service. Working with advice of the Enlightened Pedro Rodríguez Campomanes, fiscal of the Council of Castile, however, Grimaldi proceeded independently.[57] José de Larrarte, the *Consulado*'s lobbyist at court, picked up rumors that changes in both the colonial mail and commercial systems might arise, but he mistakenly concluded that the matter had been suspended.[58]

The royal regulation establishing a modernized mail system operated by the crown from La Coruña appeared on August 24, 1764, shocking both the *Consulado* and Larrarte.[59] Small ships would depart monthly for Havana and from there others would fan out across the empire. The return mail moved from Havana back to La Coruña. To help mitigate costs, the vessels

---

February 7, 1763, AHN, Estado, leg. 2944. The projects of Ortiz de Landazuri, undated, and Los Llanos, 1755, can be found in the Biblioteca del Palacio, Sección Miscelánea Ayala, sig. 2867, fols. 49–53 and 101–15. See also Josep M. Delgado Ribas, "La paz de los siete años (1750–1757) y el inicio de la reforma comercial española," in Antonio Morales Moya (coordinator), *1802: España entre dos siglos, ciencia y economía* (Madrid: Sociedad Estatal de Conmemoraciones Culturales, 2003), pp. 336–37; Téllez Alarcia, *El ministerio Wall*, p. 218.

[54] *Consulta*, commerce of America, Madrid, February 14, 1765, AHN, Estado, leg. 2314.

[55] D'Ossun to Choiseul, Madrid, January 23, 1764, AAE:CPE, vol. 539, fols. 64–69.

[56] State administered the mail service both "inside and outside the Kingdom" (*la superintendencia general de correos de dentro y fuera del reyno*). Royal declaration, Aranjuez, May 15, 1754. Archivo General de Marina Don Álvaro de Bazán, leg. 5059.

[57] Campomanes had authored an extensive study in 1761 on the mail system of Spain and the Indies. *Itinerario de las Carreras de Posta de dentro, y fuera del reyno* ... (Madrid 1761).

[58] Royal mail reform has been treated in G. Douglas Inglis and Allan J. Kuethe, "The Consulado de Cádiz y el Reglamento de Comercio Libre de 1765," in *Andalucía y América en el siglo XVIII: Actas de las IV Jornadas de Andalucía y América* (Sevilla: Escuela de Estudios Hispano-Americanos, 1985), pp. 79–87.

[59] *Reglamento provisional que manda S.M. observar para el establecimiento del Nuevo Correo mensual que ha de salir de España a las Indias Occidentales*, San Ildefonso, August 24, 1764, AGI, Correos, leg. 484.

employed could transport merchandise, a concession that opened another small breech in the Cádiz monopoly. To impose a change of this magnitude in a sudden, arbitrary manner was reminiscent of the early years of Philip V and Alberoni. The king's ministers simply bypassed the *Consulado*, the corporation that had the most at stake historically and institutionally, which found itself on the outside without a voice. Manuel Larrarte, who succeeded his father, tried desperately to secure support from Arriaga to approach Grimaldi. He realized that his cause was lost, however, when Grimaldi coolly returned the box of chocolates sent by the guild for Christmas as part of its customary annual offerings to the administrative elite.[60] The crown's manner in implementing this reform revealed a brash, aggressive Charles III, who had arrived from Italy with little respect for the customary decorum of Spanish politics. An education awaited him in 1766 with the Madrid uprising.

The royal decree October 16, 1765, constituted Charles's first major attempt at commercial reform in the Spanish Atlantic world. Signed personally by the king and addressed to Esquilache, it opened Havana to direct commerce with nine ports of Spain.[61] The legislation, extending the same privileges to Santo Domingo, Puerto Rico, Margarita, and Trinidad, responded to the recommendation of the special commission on commerce.[62] Interisland trade was permitted in colonial but not European products.[63] Finally, an ad valorem levy of 6 percent on Spanish merchandise and 7 percent on foreign goods (called the *almojarifazgo*) replaced the *palmeo*. A second decree of October 16, 1765, completed Cuban revenue reform. It increased the *alcabala* to 6 percent and established a 6 percent export tax on sugar. The sugar tax amounted to a consolidation and reduction of previous levies, representing both a concession to the emerging planter aristocracy and an effort to stimulate production.[64] The remnants of the Havana Company, which by this time had lost its special privileges, were now compelled to compete with other players on an equal basis.[65]

Shattering a monopoly that had endured over two centuries, the historic October decree was a daring reform of trade policy. What distinguished 1765

---

[60] Inglis and Kuethe, "El Consulado de Cádiz," pp. 79–80.

[61] Bilbao was excluded from the enfranchised ports and would be excluded again in 1778 because it functioned under its own separate *fuero*. Xabier Lamikiz, *Trade and Trust in the Eighteenth-Century Atlantic World: Spanish Merchants and Their Overseas Networks* (Suffolk: Royal Historical Society, Boydell Press, 2010), p. 33.

[62] This legislation is treated in Vicente Rodríguez Casado, "Comentarios al Decreto y Real Instrucción de 1765 regulando las relaciones comerciales de España e Indias," *Anuario de historia del derecho español*, 13 (1936–1941), pp. 100–35. A copy can be found in Ricardo Levene, ed. *Documentos para la historia argentina*, (Buenos Aires 1915), pp. 5, 197–98.

[63] Royal decree and instruction, San Lorenzo, October 16, 1765, AGI, SD, leg. 2188.

[64] The first decree, the product of a meeting of the Junta de Ministros, was addressed to Ricla. The second was directed to Arriaga, AGS, Hacienda, leg. 2342.

[65] Leví Marrero, *Cuba: Economía y sociedad*, XII (San Juan: Editorial San Juan, 1985), pp. 2–12.

from Ensenada's earlier efforts to liberalize trade in 1754 was the new chemistry at court, which momentarily opened space for radical change. Esquilache exploited the crisis mentality arising from the loss of Havana to crack the Cádiz monopoly, an achievement that had escaped all earlier reformers. With Charles III standing approvingly in the background, this breakthrough resembled the establishment of the reformed mail system. The *Consulado* was not consulted; indeed it was kept in the dark. Nor did Esquilache bring the Council of the Indies into the deliberations, as custom demanded. Moreover, the deeply troubled Arriaga was essentially bypassed; the venerable Minister of the Indies only saw the royal legislation a few days before it was promulgated. Arriaga bitterly opposed the liberalization of the port system, but he could approve the replacement of the *palmeo* with an ad valorem tax on merchandise.[66] Perhaps the greatest humiliation that Arriaga endured was sending the reformist legislation to the colonies under his own signature.[67]

These comprehensive reforms in Cuba took a mere two years. The army was reorganized, taxes increased, the royal administration tightened, and commercial policy liberalized. Ricla obtained permission to return to Spain, where he entered into the politics at court, eventually becoming minister of War. Esquilache assigned O'Reilly to Puerto Rico, where he continued to perform as one of the army's most promising officers.[68] He also selected a fellow Italian, the able Antonio Bucareli, to succeed Ricla as governor of Havana, placing the delicately balanced reform program in capable hands. Charles's successes in implementing a bold reformist agenda contrasted sharply with London's failure to implant similar measures in its North American colonies.

The British countered Spanish commercial reform with the Free Port Bill of 1766. The bill opened four ports in Jamaica and two in Dominica for an initial period of seven years to any foreign vessels. The principal target for the bill were Spanish traders in the Caribbean, who might trade bullion and other products (with the exception of sugar, molasses, coffee, tobacco, and manufactured goods) in exchange for slaves, British manufactures, and local produce. Jamaica had suffered a commercial downturn during the Seven Years' War, and trade remained sluggish after the conflict ended. Jamaican planters lobbied hard in Parliament to open its ports to foreign traders in an effort to reverse the downturn. The aim was to convert Jamaica and Dominica into clearinghouses for the trade in British products and slaves for foreign tropical produce and bullion, particularly as Spain deregulated trade between its

---

[66] Opinion (dictamen), Arriaga, Madrid, July 3, 1765, and Arriaga to Grimaldi, San Ildefonso, September 27, 1765, AGI, SD, leg. 2188.

[67] Esquilache to Arriaga, San Lorenzo, October 27, 1765, AGI, SD, leg. 2188.

[68] Torres Ramírez, *Alejandro O'Reilly*, pp. 49, 55–94.

Caribbean islands and the metropolis.[69] An unexpected stimulus to inter-American commerce developed soon after, when a sequence of devastating hurricanes struck Cuba, Santo Domingo, and Puerto Rico, forcing the royal authorities to improvise in securing sustenance for the beleaguered islands.[70]

THE GÁLVEZ VISITA TO NEW SPAIN

As Ricla and O'Reilly finalized their work in Cuba, Esquilache turned his attention to New Spain, by far the richest of Spain's New World possessions. In the fall of 1764, he dispatched Lieutenant Genereal Juan de Villalba y Angulo and a large cadre of military personnel to reorganize the Mexican army. Esquilache later sent him a copy of the Cuban regulation for disciplined militia to serve as a model.[71] Villalba promptly expanded the fixed garrison from an infantry battalion and a corps of dragoons to three full regiments, two of them dragoons, the other infantry. For volunteer forces, he raised a disciplined militia of six regiments, three battalions, and two separate companies of infantry as well as two mounted regiments and a corps of lancers. *Pardos* comprised two of the infantry battalions and one of the separate companies, *morenos* the other.[72] As in Cuba, the colonial military establishment grew rapidly and involved creoles and people of color among the native population.

Esquilache instituted the office of visitor-general to reform revenue collection, establish the tobacco monopoly, and improve the royal administration by introducing an intendant system on the Spanish model. After his first choice, Francisco Carrasco, the superintendant of tobacco revenues and a prominent figure at court, declined the mission for personal reasons, he summoned to the task Francisco Anselmo Armona, the intendant of Murcia.[73] By dispatching Armona and Villalba together, Esquilache aimed to foster close coordination between the two wings of reformist action as had occurred with Ricla and O'Reilly in Cuba. Armona, however, had reservations about taking the position.[74]

[69] Adrian Pearce, *British Trade with Spanish America, 1763–1808* (Liverpool: Liverpool University Press, 2007), pp. 42–51.

[70] Sherry Johnson, *Climate & Catastrophe in Cuba and the Atlantic World in the Age of Revolution* (Chapel Hill: University of North Carolina Press, 2011), chaps. 3–5.

[71] Christon I. Archer, "Charles III and Defense Policy for New Spain, 1759–1788," in Gaetano Massa, ed., *Paesi Mediterranei e America Latina* (Roma: Centro di studi americanistici America in Italia, 1982), p. 193.

[72] McAlister, The *"Fuero Militar,"* pp. 3- 4, 94. See also Ben Vinson III, *Bearing Arms for His Majesty: The Free-Colored Militia in Colonial Mexico* (Stanford: Stanford University Press, 2001), pp. 37–45.

[73] Priestley, *José de Gálvez*, p. 133.

[74] The following text is based on the manuscript account of Armona´s brother, José Antonio de Armona y Murga, in *Noticias privadas de casa, útiles para mis hijos: recuerdos históricos de mi carrera ministerial en España y América,* 2 vols. (Madrid: Ayuntamiento de Madrid, 1989 ed.), I, pp. 50–57. The authors wish to thank Juan Bosco Amores for providing this data. The original manuscript is in the Biblioteca Nacional de España, MSS/23088.

A well-connected Basque from Álava, Armona had serious misgivings about the feasibility of the enterprise, which he considered "useless." He feared that he would be "like a Quijote trying to right wrongs and do in scoundrels" but without the means to keep the viceroy from tying him up in litigation for "ten or twelve years."[75] Accordingly, he attempted to slip out of the assignment as had Carrasco before him. This time, however, Esquilache was adamant. He promised Armona the Ministry of the Indies upon his return in three or four years but threatened him with imprisonment for disobedience if he persisted in his negative mindset. This sort of high-handed behavior was precisely what the *madrileño* elite despised about the Sicilian, as he would discover in good time.

Under enormous pressure, Francisco Armona eventually relented. Two of his personal friends intervened to diffuse the issue, the Duke of Medinaceli, a grandee who would never have condescended to accept a position as minister, but who hung out at court as first equerry of the king, and his wife's uncle, Don Diego Merlo, who served as first chamberlain. In the end, however, it was a fellow Basque, Miguel de Múzquiz, who did the most to change Armona's mind. First officer in the Secretariat of Finance, and that ministry's future secretary of the Office, Múzquiz was a gentle soul who persuaded him to swallow his pride and meet with the Junta de Ministros at Aranjuez.

During this period of intense activity, the junta gathered every other day in the quarters of Grimaldi, as first secretary of the Office. Fearful of change, Arriaga spoke very little, "with tense difficulty, timidly," expressing concern that the reforms would provoke turmoil.[76] He proposed adding several articles to the instruction that Esquilache had prepared in order to reinforce the powers of Viceroy Marqués de Cruillas (1760–1766), whom, incidentally, he had appointed. And despite his fragile demeanor in the face of the two domineering Italians, Arriaga stubbornly held his ground. For his part, Armona remained concerned that the separation of the military command from the office of viceroy and his own role as an independent sort of intendant could come to no good.

Without much ado, Esquilache and Grimaldi simply ignored Arriaga and sent Armona on his way without modifying the original instructions. To manage the problem of the viceroy, Esquilache found another method. He armed Armona with outrageous secret royal orders charging Cruillas with embezzlement and theft, supposedly to the tune of some 2.5 million silver pesos, in connection with the expenditures for the defense of Veracruz while the British occupied Havana. Armona left with Villalba in September, but he died during the passage to New Spain, resulting in a disjuncture between the military reorganization and collateral financial and administrative reforms. Armona's death then led to the selection of the soon-to-be

[75] Ibid.
[76] Ibid.

controversial José de Gálvez. In both instances, Esquilache sent to notification of the appointments, the royal instructions, and the lists of personnel for the mission, leaving the Ministry of the Indies merely to process the paperwork.[77]

Gálvez, a native of the village of Macharaviaya near Málaga, had studied law and established a practice in Madrid. He improved his ties to the court through his marriage to a well-connected French woman, and later secured employment as *asesor* for the French embassy.[78] On the eve of Spain's intervention into the Seven Years' War, Gálvez came to the attention of the royal administration through a paper that he entitled "Discurso y reflexiones de un vasallo sobre la decadencia de nuestras Indias españoles," which advocated a number of reforms within the Spanish Atlantic, including greater commercial deregulation and an end to the Cádiz monopoly.[79] Gálvez did not reach the colony to begin his *visita* until July 1765, well after Villalba had launched the military reform.

Mexico was by far Spain's richest colony and it sent enormous quantities of silver to the outside. As Figure 7.2 indicates, the Mexican treasuries provided increasingly large amounts for the mother country and to support strategic defenses in the region. The latter included a massive arch of military strongpoints extending from Cumaná on the South American mainland to San Juan, then westward across the Caribbean to Havana, across the Gulf of Mexico to New Orleans, and from Texas to California. In times of peace, remittances to Spain tended to outstrip the amounts spent on Caribbean defenses, while in wartime spending on local defense took precedence. According to Figure 7.2, the *situados* rose to new highs during each of the century's major conflicts – the War of Jenkins' Ear, the Seven Years' War, and especially during the War of the American Revolution, when the *situado* peaked at just over 10 million pesos in 1783.

After the Seven Years' War, reformers decided to fortify the Cabaña on the eastern side of the Havana harbor to protect Morro Castle, as well as Aróstequi Heights to protect the city from the west and Soto Hill on the western side of the bay near the shipyard. Vast sums also went to rebuild the fortifications at San Juan, Puerto Rico. A decade later, the *situados* diverted 38.6 million Mexican pesos during the war to fund the thirteen British

---

[77] Esquilache to Arriaga, San Ildefonso, two letters, July 30, 1764, AGI, Mexico, leg. 1245. As the jacket on the Armona file explained, "This appointment was made by the Minister of Finance and *Señor* Squilache transmitted it to that of the Indies in *oficio* of July 30 of 1764." For a discussion of Armona's instructions and a translation, see Priestley, *José de Gálvez*, pp. 123–34, 404–17.

[78] José Miguel Morales Folguera, María Isabel Pérez de Colosía Rodríguez, and Juan Andrés Blanco Rodríguez, et al., *Los Gálvez de Macharaviaya* (Málaga: Junta de Andalucía, 1991), especially pp. 242–46.

[79] Luis Navarro García, "El primer proyecto reformista de José de Gálvez," in *Homenaje al Dr. José Antonio Calderón Quijano* (Sevilla: Escuela de Estudios Hispano-Americanos, 1997), pp. 387–402. A copy can be found in the Biblioteca del Palacio, Miscelánea de Ayala, vol. 1.

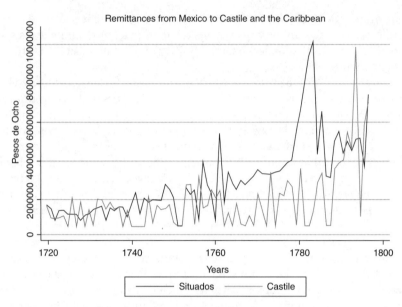

Remittances from Mexico to Castile and the Caribbean

FIGURE 7.2 Remittances from the Caja of Mexico

colonies and to provide support for the armada, the expeditionary army commanded by Bernardo de Gálvez in Florida and Louisiana, and the military garrisons in Cuba.[80] Mexico also financed the naval shipyard in Havana at the cost of nearly 600,000 pesos annually, and it provided another half million to purchase Cuban tobacco for the royal monopoly in Spain.[81] Moreover, it still remitted handsome sums to the *Depositaría de Indias* in Cádiz, thus providing critical support for the Royal Treasury. During the periods of relative peace, these remittances reached over 10 million pesos (1793).[82] It can be argued that when Gálvez began his *visita general*, Mexico City's central treasury rivaled the general treasury in Madrid in tax income, making New Spain the brightest star in the colonial crown, and it remained so until the wars of independence early in the next century.[83] As a result, Mexico stood as the crucial theater for revenue reform, which the crown entrusted to José de Gálvez.

[80] Carlos Marichal and Matilde Souto Mantecón, "Silver and Situados: New Spain and the Financing of the Spanish Empire in the Caribbean in the Eighteenth Century," *HAHR*, **74** (Nov. 1994), p. 607.

[81] An annual average of 590,000 pesos derives from the peacetime expenditures over the years 1763–1778. AGI, SD, legs. 1865–1867. Leví Marrero, *Cuba: Economía y sociedad*, XI (San Juan: Editorial San Juan, 1984), p. 30.

[82] Leví Marrero, *Cuba: Economía y sociedad*, XI, p. 613.

[83] Ibid., p. 611.

Beginning in Veracruz and systematically extending his mission throughout the colony, Gálvez imposed a series of measures designed to enhance royal income, including the introduction of royal monopolies for tobacco and aguardiente. Building upon measures that Ensenada introduced through Revillagigedo in 1753 to replace tax farmers with salaried appointees, he purged the *alcabala* administration of corrupt officials and replaced them with new men he had brought from Spain.[84] Apart from their routine communication with the Ministry of the Indies, both Villalba and Gálvez would maintain direct lines of correspondence with Esquilache.[85]

In the initial phase of his work, Gálvez consulted with local interests in establishing the aguardiente monopoly in Veracruz.[86] It was impossible for him to co-opt the Mexican elites as Ricla had done in Cuba, however, because Gálvez lacked authorization to promise commercial concessions. While the Junta de Ministros sought to deregulate the colonial commercial system, it was not prepared to include Mexico under that umbrella. The junta's new strategy represented a fundamental change from reformist policy since the time of Campillo y Cossío and Ensenada, and from the Select Committee report of February 1765, which emphasized modernizing the mercantile system to maximize economic benefits for Spain and for the Royal Treasury. Reverses suffered in the Seven Years' War had altered that perspective with strategic priorities often overtaking purely commercial concerns. The crown wanted to ensure the economic development of vulnerable imperial peripheries such as Havana, San Juan, Louisiana, or even far away Buenos Aires to enable them to pay for their own defenses. Commercially powerful Mexico might suffocate its weaker colonial competition, particularly if the viceroyalty could compete freely within an imperial free trade system. Mexico's economic well-being had to be sacrificed to leave room for expansion in the weaker colonies.[87] As early as January 1764, Grimaldi told D'Ossun that Esquilache's plans for imperial free trade did not immediately

---

[84] The classic work on this process is Priestley, *José de Gálvez*. More recent works include D.A. Brading, *Miners & Merchants in Bourbon Mexico, 1763–1810* (Cambridge: Cambridge University Press, 1971), pp. 25–51, and Linda K. Salvucci, "Costumbres Viejas, 'hombres nuevos': José de Gálvez y la burocracia fiscal novohispana (1754–1800)," *Historia mexicana*, 33 (October–December 1983), pp. 224–60, and Stanley J. Stein and Barbara H. Stein, *Apogee of empire: Spain and New Spain in the Age of Charles III, 1759–1789* (Baltimore: Johns Hopkins University Press, 2003).

[85] See AGI, Mexico, leg. 1245.

[86] José Jesús Hernández Palomo, *El aguardiente de caña en México* (Sevilla: Escuela de Estudios Hispano-Americanos, 1974), pp. 68–70.

[87] For a more detailed treatment of this transformation, see Kuethe, "Imperativos militares en la política comercial de Carlos III," in Kuethe and Juan Marchena Fernández (eds.), *Soldados del rey: El ejército borbónico en América colonial en vísperas de la independencia* (Castellón: Universitat Jaume I, 2005), pp. 149–59.

include Mexico.[88] Royal policy would keep the Veracruz trade narrowly channeled into the traditional structures of the monopoly port and convoy system, supplemented by register ships, even at the expense of overall volume of trade and potential tax revenues.

Mexico's lack of good port facilities made it easier for the crown to maintain the monopoly convoy system. As Gálvez confirmed during his visit to the region, Veracruz was "the only throat for all of the kingdom."[89] Seeking to make effective tax collections on trade, Gálvez exploited this geographical reality by his instructions of February 11, 1767, which imposed (for the first time) a 4 percent *alcabala* on goods sold in Veracruz. He also installed a rigorous system of registration for goods destined for Jalapa, before fraud could develop, and he suspended a plethora of customs officials, whom he accused of corruption.[90] Gálvez's February instructions evoked strong protests from the *Consulados* of both Mexico and Cádiz, which they forwarded to the Council of the Indies.[91] The *visitador*'s views about Mexico's geo-economic reality would remain dominant in court circles for another two decades.[92]

After the moderating hand of Esquilache had disappeared in early 1766, Gálvez's reforms quickly assumed a harsh, uncompromising tone accentuated by an anti-American bias obvious in his treatment of creole officials in the colonial administration.[93] This bias cast a shadow over the visitor-general's work in Mexico and would later influence his controversial service in Madrid.[94] Moreover, when Gálvez's purged Mexican treasury officials, their replacements were not chosen by merit, as they very frequently were merely cronies from his *malagueño* regional base.[95]

Mexicans paid more taxes and tolerated new monopolies but received little in return, except for appointments to the disciplined militia officer corps. Although some found the uniform and the accompanying military privileges attractive, most men resented sacrificing Mexican resources to support the entire Caribbean defense network. For *habaneros*, who were net beneficiaries of the pattern of royal spending, it must have seemed easy to be "faithful"

---

[88] D'Ossun to Choiseul, Madrid, January 23, 1764, AAE:CPE, vol. 540, fols. 64–69. For a broad perspective on this point, see John Fisher, "Imperial Free Trade and the Hispanic Economy, 1778–1796," *Journal of Latin American Studies*, 13 (May 1981): pp. 22–23.

[89] Gálvez to Arriaga, Mexico, February 27, 1767, AGI, Mexico, leg. 1249.

[90] Gálvez, instructions, February 11, 1767, AGI, Mexico, leg. 1245.

[91] *Consulado* of Mexico to Arriaga, Mexico, May 27, June 26, and October 29, 1767 and petition, *Consulado* of Cádiz, Cádiz, February 29, 1786, AGI, Mexico, leg. 1250.

[92] Royal order, San Lorenzo, October 19, 1787, AGI, Mexico, leg. 2505. This order to reexamine commercial policy for Veracruz confirmed the conviction that Mexico, "by having only one port in all of its north coast … makes contraband difficult."

[93] Brading, *Miners and Merchants*, pp. 34–44.

[94] Litigation involving the fate of the discharged men lingered until at least 1775. Salvucci, "Costumbres viejas," pp. 233–36

[95] Ibid., pp. 227–28, 247–49.

vassals, but taxpaying Mexicans understandably showed much less enthusiasm. Unlike the sort of orderly military preparations that unfolded over the years in Cuba, Spanish officers would face never-ending frustrations as they struggled to impart a sense of duty and military spirit to an unwilling Mexican population.[96]

Meanwhile, Esquilache further consolidated his power to control key political and economic reforms in the Spanish Atlantic. By a series of royal orders issued in late 1764 and early 1765, the Ministry of War formalized responsibility for all veteran troops operating in America, both the permanent units and the rotating Spanish battalions. Through this arrangement, Esquilache controlled directly the administration of the main fighting forces in the New World and their costly budgets. Ricla, Villalba, and the numerous other military authorities now reported to the Ministry of War, which signaled another important erosion of Arriaga's effective powers as Minister of the Indies.[97] Moreover, Esquilache added the office of director general of tobacco revenues to his portfolio, a step that provided control over a very lucrative source of American revenues.[98]

Apart from reform initiatives in Cuba and Mexico, the royal administration proceeded on a piecemeal basis to strengthen Madrid's control over less-critical portions of the empire. O'Reilly had hoped to receive the Mexican assignment, but while he still labored in Cuba, the government selected Villalba. Esquilache sent him instead to apply the Cuban military system in strategic Puerto Rico. Given the small, fragmented population, O'Reilly raised only a series of separate companies.[99] Orders also went out to the authorities in Buenos Aires, Caracas, and Peru to reorganize their militia. The Junta de Ministros ordered Viceroy Manuel de Amat of Peru in 1763 to establish a disciplined militia of 22,000 men.[100] Juan Manuel Campero, the new governor of Tucumán, personally delivered a reform plan to Amat en route to his assignment. Caracas simply received a copy of the 1734 ordinance for Spain. In Buenos Aires, where more immediate concerns loomed

---

[96] Christon I. Archer, *The Army in Bourbon Mexico, 1760–1810* (Albuquerque: University of New Mexico Press, 1977).

[97] Esquilache to Arriaga, San Ildefonso, October, 1764, AGI, SD, leg. 2078; Ricla to Arriaga, Havana, May 15, 1765, AGI, SD, leg. 2120; Esquilache to Villalba, El Pardo, February 8, 1765, AGI, Mexico, leg. 1245; Arriaga to Viceroy Pedro Messía de la Cerda, Madrid, December 7, 1764, AGI, SF, leg. 942.

[98] As the royal *cédula*, Madrid, January 2, 1766, explained, "it is my royal will that the ... tobacco administration of the three ... Kingdoms of New Spain, Santa Fe, and Peru be governed and come under the orders and dispositions that the Marqués de Squilache issues ... to whom the faculties that he might require are conceded." AGI, IG, leg.1744.

[99] Torres Ramírez, *La Compañía Gaditana*, pp. 49, 55–94. For an overview of the extension of the disciplined militia system, see Kuethe, "Las milicias disciplinadas," in Kuethe and Marchena, *Soldados del rey*, pp. 101–26.

[100] Leon G. Campbell, *The Military and Society in Colonial Peru, 1750–1810* (Philadelphia: American Philosophical Society, 1978), p. 48.

over the renewed frontier dispute with Brazil, the royal instruction of July 7, 1764, ordered Governor Pedro de Cevallo to raise units on the Cuban model as the population permitted. Esquilache sent 2,000 muskets and 151 officers and enlisted men to train this militia. The *situado* supporting these military innovations would come from Potosí.[101] In each of these three cases, the crown relied on local authorities to reform the militia, which became the standard method for military reorganization, rather than dispatching a separate commission as it had done in Cuba, Mexico, and Puerto Rico. The crown took no immediate action in Cartagena, Santo Domingo, or Panama. Santo Domingo lacked the strategic importance of a Havana or a San Juan, while Cartagena and Panama had lost status with the end of the *Galeones*. In addition, uncontrolled contraband undermined most of debt-ridden New Granada's commerce.[102] Ideally, revenue reform would precede costly military innovations. The tobacco monopoly would provide most of the revenue to cover the costly modernization of the army. A royal decree of December 26, 1765, formally established the tobacco monopoly in New Granada, "as it was done in New Spain," while the existing monopoly in Peru would also be reorganized to conform to the Mexican model. The *cédula* justified placing the operations of the monopoly in each of the three viceroyalties under Esquilache's authority because of unspecified foreign threats and rising military costs.[103] In 1760, Esquilache had transferred the Cuban monopoly from the Havana Company to entrepreneur José Villanueva Pico, but before the new arrangement could take effect the British had invaded.[104] In the aftermath of the British occupation, he ordered Ricla to reestablish the factory under direct royal administration. Ricla's successor, Antonio Bucareli, perceptively described the institution as "the monarchy's most precious jewel."[105] In a concession to the oft-favored Cubans, however, the monopoly

---

[101] Kuethe, "La milicias disciplinadas," pp. 113–14.

[102] Lance Grahn, *The Political Economy of Smuggling: Regional Informal Economies in Early Bourbon New Granada* (Boulder: Westview Press, 1977). See also, Allan J. Kuethe, "The Early Reforms of Charles III in the Viceroyalty of New Granada, 1759–1776," in *Reform and Insurrection in Bourbon New Granada and Peru*, eds. John Fisher, Allan J. Kuethe, and Anthony McFarlane (Baton Rouge: Louisiana State University Press, 1990), pp. 19–40.

[103] As the royal edict stated, "To defray the excessive expenditures that it has been necessary to make in the kingdoms of the Indies ... to protect them from enemy invasions so that my vassals can enjoy tranquility and security ... I found it appropriate to order the tobacco monopoly established in New Spain as the most useful means to meet the urgencies of the crown without burdening the vassals in commerce. And having taken stock of this measure's good results, and that it would be advantageous to extend it to the Kingdom of Santa Fe, I have resolved through my Royal Decree of December 26 of the past year that the tobacco monopoly also be installed [there] as it was in New Spain ... and [in] that of Peru, where it also had been established but poorly planned." Royal *cédula*, Madrid, January 2, 1766, AGI, IG, leg. 1744.

[104] McNeill, *Atlantic Empires*, p. 115.

[105] Leví Marrero, *Economía*, XI, p. 1.

would only supply tobacco to Spain, while leaf for local consumption would continue to be sold on the free market.[106]

While Viceroy Pedro Messía de la Cerda undertook the establishment of the tobacco monopoly in New Granada, he concurrently turned management of the aguardiente monopoly from private concessionaries to salaried public officials.[107] In 1764, he dispatched Juan Díaz de Herrera to the Presidency of Quito to reclaim the administration of the *alcabala* from tax farmers and the aguardiente monopoly from private operators and to place them both under direct royal control.[108] The treasuries of Quito and Santa Fe would continue to send annual *situados* to support Cartagena's defenses.[109]

RESISTANCE TO REFORM IN THE SPANISH ATLANTIC WORLD

The first great American challenge to the reforms of Esquilache came in the Andean provincial city of Quito, when two popular uprisings broke out over Juan Díaz de Herrera's attempts to establish an aguardiente monopoly and to place the *alcabala* under direct royal administration.[110] For many of Quito's elite and plebeian citizens, the reforms of the *alcabala* and the aguardiente monopoly posed serious dangers to their material welfare amidst a long-term decline of the formerly dominant textile economy. Many elite land owners turned from textile manufacturing to growing sugar cane and manufacturing it into aguardiente, a popular drink among the city's plebeians, and the new state monopoly threatened to cut into profits. Moreover, government attempts to control the production and sale of cane liquor provoked immediate anger among the plebeian consumers in the city's neighborhoods (*barrios*). Some even owned bootleg bars or stores that sold aguardiente and maize beer (*chicha*) in the city. The reform of the sales tax also threatened to disrupt the urban marketplace by raising the levy on small freeholders in the city's suburban parishes who produced food for the city. Moreover, the

---

[106] Ibid., pp. 1–8.
[107] Miklos Pogonyi, "The Search for Trade and Profits in Bourbon Colombia, *1765–1777*," (Ph.D. diss., University of New Mexico, 1978), pp. 163, 181. Messía de la Cerda's predecessor, José de Solís, had already removed from the control of private concessionaries the aguardiente monopolies of Santa Fe (1757) and Mompós (1760).
[108] File, revenue reform in Quito, 1764–1765, AGI, Quito, leg. 398.
[109] José Manuel Serrano Álvarez, *Fortificaciones y tropa: El gasto militar en Tierra Firme, 1700–1788* (Sevilla: Diputación de Sevilla, Universidad de Sevilla Consejo Superior de Investigaciones Científicas, Escuela de Estudios Hispano-Americanos, 2004).
[110] For studies of the Quito Insurrection of 1765, see Kenneth J. Andrien, "Economic Crisis, Taxes, and the Quito Insurrection of 1765, *Past & Present: A Journal of Historical Studies*, no. **129** (November 1990), pp. 104–31; idem, *The Kingdom of Quito, 1690–1830: the State and Regional Development* (Cambridge 1995), pp. 180–89; Anthony McFarlane, "The Rebellion of the Barrios: Urban Insurrection in Bourbon Quito," *HAHR*, **49** (May 1989), pp. 283–330; and Martin Minchom *The People of Quito, 1690–1810: Change and Unrest in the Underclass* (Boulder: Westview Press, 1994), pp. 222–32.

new administration tightened regulations on the smuggling of untaxed goods brought into the city by peddlers (many of them indigenous and not theoretically subject to paying the sales tax). By 1765, the urban plebe and disgruntled elites were prepared to join forces in an unprecedented popular alliance against crown reforms.[111]

On May 22, 1765, the angry citizens of Quito staged a massive uprising directed against the building housing the aguardiente monopoly and the *aduana* in the city's Plaza de Santa Barbara. The city's butchers, peddlers, small farmers, and shop owners apparently led the attacks, and the rioters proceeded to drink the product and then destroy the buildings in a disciplined, methodical manner. Although the crowd ultimately disbanded after the audiencia granted them a pardon and agreed to abolish the fiscal innovations, an uneasy calm prevailed in the city. Simmering antagonisms erupted into a second riot on June 24 during the feast of Saint John, as a popular force of several thousand besieged peninsulars and government officials in the central square, where they fought until nearly four the next morning when the authorities capitulated. With the local creole elite and the Jesuits serving as mediators, the audiencia acceded to the rioters' demands – the justices surrendered all weapons to the protestors, all peninsular Spaniards left the city within seven days, and the crowd received a full pardon from any prosecution. The uprising effectively suspended royal government in Quito, as power rested with an uneasy coalition of creoles and plebeians.[112]

Tensions within the coalition government ultimately undermined its power and hastened the return of royal control. The violence of the two uprisings and the increasing radicalism of the plebeians alienated creole elites, and latent distrust between mestizos and Amerindians in the city also weakened the popular government. In short, the class and ethnic tensions present in *quiteño* society gradually undermined the fragile popular coalition governing the city after the audiencia conceded to the demonstrators their principal demands. On September 1, 1766, when a royal army entered Quito under the command of the conciliatory governor of Guayaquil, Juan Antonio de Zelaya, the divided citizenry of Quito welcomed the soldiers warmly, and this serious threat to royal authority ended.[113]

Resistance from within Spain, the *motín* of Esquilache, also blunted the momentum of reform. The uprising began in Madrid on the evening of March 23, 1766, Palm Sunday, when approximately 6,000 people gathered in the Plaza Mayor to march on the house of the king's unpopular Italian minister, the Marqués de Esquilache. The demonstration took place against a background of high food prices, rising taxes to pay for the recent war, and

---

[111] Andrien, "Economic Crisis, Taxes," pp. 111–12, 117–19.
[112] Ibid., pp. 120–25; McFarlane, "Rebellion of the Barrios," pp. 300–17.
[113] Andrien, "Economic Crisis, Taxes," pp. 125–29; McFarlane, "Rebellion of the Barrios", pp. 317–24.

Esquilache's municipal reforms, including an incendiary edict issued on March 20 forbidding *madrileños* from wearing their traditional long capes and large-brimmed hats, ostensibly to prevent criminals from hiding weapons or stolen goods. After looting the house of Esquilache, who had taken refuge in the Royal Palace, the crowd's numbers swelled to over 15,000, and it began attacking coaches, breaking windows in the houses of the wealthy, freeing jailed prisoners, and smashing city street lights in Madrid, newly installed by order of Esquilache.[114] The next day the violence escalated as upwards of 25,000 people swarmed into the Puerta del Sol and then marched to the Royal Palace, where they confronted the king's Walloon Guards, a widely despised group of foreign troops. Dozens of demonstrators and ten of the guardsmen died, and the angry crowd dragged the bodies of the dead soldiers through the streets, burning two.[115] The crowd had initially demanded the removal and exile of the foreigner Esquilache and a lowering of food prices, but by the second day they called for the resignation of all foreign ministers, revocation of the dress regulations, and the abolition of the Walloon Guards. Although his ministers were divided over how to respond, the king appeared in person from a balcony of the Royal Palace and acceded to all the crowd's demands, which quieted the assembled multitude.

Nonetheless, at midnight a shaken Charles left the city with his aged and frail mother and his children through a tunnel at the back of his palace, where waiting coaches transported them to Aranjuez. The contemporary account of the Conde de Fernán-Núñez captures well the intense drama of the moment and the humiliation that Madrid inflicted upon its ruler:

Not believing it advantageous for his [royal] image to remain any longer in Madrid, and wishing to punish its inhabitants [by his absence], H.M. resolved to retire to Aranjuez that same night, and having executed all the steps in the greatest secrecy, he left with the whole royal family through the vaults (*bóvedas*) of the Palace, and boarding the carriages outside of the San Vicente Gate, he set out for Aranjuez to where he had deployed the Walloon Guard for his protection. As the tunnels (*callejones bajos*) were narrow, it was necessary to saw off the poles of the Queen mother's litter ... so that it could get through. But despite everything, she got off and made the trip like the others, although they say that she spared nothing in urging the king not to go.[116]

---

[114] The street lights were part of the municipal reforms sponsored by Esquilache. The crown hired Italian architect Francisco Sabatini to modernize various aspects of the city's water supply, waste disposal, and safety, which is why the government forced citizens to pay for lights. This probably explains why the crowd destroyed the seemingly innocuous street lights during the *motín*, along with attacking the house of Sabatini. See Antonio Domínguez Ortiz, *Carlos III y la España de la ilustración* (Madrid: Alianza Editorial, 1988), pp. 65–66.

[115] John Lynch, *Bourbon Spain, 1700–1808* (Oxford: Basil Blackwell, 1989), p. 262.

[116] Quoted in María Ángeles Pérez Samper, *Isabel de Farnesio* (Barcelona: Plaza y Janés, 2003), p. 482.

Although the king and his family had escaped the turbulent capital successfully, Charles clearly recognized the gravity of this dangerous political situation.

With his departure from Madrid, Charles received a profound, but most unwelcome, education in the politics of Madrid. The brash, cocky king who had arrived from Italy intending to initiate ambitious reform programs became a much more cautious, prudent statesman. This transition revealed the true strength of a monarch, who was able to learn from and adjust to the realities that he confronted. Over the long haul, he would accomplish much, but his reformist agenda would unfold slowly, carefully contoured to the political realities that he confronted. In his flight from Madrid, Charles wisely employed his Royal Guards to defend the road to Aranjuez, a precaution that his bungling French cousin failed to take twenty-three years later when he fled to Versailles.

On March 25, news of the king's flight and word that the government had ordered troops to assemble in Madrid led groups of protestors to mobilize and seize arms to defend against an expected attack. Many cried out, "God save the king, death to Esquilache." In a mark of apparent contempt, crowd leaders sent a newly freed convicted criminal, Diego de Avendaño, to Aranjuez with their early demands to the king, along with the additional requirement that he return to Madrid and grant an official pardon to everyone who had participated in the *motín*.[117] While in Aranjuez, Charles also received a surprising letter from Bishop Antonio Rojas y Contreras, the aristocratic president of the Council of Castile, supporting the aims of the crowd and urging the dismissal of Esquilache. The bishop also encouraged the full Council to recommend the same action to the monarch.

On March 26, when Avendaño returned from Aranjuez, he announced the king's capitulation. Esquilache left for Italy and the crowd dispersed. The demonstrators suffered twenty-one dead, forty-nine wounded, and government troops lost nineteen. Moreover, when news of the Madrid uprising spread to the provinces, additional *motines* erupted in a series of key provincial cities such as Bilbao, Saragossa, Barcelona, and Cádiz. The political fallout only worsened when the aristocratic bishop of Cuenca, Isidoro de Carvajal y Lancaster, wrote a letter (well distributed among political elites in the capital) supporting the demands of the Madrid crowd, even citing failures of colonial policy, such as the loss of Havana, as evidence of God's wrath against the reformers.[118] The whole affair left the king and his reformist ministers shaken; their regalist agenda appeared derailed by this powerful outpouring of popular hostility, which even some influential members of the aristocracy now openly supported.[119]

[117] Stein and Stein, *Apogee of Empire*, pp. 86–87.
[118] Ibid.
[119] There is a large body of work treating the *motín* of Esquilache, but it is very well summarized in Domínguez Ortiz, *Carlos III y España*, pp. 63–84.

For Charles, the humiliation was profound. Feeling compelled to flee the palace under cover of darkness was a severe blow to his image as king. As the Conde de Aranda forcefully pacified Madrid, French Ambassador D'Ossun urged Charles to return immediately to face down the opposition, but he refused.[120] Instead, the king waited until the court moved to Oriente Palace for the winter, and he only entered the city after having extracted an apology from the corporations of Madrid, a document that Aranda carefully orchestrated.[121] Finally, having to dismiss his favorite minister was undoubtedly an extremely bitter pill. Predictably, Charles remained faithful to Esquilache. The king supported the Italian's heavy tobacco habit during later years by supplying him with Cuban leaf, and he eventually found him a job as ambassador to Venice.[122] The king received yet another blow when his aging mother, Elizabeth Farnese, died at Aranjuez four months after the uprising.[123] As she wished, her interment took place at La Granja de San Ildefonso, where she had deposited the remains of Philip twenty years earlier. Upon her death, the last vestiges of a royal policy that gave primacy to dynastic concerns disappeared.

Despite these highly visible setbacks, King Charles and his ministers realized that only bold action, not timid resignation, would allow them to regain the political initiative in the wake of the uprisings. Contemporaries (and even some later historians) saw evidence that the *motín* of Esquilache was planned by sinister elements, not a spontaneous outpouring of popular opposition. Conspiracy advocates argued that the protests had spread quickly to other cities from Madrid, and that, before the outbreak of violence, broadsheets (*pasquines*) had called for popular protests against the dress regulations during the weeks leading up to Palm Sunday. Moreover, the apparent support of aristocratic factions for the demonstrators' demands, and the participation of agitators who spurred the crowds to action in taverns and public places, all pointed to an elite-led conspiracy.[124] The British ambassador, Lord Rochford, even hinted that the French had worked behind the scenes with Spanish aristocrats to engineer the uprising in Madrid.[125] To get to the bottom of the problem, the king set up a commission of inquiry, headed by the Conde de Aranda, to determine which groups had manipulated the people into rioting. The king and his ministers badly needed a conspiracy, and even

---

[120] D'Ossun to Choiseul, Aranjuez, May 12, June 2, June 19, June 24, and July 7, 1766, and Choiseul to d'Ossun, Versailles, June 29, 1766, AEE:CPE, vol. 546, fols. 81, 132, 141, 165–66.
[121] D'Ossun to Choiseul, Aranjuez, May 17, June 2, June 9, June 23, and July 11, 1766, AAE: CPE, vol. 546. His Majesty received the petition on June 7. The royal entourage avoided Madrid on its summer journey to La Granja de San Ildefonso by passing through the Escorial.
[122] Esquilache to Governor of Cuba Antonio Bucareli, Messina, September 1771, AGI, IG, leg. 1629.
[123] Pérez Samper, *Isabel de Farnesio*, pp. 486–88.
[124] Domínguez Ortiz, *Carlos III y España*, pp. 76–77.
[125] Lynch, *Bourbon Spain*, pp. 264–65.

more importantly, a scapegoat to justify a return to unpopular reformist policies. They would soon find it in the powerful Jesuit order.

The role of the *Consulado* of Cádiz remains uncertain, but it is curious that the two principal reformist ministers of the period, Ensenada and Esquilache, both fell at the moment when commercial deregulation was in play. Fernando de Silva Álvarez de Toledo, the Duke of Alba (formerly Huéscar), who owned vast tracts of land near Seville that benefitted from the *tercio* reserved for local produce on the fleets, aroused suspicion, but no concrete evidence appeared.[126] Alba formed part of an inner circle of advisors, primarily from the Council of State, upon whom Charles depended during the dark months after the riots, and he urged the monarch to transfer his capital to Seville, a proposition that Charles, who had spent five years of his youth there, considered seriously.[127] Ensenada believed that his moment for a full restoration had finally arrived, but on April 19, he received orders to return to his exile, this time in Medina del Campo.[128] The aged minister's enemies controlled the now influential Council of State, led by Alba and Wall, and he had outlived his political usefulness to Charles. Ensenada would remain at Medina del Campo until his death in 1781. Meanwhile, the venerable Fray Arriaga, whom Esquilache had pushed into the background, suddenly emerged as a powerful, respected figure. Like Grimaldo following the exile of Alberoni, Arriaga must have felt a deeply satisfying sense of redemption.

CAROLINE CLERICAL REFORM AND THE JESUITS

The crown's attack on the Society of Jesus in 1767 formed part of the larger regalist effort to reform the Roman Catholic Church and subordinate it to the Bourbon state. The ministers of Charles III were all pious Roman Catholics, but they wanted to limit the temporal power of the papacy, the influence of the Roman Curia in national affairs, and the accumulation of wealth by the Church in Spain and the Indies.[129] This reformed "national church" would work in tandem with the monarchy to implement crown policies and ensure social stability.[130] An important component in advancing crown power over

---

[126] Conde de Fernán-Núñez, *Vida de Carlos III*, eds. A. Morel-Fatio and A. Paz y Meliá, 2 vols. (Madrid: F.Fe, 1898), I, p. 206; Manuel Danvila, *Reinado de Carlos III*, 6 vols. (Madrid: El Progreso Editorial, 1892–1896), II, pp. 317, 568.

[127] D'Ossun to Choiseul, Aranjuez, April 10, May 9, June 9, 19, and 23, and July 5, 1766, AAE: CPE, vol. 545, fols. 42–43, 81, 265, 268, 355–56.

[128] No clear explanation for Charles's thinking ever appeared. Gómez Urdáñez, *Castilla*, p. 516.

[129] According to the *catastro* (land register) of the Marqués de la Ensenada, the church in Castile owned one-seventh of the land but accounted for one-fourth of the agricultural production. It also owned one-tenth of the grazing animals, and numerous liens and loans on property. Domínguez Ortiz, *Carlos III y la España*, p.144.

[130] Charles C. Noel, "Clerics and Crown in Bourbon Spain, 1700–1808: Jesuits, Jansenists, and Enlightened Reformers," in James E. Bradley and Dale K. Van Kley, eds., *Religion and*

the church was control over naming key appointments to the secular hierarchy, embodied in the Concordat of 1753. The regular clergy, however, remained more independent, and by the eighteenth century the orders had acquired a reputation for being lazy, corrupt, and a drain on the resources of society.[131] A generation earlier, Juan and Ulloa had railed against the abuses of the orders in the Andes, and their report and others contributed to the decision to secularize the *doctrinas de indios* by 1753. The Jesuits, however, had largely avoided such crown attacks until the downfall of Ensenada and Rávago lost them the advocacy of the so-called Jesuit Party in Madrid. Without their protectors, the Jesuits suddenly became a visible target for the regalist ministers of Charles III, who harbored no love for the Society or the papacy.

Bourbon regalists were aided in their efforts to create a reformed national church by the Jansenists, who wanted to purge Catholicism of the more emotional forms of Baroque popular piety with its emphasis on the cult of saints, lavish religious festivals, and ornate decoration. Jansensism was a European reform movement with particular strength in France, but Jansenists in Spain also favored a return to the simplicity of the early church. Although always a diverse minority within the Spanish Church, Jansenists believed in a more direct relationship between men and their God, emphasizing the importance of divine grace rather than free will and good deeds in achieving salvation. They also wanted to weaken the authority of the papacy and the Inquisition. Instead, Jansenists promoted episcopal power, and they often found it useful to ally with Bourbon regalists in their efforts to reform the church.[132] Like their reforming allies at court, Spanish Jansenists were attracted to many of the ideas of the Enlightenment, and they wanted to reform morality and to gain greater control over the educational system as a vehicle to promote social and religious change.[133] The chief obstacle to these changes were more conservative political and clerical groups, particularly the Jesuits, whose adherence to the papacy and influence over university education made the Society a natural enemy of the Jansenists.[134]

By the mid-eighteenth century, the Jesuits had accumulated a powerful array of political and clerical enemies. The Order advocated the importance of human free will in achieving salvation over divine grace or predestination, which put them at loggerheads with the Jansensists and even some other

Politics in Enlightenment Europe (Notre Dame: University of Notre Dame Press, 2001), pp. 131–32.

[131] The census of 1768 counted 55,453. regular clergymen and 27,665 nuns in Spain. Along with 51,048 secular clergy, the total number of religious in the country were 151,829, not counting sacristans, administrators, and auxiliary clergy. Dominguez Ortiz, *Carlos III y la España*, p. 145.

[132] Ibid., pp. 126–27.

[133] Ibid., pp. 127–29.

[134] Ibid., pp. 142–43.

orders, such as the Dominicans and Augustinians.[135] Many Jesuits also advocated the doctrine of probabilism, which provided a way of approaching difficult matters of conscience or a dispute over church doctrine. According to probabilism, a Catholic may safely follow an act or doctrine approved by a church leader, even if the weight of evidence (scientific or theological) supports a contrary opinion or theological interpretation. For a missionary order such as the Jesuits – with evangelical enterprises stretching from Mexico to China – probabilism allowed them to borrow a great deal from advanced indigenous civilizations and exercise greater flexibility in converting people of different cultural backgrounds. For other religious orders, secular clergymen, and especially the Jansenists, probabilism only promoted moral and theological laxity within the church. While not all Jesuits defended probabilism, the doctrine was still closely associated with the order.[136] In addition, the fact that some Jesuits had defended the overthrow of immoral governments made them susceptible to charges of advocating regicide and revolution, a charge that alienated regalists in Spain and particularly alarmed King Charles III.[137] Finally, the near monopoly that the Society traditionally had over the position of royal confessor with its extensive powers of ecclesiastical patronage, and its domination of the prestigious *colegios mayores* at Spanish universities, had led to deep resentment among many clergymen and the laity. [138]

THE LONG DISPUTE WITH THE JESUITS OVER THE DIEZMO

Another major, long-simmering source of friction between the crown and the Society of Jesus was their long, acrimonious struggle over whether or not the order was exempt from paying the tithe (*diezmo*) on its extensive land holdings in the New World, a dispute that reached its resolution only a few months before the expulsion order. The tithe was a tax of 10 percent on all rural produce, which was used to support the Roman Catholic Church. In 1501, Pope Alexander VI declared the crown the "absolute owner" of tithes collected in the Indies, because of the bountiful harvest of indigenous souls to be converted and brought into the church. Two-ninths (*dos novenos*) of every tithe collection went directly to the royal treasuries of the Indies, while the rest was divided to support the various activities of the secular clergy.[139] Every owner of a productive land holding paid the tithe, but the Jesuits claimed that Pope Pius IV in 1561 had made them exempt from paying the tax in order to

---

[135] Ibid., pp. 86–87.
[136] Ibid.; Pablo Macera, "El probabilismo en el Perú durante el siglo XVIII," in *Trabajos de Historia*, tomo II (Lima 1977), 79–137.
[137] Domínguez Ortiz, *Carlos III y la España*, p. 87.
[138] Ibid., p. 88.
[139] C. H. Haring, *The Spanish Empire in America* (New York: Harcourt Brace and World, 1947), pp. 167–69.

help support their many missions to evangelize indigenous peoples in the Indies. This concession had been confirmed by Gregory XIII in 1568 and Gregory XIV in 1591 and ratified by King Philip II in 1572.[140] As a result, the Jesuits paid no tithes on their extensive rural landholdings in the New World, despite repeated protests from viceregal authorities and from the hierarchy of the secular clergy in the Indies.

The Jesuits successfully defended this exemption until the cathedral chapters of Mexico City and the Philippines brought the matter before the Council of the Indies in 1748. In response to this legal challenge from the cathedral chapters, Padre Pedro Ignacio de Altamirano, the Jesuit *procurador general de las Indias*, argued in a memorial to the Council that his order was the "absolute owner of its tithe revenues in the Indies" because of concessions that both the papacy and the crown had granted over 200 years before.[141] Although normally sympathetic to the Jesuits, King Ferdinand realized that the amounts of lost tithe revenues were considerable, and Padre Altramirano's claims constituted a powerful challenge to the crown's *real patronato*. As a result, King Ferdinand convened a special junta composed of four members of the Council of Castile and the *fiscal* of the Council of the Indies to study the matter. In its *consulta* of December 10, 1749, the junta argued that the Jesuits must pay the tithe on the fruits of their estates and any future lands that they might acquire.

According to the *consulta*, Pope Alexander VI had given Ferdinand, Isabel, and their successors the right to collect the tithe for the maintenance of the church in the Indies, and no subsequent pope had the right to exempt any group from paying the tax, including the Jesuits. On the other hand, the Jesuits could not be expected to pay the tax retroactively, because the amount they would owe was simply enormous. Moreover, the junta also applauded the meritorious evangelization efforts of the Society in the Indies, which their extensive landholdings supported. As a result, the junta recommended charging the Jesuits a *diezmo* of 3 1/3 percent (*uno a treinta*) rather than the full 10 percent paid by everyone else.[142] The crown concurred with the recommendation of the king's special junta, stating that beginning on January 1, 1750, the Jesuits would pay the 3 1/3 percent on all future harvests from its landholdings. The edict also demanded that all parties accept the king's judgment and maintain absolute silence on the matter in the future. His Majesty would tolerate no future litigation or discussion concerning the Jesuits and the tithe.[143]

---

[140] Royal *cédula*, Buen Retiro, February 24, 1750, AGI, IG, leg. 3085A.

[141] *Consulta*, Madrid, December 10, 1749; royal *cédula*, Buen Retiro, February 24, 1750, AGI, IG, leg. 3085A.

[142] *Consulta*, Madrid, December 10, 1749, AGI, IG, leg. 3085A.

[143] Royal *cédula*, Buen Retiro, February 24, 1750 AGI, IG, leg. 3085A,. This discussion of the Jesuits and the tithe occurred just as the King had convened the Junta Particular de Ministros at the home of José de Carvajal y Lancaster in November of 1748 to consider reforms of the

Despite the crown's definitive decision, disputes continued. On March 13, 1755, the *cabildos eclesiásticos* of the cathedrals of Mexico City, Puebla , and Quito wrote the crown that the Society had refused to pay the tithe as ordered in the edict of February 24, 1750.[144] Authorities in Mexico and Quito then sent an inventory of the large estates of the Jesuits in both provinces to indicate just how much revenue the crown was losing. According to data later compiled from the government agency administering the properties in Quito, total income from all the Jesuit properties ranged from 168,000 pesos in 1766 to 223,000 pesos in 1765.[145] In some years the Jesuits recorded handsome profits nearing 60,000 pesos, while in others their expenses exceeded income. These networks of estates supported the thirteen Jesuit colleges operating in the district and frontier missions along the Mainas and Marañon Rivers. The memorial from Mexico showed that the income from Jesuit properties reached 425,000 pesos annually, which dwarfed the amounts recorded in the Society's extensive holdings in the Audiencia of Quito.[146] In both New Spain and Quito, however, the amounts of tithe revenue the Society owed to the crown were substantial, and by claiming an exemption, the Society was costing the crown dearly in lost revenues.

In three separate (unsigned) letters, the Jesuits disputed the claims of their great wealth and any allegations about the order's failure to pay the tithe at 3 1/3 percent. The letters began by defending the Society's past exemptions from the tithe, although each letter also accepted the right of the king of Spain to levy the tax on them. According to the letters, authorities in the Indies had defamed the Society with: "impostures and slanders that are destroying the

regular orders in the Indies. Among the issues discussed at that meeting was limiting the amount of real estate (*bienes raíces*) that the orders could purchase in the Indies. The archbishops elect of Lima and Mexico City argued strongly for limiting the excessive wealth of the orders. Given that the Jesuits had the largest landholdings among the orders, placing limits on *bienes raíces* would have dealt the order a potentially more devastating blow than forcing them to pay the full tithe. In the end, the committee remained divided on the issue, and it dropped the matter. The strong support of the Marqués de la Ensenada and Francisco de Rávago probably protected the Jesuits from any such radical reform of crown policy concerning clerical land holding. Junta Particular de Ministros, Madrid, Biblioteca del Palacio Real, II, 1601E, ff. 22–39.

[144] Royal *cédula*, Buen Retiro, February 19, 1756, AGI, IG, leg. 3085A.

[145] Kenneth J. Andrien, *The Kingdom of Quito, 1690–1830: The State and Regional Development* (Cambridge: Cambridge University Press, 1995), pp. 102–106, 223–29.

[146] "Copia de lo mas substancial del testimnio dada por el essmo Joseph Pazmiño comprovado de otros tres, su fha en la Cuidad de San Francisco de Quito a 5 dias del mes de Abril de 1763, por donde consta las matrículas o breve resumen de las haciendas que la religión de la Compañía de Jesús posehe en las cinco leguas inmediatas de la misma ciudad, cuya aberiguación se hizo de orden de su Almo Obispo, a pedimiento de aquel Ven Cabildo a fin de dar cuenta a SM del grave perjuicio, que a los dos messas y reales novenas se les sigue con la adquisición de tan numerosas y vastas Haciendas en toda la provinicia que contienen una infinidad de Gente empleada, y especialmente con el Privilegio que la Religión de la Compañía de Jesús desfruta moderamente de pagar Diezmo de treinta y uno de todos los frutos de sus fincas." Third Anonymous Letter of Jesuit, n.p., n.d., AGI, IG, leg. 3085A.

reputation and good name of the order."[147] The Jesuits, however, had grown used to such slanderous remarks, which they tolerated with resignation, even though "the love for the truth and the right to self defense do not permit that those memorials, [so] injurious to the integrity, rectitude, and good reputation, pass in silence."[148] According to the letters, some of their critics had even falsely implied that the tithe assessment of 3 1/3 percent had been granted only because of the sinister intervention on behalf of the Society by Padre Rávago, King Ferdinand's Jesuit confessor.[149] The third letter argued that the secular hierarchy in Mexico was guilty of breaking the officially imposed silence on the tithe controversy, when the spokesman for the Church in the Archdiocese of Mexico, Joseph Miranda, wrote to the crown on June 26, 1760, claiming (falsely) that the Jesuits refused to pay the tax. Miranda also had claimed that the order owned twenty-four haciendas in New Spain and thirteen smaller holdings (*ranchos*). The Jesuit author of the letter argued, however, that this was a gross exaggeration. Some of the properties had two or three different names, so Miranda thought that each name referred to a different estate, when it did not. Miranda also claimed that the total income from the Mexican properties reached 425,000, but he failed to mention that annual expenses reached 439,000 pesos, leaving a deficit of nearly 14,000 pesos annually, not large profits remitted to Rome.[150] In short, the order claimed that all the arguments lodged against them were slanderous lies designed merely to discredit the good name of the Society of Jesus.

When authorities in Santiago de Chile, Mexico City, Puebla, Guatemala, Durango, and Lima lodged additional complaints in 1765 about the Jesuits refusing to pay the tithe assessments, King Charles III passed the matter once again to the Council of the Indies. The *fiscal* of the Council argued that the edict of 1750 setting the tithe at 3 1/3 percent was merely a concession by King Ferdinand VI to the Society, which could be revoked at any time by the crown.[151] In a final edict on the matter of December 4, 1766, the king revoked the order of 1750 setting the tithe for the Jesuits at 3 1/3 percent, commanding instead that the Society pay the full 10 percent tithe on all of its properties, including those rented out to laymen. This new regulation served to provide for the church's financial stability in the Indies and to defend his *real patronato*, which was:

gravely harmed by the ... decree, as well as the churches, contrary to the righteous and pious intentions of the King my brother, who erroneously issued it, advised by importune pleadings, capricious and indecent offerings, complicated with the evils of false accounts that betoken the nullity of ... the very decree.[152]

---

[147] Ibid., First Anonymous Letter of Jesuit, n.p., n.d.
[148] Ibid.
[149] Ibid.
[150] Ibid., Third Anonymous Letter of Jesuit, n.p., n.d.
[151] *Consulta de parte*, Madrid, July 15, 1765, AGI, IG, leg. 3085A.
[152] Royal *cédula*, Madrid, December 4, 1766 AGI, IG, leg. 3085A.

According to King Charles, it had never been his brother's intention to make a permanent concession to the Jesuits, whose contributions to society did not exceed those of the other regular clergy in the Indies.[153] This edict finally ended the long controversy with the order over its tithe contributions. It came just three months before the order expelling the Jesuits from the Spanish empire. The Jesuits had engaged in a long and ultimately futile effort to avoid paying tithes. By the time of the Madrid uprising in 1766, they had few defenders and numerous enemies.

THE EXPULSION OF THE JESUITS

Much of the work of the commission appointed by Charles III to investigate the *motín* of Esquilache fell to the regalist *fiscal* of the Council of Castile, Pedro Rodríguez Campomanes, who quickly decided to assemble a case blaming the Jesuits for the uprising. His influential report appeared on December 31, 1766. Lacking any real concrete evidence linking the Society to the disorders, Campomanes merely summarized popular fears and suspicions about the order.[154] He accused the Jesuits of exercising sinister domination over higher education to promote their views and of using their domination of key advisory positions in the government to advance their own nefarious designs for "world domination." Compomanes also condemned the order for having lavish landholdings, illicit commercial interests, and manufacturing enterprises in Spain and the empire, which they had accumulated by using unfair tax exemptions.[155] Moreover, the order remitted profits from their New World enterprises to Rome, enriching the papacy with wealth that rightly belonged to the monarchy. In the end, Campomanes reiterated most of the claims found in anti-Jesuit literature of the period, which he used to construct a passionate but flimsy case linking the order to the popular uprisings against the crown.[156]

---

[153] Ibid.

[154] The report of Campomanes has been edited in a modern publication. See Pedro R. de Campomanes, *Dictamen fiscal de expulsión de los Jesuitas de España (1766–1767)*, ed. and intro. by Jorge Cejudo y Teófanes Egido (Madrid: Fundación Universitaria Española, 1977).

[155] For an excellent summary of Campomanes and his arguments, see Stein and Stein, *Apogee of Empire*, pp. 101–07.

[156] Contemporaries and later historians have debated whether the uprising was a spontaneous action of the Madrid populace or whether other partisan groups opposed to Esquilache in particular and reform in general organized and perhaps even manipulated popular discontent for their own political ends. Among the groups most often cited as conspirators are: the French, members of the high nobility, and members of the church, including the Jesuits. For more recent summaries of these positions, see Laura Rodríguez, "The Riots of 1766 in Madrid," *European Studies Review*, 3:3 (1973), pp. 232–37; and Lynch, *Bourbon Spain*, pp. 264–26, who present a case for implicating all three groups. Stein and Stein, *Apogee of Empire*, pp. 92–101, argue for the complicity of the elites who opposed reform. Domínguez Ortiz, *Carlos III y España*, pp. 76–78, argues that the evidence is still inconclusive about the

Campomanes's explosive report gave the king and his ministers a convenient, unpopular scapegoat for the popular unrest, which absolved the government, the nobility, most of the church, and the common people from any responsibility in provoking the *motín* of Esquilache. After consulting with persons of "experience and high character," the king issued a royal decree on February 27, 1767, ordering the expulsion of the Jesuits in order to protect the people and secure respect for the crown.[157] He remitted the edict secretly to the Conde de Aranda, who sent out clandestine orders on March 1 to the viceroys, captains general, and governors of the Indies and the Philippines to execute the decree. Aranda's letter called for secrecy in complying with the royal will, but he ordered that it all be accomplished without disturbing the peace or provoking any resistance from the local populace. He also instructed civil authorities to inform the clergy of each region and the other religious orders that the edict applied only to the Jesuits. The king had full confidence in the loyalty and fidelity of the other regular orders.[158]

Although Aranda allowed each official in the Indies discretion over the details of the expulsion, he provided another letter offering basic instructions for how to carry out the operation, which he instructed should be opened only on the day before executing the task. Aranda told the officials to keep the entire matter secret until the morning before the operation, when each official would muster troops to close off all roads leading to the Jesuit *colegios* (colleges). After surrounding each *colegio*, the Jesuits would be confined in their chapter house as a group (including even the brother cook), and anyone temporarily outside the *colegio* must be summoned to return immediately. All official papers, accounts, or books should be sequestered, along with all the vestments and jewels, with an inventory taken of everything. He demanded that the Jesuits be well treated, and all novices who had not taken vows could choose to leave the order and take up positions as secular clergy. Each Jesuit could take only his personal possessions – clothes, prayer books, tobacco, or chocolate – on the trip to the nearest port, without communicating with any other religious or lay person. At the port of embarkation, officials would keep a list of the Jesuits, their names, countries of origin, and rank within the order. Any elderly or ill Jesuits could be kept behind and given medical attention, and the *procurator* of each *colegio* must delay leaving for two months in order to give an accounting of the administration of the Jesuit properties and to answer any questions about the confiscated assets. Colonial authorities would

existence of a conspiracy, and he believes the *motín* was a spontaneous outpouring of economic discontent and xenophobia directed against the king's foreign ministers.

[157] Royal *cédula*, el Pardo, March 27, 1767 AGI, IG, leg. 3087.

[158] Conde de Aranda to the viceroys of Mexico, Peru, Santa Fe, the governor of Buenos Aires, the commander of Chile and the governor of the Philippines, Madrid, March 1, 1767 (*circular reservada*) AGI, IG, leg. 3087.

turn over all Jesuit schools or seminaries to other regular orders or to the secular clergy.[159]

The king issued the formal royal edict of expulsion on March 27, 1767, and six days afterward royal troops in Spain began rounding up members of the order throughout the country.[160] The edict did not provide any specific reasons for the action, arguing that its purpose was to maintain the subordination, tranquility, and justice of his towns and cities and to protect his people and secure respect for the monarchy. The king gave the commission to enforce the expulsion of the Jesuits to the Conde de Aranda, who would also oversee the administration of all Jesuit properties as president of the Council of Castile. Each Spanish Jesuit would receive an annual pension of 100 pesos, with 90 pesos going to each lay brother; foreign Jesuits resident in any dominions under royal control would be sent home, without any pension. Novitiates could either leave the order and remain as secular clergymen or stay with their Jesuit brothers, but if they went into exile, they received no pension from the crown. Any Jesuit who attempted to return to any lands under the control of the Spanish monarchy would face criminal charges. In order to maintain order and tranquility throughout his dominions, the king and the Council of the Indies ordered that no one write, discuss, or initiate any disturbance regarding the expulsion of the Society. Even bishops and high secular clerics must never speak of the expulsion nor say anything about the order without special permission of the crown. Anyone failing to adhere to this silence would be prosecuted as a criminal.[161] Enforcement of the *cédula* of expulsion throughout the Indies generally took place with military precision, provoking only limited disruptions of public order, principally in New Spain.[162]

---

[159] "Instrucción de lo que deberán executar los Comisionados para el estrañamiento y ocupación de bienes y haciendas de los Jesuitas en estos Reynos de España y Islas adjacentes, en conformidad do lo resuelto por S.M.," Madrid, March 1, 1767 AGI, IG, leg. 3087.

[160] For the expulsion of the Jesuits in Spain, see: Inmaculada Fernández Arrillaga, *El Destierro de los jesuitas Castellanos, (1767–1815)* (Salamanca: Junta de Castilla y León, 2004); Two edited volumes deal with the expulsion and exile of the Jesuits: Manfred Tietz, ed., *Los jesuitas españoles expulsos: Su imagen y contribución al saber sobre el mundo hispánico en la Europa del siglo XVIII* (Frankfort and Madrid: Iberoamericana, 2001) and Enrique Giménez López, ed., *Expulsión y exilio de los Jesuitas Españoles* (Murcia: Universidad de Alicante, 1997). On the expulsion of the Jesuits in California, see: Salvador Bernabéu Albert, *Expulsados del infierno. El exilio de los misioneros jesuitas de la península californiana (1767–1768)* (Madrid: Consejo Superior de Investigaciones Científicas, 2008).

[161] Royal *cédula*, el Pardo, March 27, 1767, AGI, IG, leg. 3087,

[162] For a discussion of how the expulsion proceeded in Peru, see: Manuel de Amat y Junient, *Memoria de gobierno*, ed. and intro. by Vicente Rodríguez Casado y Florentino Pérez Embid (Sevilla: Escuela de Estudios Hispano-Americanos, 1947), pp. 128–45; Rubén Vargas Ugarte, *Historia de la Compañía de Jesús*, IV (Burgos: Consejo Superior de Investigaciones Científicas, 1965), pp. 163–79.

CONCLUSION

The deregulation of trade and the expulsion of the Jesuits proved turning points in the reform and renovation of the Spanish Atlantic world. The early reign of Charles III began with high hopes for reform as the new king's regalist ministers planned sweeping changes in the empire, only to suffer a humiliating defeat in the Seven Years' War. The loss of Havana shocked many at court, but working through Esquilache and his other ministers, the king was able to exploit the crisis mentality that ensued to plan some important commercial, military, and political changes, culminating in the proclamation of imperial free trade for several Caribbean colonies in the Indies. This initial optimism faded, however, with the outbreak of the *motín* of Esquilache in 1766. The uprisings in Madrid and elsewhere in Spain demonstrated the widespread discontent with the reform policies pursued by the monarchy, discrediting King Charles and his ministers. Moreover, the king was forced to flee Madrid and acquiesce to all the demands posed by the protestors as popular groups, some members of the aristocracy, the bureaucracy, and the clergy came out against crown reform policies. Charles was even forced to dismiss his close advisor and collaborator in reform, the Marqués de Esquilache. The king and his ministers emerged humiliated, with their hold on power badly shaken by the popular outburst and the broad coalition arrayed against them. To save face, however, Charles and his ministers seized the political initiative by forming a commission to investigate the uprising in Madrid, which placed the blame for the unrest squarely on the Society of Jesus. Claims of a Jesuit-led conspiracy allowed the crown to find a scapegoat without confronting directly the broad array of popular and conservative political forces opposed to reform. It also allowed King Charles and his allies to remove a key anti-regalist force in Spain and its empire when the order was expelled in 1767. The crown forbade any mention of the Jesuits, and the edict of expulsion prohibited members of the order from returning to their homelands in Spain or the Indies. It was not until 1798 that the crown relented, and the Spanish Jesuits (now mostly old men) began filtering back to their families and homelands.[163]

The expulsion gave King Charles III and his ministers a much-needed victory after setbacks in the Seven Years' War and the uprisings in Spain, which allowed this most able of the Bourbon monarchs to push reform to its apogee during the eighteenth century. Expelling the Society of Jesus removed a politically and economically powerful opponent of regalist reform initiatives, and it gave the crown access to their wealthy possessions in Spain and the Indies. Moreover, it demonstrated the confidence and assertiveness of the monarchy in the face of strong opposition to reform in both Spain and the

[163] Royal order, Madrid, March 14, 1798, AGI, IG, leg. 3084.

Indies. Nonetheless, powerful vested interests continued to oppose reform and despite bold initiatives, conservative opposition groups would still work to undermine or at least blunt reform initiatives throughout the Spanish Atlantic world. In addition, Spain's enemies, particularly Great Britain, had a stake in promoting commercial ties with the Spanish Indies and in thwarting efforts by reformers to keep foreigners out of the transatlantic trade. The political interplay among these various groups favoring and opposed to reform would ultimately determine the successes and failures of Bourbon reformers during the remainder of the reign of Charles III.

8

The Reorganization of Spain's Atlantic Empire, 1767–1783

Despite suffering setbacks with the loss of Havana and the *motín* of Esquilache, the reign of Charles III would mark the pinnacle of colonial reorganization and the resurgence of Spanish military power in the Atlantic world. The pace and character of reform varied during Charles's rule, influenced by the nature of the challenges Spain faced, the opportunities for change, the power of vested interests in Spain and the Indies, pressures from rival powers, the character of the king's ministers, and the level of commitment and enthusiasm of Charles himself. Following the Seven Years' War, the king and his Sicilian de facto prime minister, the Marqués de Esquilache, pushed a reformist agenda aggressively, but the pace faded after the popular unrest in March 1766, which led to the Italian's ouster. The opportunity for revenge offered by the colonial rebellion against Great Britain in North America opened the door to a renewal of a reformist agenda under José de Gálvez. Despite the uneven results of the Gálvez reforms, Spain would register military advances both on land and at sea, scoring a telling series of victories against Great Britain in the War of the American Revolution.

Charles was the most ambitious and capable of the Bourbon monarchs. A proponent of the liberating ideals of the Enlightenment, he brought a freshness of mind to the throne, enabling him to challenge entrenched partisan groups and experiment boldly in search of realistic alternatives to modernize Spain and its empire. The policies he pursued were typical of the European enlightened absolutism of his time, which championed both reform from above and the use of human reason to attain progress. Charles sought to curtail the power of a conservative aristocracy and of the various privileged groups opposed to reform in both Spain and the Indies. Although a pious man, he also curbed the temporal power of a reactionary clergy and expelled the ultramontane Jesuit order. Championing efficient government, Charles centralized and rationalized royal administration, codified laws, and tightened tax collection. To promote economic development, he constructed roads, colonized frontiers, and fostered native industry, principally through state enterprise. He supported science, built a reservoir, and created a modern banking system. He also beautified Madrid, embracing architectural good sense and elegant interior design.[1] Most importantly, he infused new energy into the challenge of colonial reform, which the crown had addressed so unevenly over the preceding decades.

Charles sought to reestablish Spain as a first-rate military power. He was highly pragmatic, and his overall program was surprisingly eclectic in the search for workable solutions. Although a modern thinker, he was still quite willing to use traditional policies in advancing his political purposes. While he curbed the ancient privileges of the church, including the *fuero eclesiástico*, Charles extended an extensive *fuero militar* to the American militia, when he sought to convert volunteer units into effective fighting forces.[2] He curtailed the sale of audiencia offices in the colonies, stressing merit in making appointments over social status and connections, but he reestablished the practice of selling army commissions to help finance his far-flung military establishment.[3] In commercial policy, he repeatedly showed the instincts of a true physiocrat as he championed deregulation; but the king also extended lucrative royal monopolies as an effective means to enhance his income to pay for growing military establishments. In the end, the single point of consistency in Charles's reforms was his search for the means to wage war more effectively.

Although Charles remained committed to reform, the *motín* of Esquilache demonstrated the widespread hostility of elites and popular groups toward change, even in Spain itself. Crown attempts to promote the unregulated sale of grain on the free market coincided with a severe draught, leading to an upsurge in grain prices and hunger among the popular classes. Rising taxes only exacerbated the problem. The xenophobic fears of the Spanish people made the king's Italian ministers, particularly the highly visible Esquilache, convenient targets for this growing popular animosity. Aristocratic members of the clergy had also registered their vocal opposition to reform. Bishop Diego de Rojas y Contreras, president of the Council of Castile, had urged that body to demand the resignation of Esquilache. The Bishop of Cuenca, Isidoro de Carvajal y Lancaster even blamed the Italian's policies for the loss of Havana, Madrid's high food prices, unnecessary taxes, unpopular urban reforms, and for displacing loyal public officials, leading to the poor

---

[1] The standard treatment of the enlightened character of regime is Richard Herr, *The Eighteenth-Century Revolution in Spain* (Princeton: Princeton University Press, 1958).

[2] Nancy M. Farriss, *Crown and Clergy in Colonial Mexico, 1759–1821: The Crisis of Ecclesiastical Privilege* (London: Athlone Press, 1986); Lyle N. McAlister, *The "Fuero Militar" in New Spain, 1764–1800* (Gainesville: University Presses of Florida, 1957).

[3] Mark A. Burkholder and D. S. Chandler, *From Impotence to Authority: The Spanish Crown and the American Audiencias, 1687–1808* (Columbia: University of Missouri Press, 1977) pp. 98–135; Allan J. Kuethe *Cuba, 1753–1815*: Crown, Military, and Society (Knoxville: University of Tennessee Press, 1986), pp. 149–50.

administration of government. Both men embodied three conservative pillars of the Bourbon regime: the aristocracy, the clergy, and the public servants drawn from the prestigious university *colegios*. All were threatened to some degree by reform. Although the role of the *Consulado* of Cádiz in the uprising remains unclear, the guild certainly sought to undo commercial reforms in the Caribbean that undermined its monopoly after the unrest abated. In short, regardless of their direct role in the *motín* of Esquilache, a number of important interest groups stood to gain from the political instability following the uprisings. The riots in Madrid and elsewhere clearly exposed fissures in Spanish society over the Bourbon reforms, encouraging the junta investigating the affair to search for a conspiracy and to find a scapegoat, the powerful Society of Jesus.[4] In the later years of Charles's reign, a wide range of interest groups in the Indies also would vigorously oppose reform, even leading to armed insurrections against the Bourbon state.

POPULAR UNREST AND THE SLOWDOWN OF REFORM AFTER ESQUILACHE

In the aftermath of the Madrid riots and the expulsion of the Jesuits, no one emerged to assume the dominant role exercised by Esquilache. The Ministry of War passed to Lieutenant General Juan Gregorio Muniain, the governor of Badajoz, while Finance went to Miguel de Múzquiz. A well-educated *navarro* of modest birthright from the Valley of Baztán, Múzquiz had risen through the Ministry of Hacienda, becoming *oficial mayor* under Esquilache.[5] He was a respected, able magistrate, inclined toward innovation, but he was also a cautious and gentle man who had no intention of following Esquilache into exile. Neither Muniain nor Múzquiz showed a strong interest in American affairs, which again remained with Arriaga. Múzquiz did monitor the financial reforms in Cuba, but input from his office declined markedly.[6] Muniain continued to receive at least some of the correspondence pertaining to the regular army, but little happened until Charles made O'Reilly inspector-general of the army of America in 1770.[7] Meanwhile, Charles appointed the dynamic Conde de Aranda president of the Council of Castile.[8]

Charles's strength as king lay in his ability to recognize and act on good ideas. He did not seem to have originated much legislation on his own, and following Esquilache's departure he lacked dynamic, imaginative ministers

---

[4] John Lynch, *Bourbon Spain, 1700–1808* (Oxford: Basil Blackwell, 1989), p. 283.

[5] José Antonio Escudero, *Los orígenes del Consejo de Ministros en España* (Madrid: Editoria Nacional, 1979), I, pp. 312–13. Muniain had experience as minister in the court of the infante Philip.

[6] This correspondence can be found in AGS, *Hacienda*, legs. 2344–50.

[7] See, for example, AGI, SD, legs. 2079, 2120, and 2121, and IG, leg. 1885.

[8] Rafael Olaechea and José Ferrer Benimeli, *El Conde de Aranda (Mito y realidad de un político aragonés)*, 2 vols. (Zaragoza: Librería General, 1978), II, pp. 34–35.

committed to reform. After his return, Ensenada had been a strong advocate of innovation, but he was now gone as well. Grimaldi, a talented administrator and graceful diplomat, was not an imaginative, original thinker, although he had taken a personal hand in reforming the maritime mail service. While he probably would have been capable of asserting leadership in the post-Esquilache period, the xenophobic tone of the 1766 riots effectively pushed him into the background. [9]

The *motín* of Esquilache and the expulsion of the Jesuits momentarily diverted the attention of Charles and his ministers from preparing the American defenses for another war with Britain, but the hostile reception that some Bourbon reform initiatives received from colonial society also played a major role. Apart from fierce opposition in Quito in 1765, disorders spread to Guatemala, the Chocó, the Governorship of Popayán, and Santiago de Chile, which led to more cautious policies from Madrid. [10] In both Guatemala and New Granada, for example, colonial officials either revoked the new measures or modified and enforced them with restraint. [11] It is no small wonder that the crown initiated no new *visitas* on the scale of those of Ricla and O'Reilly and Gálvez and Villalba.

The most serious resistance took place in the richest of Spain's possessions, New Spain, where armed conflicts erupted against the reforms of José de Gálvez in the mining zones north of Mexico City. [12] Gálvez and the viceroy, the Marqués de Croix, had anticipated resistance to the order expelling the Jesuits in Mexico City and Puebla, but the secrecy of their planning and their use of large numbers of troops allowed the process to proceed without serious protest. [13] Violence did accompany the expulsion, however, in the mining areas around San Luis Potosí and Guanajuato and spread westward to

---

[9] John Lynch, in *Bourbon Spain*, p. 251, postulated that Grimaldi "never had an original idea in his life," which may overstate the case, at least when the Genoese is compared to Arriaga.

[10] D. A. Brading, *Miners and Merchants in Bourbon Mexico, 1763–1810* (Cambridge: Cambridge University Press, 1971), p. 233: Miles Wortman, "Bourbon Reforms in Central America, 1750–1786" *The Americas*, 32 (1975), pp. 227–29; Gustavo Arboleda, *Historia de Cali desde los orígenes de la ciudad hasta la expiración del período colonial*, 2 vols. (Cali: Arboleda Emprenta, 1956), II, pp. 236–332; William F. Sharp, *Slavery on the Spanish Frontier: The Colombian Chocó, 1680–1810* (Norman: University of Oklahoma Press, 1976), pp. 160–69; Guillermo Céspedes del Castillo, "La renta del tabaco en el virreinato del Perú," *Revista histórica*, 21 (1954), p. 149.

[11] Brading, *Miners and Merchants*, p. 233; Wortman, "Bourbon Reforms," pp. 227–29; Arboleda, *Historia de Cali*, II, pp. 236–332; Federico, González Suárez, *Historia general de la República de Ecuador*, 7 vols. (Quito: Casa de la Cultura Ecuatoriana, 1970 [1890–1891]), V, pp. 222–23.

[12] Herbert Ingram Priestley, *José de Gálvez: Visitor-General of New Spain (1765–1771)* (Berkeley: University of California Press, 1916), pp. 140–42, 150, 158, 162, 175–209.

[13] Mexico City and Puebla were the centers of Jesuit activity and had experienced some recent unrest, so they mustered two battalions of the regular army, one battalion of militia, a battalion of the *pardo* militia, two companies of the merchant guard, three companies drawn from the guilds, and two squadrons of dragoons. A similar force aided in rounding

Michoacán. Unrest about higher taxes, the recruitment of militiamen, land disputes, and the imposition of the tobacco monopoly had created social tensions, which erupted into violent popular protests in these areas. Some of that violence was triggered by efforts to expel the Jesuits, while the removal of the Society proved only a minor side issue in other regions. Nonetheless, when local governments proved unable to put down the disorders in most towns and cities, the viceroy sent a military force under the command of Gálvez to restore order, reestablish royal authority, and punish the guilty.[14]

The violent protests in New Spain began near the important mining city of San Luis Potosí, where attempts to expel the Jesuits on June 26, 1767, occurred after weeks of unrest in the city and its hinterland. Three separate riots had erupted in nearby Cerro de San Pedro in May and early June over government attempts to restrict possession of guns and arrest vagabonds, and over a land dispute between locals and a Carmelite convent. In each case, local authorities appeased the rioters by suspending local taxes and returning the disputed lands, but only a very tentative order returned to the region.[15] As a result of these outbreaks, the mayor of San Luis Potosí, Andrés Urbina, feared that violence might accompany the order to expel the Jesuits, so he called on a local landowner, Francisco Mora, to bring armed workers from his lands to enforce order on the day set for the expulsion, June 25, 1767. When the mayor and Mora attempted to remove the Jesuits from their *colegio*, however, a mob seized the priests and returned them to their religious house. Mora and Urbina barely escaped with their lives. Then, the protestors broke into the jail and freed prisoners, captured arms and powder in the city armory, and looted several stores and merchant warehouses.[16] Mora tried to negotiate with the protestors about allowing the expulsion to take place on July 9, but local indigenous groups from the surrounding hill towns invaded the city and foiled the plan, even though Mora's forces drove them out the next day. By this time, disorders and violence had spread to the surrounding towns of Guadalcázar, Venado, Hedionda, and San Felipe. Mora and the authorities wisely decided to await the arrival of royal troops under Gálvez before attempting to remove the Jesuits from the city.[17]

Similar outbreaks of violence occurred in the important mining town of Guanajuato, where local citizens opposed key elements of the Bourbon reforms, particularly the tobacco monopoly, the reform of the *alcabala*, and the recruitment of local citizens into the newly formed militia regiments. The

up the Jesuits in Puebla. See Felipe Castro Gutiérrez, *Nueva ley, Nuevo rey: Reformas borbónicas y rebelión popular en Nueva España* (Michoacán: El Colegio de Michoacán, Universidad Nacional Autónoma de Mexico, Instituto de Investigaciones Históricas 1996), p. 181.

[14] Priestley, *José de Gálvez*, pp. 212–23.
[15] Castro Gutiérrez, *Nueva ley, Nuevo rey*, pp. 120–27; Priestley, *José de Gálvez*, pp. 217–18.
[16] Castro Gutiérrez, *Nueva ley, Nuevo rey*, pp. 132–36.
[17] Ibid., pp. 137–40.

elite of the city – including leading miners, the cabildo, local Inquisition Commissioner Juan José Bonilla, and the heads of the regular orders – argued that the mining economy was in decline because of the need for costly drainage projects, ever deeper mine shafts, a scarcity of investment capital, the low quality of silver ore, and shortages of key products caused by the rigorous collection of the sales tax. The viceroy responded to their entreaties by exempting miners from serving in the militia, which local officials found woefully inadequate.[18] On July 17, 1766, over 6,000 miners descended on the city where they attacked the local offices (*estanquillos*) of the tobacco monopoly and the *aduana* building, which oversaw the collection of the sales tax. They even took the chief administrator of the *aduana* hostage, and later the mayor as well. The miners then marched to the cabildo and demanded the closure of the *estanquillos*, a return to the old way of collecting the *alcabala*, and an end to militia recruitment in the region. The terrified city council conceded to all the demands, and an uneasy calm returned to the city.[19]

In this tense environment, efforts to expel the Jesuits from Guanajuato provoked a new wave of violent protests. Torrential rains kept the two commissioners entrusted with the expulsion, Fernando Torija and Felipe Berri, from arriving in Guanajuato until six days after the expulsion had taken place elsewhere in New Spain. As a result, local citizens knew of their likely mission, and when the two commissioners and a force of six militiamen attempted to approach the Jesuit *colegio*, a large crowd assembled to stop them. Berri apparently panicked and ordered the soldiers to open fire, killing fourteen of the protestors. The beleaguered militiamen, Torija, and Berri fled to the city offices, and then only survived because a local priest and a group of friars and the Jesuit priests managed to calm the crowd.[20] The next day, Berri returned with a force of fifty-six militiamen, but they faced 8,000 miners, who had descended on the city. The miners attacked the Royal Treasury, the customs house, and the residences and stores of local peninsular Spaniards (called *gachupines*).[21] The local priest and members of the cabildo then accepted the demands of the crowd – the commissioners had to exit the city, leaving the Jesuits behind, and all members of the protest would receive a pardon.[22] When the commissioners and the militiamen attempted to leave Guanajuato on July 3, however, a large crowd attacked them outside of the city. They were saved once again by the intercession of a group of priests, who formed a cordon around the men to protect them. The attackers then dispersed, and Berri, Torija, and the militiamen made their escape.[23]

[18] Ibid., pp. 153–54.
[19] Ibid., p. 156.
[20] Ibid., pp. 156–57.
[21] Ibid., p. 158.
[22] Ibid., p. 159.
[23] Ibid., pp. 159–60.

Popular unrest spread to Michoacán over the recruitment of local men into the militia in September 1766. After the militia recruiting team arrived in the town of Pátzcuaro, a crowd of 500 mulattos and indigenous men from the city barrios and the surrounding towns assembled to protest a rumored impressment of local citizens.[24] The viceroy sent the local bishop to investigate the disorder, and the prelate claimed that peace had returned to Pátzcuaro. On December 5, however, a group of fifty men assaulted a militia recruiter in Uruapan, and after subjecting the soldier to insults and humiliation, the protestors stoned the houses of local *gachupines*.[25] The popular anger turned from defensive protests against the militia reforms into more serious defiance of royal authority with the election of an indigenous governor, Pedro de Soria Villaroel, in early 1767. According to Spanish accounts, Soria attempted to forge cross-community ties to recreate the pre-Columbian Tarascan alliance and challenge royal authority in the region. José de Gálvez claimed that 113 indigenous communities owed allegiance to Soria, who entered into divisive disputes with local Spanish officials over the collection of tribute. When Spanish officials arrested Soria, over 400 of his followers stormed the jail, freed the leader, and took over the town. Violence later spread to the countryside and to several smaller towns in the region.[26]

Amid this widespread disorder, the official in charge of expelling the Jesuits, Tiburcio Sedano arrived from Valladolid on July 3, 1767. Gálvez had already written to Soria demanding his full cooperation and allegiance under threat of serious punishment.[27] A large crowd armed with stones and arrows confronted the royal troops and Sedano, blocking them from proceeding to the Jesuit residence. Members of the city council, clergymen, and Soria tried to quiet the crowd and to prevent violence, and in the end, the protestors dispersed without further incident. In the subsequent weeks, community leadership passed from Soria to two radicals, Juan Antonio Castro and Lorenzo Arroyo. These two men organized an uprising of 600 indigenous and mestizo men in Pátzcuaro, demanding that all *gachupines* leave the region. In the subsequent days, Castro and Arroyo formed a permanent armed guard to patrol the city, but a group of militiamen unexpectedly came upon Castro and captured him. The militia then conveyed their prisoner to nearby Ariztimuño, where the local mayor had Castro summarily executed. The whole region remained in a tense standoff, as the local people periodically disrupted the peace, and Spanish authorities remained too weak to restore order.[28]

[24] Ibid., pp. 165–66.
[25] Ibid., p. 168.
[26] Ibid., pp. 168–71.
[27] Ibid., p. 171.
[28] Ibid., pp. 172–73.

José de Gálvez set out from Mexico City on July 9, 1767, vested with full powers from the viceroy to quell the unrest in the northern mining zones, expel the Jesuits, and punish anyone guilty of disturbing the public order. Gálvez and his troops arrived on June 25 in San Luis de la Paz. They proceeded to San Luis Potosí on July 24 and then went on to Guanajuato, arriving on October 16. Finally, Gálvez advanced to Valladolid on November 14, where the prisoners from the uprisings in Michoacán had been jailed.[29] At each of these stops and in any surrounding towns where uprisings had taken place, Gálvez first oversaw the expulsion of the Jesuits and then presided over the trials of anyone arrested for promoting violence against the crown and public order. Convicted leaders such as Soria were condemned to death and their heads displayed on pikes as grim reminders of the price enacted for rebellion against the crown. In all, Gálvez brought 3,000 people to trial; he condemned 85 to death, 73 to be severely whipped, 674 to term or life imprisonment, and 117 to banishment.[30] The self-righteous Gálvez felt no pangs of remorse for meting out such punishments; as he wrote, "I have not upon my conscience the slightest scruple of having exceeded the limits of justice, for I mitigated my sentences always with clemency and mercy."[31] Before leaving San Luis Potosí and Guanajuato, Gálvez also levied taxes to repair or replace any public buildings damaged in the disturbances, and he reorganized local governments to make them more likely to maintain public order. Although the punitive expedition of José de Gálvez restored public order and punished many of those guilty of disrupting public order, the revolts of 1767 demonstrated the continuing, widespread opposition to reform in the Spanish Atlantic world, which slowed the implementation of any bold new innovations after 1766.

Quite apart from the outbreaks of popular unrest in New Spain, the diplomatic machinations of France also helped to account for the waning impulse for reform. The Family Compact had committed Spain and France to reopening the struggle with Great Britain as early as 1768.[32] Despite distractions, Charles remained faithful to that goal, but the French did not. When addressing the Spanish court, Choiseul articulated a tougher line than he was prepared to support. He spoke bravely about the next war and urged Spain to rebuild its colonial establishment, but in his private correspondence with his friend Grimaldi, he urged restraint.[33] Choiseul's duplicity arose in

[29] Ibid., pp. 175–221.

[30] Priestley, *José de Gálvez*, p. 228.

[31] Ibid., 228–29.

[32] Choiseul to D'Ossun, Versailles, November 13, 1763, AAE:CPE, vol. 539, fol. 318; Allan Christelow, "French Interest in the Spanish Empire during the Ministry of the Duc de Choiseul, 1759–1771," *HAHR*, 21 (November 1941), p. 523; A. S, Aiton, "Spanish Colonial Reorganization under the Family Compact, *HAHR*, 12 (August 1932), p. 271.

[33] Louis Blart, *Les Rapports de la France et de L'Espagne après le Pacte de Famille, jusqu'a la fin du Ministère du Duc de Choiseul* (Paris: F. Alcan, 1915), pp. 77–78, 94; E. Daubigny, *Choiseul et la France d'Outre-Mer après le Traité de Paris* (Paris: Hachatte, 1892), p. 275.

part from his hope that France might pry her way into a privileged position within the commercial system of Spanish America by acting the part of a faithful ally. This aspiration, however, met steady frustration because Esquilache and Charles refused to allow Spain to become an economic dependency of France, and they repeatedly denied special commercial concessions.[34] The French also viewed with concern Esquilache's moves to encourage the sugar industry in Cuba and elsewhere, a development that promised long-run competition for French interests in Saint Domingue and Martinique.[35] Thus, despite their superficial belligerency, the French were reluctant to support any conflict that promised small benefit for their national interests. The immediate result was to postpone any Franco-Spanish war against Britain. This French diplomatic retreat also helps explain the lack of urgency about any colonial reorganization with the threat of war with Britain looming.[36]

The final step in the French diplomatic retreat came during the Malvinas Islands crisis of 1770. The crisis arose when the British established a settlement on the islands, which Spain viewed as definitely within its defensive perimeter. Madrid and Versailles had anticipated potential British intrusions into the area, which they feared would threaten Spain's commercial and military security.[37] In 1770, Governor Francisco Bucareli, striking from Buenos Aires, took possession of the settlement militarily, igniting a heated international confrontation.[38] His pride aroused, Charles reacted belligerently, fully expecting to receive the French support that he would need to prevail.[39] Although reluctant, Choiseul appeared willing to back Spain, but Louis XV faced political and financial chaos at home. France found itself embroiled in the turmoil that Chancellor René Maupeoux's attempts to reform the *parlements* had provoked, leading Louis to dismiss Choiseul and to urge his cousin to seek peace: "war would be horrible for me and for my people ... if Your Majesty could make some sacrifice to preserve the peace ... that would be a great service to the human race and to me in particular."[40] Charles had no choice but to back down and to restore the colony. Although

---

[34] Christelow, "French Interest," pp. 518–37; D'Ossun to Choiseul, Madrid, March 8 and April 2, 1764, AAE:CPE, vol. 540, fols. 182–86, 225–26.

[35] Christelow, "French Interest," pp. 528–29.

[36] Frances PL. Renaut, *Pacte de Famille et l'Amerique: La Politique Coloniale Franco-Espagnolede 1760 á 1792 (Paris: Lerroux, 1922)*, pp. 107–08, 112–14. The Madrid riots and the exile of Esquilache contributed to this mellowing of French policy, for the French feared that the Spanish drive for reform would weaken and that an unprepared Spain might pull France down in a confrontation with the British. Blart, *Les Rapports*, pp. 86–94.

[37] Memoire, D'Ossun, Madrid, April 28, 1766, AAE:CPE, vol. 545; Grimaldi to Arriaga, El Pardo, February 12, 1768, AGI, IG, leg. 412.

[38] Julius Goebel, *The Struggle for the Falkland Islands: A Study in Legal and Diplomatic History* (New Haven: Yale University Press, 1927), pp. 271–410.

[39] Blart, *Les rapports*, pp. 166–75.

[40] Louis XV to Charles III, Versailles, December 21, 1770, AHN, Estado, leg. 2850.

the British agreed to evacuate their people eventually, this compromise left the future legal status of the islands muddled.[41]

THE RENEWAL OF REFORM

Although the pace of reform slowed after the Esquilache riots, military innovations continued to advance. Charles appointed the vigorous Alejandro O'Reilly as inspector-general of the army of America in 1770, during the Malvinas crisis. This position provided him institutional autonomy from the Ministry of the Indies, and it definitely removed control of the American regular army from the Ministry of War. From his new position, O'Reilly extended the military reform to Santo Domingo and New Granada's Caribbean provinces in 1773 and to Guayaquil in 1775. He also renewed efforts to reform the Caracas militia. Further, the veteran garrisons of New Granada also underwent reorganization as the contingent in Cartagena was upgraded to a regiment, and O'Reilly reestablished the Fixed Battalion of Panama, which had withered away over time.[42]

The acquisition of Louisiana transformed the military focus from keeping the French out of Texas to containing the British east of the Mississippi River. To adjust the defenses of the northern frontier to this new reality, Madrid detached Field Marshal Marqués de Rubí from the Villalba expedition to review the presidio system.[43] Following an inspection conducted between 1766 and 1768, Rubí advocated rationalizing the defense line, which would run from the Concepción River in Sonora to the Guadalupe River in Texas, reducing the number of presidios from twenty-four to fifteen with an accompanying decrease in costs.[44] The critical adjustment entailed shifting Texas's defenses southward to run from La Bahía on the Gulf westward along a route essentially following the Río Grande River. San Antonio and Santa Fe would remain north of the line, but the two presidios in the east, the long-time stronghold of Los Adaes and San Agustín de Ahumada would be abandoned, along with San Sabá, located well above San Antonio, which had been

---

[41] Goebel, *The Struggle*, pp. 314–15, 358–60, and 407–10.

[42] Arriaga to the Governor of Caracas, San Ildefonso, September 20, 1773, in Santiago-Gerardo Suárez (ed.), *Las fuerzas armadas venezolanas en la colonia* (Caracas: Academia Nacional de Historia, 1979), pp. 160–61; María Rosario Sevilla Soler, *Santo Domingo: Tierra de frontera (1750–1800)* (Sevilla: Escuela de Estudios Hispano-Americanos, 1980), pp. 325–26, Allan J. Kuethe, *Military Reform and Society in New Granada, 1773–1808* (Gainesville: University Presses of Florida, 1978), chaps. 1–3.

[43] This step came via royal order of August 7, 1765, reproduced in Rubí's diary, "Itinerary of Señor Marqués de Rubí . . .," in Jack Jackson, (ed. and intro.), *Imaginary Kingdom: Texas as Seen by the Rivera and Rubí Military Expeditions, 1727 and 1767* (Austin: University of Texas Press, 1995), p. 91.

[44] Jackson, "Historical Background," in *Imaginary Kingdom*, pp. 71–88, provides a useful summary of this transformation. Rubí calculated that his plan would reduce costs from 453,000 to 373,000 pesos.

established to check French expansion from the north. They had little value, Rubí reasoned, with the French gone from Louisiana. With input from Viceroy Marqués de Croix, Rubí's report emerged as the regulation of 1772, which Hugo O'Connor subsequently implemented.[45] As expenditures on Texas declined, New Orleans became the recipient of handsome subsidies from Veracruz, which reached it through Havana.[46]

Louisiana won "free trade" access to the ports of Spain in 1768 and Yucatán followed in 1770.[47] These steps amounted to a follow-through on the work of the 1764–1765 select committee on commerce, which had included Louisiana and Campeche among those jurisdictions that it recommended for liberalized privileges. No new thinking was involved; but Grimaldi at State, not Arriaga, managed both advances.[48] And in 1772, the Canary Islands joined the list of Spanish ports authorized for the Caribbean trade.[49]

Under the leadership of the dedicated reformer, Tomás Ortiz de Landazuri, treasury organization also made modest advances. As *contador general de Indias*, Ortiz de Landazuri convinced Arriaga in 1767 to replace the Junta de Real Audiencia of Chile, which was dominated by local interests, with a *contaduría mayor*, both to modernize that colony's fiscal system and to invigorate the collection of taxes. Already in place in Havana and Caracas, this institution was also extended to Buenos Aires that same year.[50] The product of officials who had reached prominence under Esquilache, these actions were small-scale, and they lacked the vision and ambition that had characterized the earlier period. Meanwhile, the Gálvez mission to New Spain continued to advance its revenue reforms. With Esquilache gone, reforming officials sustained their work within limited spheres; but only the return of energetic leadership would revitalize more comprehensive fiscal innovations.

The one exception was the armada, where Charles sustained an unflagging commitment to development. The new monarch reoriented naval strategy away from its defensive mindset toward more offensive strategies and tactics.

---

[45] John Francis Bannon, *The Spanish Borderlands Frontier, 1513–1821* (Albuquerque: University of New Mexico Press, 1973), pp. 172–81.

[46] José Manuel Serrano Álvarez and Allan J. Kuethe, "La Texas colonial entre Pedro de Rivera y el marqués de Rubí, 1729–1772: Aportaciones económicas al sistema presidial," *Colonial Latin American Historical Review*,14 (Summer 2005), pp. 308–10.

[47] J. Muñoz Pérez, "La publicación del Reglamento de Comercio Libre de Indias de 1778," *Anuario de estudios americanos*, 4 (1947), pp. 640–42.

[48] Files, commercial privileges for Louisiana and Yucatán, 1768 and 1770, AGI, SD, leg. 2585, and IG, leg. 2410.

[49] Royal *cédula*, Madrid, July 24, 1772, AGI, IG, leg. 3093.

[50] John Lynch, *Spanish Colonial Administration: The Intendant System in the Viceroyalty of the Río de la Plata* (London: Athlone Press, 1958), p. 120. Ortiz de Landazuri, who had served on the 1764 select committee on commercial reform and who exerted a continuing influence on mercantile policy, may well have been responsible for the strides at this time toward the further liberalization of trade regulations. Muñoz Pérez, "La publicación," pp. 27 ff.

This shift quickly became apparent as the smaller, mobile craft utilized in earlier years gave way to the construction of larger vessels, including two triple-deckers with over 100 cannons. The *Santísima Trinidad*, for example, launched in Havana in 1769, was a massive vessel of 120 guns, and it was subsequently modified to include a fourth deck and another 16 cannons. This colossus, although limited at sea because of its tall frame, symbolized the resurgence of Spanish sea power. By 1779, new construction at Havana and the arsenals at Cartagena de Levante, Cádiz, and El Ferrol had brought the operative fleet up to some sixty ships of the line.[51]

The fall of Esquilache and the ensuing conservative backlash left Gálvez exposed in Mexico without protection at court and vulnerable to the enemies of reform. Gálvez's controversial decree of February 11, 1767, which centralized revenue collection at Veracruz, reached Madrid at the peak of the reaction against Esquilache's initiatives. Arriaga followed customary procedure and referred the question to the Council of the Indies, a conservative stronghold of the Spanish elite. Its grand chancellor was the conspiratorial Duke of Huéscar (later Duke of Alba) and the Marqués de San Juan de Piedras Albas was president; both were staunch conservatives.[52] Only Comptroller General Tomás Ortiz de Landazuri, who had served on the 1764–1765 select committee reviewing commercial policy, was a reformer, but he disliked Gálvez's high-handed methods and his inclination to exclude Mexico from imperial free trade.[53] Arriaga worked throughout the year with the Council to prepare a case against Gálvez to destroy his *visita*.[54] On February 10, 1768, in a stinging rebuke to the controversial reform mission to Mexico, the Council issued a *consulta* that urged Charles to revoke the February 1767 instruction to Veracruz.[55]

To avoid political controversy over the Gálvez *visita*, Charles elected to delay by asking Viceroy Marqués of Croix, an Esquilache appointee, to assess the issue.[56] Croix's report arrived at court in late 1768, and it rendered a favorable appraisal of Gálvez's work.[57] At this point, Charles stunned the Council of the Indies by withdrawing the question from its purview and

[51] Brian Lavery, *The Ship of the Line*, I, *The Development of the Battle Fleet, 1650–1850* (London: Conway Maritime Press, 1983), p. 111. For an inventory of the ships constructed during this period, see John D. Harbron, *Trafalgar and the Spanish Navy* (London: Conway Maritime Press, 1988), pp. 170–71.

[52] Luis Navarro García, *La Casa de Contratación en Cádiz* (Cádiz: Instituto de estudios Gaditanos, 1975), p. 55.

[53] Opinión (Opinion), Ortiz de Landazuri, Madrid, December 22, 1767, AGI, Mexico, leg. 1250. See also AGI, IG, leg. 38.

[54] Arriaga to Piedras Albas, San Ildefonso, September 10, 1767, and Madrid, December 14, 1767, AGI, Mexico, leg. 1250.

[55] *Consulta*, Council of the Indies, February 10, 1768, AGI, Mexico, leg. 1249.

[56] Royal order, Aranjuez, April 18, 1768, AGI, Mexico, leg. 1250.

[57] Croix a Arriaga, Mexico, September 28, 1768, AGI, Mexico, leg. 1250.

remanding it to the jurisdiction of the *fiscales* of the Council of Castile.[58] These magistrates were José de Moñino, the future Conde de Floridablanca, and Pedro Rodríguez Campomanes, who had assisted Grimaldi in reforming the mail service and had prepared the report blaming the Jesuits for the *motín* of 1766.[59] The *fiscales* issued an exhaustive, 621-page opinion on April 20, 1771, that upheld Gálvez.[60] As a result, when the vindicated Gálvez returned to Spain later that same year, Charles appointed him to the Council of the Indies, which allowed him to confront directly the reactionary forces set against modernization.[61]

Despite real accomplishments, the Gálvez mission had achieved far less than originally planned. Esquilache's instructions specified that the visitor general should determine "whether it will be useful ... to establish one or more intendancies in New Spain on the same model as those of Spain."[62] This reform went beyond the Cuba model by including administration and justice in addition to finance, which entailed a controversial administrative reorganization. Gálvez's 1768 plan for intendancies floundered indefinitely after active opposition from Viceroy Croix's replacement, Antonio Bucareli, and fierce anti-reformist opposition in Spain.[63] Madrid simply lacked the strong leadership to drive through such a controversial reform. The momentum for ambitious administrative reforms would not resume until Gálvez himself became Minister of the Indies in 1776 and the threat of war with Britain loomed.

After the king's rescue of the Gálvez *visita*, commercial reform slowly advanced. The most significant step came by royal order of April 23, 1774, which authorized craft operating under the 1765 regulation to call at multiple ports.[64] The difficulty with exploiting trade liberalization had been the policy's inflexibility. Upon their arrival, Spanish and colonial merchants

---

[58] Arriaga to the *fiscales* of the Council of Castile, Palace, March 3, 1769, AGI, Mexico, leg. 1250.

[59] Campomanes was on record as an advocate of commercial reform. Pedro Rodríguez de Campomanes, *Reflexiones sobre el comercio español a Indias* (1762), ed. by Vicente Llombart Rosa (Madrid: Instituto de Estudios Fiscales, 1988).

[60] Opinión, Pedro Rodríguez Campomanes and José de Moñino, Madrid, April 20, 1771, AGI, Mexico, leg. 1250.

[61] Mark A. Burkholder, *Biographical Dictionary of the Councilors of the Indies, 1717–1808* (Westport: Greenwood Press, 1986), p. 45.

[62] Instruction, Palace, March 14, 1765, art. 31, AGI, Mexico, leg. 1249. Cited in Allan J. Kuethe and Lowell Blaisdell, "French Influence and the Origins of the Bourbon Colonial Reorganization." *HAHR* 71, no. 3 (August 1991), p. 595.

[63] Brading, *Miners and Merchants*, pp. 45–47.

[64] *Expediente*, multiport trade, 1774, AGI, IG, leg. 2411. For a detailed treatment of this reform, see Kuethe, "The Regulation of 'Comercio Libre' of 1765 and the Spanish Caribbean Islands," in *Primer Congreso Internacional de História Económica y Social de la Cuenca del Caribe, 1763–1898*, edited by Ricardo E. Alegría (San Juan: Centro de Estudios Avanzados de Puerto Rico y el Caribe, San Juan de Puerto Rico, 1992), pp. 204–207.

declaring for a certain port might find the local demand insufficient to sell all of their cargo, and the law did not give them the right to continue on to other ports where they might market their produce successfully. The *Consulado* opposed such an innovation, which threatened to weaken further its position, but the influence of the aging Fray Arriaga had faded. As a result, the cautious Múzquiz guided the necessary legislation through. Eight years had passed since the downfall of Esquilache, and the new commercial system had produced impressive results in Havana, especially the trade carried in small, mobile Catalonian *saetías*, which had attracted keen interest at court.[65] Under these circumstances, the *Consulado's* protests went unheeded. Meanwhile, Ortiz de Landazuri's patient work led later in 1774 to the legalization of trade in colonial products among Peru, New Spain, Guatemala, and New Granada on the Pacific.[66] Finally, Cumaná joined the Caribbean system of deregulated trade in July of that same year.[67]

THE EXTINCTION OF THE SOCIETY OF JESUS

King Charles doggedly pursued his reforms of the church, focusing principally on his continuing attack on the Jesuit order. Not content with expelling the Jesuits from their domains, the governments of Portugal, France, and Spain lobbied the papacy for a complete dissolution of the order. The Spanish Bourbon family took the lead in this effort. After the expulsion of the order from Spain and the Indies, the Kingdom of Naples followed suit in November 1767, and the Duchy of Parma did likewise in February 1768, effectively removing the order from the Italian peninsula. King Charles III's younger brother Philip still ruled Parma, while his son reigned in Naples, and by late 1768 both kingdoms joined Spain in lobbying to extinguish the order. Pope Clement XIII resisted these efforts, claiming the Jesuits had done a great deal of good for the church and deserved no such fate. Nonetheless, when the Bourbon monarchs seized Avignon in France, and Pontecorvo and Benevento, which were papal enclaves in the Kingdom of Naples, the pope agreed to convene the College of Cardinals to consider the dissolution of the Society. He died the day it was scheduled to meet. The matter then passed to his successor, Lorenzo Ganganelli, taking the name Clement XIV, who chose to conciliate the Bourbon monarchs and recover the papacy's lost territories.

Pope Clement XIV issued his papal brief (*breve*) *Dominus ac Redemptor* on July 21, 1773, dissolving the Jesuit order, and it was published in Madrid on September 12, 1773.[68] The brief began with a history of the Society of Jesus from its approval by Pius III in 1540, but it then went on to list the many

---

[65] Leví Marrero, *Cuba: Economía y sociedad*, XII (San Juan: Editorial San Juan, 1985), pp. 27–28.

[66] File, intercolonial trade, 1774, AGI, Mexico, leg. 2521.

[67] Royal *cédula*, July 14, 1774, AGI, SF, leg. 542.

[68] "Breve de Nuestro Muy Santo Padre Clemente XIV. Por el qual su santidad suprime, deroga, y extingue el instituto y orden de los Clérigos Regulares, denominados de la Compañía de Jesus,

complaints lodged against the order, particularly its "covetousness of temporal goods, out of which arose, as everyone knows, those upsets that caused great grief and disquiet for the Apostolic See as well as the measures that some sovereigns took against the Company."[69] According to the document, under his predecessor Clement XIII, the clamor and complaints against the order grew daily, which aroused "seditions, tumults, discords, and scandals ... fracturing and breaking entirely the tie to Christian charity."[70] Moreover, the kings of France, Spain, Portugal, and the Two Sicilies already had expelled the order from their domains. As a result, the pope declared that using the apostolic power of his office

we suppress and extinguish the aforementioned Company; we abolish and annul all and each of its offices, ministries, and positions, houses, schools, colleges, orphanages, farms, and whatever possessions located in whatever province, kingdom, or dominion, and that by whatever means they relate to it, and statutes, usages, customs, decrees, and codes, although they may be affirmed by oaths [and] Apostolic confirmation ... and likewise all and each one of its privileges and general reprieves.[71]

Members of the order faced a stark choice: leave their houses and either join another regular order or the secular clergy. Overall, the extinction of the order affected the lives of more than 22,000 men in the Society of Jesus. The papacy would dispose of the Jesuit missions. Finally, the papal order extinguishing the Society was final; it could not be delayed, appealed, or overturned at any future date.[72]

Since the expulsion of the Jesuits from the Spanish Empire in 1767, the material possessions or *temporalidades* of the order had reverted to the crown and were administered by the Conde de Aranda and the Council of Castile. With the extinction of the order in 1773, Pope Clement XIV now claimed jurisdiction over the *temporalidades* in Spain and the Indies, and he established a special committee headed by Cardinal Antonio Casali to make an inventory of the Jesuit wealth and establish a series of special papal committees to decide how to manage or sell Jesuit assets and the order's missions, *colegios*, seminaries, and schools. This unwelcome assertion of papal authority prompted King Charles III to refer the issue of managing Jesuit assets to the Council of the Indies.[73] The *fiscal* of the Council immediately disputed the

que ha sido presentado en el Consejo para su publicación. Año 1773 en Madrid. En la Imprenta de Pedro Marion." The original brief was issued in Rome on July 21, 1773, and published in Madrid on September 12, 1773, AGI, IG, leg. 3087.

[69] Ibid., p. 33.

[70] Ibid., p. 28.

[71] Ibid., pp. 33–34.

[72] Ibid., pp. 36–47.

[73] Pope Clemente XIV, "Para futura memoria," to Cardinal Negroni, Rome, 1773 AGI, IG, leg. 3087.

jurisdiction of Cardinal Casali's committee, arguing that the Council of Castile controlled the administration of the Jesuit assets. He contended that only the king of Spain had the power to enforce religious policy in Spain and its overseas possessions, regardless of the papal order sent out by his nuncio in Madrid, the Conde de Vincenti. This included authority to dispose of the houses, goods, lands and effects of the Jesuits. According to the Council's *fiscal*, the king controlled

all the worldly properties that the extinguished possessed in their respective territories, [so you may] dispose of them as you chose by the authority of his universal patronage, without prejudice to the faculties that the diocesans possess to intervene in purely spiritual affairs that pertain to them, for to understand otherwise would notoriously prejudice the very royal prerogative ... without which this brief would by no means be able to change or invalidate the measures that were taken beforehand by His Majesty.[74]

Three years later, the secretary of the Office for the Indies, José de Gálvez, who then had jurisdiction of the Jesuit *temporalidades* in America, wrote to the Council of the Indies imposing a complete ban on any discussion of the Jesuits, including the disposition of their properties.[75] The Council concurred. By 1776, even the pope had relented and agreed to impose silence on the matter.[76] The papacy was never able to enforce its claims on Jesuit properties in the Spanish Atlantic world, which remained administered by crown authorities.

The administration of the lucrative Jesuit holdings in both Spain and the Indies proved much more difficult than the crown had anticipated, and the stakes were enormous. The Society of Jesus had owned agricultural properties in Peru worth an estimated 6 million pesos, while estimates for their holdings in New Spain reach 8.5 to 10 million pesos, and for New Granada nearly 1 million pesos.[77] The crown initially gave Conde de Aranda and the Council of Castile supervisory authority over Jesuit assets in Spain and the Indies, but the task proved well beyond the capabilities of Aranda and that body. There was similar confusion in the actual administration of the properties in the various provinces of the Indies. Under an order of the Council of Castile on

---

[74] Informe del Fiscal para Consulta del Consejo, Madrid, November 23, 1773, AGI, IG, leg. 3087.

[75] José de Gálvez to Council of the Indies, El Pardo, February 22, 1776, AGI, IG, leg. 3087.

[76] Letter from Pope Pius VI to the Spanish crown, Rome, January 23, 1776, AGI, IG, leg. 3087.

[77] Kendall W. Brown, "Jesuit Wealth and Economic Activity within the Peruvian Economy: The Case of Southern Peru," *The Americas*, 44, no. 1 (July 1987), p. 42. Brown is citing the following works providing these estimates: Pablo Macera dall'Orso, "Instrucciones para el manejo de las haciendas jesuitas del Perú (ss. XVII-XVIII)," *Nueva Corónica*, 2 (1966), pp. 8–9; James Denson Riley, "The Management of the Estates of the Jesuit *Colegio Máximo de San Pedro y San Pablo* of Mexico City in the Eighteenth Century," (Ph.D. Diss., Tulane University, 1972), p. 247; and Germán Colmenares, *Haciendas de los Jesuitas en el Nuevo Reyno de Granada , siglo XVIII* (Bogotá: Universidad Nacional, 1969), pp. 18, 22.

February 24, 1768, the viceroys and governors set up a junta superior in each capital city composed of the viceroy, captain general or governor, two members of the local audiencia, its *fiscal*, and a treasury official. Below this junta were juntas *municipales* and juntas *provinciales*, composed of the local governor or *corregidor*, a parish priest named by the bishop, and a *regidor* of the cabildo. The result of the proliferation of committees was confusion, a lack of uniform policies, and little supervision of local officials, leading to corruption and inefficiency.[78]

Given the administrative difficulties experienced in the Indies, in 1783 the crown separated the administration of Jesuit *temporalidades* in Spain from the Indies, which it placed under the Secretariat of the Indies in 1783.[79] The next year the ministry created the office of *director de temporalidades* for the Indies, with an office staff to organize the accounts of the Jesuit assets and ensure that the monies remitted each year from the Indies went to pay the pensions of the Jesuits in exile, with any remaining funds going to the Royal Treasury.[80] The director was to oversee the collection of 2.5 million copper *reales* annually to pay for the pensions of the exiled Jesuits and to repay 11,255,000 *reales* in debts owed to the Spanish treasury. In the Indies, the juntas *muncipales* were disbanded, and the juntas *superiores* and juntas *provinciales* administered only judicial cases arising from the administration of Jesuit wealth. The administration of economic assets fell to a newly created *administrador-tesorero de temporalidades* in each capital city, along with a comptroller, who would oversee *administradores subalternos*. The latter would do the actual collection of revenues at the local level (often in conjunction with local cabildos and *corregidores*).[81] Apart from a brief period when the Ministry of the Indies administered the assets, the amounts remitted to Spain from *temporalidades* in the Indies remained disappointing. Even during the years of peak remittances, the amounts collected largely came from the sale of Jesuit assets, not the skillful management of the properties, ensuring that the revenues from the Indies would diminish over time. For the crown, the lure of controlling the vast wealth of the Jesuits proved illusory in the long run.

RENEWAL OF REFORM AND RESISTANCE
IN THE SPANISH ATLANTIC

Despite the crown's frustrations with the administration of Jesuit properties, reformers soon forged ahead once again with additional commercial and

---

[78] Antonio Porcel to the Suprema Junta del Estado, Madrid, October 24, 1787, AGI, IG, leg., 3085B.

[79] Reglamento de la Dirección de Temporalidades de los Dominios de las Indias y Filipinas, Aranjuez, June 22, 1784, AGI, IG, leg. 3084.

[80] Ibid.

[81] Antonio Porcel to the Suprema Junta del Estado, Madrid, October 24, 1787, AGI, Lima, leg. 3085B.

administrative reforms. News of Lexington and Concord, which raised hopes for revenge against the British, coincided with the death of the venerable Fray Julián de Arriaga in January 1776, allowing the king to appoint José de Gálvez as the new secretary of the Office for the Indies. Galvez's extensive American experience and proven success as a reformer enabled him to assert unprecedented personal dominance over the ministry. He did not receive the naval portfolio, which went to Pedro González Castejón. Nonetheless, the death of the Duke of Alba, who was acting president of the Council of the Indies, allowed Charles to name Gálvez governor of the Council on February 26, 1776.[82] The death the following year of Tomás Ortiz de Landazuri (*contador general de Indias*) enabled Gálvez to secure that key position for one of his allies, Francisco Javier Machado Fiesco.

Events during the preceding year, moreover, had removed two potential rivals. O'Reilly's power collapsed in 1775 after his monumental failure as commander of an expedition against the Dey of Algiers. Faced with an angry public outcry against the Irishman, Charles assigned him to inspect the Chafarinas Islands off the coast of Africa; and in 1776, the king named him captain general of Andalusia, far from Madrid.[83] Building xenophobia in Spain following the Algerian debacle also forced the king to remove Grimaldi from State. Charles assuaged the loyal Italian's humiliation, however, by naming him ambassador to the papacy.[84]

Charles replaced Grimaldi with the talented Conde de Floridablanca, who quickly emerged as the dominant force in the new reformist government. The first among the six secretaries of the Office, Floridablanca would skillfully guide Spain through the troubled waters of the American Revolutionary period and well beyond, as his shrewd diplomacy promoted Spain's interests at the expense of its historic British foe. A magistrate of the first order, his commanding presence was captured very effectively by the brush of Francisco de Goya y Lucientes, the brilliant court painter of the era (see Figure 8.1). Floridablanca's rival to succeed Grimaldi had been the ambitious Conde de Aranda. To rid Madrid of his meddling, Floridablanca assigned him to the embassy at Versailles. Within this context, Gálvez, as both secretary of the Office for the Indies and as governor of the Council, enjoyed considerable autonomy. Furthermore, he benefitted from the support of Múzquiz, the senior member of the cabinet, who enjoyed a favorable personal relationship with the king.[85]

---

[82] The Duque de Alba was acting president by virtue of being hereditary grand chancellor of the Indies. As head of the royal household and dean of the Council of State, he had remained an important political figure at court.

[83] Bibiano Torres Ramírez, *Alejandro O'Reilly en las Indias* (Sevilla: Escuela de Estudios Hispano-Americanos, 1969), pp. 10–11.

[84] Escudero, *Los orígenes*, I, pp. 344–60.

[85] Anthony H. Hull, *Charles III and the Revival of Spain* (Washington, D.C.: University Press of America, 1981), pp. 193, 304.

FIGURE 8.1 José Moñino, Conde de Floridablanca (1728–1808) in the Museo del Prado, wearing the insignia of the Order of Charles III, apparently painted by Francisco de Goya y Lucientes, although some authorities claim it was done by (a) student(s) in his studio. (See plate section for color version)

The new Minister of the Indies changed the tempo and tone of government, essentially discarding the customary formula of consultation and compromise with the American elites in favor of a more authoritarian approach. He could justify this change by the urgencies that the looming, long-awaited reckoning with the British imposed. He unleashed a far-reaching program featuring reform in the areas of administration, commercial policy, and revenue collection, and he renewed and extended the military reorganization. Gálvez demonstrated impressive initiative and ambition, but he often lacked the tactful good sense needed to pursue change without provoking bitter resistance. During his years of leadership, he would achieve much but at a very high price.

Gálvez first turned to administrative initiatives aimed at strengthening the peripheries, an objective dating back to the early years of Charles's reign and before. To shore up the northern rim of the empire, he established the Commandancy General of the Interior Provinces, which united New Spain's northern frontier from Texas to California. Gálvez considered establishing yet another viceroyalty in the region, but the frontier lacked the resources to support the necessary enlargement of the bureaucracy.[86] Gálvez also introduced an intendancy into Caracas, the first extension of that institution since Sonora. And given the growing economic and military importance of northern South America, he elevated Caracas into a captaincy general the following year, uniting Maracaibo, Cumaná, and Guayana under that same authority.[87]

The most far-reaching administrative innovation was the establishment of the Viceroyalty of the Río de la Plata in 1776 with its capital in Buenos Aires, the emerging commercial center in the southern cone of South America. While authorities in the Río de la Plata had called for the establishment of a viceroyalty to protect Spain's exposed southern flank, insufficient funds always had made the idea impractical. Portuguese commercial incursions from Brazil through the Colônia do Sacramento finally forced the crown to outfit a military expedition to clear out the interlopers.[88] Gálvez gave command of the military force to the former Governor of Buenos Aires, Pedro de Cevallos,

---

[86] Lynch, *Spanish Colonial Administration*, pp.38–43; Luis Navarro García, *Don José de Gálvez y la Comandancia General de las Provincias Internas del norte de Nueva España* (Sevilla: Consejo Superior de Investigaciones Científicas, 1964), chap. 5.

[87] Luis Navarro García, *Intendencias de Indias* (Sevilla: Escuela de Estudios Hispano-Americanos, 1959), p. 34; Mario Briceño Parozo, "Ámbito institucional de la Capitanía General de Venezuela," *Memoria del Tercer Congreso Venezolano de Historia*, 3 vols. (Caracas: Academia Nacional de Historia, 1979), II, pp. 299–317. By 1776, Gálvez had already unified the area commercially, extending the trade range of the Caracas Company to include the provinces of Guayana and Cumaná and the islands of Margarita and Trinidad. Maracaibo had been brought under the Caracas Company in 1752. Royal order, San Lorenzo, November 16, 1776, AGI, Caracas, leg. 924.

[88] John Lynch, *Spanish Colonial Administration*, pp. 40–41.

who argued that he needed political and fiscal authority over Buenos Aires, Paraguay, Tucumán, and the Audiencia of Charcas, including the mining center at Potosí. The crown granted these powers in 1776. With the successful conclusion of the military campaign, Cevallos in July 1777 urged Gálvez to make the arrangement permanent, erecting a new, fourth Viceroyalty of the Río de la Plata.[89] King Charles had long wanted a secure southern cone from British and Portuguese commercial ambitions, and Gálvez quickly approved the permanent creation, thus partially dismembering the Viceroyalty of Peru.

The Madrid government approved the establishment of the intendant system in the Río de la Plata in 1782, the most extensive use of that administrative innovation yet in the Indies. The Ordinance of Intendants established eight intendancies in the new viceroyalty, and in 1784 the crown founded a ninth intendancy in Puno. The new officials had a generous salary and exercised control over general administration, finance, the military, and certain judicial matters relating specifically to matters under the intendants' direct control. The intendants also exercised much authority over ecclesiastical patronage. The intendant of the province of Buenos Aires was designated as a superintendant, with the remaining officials given lesser titles as provincial intendants. After a series of conflicts with the viceroy, however, the superintendancy was abolished in 1784, and the viceroy assumed those duties. The ordinance eliminated the offices of governor and *corregidor* and replaced them with subdelegates, paid with 3 percent of the tribute receipts collected in their districts. These subdelegates lacked the judicial authority accorded to earlier offices. The intendants represented a new administrative layer, linking the viceroy and the audiencias with provincial administrators.[90]

Gálvez quickly signaled his determination to expand dramatically the deregulation of colonial commerce. The royal decree of October 3, 1776, brought Santa Marta and Ríohacha into the Caribbean free trade system, while another of July 10, 1777, added Mallorca to the enfranchised ports of Spain. Given the successes of the Cuban experiment, an informed observer at court, the Marqués de Echandía, cautioned the *Consulado* of Cádiz that any resistance to further liberalization was hopeless.[91] Moreover, pressure had begun to build within other regions of Spain for broader commercial opportunities. Burgos, Zamora, and Salamanca all supported a petition from Santander for wider opportunities in the colonies. On February 2, 1778, Gálvez opened all of South America below New Granada, including Buenos Aires, Chile, and Callao, to the October 1765 system. And responding to welcomed pressure from Aragón and Granada, he added Murcia, Tortosa, and Almería to the list of authorized ports in Spain.[92]

---

[89] Ibid.
[90] Ibid., pp. 62–90.
[91] *Consulado* to Echandía, Cádiz, July 18, 1777, AGI, Consulados, book 88.
[92] The files for these petitions, royal decrees, and royal orders are located in AGI, IG, legs 2411–12.

The famous Regulation of Free Trade of October 12, 1778, represented a renewed effort to undercut contraband, broaden markets, and draw the colonial economies into a tighter commercial dependence on the metropolis.[93] In most respects, it amounted to a continuation of commercial liberalization that had already taken place, although it finally included Cartagena, Panama, and Guayaquil in the new system, and it systematized tax rates. The crown still excluded New Spain, where smuggling was viewed as a lesser threat than in the other colonies and where the powerful *Consulado* of Mexico City successfully defended its privileges. It also excluded Caracas, where the *Real Compañía Guipuzcoana de Caracas* still held sway. The cacao trade with Veracruz posed an additional complication. In the preparation for the historic regulation and shortly before his death in 1777, Ortiz de Landazuri wrote a preliminary draft for Gálvez's review.[94] Remaining faithful to the spirit of the 1765 recommendation by the select committee on which he had served, Ortiz de Landazuri had included Mexico and Venezuela among those jurisdictions participating in the deregulated system, This undoubtedly would have maximized the volume of commerce between America and the peninsula to the benefit of the Spanish economy.

Defense imperatives still led Gálvez to oppose including Mexico and Venezuela in the system of imperial free trade in 1778. As Spain drew ever closer intervening in the War of the American Revolution, policies favoring the peripheries remained a top priority. Moreover, Gálvez was convinced that Spain would continue to capture the mass of Mexican silver through the established convoy system. During his research in preparing the October regulation, Ortiz had assessed the annual loss to contraband from 1747 to 1761. This amount he calculated at 12 million pesos, but most of it he attributed to New Granada and Peru. Mexico, he believed, accounted for only 1 million.[95] Confident that the Mexicans had only one workable outlet, Gálvez struck from the preliminary draft those articles including Veracruz and La Guaira in the free trade zone. La Guaira, it should be remembered, continued a vigorous cacao trade with Mexico, where the Caracas Company still retained rights. Article 6 of the final draft simply provided that the crown would define a separate policy for Mexico, although it would come under the modernized taxation rates.[96]

---

[93] Muñoz Pérez, "La publicación," pp. 28 ff; John Fisher, "Imperial 'Free Trade' and the Hispanic Economy, 1778–1796," *The Journal of Latin American Studies*, 13 (1981), pp. 21–23.

[94] Gálvez to Ortiz, San Ildefonso, August 18, 1776, AGI, IG, leg. 2411; Ortiz to Martín Cuetro, Madrid, December 7, 1776, AGI, IG, leg. 2046A.

[95] Ortiz, report on the American products in silver, gold, and produce by kingdom, December 6, 1776, AGI, IG, leg. 2411.

[96] Ortiz, regulations for American commerce, Madrid, December 6, 1776, with the Gálvez annotations and deletions, AGI, IG, leg. 2411. The *Reglamento y aranceles reales para el*

TABLE 8.1 *Imports from America to Spain*

Year	Value of Imports	Index: 1747/78=100	Index: 1766/78=100
1782	111,983,765	26	23
1783	541,954,787	124	110
1784	1,201,263,356	276	245
1785	1,148,573,947	263	234
1786	791,085,627	181	161
1787	779,167,112	179	159
1788	805,032,460	185	164
1789	721,253,993	165	147
1790	780,816,540	179	159
1791	1,013,594,889	232	207
1792	780,469,956	179	159
1793	809,609,849	186	165
1794	1,039,284,940	238	212
1795	820,223,396	188	167
1796	1,041,222,273	239	212
Total	12,454,095,293	190	169

Source: Antonio García Baquero, "Los resultados del libre comercio y 'el punto de vista': Una revision desde la estadística," *Manuscrits* 15 (1997): pp. 303–22.

Comercio libre produced a dramatic upsurge in exports from the Indies to Spain by 1783, once hostilities with Great Britain had effectively ended. According to the data in Table 8.1, the volume of imports from America surged from 111,983 765 *reales de vellón* in 1782 to over 1,201,263,356 *reales de vellón* in 1784. As Table 8.1 indicates, this represented an index of growth from 23 percent in 1782 (using the years 1766–1778 as the base year of 100 percent) to 245 percent in 1784, a phenomenal rate of growth in both the volume and value of colonial trade. Moreover, although the value of American imports varied (sometimes considerably) from year to year, the overall trend in trade was still unquestionably positive (see Table 8.1). In a report to the Council of State, Diego Gardoqui (Minister of Finance) reported that between 1787 and 1792 Spain ran an annual trade deficit within Europe of 404 million copper *reales*, and over half of this amount was to pay for goods re-exported to the Indies. The favorable balance of trade with the Indies produced enough revenue to eliminate this deficit, however, generating an overall trading surplus of 184 million *reales de vellón* each year.

comercio libre de España a Indias de 12 de octubre de 1778 has been reprinted by the Escuela de Estudios Hispano-Americanos (Seville 1977). Ortiz's draft also included the ports of Venezuela. The revised draft reserved those ports for the Caracas Company but "without exclusive privilege."

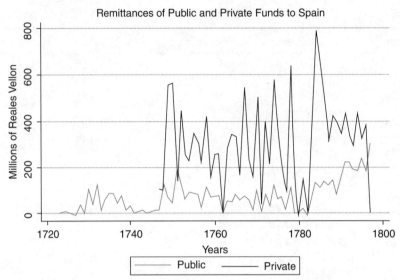

Remittances of Public and Private Funds to Spain

FIGURE 8.2 Remittances of Public and Private Revenue to Spain

Figure 8.2, showing remittances of public and private funds sent from the Indies to Spain demonstrates that trade tended to decline during the 1750s, but it retained a generally upward trajectory from 1765 to 1785 despite annual fluctuations, particularly in the remittance of private funds. Public revenues sent from the Indies followed a clear upward trajectory from 1784 until the outbreak of war with Great Britain in 1796. The figures for private remittances are very difficult to measure with accuracy, but the available estimates in Figure 8.2 indicate an unmistakable overall upward trend for the period after the proclamation of imperial free trade, peaking in the mid-1780s despite a serious drop during the War of the American Revolution. After the outbreak of war with Britain in 1796, remittances declined once again. Moreover, the range of American products imported into Spain was quite varied. The Indies shipped large quantities of bullion (mostly silver) on both the public and private accounts, along with impressive quantities of sugar, hides, wood, cacao, cascarilla, and tobacco. In addition, merchants from the Indies sent smaller quantities of spices, herbs, miscellaneous medicinal products, coffee, tea, lead, tine, wheat, barley, and animal products.[97] In short, the largely unrestricted sailings of individual trading vessels allowed merchants in the Indies to send not only bullion, but to ship more perishable products as well, allowing for a wider range of commodities sent to Spain.

[97] John Fisher, *Commercial Relations Between Spain and Spanish America in the Era of Free Trade* (Liverpool: Liverpool University Press, 1985), pp. 66–71.

The regulation of 1778 had been drafted in secrecy, as the secretary of the Office for the Indies guarded against possible reactions both within and outside of Spain. Gálvez had his brother, Miguel, handle the actual printing.[98] After delays because of treaty obligations and later opposition from powerful vested interests and conservatives at court, the Spanish crown finally promulgated a comprehensive reform of the colonial commercial system. When he published the landmark regulation, the controversial Gálvez showed a keen awareness of his debt to his reformist predecessors. He ordered copies sent at once to Ensenada, Esquilache, and Grimaldi. The aging Ensenada, who was barely able to pen a thank you note, still languished in exile at Medina del Campo.[99] Well supplied with Cuban tobacco, Esquilache remained Spain's ambassador to Venice, and Grimaldi was still ambassador to the papacy.[100] When Ortiz de Landazuri died, Gálvez even placed his daughter, who resided in Peru, under his personal protection.[101] These admirable gestures revealed a level of sensitivity and gentility seldom visible during his public political career.

Reminiscent of the work of Ricla and O'Reilly in Cuba and of himself in Mexico, Gálvez launched a succession of controversial *visitas* to Peru, New Granada, Quito, and Chile, where the high-handed, arbitrary tactics of his appointees resembled his own behavior. These included the missions of Regents-Visitors José Antonio de Areche to Peru and Juan Francisco Gutiérrez de Piñeres to New Granada in 1777 to reorganize colonial finance and administration. Tomás Álvarez de Acevedo and José García-Pizarro led *sub-visitas* to Chile and to Quito. Acting through this cadre, Gálvez abruptly brought new rigor to the enforcement of existing revenue regulations and widely raised monopoly prices and increased the *alcabala*.[102] They also took more accurate censuses of the indigenous population to ensure that tribute levies were collected efficiently. To assert effective control over the machinery of the colonial government, his regents-visitor ruthlessly purged the colonial audiencias, the royal treasuries, and even the lower level administrative offices of deeply entrenched colonial elites or their Spanish surrogates. Having grown accustomed to a voice in the political process through

---

[98] José de Gálvez to Miguel de Gálvez, San Ildefonso, September 24, 1778, AGI, IG, leg. 2409.

[99] He died in 1781.

[100] Ensenada to Gálvez, Medina del Campo, October 29, 1778; Grimaldi to Gálvez, Rome, December 3, 1778; and Esquilache to Gálvez, Venice, November 28, 1778, all in AGI, IG, leg. 2409.

[101] Viceroy Manuel Guirior to Gálvez, Lima, February 20, 1779, AGI, Lima, leg. 659.

[102] Jacques A. Barbier, *Reform and Politics in Bourbon Chile, 1755–1796*, (Ottawa: University of Ottawa Press, 1980), pp. 113 ff; Kuethe, *Military Reform and Society*, pp. 118–25; John Leddy Phelan, *The People and the King: The Comunero rebellion in Colombia, 1781* (Madison: University of Wisconsin Press, 1978), chaps. 1–2; John R. Fisher, *Bourbon Peru, 1750–1824* (Liverpool: Liverpool University Press, 2003), pp. 29–34.

Income of Cuenca, Guayaquil, and Quito, 1765–1804

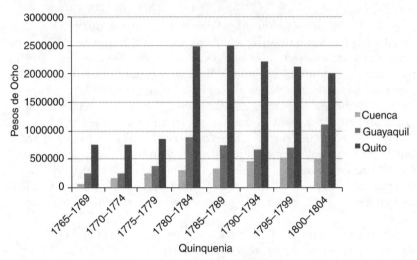

FIGURE 8.3 Income of Cuenca, Guayaquil, and Quito, 1765–1804

bureaucratic participation, these elites now almost invariably found themselves replaced by Spanish-born officials, while many others were added.[103]

The net result of these innovations was a dramatic upsurge in tax revenues in most regions, even in the Audiencia of Quito, which remained mired in a century-long economic decline of its dominant economic sector: textile production. During the tenure of President-Regent and Visitor José García de León y Pizarro in Quito, tax revenues experienced a dramatic upsurge, clearly demonstrating the effectiveness of this new colonial state apparatus in the district (see Figure 8.3). Treasury receipts in the Cuenca district, where the reforms had a lesser impact, grew from less than 65,000 pesos in the period from 1765 to 1769 to more than 526,000 pesos between 1800 and 1804. Meanwhile, income flowing into the Guayaquil treasury soared from more than 249,000 pesos to more than 1.1 million pesos during the same time period. Both regions experienced substantial economic growth, which the reinvigorated state apparatus tapped with greater efficiency, draining investment capital that might have gone into entrepreneurial activities to sustain local economic prosperity. The increase in government revenues was

---

[103] John Leddy Phelan, "El auge y la caída de los criollos en la Audiencia de Nueva Granada, 1700–1781," *Boletín de historia y antigüedades*, 59 (1972), pp. 597–618; Jacques A. Barbier, "Elite and Cadres in Bourbon Chile," *HAHR*, 52 (Aug., 1972), pp. 432–433; Leon G. Campbell, *The Military and Society in Colonial Peru, 1750–1810* (Philadelphia: American Philosophical Society Press, 1978), p. 74. See also, Burkholder and Chandler, *From Impotence to Authority*, pp. 101–06.

most striking, however, in the economically depressed north-central high-lands, the center of a decaying woolen textile industry. Income flowing into the Quito treasury (bolstered by remittances from Guayaquil and Cuenca) shot upwards from less than 746,000 pesos in the aftermath of the Quito Insurrection (1765–1769) to more than 2.5 million pesos between 1785 and 1789.[104] Such heavy fiscal exactions on the declining north-central highlands undoubtedly exacerbated the downward economic spiral of the region, but they filled the region's royal coffers.

Unlike the Audiencia of Quito, where enhanced fiscal pressures did not disrupt the public order, in upland Santa Fe de Bogotá and the central and southern Andes, Bourbon innovations sparked violent and bloody uprisings. Earlier efforts to remove Upper Peru from the Viceroyalty of Peru had already disrupted regional trade patterns and led to regional economic dislocation, which only worsened with the rise in taxes, leading to local fears and dis-content with crown policies. These disruptions of the traditional political, social, and economic orders paved the way for the Great Age of Andean Rebellions, beginning in 1781 in Chayanta (north of Potosí), Tinta (near Cuzco), and the La Paz region, and included the revolt of the Comuneros of New Granada in 1781. These dangerous upheavals (even more serious than the disorders faced by Gálvez during his *visita* in New Spain) caused great loss of life and reminded the monarch of the practical limitations inhibiting sudden increases of tax revenues.[105] Gálvez well might have lost his job had not Charles been a man of patience, and had not the minister's nephew, Bernardo, been winning glory for Spain in Florida at the same time.

The first phase of the resistance against the reforms began inauspiciously as a series of local protests by the Aymara people of Macha (in Chayanta, north of Potosí) under the leadership of an illiterate Andean peasant, Tomás Katari. Katari and the people of Macha wanted to gain redress over abuses in tribute collection and the forced allocation of European wares (*repartimiento de comercio* or *repartos*). Despite his humble origins, Katari would inaugurate a remarkable struggle leading to unprecedented claims for indigenous autonomy and political power in the region. Between 1777 and 1780, Katari led the ten ethnic communities of Macha in a series of legal confronta-tions with the local *corregidor* and the Audiencia of Charcas, which promp-ted him to make the long trek from Chayanta to Buenos Aires, where he took his case directly to the viceroy, a supporter of reform in the Indies. Although authorities in Buenos Aires initially supported Katari against entrenched

[104] Kenneth J. Andrien, *The Kingdom of Quito, 1690-1830: The State and Regional Development* (Cambridge: Cambridge University Press, 1995), pp. 196–201.

[105] Phelan, *The People*, chaps. 3–16; Scarlett O'Phelan Godoy, *Rebellions and Revolts in Eighteenth-Century Peru and Upper Peru* (Cologne: Böhlau Verlag, 1985), chaps. 4–5; David Cahill, *From Rebellion to Independence in the Andes: Soundings from Southern Peru, 1750-1830* (Amsterdam: Aksant, 2002), chaps. 6–7.

traditional groups in Charcas, local authorities remained opposed to his popular movement, ultimately leading to violent confrontations. The protests led to the expulsion of Spanish authorities from the region, the assumption of power by Katari, and then to a widespread insurrection of the Aymara peoples against the Spanish colonial regime. Even after local Spanish authorities murdered Katari in December 1780, rebellion engulfed the region, as the Aymara army even attempted an unsuccessful siege of La Plata. Within a year, however, Spanish troops had defeated the Aymara rebels.[106]

Simultaneously with the unrest in Chayanta, an even more violent and serious insurrection threatened Spanish power southeast of Cusco in Tinta, led by José Gabriel Condorcanqui, who took the name Tupac Amaru II after the Inca leader executed in 1572. The Bourbon reforms had provoked economic hardship and high taxes, and local political corruption in tribute assessments and *reparto* allocations led to hostility toward the Spanish regime. After Tupac Amaru and his troops executed the corrupt local *corregidor*, Antonio de Arriaga, a widespread rebellion inflamed the whole Cusco region as the rebel leader attempted to forge a broadly based coalition of the region's diverse ethnic population. The leadership of his army consisted of nineteen Spaniards and creoles, twenty-nine mestizos, seventeen Andeans, and four blacks and mulattos. The bulk of his troops were indigenous tribute payers. Tupac Amaru used a diverse set of Andean and Christian symbols in forging a program designed to attract a broad regional coalition to protest abuses of the colonial regime. He took the title of *Sapa Inca*, dressed in traditional Inca royal tunics, and drew upon popular messianic beliefs that foretold of the return of the last ruler, Tupac Amaru, who would expel the Spanish authorities and bring justice and social order to the Andes. Spanish authorities in Cusco raised an army of creole militiamen and loyal Andeans, but Tupac Amaru's troops defeated the Spanish force at Sangaragá, where the bulk of the royal army perished.

After their victory, many of the indigenous rank-and-file took out years of pent-up anger and frustration by killing creoles, peninsulars, and noncombatants indiscriminately. These atrocities led most creoles to abandon the movement and join forces with the royalists, and numerous competing Andean ethnic leaders refused to recognize the leadership of Tupac Amaru, either remaining neutral or joining the royalist military effort to suppress the rebellion. Tupac Amaru ultimately prepared to lay siege to Cusco with 30,000 rebel soldiers. When Spanish troops stopped the rebels from surrounding the city, Tupac Amaru abruptly retreated with his army to Tinta, where a Spanish force from Cusco ultimately defeated and captured the rebel leader, who was publically executed in Cusco in 1781. He was drawn and

---

[106] The best new work on the Katari movement is Sergio Serulnikov, *Subverting Colonial Authority: Challenges to Spanish Rule in Eighteenth-Century Mexico* (Durham: Duke University Press, 2003).

quartered in the main square in Cusco, and his body parts displayed pub-lically as a grim reminder of the price exacted on those who rebelled against the crown. Nonetheless, his army continued to harass Spanish authorities in the region under the command of his cousin, Diego Cristóbal Tupac Amaru.[107]

Diego Cristóbal led his Quechua-speaking rebel forces to Upper Peru, where they took Puno in May 1781 and established connections with Aymara rebels led by the Katari brothers and a second large Aymara force operating around La Paz under the command of an illiterate Andean petty merchant, Julián Apasa. Apasa initially pretended to be the incarnation of the deceased leader, Tomás Katari, which allowed him to raise an army and later to take the name Tupac Katari. When the Spaniards captured one of the original Katari brothers and another died in battle, the Aymara forces fell under the single command of Julián Apasa-Tupac Katari. Although the kins-men of Tupac Amaru nominally led the rebellion, relations between the Quechua and Aymara commanders were often strained. They had to speak with each other through interpreters, and friction and animosity impeded joint operations. The Quechua forces operated out of Puno, while Tupac Katari and the Aymara army besieged La Paz twice without success. When Spanish forces raised the second siege of the city in May 1781, bitter divisions emerged between the two camps, and the Tupac Amaru clan decided to abandon their Aymara allies and seek a surrender and pardon from Spanish authorities. Tupac Katari was unaware of the Quechua army's surrender, and a few days after learning of the betrayal, he was lured into a trap, captured, and later executed, effectively ending the rebellions against Spanish authority. Despite its victory, Spanish authority in the Andes had been deeply shaken by these three bloody rebellions.[108]

The fourth major upheaval against Bourbon innovations began in New Granada in March 1781 in the town of Socorro in Tunja Province (in upland, central Colombia), and the Comunero Rebellion soon engulfed much of the viceroyalty's interior. The rebellion broke out in response to the ambitious attempts by Regent-Visitor Juan Francisco Gutiérrez de Piñeres to enforce strict tax and monopoly laws, reduce inefficiency and waste, and eliminate fraud and corruption. The Socorro region was very adversely affected by efforts to raise taxes on local cotton production and restrict the cultivation of tobacco to a zone near the city of Girón. The insurgents in Socorro arose to challenge the new revenue measures, and in April 1781 over 4,000 protestors

---

[107] The newest treatment of the Tupac Amaru Revolt is Ward Stavig, *The World of Tupac Amaru: Conflict, Community, and Identity in Colonial Peru* (Lincoln: University of Nebraska Press, 1999).

[108] The newest treatment of the Tupac Katari Revolt is Sinclair Thomson, *We Alone Shall Rule: Native American Politics in the Age of Insurgency* (Madison: University of Wisconsin Press, 2002).

gathered in the city to select a council of leaders headed by Juan Francisco Berbeo, a local creole who commanded the rebel forces. To complicate matters, the viceroy, Manuel Antonio Flores, had deployed the bulk of the army to defend Cartagena from a threatened British attack after Spain entered the War of the American Revolution. When Gutiérrez de Piñeres and the authorities in Bogotá heard of the insurgency in Socorro, they sent a small military force to crush the rebels, but the insurgents defeated the royal troops decisively at the Battle of Puente Real. After this victory, the rebel army swelled to over 15,000 men, and it encamped outside the now nearly defenseless viceregal capital. The rebels issued their demands in the thirty-four Capitulations of Zipaquirá, which dealt with the full range of Comunero complaints against Bourbon fiscal and administrative innovations. Royal power effectively rested with the archbishop of Bogotá, Antonio de Caballero y Góngora, who took charge of negotiations with the rebels. Without a military force to defend the city, Caballero y Góngora and the civilian authorities in Bogotá hastily accepted the Capitulations and issued a pardon to the rebels. Once the rebels had returned home and a column of troops had arrived from Cartagena, however, the government repudiated its agreement. When it became clear that the royal administration did not intend to honor the terms of the Capitulations, a lieutenant of Berbeo, José Antonio Galán, attempted without success to resuscitate the insurrection. Galán was later captured and executed in Santa Fe, and the Comunero Rebellion effectively ended.[109]

While these areas of the South American highlands were caught up in the uprisings against the new reformist agenda, coastal regions uniformly remained stable. They also served as bases for the eventual military pacification of the interior. As the beneficiaries of the patterns of military spending, those populations had little reason to protest revenue reform, and they hosted intimidating military establishments. Moreover, the deregulation of commercial policy in 1778 surely attracted at least some coastal interests to the reformist agenda.

In the uplands, both the Governorship of Popayán in southwestern New Granada and the Presidency of Quito were exceptions, both remaining tranquil. Part of the explanation surely lies in the memory of the failed uprisings of 1765. Another factor discouraging popular mobilizations, however, was the fixed, inland garrisons established in both jurisdictions in the aftermath of those disorders. Moreover, Viceroy Manuel Flores had extended the disciplined militia system to Popayán in 1777. And as a precaution, the president-regent in Quito, José García de León y Pizarro, had reorganized the militia of the *quiteño* uplands in conjunction with his duties as visitor-general. By comparison, other inland authorities had lacked similar instruments when

---

[109] Kuethe, *Military Reform and Society*, pp. 87–88.

the populace challenged their authority.[110] In Chile, where the local elites skillfully subverted the work of Álvarez to their own ends, no occasion arose to protest violently.[111]

SPAIN AND THE WAR OF THE AMERICAN REVOLUTION

As the reformist program of Gálvez evolved, military triumphs against the British foe vindicated the controversial agenda of Charles III. After careful preparation, Madrid entered the War of the American Revolution on its own terms on June 21, 1779. Versailles had allied with the colonial insurgents a year before.[112] The conflict featured impressive military actions taken on the offensive and backed by a resurgent armada. Spain swept the British from the Gulf of Mexico and defended successfully its strongholds in Central America. While it failed to expel its rival from Gibraltar in Europe, it retook Minorca in the Mediterranean.[113] Cuban authorities sent the regular army on the offensive, while the disciplined militia manned the home defenses. Moreover, several thousand reinforcements arrived from Europe.[114] The force that Bernardo de Gálvez, José's nephew, led to victory in a spectacular campaign across the northern rim of the Gulf numbered 7,400 men when it successfully laid siege to Pensacola in May 1781.[115] To assemble an army of this size was a remarkable achievement for a regime that had failed so miserably in 1762, demonstrating the success of military reform. Ricla's strategy had worked.

Although the main force was diverted to Guarico for a planned Franco-Spanish invasion of Jamaica in 1782, while other troops held Florida, Governor Juan Manuel Cagigal still found enough men to seize Providence in the Bahamas. Again the disciplined militia defended the home front while the regulars assumed the offensive.[116] In April 1782, the victory of Admiral and Commander of the Leeward Islands Squadron George Rodney over the French fleet at Les Saintes saved Jamaica, but Spanish gains nevertheless remained impressive.

---

[110] Kuethe, *Military Reform and Society*, pp. 48–51, 63–78, 90–91. In Peru, the massive militia raised by Viceroy Amat excelled in producing uniforms for officers but had very little military capacity. Campbell, *The Military and Society*, chap. 3.

[111] Barbier, *Reform and Politics in Bourbon Chile*, passim.

[112] Thomas E. Chávez, *Spain and the Independence of the United States: An Intrinsic Gift* (Albuquerque: University of New Mexico Press, 2002), chaps. 4–8.

[113] Ibid., chaps. 9–10.

[114] Some 7,600 embarked, but the crossing took three months and many were lost.

[115] Kuethe, *Cuba, 1753–1815*, chap. 4. The army contained 725 soldiers that the French provided.

[116] Ibid., pp. 117–18; James A. Lewis, *The Final Campaign of the American Revolution: The Rise and Fall of the Spanish Bahamas* (Columbia, S.C.: University of South Carolina Press, 1991).

Despite these victories on land, the armada earned only a mixed record. By the time of Madrid's declaration of war, Spanish naval forces featured some sixty ships of the line and over thirty frigates.[117] Charles, through his ministers, expected the fleet deployed in Havana to attack British targets, such as the Jamaican sugar convoys, but its tradition-bound officers, who thought defensively, fabricated resourceful justifications to remain in port. Moreover, the fleet that supported Galvez's Florida campaign did so only reluctantly. Nevertheless, early in the war, Spanish forces together with the French deployed sixty-six ships of the line at Brest, threatening an invasion of Great Britain, while subsequently the two navies' actions divided and distracted the British sufficiently to slow fatally the relief that Cornwallis needed at Yorktown.[118]

On another level, Spain furnished substantial material and financial assistance both to the rebellious English colonists as co-belligerents and to its French allies. Beginning even before it entered the conflict openly, Madrid transferred money and war material to the insurgents. While it made these transfers principally through its bases at New Orleans and Havana, the Madrid government sent some support directly to Boston from Cádiz.[119] Madrid calculated this assistance at some 611,000 pesos, two-thirds of it subventions, the rest in loans.[120] Moreover, Spain lent at least 5 million pesos to France, in silver transferred from Veracruz to Havana, which then went out to French forces operating in the American theater. Certainly, the most significant example was the 500,000 pesos that Special Agent Francisco de Saavedra raised in Havana and sent north with the fleet of Admiral de Grasse to finance the French and American forces at Yorktown.[121]

Spain's strong financial position rested on the output of Mexico's silver mines, and the military advances supported by this bullion vindicated the reformist program of Charles III in a very tangible way. Spain's successes, capping nearly a century of conflict, left it as the only one of the three colonial

---

[117] "Administration of Florida Blanca" (memoirs), in William Coxe, *Memoirs of the Kings of Spain of the House of Bourbon* ... 2nd. ed., V (London: Longman, Hurst, Rees, Orme, and Brown, 1815), appendix 1, pp. 91–93. See also note 51.

[118] John A. Tilley, *The British Navy and the American Revolution* (Columbia, S.C.: University of South Carolina Press, 1987), pp. 127–268; N. A. M. Rodger, *Command of the Ocean: A Naval History of Britain, 1649–1815* (New York: W. W. Norton, 2006), pp. 343–54.

[119] Governor Diego de Navarro to Gálvez, Havana, July 14, 1780 and June 9, 1781, AGI, SD, legs. 1233, 2597. Additional information can be found in AGI, Mexico, 2049, 2051.

[120] José Antonio Armillas Vicente, "El nacimiento de una gran nación. Contribución española a la independencia de los Estados Unidos de América del Norte," *Cuadernos de investigación del Colegio Universitario de Logroño* (Logroño: Colegio Universitario, 1977), pp. 91–98.

[121] James A. Lewis, "Las Damas de La Habana, el Precursor, and Francisco de Saavedra: A note on Spanish Participation in the Battle of Yorktown," *The Americas* 37 (July 1980), pp. 83–86, 90–98. Records of these transactions are located in AGI, SD, leg. 1974.

powers retaining a position on the North American continent below Canada. For Charles III, this reality was nothing short of sweet revenge.

CONCLUSION

Although the Bourbon reforms in the Spanish Atlantic world reached new heights during the period from 1759 to 1783, this innovating impulse emerged from a long and complicated political process in which foreign and domestic interest groups with very different political agendas contested for power. Spain's rivals for empire in the Atlantic, particularly France and Great Britain, influenced the course of reform by attempting to gain commercial inroads into the rich Spanish possessions in the Indies through the contraband trade, but also by waging wars that drew the attention of policy makers in Madrid from their objectives. After defeats in the Seven Years' War, King Charles and his ministers renewed their vigorous efforts to strengthen imperial defenses and promote reforms capable of financing them. Conservative interest groups in Spain with very different visions about the future of the empire, however, concurrently worked to undermine the process of Enlightened reform. Moreover, the Spanish Enlightenment itself represented a fusion of ideas from Europe, along with a variety of political currents from the Indies, which often led to conflicts even in reformist circles about the best way to renovate the Spanish empire. As historian Gabriel Paquette has noted, "the idiosyncratic and uneven nature of policy resulted from the diversity, not the paucity of competing ideas which the Spanish crown sought to implement, often simultaneously in various colonies."[122] Finally, a diversity of political ideas about reform existed in the Spanish Indies themselves, leading some interest groups to embrace reforms, such as commercial deregulation, while other innovations led to political opposition from a wide range of social groups, threatening Madrid's plans for modernization.

Crown officials in New Spain had the talented and ruthless José de Gálvez on the scene in the 1760s, and his punitive expedition put down the popular uprisings with brutal efficiency. However, the outbreak of violent rebellions in the Andes and New Granada, which were much more serious affairs, shook the foundations of Spanish power in both regions. Neither defeat in war nor popular upheaval in the Indies derailed reform for long, but these political conflicts did shape the direction of policy in each region of the empire. The intendant system, for example, was never imposed throughout the Viceroyalty of New Granada in the wake of the Comunero Rebellion. It is hardly surprising that the Bourbon reforms appear a diverse and sometimes contradictory hodgepodge of policies that varied markedly in different regions of the empire. The

---

[122] Gabriel Paquette, *Enlightenment, Governance, and Reform in Spain and its Empire, 1759–1808* (Surry: Ashgate Press 2008), p. 153.

reforms materialized in highly contested political arenas in Spain and the Indies, where interest groups representing very different ideas and political visions about the future of the Spanish Atlantic world clashed. Politics is an inherently messy process, and the Bourbon reforms reflect the disorder, muddle, and even chaos that conflicted political arenas invariably produce.

9

Adjustments and Refinements in the Reformist Agenda, 1783–1796

The period following Spain's victory in the War of the American Revolution allowed Madrid to consolidate and to refine gains made in its reformist agenda by advancing additional administrative, fiscal, military, and commercial innovations. Underlying tensions arose from problems with finance, however, particularly owing to mushrooming military expenditures for both land forces and the armada. Although humbled and stripped of its North American colonies, Great Britain still possessed a superior navy, which posed a continuing military threat in the Atlantic world, but new thinking was in order. In confronting the challenges that faced it, Spain enjoyed capable leadership from the Conde de Floridablanca and his ally in the royal cabinet, Pedro López de Lerena. Skillfully working its way through the incredibly complex issues that it faced, the Madrid government would push reform of the imperial system to its pinnacle. Bolstered by a highly productive empire, Spain once again would stand among the great powers of the western world. While the crown used the American revenues to advance Spain's military standing, however, little was invested to develop the economic infrastructure of the metropolis or the Indies. As a result, Madrid's successes in reorganizing its empire over the eighteenth century would ultimately fall victim to international conflict, first to the wars of the French Revolution and ultimately to two disastrous conflicts with the British beginning in 1796, which would put a definitive end to the reforming impulse in the Spanish Atlantic world.

Despite these coming military challenges, the future appeared secure as the Treaty of Paris ended the successful War of the American Revolution and confirmed the expulsion of the British from all of the North American continent south of Canada. The treaty also provided for the transfer to Spain of both East and West Florida, which reestablished its territorial monopoly on the Gulf of Mexico. Madrid returned Providence in the Bahamas to London; but in Europe, it at long last retrieved Minorca. Nonetheless, nagging grievances remained. The enterprise to retake Jamaica had failed, leaving the

British with an imposing presence in the heart of the Caribbean, which they could use to penetrate Spanish American marketplaces and threaten Spain's empire militarily. Moreover, while Spain allowed some British logging in Central America between the Belize and Río Honda Rivers, it failed to win its claims for fishing rights off Newfoundland.[1] Gibraltar also continued to be a major aggravation on the Iberian mainland. As a result, ongoing challenges persisted for Spain, despite impressive military successes.

Although Spain's victories in the recent war vindicated the reforms of Charles III, powerful foreign and domestic enemies to innovation remained. The British controlled the sea lanes in the Atlantic, and they remained aggrieved over Spanish and French assistance to the successful rebellion of their thirteen North American colonies. A wide variety of political groups in the Indies still opposed higher taxes, restrictions on commerce, and the political disorders accompanying administrative and clerical innovations. Moreover, the high-handed polices of the *visitadores* dispatched by Gálvez had left seething animosities in the wake of the rebellions in New Granada and the Andes. In Spain, conservative political groups in Madrid, some members of the clergy, and popular groups also remained angry and opposed to many crown innovations. In addition, the heavy debts incurred during the War of the American Revolution promoted divisions even among reformers about the pace and direction of the changes needed to place the crown on a stable course financially, while still maintaining the army and navy needed to keep Spain's enemies at bay. It is no small wonder that when the French Revolution disrupted the peace of Europe – with ramifications throughout the Atlantic world – the exigencies of war would overwhelm the reforming impulse by 1796, as Spain was swept up in yet another dangerous conflict with Great Britain.

THE FINANCIAL PRICE OF WAR

Both Spain and its French ally had accumulated alarming deficits on their way to victory against Britain. The debt that Versailles faced would bring down French absolutism within four years after the peace, as its exhausted treasury could no longer find the means to meet the monarchy's obligations. That crisis would lead to revolution, the abolition of the monarchy, and the shocking execution of King Louis XVI. Despite its fiscal difficulties, however, Versailles repaid Madrid for at least some of the financial obligations incurred during the war.[2] The Spanish crown faced nothing as desperate as France, largely

---

[1] A copy of the peace treaty is located in Alejandro de Cantillo, comp., *Tratados, convenios y declaraciones de Paz y de comercio ... desde el año 1700 ...* (Madrid: Imprenta de Alegría y Charlain, 1843), pp. 586–90.

[2] Aranda, for example, recovered over 1 million pesos. "*Informe general,*" August 14, 1789, AGI, SD, leg. 1974. This same *legajo* contains the records for other, smaller payments.

because of its productive empire, but fundamental adjustments to control and manage its debt bore far-reaching implications for colonial governance and for the armed forces.[3]

Madrid had long financed its deficits for the American theater principally through loans or forced donations from the *Consulado de Cargadores a Indias*. Although the crown usually put up taxes administered by the guild as collateral against its loans and eventually paid something, there was little expectation that full repayment would ever materialize. Instead, the crown traditionally granted the merchant guild special trade concessions, which had permitted the monopoly to thrive over the centuries. Charles III aimed to break this dependency and to free his hand politically. During the hostilities between 1762 and 1763, the king had avoided compromising commitments to the *Consulado* by drawing on the war chest of more than 270,000,000 copper *reales* inherited from his half-brother.[4] The reformist monarch thus enjoyed considerable latitude as he addressed the deregulation of colonial commerce, a process that reached its climax through the promulgation of the famous Regulation of Free Trade of 1778. As events developed after 1779, it

[3] For studies on military spending, see John Jay TePaske, "La política española en el Caribe durante los siglos XVII y XVIII," in *La influencia de España en el Caribe, la Florida, y la Luisiana, 1500–1800*, eds. Juan Marchena Fernández y Antonio Acosta (Madrid: Instituto de Cooperación Iberoamericana, 1983), pp. 61–87; Juan Marchena Fernández, "La financiación militar en Indias: Introducción a su estudio," *Anuario de estudios americanos*, XXXVI (1979), pp. 81–110; Allan J. Kuethe and G. Douglas Inglis, "Absolutism and Enlightened Reform: Charles III, the Establishment of the *Alcabala*, and Commercial Reorganization in Cuba," *Past & Present: A Journal of Historical Studies*, núm. 109 (November 1985), pp. 141–42; Kuethe, "Guns, Subsidies, and Commercial Privilege: Some Historical Factors in the Emergence of the Cuban National Character, 1763–1815," *Cuban Studies*, XVI (1986), pp. 128–38; Alvaro Jara, "El financiamiento de Cartagena de Indias: Los excedentes de las cajas de Bogotá y de Quito, 1761–1802," *Historia* (Santiago de Chile), XXVIII (1994); Carlos Marichal, *De Colonia a Nación: impuestos y política en México, 1750–1860* (México: Colegio de México, 2001); José Manuel Serrano Álvarez, *Fortificaciones y tropas. El gasto militar en Tierra Firme, 1700–1788* (Sevilla: Diputación de Sevilla, Universidad de Sevilla: Consejo Superior de Investigaciones Científicas, Escuela de Estudios Hispano-Americanos, 2004); Serrano, "Situados y rentas en Cartagena de Indias durante el siglo XVIII." *Temas americanistas*, núm. 17 (2004); Matilde Souto, *Mar abierto: la política y el comercio del consulado de Veracruz o el ocaso del sistema imperial* (México: Colegio de México, 2001); Johanna von Grafenstein, *Nueva España en el Circuncaribe, 1779–1808: Revolución, competencia colonial y vínculos intercoloniales* (México: Universidad Nacional Autónoma, 1997); Herbert S. Klein, "Un comentario sobre sistemas y estructuras fiscales del imperio español," in Ernest Sánchez Santiró, Luis Jáuregui, Antonio Ibarra, coordinadores, *Finanzas y política en el mundo iberoamericano: Del antiguo régimen a las naciones independientes, 1754–1850* (México: Facultad de Economía-UNAM, Instituto Mora,Universidad Autónoma del Estado de Morelos, 2001).

[4] Jacques A. Barbier, "Towards a New Chronology for Bourbon Colonialism: The 'Depositaría de Indias' of Cádiz; 1722–1789" *Iber-Amerikanisches Archiv*, 6 (1980), pp. 344–45; Jacques A. Barbier and Herbert S. Klein "Las prioridades de un monarca ilustrado: el gasto publico bajo el reinado de Carlos III," *Revista de Historia Económica*. 3 (Fall 1985), p. 476.

took a new institution – the Banco Nacional de San Carlos – to manage the deficit.

The establishment of the bank was the work of Secretary of the Office for Finance Miguel de Múzquiz. The idea for such an institution came from Francisco Cabarrús, a financial guru of Madrid, who first proposed the idea in late 1781. Múzquiz at first hesitated to undertake such an innovative, daring step. Nonetheless, encouraged by the king and Floridablanca, he finally acquiesced and established the Banco de San Carlos in June 1782. The bank would finance debt by issuing *vales reales* (royal promissory notes), which were money-like, interest-bearing annuities. After the war ended, the treasury raised taxes and gradually retired the public debt owed to purchasers of the *vales*.

The bank faced strong opposition led by the *Cinco Gremios Mayores* of Madrid, which feared that any modernization of the financial system would threaten its privileged relationship to the monarchy.[5] This resistance offers yet another example of the obstacles that impeded enlightened innovation. Once again, however, the reformers used military exigencies to justify their policies.

In declining health, Múzquiz summoned maximum energy as he launched the new bank project. At a time when the complexities of royal administration had increased the workload of the Office of Finance, Múzquiz still held War, which he had accepted after the death of Ricla in 1780. While Finance and War held an intimate relationship within the apparatus of the modern state, Múzquiz was not a soldier, and he received advice on technical matters from Floridablanca and even from Aranda, who remained in Paris.[6] The workload was nevertheless crushing and may well have contributed to the death of Múzquiz in 1785.

Reality dictated that an increase in American specie would be needed to underpin the *vales* issued by the bank. As the preamble to the enabling *cédula* explained,

The issuance of *vales* and half *vales* by the Treasury, which the urgencies of the present war have necessitated in order to avoid oppressive levies upon my faithful vassals, concurrently requires the establishment of a ready and effective means to convert those *vales* into gold or silver money when their owners require it.[7]

Under these circumstances, and given the relatively inelastic nature of peninsular revenues, the remission of American silver assumed new importance.[8] This also

---

[5] José Antonio Escudero, *Los orígenes del Consejo de Ministros en España* (Madrid: Editora Nacional, 1979), I, pp. 386–89. "An agency of the commercial patriciate of Madrid, the *Cinco Gremios* dominated wholesale and retail trade in manufactures in the capital and were involved in the same joint-stock companies," David R. Ringrose, *Madrid and the Spanish Economy, 1650–1850* (Berkeley: University of California Press, 1983), p. 321.

[6] Escudero, *Los orígenes*, I, p. 387.

[7] Royal *cédula*, Aranjuez, June 2, 1782, AGI, IG, leg. 1849.

[8] For an overview of the relative inelasticity of Spanish finances during this period, see Renate Pieper, "Contiendas imperiales y política fiscal: España y Gran Bretaña en el siglo

FIGURE 9.1   Spanish American Gold and Silver Production

suggested the need for closer institutional coordination between Spain and America, but such cooperation would take time to develop, especially in view of the confrontational policies pursued by José de Gálvez.

One of the most important sources of revenue in the Spanish Atlantic world was the rising levels of gold and silver production in the mines of the Indies. According to Richard Garner, in the first half of the colonial period (circa 1560–1685), Spanish American mines provided approximately 25,000 tons of silver alone to the Atlantic world and to Asia, while during the second half of the period (1686–1810), that amount more than doubled.[9] As Figure 9.1 indicates, remittances of gold and silver rose steadily from 1700 to the 1750s, when silver shipments began to dip slightly. From the 1760s on, however, transmittals of both gold and silver rose steadily to reach a high of nearly 345 million pesos. Although they fell to slightly more than 336 million pesos in the decade from 1790 to 1800, these levels still remained impressively high. The quantity of silver bullion dwarfed the amount of gold sent from the Indies, but the remission of both precious metals allowed the crown to maintain its fiscal solvency during the reign of Charles III, despite the outbreak of expensive wars that threatened to drain the Royal Treasury. Indies

XVIII," in Ernest Sánchez Santiró, Luis Jáuregui, Antonio Ibarra, coordinadores, *Finanzas y política en el mundo iberoamericano: Del antiguo régimen a las naciones independientes, 1754–1850* (México: Facultad de Economía-UNAM, Instituto Mora, Universidad Autónoma del Estado de Morelos, 2001), pp. 63–76.

[9] Richard Garner, "Long-Term Silver Mining Trends in Spanish America: A Comparative Analysis of Peru and Mexico," *American Historical Review*, 93 (October 1988), p. 899.

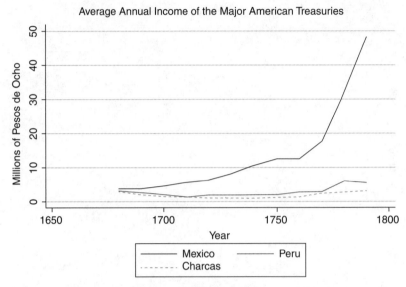

FIGURE 9.2 Average Annual Income of the Major American Treasuries

revenues, particularly the steady transfer to Iberia of precious metals, made the difference between fiscal solvency and the bankruptcy that afflicted Spain's French allies. They also proved the difference between defeat and victory in the War of the American Revolution.

While all the realms of the Indies contributed precious metals and other tax revenues to sustain the Spanish treasury, Mexico dramatically outstripped all other regions of the empire in producing revenue for the crown. The mines of New Spain enjoyed higher grades of silver ore and lower operating costs, making it the New World's premier mining center in the eighteenth century and leading to an impressive century-long upsurge in tax revenues in the northern viceroyalty.[10] Miners in New Spain paid a tax of only one-tenth of production (*diezmo*), while South American miners paid twice that amount (*quinto*), and the price of mercury was higher in South America. As Figure 9.2 (showing the average annual income of the treasuries of Mexico, Peru, and Charcas) indicates, all three regions produced similar amounts of revenue in the late seventeenth century; but after 1700, income levels in the Mexican treasuries increased dramatically and quickly surpassed all other regions of the American empire. From the 1760s on, income flowing into the Mexican treasuries shot upward abruptly, dwarfing the amounts produced in Peru and Charcas, while New Granada never contributed large amounts of public

[10] Garner argues that New Spain's silver production grew at an annual rate of 1.2–1.4% from 1725 to 1809.

revenues.[11] The reforms initiated by the Gálvez *visita* and later administrative and fiscal innovations had clearly engineered a bonanza in tax revenues flowing into the treasuries of New Spain. Moreover, Mexican income supplied subsidies to the defense of the Caribbean and contributed a great deal to the dramatic victories of Spain in Florida and the circum-Caribbean. In the period from 1763 to 1767, New Spain also sent nearly 43 million *reales de vellón* to Spain, accounting for 12.5 percent of the monies sent from the Indies to the metropolis. That amount rose to more than 186 million copper *reales* in the period from 1773 to 1777, and it shot up to more than 472 million *reales* in the years between 1793 and 1796, accounting for 81.4 percent of all Indies revenues shipped to Spain.[12] New Spain had clearly become a sub-metropolis, financing the defense of strategic sea lanes in the Caribbean and sustaining the Royal Treasury in Madrid.

JOSÉ DE GÁLVEZ AND REFORM IN AMERICA

Flush with the triumph over the British in America, highlighted by the victories of his nephew Bernardo, José de Gálvez forged ahead with his controversial agenda despite the costs and risks entailed. Gálvez enjoyed the friendship and patronage of the king's confidant, Múzquiz, who apparently protected him in the royal cabinet.[13] Gálvez was successful initially in covering up the blunders of his *visitadores* in South America and blaming others, particularly Viceroy Manuel Guirior in Peru. A frank assessment from the inspector general of the Peruvian militia, Juan Manuel Fernández Palazuelos, addressed to Aranda in May 1781, pinpointed the obstacles to the truth:

Dn. José de Gálvez was crazy in Mexico and his keeper was Dn. José Antonio de Areche . . . . With the governorship of the Council and the Secretariat of the Universal Office in Gálvez's hands, there is no means through which His Majesty can discover the truth about these events . . . . The distances and the many hands through which the correspondence must pass does not, sir, permit a greater illumination of this business.[14]

Despite his foibles and the controversy surrounding his appointees, the reputation of Gálvez remained temporarily protected.

[11] Herbert S. Klein, *The American Finances of the Spanish Empire: Royal Income and Expenditures in Colonial Mexico, Peru, and Bolivia, 1680–1809* (Albuquerque: University of New Mexico Press, 1998), pp. 35–47, 58–66, 78–95.
[12] Carlos Marichal, "Beneficios y costas fiscales de colonialismo: Las remesas Americanas a España, 1760–1814," *Revista de Historia Económica*, XV:3 (Fall-Winter 1997), pp. 482–84.
[13] Anthony H. Hull, *Charles III and the Bourbon Revival in Spain* (Washington, D.C.: University Press of America, 1981), pp. 193, 304; Escudero, *Los orígenes* I, pp. 351–55, 386, 394.
[14] Quoted in Escudero, *Los orígenes* I, pp. 388.

The fates of Governor Juan Manuel de Cagigal (of Havana) and Lieutenant Colonel Francisco Miranda offer an intriguing illustration of Gálvez's ability to manage information. Both Cagigal and Miranda were excellent officers, whose achievements at Pensacola and then in conquering Providence threatened to detract from Gálvez's family's glory, which both Bernardo and José jealously protected. Charging both men with leaking strategic information to the enemy and smuggling, the Minister of the Indies railroaded them out of the royal service. Although Miranda escaped confinement, Cagigal suffered lengthy imprisonment. After José's death, Cagigal's distinguished family secured his release from prison and his complete exoneration. By then, Miranda was on his way to winning glory in the Venezuelan movement for independence.[15] Given Gálvez's control over both the Secretariat and the Council of the Indies, it is doubtful that Charles III was ever aware of the injustices perpetrated in his name.

Gálvez showed little inclination to adjust his spendthrift agenda to the new political realities that emerged in America after 1783. The millions of silver pesos diverted to support armies deployed to suppress angry taxpayers in the uplands of Peru and New Granada could have been remitted to Spain, where specie was in short supply and needed to uphold the *vales reales*.[16] Colonies were supposed to be profitable, and while past radical measures were justified by the necessities of war, those conditions had passed. Yet Gálvez did not retreat from unnecessary confrontations with the colonial establishment, nor did he reduce military expenses and consolidate gains from less controversial fiscal and commercial innovations. Such moderation would come eventually, despite Gálvez, but in the meantime the Minister of the Indies pressed stubbornly ahead with his hardfisted agenda.

An especially nagging problem in financing the colonial defense system was perpetual complaints about the inadequacy of monies transferred from wealthy inland areas to militarily strategic but poorer peripheries. Mexico, for example, continued to send millions of pesos to Havana annually for redistribution throughout the Gulf of Mexico, the Caribbean islands, and Florida; Peru financed Panama; Upper Peru funded Buenos Aires, and Quito and Santa Fe supported Cartagena. Yet these transfers, or *situados*, never seemed enough for the revenue-hungry coastal strongholds, and they almost always arrived late.[17] This compelled hard-pressed coastal bureaucrats to borrow at usurious rates from local merchants, and to purchase their goods at inflated prices. These obligations were not only repaid in specie from the *situados*, but also by permitting young creoles entrance into the army officer

---

[15] See Manuel Hernández González, *Francisco de Miranda y su ruptura con España* (Caracas: Academia Nacional de Historia, 2006).

[16] Juan Marchena Fernández, "Financiación militar y situados," in *Temas de historia militar* (Madrid: Servicio de Publicaciones del EME, 1988), I, especially pp. 288–89.

[17] Ibid.; Serrano Álvarez, *Fortificaciones y tropas*, passim.

corps in increasing numbers.[18] By the mid-1780s, American officers threatened to outnumber Europeans in the regular army, signaling yet another grave erosion of Spanish authority. By the end of the century, the ratio would overwhelmingly favor Americans, and the debt to colonial merchants continued to grow despite huge amounts of revenue generated in the colonies. Creoles not only financed the American army; they commanded it.[19] In addition, military privilege converted both the regular army and the militia into autonomous, self-policing institutions.[20]

To tighten his grip on the colonies, Gálvez aggressively advanced the completion of administrative reorganizations that he had begun before the war. As local circumstances and preparations permitted, he extended the intendant system of provincial administration to the Viceroy of Peru in 1784 and to Mexico, Guatemala, and Chile in 1786.[21] Moreover, he placed these officials under the supervision of superintendants, officers who stood autonomously from the viceroys and the normal give-and-take in colonial politics.[22] The Madrid government also created a new audiencia in Caracas in 1786 after extinguishing the Caracas Company, and a new tribunal in Cusco (1787) in the wake of the Tupac Amaru revolt. The government continued its policy of excluding creoles, even the sons of distinguished colonial families, from appointment in the intendancies and the new audiencias. José de Baquíjano y Carrillo (a prominent creole intellectual, a member of the Order of Charles III, and the third Conde de Vistaflorida) of Lima, for example, spent most of his adult life in pursuit of an audiencia judgeship, attaining it only in 1806.[23] The reformed administrative apparatus was sure to increase revenues, but over time local expenditures would consume most of them.

---

[18] For a case study of this phenomenon, see Juan Marchena Fernández, *La institución militar en Cartagena de Indias en el siglo XVIII* (Sevilla: Escuela de Estudios Hispano-Americanos, 1982), chap. 5.

[19] Juan Marchena Fernández, *Oficiales y soldados en el ejército de America* (Sevilla: Escuela de Estudios Hispano-Americanos, 1983) chap. 3; Allan J. Kuethe, *Cuba, 1753–1815: Crown, Military, and Society* (Knoxville: University of Tennessee Press, 1986), pp. 118–22, 148–54.

[20] L.N. McAlister, *The "Fuero Militar" in New Spain, 1764–1800* (Gainesville: University Presses of Florida, 1957); Allan J. Kuethe, *Military Reform and Society in New Granada, 1773–1808* (Gainesville: University Presses of Floria, 1978), pp. 5–6, 27–28, 108–17, 158.

[21] Luis Navarro García, *Intendencias de Indias* (Sevilla: Escuela de Estudios Hispano-Americanos, 1959):, pp. 44–51; J. R. Fisher, *Government and Society in Colonial Peru: The Intendant System, 1784–1814* (London: Athlone Press, 1970).

[22] D. A. Brading, *Miners & Merchants in Bourbon Mexico, 1763–1810* (Cambridge: Cambridge University Press, 1971), p. 45. Horst Pietschmann, *Las reformas borbónicas y el sistema de intendencias en Nueva España: Un estudio político administrativo* (Mexico: Fondo de Cultura Económica, 1996) (German edition 1972), pp.150–52, has argued that the establishment of intendancies did not necessarily imply a weakening of the viceregal office as viceroys had never had full autonomy over the Royal Treasury.

[23] Mark A. Burkholder, *Politics of a Colonial Career: José Baquíjano and the Audiencia of Lima* (Albuquerque: University of New Mexico Press, 1980).

Even following the Comunero Rebellion, Gálvez remained determined to press his reformist agenda to its limits in New Granada. Archbishop-Viceroy Antonio Caballero y Góngora had negotiated a truce with the Comuneros, only to renege once he had positioned a battalion of troops in Santa Fe. In 1783 he expanded this force, which was converted into a fixed, auxiliary regiment of 1,300 men. Moreover, he established a disciplined militia in the uplands, and he placed these new units under the command of reliable, Spanish-born officers. The archbishop-viceroy also fortified the capital to protect royal authority from its own subjects. He established a gunpowder factory and expanded the viceregal staff to man the burgeoning administration. When José García de León y Pizarro completed his successful mission in Quito to assume a position on the Council of the Indies, moreover, he bore instructions from Gálvez to consult with the archbishop-viceroy to draft plans for an intendant system. This meeting occurred in 1785 and the plan was on Gálvez's desk when he died in 1787.[24]

With bayonets assembled to enforce the royal will, Caballero y Góngora collected crown revenues vigorously, including an expansion of the tobacco and aguardiente monopolies.[25] As a result of these reforms, royal income in New Granada peaked at the end of his administration in 1789, registering a total of 3,354,000 pesos.[26] As the reforms in New Granada demonstrate, under the orders of Gálvez, the archbishop-viceroy had not practiced moderation after quelling the Comunero Revolt, but instead had bulled ruthlessly forward. On the other hand, while revenues rose under his tenure, so too did the cost of collecting them, leaving a yawning deficit of 2 million pesos in the income-starved jurisdiction by the end of the 1780s.[27]

---

[24] García-Pizarro to Gálvez, Cartagena, December 20, 1785, AGI, Quito, leg. 264; Antonio Caballero y Góngora, "Relación del estado del Nuevo Reino de Granada ... 1789," in José Manuel Pérez Ayala, *Antonio Caballero y Góngora, virrey arzobispo de Santa Fe, 1723–1796* (Bogotá: Imprenta Municipal, 1951), p. 371. A copy of the intendancy plan can be found in the Archivo Histórico Nacional de Colombia, Virreyes, vol. 17, fols. 1249–72.

[25] Allan J. Kuethe, *Military Reform and Society*, chap. 5. In his highly influential, *The People and the King: The Comunero Revolution in Colombia*, John Leddy Phelan maintained that the intensity of the elite and popular resistance in the viceregal interior led a chastened Gálvez to retreat meaningfully from his aggressive agenda in New Granada and to back Caballero y Góngora as he worked through the customary means of consultation and compromise to hammer out a satisfactory outcome that both reestablished the peace and fostered harmony over the long haul. Phelan's reading of the outcome of the Comunero Rebellion essentially awarded victory to the insurgents, albeit with moderate advances for royal authority, making the viceroyalty unique among the American colonies in successfully blunting the Gálvez agenda. This interpretation missed the mark on two key points. Phelan was unaware that Gálvez planned to impose the intendant system and that revenues peaked in 1789 as the result of severe collection practices under Caballero y Góngora.

[26] Caballero y Góngora, "Relación," p. 374.

[27] Allan J. Kuethe, "More on the 'Culmination of the Bourbon Reforms:' A Perspective from New Granada," *HAHR*, 58 (1978), pp. 477–80.

To aggravate matters, Gálvez ordered the archbishop-viceroy to subdue the Cuna Indians of Darién while the army was concurrently engaged in a holding action against the inhabitants of Ríohacha's Guajiro Peninsula. Both frontiers were inhabited by unpacified indigenous peoples who traded freely with the British. In Ríohacha, the Guajiros allowed contraband to come freely into and out of the viceroyalty, while Spain's inability to control Darién threatened the security of the strategic Isthmus of Panama. At its peak between 1785 and 1789, the Darién expedition featured four fortified settlements backed by some 1,000 soldiers drawn from the viceroyalty's veteran garrisons and from the disciplined militia. As he left the viceroyalty, Caballero y Góngora claimed victory, for he had induced Chief Bernardo to come to the seaside village of Turbaco, near Cartagena, and sign a solemn treaty of peace in 1787. In the end, the Cunas simply pulled back, waiting for the Spanish to leave. As for the Guajiros, they had repelled a similar attempt to take control of their lands during 1775 and 1776, driving the viceroyalty's armed forces to the peripheries of their peninsula.[28]

Gálvez's costly and confrontational reform program proved unsustainable, particularly as information about events in South America gradually reached Madrid. A major jolt to the minister's reputation occurred with the return of Manuel Guirior in 1784. Guirior, who had powerful friends at court, blamed the bungling of Visitador José Antonio de Areche in advancing the policies of his mentor, Gálvez, for the outbreak of rebellion. The former viceroy, like many other prominent naval officers of the time, was a *bailío*, having received his training and formation as a knight in the Order of San Juan de Jerusalem in Malta, whose prominent voice in Madrid could not be suppressed.[29] The French, who had been cool toward Gálvez for some time, put off by his intractable, indeed "violent," character, watched the transformation of his status with great interest.[30] In January 1785, Ambassador Bourgoing reported to Foreign Minister Vergennes:

The information coming out of that Royal Office [Secretariat of the Indies] completely vindicates Mr. Guirior and so gravely implicates Mr. Areche that the Prosecutor General of the Council of the Indies is coming to discover that it is he himself [Areche] who deserves the characterization as traitor to the nation, which he had pinned on the viceroy, and that accordingly capital punishment would be justified. One can imagine Mr. Gálvez's perplexity in the face of the crisis in which one of his

---

[28] Kuethe, *Military Reform and Society*, chap. 6.

[29] This little known dimension of the power structure in Madrid has been identified by María Baudot Monroy and Marta García Garralón, "El éxito del modelo de gestión de la Marina maltesa y su relación con la Real Armada española del siglo XVIII," in Agustín González Enciso, ed., *Un estado militar: España, 1650–1820* (Madrid: Actas, San Sebastián de los Reyes, 2012), pp. 210–52. See also María Baudot Monroy, *"Julián de Arriaga y Rivera. Un Vida al Servicio de la Marina (1700–1776)"* (Ph.D. diss., Universidad Nacional de Educación a Distancia, 2010), pp. 24–26.

[30] Bourgoing to Vergennes, Madrid, April 20, 1785, AAE:CPE, vol. 616, fols. 415–17.

creatures finds himself [but] whose misdeeds were simply following the orders of that minister.[31]

Moreover, the minister's position was weakened when his nephew, Bernardo, died in Mexico, shortly after he had elevated him to viceroy. This personal tragedy removed a visible reminder of the Gálvez family's glory. The news arrived at court almost simultaneously with the embarrassing revelations concerning Peru.[32] Finally, when Miguel de Múzquiz died in January 1785, the secretary of the Indies lost his principal supporter within the royal cabinet.

COMPETING VIEWS OF REFORM IN SPAIN

The death of Múzquiz, following a lengthy, visible deterioration of his health, opened the way for a profound reorientation of royal policy with far-reaching implications for the American empire. Charles had elevated Múzquiz to Conde de Gausa in 1783, and he awarded him the cross of the Order of Charles III.[33] Much like Arriaga, Múzquiz had commanded a personal respect rarely enjoyed at court, and the king was clearly moved by his passing.[34] Floridablanca secured the succession of a disciple, Pedro López de Lerena, to the Secretariat of Finance and to an interim appointment to Secretariat of War.[35] An accountant and a long-time associate of Floridablanca, Lerena had risen to become intendant of Andalusia, but his appointment astonished the court because of his humble origins, even given the relatively relaxed standards in the new, enlightened climate.[36] It is worth remembering that despite their titles, few ministers of Charles III were true aristocrats. As the English traveler Joseph Townsend observed during his visit in 1786–1787:

It must be striking to an Englishman to see all the most important offices occupied by men who have been taken from the lower ranks, and not to find among them one man of fashion, not one grandee of Spain. These are all precisely where they ought to be: lords of the bed-chamber, grooms of the stole, masters of the horse, all near the throne, partaking of its splendor, whilst the drudgery and responsibility of office is left to others who are better qualified to bear that burden. In England it is far otherwise: our

---

[31] Bourgoing to Vergennes, Madrid, January 17, 1785, AAE:CPE, vol. 616, fols. 47–51.

[32] Ibid.

[33] Escudero, *Los orígenes* I, p. 394.

[34] Hull: *Charles III*, p. 304.

[35] Ibid., pp. 351, 395–96.

[36] Francisco Montes, as royal treasurer, was the hope of conservative forces for Hacienda, but he was outside the reformist loop. As former prior of the Consulado he, not surprisingly, had been cool toward the Banco de San Carlos and currently stood in opposition to the establishment of the Philippines Company. When asked by the French ambassador if he considered the Conde de Aranda for War, Floridablanca retorted that he had no intention of bringing him back. Bourgoing to Vergennes, Madrid, January 31 and February 7, 1785, AAE:CPE, vol. 616, fols. 90–92, 112–117.

men of fashion, from their infancy, are trained to high pursuits ... [and] many of the greatest men, and the most able ministers, are to be found among our principal nobility.[37]

In the words of John Lynch, "this minor aristocracy was becoming an aristocracy of merit, and it held a new concept of office as a professional career."[38]

In Lerena, Floridablanca had a man personally indebted to him handling two critical areas of royal administration. This would pay dividends as the great minister aggressively sought to reorient royal policy in accord with the new political realities that confronted Spain after 1783. Through Lerena, new policies took shape that would culminate eventually in the formation of the Junta Suprema de Estado in 1787. This new orientation, affecting both Spain and the empire, appeared forcefully with the Royal Decree of June 29, 1785, which emphasized the imperative of cutting spiraling administrative costs:

The unavoidable, enormous expenditures that the urgencies of the last war occasioned for me, and my special care not to burden my beloved vassals with new taxes, have overburdened the Crown to the point that, not sufficing its income to satisfy its obligations and the charges and interest upon them, it has been necessary to find the means not only to pay these, but also to establish a fund applicable to the liquidation of the principle. To realize these objectives, I have preferred to eliminate or to reduce expenditures of all kinds and from all areas, avoiding new taxes for now, and organizing a more upright, more workable, and more equitable administration of the Crown's revenues than what has heretofore existed.[39]

Lerena sent a royal order to Gálvez with an *Instrucción Provisional* dated September 21, detailing the means to implement the royal decree. This invasion of what had been the secretary's of the Indies terrain anticipated the eventual unification of finance for Spain and for the Indies under a single hand.

Lerena also advanced a series of measures tightening the coordination of Spain and the Indies during 1785. In September, he requested the financial accounts for each five-year period since 1766, and he sent to Gálvez, "for your information," the regulation that he had just promulgated for managing royal income in the four kingdoms of Andalusia.[40] Moreover, in his capacity as secretary of the Office for War, Lerena had requisitioned copies of the regulations for the American garrisons, a step he later repeated from his other ministry. An annoyed Gálvez, who clearly resented these intrusions into his domain, responded sharply:

---

[37] Quoted in Escudero, *Los orígenes* I, p. 493.
[38] Lynch, *Bourbon Spain*, p. 293.
[39] Lerena to Gálvez, San Ildefonso, October 4, 1785, with the royal decree of June 29 and the *instrucción provisional* of September 21, AGI, IG, leg. 1337.
[40] Royal order (circular), September 18, 1785, and Lerena to Gálvez, Palace, December 28, 1785, AGI, IG, leg. 1337.

Your Excellency requests samples of the very same regulations that I have already sent, and as I know that one of the communications will come to me via the Secretariat for Finance and the other through that for War, Your Excellency should determine in which of them they can be found and order the copies that you want.[41]

Charles soothed the wounded pride of his prickly but faithful minister by elevating him to Marqués de Sonora in August.[42]

Lerena's initiatives represented a concerted attempt by the king's ministers to solve the dilemma of how to keep military costs in proper proportion to royal income. Although costs associated with the armada continued to soar, garrisons permanently stationed in America offered a handy, necessary target for a new attempt at cost management.[43] In 1786, the crown took the revolutionary step of discontinuing the use of rotating regiments to help garrison the colonies, substituting for them an expansion of the fixed units.[44] By diminishing the role of Spanish troops, this decision abrogated the safeguards that the reformers of 1719 and 1763 had prescribed to ensure Spanish (over creole) control in the American *plazas fuertes*, but it responded to the new realities that imperial finances imposed. Madrid did in fact realize that its innovation entailed risks, but it hoped to minimize them through prudent recruitment.[45]

Cuba, Mexico, New Granada, and the Río de la Plata converted their allocations of rotating battalions into permanent units in the subsequent

---

[41] Lerena to Gálvez, Palace, June 8, and San Ildefonso, October 1, 1785, and Gálvez to Lerena, San Lorenzo, October 18, 1785, AGI, IG, leg. 1337.

[42] A copy of the royal order, dated August 25, 1785, can be found in Escudero, *Los orígenes*, I, pp. 398–99.

[43] Jacques A. Barbier, "Indies Revenues and Naval Spending: The Cost of Colonialism for the Spanish Bourbons, 1763–1805," *Jahrbuch für Geschichte von Staat, Wirtschaft, und Gesellschaft Lateinamerikas*, XXI (1984), pp. 179–81.

[44] From the desk of Gálvez, a royal order of April 16 addressed to Alejandro O'Reilly, acting as subinspector general of the army of America, explained: "In order to avert as much as possible the inconveniences and the considerable costs occasioned by the transfer of army regiments from Spain to garrison the *plazas* of the Indies, the King has decided that fixed units be formed in place of them, and that accordingly this should begin with a regiment of three battalions to become the second fixed [regiment] of Havana and the island of Cuba, to which effect H.M. wants Your Excellency to propose to him through my ministry the quickest and most expeditious manner ... to raise it." AGS, GM, leg. 6880.

[45] By order of July 3, 1786, Lerena sent Gálvez an unprinted regulation of sixteen articles detailing a new method for maintaining the fixed units in America, which included a formula for periodically extracting fifty men from individual peninsular regiments and maintaining recruitment parties in the Canary Islands. To compensate for what Spain could not provide itself, a third of the soldiery might be creoles. In reality, the creole population of the officer corps already surpassed 40% and native enlisted men surely represented much more. Gálvez evidently understood the impracticality of the new measures, and he failed to execute Lerena's intrusive order. A clerk, inventorying the minister's papers following his death, found the folder that contained the order still unopened, "How it was found among the papers of the deceased Señor Marqués de Sonora following his death." AGI, IG, leg. 1339.

years.[46] In the case of Cuba, for example, a new fixed regiment replaced the two Spanish battalions that had customarily been deployed in Havana since 1763, while in New Granada, the fixed garrison of Cartagena was expanded to two battalions and the Regiment of the Princess sent home. By minimizing transportation costs, these measures surely reduced colonial expenditures momentarily, but they bore implications for the social composition of the armed forces.[47]

The death of José de Gálvez on June 17, 1787, opened the way for a final adjustment of colonial policy under Charles III.[48] The achievements under Gálvez had been monumental, especially in the areas of commerce and administration, but they also proved financially and politically costly. The challenge for his successor would be to preserve recent gains while minimizing the negatives. The prudent adjustments executed by Lerena even before Gálvez's passing now accelerated as Floridablanca addressed those objectives more directly.

This process began with a decree of July 8, 1787, when Charles, acting through Floridablanca, established the Junta Suprema de Estado. This step institutionalized inter-ministerial collaboration, which had characterized the early phase of his regime with the formation of the Junta de Ministros. The Junta Suprema, which brought together all ministers on a weekly basis, amounted to the formal establishment of a Spanish cabinet. The decree provisionally divided the administration of the Indies into two parts: War, Finance, and Commerce; and Grace and Justice.[49] Secretary of the Navy Antonio Valdés y Bazán acceded to the former, while Antonio Porlier received the latter. Fiscal of the Council of the Indies at the time of his elevation, Porlier had broad American experience, having been *procurador* for the audiencias of Buenos Aires, Lima, and Mexico. Fray Valdés, like Arriaga before him, was a *bailío* in the order of San Juan de Jerusalem and had succeeded Pedro González de Castejón at Marine in 1783. He too had served in America, even having been taken prisoner at Havana in 1762.[50] Despite his broadened portfolio, Valdés, who projected the confident, serene, but determined image of a naval commander, would

---

[46] Christon I. Archer, *The Army in Bourbon Mexico,1760–1810* (Albuquerque: University of New Mexico Press, 1977), p. 27; Laurio H. Destefani, "La defensa militar del Río de La Plata en la época hispana," *Memoria del Tercer Congreso Venezolano de Historia*, I (Caracas: Academia Nacional de Historia, 1979), p. 515; Kuethe, *Military Reform*, p. 147; *Cuba, 1753–1815*, pp. 128–29.

[47] This reduction is evident in Cuba. AGI, SD, legs. 1852–57. For New Granada, see Kuethe, *Military reform*, chap. 7.

[48] Jacques A. Barbier, "The Culmination of the Bourbon Reforms, 1787–1792," *HAHR*, 57 (February 1977), especially, pp. 52, 62–63.

[49] AHN, Estado, Libro 1. Escudero, *Los orígenes*, II (Madrid 1979), is a reproduction of the version published for the first time in 1795, which corresponds closely but not completely to the manuscript version.

[50] Agustín Guimerá Ravinda, "Estado, administración y liderazgo naval: Antonio Valdés y Charles Middleton (1778–1808)," in González Enciso, *Un estado militar*, pp. 184–86; John

consistently make the armada his first priority (see Figure 9.3). To replace Gálvez as governor of the Council of the Indies, Floridablanca named his brother, Francisco Moñino, who had first entered that institution in 1778.[51] Finally, the badly over worked Lerena had persuaded the king in May to relieve him of his interim assignment to War, which Charles filled with Jerónimo Caballero.[52]

For colonial affairs, the decree set a clear tone of moderation, which suggested a profound reorientation of colonial policy.

I desire that all I command the *Junta* be observed with great care regarding the government and the prosperity of my vassals in the Indies, who being farther away require more vigilance and attention in order to secure for them all possible advantages appropriate to the nature of the land, viewing them in the same way as my other vassals, with whom they should form one unified Monarchy, without special predilection.[53]

This represented a significant departure from the confrontational, anti-American orientation that had characterized the Gálvez years and a return to the principles of "justice, prudence, and finesse" articulated so eloquently by Admiral Andrés de Pez sixty years before. America could not be controlled at the point of a bayonet but by a sense of community and allegiance to the Spanish crown.

While the conciliatory tone taken by the junta signaled a fundamental reorientation, it did not go so far as to embrace the equality of Spain and the Indies. Political control dominated all other agendas. Regarding the army, this was evident from the July instruction to the junta, which preserved the long-standing strategy of favoring Spaniards for officers, emphasizing that the authorities

should be inclined to prefer and appoint all the Europeans to be found for leaders and senior officers of those [American] units: and it should also be required that those same Spanish troops be moved and renewed from time to time, not only with those that come from Europe to relieve them, as currently practiced, but be transferred as often as possible from one territory or *plaza* in the Indies to another in order to curtail the relationships, friendships, and other entanglements [of the sort] that undermine discipline and foster desertions more there than in Spain.[54]

Nonetheless, by the 1790s Americans would assume a majority in officer corps of the American army. This majority first emerged in the lower ranks, but as time passed Americans progressively gained strength at the top.[55]

D. Harbron, *Trafalgar and the Spanish Navy* (London: Conway Maritime Press, 1988), p. 43; Escudero, *Los orígenes*, I, pp. 390–91, 447.

[51] Mark A. Burkholder, *Biographical Dictionary of Councilors of the Indies, 1717–1808* (Westpor: Greenwood Press, 1986), pp. 81–82.

[52] Escudero, *Los orígeneres*, I, pp. 401–03.

[53] Royal decree, Palace, July 8, 1787, AHN, Estado, libro 1, reproduced in Escudero, *Los orígenes*, I, pp. 423–25.

[54] Instruction, Junta de Estado, Palace, July 8, 1787, AHN, Estado, libro 1, art. 152.

[55] Marchena Fernández, *Oficiales y soldados*, pp. 112–13, 120–21. See also, Kuethe, *Cuba: 1753–1815*, chaps. 5–6.

El Exmo. Sr. Br. Fr. D. Antonio Valdes Fernandez Bazan Gran Cruz, y Comendador del Orden de S. Juan, del Consejo de Estado, Gefe de Esquadra, y Secretario de Estado, y del Despacho Universal de Marina. Obtubo este Empleo en 2 de Marzo de 1783 habiendo seguido todas las gradas de su Carrera Militar desde 26 de Octubre de 1752 e q. sentó plaza de Guardia Marina. Mando varios buques y Divisiones de la Armada, fue Sub Inspector de Arsenales Insper. Gr.l de Marina, desempeño importantes Comis. del R. Servicio y entre ellas la de restablecer en el año de 1782 la fundicion de Artilleria de hierro de las fabricas de la Cavada. Nacio en Burgos á 25 de Marzo de 1744.

FIGURE 9.3 Fray Antonio Valdés y Bazán (1744–1816) in the Museo Naval, painted by Rafael Tegeo in 1828 from an original painted by an unknown artist. (See plate section for color version)

REFINEMENTS IN COLONIAL POLICY

Reflecting the new orientation, junta policy as it developed over the succeeding years assigned higher importance to peninsular strategic interests while aiming to moderate many aspects of the Gálvez political and military program in the colonies. Its tone reflected a determination to maximize the remission of revenues to the metropolis, to refine commercial reform, and at the same time to reassure the colonial establishment through more even-handed policies, particularly in fiscal administration. Although continuity with the Gálvez era remained strong, the practical-minded, moderate tone of Valdés, Porlier, and the Junta Suprema, acting in accord with their instructions, led to major adjustments in colonial policy. This would quickly became evident as Valdés attempted both to temper Gálvez's confrontational practices and to reassure alienated inland creoles, while concurrently seeking the means to reduce military expenditures and thus maximize remissions to Spain.[56] In short, the crown hoped to consolidate gains that Gálvez had made to reap the benefits of colonialism while cutting waste, and – insofar as royal interests permitted – reducing friction with the colonies. Seen in a larger perspective, this reorientation marked the beginning of a new period in colonial history that continued without interruption through the death of Charles III and the succession of his son.

The shift in colonial policy reflected fundamental changes in military strategy. Floridablanca's Instruction contained self-confidence and aggressiveness, showing that Spain had not yet attained its military goals. The last war, it stated, had demonstrated that Spain must turn to offensive warfare. In any future conflict, Spain would attack England itself in conjunction with the French fleet and army, invading through Plymouth and Wales. The emphasis on England did not mean that Madrid had forsaken its traditional agenda of recapturing Jamaica and Gibraltar and expelling foreign wood cutters from Central America, but now the route to victory lay through London.[57] It is impossible to know if Charles's planned invasion of Britain might have transpired, since late in 1788 the king suffered a chill while hunting that developed into a fatal fever. Moreover, by the time that proper cause for war developed with the Nootka Sound crisis of 1789–1790, France had succumbed to revolution and become hopelessly alienated from Bourbon Spain. Nonetheless, as the Junta Suprema de Estado took stock of colonial policy, it acted on the assumption that the next conflict would involve Europe primarily, adding one more reason to maximize colonial remittances to the peninsula.

During late 1787 and 1788, one clear manifestation of the new politics was the recall in August 1787 of ex-visitor general and current Superintendant Jorge Escobedo, who had replaced Areche and whose uncompromising fiscal policies had generated intense controversy in Lima. Moreover, the superintendancies of

---

[56] Jacques A. Barbier, "The Culmination of the Bourbon Reforms, 1787–1792," *HAHR*, 57 (1977), pp. 51–68. Barbier's pioneering article stimulated debate over the extent of continuity and discontinuity in colonial policy following the death of Gálvez. See John Fisher, "Critique of Jacques Barbier's 'The Culmination of Bourbon Reforms, 1787–1792'" and Jacques A. Barbier "Jacques Barbier's Reply," *HAHR*, 58 (1978), pp. 83–90, and Kuethe, "More on the 'Culmination of the Bourbon Reforms,'" pp. 477–80.

[57] "Instrucción reservada," Palace, July, 1787, AHN, Estado, book 1, fols. 182–85. The version of this document published in 1795,when Spain was allied with the British, deleted these articles and that revision has reappeared in Escudero, *Los orígenes*, II.

Peru, New Spain, and Río de la Plata were abolished, and their powers given to the viceroys.[58] Less dramatic but equally significant were numerous adjustments at the local level to defuse antagonisms that had developed between the royal administration and the colonial elites.[59] Americans also gained some limited access to the colonial audiencias, but they never attained the level of power enjoyed earlier in the century.[60] The accession of Charles IV did not perceptively alter this new orientation in colonial administration. Although the new king lacked his father's vision, freedom of mind, and personal strength, he was quite content to retain the powerful cabinet that he'd inherited and continue the more moderate colonial reform policies begun in the later years of Charles III.

The Junta Suprema's new strategy was clearly evident in the work of Fray Francisco Gil y Lemos, who served as Viceroy of New Granada for seven months in 1789 before moving on to Peru.[61] Gil y Lemos bore instructions from the junta to implement more pragmatic colonial policies in the region, and he did so quickly. His most important action was to shelve Gálvez and the archbishop's plan to establish an intendant system in New Granada. It was never revived. Encountering the enormous debts left by his spendthrift predecessor, the viceroy slashed the size of the bloated viceregal staff and reduced the veteran garrison of Santa Fe de Bogotá. He then disbanded the interior militia, ended the extensive plans to fortify Santa Fe, and stopped construction of a gun powder factory. Moreover, Gil y Lemos halted the expensive Darién pacification campaign against the Cuna Indians and cancelled dyewood concessions in Santa Marta and Riohacha that Caballero y Góngora had granted to foreign merchants in exchange for flour to feed the army in Darién – concessions that had become the source of illicit commercial penetration.[62]

A similar retreat from the draconian and extractive policies of the Gálvez years occurred farther south in the viceroyalty, in the Audiencia of Quito. Gálvez had dispatched a loyal protégé, José García de León y Pizarro, to Quito as *visitador* and president-regent in 1787, and he oversaw a dramatic expansion of the royal bureaucracy and the militia, which he used to extract unprecedented

---

[58] Fisher, *Government and Society*, pp. 60–61; Brading, *Miners and Merchants*, pp. 66–67.

[59] Suspended in New Spain, for example, was the Gálvez plan to abolish the *repartimiento de mercancías*, which threatened the powers of the *alcaldes mayores* and their merchant allies. Stanley J. Stein, "Bureaucracy and Business in the Spanish Empire: Failure of a Bourbon Reform in Mexico and Peru," *HAHR*, 61 (February 1981), pp. 15–16. See also Brading, *Miners and Merchants*, pp. 70–71.

[60] Mark A. Burkholder and D. S. Chandler, *From Impotence to Authority: The Spanish Crown and the American Audiencias, 1687–1808* (Columbia: University of Missouri Press, 1977) p. 120.

[61] Gil, like Valdés, was a navy officer and a *bailío* in the order of San Juan de Malta. Bibiano Torres, *La marina en el gobierno y administración de Indias* (Madrid: Editorial MAPFRE, 1992), pp. 145–46.

[62] Kuethe, *Military Reform and Society*, pp. 145–56.

levels of revenue from the depressed economy of the region (see Figure 7.2). Despite these successes and his lavish use of bureaucratic patronage to quell local opposition, a few years after García Pizarro left Quito, complaints arose about his blatant nepotism, corruption, and tyrannical rule.[63] As a result, on October 9, 1788, the crown ordered a special investigation (*pesquisa*) of specific allegations raised against him while he ruled the Kingdom of Quito. When the Viceroy Gil y Lemos received the order to begin the *pesquisa*, he entrusted the task to Fernando Quadrado y Valdenebro, a straight-laced justice of the Quito audiencia renowned for his personal and professional integrity.[64]

This *pesquisa* faced formidable opposition from President Villalengua, the son-in-law, successor, and political heir of García Pizarro, who had no intention of allowing his predecessor's policies to become discredited. The president attacked Quadrado for partisanship, claiming that he only solicited testimony from malcontents opposed to local political leaders. Quadrado struck back at Villalengua and his allies, charging that they were "a powerful family, no less for its riches than for … their authority at court."[65] The *pesquisa* soon degenerated into a series of charges and counter charges, leaving the entire kingdom embroiled in political factionalism by 1790. Indeed, it was apparent that only the Madrid government's intervention could resolve the political deadlock in Quito. After a careful review of the evidence, members of the Council of the Indies decided not to mete out any punishments. Instead, the Council quietly transferred Villalengua to Guatemala as president-regent of the audiencia, removing him from the scene. As for Fernando Quadrado, the Council commended his efforts to uncover the truth about corruption in Quito and Guayaquil, but they also acknowledged that he had far exceeded his instructions by probing into every aspect of the García Pizarro clan's activities in Quito. In the end, the Council ordered the new president, Juan Antonio Mon y Velarde, to complete the investigation quietly and to promote harmony in the Kingdom of Quito.[66]

Shortly after arriving in Quito, Mon y Velarde wrote the crown recommending a leaner, more efficient bureaucracy and a state-sponsored program to promote economic growth in the depressed region. The new president first attacked administrative problems in the kingdom's fiscal bureaucracy. He charged that accounts from virtually every agency

---

[63] Francisco de Gil y Lemos to Fernando Quadrado, Santa Fe, January 26, 1789, AGI, Quito leg. 272. Cited in Kenneth J. Andrien, "The Politics of Reform in Spain's Atlantic Empire during the Late Bourbon Period: The Visita of José García de León y Pizarro in Quito," *Journal of Latin American Studies* 41:4 (November 2009), pp. 652–54.

[64] Ibid.

[65] Fernando Quadrado to Francisco de Gil y Lemos, Quito, June 18, 1789 AGI, Quito leg. 267; *carta reservada*, Fernando Quadrado to Francisco de Gil y Lemos, Quito, March 21, 1789 AGI, Quito, leg. 267.

[66] Ibid.

were in arrears, making it impossible to audit their honesty and efficiency.[67] To deal with these abuses, Mon y Velarde proposed a complete
revamping of the fiscal bureaucracy by cutting waste, lowering salaries,
eliminating superfluous jobs, and demanding more efficient record keeping. Without such drastic reforms, the president claimed, this top-heavy
fiscal bureaucracy would bring further ruin to the economy and society of
the Kingdom of Quito.[68]

Apart from administrative changes, Mon y Velarde also advocated an
ambitious economic development program for the region to reverse the
appalling, century-long decline of woolen textile production. The president recognized that regional economic decline stemmed from the introduction of cheap European cloth from the early eighteenth century. While
Mon y Velarde commended the crown for limiting imports of cheap
European *paños de segundo* into Lima, he also recognized that this policy
was insufficient to promote the kingdom's economic recovery. To ameliorate this dismal state of affairs, he argued for stricter prohibitions on
European cloth imports to South American markets, investment in roads
and other infrastructure, loosening monopoly controls (primarily over
cascarilla production), tax incentives to free up investment capital, and
technical assistance to rejuvenate the moribund mining industry. Without
such state-sponsored assistance, Mon y Velarde predicted that the economy would languish, tax revenues would decline (especially those levied on
the oppressed Amerindian population), and overseas commerce would
slowly wither.[69]

The president never served in Quito long enough to mobilize sufficient
political support to implement these plans. After less than one year in power,
he was promoted to the Council of the Indies and left the kingdom for
Spain.[70] On route, he died in Cádiz, and thus he never had the opportunity
to argue his views on reform as a member of the Council. At the same time,
there was no enthusiasm in Madrid for resuscitating colonial woolen

---

[67] Before his posting in Quito, Mon y Velarde had served as *oidor* in New Granada and *visitador* in
Antioquia (1785 to 1788), where he imposed programs to develop a vigorous local economy.
Building on recommendations from the governor of Antioquia, Francisco Silvestre, the *visitador*
had improved local administration, promoted public order, called for the creation of a bishopric,
and most importantly, encouraged mining, commerce, and agriculture. Ann Twinam, *Miners,
Merchants, and Farmers in Colonial Colombia*, (Austin: University of Texas Press, 1982), pp. 32–
33, 50–60, 124–28, 106–08; Burkholder and Chandler, *Biographical Dictionary of Audiencia
Ministers*, p. 219; and Anthony McFarlane, *Colombia before Independence: Economy, Society,
and Politics under Bourbon Rule* (Cambridge: Cambridge University Press, 1993), pp. 137–40.
[68] The president also found the militia system equally wasteful and warranting drastic cutbacks.
Juan Antonio Mon y Velarde to Pedro de Lerena, Quito, March 3, 1791 AGI, Quito, leg. 249.
[69] Ibid. These plans are also summarized in Washburn, *"The Bourbon Reforms: As Social and
Economic History of the Audiencia of Quito, 1760–1810"* (Ph.D. diss., University of Texas,
1984), pp. 157–59.
[70] Burkholder and Chandler, *Biographical Dictionary of Audiencia Ministers*, p. 219.

manufacturing in Quito. As Archbishop-Viceroy Antonio Caballero y Góngora observed, the decline of Quito's textile industry was fitting and just, because agriculture and mining were the "appropriate function of the colonies," while manufactured goods such as cloth "ought to be imported from Spain."[71] As a result, crown policies may have moderated after the death of Gálvez, but authorities in Madrid remained steadfast in their unwillingness to implement the economic policies advocated by Mon y Velarde in Quito that threatened peninsular interests.

Although unwilling to encourage textile manufacturing centers such as Quito, the curtailment of the bureaucracy and the reduction of the militia in New Granada signaled a relaxation in the unremitting drive to increase revenues. By reducing political tensions, the crown would require fewer costly troops to sustain its authority, a strategy that diminished both expenses and political risks. The resulting economies compensated for laxer enforcement practices. Meanwhile, the tobacco and aguardiente monopolies continued to grow and became major sources of revenue. The new strategy proved financially wise in the long run, for in the 1790s the Viceroyalty of New Granada both paid off its enormous internal debt and eventually accumulated modest surpluses for the Spanish treasury.[72] When he next became viceroy of Peru, Gil advanced much the same agenda.[73] Nonetheless, the basic fiscal administration that Gálvez had installed remained in place, including the intendancies, where they already existed. Tax rates were not reduced nor were the lucrative royal monopolies disbanded.[74]

Even though the crown pursued more moderate, cost-saving policies in New Granada and elsewhere, it vigorously promoted the colonial mining sector to boost remittances of silver from the Indies to Spain. After all, silver mining was still fundamental for gaining the riches to support the imperial ambitions of Madrid, and Gálvez's policy in New Spain reflected this lust for American silver. In 1783, he established ordinances for the Real Cuerpo de Minería, complete with a separate *fuero*. The ordinances capped ambitious initiatives to reorganize and to stimulate the silver mining industry of New Spain, dating back to his *visita* during the 1760s. Gálvez then named Fausto D'Elhúyar of Logroño director of the mining tribunal in 1786 and sent him a

---

[71] Quoted in John Lynch, "The Origins of Spanish American Independence," in Leslie Bethell, ed., *The Independence of Latin America* (Cambridge: Cambridge University Press, 1987), p. 16.

[72] McFarlane, *Colombia Before Independence*, p. 225.

[73] Leon G. Campbell, *The Military and Society in Colonial Peru, 1750–1810* (Philadelphia: American Philosophical Society, 1978), pp. 211–12; Fisher, "Critique," *HAHR*, 58 (1978), 84–85.

[74] In the name of free enterprise, the abolition of crown monopolies in Venezuela and the Philippines was indeed considered, and all other jurisdictions were ordered to report on such a possibility. When it became evident that no compensatory source of revenue was available, the idea was abandoned. Jacques A. Barbier, "Venezuelan 'libranzas,' 1788–1807: From Economic Nostrum to Fiscal Imperative," *The Americas*, 37 (1981), p. 467.

cadre of Saxon technicians to assist in introducing modern technology, including the recently developed Von Born method of amalgamation.[75] An earlier initiative had featured an expedition to New Granada under Fausto's older brother, Juan José, and Baron Thaddeus von Nordenflicht led another to Peru.[76] As in Mexico, Gálvez sent Saxon technicians along with both missions. Mining had never amounted to much in New Granada, but the crown hoped to revive seventeenth-century works in Mariquita through employing modern mining techniques.[77] The Madrid government had higher expectations for Peru, where the once spectacular industry had faded to a distant second place behind Mexico.[78] Efforts in Peru to establish a mining tribunal modeled on the Mexican precedent led to fierce opposition from the *limeño* mercantile elite, which was determined to sustain financial and juridical hegemony over the silver mining industry. Given the conciliatory tone that the Junta Suprema de Estado had adopted, Valdés retreated, and Von Nordenflicht's mission languished without strong support from Madrid.[79] In New Spain, such opposition did not appear, and its mining mission labored productively in collaboration with the mining elite. The same cooperation was obtained in New Granada, but with scant success in stimulating regional production.

Meanwhile, the Junta Suprema pushed forward confidently with commercial reforms, responding to pressures within Spain and the Indies to draw the colonies into a tighter economic dependence and to make colonial trade more profitable. The principal competition for colonial trade continued to come from the British. While their free port at Jamaica attracted Spanish traders, English smugglers also plied their craft individually.[80] Moreover, London still retained its infuriating, historic prerogatives in Spain's Iberian ports.[81] The French had seen their rights eroded,

---

[75] Walter Howe, *The Mining Guild of New Spain and Its Tribunal General, 1770–1821* (Cambridge: Harvard University Press, 1949), pp. 22–62, 166–67, 177–78. The reformist mission did not arrive until August 1788.

[76] Arthur P. Whitaker, "The Elhúyar Mining Missions and the Enlightenment," *HAHR*, 31 (November 1951), pp. 557–85.

[77] Sandra Montgomery Keelan, "The Bourbon Mining Reform in New Granada, 1784–1796," in John R. Fisher, Allan J. Kuethe, and Anthony McFarlane, eds., *Reform and Insurrection in Bourbon New Granada and Peru* (Baton Rouge: Louisiana State University Press, 1990), pp. 41–53.

[78] J. R. Fisher, *Silver Mines and Silver Miners in Colonial Peru, 1776–1824* (Liverpool: Liverpool University Press, 1977), chap. 1.

[79] Fisher, "Critique," pp. 83–86.

[80] Adrian J. Pearce, *British Trade with Spanish America, 1763–1808* (Liverpool: Liverpool University Press, 2007), pp. 80–84.

[81] Floridablanca lamented "the special privileges that the English nation had, especially in Andalusia, at the time of Spain's greatest weakness [and] the treaties on inspections, manifests, and trading vessels that harmed us so much." Junta de Estado, Palace, July 8, 1787, AHN, Estado, book 1, art. 401.

and the 1778 regulation had abolished the *palmeo*, which had served their interests so well in Cádiz.[82] Floridablanca showed no inclination to negotiate a new commercial treaty with Paris because, as he asserted in his instruction to the junta, "the old treaties are not very advantageous; but they have become more relaxed or at least more equitable, [with] many points obscured, and thus it is not advantageous to retreat even a single step from the unshackled condition that we have acquired and will be able to acquire in the future."[83] As late as 1788–1789, with its finances collapsing, Versailles continued to protest the constraints that Madrid persisted in imposing upon its textiles from entering American markets.[84]

The regulation of 1778 had made Spain's merchants more competitive, and its corsairs and coastguards continued to inflict their damages on contrabandists; but the Junta Suprema decided to advance the deregulation of commerce initiated in 1765 by including Veracruz and La Guaira in the new system. Pressure in Spain to do so had begun to build. The 1778 regulation had failed to produce the instant panacea that Spanish producers and merchants had envisioned. While the total volume of legal trade expanded substantially during the postwar period, the increased competition among the ports of Spain drove down prices as colonial markets became saturated.[85] This was a natural outgrowth of competition and probably reflected favorably on Spain's ability to compete with foreign rivals in its own empire. At the same time, a lack of information about conditions in specific colonies and in the several regions of Spain itself often led to markets being oversupplied. Catalonians shipping wine to Lima, for example, might find upon their arrival that *gaditanos* had already beaten them to that distant outlet, leaving them little choice but to sell at a loss or to wait many, many months in the hope that demand might improve. Under the traditional monopoly port system, especially after the improved mail service installed in 1764, it had been much easier to measure demand in America and therefore curtail risk. In fact, even Mexico quickly became saturated. In 1784, following the reestablishment of the peace, Madrid had imposed specific tonnage limits for Veracruz to be divided among the authorized Spanish ports, but Spanish traders all too often found the

---

[82] France and Spain had entered into a new commercial treaty in 1768 while the Third Family Compact was still riding high, but the French only gained equality with England in the peninsular trade, without new rights in America. Allan J. Kuethe and Lowell Blaisdell, "French Influence and the Origins of the Bourbon Colonial Reorganization, *HAHR*, 71 (August 1991), pp. 602–603.

[83] Junta de Estado, Palace, July 8, 1787, AHN, Estado, book 1 art. 352.

[84] George Verne Blue, "French Protests against Restrictions on Trade with Spanish America, 1788–1790," *HAHR* 13 (August 1933), pp. 336–38.

[85] For Peru, see Patricia H. Marks, "Confronting a Mercantile Elite: Bourbon Reformers and the Merchants of Lima, 1765–1796," *The Americas*, 60 (April 2004), pp. 536–37.

Mexican marketplace oversupplied.[86] This development suggests that Charles and his ministers may well have underestimated the ability of profit-hungry entrepreneurs to overcome the barriers imposed by geography.

Other commercial problems arose from the tax structure, which curtailed profits and discouraged trade. The military-minded regime of Charles III aimed most of all to enhance financial support for its far-flung armed forces. The 1778 regulation gave lip service to fomenting Spanish industry and agriculture, but in fact collecting revenue trumped other policy considerations. Ortiz de Landazuri favored moderating overall tax rates to enhance the competitiveness and profitability of Spanish industry, but he died in 1777. The actual export levies set by Gálvez (in consultation with Múzquiz and Floridablanca) did little to help Spanish goods to compete in colonial markets.[87] On key products such as wines, which had been taxed on a fixed basis under the Project of 1720, the rates in fact decreased, but the official values assigned in the regulation were inflated, leading to an overall increase. Moreover, the levies on important luxury items, which had been relatively low when assessed by volume, rose when converted to an ad valorem basis, even as defined by Ortiz. Additional wartime and local impositions only added to the overall tax burden.[88] Hence, although royal revenues and the volume of trade increased impressively, this did not necessarily reflect higher profits for Spanish traders or producers.

Over time the apparent successes of Catalonian textiles also appeared largely illusory. The 1778 regulation gave lower tax rates (3 rather than 7 percent) to goods defined as native products, but cloths could qualify for these Spanish rates if they were *pintadas, o beneficiadas* in Spain. Under this loose definition, textiles merely had to be embellished in some respect – perhaps trimmed with lace – to qualify for low Spanish rather than higher foreign tax rates. Many of the so-called Catalonian manufactures were made in France with only some small refinement added in Barcelona. This worked to the

---

[86] José Joaquín Real Díaz, *Las ferias de Jalapa* (Sevilla: Escuela de Estudios Hispano-Americanos, 1959), pp. 112–13; Delgado Ribas, "El impacto de las crisis coloniales en economía catalana (1787–1807)," in *La economía española al final del Antiguo Régimen, vol. 3. Comercio y colonias*, ed. Josep Fontana (Madrid: Allianza Editorial, 1982), p. 105; John Fisher, *Commercial Relations between Spain and Spanish America in the Era of Free Trade, 1778–1796* (Liverpool: Liverpool University Press, 1985), pp. 18 (nt. 16), 45–46. For a revisionist discussion of how the deregulation of commerce led to greater risk and market saturation in New Spain, see Jeremy Baskes, "Risky Ventures: Reconsidering Mexico's Colonial Trade System," *Colonial Latin American Review* 14:1 (June 2005), pp. 27–54.

[87] Gálvez to Múzquiz, San Ildefonso, September 24, 1778, AGI, IG, leg. 2409.

[88] J. M. Delgado Ribas, "El modelo catalán dentro del sistema de libre comercio (1765–1820)" in Josef Fontana and Antonio Miguel Bernal, eds. *El comercio libre entre España y América (1765–1824)* (Madrid: Fundación Banco Exterior, 1987), pp. 53–57; J. M. Delgado Ribas, "*Catalunya y el sistema de libre comercio (1778–1818): Una reflexión sobre las raíces del reformismo borbónico.*" Ph.D. diss. Abstract, University of Barcelona, 1981, pp. 27–30.

advantage of the Royal Treasury, which collected taxes on foreign textiles as they entered Spain and again as they left for the colonies, but it was probably unfavorable for infant Spanish industries, which remained at a competitive disadvantage.[89] Given the high expenses incurred in the War of the American Revolution, the treasury faced a large postwar deficit and consequently short-term fiscal priorities continued to dwarf long-term economic development considerations.

Spanish businessmen also suffered from a shortage of readily available investment capital during the postwar period. The issuance of large quantities of *vales reales* during the war through the Banco Nacional de San Carlos and the expenditure of huge sums of money in the American theater drained venture capital that might productively have underwritten colonial commerce. It is hardly surprising that in 1785, soon after the death of Miguel de Múzquiz (Gálvez's principal ally in the royal cabinet), Lerena succeeded in forcing the Minister of the Indies to order the American authorities to remit all surplus revenues to Spain.[90] This measure proved too little too late. An impressive number of Spanish businesses, the victims of unfavorable competition, heavy taxes, and highly priced credit, folded during the mid-1780s. This process culminated in a severe recession in 1787, which coincided with the death of Gálvez and the creation of the Junta Suprema.[91]

The junta worked through 1788 to formulate an appropriate way to incorporate Mexico and Venezuela into the system of "free trade."[92] On February 28, 1789, the crown promulgated the reform, which opened the way for Spanish merchants to penetrate those colonies more freely, to undermine the monopoly of the *Consulado* of Mexico City, and to participate directly in the lucrative Veracruz market.[93] Moreover, in a separate action

---

[89] This process nevertheless obviously produced mixed results, for the people involved in finishing foreign manufactures for export developed quasi industries of a sort. Carlos Martínez Shaw, "El libre comercio y Cataluña: Contribución a un debate," in Fontana and Bernal, *El comercio libre*, pp. 45–49.

[90] Jacques A. Barbier and Herbert S. Klein, "Revolutionary Wars and Public Finances: The Madrid Treasury, 1784–1807," *Journal of Economic History*, XLI (June 1981): p. 331; Jacques A. Barbier, "Towards a New Chronology," p. 347.

[91] Delgado Ribas, "El impacto de las crisis," pp. 102–18. For an overview of the crisis in the Spanish economy and its relationship to the American trade, see also Barbara H. Stein and Stanley J. Stein, "Concepts and Realities of Spanish Economic Growth, 1759–1789" in *Historia ibérica*, I (1973): pp. 103–19.

[92] Barbier, "The Culmination," pp. 62–63.

[93] Royal order, Palace, February 28, 1789, AGI, Mexico, leg. 2505. This step found little support from the *Consulado* of Mexico, which preferred the security offered by a controlled commerce. Javier Ortiz de la Tabla Ducasse, *Comercio exterior de Veracruz, 1778–1821: Crisis de dependencia* (Sevilla: Escuela de Estudios Hispano-Americanos, 1978), p. 10. The effects of this measure are developed at length in Brading, *Miners and Merchants*, and in Brian R. Hamnett, *Politics & Trade in Southern Mexico, 1750–1821* (Cambridge: Cambridge University Press, 1971).

to bolster Spanish traders, the junta adjusted tax rates downward and established a system to provide the ports of Spain semi-annual reports on American market conditions.[94] Finally, since deregulation made its mission obsolete, the crown abolished the *Casa de la Contratación* in 1790.[95]

In a *cédula* of February 28, 1789, the junta opened the slave trade of Cuba, Santo Domingo, Puerto Rico, and Caracas to all Spanish subjects, finally implementing the recommendation that O'Reilly had made for Cuba twenty-five years earlier. Moreover, owing to the October 1, 1777, settlement with Portugal, which ceded the islands of Anno Bom and Fernando Pó off the West African coast to Spain, this privilege could be exercised without recourse to European middlemen.[96] The 1789 liberalization of the slave trade came only after vigorous *habanero* lobbying but, as usual with Cuban-inspired reformist initiatives in the Caribbean, the legislation came to have much broader application. For Madrid the step made good political and economic sense. It rewarded Cuba, whose militia had brought glory during the recent war, and whose burgeoning sugar industry promised to enhance royal revenues. The measure also promoted the movement toward greater commercial deregulation. To avert the cost of running empty ships, departing slave vessels could carry cargoes on their outbound voyages, a step that legalized coveted access to the British Free Ports of the Caribbean. The *cédula* also abolished the levy on slave importations. Moreover, in a landmark concession, the edict permitted foreigners entry into this trade for a period of two years. Then too, the junta extended these same liberties to New Granada and to Buenos Aires in 1791, while approving foreign participation for six more years, a concession that subsequently became permanent.[97]

While these adjustments in colonial policy promised relief for the Royal Treasury in Spain and cooled the political tensions generated in America during the war, they alone could not balance the royal budget. Spiraling costs to support the armada constituted a critical dimension of the struggle to bring military and administrative outlays under control and to reorient imperial policy from a war time to a peacetime footing. As the 1780s progressed, Charles III continued to view the fleet as an essential instrument for his military ambitions, and this did not change when the throne passed to his son. According to the data in Figure 9.2, in 1760, Charles III's first year on the throne, the crown spent 66,077,000 copper *reales* on the armada,

---

[94] Delgado Ribas, "Catalunya y el sistema," pp. 42–43.

[95] Jacques A. Barbier, "Towards a New Chronology," pp. 338–39.

[96] Dauril Alden, *Royal Government in Colonial Brazil* (Berkeley: University of California Press, 1968), p. 267.

[97] Proceedings, Junta de Estado, February 19, 1789, AHN, Estado, book 3. This order can be found in Ricardo Levene, *Documentos para la historia argentina*, VI, *Comercio de Indias: Comercio libre (1778–1791)* (Buenos Aires 1915), pp. 394–99. See also James Furguson King, "Evolution of the Free Slave Trade Principle," *HAHR*, 22 (February 1942), pp. 34–56.

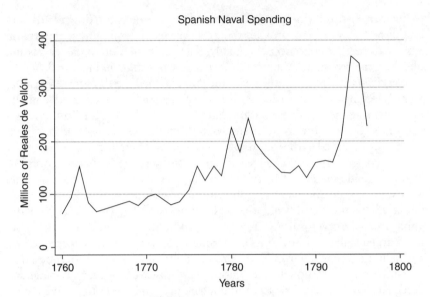

FIGURE 9.4 Spanish Naval Spending

which amounted to 15.3 percent of the crown's total expenditures.[98] By 1788, that figure had risen to 158,522,000 *reales*, and it accounted for 24.5 percent of total royal expenses (see Figure 9.2).[99] In September 1788, two months before Charles's death, Valdés reported to the Junta Suprema that the armada numbered seventy-one ships of the line and forty-three frigates.[100] Within a year, these strengths had increased to seventy-six and fifty-one respectively.[101]

During the reign of Charles IV, the cost of building and supporting this large armada led naval spending to spiral to 367,579,000 *reales*, a high for the century, amounting to nearly 39 percent of the royal budget.[102] Given the enormous costs involved in putting ships to sea and the difficulties of securing a sufficient number of sailors to man them, Madrid could not hope to arm more than two-thirds of its force at any time. As a result, the navy held a portion in reserve to anticipate possible losses sustained in combat, while

[98] Jacques A. Barbier, "Indies Revenues and Naval Spending: The Cost of Colonialism for the Spanish Bourbons, 1763–1805," *Jahrbuch für Geschichte von staat, wirtschaf und gessellschaft Lateinamerikas*, 21 (1984), pp.176–77.

[99] Ibid.

[100] Minutes, Junta de Estado, September 15, 1788, AHN, Estado, book 2.

[101] G. Douglas Inglis, "The Spanish Naval Shipyard at Havana in the Eighteenth Century," in *New Aspects of Naval History: Selected Papers from the 5th Naval History Symposium* (Baltimore: Nautical and Aviation Publishers, 1985), p. 53.

[102] Barbier, "Indies Revenues and Naval Spending," p. 177.

other vessels necessarily underwent maintenance and repair. It took 850 men and 40 officers to man a triple-decked warship. In addition, the mere expense of maintaining four arsenals to repair existing ships was daunting, and those vessels venturing into strategic tropical waters required special attention, for their iron and wood decayed rapidly while shipworms bored into their bottoms.[103] Moreover, the demand for new construction was permanent, as aged vessels had to be replaced and new craft built to be held in reserve.

The armada habitually consumed all of the surpluses remitted from America to the *Depositaría de Indias* and more.[104] Given the competition for those surpluses within Spain itself, and in particular the needs of the Banco de San Carlos, this situation was untenable over the long run. Moreover, when British intrusions at Nootka Sound seemed to provide justification for war, Madrid prepared the armada for the long-anticipated invasion of Britain; but when Floridablanca urged France to uphold its treaty obligations, the severely weakened Louis XVI dared not ask the revolutionary National Assembly to declare war. As in 1770, the frustrated Spanish monarch had no choice but to back down, leaving its expensive navy to languish in port.[105]

Lerena at Finance and Valdés at Marine battled annually within the junta over naval expenditures, and to his credit the finance minister succeeded during the 1780s in keeping the armada's budget under 200 million copper *reales*. Lerena's push for austerity finally bore fruit; the armada's costs had stabilized while colonial remissions mushroomed. As a result, in the quinquennium 1785 to 1789, Indies revenues exceeded naval expenditures for the first and only time during the reign of Charles III.[106] As allocations for the armada leveled off, Valdes's urgent measures in the Junta Suprema to maximize remissions of colonial revenue to Cádiz surely reflected, at least in part, his determination to secure additional funding for the fleet.[107] Moreover, those same urgencies related directly to the junta's renewed effort to "restore the commerce of America to necessary levels" by bringing Veracruz and La Guaira under the 1778 regulation.[108]

In keeping with this move to lower administrative costs and increase remittances of colonial revenue, Madrid made the surprising decision to halt new shipbuilding in Havana. Although those vessels already under

[103] N.A.M. Rodger, *The Command of the Ocean: A Naval History of Britain, 1649–1815* (New York: W. W. Norton, 2004), p. 303. Rif Winfield, *British Warships in the Age of Sail, 1793–1817* (London: Chatham Publishing, 2005), pp. 1 ff. details refitting cost for specific ships.

[104] Barbier, "Indies Revenues and Naval Spending," pp. 179–81.

[105] Minutes, Junta de Estado, March 22, April 26, May 16, May 31, and July 5, 1790, AHN, Estado, book 3; Warren L. Cook, *Flood Tide of Empire: Spain and the Pacific Northwest, 1543–1819* (New Haven: Yale University Press, 1973), chap. 6.

[106] Barbier, "Indies Revenues and Naval Spending," p. 181.

[107] Ibid., pp. 177–84.

[108] Lerena to the Junta Suprema de Estado, Aranjuez, April 28, 1788, AHN, Estado, book 3.

construction would be finished, the Cuban shipyard thereafter became little more than a naval garage limited to repairing and servicing of ships operating in American waters. In 1795, the seventy-four-gun *Asia* was the last ship of the line to emerge from what had been the most productive shipyard of the empire under Charles III.[109] The closure of Havana's shipbuilding facility, with all new construction transferred to the peninsula, was a dramatic manifestation of the junta's determination to maximize the remission of silver to Spain in order to back the *vales reales* of the Banco de San Carlos and to stimulate the Spanish economy.

A decree of April 25, 1790, completed the ministerial reorganization by dissolving the Secretariat for the Indies, integrating its several functions into the appropriate Spanish offices. Colonial affairs were now divided among Valdés at Marine, Lerena at Finance, Porlier at Grace and Justice, and the Conde de Campo-Alange, who replaced Jerónimo Caballero at War.[110] Within their respective ministries, however, both Finance and Grace and Justice would remain separated from Spanish affairs. Floridablanca at State continued to preside over the Junta Suprema, while Valdés acted as alternative.[111] This reorganization represented the final step toward coordinating the affairs of America and Spain and improving the administration of the Indies.[112]

As Floridablanca's esteem for López de Lerena's services grew, the Finance minister gained both the status of hidalgo and a habit in the Order of Santiago. In March 1791, Floridablanca secured for him a title of Castile as he became the first Conde de Lerena.[113] Moreover, he married María Pescattori Díaz de Lavandero, the daughter of the Marquéz de San Andrés. The widow of José de Gálvez acted as his *madrina* in the wedding, which suggests that differences over policy did not necessarily translate into permanent familial animosity.[114] Lerena's fading health, however, led Charles to replace him on an interim basis in October 1791 with the able Diego de Gardoqui, who had recently served as *chargé d'affaires* in the United States of America.[115] Lerena died the following January.

---

[109] Allan J. Kuethe and José Manuel Serrano, "El astillero de La Habana y Trafalgar," *Revista de Indias*, 67 (September.-December 2007), pp. 770–72.

[110] Caballero had assumed those duties in May 1787, relieving a much overworked López de Lerena.

[111] AHN, Junta de Estado, book 3. Ibid.

[112] Barbier, "The Culmination ," pp. 51–68.

[113] http://www.euskalnet.net/laviana/gen_hispanas/lerena.htm. Accessed September 24, 2010.

[114] Eric Beerman, "El conde de Aranda y la tertulia madrileña (1788–1790) de la viuda de Bernardo de Gálvez," in José A. Ferrer Benimeli (director), *El conde de Aranda y su tiempo*, vol. 2 (Zaragoza Institución "Fernando el Católico," Diputación de Zaragoza, 2000), p. 359.

[115] Escudero, *Los orígenes*, I, pp. 534–38; Light Townsend Cummins, *Spanish Observers and the American Revolution, 1775–1783* (Baton Rouge: Louisiana State University Press, 1991), p. 193; Manuel Ballesteros Gaibrois, "El vasco Diego de Gardoqui, primer embajador

SPAIN AND THE WARS OF THE FRENCH REVOLUTION

Developing against the backdrop of increasing anguish over revolutionary events in France, a palace coup by conservatives on February 28, 1792, toppled Floridablanca, leading to the brief triumph of the Conde de Aranda and his Aragonese faction. It also brought a sudden end to the Junta Suprema de Estado. Aranda had arranged for his return from Paris in 1787, and once in Madrid he conspired endlessly to undermine his rival, Floridablanca. As Minister of State, however, he stood on perilously weak ground with Queen María Luisa and her ambitious favorite, Manuel Godoy. Maria Luisa, daughter of Philip, the Duke of Parma, and the granddaughter of Elizabeth Farnese, was a restless, headstrong woman much given to intrigue who had long resented Floridablanca.

Banished from court like most other reformers before him, the fallen minister initially took refuge in Hellín, Murcia, his homeland. However, Charles soon ordered him imprisoned in Pamplona, where he remained until 1794, when he was allowed to return to Murcia. Floridablanca's formal rehabilitation did not come until March 1808. No other changes occurred in the cabinet until eight months later when Godoy displaced Aranda. Since King Charles IV had also come to depend upon him, the queen's favorite became de facto prime minister.[116]

Before his downfall, Aranda resuscitated the nearly moribund Consejo de Estado, a traditional arm of the higher aristocracy, which had replaced the Junta Suprema. Additional members joined the secretaries of the Office during their weekly meetings, and the king sometimes attended in person. This institutional reorganization was unfortunate, as the increase in the number of voices and the presence of Charles slowed the coordination of royal policy for Spain and Indies, which had proceeded so effectively over the preceding five years. Nevertheless, colonial governance experienced more continuity than change, particularly in the delicate area of commercial policy.[117]

Despite an impressive rise within the Spanish Atlantic following the liberalization of 1778, Spain still had not recaptured the lion's share of the colonial trade by the 1790s. British commerce with the Indies grew to astonishing levels, which paralleled the remarkable advances that Madrid had recorded. This success partially resulted from lingering connections established between Jamaican and Spanish American merchants when Madrid authorized neutral trade during the War of the American Revolution. Moreover, Britain

de España ante Los Estados Unidos de América," in Ronald Escobedo Mansilla, Ana de Zaballa Beascoechea, and Óscar Álvarez Gila, *Euskal Herria y el Nuevo Mundo: La contribución de los Vascos a la formación de las Américas* (Vitoria: Servicio Editorial, Universidad del País Vasco, 1996), pp. 305–18.
[116] A summary of these transitions can be found in Escudero, *Los orígenes*, I, pp. 473–88, 517–19, 540–59.
[117] Barbier, "The Culmination," pp. 66–67.

established additional free ports in the West Indies between 1787 and 1793, luring into its commercial network even more Spanish-American dealers. At the same time, the implementation of the free slave trade in 1789 for the Greater Antilles, Caracas, and soon afterward for New Granada and Río de la Plata, opened wider the gates to international commercial transactions. Finally, the British alliance during Spain's war with revolutionary France (1793–1795) further eroded barriers that Madrid had once hoped to sustain to British commercial penetration.[118]

Policy makers fought foreign commercial penetration by ending the fleet system to New Spain, but they also acted to empower regional elites through institutionalizing new centers of legal commercial activity. Bringing Mexico into the system of imperial free trade did not indicate that the post-Gálvez governments had abandoned the crown's previous commitment to develop the exposed imperial peripheries. Such strategic priorities had by no means vanished from commercial policy. Indeed, the liberalization of the slave trade in 1789 reflected Madrid's long-standing commitment to develop its vulnerable frontier holdings. By this time, royal strategy had evolved from containing Mexico to encouraging the development of the imperial peripheries directly through institutional reforms. The Regulation of Free Trade had provided for the establishment of *consulados* in the enfranchised ports of Spain.[119] Now the time had come to extend that liberalization to the colonies and to weaken the suffocating grip of the Lima and Mexico City merchant guilds. As a result, between 1793 and 1795, Madrid established eight new *consulados* in America.[120]

By 1793, Havana, Caracas, and Buenos Aires had registered striking economic and demographic advances, and the crown hoped to draw these regions further into the imperial commercial system.[121] Moreover, the slave uprising of 1791 in Saint Domingue effectively removed that island as a competitor to Cuba, whose economic potential now seemed limitless. New Granada and Chile remained peripheries of the Spanish Atlantic system, and

---

[118] As Adrian Pearce has observed, this period "marked the consolidation of Hispanic America as Britain's most important commercial partner in the West Indies after the United States – a position from which there would be no subsequent retreat." Pearce, *British Trade with Spanish America*, p. 101.

[119] *Reglamento para el comercio libre 1778* (Madrid 1778), art. 53.

[120] Gabriel B. Paquette, "State-Civil Society Cooperation and Conflict in the Spanish Empire: The Intellectual and Political Activities of the Ultramarine Consulados and Economic Societies, c. 1780–1810," *Journal of Latin American Studies*, 39 (May 2007), p. 270.

[121] Susan Migden Socolow, *The Merchants of Buenos Aires, 1778–1810* (Cambridge: Cambridge University Press, 1978), pp. 170–73 and "Buenos Aires: Atlantic Port and Hinterland in the Eighteenth Century," in Franklin W. Knight and Peggy K. Liss (eds.), *Atlantic Port Cities: Economy, Culture, and Society in the Atlantic World, 1650–1850* (Knoxville: University of Tennessee Press, 1991), pp. 240–61.

that was not likely to change.[122] Nonetheless, the crown aimed to use an expanded system of *consulados* to consolidate gains already made while stimulating progress in the less developed sectors. By co-opting the local merchant and planter elites into the imperial commercial system, the new guilds promised to facilitate mercantile administration and to strengthen Madrid's ties to its emerging possessions.[123]

The breakthrough in this effort to wrest the control of trade from traditional monopolies and to draw the outer regions closer to the royal administration came in Caracas and its satellite port, La Guaira. Under the Regulation of Free Trade, the Caracas Company had lost its "exclusive privileges," and the annual quota for "Venezuela, Cumaná, Guayana, and Maracaibo" was subsequently divided between it and the enfranchised ports of Spain.[124] In 1785, the crown folded the declining Caracas Company into the newly established Philippines Company.[125] Later that same year, Intendant Francisco Saavedra, a fast-rising disciple of José de Gálvez, urged the *malagueño* to fill the resulting institutional void by creating a *consulado* modeled on those recently established in Spain.[126] Saavedra had served as the controversial minister's special envoy to the Caribbean during the War of the American Revolution to coordinate financial cooperation between Madrid and Versailles, and he had arranged the loan from the Havana elite that financed the French action at Yorktown.[127] Gálvez, long committed to undermining the *Consulados* of Mexico City and Lima, responded quickly and

---

[122] John Fisher, "The Effects of Comercio Libre on the Economies of New Granada and Peru," in Fisher, Kuethe, and McFarlane, *Reform and Insurrection*, pp. 149–57 showed that the commercial results were anemic. And Jacques A. Barbier concluded that under the Bourbon program, Chile "never became an asset, only less of a burden." *Reform and Politics in Bourbon Chile, 1755–1796* (Ottawa: University of Ottawa Press, 1980), p. 190.

[123] As Gabriel B. Paquette has perceptively argued, "The Crown's decision to charter additional colonial *consulados* was underpinned by two factors: first, the regalist intention to supplant the entrenched corporations of its American empire with institutions more amenable to metropolitan manipulation; the second, the recognition of mutual interest uniting the metropolitan state and the emerging elites of the imperial periphery. The *comercio libre* legislation and new *consulados*, then, were two mechanisms by which the Crown planned to wrest control of its American markets and supersede monopoly corporations that thwarted its aims." Paquette, "State-Civil Society," p. 270.

[124] *Reglamento para el comercio*, art. 5; Real Díaz, *Las ferias*, pp. 112–13.

[125] Roland Dennis Hussey, *The Caracas Company, 1728–1784* (Cambridge: Harvard University Press, 1934), pp. 296–98.

[126] Saavedra to Gálvez, Caracas, May 2, 1785. Reproduced in Eduardo Arcila Farías, intro. and comp., *El Real Consulado de Caracas* (Caracas: Instituto de Estudios Hispanoamericanos, Facultad de Humanidades y Educación, Universidad Central de Venezuela, 1957), pp. 217–19.

[127] James A. Lewis, "Las Damas de La Habana, el Precursor, and Francisco Saavedra: A Note on Spanish Participation in the Battle of Yorktown," *The Americas* (July 1980), pp. 83–99. See also, Francisco Morales Padrón (ed.), *The Journal of Don Francisco Saavedra de Sangronis, 1780–1783*, trans. By Aileen Moore Topping (Gainesville 1989).

affirmatively, and he sent along copies of the instruments that Málaga and Seville had recently developed for their guilds.[128] During the ensuing several years, Caracas worked to draft an appropriate policy. This tedious process, which balanced the interests of the planters and the merchants, finally produced a document that Saavedra took with him when he returned to Spain in 1788.[129]

In Madrid, Diego de Gardoqui brought to fruition the legal enfranchisement of *consulados* for Caracas and the seven other cities. When Charles IV assigned the affairs of the Indies to the functional secretaries of the Office in 1790, colonial commerce went to Finance. When that ministry subdivided its American workload between three officials, Gardoqui, whom Lerena recruited, received commerce for the Indies along with Spanish and American *consulados*.[130] Other petitions soon joined that of Caracas on Gardoqui's desk as more and more jurisdictions sensed the opportunity to advance their interests.[131] At Lerena's urging, Charles elevated Gardoqui to relieve the ailing magistrate; but he retained personal control over his former assignment.[132] Named proprietary minister after Lerena's death, he advanced the question of American *consulados* from that portfolio to the Consejo de Estado.[133] Caracas's quest, which Saavedra continued to champion, found expression by royal *cédula* of June 3, 1793.[134] A charter for Guatemala, whose merchants had aggressively petitioned in 1787 for the right to form a guild, followed later that year.[135] In a similar vein, the crown authorized *consulados* for Buenos Aires and Havana in 1794.[136]

Much to the frustration of an impatient Caracas, Gardoqui had proceeded deliberately, preferring to accumulate petitions from interested groups and to

---

[128] Gálvez to Saavedra, San Ildefonso, September 5, 1785. Reproduced in Arcila Ferías, *El Real Consulado*, p. 220. For Mexico City, see Hamnett, *Politics & Trade*, p. 71; and Brading, *Miners & Merchants*, pp. 114–17. For Lima, see Marks, "Confronting a Mercantile Elite," pp. 538–40, 548–54

[129] Arcila Farías, *El Real Consulado*, p. 19.

[130] Escudero, *Los orígenes*, I, pp. 512–13.

[131] Germán Tjarks, *El Consulado de Buenos Aires y sus proyecciones en la historia del Río de La Plata*, I (Buenos Aires: Universidad de Buenos Aires, 1962), pp. 52–54.

[132] Escudero, *Los Orígenes*, I, p. 515.

[133] Tjarks, *El Consulado de Buenos Aires*, pp. 56–57.

[134] Arcila Farías, *El Real Consulado*, pp. 20–21; Royal order (Gardoqui to Consulado), Aranjuez, June 24, 1793, in ibid., pp. 75–76.

[135] The petition can be found in Robert Sidney Smith, "Origins of the Consulado of Guatemala, *HAHR*, 24 (May 1946), pp. 160–61. See also Ralph Lee Woodward, *Class Privilege and Economic Development: The Consulado de Comercio de Guatemala, 1793–1871* (Chapel Hill: University of North Carolina Press, 1966), pp. 6–9.

[136] Peter James Lampros, *"Merchant-Planter Cooperation and Conflict: The Havana Consulado, 1794–1832"* (Ph.D. diss., Tulane University, 1980); Tjarks, *El Consulado de Buenos Aires*, p. 57.

authorize the drafting of regulations suited to individual jurisdictions.[137] Caracas and Havana, for example, carefully balanced planter and merchant interests, whereas Guatemala and Buenos Aires produced instruments structured primarily for commerce.[138] This mode of operation conformed to the moderate tone of the colonial administration after the establishment of the Junta Suprema in 1787, which emphasized consultation and compromise. The Consejo de Estado, however, had little tolerance for historic commercial monopolies. Despite the protests of Mexico City, it acted in 1795 upon petitions from Guadalajara and Veracruz to erect two more guilds, while it likewise extricated Santiago de Chile from the grip of Lima.[139] In an attempt to draw the merchants of Cartagena more fully into the imperial system, the *consejo* also sanctioned their proposal for a *consulado*.[140]

As instruments of both the local elite and the royal administration, the new *consulados* promoted collaboration on the peripheries in the Spanish Atlantic world, shaping "both the formulation and implementation of metropolitan policy."[141] Despite their differing personalities, these guilds promised to assist the crown in administering commerce, adjudicating legal disputes, promoting economic development, improving infrastructure, and frustrating contraband. To finance the *consulados*, their charters permitted collecting a small tax on imports and exports.[142] How much further Madrid might have advanced this system is unknown, as the First British War erupted in October 1796, plunging Spain into a crisis from which it never recovered.

As Madrid entered 1796, it could view the American empire with considerable satisfaction. The royal dominions stretched from Upper California across the continent to Louisiana, then around the Gulf of Mexico to East Florida, and from there they reached south, deep into the cone of South America. Spain's historic rivals had lost most their continental empires, although the incident at Nootka Sound served notice that the British still posed a problem in the extreme north. Moreover, the boundary differences with the Portuguese in Brazil had been stabilized. At the core of the reformist struggle, the commercial system, after a long, complicated struggle had been

---

[137] Unsigned intra-ministerial note, June 1793, *apoderado* (lobbyist) of Caracas Narciso Saénz to the crown, Madrid, July 17, 1792, and deputies of commerce, Caracas, January 25, 1793, all AGI, Caracas, leg. 908. A copy of the Caracas ordinance can be found in leg. 901.

[138] Lampros, "Merchant-Planter Cooperation," p. 19; Ralph Lee Woodward, *Class Privilege and Economic Development*, pp. 9–10; Tjarks, *El Consulado de Buenos Aires*, pp 47–57.

[139] Hamnett, *Politics & Trade*, pp. 98, 143; Marks, "Confronting a Mercantile Elite," pp. 526–30.

[140] Justo Cuño Bonito, "El Consulado de Comercio. Cartagena de Indias y su papel económico y político en el conflicto de independencia (1795–1821)," *Studia histórica. Historia contemporánea*, 27 (2009), pp. 315–26; McFarlane, *Colombia before Independence*, pp. 181–84.

[141] Paquette, "State-Civil Society," p. 263

[142] Ibid., pp. 267–78. For an example of how such alliances between crown and colonial elites might work, see Dominique Goncalvès, *Le Planteur et le Roi: L'Aristocratie Havanaise et la Couronne D'Espagne (1763–1838)* (Madrid : Casa de Velásquez, 2008), part 2.

deregulated, with the historic monopoly of Seville/Cadiz broken and the American trade opened up to the other ports of Spain. In America, eight new *consulados* extended the reach of the crown into the colonial peripheries as never before, and the expectation of further development and diversification were high.

The empire also appeared well defended, with its multiple *plazas fuertes* manned by carefully allocated fixed regiments and battalions of horse and foot, all backed by disciplined militiamen trained by veteran officers and enlisted men, well equipped, and fortified with military corporate privileges. Artillery companies manned the impressive fortifications.[143] Moreover, a line of carefully placed presidios defended Mexico's northern frontier. Enhanced administrative instruments, added from 1739 forward, supported these defenses. They included two new viceroyalties, the Captaincy General of Caracas, and the Commandancy General of the Interior Provinces of Northern New Spain. Moreover, the reformist intendant system of provincial administration now functioned everywhere except New Granada. By 1794, the Spanish Armada, second largest navy in the world, totaled seventy-nine ships of the line and fifty-three frigates. Scores of lesser vessels rounded out the fleet.[144] Compared to what Spain could put to sea in 1714, this naval presence was astonishing. The dreams of Tinajero and Patiño had clearly been realized.

The rising levels of tax revenue remittances from the Indies into the General Treasury in Madrid also attest to the financial success of the reform effort by the 1790s. Income from the Indies rose from 58,056,000 copper *reales* in 1763 to more than 312, 290,000 *reales* in 1796.[145] Administrative, fiscal, commercial, and clerical reforms apparently had a strong cumulative effect on producing ever larger remittances. Figure 9.4, which presents a three-year moving average of Indies income flowing into the General Treasury in Madrid, demonstrates the high levels of these revenue shipments from Spain's American possessions. The graph clearly delineates three major periods of where remittances increased markedly, from 1733–1740 and 1749–1762, and after 1783. The first corresponds to the implementation of initiatives under Patiño's ministry, which had begun under Alberoni; they were only reversed by the outbreak of the War of Jenkins' Ear in 1739, which evolved into the War of the Austrian Succession, ending in 1748. The second increase in remittances corresponds to the advent of peace and the revival of trade in the Spanish Atlantic world and also to the reform initiatives that Carvajal and Ensenada sponsored, which kept remittances at their highest levels in the century, until the Seven Years' War disrupted commerce in the

---

[143] A compilation of these units can be found in Julio Albi, *La defensa de las Indias (1764–1799)* (Madrid: Instituto de Cooperación Iberoamericana, Ediciones Cultura Hispánica,1987), pp. 237–45.

[144] Barbier, "Indies Revenues and Naval Spending," pp. 173–74.

[145] Marichal, "Beneficios y costos fiscales," p. 479.

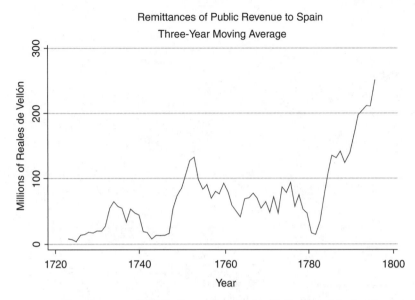

FIGURE 9.5 Remittances of Public Revenue to Spain, Three-Year Moving Average

Spanish Atlantic and Indies revenues registered in Madrid declined. Colonial remittances rose again during the 1770s, only to drop during the War of the American Revolution. Then they rose steadily to the highest levels ever attained, even during the war with France (1793–95). From the crown's viewpoint, the whole century-long process of the reform and renovation of the Spanish Atlantic world paid huge fiscal dividends.

Remittances from the Indies not only rose considerably during the eighteenth century, they also formed an increasingly large share of the crown's total income. In 1763, the 58,056,000 copper *reales* arriving from the Indies and recorded by the General Treasury accounted for just over 12 percent of the royal income. By the year that war broke out with Great Britain in 1796, the 312,292,000 *reales* in Indies revenues amounted to well over 33 percent of the king's income.[146] As Figure 9.5 of remittances from the Indies and the total revenues recorded at the General Treasury clearly demonstrates, Indies remittances not only pushed up total income in the Madrid treasury, but they also accounted for an ever larger percentage of the crown's total revenues after the War of the American Revolution, oscillating between 23 and 34 percent. The reforms not only paid dividends for the Spanish treasury, but they also helped the crown attain greater fiscal stability.

Despite these impressive fiscal benefits, long-term financial difficulties still plagued the crown in the 1790s. In a path-breaking article in 1981, Jacques

---

[146] Ibid.

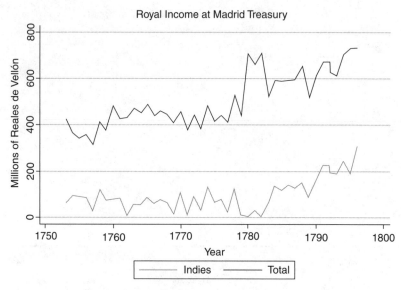

FIGURE 9.6 Royal Income at Madrid Treasury

A. Barbier and Herbert S. Klein demonstrated that the Spanish crown was living at the full extent of its means by the end of the eighteenth century, and its sources of income, other than Indies remittances, were quite inelastic.[147] Any extraordinary expenses arising from war could not be met by any significant increase in tax income. Taxes were fixed, wealthy citizens and corporate groups often enjoyed exemptions, and the crown lacked the power and the will to reform the tax code and break with the structures of the Old Regime. The War of the American Revolution could only be underwritten by issuing *vales reales* from the Banco de San Carlos and by borrowing from foreign bankers. This simple fact led Lerena to undertake austerity measures after the war had ended in order to pay down the crown's deficit by cutting spending (particularly on the military), judiciously issuing *vales reales*, and trying to maximize remittances from the Indies.[148] When war with France broke out in 1793, the crown financed it with 48,110,000 copper *reales* from a Dutch loan, from looting every source of income in the treasury, and through issuing large amounts of *vales reales*.[149] By the end of that conflict, sources of credit were exhausted. When war commenced with Great Britain in 1796, royal credit had collapsed and, following up on its decisive naval victory at Cape Saint Vincent, the British fleet blockaded Cádiz and curtailed the remittance of royal revenues from the Indies.

---

[147] Barbier and Klein, "Revolutionary Wars," pp. 318–21.
[148] Ibid., p. 324.
[149] Ibid.

Even more disturbing than the inelastic nature of the sources of income for the General Treasury was the crown's decision, even during peacetime, to expend so much of its treasure on defending the realm. The costs of the armada were enormous, and efforts by Lerena to contain them proved futile by the 1790s (see Figure 9.1). Moreover, the crown also spent a great deal on land defenses both in Europe and in America. Throughout the Indies, the fortifications, the regular army, and the militia soaked up huge amounts of treasury income. Consequently, although New Spain generated high levels of tax income, a large percentage of that wealth, which might have been remitted to Madrid, remained in America. During the reign of Charles III, the Spanish treasury routinely spent between 50 and 66 percent of the crown's annual income on the army and the navy.[150] When taken in conjunction with the amounts spent servicing the debt (which was accumulated paying for wars) the General Treasury spent nearly 80 percent of the crown's income on military-related expenditures.[151] War and reform were bound together throughout the century, as the fiscal rewards of reform went to pay for the persistent conflicts that disrupted the Spanish Atlantic world.

Yet there were other pressing concerns. The painful war with France delivered shocking evidence that the king's old regime soldiers were no match for the revolutionary armies. After an exhilarating penetration of French territory at the start of the war, Spanish forces were hurled back, deep into Spain, as French forces advanced to the Ebro less than 200 miles from Madrid. The peace settlement cost Spain Santo Domingo and reminded Madrid of the historic axiom that, given the size of its northern neighbor, peace along the Pyrenees was imperative.[152] These realities would soon intimidate Spain into joining the fearful French revolutionaries against the British in two disastrous wars in 1796–1802 and 1804–1808, bringing the period of reform to a sputtering conclusion.

Moreover, the fleet so carefully assembled during the reign of Charles III would suffer a disastrous loss at the hands of the British at Cape Saint Vincent in 1797. More would be destroyed in 1805 in another, even more devastating reverse at Trafalgar. Apart from these defeats, these conflicts demonstrated that the Achilles' heel for Spanish naval power was its dependence upon remissions from America for finance. If the flow of treasure were interrupted for an extended period, the whole edifice might collapse. Closing the Havana

[150] Jacques A. Barbier and Herbert S. Klein, "Las prioridades de un Monarca Ilustrado: El gasto público bajo el Reinado de Carlos III," *Revista de Historia Económica*, III:3 (1985), pp. 481, 493–94.

[151] Ibid.

[152] A handy overview of this conflict can be found in Lynch, *Bourbon Spain*, pp. 388–94. See also, Luis Sierra Nava, "La cesión de Santo Domingo a Francia en la Paz de Bâle: Trueque de intereses comerciales, en las correspondencias de Godoy con sus plenipotenciarios Iriarte e Iranda con una referencia a la devolución de las Vascongadas (1795)," en Escobedo, Zaballa, and Álvarez, *Euskal Herria*, pp. 319–37.

shipyard to new construction only worsened the problem, since all funds for shipbuilding must now cross the ocean to Spain.

In addition, colonial armies, had become Americanized despite royal safeguards to the contrary, and the militia, which grew in relative importance as Spain's continental commitments denied it the ability to reinforce the colonial garrisons, was a force that Americans had financed and populated from the start. Certainly, the return to the historic formula of consultation and compromise in the political process seemed to have healed the wounds opened by the intemperate policies of the Gálvez years, but even so, deep concern arose over the appearance of French revolutionary propaganda during 1795 in Mexico City, Santa Fe, Caracas, Quito, Cuzco, and elsewhere.[153] Ultimately, Americans, financing and populating the armed forces, controlled their own destinies.

CONCLUSION

War and reform coexisted throughout the Spanish Atlantic during the eighteenth century, particularly during the reigns of Charles III and Charles IV. War or the fear of war spurred regalist reformers in Spain to devise new ways to administer and gain tax revenues throughout the Spanish Atlantic world. Moreover, wars often interrupted reform efforts and forced the king's ministers to deal with pressing military concerns. In addition, reformers justified innovations because of the exigencies of war or the looming threat of armed conflict. Finally, the dangers posed by Spain's rivals, particularly Great Britain, convinced both kings that high levels of spending on the army and navy were essential to maintaining the security of the empire, which consumed the resources gained by political, economic, social, and financial innovation in the Indies. With the outbreak of war with Britain in 1796, the enemy navy disrupted all commerce within the Spanish Atlantic world, leading the crown to abandon its century-long effort to reform the empire as the fiscal exigencies of war outweighed all other policy concerns. Naval defeats first at Cape St. Vincent and later at Trafalgar severely weakened the Spanish navy, which Charles III had so assiduously assembled during his long reign. In the end, war consumed and then destroyed the fruits of reform.

As the political struggles in late eighteenth-century Spanish Atlantic world indicate, the Bourbon Reforms emerged from a long and complex political process in which interest groups with very different visions about the future of the empire and very diverse political agendas contested for power. The Spanish Enlightenment represented a fusion of ideas from Europe along with a variety of political currents from the Indies, which often identified the political, social, and economic ills of the colonial order. Reformist tracts

---

[153] The *Consejo de Estado* anguished over these incidents. See Barbier, "The Culmination," p. 67.

written by peninsular intellectuals (such as the *proyectistas*), colonial clergymen, Amerindian ethnic leaders, creole elites, and colonial bureaucrats all
entered into the public debate about the reform and renovation of the
empire.[154] Policy makers in Madrid drew on all this information to fashion
imperial reforms, but the process always involved considerable give and
take.[155] Reform in the Indies also emerged from highly contentious political
arenas, which established the context for political, social, economic, and
cultural changes. It is no small wonder that the Bourbon Reforms appear a
diverse and even contradictory set of policies that sometimes differed markedly in various regions of the Indies. The reforms emerged from an intensely
political process, which represented different ideas and political agendas in
various areas of the complex and diverse Spanish Atlantic world.

[154] See Kenneth J. Andrien, "The *Noticias secretas de América* and the Construction of a
Governing Ideology for the Spanish American Empire," *Colonial Latin American Review*,
7:2 (1998), pp. 175–92.
[155] For a summary of the early political ideas about reforming the empire by José de Gálvez,
see Luis Navarro García, *La política Americana de José de Gálvez* (Málaga: Editorial
Algazara, 1998).

Conclusion: War and Reform in the Spanish Atlantic World

War and reform evolved into central, interconnected themes of the Spanish Atlantic world during the eighteenth century. War influenced the direction and outcome of Bourbon reforms, and policy innovations periodically sparked military conflicts with Spain's rivals. Spain's competition with France, the Netherlands, and Great Britain, more specifically, led to frequent hostilities, sometimes over European affairs and other times over colonial rivalries. The Spanish crown viewed commerce with the Indies as a closed metropolitan monopoly, guaranteed by the papal donation of 1493. As a result, the Spanish claimed complete sovereignty over the lands in the Indies and the surrounding sea lanes, and they wanted to shut out all foreign intruders.[1] For their part, other European powers, particularly the British, had long sought direct access to Spanish American markets, and they viewed Spain's monopolistic policy as an unfair restriction of trade. The recurrent outbreaks of war that resulted from disputes over access to Spain's colonial markets in the Atlantic, often complicated by conflicting dynastic ambitions in Europe, sometimes derailed reform and interrupted policy designs in its empire, and they frequently led to the abandonment or discrediting of reformist objectives. On other occasions, however, war could impel reform, as Bourbon ministers enacted policies to prepare Spain for looming conflicts with her enemies. From the end of the War of the Spanish Succession in 1713, reformers repeatedly promoted a series of innovations to modernize the Spanish Atlantic world, at least until the outbreak of war with Great Britain in 1796. In that conflict, the British navy cut the sea lanes between Spain and America, leading to a precipitous decline in tax remittances and trade from the Indies and ultimately to the slow strangulation of the eighteenth-century reforming impulse.

---

[1] Elizabeth Mancke, "Negotiating an Empire: Britain and its Overseas Possessions," in Christine Daniels and Michael V. Kennedy, eds., *Negotiated Empires: Centers and Peripheries in the Americas, 1500–1820* (New York and London: Routledge, 2002), pp. 235–38.

The Bourbon reform process can best be understood by focusing on the interplay between events in Europe and in the Indies, which together shaped efforts to renovate the Spanish Atlantic world. The Indies and Spain were joined by a common legal system, ideology of empire, and bureaucratic ties, and they also faced similar challenges of dynastic ambition, warfare, commercial policy, and the flow of ideas and people across the Atlantic Ocean. At the same time, reformers and entrenched interest groups opposed to change fought continuously to promote or to impede the reform process between 1713 and 1796. Such debates over the course of royal policy could only be resolved in unpredictable political arenas on both sides of the Atlantic, and such political contestation – interrupted by periodic outbreaks of warfare with European rivals – shaped the long-term fate of the Bourbon reforms. Political disputes also frequently led to markedly different policy outcomes in different provinces of the American empire. Efforts to reform the sales tax and impose a royal monopoly on cane liquor (aguardiente), for example, led to popular insurrections in Quito and Colombia, while the policies provoked little controversy in Peru and most of New Spain. Political conflicts also led to untidy results, as vested interest groups fought to control and shape royal polices for their own ends, leading to disputes, compromises, and in some cases, even violence. All played a role in defining the nature and evolution of reform over the eighteenth-century empire. Events in Spain and the Indies were thus inextricably joined to each other and to the political, social, and economic currents present throughout the rest of the Atlantic world.

THE EARLY BOURBON REFORMS, 1715–1754

At the end of the War of the Spanish Succession, the ministers of King Philip V recognized the pressing the need to reform and to revitalize the Spanish Atlantic world. Commerce with the Indies was a key to the recovery of Spain, but major problems faced reformers. Rampant contraband flourished during the succession war when Spain could not supply its overseas possessions. In this period, French traders captured colonial markets in the Pacific, while French, British, and Dutch smugglers plied Spanish markets in the Caribbean and the South Atlantic. Moreover, the Utrecht settlement allowed the British South Sea Company to gain the slave *asiento* to Spanish America and to send one annual ship of 500 tons to participate in the trade fairs (alongside Spanish ships) in New Spain and South America, while it bound Spain to conserve its historic commercial system and to uphold its standing treaty obligations. British, French, Dutch, and Hanseatic merchant houses also supplied manufactured goods to their Spanish allies in the merchant guild of Seville and later Cádiz, who in turn transshipped the merchandise to the Indies through the legal trading system. Indeed, these Spanish guild members were sometimes called *prestanombres* (literally meaning they lent out their names) and many served as little more than front men reshipping foreign merchandise to markets in the Americas. Such foreign penetration of the legal trading system undermined the hope of using the transatlantic trade to revive the Spanish economy, as profits from American commerce primarily enriched Madrid's foreign competitors.

Foreigners gained their advantageous position because of the weakness of Spanish manufacturing, but also because of special treaty privileges granted during the seventeenth century to the British, French, Dutch, and Germans. The British, for example, received broad immunities from customs inspections of their ships anchoring in Spanish ports and of merchandise in warehouses in Spain. These protections were upheld by a special judge nominated by the British and technically confirmed by the Madrid government, who decided all cases involving British merchants on Spanish soil. A resident British consul in Cádiz, the only port licensed to trade with America between 1717 and 1765, complemented the powers of this special judge, which effectively gave British subjects extraterritoriality, allowing them exemptions from Spanish justice, as well as low tariff rates on their imports into Spain. Along with the concessions granted to London under the Utrecht peace accords, these treaty privileges allowed British goods to gain indirect access to rich markets in the Spanish Indies. The Dutch, French, and Germans enjoyed similar concessions. These special, damaging privileges allowed foreign commercial houses to supply the majority of the goods traded through the legal commercial system in America. Along with profits reaped in contraband commerce with the Indies, foreign powers thus gained the lion's share of the commercial wealth drawn from Spain's trade with its overseas empire.

In order to study attempts at reforming the Spanish Atlantic world, this book has examined a series of case studies that shaped the progress of royal policy in different areas of Spain and the Indies during the eighteenth century. Each was a turning point for the colonial world, and the success or failure of Bourbon initiatives resulted from just such moments of political struggle. These case studies also identify a new chronology, demonstrating that the early Bourbon reforms advanced in two distinct but interlocked phases, 1715–1736 and 1737–1754, with each preparing the way for the next.

Reform began with the initiatives of Cardinal Julio Alberoni, the influential Italian who guided policy decisions for the first Bourbon monarchs, Phillip V and his second wife, Elizabeth Farnese, from 1714. Alberoni made a major effort to assert control over Spain's principal seaports and to expunge foreign interests from Spanish commerce, particularly trade with the Indies. His chief reforms specifically dealing with America involved the transfer of the *Casa de la Contratación* and the *Consulado* from Seville to Cádiz in 1717, the foundation of the Viceroyalty of New Granada and the establishment of the tobacco monopoly in Cuba that same year, and the reorganization of strategic Havana's military in 1719. The reforming impulse ended abruptly, however, with Spain's humiliating defeat in the War of the Quadruple Alliance, which discredited Alberoni, leading to his fall and exile.

After a short respite following the downfall of Alberoni, reform began anew under the guidance of Alberoni's protégé, José Patiño, King Philip's chief minister between 1726 and 1736. Patiño brought new strength to the ministry governing the Indies, resuscitated the Alberoni agenda, rebuilt the fleet lost at the Battle of Cape Passaro during the War of the Quadruple Alliance, and sought to curtail the foreign contrabandists operating in the Indies by funding an enlarged coast guard, particularly in the Caribbean. He also licensed privateers to harass the shipping of Spain's rivals. The principal complication faced by reformers during this first reform period was the European dynastic designs of King Philip and his wife, who sought Italian kingdoms for their children, leading to European conflicts that distracted Madrid from its task of reorganizing the relations between Spain and its overseas possessions.

The second phase emerged in the late 1730s when a new generation of innovators guided royal policy, led first by José de la Quintana and José de Campillo and later by the Marqués de la Ensenada, whom José de Carvajal y Lancaster joined during the time of King Ferdinand VI. Under their leadership, the crown ended the systematic sale of appointments to colonial offices, curtailed the autonomy of the *Consulado* of Cádiz, and opened the door to the widespread use of register ships during War of Jenkins' Ear and afterwards. Following that conflict, the Treaty of Madrid revoked the commercial concessions that Britain's South Sea Company had enjoyed since Utrecht, and it thus finally allowed Spain to modernize its colonial commercial system, although internally it still faced the objections of vested interests in the *Consulado* and its conservative allies among the political class in Spain.

At the same time, Ensenada and his entourage advanced major administrative and military initiatives, and they also promoted an ambitious clerical reform – the removal of the regular clergy from their lucrative indigenous parishes between 1749 and 1753. This attack on the wealth and power of the regular orders in the Indies marked the rising tide of regalism over the more decentralized, patrimonial monarchy of the Spanish Habsburgs. Indeed, Ensenada even nurtured plans to resuscitate José de Campillo's vision for free trade within the empire. This third period of reform ended before Ensenada could enact commercial reform, when a palace coup, engineered by his opponents and their powerful foreign allies, toppled the great minister in 1754. The fall of this powerful advocate of change dulled the reformist impulse during the remaining years of the rule of Ferdinand VI.

Previous historians have devoted scant attention to the first two periods of reform and instead have largely focused on the reign of Charles III as the only significant era of change in the century. The contributions of Alberoni, Patiño, and even Ensenada have been downplayed or even ignored by most scholars. One influential treatment of the Bourbon period, for example, characterized Alberoni as a "mere pygmy" and argued that Patiño was "not an original thinker or even a reformer. He was a conservative."[2] Although historians may differ in their assessment of these ministers, a principal reason for ignoring or minimizing the early Bourbon reforms has been the relative lack of documentation in the Spanish archives for the reign of Philip V, leading most scholars to conclude that little innovation actually occurred at that time. Much of the Spanish documentation from this period burned in the fire at Madrid's Royal Palace in 1734. The present study has relied heavily on French diplomatic documentation to reconstruct the early reforms, the controversies that accompanied them, and the diverse political outcomes they produced. Indeed, it has been shown here that Philip V's ministers addressed a full range of problems, including commercial, administrative, military, fiscal, and ecclesiastical concerns, although on a more limited basis than those later addressed under Charles III. Clearly, the pressing issues that Alberoni, Patiño, and Ensenada confronted did much to prepare the way and afford greater political latitude for the crown ministers that followed them.

CHARLES III AND THE PINNACLE OF REFORM

Reform regained momentum during the reign of Ferdinand's successor, King Charles III, particularly after the loss of Havana to a British expeditionary force during the Seven Years' War. The fall of this major Caribbean stronghold impelled Charles and his advisors in Madrid to shore up defenses in the Indies, and it opened the door to the resumption of Ensenada's reformist agenda. The expenses incurred with higher military outlays prompted the crown to tighten administrative controls and raise taxes throughout the empire. It also required even more systematic efforts to curtail contraband and the penetration of foreign merchants into the legal trade, and to liberalize commercial policy. Moreover, Charles continued Madrid's attack on the influence of the religious orders when he expelled the wealthy and powerful Society of Jesus from Spain and the empire in 1767, giving the crown control of the orders' lucrative estate complexes in the Indies. Following the removal of the religious orders from their indigenous parishes under Ensenada, the expulsion of the Jesuits demonstrated the triumph of regalism over entrenched vested interests, such as those of the Roman Catholic Church. In short, the crown advanced policies aimed at enhancing the power of the centralizing Bourbon state and its capacity to wage war effectively.

---

[2] John Lynch, *Bourbon Spain, 1700–1808* (Oxford, Basil Blackwell, 1989), pp. 76, 91; Most of the early literature on the Bourbon reforms emphasizes the reign of Charles III as the only significant era of change; one exception is John R. Fisher, *Bourbon Peru, 1750–1824* (Liverpool: University of Liverpool Press, 2003). Even the recent synthesis by J. H. Elliott, follows the more traditional chronology of reform beginning in responses to losses in the Seven Years' War. See Elliott, *Empires of the Atlantic World: Britain and Spain in America, 1492–1830* (New Haven: Yale University Press, 2006), pp. 302–25.

Charles III and his ministers began this third and most ambitious phase of the reform process by sending out royal *visitadores* first to Cuba and New Spain and, later, on the eve of his intervention in the War of the American Revolution, to the other jurisdictions of the Indies to garner information and to launch administrative, fiscal, military, and commercial reforms. The crown had already ended the sale of appointments to high-ranking colonial offices during the reign of Ferdinand. Madrid then began replacing creole office-holders with younger, better-trained, peninsular-born bureaucrats theoretically more loyal to the crown, and this process accelerated considerably under Charles. Crown officials at court also created new, high-powered administrative units in formerly peripheral regions of South America, which had evolved over time into potentially important possessions economically and militarily but remained dominated by contraband trade. Madrid had already reestablished the Viceroyalty of New Granada in northern South America in 1739. In 1776, the government of Charles III created the Viceroyalty of the Río de la Plata in South America's southern cone, and one year later it established the Captaincy General of Caracas. And to New Spain and most of South America, the crown dispatched intendants, who were responsible for provincial administration, including finance, justice, and defense. Many of these officials were military men, but in all cases they served as a link between local authority in the provinces and the high courts or audiencias in the major regional capitals. As part of this intendancy reform, the crown abolished the controversial position of *corregidor de indios*, replacing these magistrates with subdelegates who reported directly to the intendant. Overall, Charles's initiatives enlarged the colonial bureaucracy, which decreased the importation of contraband goods and the illicit outflow of silver through the Caribbean and South Atlantic.

To gain greater control over commerce, the crown began liberalizing trade policies, allowing the Caribbean islands to trade freely with most Spanish ports in 1765. Over the century, a combination of the treaty obligations imposed at Utrecht, the enormous power of the *Consulado* of Cádiz, and the enemies of deregulation at court had impeded the modernization of the colonial commercial system, but by 1778 new circumstances, including the successes recorded in the Caribbean since 1765 and the urgency imposed by looming international conflict opened the door to the extension of imperial free trade to the entire empire, excepting only Mexico and Venezuela. By 1789, even these provinces were brought into the liberalized system.

The decision to exclude New Spain from *comercio libre* in 1778 undoubtedly stemmed partly from the opposition of the *Consulados* of Mexico City and Cádiz, but the crown's decision to strengthen the imperial peripheries played a more important role. Given that contraband commerce could be minimized by funneling Mexico's trade through Veracruz, the crown was willing to sacrifice taxes on the commercial upsurge that would have ensued if its richest colony had been incorporated fully into the system of free trade a decade earlier. Madrid's priority was to protect and promote economic development on the empire's frontiers by curtailing contraband and stimulating trade between the ports of Spain and the emerging peripheries in the Indies such as New Granada and the Río de la Plata. Having New Spain's vibrant mining and tropical exports flood Spanish markets risked overwhelming the still fragile economies of its Caribbean and South Atlantic possessions. Consequently, Mexico waited eleven more years until new realities would permit Charles IV to bring it into the system of imperial free trade.

The defeat at Havana in 1762 allowed Charles to follow his own militaristic instincts by elevating defense imperatives to the top of his reformist agenda for America. The king used the momentary loss of this strategic Caribbean stronghold as justification to push aside political enemies, arguing that Spanish security superseded all other concerns. Madrid enhanced local defenses by strengthening the regular army and by forming a disciplined militia comprised largely of loyal colonial subjects in strategic localities. At the same time, it expanded the fleet aggressively. In a further effort to limit the power of the religious orders, the crown used the regular army and the militias to patrol the imperial frontiers, supplanting the traditional role of the missions in securing contested peripheral areas and converting the *indios bárbaros*. Forts manned by soldiers, rather than the missions of the regular clergy, served as the crown's primary representative among the indigenous peoples, and in 1776 it elevated the northern Mexican frontier to a commandancy general. To fund these costly undertakings, royal officials raised new taxes, collected existing levies more effectively, and created royal monopolies for the sale and distribution of coveted commodities such as tobacco and aguardiente. These fiscal policies led to a dramatic increase in royal revenues from colonial treasuries, particularly in New Spain. It was a time of sweeping imperial innovations, which only escalated after Spain's triumph in the War of the American Revolution, as Charles's military ambitions grew.

Successive Bourbon monarchs and their regalist ministers willingly subordinated commercial imperatives and the economic development of Spain itself to colonial military priorities and to the armada, something especially true under Charles III. Charles never forgot his humiliation during the War of the Austrian Succession, when a threatened British naval bombardment of Naples forced the young king of the Two Sicilies to withdraw his forces supporting the Spanish army fighting to advance his parents' dynastic ambitions in northern Italy, and his defeat at Havana only deepened his preoccupation. Consequently, throughout his reign in Spain, Charles allowed preparations for war to trump all other priorities, and the bulk of the Indies revenues, enhanced abundantly by a century of reform, went into expanding the armed forces, particularly the navy. Given the weakness of the Spanish merchant marine, however, the armada always lacked sufficient numbers of experienced, well-trained sailors to man the newly constructed vessels properly. Expanding commerce by including New Spain in *comercio libre* in 1778 might have promoted such an expanded merchant marine, but strategic priorities came first. Charles was focused narrowly on preparing for war, even holding out hopes of launching a joint invasion of the British Isles with French allies until the very end of his reign. Moreover, Charles really had no long-term plans for the modernization of Spain and her economy; the king dreamed single-mindedly of restoring Spanish military greatness. Ironically, much of the navy that the king had nurtured so carefully went down to the bottom of the sea in battles against the British at Cape St. Vincent (1797) and Trafalgar (1805), and during the French occupation (1808–1814).

Reform survived the death of Charles III in 1788, continuing aggressively during the early years of his son, Charles IV, particularly in the area of commerce. Yet funding for Spain's army and navy depended far too much on reliable remittances of American revenues. War with Great Britain in 1796 led to a blockade that interrupted and then effectively cut regular commercial ties between Spain and the Indies. Thereafter, the financially strapped Spanish crown promulgated policies needed to fund this bitter and ultimately unsuccessful conflict, which consumed the lion's share of the New World revenues enhanced over a century of reform, but they were not enough to stave off defeat in the early nineteenth century.

FINAL REFLECTIONS

The century-long process of reform in the Spanish Atlantic world involved a major expansion of royal power at the expense of vested interest groups, both domestic and foreign. Before the reform period, Spain and its overseas empire had formed a "composite monarchy," comprised of distinct provinces or kingdoms, united only by a common monarch.[3] The Hapsburgs had recognized a broad array of local privileges (*fueros*) granted to towns, provinces, and the principalities and kingdoms in their Iberian possessions, and they made little effort to centralize their political powers. In addition, the crown gave concessions to high-ranking corporate groups, such as the nobility, the crusading orders, merchant guilds (*consulados*), sheep growers (*mesta*), and the church to ensure political stability within the kingdoms of Spain. Whenever the Hapsburg kings deviated from this tradition of composite monarchy, political instability and even armed insurrections erupted. The revolt of the Catalans (and later the Portuguese) in 1640, for example, was sparked by the Union of Arms, a policy of the Count Duke of Olivares to have all the provinces of the Spanish empire contribute to supporting a common army. This failed attempt at fiscal and political centralization nearly ended the union of the crowns established by Ferdinand and Isabel in the fifteenth

[3] J. H. Elliott, "A Europe of Composite Monarchies," *Past & Present*, 42 (February 1969), p. 51.

century. The political, commercial, and religious reforms of the eighteenth
century, however, sought to replace this idea of composite monarchy by
centralizing power in a renewed Bourbon state, reflecting the rise of regalism
over the decentralized, patrimonial rule of the Habsburgs.

Reform also provoked conflict with Spain's European rivals. As Spanish
reformers tried to limit foreign influence in Spanish ports, use an expanded
coast guard and privateers to control contraband commerce, and expand the
bureaucracy in the New World to limit foreign penetration of markets in the
Indies, war often ensued. Britain and France joined forces against Spain
(along with Savoy and Austria) in the War of the Quadruple Alliance
(1718–1720). During the War of Jenkins' Ear (1739–1748), the British
invaded the Caribbean, capturing Portobelo and attacking Cartagena de
Indias. A decade later France and Spain battled Britain in the Seven Years'
War (1756–1763). All of these conflicts resulted in large measure from efforts
by Spain's rivals to expand their access to commercial markets in the Spanish
Atlantic world, lured by American resources, particularly silver. Reformers in
Spain either found their efforts thwarted by failures in war, such as the
disastrous defeats in the War of the Quadruple Alliance, or they used
the threat of war to push through an ambitious array of innovations, as the
ministers of Charles III did following the loss of Havana in 1762 and, later, in
anticipation of Madrid's intervention in the War of the American
Revolution. In short, war was a constant theme in the eighteenth-century
Atlantic world, and it was intimately linked with efforts to reform and
renovate the Spanish empire.

As the political struggles over these changes indicate, enlightened reform
emerged from a long, complicated political process in which the crown,
colonial interest groups, and the church contested for power, while concurrently foreign rivals attempted to gain greater access to the rich markets of
Spanish America. The many ebbs and flows of royal policy made the whole
process of imperial reorganization appear a stumbling and even contradictory
hodgepodge of policies. While historians will search in vain for a "master
plan" for the Bourbon reforms, the political, social, economic, and religious
innovations that evolved over the course of the century were anything but a
mere hodgepodge of unrelated programs. Bourbon ministers merged enlightened ideas from Europe with a variety of discourses on reform from the Indies
about local political, social, and economic ills to fashion pragmatic imperial
reforms. The crown's ministers used the newest ideas and approaches available to them, but the process always involved considerable compromise.
Politics in the Spanish Atlantic world was an inherently disorderly process,
with a host of different groups fighting to shape, impede, or even destroy
efforts to modernize. Over time the process of reform shifted, as crown
ministers resolved or at least improved some difficult problems and turned
to new pressing concerns. Once Patiño's coast guards regained some measure
of control over sea lanes in the Caribbean, for example, Ensenada could begin

using individual register ships to replace the *Galeones* serving South America. The success of these reforms allowed policy makers under Charles III to realize the dream advanced by José de Campillo in his *Nuevo sistema económico para América* through implementing free trade within the empire between 1765 and 1789. In short, Enlightened reform emerged piecemeal from highly contested changing political environments throughout Spain's Atlantic empire over the course of the eighteenth century, which gave the reform process its apparently halting and even muddled appearance.

Timeline for the Spanish Atlantic World in the Eighteenth Century

I. ALBERONI, PATIÑO, AND THE BEGINNINGS OF ATLANTIC REFORM, 1713–1736

1713   The Peace of Utrecht ends the War of Spanish Succession
1714   Philip loses his first wife, Marie Louise of Savoy, to tuberculosis
1714   Ministry of the Indies created under Bernardo Tinajero

The Leadership of Abad (later Cardinal) Julio Alberoni, 1715–1719

1714	(December 23) The fateful meeting of the new queen, Elizabeth Farnese, and Anne Marie de la Trémoille-Noir, Princess Ursins at Jadraque. Ursins leaves for France with her entourage of French advisors to the king
1715	Alberoni suppresses the Ministry of Marine and the Indies, dismissing pro-French minister Bernardo Tinajero
1716	Alberoni begins harassing foreign merchants to regain control over Spain's ports
1716	A secret Triple Alliance is formed, consisting of France, England, and the Netherlands against Spain
1717	(January 28) Appointment of José Patiño as marine intendant and President of the *Casa de la Contratación*
1717	(April 11) Installation of the tobacco monopoly in Cuba
1717	(May 8) Transfer of the *Consulado* from Seville to Cádiz
1717	(May 27) Establishment of the Viceroyalty of New Granada
1717	(August 11) Battle of Cape Passaro near Sicily, where Admiral Bing defeats Spanish fleet
1717	(August 21) *veguero* rebellion begins in Cuba, opposing the tobacco monopoly
1718–1720	War of the Quadruple Alliance
1719	Reorganization of Havana's fixed garrison into a modern battalion

1719   (December 5) Alberoni leaves Madrid and the court for exile in
            Italy followed upon by the reemergence of José de Grimaldo

Conservative Period, 1720–1726

1720   (April 5) Promulgation of the Project of 1720 and the assessment of
       export duties by volume (the *palmeo*)
1720   (May 31) Establishment of the royal mail system under the control of
       the *Consulado* of Cádiz
1721   Reestablishment of the Ministry of Marine and the Indies
1723   Viceroyalty of New Granada suppressed
1724   King Philip V abdicates in favor of his son Louis, who dies after an
       eight-month reign, leading to Philip's return to the throne
1724   Suppression of the tobacco monopoly in Cuba
1725   Duke of Riperdá negotiates Treaty of Vienna with Austria
1726   (May) Riperdá falls from power followed by the dismissal of
       Grimaldo in September

The Ministry of José Patiño, 1726–1736

1726   Patiño emerges as secretary for the Office of Marine and the
            Indies and Finance
1727   Patiño restores the tobacco monopoly in Cuba
1728   *Real Compañia Guipuzcxoana de Caracas* established,
            breaking the *Consulado*'s monopoly over trade with the Indies
1729–1733   The court resides in Seville
1729   (September 23) Patiño's government grants the *Consulado* the
            right to define its own membership
1729   (November 9) Treaty of Seville temporarily normalizes
            Madrid's relations with London and Versailles
1732   Patiño convinces the *Consulado* to impose a 4 percent tax to
            finance a coast guard in the Caribbean
1733   (November 7) First Family Compact signed
1734   Patiño initiates the process of restoring the Viceroyalty of New
            Granada, which is completed on February 25, 1739
1736   (November 3) Death of Patiño

II. THE SECOND WAVE OF REFORM, 1736–1763

1737–1743   Crown conflicts with *Consulado* of Cádiz over loans,
            contraband, and guild leadership and membership
1739   Outbreak of the War of Jenkins's Ear, which then merged with
            European dynastic conflicts to become the War of the Austrian
            Succession

1740	End of the *Galeones* with new reliance on register ships to supply South America
1740	Establishment of the Royal Havana Company
1741	Unsuccessful siege of Cartagena by the British
1741	Caracas Company awarded monopoly trading rights
1741	(October 11) José de Campillo y Cossío becomes Minister for Marine and the Indies
1742	Outbreak of Juan Santos Atahualpa rebellion in eastern slopes of the Andes
1743	*Nuevo sistema de gobierno económico para la América* by Campillo y Cossío circulates in governing circles
1743	(April 12) Death of Campillo y Cossío
1743	Marqués de la Ensenada appointed to Ministries of War, Finance, and Marine and the Indies
1743	(October 25) Second Family Compact signed
1746	Death of King Philip V and accession of Ferdinand VI
1746	José de Carvajal y Lancaster assumes Ministry of State
1746	Lima earthquake and devastation of the port of Callao
1749	Secularization of the indigenous parishes in the archdioceses of Lima, Mexico City, and Santa Fe de Bogotá
1749–1751	León's rebellion in Venezuela
1750	Crown ends the sale of bureaucratic appointments in the Indies
1750	(October 5) Treaty of Madrid formally ends *asiento* of South Sea Company to supply slaves and the right to participate in the trade fairs at Veracruz and Portobelo
1753	Secularization of all indigenous parishes of the Indies
1754	Death of Carvajal and downfall of Ensenada
1754	Julián de Arriaga named Minister of Marine and the Indies
1754	Reestablishment of the *Flota* to New Spain, ending plans to liberalize trade
1759	Death of Ferdinand VI and the temporary regency of Elizabeth Farnese

III. PINNACLE OF THE BOURBON REFORMS, 1763–1796

1759	(November) Charles III arrives in Madrid from Naples
1761	(August 15) Third Family Compact signed
1762	Spain enters the Seven Years' War and loses Havana
1763	Treaty of Paris and return of Havana to Spain at the price of Florida
1763–64	Creation of disciplined militia units in Cuba with the *fuero militar*
1764	Establishment of an intendancy in Cuba
1765	(August 24) Creation of a modernized royal mail system

1765	(October 16) Regulation of free trade opens Havana, Santo Domingo, Puerto Rico, Margarita, and Trinidad to nine ports in Spain
1765–1766	(May 22 to September 1) Quito Insurrection against direct royal administration of the *alcabala* and the aguardiente monopoly
1765–71	Gálvez *visita* to New Spain
1766	(March 23) Esquilache riots begin in Madrid
1766	Death of Elizabeth Farnese
1767	(February 27) Expulsion of the Jesuits
1776	Death of Julián de Arriaga
1776	José de Gálvez named Minister of the Indies and Governor of the Council of the Indies
1776	Creation of the Viceroyalty of the Río de la Plata
1777	Conde de Floridablanca named Minister of State
1777	Caracas elevated to a captaincy general
1777	*Visitas* to Peru, New Granada, Chile, and Quito
1778	(October 12) Regulation of imperial free trade for all but Caracas and New Spain
1779	Spain enters the War of the American Revolution
1781	Andean rebellions and Comunero revolt in New Granada
1782	Intendancy system extended to Río de la Plata
1782	Banco de San Carlos established
1783	Ordinances issued for Mexico's Real Cuerpo de Minería
1783	(September 3) Treaty of Versailles ends the War of the American Revolution
1784	Intendancy system introduced in Peru
1786	Intendancy system extended to New Spain, Guatemala, and Chile
1787	Death of José de Gálvez
1787	Creation of the Junta Suprema de Estado
1788	Death of King Charles III and the succession of his son as Charles IV
1789	New Spain and Venezuela drawn into the system of imperial free trade, followed by the liberalization of the slave trade
1792	(February 28) Fall of Floridablanca
1792	Installation of the Consejo Supremo de Estado
1793–95	Eight additional *Consulados* erected in America
1793–95	War with revolutionary France
1796	War with Great Britain

Bibliography

Archives

Archives des Affaires Etrangéres, Paris
    Correspondance Politique Espagne
    Memoirs et documents i Fonds Divers Espagne
    Traites
Archives Nacionales de France
    Correspondance Consulaire
Archivo de San Francisco de Lima
    Registro II
Archivo General de Indias, Seville
    Buenos Aires
    Caracas
    Consulados
    Correos
    Guadalajara
    Indiferente General
    Lima
    Mexico
    Panamá
    Papeles de Cuba
    Quito
    Santa Fe
    Santo Domingo
    Ultramar
Archivo General de la Marina Alvaro Bazán
Archivo General de Simancas
    Guerra Moderna
    Hacienda
    Marina
Archivo Histórico Nacional de Colombia, Bogotá
    Virreyes
Archivo Histórico Nacional, Madrid
    Estado
Biblioteca del Palacio, Madrid
    Miscelánea Ayala

Printed Materials

http://www.euskalnet.net/laviana/gen_hispanas/lerena.htm

Acosta Rodríguez, Antonio, Adolfo González Rodríguez, and Enriqueta Vila Vilar, eds. *La casa de la contratación y la navegación entre España y Las Indias*. Seville: Universidad de Sevilla, 2003.

Adelman, Jeremy. *Sovereignty and Revolution in the Iberian Atlantic*. Princeton: Princeton University Press, 2006.

Aiton, Arthur S. "The Asiento Treaty as Reflected in the Papers of Lord Shelburne." *The Hispanic American Historical Review* 8, no. 2 (May 1928): 167–77.

"The Diplomacy of the Louisiana Cession." *The American Historical Review* 36, no. 4 (July 1931): 701–20.

"Spanish Colonial Reorganization under the Family Compact." *Hispanic American Historical Review* 12, no. 3 (August 1932): 269–80.

Albi, Julio. *La defensa de Las Indias (1764–1799)*. Madrid Institución de Cooperación Ibero Americano, 1987.

Albi de la Cuseta, Julio, Leopoldo Stampa Piñero, and Juan Silvela y Miláns de Bosch, *La caballería española: Un eco de clarines*. Madrid: Tabapress, 1992.

Alden, Dauril. *Royal Government in Colonial Brazil*. Berkeley: University of California Press, 1968.

Altman, Ida. *Emigrants and Society: Extremadura and America in the Sixteenth Century*. Berkeley and Los Angeles: University of California Press, 1989.

Transatlantic Ties in the Spanish Empire: Brihuega Spain and Puebla Mexico, 1560–1620. Stanford, CA: Stanford University Press, 2000.

Álvarez de Morales, Antonio. "Los proyectos de reforma del ejército del conde de Aranda." In *Estudios sobre ejército, política y derecho en España (Siglos XII-XX)*, 151–160, edited by Javier Alvarado Planas and Regina María Pérez Marcos. Madrid: Ediciones Polifema, 1996.

Alvarez de Toledo, Cayetana. *Politics and Reform in Spain and Viceregal Mexico: The Life and Thought of Juan de Palafox, 1600–1659*. Oxford: Clarendon Press, 2004.

Amat y Junient, Manuel de. *Memoria de gobierno*. Edited by Vicente Rodríguez Casado and Florentino Pérez Embid. Seville: Escuela de Estudios Hispano-Americanos, 1947.

Amich, José. *Historia de las misiones del Convento de Santa Rosa de Ocopa*. Iquitos: Editorial Universo, S. A., 1988.

Andrien, Kenneth J. "The Coming of Enlightened Reform in Bourbon Peru: Secularization of the Doctrinas de Indios, 1746–1773," In *Enlightenment, Governance, and Reform in Spain and Its Empire, 1759–1808*, edited by Gabriel B. Paquette, 183–202. Basingstoke: Palgrave-MacMillan, 2008.

Crisis and Decline: The Viceroyalty of Peru in the Seventeenth Century. Albuquerque: University of New Mexico Press, 1985.

"Economic Crisis, Taxes, and the Quito Insurrection of 1765." *Past and Present* 129 (November 1990): 104–31.

The Kingdom of Quito, 1690–1830: The State and Regional Development. Cambridge: Cambridge University Press, 1995.

"Legal and Administrative Texts," in Joanne Pillsbury ed., *Guide to Documentary Sources for Andean Studies, 1530–1900*, 107–119. Norman: University of Oklahoma Press, 2008.

"The Noticias Secretas de América and the Construction of a Governing Ideology for the Empire." *Colonial Latin American Review* 7, no. 2 (December 1998): 175–92.

"The Politics of Reform in Spain's Atlantic Empire During the Late Bourbon Period: The Visita of José García de Leon Y Pizarro in Quito." *Journal of Latin American Studies* 41, no. 4 (November 2009): 637–62.

"The Sale of Fiscal Offices and the Decline of Royal Authority in the Viceroyalty of Peru, 1633–1700," *HAHR* 62(February 1982): 49–71.

Arboleda, Gustavo. *Historia de Cali desde los orígenes de la ciudad hasta la expiración del período colonial.* 2 vols. Cali: Biblioteca de la Universidad del Valle 1956.

Archer, Christon I. *The Army in Bourbon Mexico, 1760–1810.* Albuquerque: University of New Mexico Press, 1977.

"Charles III and Defense Policy for New Spain, 1759–1788." In *Paesi Mediterranei E America Latina*, 158–201, edited by Gaetano Massa. Rome: Centro di Studi Americanistici America in Italia, 1982.

Arcila Farías, Eduardo. *El Real Consulado de Caracas.* Caracas: Instituto de Estudios Hispanoamericanos, 1957.

Armillas Vicente, José Antonio. "El nacimiento de una gran nación. Contribución española a la independencia de los Estados Unidos de América del Norte." In *Cuadernos de investigación del Colegio Universitario de Logroño*, 91–98. Logroño: Colegio Universitario de la Rioja, 1977.

"La política exterior de los primeros Borbones." In *Historia general de España y América: La España de las reformas hasta el final del reinado de Carlos IV*, edited by Carlos E. Corona Baratech and José Antonio Armillas Vicente, 267–98. Madrid: Ediciones Rialp, 1984.

Armitage, David. "Three Concepts of Atlantic History." In *The British Atlantic World, 1500–1800*, edited by David Armitage and Michael J. Braddick, 11–27. Basingstoke: Palgrave-MacMillan, 2002.

Armona y Murga, José Antonio de. *Noticias privadas de casa, útiles para mis hijos: Recuerdos históricos de mi carrera ministerial en España y América.* Madrid: Private Manuscript, 1787.

Bailyn, Bernard. *Atlantic History: Concepts and Contours.* Cambridge: Harvard University Press, 2005.

Bakewell, Peter J. "Registered Silver Production in the Potosí District, 1550–1735." *Jahrbuch für Geschichte von Staat, Wirtschaft, und Gesellschaft Lateinamerikas* 12 (1975): 94–97.

Ballesteros Gaibrois, Manuel. "El vasco Diego De Gardoqui, primer embajador de España ante Los Estados Unidos de América." In *Euskal Herria y el Nuevo Mundo: La contribución de los Vascos a la formación de las Américas*, edited by Ronald Escobedo Mansilla, Ana de Zaballa Beascoechea and Óscar Álvarez Gila, 305–18. Vitoria: Servicio Editorial Universidad del Pais Vasco, 1996.

Bannon, John Francis. *The Spanish Borderlands Frontier, 1513–1821.* Albuquerque: University of New Mexico Press, 1973.

Barbier, Jacques A. "Comercio Neutral in Bolivarian America: La Guaira, Cartagena, Callao, and Buenos Aires." In *América Latina en la época de Simón Bolívar,* edited by Reinhard Liehr, 363–77. Berlin: Colloquium Verlag, 1989.

"Comercio secreto: The Economic and Political Significance of a Fiscal Expedient, 1800–1808." Paper presented at the International Congress of Americanists. Amsterdam, 1987.

"The Culmination of the Bourbon Reforms, 1787–1792." *Hispanic American Historical Review* 57, no. 1 (February 1977): 51–68.

"Elite and Cadres in Bourbon Chile." *The Hispanic American Historical Review* 52, no. 3 (August 1972): 416–35.

"Imperial Policy toward the Port of Veracruz, 1788–1808: The Struggle between Madrid, Cádiz, and Havana Interests." In *The Economies of Mexico and Peru During the Late Colonial Period, 1760–1810,* edited by Nils Jacobsen and Hans-Jürgen Puhle, 240–51. Berlin: Colloquium Verlag, 1986.

"Indies Revenues and Naval Spending: The Cost of Colonialism for the Spanish Bourbons, 1763–1805,." In *Jahrbuch Für Geschichte Von Staat, Wirtschaft Und Gesellschaft Lateinamerikas* 21 (1984): 171–88.

"Jacques Barbier's Reply." *The Hispanic American Historical Review* 58, no. 1 (February 1978): 87–90.

"Peninsular Finance and Colonial Trade: The Dilemma of Charles IV's Spain." *Journal of Latin American Studies* 12, no. 1 (May 1980): 21–37.

Reform and Politics in Bourbon Chile, 1755–1796. Ottawa: University of Ottawa Press, 1980.

"Towards a New Chronology for Bourbon Colonialism: The 'Depositaría de Indias' of Cádiz, 1722–1789." *Ibero-Amerikanisches Archiv* 6, no. 4 (1980): 335–53.

"Venezuelan Libranzas, 1788–1807: From Economic Nostrum to Fiscal Imperative." *The Americas* 37, no. 4 (April 1981): 457–78.

Barbier, Jacques A., and Herbert S. Klein. "Las prioridades de un monarca ilustrado: El gasto publico bajo el reinado de Carlos III." *Revista de Historia Económica* 3, no. 3 (Fall 1985): 473–95.

"Revolutionary Wars and Public Finances: The Madrid Treasury, 1784–1807." *Journal of Economic History* 41, no. 2 (June 1981): 315–37.

Baskes, Jeremy. "Coerced or Voluntary: The Repartimiento and Market Participation of Peasants in Late Colonial Oaxaca," *Journal of Latin American Studies* 28 (1996): 707–733.

"Colonial Institutions and Cross-Cultural Trade: Repartimiento, Credit, and Indigenous Production of Cochineal in Eighteenth-Century Oaxaca, Mexico," *Journal of Economic History* 65:1 (March 2005): 186–210.

"Indians, Merchants, and Markets: A Reinterpretation of the Repartimiento and Spanish-Indian Relations in Colonial Oaxaca, 1750–1821. Stanford: Stanford University Press, 2000.

"Risky Ventures: Reconsidering Mexico's Colonial Trade System." *Colonial Latin American Review* 14, no. 1 (June 2005): 27–54.

Baudot Monroy, María. *"Julián de Arriaga y Rivera: Una vida al servicio de la Marina."* PhD diss., Universidad Nacional de Educación a Distancia, 2010.

"Orígenes familiares y carrera profesional de Julián de Arriaga, Secretario de Estado de Marina e Indias (1700–1776)." *Espacio, Tiempo y Forma, Serie IV, Historia Moderna,* 17 (2004): 163–85.

Baudot Monroy, María, and Marta García Garralón, "El éxito del modelo de gestión de la Marina maltesa y su relación con la Real Armada española del siglo XVIII," In *Un estado militar: España, 1650–1820,* edited by Agustín González Enciso, 210–52. Madrid: Actas Editorial, 2012.

Baudrillart, Alfred. *Phillippe V et la Cour de France.* Paris: Firmin/Didot et cie, 1890.

Beerman, Eric. "El conde de Aranda y la tertulia madrileña (1788–1790) de la viuda de Bernardo de Gálvez," In *El conde de Aranda y su tiempo,* edited by José A. Ferrer, 349–62. Benimeli Zaragoza: Institución Fernando el Católico, 2000.

Belanger, Brian. "Secularization and the Laity in Colonial Mexico: Querétaro, 1598–1821." PhD diss., Tulane University, 1990.

Bély, Lucien. *Espions et Ambassadeurs au Temps de Louis XIV.* Paris: Fayard, 1990.

Benjamin, Thomas. *The Atlantic World: Europeans, Africans, Indians, and Their Shared History.* Cambridge: Cambridge University Press, 2009.

Bernabéu Albert, Salvador. *Expulsados del infierno. El exilio de los misioneros jesuitas de la península californiana (1767–1768).* Madrid: Consejo Superior de Investigaciones Científicas, 2008.

Bernal, Antonio-Miguel. *La financiación de la carrera de Indias (1492–1824). Dinero y crédito en el comercio colonial español con América.* Seville: Escuela de Estudios Hispano-Americanos, 1992.

Bernard, Gildas. "La Casa de la Contratación de Sevilla, luego de Cádiz en el siglo XVIII." *Anuario de Estudios Americanos* 12 (1959): 253–86.

Le Secrétariat D'état et le Conseil Espagnol des Indes (1700–1808). Geneva: Dioz, 1972.

Béthencourt Massieu, Antonio de. "La Guerra de la Oreja: El corso marítimo." In *España y el mar en el siglo de Carlos III,* edited by Vicente Palacio Atard, 337–45. Madrid: Marinvest, 1989.

"Las aventuras italianas de Felipe V." In *España y el mar en el siglo de Carlos III,* edited by Vicente Palacio Atard, 323–35. Madrid: Marinvest, 1989.

Patiño en la política internacional de Felipe V. Valladolid: Facultad de Filosofía y Letras de la Universidad de Valladolid, 1954.

Relaciones de España bajo Felipe V. Valladolid: Universidad de Valladolid, 1998.

Blart, Louis. *Les Rapports de la France et de L'espagne après le Pacte de Famille, jusqu'à la fin du Ministère du Duc de Choiseul.* Paris: F. Alcon, 1915.

Bleichmar, Daniela, Paula De Vos, Kristin Huffine, and Kevin Sheehan, eds. *Science in the Spanish and Portuguese Empires, 1500–1800.* Stanford, CA: Stanford University Press, 2009.

Blue, George Verne. "French Protests against Restrictions on Trade with Spanish America, 1788–1790." *The Hispanic American Historical Review* 13, no. 3 (August 1933): 336–44.

Bolton, Herbert. "The Epic of Greater America." *American Historical Review* 38, no. 3 (April 1933): 448–74.

Boyd-Bowman, Peter. *Índice geobiográfico de cuarenta mil pobladores españoles de América en el siglo XVI.* Bogotá: Instituto Caro y Cuervo, 1964.

Brading, D. A. "Bourbon Spain and Its American Empire." In *Colonial Spanish America*, edited by Leslie Bethell, 112–62. Cambridge: Cambridge University Press, 1987.

Church and State in Bourbon Mexico: The Diocese of Michoacán, 1749–1818. Cambridge: Cambridge University Press, 1994.

The First America: The Spanish Monarchy, Creole Patriots, and the Liberal State, 1492–1867. Cambridge: Cambridge University Press, 1991.

Miners and Merchants in Bourbon Mexico. Cambridge: Cambridge University Press, 1971.

"Tridentine Catholicism and Enlightened Despotism in Bourbon Mexico." *Journal of Latin American Studies* 15, no. 1 (May 1983): 1–22.

Brandon Lowry, Lyn. "*Forging an Indian Nation: Urban Indians under Spanish Colonial Control (Lima, Peru, 1535–1765).*" PhD diss., University of California at Berkeley, 1991.

Briceño Parozo, Mario. "Ámbito institucional de la Capitanía General de Venezuela." In *Memoria del Tercer Congreso Venezolano de Historia.* Caracas: Academia Nacional de Historia, 1979.

Brown, Kendall W. "Jesuit Wealth and Economic Activity within the Peruvian Economy: The Case of Southern Peru." *The Americas* 44, no. 1 (July 1987): 23–43.

"Marie-Anne de la Tremouille," In *Women in World History: A Biographical Encyclopedia*, 16 vols., edited by Anne Commire and Deborah Klezmer, vol. 10, 358–62. Waterford, CT: Yorkin Publications, 1999–2002.

Brown, Vera Lee. "Contraband Trade: A Factor in the Decline of Spain's Empire in America." *The Hispanic American Historical Review* 8, no. 2 (May 1928): 178–89.

"The South Sea Company and Contraband Trade." *The American Historical Review* 31, no. 4 (July 1926): 662–78.

Browning, Reed. *The War of the Austrian Succession.* New York: St. Martin's Press, 1993.

Burkholder, Mark A. *Biographical Dictionary of Councilors of the Indies, 1717–1808.* New York: Greenwood Press, 1986.

"The Council of the Indies in the Late Eighteenth Century: A New Perspective." *The Hispanic American Historical Review* 56, no. 3 (August 1976): 404–23.

Politics of a Colonial Career: José Baquíjano and the Audiencia of Lima. Albuquerque: University of New Mexico Press, 1980.

Burkholder, Mark A., and D. S. Chandler. *Biographical Dictionary of Audiencia Ministers in the Americas, 1687–1821.* Westport, CT.: Greenwood Press, 1982.

From Impotence to Authority: The Spanish Crown and the American Audiencias, 1687–1808. Columbia: University of Missouri Press, 1977.

Bustos Rodríguez, Manuel. *Cádiz en el sistema atlántico: La ciudad, sus comerciantes y la actividad mercantil (1650–1830).* Cádiz: Universidad de Cádiz Servicio de Publicaciones, 2005.

"Prólogo," In *La Casa de Contratación y la Intendencia General de la Marina en Cádiz* by Ana Crespo Solana. Cádiz: Servicio de Publicaciones, Universidad de Cadiz, 1996.

Caballero y Góngora, Antonio. "Relación del estado del Nuevo Reino de Granada1789." In *Antonio Caballero y Góngora, virrey arzobispo de Santa Fe, 1723–1796*, edited by José Manuel Pérez Ayala, 297–408. Bogotá: Imprenta Municipal, 1951.

Cahill, David. *From Rebellion to Independence in the Andes: Soundings from Southern Peru, 1750–1830*. Amsterdam: Aksant, 2002.

Cala, Fray Isidoro. "Planctus indorum christianorum en america peruntina." In *Una denuncia profética desde el Perú a mediados del siglo XVIII: El Planctus indorum christianorum en America Peruntina*, edited by José María Navarro. Lima: Pontífica Universidad Católica del Perú, 2001.

Campbell, Leon G. *The Military and Society in Colonial Peru, 1750–1810*. Philadelphia: American Philosophical Society, 1978.

Campillo y Cossío, José del. *Nuevo Sistema Económico para America*. Edited by Manuel Ballesteros Gaibrois. Oviedo: Grupo Editorial Asturiano, 1993.

Nuevo sistema de gobierno económico para la América: Con los males y daños que le causa el que hoy tiene.... Madrid: Imprenta de Benito Cano, 1789.

Campomanes, Pedro Rodríguez de. *Dictamen fiscal de expulsion de los Jesuitas de España (1766–1767)*. Edited by Jorge Cejudo y Teófanes Egido. Madrid: Fundación Universitaria Española, 1977.

Itinerario de las Carreras de Posta de dentro, y fuera del reyno.... Madrid, 1761.

Reflexiones sobre el comercio español a Indias (1762). Madrid: Instituto de Estudios Fiscales, 1988.

Cañizares Esguerra, Jorge. *How to Write the History of the New World: Historiographies, Epistemologies, and Identities in the Eighteenth-Century Atlantic World*. Stanford, CA: Stanford University Press, 2001.

Cánovas Sánchez, Francisco, José Antonio Escudero, and José María García Marín, et al. "La época de los primeros Borbones, vol. I, La nueva monarquía y su posición en Europa (1700–1759)." In *Historia de general de España*, edited by José María Jover Zamora. Madrid: Espasa Calpe, 1985.

Cantillo, Alejandro de. *Tratados, convenios y declaraciones de paz y de comercio que han hecho con las potencias estranjeras los monarcas españoles de la casa de Borbon: desde el año 1700 has el dia: puestos en órden é ilustrados muchos de ellos con la historia de sus respectivas negociaciones*, Madrid: Imprenta de Alegría y Charlain, 1843.

Carvajal y Lancáster, José de. *Testamento político o idea de un govierno católico (1745)*, ed. by José Miguel Delgado Barrado. Córdoba: Universidad Servicio de Publicaciones, 1999.

Castellano, Juan Luis. *Gobierno y poder en la España del siglo XVIII*. Granada: Editorial Universidad de Granada, 2006.

Castillero Calvo, Alfredo. "Las fortificaciones." In *Historia general de Panamá*, edited by Alfredo Castillero Calvo. Panama City: Comité Nacional del Centenario de la República, 2004.

Castro, Adolfo de. *Vida del Almirante D. Andrés de Pes, ministro de marina*. Cádiz: Federico Joly, 1879.

Castro, Concepción de. *A la sombra de Felipe V: José Grimaldo, ministro responsable (1703–1726)*. Madrid: Marcial Pons, 2004.

Castro Gutiérrez, Felipe. *Nueva ley y Nuevo rey: Reformas borbónicas y rebelión popular en Nueva España*. Zamora: Colegio de Michoacán, 1996.

Céspedes del Castillo, Guillermo. "La renta del tabaco en el virreinato del Perú." *Revista histórica* 21 (1954): 138–63.

Chaunu, Huguette et Pierre. *Seville et L'atlantique, 1504–1650*. Paris: Colin, 1955–1959.

Chávez, Thomas E. *Spain and the Independence of the United States: An Intrinsic Gift*. Albuquerque: University of New Mexico Press, 2002.

"New Light on Felipe de Rábago y Terán," *Southwest Historical Quarterly* 111 (Oct. 2007): 161–163.

Spanish Texas, 1519–1821. Austin: University of Texas Press, 1992.

Christelow, Allan. "French Interest in the Spanish Empire During the Ministry of the Duc de Choiseul, 1759–1771." *The Hispanic American Historical Review* 21, no. 4 (November 1941): 515–37.

Colección de los tratados de paz, alianza, comercio & c: Ajustados por la Corona de España con las potencias extrangeras desde el reynado del Señor Don Felipe Quinto hasta el presente, II. Madrid: Imprenta real, 1800.

A Collection of All the Treaties of Peace, Alliance, and Commerce, between Great Britain and Other Powers from the Treaty Signed at Munster in 1648, to the Treaties Signed at Paris in 1783, Vol. 2. Edited by Charles Jenkinson. London: Printed for J. Debret, 1785.

Colmenares, Germán. *Haciendas de los Jesuitas en el Nuevo Reyno de Granada , siglo XVIII*. Bogotá: Universidad Nacional de Colombia, 1969.

Cook, Noble David. *Born to Die: Disease and the New World Conquest, 1492–1650*. Cambridge: Cambridge University Press, 1998.

Cook, Warren L. *Flood Tide of Empire: Spain and the Pacific Northwest, 1543–1819*. New Haven, CT: Yale University Press, 1973.

Coxe, William. *España bajo el reinado de la casa de Borbón...*, II. Madrid: Estab. Tip. de D.F. de P. Mellado, 1846.

Memoirs of the Kings of Spain of the House of Bourbon from the Accession of Philip V to the Death of Charles III, 1700 ... to ... 1788, Vol. III. 2nd edn., London: Longman, Hurst, Rees, Orme, and Brown, 1813.

Crespo Solana, Ana. *Entre Cádiz y los Países Bajos: Una comunidad mercantil en la ciudad de la ilustración*. Cádiz: Fundación Municipal de Cultura,2001.

La Casa de Contratación y la Intendencia General de la Marina en Cádiz. Cádiz: Universidad de Cádiz, 1996.

Crosby, Alfred. *Ecological Imperialism: The Biological Expansion of Europe, 900–1900*. Cambridge: Cambridge University Press, 1986.

Cummins, Light Townsend. *Spanish Observers and the American Revolution, 1775–1783*. Baton Rouge: Louisiana State University Press, 1991.

Cuenca-Esteban, Javier. "Statistics of Spain's Colonial Trade, 1747–1820: New Estimates and Comparisons with Great Britain," *Revista de historia económica* 26:3 (Autumn-Winter 2008): 323–354.

Cuño Bonito, Justo. "El Consulado de Comercio. Cartagena de Indias y su papel económico y político en el conflicto de independencia (1795–1821)." *Studia histórica. historia contemporánea* 27 (2009): 311–48.

Curtain, Philip. *The Atlantic Slave Trade: A Census.* Madison: University of Wisconsin Press, 1969.

Danvila, Manuel. *Reinado de Carlos III.* Madrid: El Progreso 1892–1896.

Daubigny, E. *Choiseul et la France d'Outre-Mer après Le Traité de Paris.* Paris: Hachette et cie, 1892.

Deans-Smith, Susan. *Bureaucrats, Planters, and Workers: The Making of the Tobacco Monopoly in Bourbon Mexico.* Austin: University of Texas Press, 1992.

Delgado Barrado, José Miguel. *El proyecto político de Carvajal: Pensamiento y reforma en tiempos de Fernando VI.* Madrid: Consejo Superior de Investigaciones Científicas, 2001.

Delgado Ribas, J. M. "Catalunya y el sistema de libre comercio (1778–1818): Una reflexión sobre las raíces del reformismo borbónico." PhD diss., University of Barcelona, 1981.

El Comerç entre Cataluña i Amèrica (Sigles XVII y XIX). Barcelona: L'Avenç, 1986.

"El impacto de la reforma del 'comercio libre' sobre el comercio colonial." In *Economic Effects of European Expansion, 1492–1824,* edited by J. Casas Pardo, 387–434. Stuttgart: F. Steiner, 1992.

"El impacto de las crisis coloniales en economía catalana (1787–1807)." In *La economía española al final del Antiguo Régimen: Comercio y colonias,* edited by Josep Fontana, 97–169. Madrid: Alianza Editorial, 1982.

"El modelo catalán dentro del sistema de libre comercio (1765–1820)." In *El comercio libre entre España y América (1765–1824),* edited by Josep Fontana and Antonio Miguel Bernal, 53–69, Madrid: Fundación Banco Exterior, 1987.

"La paz de los siete años (1750–1757) y el inicio de la reforma comercial española." In *1802,* 321–76, Madrid: Ministerior de Educación, Cultura y Deporte, 2003.

"La paz de los siete años (1750–1757) y el inicio de la reforma del comercio colonial español," In *1802: España entre dos siglos: ciencia y economía,* coordinated by Antonio Morales Moya, 321–43. Madrid: Sociedad Estatal de Conmemoraciones Culturales, 2003.

"'Libre comercio': Mito y realidad." In *Mercado y desarrollo económico en la España contemporánea,* edited by T. Martínez Vera. Madrid: Siglo XXI de España, 1986.

Denson Riley, James. "The Management of the Estates of the Jesuit *Colegio Máximo de San Pedro y San Pablo* of Mexico City in the Eighteenth Century." PhD diss., Tulane University, 1972.

Destefani, Laurio H. "La defensa militar del Río de la Plata en la época hispana." In *Memoria del Tercer Congreso Venezolano de Historia.* Caracas: Academia Nacional de Historia, 1979.

Dilg, George Robertson. "The Collapse of the Portobelo Fairs: A Study in Spanish Commercial Reform, 1720–1740." PhD diss., Indiana University, 1975.

Domínguez Ortiz, Antonio. *Carlos III y la España de la ilustración.* Madrid: Alianza Editorial, 1988.

Los extranjeros en la vida española durante el siglo XVII y otros artículos. Seville: Diputación de Sevilla, Área de Cultura y Ecología, 1996.

Dueñas, Alcira. "Andean Scholarship and Rebellion: Indigenous and Mestizo Discourses of Power in Mid-and Late-Colonial Peru." PhD diss., Ohio State University, 2000.

———. *Indians and Mestizos in the "Lettered City": Reshaping Justice, Social Hierarchy, and Political Culture in Colonial Peru.* Boulder: University of Colorado Press, 2010.

Dym, Jordana, and Christophe Belaubre. *Politics, Economy, and Society in Bourbon Central America, 1759–1821.* Boulder: University Press of Colorado, 2007.

Earle, Rebecca. "Information and Disinformation in Late Colonial New Granada." *The Americas* 54 (October 1997): 167–84.

Eissa-Barroso, Francisco A. "'Of Experience, Zeal, and Selflessness': Military Officers as Viceroys in Early Eighteenth-Century Spanish America." *The Americas* 68 (January 2012): 317–45.

Elliott, J. H. *The Count-Duke of Olivares: The Statesman in an Age of Decline.* New Haven, CT: Yale University Press, 1986.

———. *Empires of the Atlantic World: Britain and Spain in America, 1492–1830.* New Haven, CT: Yale University Press, 2006.

———. "A Europe of Composite Monarchies." *Past and Present* 137 (November 1992): 48–71.

Eltis, David. *The Rise of Atlantic Slavery in the Americas.* Cambridge: Cambridge University Press, 2000.

Erlanger, Philippe. *Felipe V, esclavo de sus mujeres.* Translated by Robert Sánchez. Barcelona: Editorial Ariel, 2003.

Escamilla González, Iván. *Los intereses malentendidos: El Consulado de Comerciantes de México y la monarquía española, 1700–1739.* Mexico City: Universidad Autónoma de México, 2011.

Escudero, José Antonio. *Los orígenes del Consejo de Ministros en España, 2 vols.* Madrid: Editora Nacional, 1979.

Estrada, Dorothy Tank. *La Educación Illustrada, (1776–1836).* Mexico: El Colegio de México, 1977.

Farriss, Nancy M. *Crown and Clergy in Colonial Mexico, 1759–1821: The Crisis of Ecclesiastical Privilege.* London: Athlone Press, 1986.

Ferguson King, James. "Evolution of the Free Slave Trade Principle in Spanish Colonial Administration." *The Hispanic American Historical Review* 22, no. 1 (February 1942): 34–56.

Fernán-Núñez, Conde de. *Vida de Carlos III.* Edited by A. Morel-Fatio and A. Paz y Meliá. Madrid: F. Fe, 1898.

Fernández Albaladejo, Pablo. "El decreto de suspensión de pagos de 1739: Análisis c implicaciones." *Moneda y crédito*, no. 142 (1977): 51–85.

Fernández Arrillaga, Immaculada. *El destierro de los Jesuitas castellanos, (1767–1815).* Salamanca: Junta de Castilla y León, 2004.

Fernández Duro, Cesáreo. *Armada española desde la unión de los Reinos de Castilla y de Aragón, VI.* Madrid: Museo Naval, 1973.

Ferry, Robert J. *The Colonial Elite of Early Caracas: Formation and Crisis, 1567–1767.* Berkeley: University of California Press, 1989.

Fisher, John R. *Bourbon Peru, 1750–1824.* Liverpool: Liverpool University Press, 2003.

Commercial Relations between Spain and Spanish America in the Era of Free Trade, *1778–1796.* Liverpool: Liverpool University Press, 1985.

"Critique of Jacques Barbier's 'The Culmination of Bourbon Reforms, 1787–1792.'" *The Hispanic American Historical Review* 58 (February 1978): 83–86.

"The Effects of Comercio Libre on the Economies of New Granada and Peru." In *Reform and Insurrection in Bourbon New Granada and Peru,* edited by Allan J. Kuethe, John R. Fisher and Anthony McFarlane. Baton Rouge: Louisiana State University Press, 1990.

"El estanco del tabaco en el Perú borbónico," in *Tabaco y economía en el siglo XVIII,* edited by Agustín González Enciso and Rafael Torres Sánchez, 35–73. Pamplona: Ediciones Universidad de Navarra, 1999.

Government and Society in Colonial Peru: The Intendant System, 1784–1814. London: Athlone Press, 1970.

"Imperial 'Free Trade' and the Hispanic Economy, 1778–1796." *Journal of Latin American Studies* 13, no. 1 (May 1981): 21–56.

"The Imperial Response to 'Free Trade': Spanish Imports from Spanish America, 1778–1796." *Journal of Latin American Studies* 17, no. 1 (May 1985): 35–78.

Silver Mines and Silver Miners in Colonial Peru, 1776–1824. Liverpool: University of Liverpool Press, 1977.

"Soldiers, Society, and Politics in Spanish America, 1750–1821." *Latin American Research Review* 17, no. 1 (1982): 217–22.

Fontana Lázaro, Josep. *La economía española al final del Antiguo Régimen, Vol. III.* Madrid: Alianza Editorial, 1982.

Fontana Lázaro, Josep, and Antono Miguel Bernal, eds. *El "comercio libre" entre España y América (1765–1824).* Madrid: Fundación Banco Exterior, 1987.

Gárate Ojanguren, Montserrat. *La Real Compañía Guipuzcoana de Caracas.* San Sebastián: Sociedad Guipuzcoana de Ediciones y Publicaciones, 1990.

García Cárcel, Ricardo. *Felipe V y los Españoles: Una visión periférica del problema de España.* Barcelona: Plaza & Janes, 2002.

García Fuentes, Lutgardo. *El comercio español con América, 1650–1700.* Seville: Diputación Provincial de Sevilla, 1980.

García-Baquero González, Antonio. *Cádiz y el Atlántico, 1717–1778. El comercio colonial español bajo el monopolio gaditano,* 2 vols. Seville: Escuela de Estudios Hispano-Americanos, 1976.

"Comercio colonial y producción industrial en Cataluña a fines del siglo XVIII." In *Actas del Coloquio de Historia Económica de España,* 268–94. Barcelona: Editorial Ariel, 1975.

"Los resultados de libre comercio y 'el punto de vista': Una revision desde la estadística." *Manuscrits* 15 (1997): 303–22.

García-Mauriño Mundi, Margarita. *La pugna entre el Consulado y los jenízaros por las exportaciones a Indias (1720–1765).* Seville: Universidad de Sevilla, 1999.

Garner, Richard. "Long-Term Silver Mining Trends in Spanish America: A Comparative Analysis of Peru and Mexico." *American Historical Review* 93, no. 4 (October 1988): 898–935.

Garrido Conde, María Teresa. *La primera creación del Virreinato de Nueva Granada (1717–1723)*. Seville: Escuela de Estudios Hispano-Americanos, 1965.

Gershoy, Leo. *From Despotism to Revolution, 1763–1789*. New York: Harper and Row, 1944.

Giménez López, Enrique, ed. *Expulsión y exilio de los Jesuitas españoles*. Murcia: Universidad de Alicante, 1997.

Giraud, Marcel. *Histoire de la Louisiane Francaise, III, L'Époque de John Law (1717–1720)*. Paris: Presses Universitaires De France, 1966.

Godoy, Scarlett O'Phelan. *Rebellions and Revolts in Eighteenth-Century Peru and Upper Peru*. Cologne: Böhlau, 1985.

Goebel, Julius. *The Struggle for the Falkland Islands: A Study in Legal and Diplomatic History*. New Haven, CT: Yale University Press, 1927.

Gómez Urdáñez, José Luis. *El proyecto reformista de Ensenada*. Lerida: Milenio, 1996.

Fernando VI. Madrid: Arlanza,2001.

Gómez Urdáñez, José Luis, and Pedro Luis Lorenzo Cadarso. *Castilla en la edad moderna*, second part, *Historia de Castilla de Atapuerca a Fuensaldaña*. Edited by Juan José García González, Julio Aróstegui Sánchez, Juan Andrés Blanco Rodríguez, et. al. Madrid: La Esfera de los libros 2008.

Gonçalvès, Dominique. *Le Planteur et le Roi: L'Aristocratie Havanaise et la Couronne D'Espagne (1763–1838)*. Madrid: Casa Velásquez, 2008.

González Suárez, Federico. *Historia general de la República de Ecuador*, Vol. 5. Quito: Casa de la Cultura, 1890–1891.

Grafe, Regina, and Alejandra Irigoin. "Bargaining for Absolutism: A Spanish Path to Nation-State and Empire Building." *Hispanic American Historical Review* 88, no. 2 (May 2008): 173–209.

"The Spanish Empire and Its Legacy: Fiscal Redistribution and Political Conflict in Colonial and Post-Colonial Spanish America." *Journal of Global History* 1, no. 2 (2006): 241–67.

Grafenstein, Johanna von. *Nueva España en el Circuncaribe, 1779–1808: Revolución, competencia colonial y vínculos intercoloniales*. Mexico: Universidad Nacional Autónoma, 1997.

Grahn, Lance. *The Political Economy of Smuggling: Regional Informal Economies in Early Bourbon New Granada*. Boulder, CO: Westview Press, 1997.

Guimerá, Agustín, ed. *El reformismo borbónico: Una vision interdisciplinar*. Madrid: Alianza, 2002.

"Estado, administración y liderazgo naval: Antonio Valdés y Charles Middleton (1778–1808)." In *Un estado militar: España, 1650–1820*, edited by González Enciso, 184–86. Madrid: Actas Editorial,2012.

Hamnett, Brian R. *Politics & Trade in Southern Mexico, 1750–1821*. Cambridge: Cambridge University Press, 1971.

Harbron, John D. *Trafalgar and the Spanish Navy*. London: Conway Maritime Press, 1988.

Haring, C. H. *The Spanish Empire in America*. New York: Harcourt, Brace, and World, Inc., 1947.

Headrick, Daniel R. *When Information Came of Age: Technologies of Knowledge in the Age of Reason and Revolution*. New York: Oxford University Press, 2002.

Hellwege, Johann. *Die Spanischen Provinzialmilizen im 18 Jahrhundert. Boppard am Rhein: H. Boldt, 1969.

Heredia Herrera, Antonia. "Asiento con el Consulado de Cádiz, en 1720, para el despacho de avisos." In *Instituto de Estudios Gaditanos.* Cádiz: Diputación Provincial, 1975.

Sevilla y los hombres del comercio (1700–1800). Seville: Editoriales Andaluzas Unidas, 1989.

Hernández González, Manuel. *Francisco de Miranda y su ruptura con España.* Santa Cruz de Tenerife: Ediciones Idea, 2006.

Hernández González, Pablo J. "La otra guerra del inglés: La resistencia a la presencia británica en Cuba (1762–1763)." 2 vols., PhD diss., University of Seville, 2001.

Hernández Palomo, José Jesús. *El aguardiente de caña en México.* Seville: Escuela de Estudios Hispano-Americanos, 1974.

Herr, Richard. *The Eighteenth-Century Revolution in Spain.* Princeton, NJ: Princeton University Press, 1958.

Hidalgo, Dennis R. "To Get Rich for Our Homeland: The Company of Scotland and the Colonization of the Isthmus of Darien." *The Colonial Latin American Historical Review* (Summer 2001): 331–46.

Howe, Walter. *The Mining Guild of New Spain and Its Tribunal General, 1770–1821.* Cambridge, MA: Harvard University Press, 1949.

Hull, Anthony H. *Charles III and the Revival of Spain.* Washington: University Press of America, 1981.

Hussey, Roland Dennis. *The Caracas Company, 1728–1784.* Cambridge, MA: Harvard University Press, 1934.

Inglis, G. Douglas. "The Spanish Naval Shipyard at Havana in the Eighteenth Century." In *New Aspects of Naval History: Selected Papers from the 5th Naval History Symposium,* 47–58. Baltimore: Nautical and Aviation Pub. Co. of America, 1985.

Inglis, G. Douglas, and Allan J. Kuethe. "El Consulado de Cádiz y el Reglamento de Comercio Libre de 1765." In *Andalucía y América en el siglo XVIII: Actas de las IV Jornadas de Andalucía y América,* 79–87. Seville: Escuela de Estudios Hispano-Americanos, 1985.

Irigoin, Alejandra, and Regina Grafe. "Response to Carlos Marichal and William Summerhill." *Hispanic American Historical Review* 88, no. 2 (May 2008): 235–45.

Israel, J. I. *Race, Class, and Politics in Colonial Mexico, 1610–1670.* Oxford: Oxford University Press, 1975.

Jackson, Jack. "Introduction" to *Imaginary Kingdom: Texas as Seen by the Rivera and Rubí Military Expeditions, 1727 and 1767,* edited by Jack Jackson, ix–xvii. Austin: Texas State Historical Association, 1995.

Jara, Álvaro. "El financiamento de Cartagena de Indias: Los excedentes de las cajas de Bogotá y de Quito, 1761–1802." *Historia (Santiago de Chile)* 28 (1994).

Johnson, Sherry. *Climate & Catastrophe in Cuba and the Atlantic World in the Age of Revolution.* Chapel Hill: University of North Carolina Press, 2011.

"Revisiting the British Capture of Havana in 1762." Paper presented at the Conference on Latin American History, American Historical Association Meeting, 2005.

Juan, Jorge, and Antonio de Ulloa. *Discourse and Political Reflections on the Kingdoms of Peru. Their Government, Special Regimen of Their Inhabitants and Abuses Which Have Been Introduced into One and Another, with Special Information on Why They Grew up and Some Means to Avoid Them.* Translated by John J. TePaske and Besse A. Clement. Norman: University of Oklahoma Press, 1978.

Kamen, Henry. "El establecimiento de los intendentes en la administracion Espanola." *Hispania*, no. 95 (1964): 368–95.

Philip V of Spain: The King Who Reigned Twice. New Haven, CT: Yale University Press, 2001.

The War of the Succession in Spain, 1700–1715. Bloomington: Indiana University Press, 1969.

Kimbell, Bennett R. "El Baluarte del Sur: Archeological and Historical Investigations of the Southeast Bastion at Presidio San Sabá," *Bulletin of the Texas Archeological Society* 81 (2010): 323–354.

Klein, Herbert S. *The American Finances of the Spanish Empire: Royal Income and Expenditures in Colonial Mexico, Peru, and Bolivia, 1690–1809.* Albuquerque: University of New Mexico Press, 1998.

"The Colored Militia of Cuba, 1568–1868." *Caribbean Studies* 4 (July 1966): 17–27.

"Un comentario sobre sistemas y estructuras fiscales del imperio español." In *Finanzas y política en el mundo iberoamericano: Del antiguo régimen a las naciones independientes, 1754–1850.* Mexico: Universidad Autónoma de México, 2001.

Klein, Herbert S., and Ben Vinson III. *African Slavery in Latin America and the Caribbean.* Oxford and New York: Oxford University Press, 1977.

Knight, Alan. *Mexico: The Colonial Era.* Cambridge: Cambridge University Press, 2002.

Koenigsberger, H. G. "Dominium Regale or Dominium Politicum Et Regale." In *Politicians and Virtuosi: Essays in Early Modern History*, edited by H. G. Koenigsberger, 1–25. London: Hambledon Press, 1986.

Kuethe, Allan J. "Alejandro O'Reilly y las reformas económicas de Carlos III en Cuba." In *Memoria del Cuarto Congreso Venezolano de Historia*, 17–34. Caracas: Academia Nacional de Historia, 1982.

"Cardinal Alberoni and Reform in the American Empire." In *Early Bourbon Spanish America: Politics and Society in a Forgotten Era (1700–1759)*, edited by Francisco A. Eissa-Barroso and Ainara Vázquez Varela, 23–38. Leiden: Brill, 2013.

"The Colonial Commercial Policy of Philip V and the Atlantic World." In *Latin America and the Atlantic World (1500–1850)*, edited by Renate Pieper and Peer Schmidt, 319–33. Cologne: Böhlau-Verlag, 2005.

Cuba, 1753–1815: Crown, Military, and Society. Knoxville: University of Tennessee Press, 1986.

"The Development of the Cuban Military as a Socio-Political Elite, 1763–1783." *The Hispanic American Historical Review* 61 (1981): 695–704.

"The Early Reforms of Charles III in the Viceroyalty of New Granada, 1759–1776." In *Reform and Insurrection in Bourbon New Granada and Peru*, edited by Allan J. Kuethe, John R. Fisher and Anthony McFarlane, 19–40. Baton Rouge: Louisiana State University Press, 1990.

"El fin del monopolio: Los Borbones y el Consulado Andaluz." In *Relaciones de poder y comercio colonial: Nuevas perspectivas*, edited by Enriqueta Vila Vilar and Allan J. Kuethe, 56–82. Seville: Consejo Superior de Investigaciones Científicas, 1999.

"Guns, Subsidies, and Commercial Privilege: Some Historical Factors in the Emergence of the Cuban National Character, 1763–1815." *Cuban Studies* 16 (1986): 128–38.

"Imperativas militares en la política comercial de Carlos III." In *Soldados del rey: El ejército borbónico en América colonial en vísperas de la independencia*, edited by Allan J. Kuethe and Juan Marchena Fernández, 149–59. Castellón: Universitat Jaume I, 2005.

"La batalla de Cartagena de 1741: Nuevas perspectivas." *Historiografía y bibliografía americanistas* 18 (1974): 19–38.

"La desregulación comercial y la reforma imperial en la época de Carlos III: Los casos de Nueva España y Cuba." *Historia Mexicana* XLI (October–December 1991): 265–92.

"Las milicias disciplinadas." In *Soldados del rey: El ejército borbónico en América colonial en vísperas de la independencia*, edited by Allan J. Kuethe and Juan Marchena Fernández, 101–26. Castellón: Universitat Jaume I, 2005.

Military Reform and Society in New Granada, 1773–1808. Gainesville: University Presses of Florida, 1978.

"More on the 'Culmination of the Bourbon Reforms': A Perspective from New Granada." *The Hispanic American Historical Review* 58, no. 3 (August 1978): 477–80.

"Proyectismo et reform commercial á l'époque de Philippe V." In *L'Amérique en projet: Utopies, controverss et réformes dans l'empire espagnol (XVI-XVIII siècle)*, edited by Nejma Kermele and Bernard Lavallé, 243–51. Paris: L'Harmattan, 2008.

"The Regulation of 'Comercio Libre' of 1765 and the Spanish Caribbean Islands." In *Primer Congreso Internacional de Historia Económica y Social de la Cuenca del Caribe, 1763–1898*, edited by Ricardo E. Alegría, 191–208. San Juan: Centro de Estudios Avanzados de Puerto Rico y el Caribe, 1992.

"Traslado del Consulado de Sevilla a Cádiz: Nuevas Perspectivas." In *Relaciones de poder y comercio colonial: Nuevas perspectivas*, edited by Enriqueta Vila Vilar, and Allan J. Kuethe, 35–55. Seville: Consejo Superior de Investigaciones Científicas, 1999.

Kuethe, Allan J., and Lowell Blaisdell. "The Esquilache Government and the Reforms of Charles III in Cuba." *Jarhbuch für Geschichte von Staat, Wirtschaft und Gesellschaft Lateinamerikas* 19 (1982): 117–36.

"French Influence and the Origins of the Bourbon Colonial Reorganization." *The Hispanic American Historical Review* 71, no. 3 (August 1991): 579–607.

Kuethe, Allan J., and G. Douglas Inglis. "Absolutism and Enlightened Reform: Charles III, the Establishment of the *Alcabala*, and Commercial Reorganization in Cuba." *Past and Present*, no. 109 (November 1985): 118–43.

Kuethe, Allan J., and José Manuel Serrano. "El astillero de la Habana y Trafalgar." *Revista de Indias* 67 (September–December 2007): 763–76.

Lamikiz, Xabier. *Trade and Trust in the Eighteenth-Century Atlantic World: Spanish Merchants and Their Overseas Networks*. Suffolk: Boydell Press, 2010.

Lampros, Peter James. "Merchant-Planter Cooperation and Conflict: The Havana Consulado, 1794–1832." PhD diss., Tulane University, 1980.

Lanning, John Tate. *Academic Culture in the Spanish Colonies*. Oxford: Oxford University Press, 1940.

Latasa, Pilar. "Negociar en red: Familia, amistad, y paisanaje. El virrey Superunda y sus agentes en Lima y Cádiz (1745–1761)." *Anuario de Estudios Americanos* 60, no. 2 (2003): 463–92.

Lavery, Brian. *The Ship of the Line, Vol. I, The Development of the Battle Fleet, 1650–1850*. London: Conway Maritime Press, 1983.

Levene, Ricardo, ed. *Documentos para la historia argentina 6, Comercio de Indias: Comercio Libre (1778–1791)*. Buenos Aires: Facultad de Filosofía y Letras, 1915.

Lewis, James A. *The Final Campaign of the American Revolution: The Rise and Fall of the Spanish Bahamas*. Columbia: University of South Carolina Press, 1991.

———. "Las Damas de La Habana, el Precursor, and Francisco de Saavedra: A Note on Spanish Participation in the Battle of Yorktown." *The Americas* 37 (July 1980): 83–99.

Liss, Peggy K. *Atlantic Empires: The Network of Trade and Revolution*. Baltimore: Johns Hopkins University Press, 1983.

Loayza, Francisco A., ed. *Fray Calixto Túpak Inka: Documentos originales y , en su mayoría, totalmente desconocidos, auténticos, de este apóstol indio, valiente defensor de su raza, desde el año 1746 a 1760*. Lima: Los Pequeños Grandes Libros de Historia Americana, 1948.

López Canto, Ángel. *Miguel Enríquez*. San Juan: Consejo Sperior de Investigaciones Científicas, 1998.

Lucena Giraldo, Manuel. *Laboratorio tropical: La expedición de límites al Orinoco, 1750–1767*. Madrid: Consejo Superior de Investigaciones Científicas, 1993.

Lucena Salmoral, Manuel. *Piratas, corsarios, bucaneros, y filibusteros*. Madrid: Síntesis Editorial, 2005.

Luxán Meléndez, Santiago de Montserrat Gárate Ojanguren, and José Manuel Rodríguez Gordillo, *Cuba-Canarias-Sevilla: El estanco español del tabaco y Las Antillas (1717–1817)*. Las Palmas de Gran Canaria: Ediciones del Cabildo de Gran Canaria, 2012.

Lynch, John. *Bourbon Spain, 1700–1808*. Oxford: Basil Blackwell, 1989.

———. "The Origins of Spanish American Independence." In *The Independence of Latin America*, edited by Leslie Bethell, 1–48. Cambridge: Cambridge University Press, 1987.

———. *The Spanish American Revolutions, 1808–1826*. New York: Norton, 1973.

———. *Spanish Colonial Administration: The Intendant System in the Viceroyalty of the Río de la Plata*. London: Athlone Press, 1958.

Macera Dall'Orso, Pablo. "El probabilismo en el Perú durante el siglo XVIII." In *Trabajos de Historia, II*, 79–137. Lima: Instituto Nacional de Cultura, 1977.

———. "Instrucciones para el manejo de las haciendas jesuitas del Perú (Siglos XVII-XVIII)." *Nueva corónica* 2 (1966): 1–127.

Mahoney, James. *Colonialism and Postcolonial Development: Spanish Colonialism in Comparative Perspective*. Cambridge: Cambridge University Press, 2010.

Malamud Rikles, Carlos Daniel. *Cádiz y Saint Malo en el Comercio Colonial Peruano (1698–1725)*. Cádiz: Diputación de Cádiz, 1986.

Mancke, Elizabeth. "Negotiating an Empire: Britain and its Overseas Possessions." In *Negotiated Empires: Centers and Peripheries in the Americas, 1500–1820*, edited by Christine Daniels and Michael V. Kennedy, 235–238. New York and London: Routledge, 2002.

Marchena Fernández, Juan. "Financiación militar y situados." In *Temas de historia militar*, 261–307, Madrid: Servicio de Publicaciones EMS, 1988.

——. "Italianos al servicio del rey de España en el ejército de América, 1740–1815." In *Italiani al servicio straniero in etá moderna: Annali di storia militare europea*, edited by Paola Bianchi, Davide Maffi and Enrico Stumpo, 135–77. Milan: Franco Angeli, 2008.

——. "La financiación militar en Indias: Introducción a su estudio." *Anuario de Estudios Americanos* 36 (1979): 81–110.

——. *La institución militar en Cartagena de Indias, 1700–1810*. Seville: Escuela de Estudios Hispano-Americanos, 1982.

——. "Los oficiales militares irlandeses en el ejército de América. 1750–1815." In *Extranjeros en el ejército. Essays on the Irish Military Presence in Early Modern Spain. 1580–1818*, edited by Enrique García Hernán and Óscar Recio Morales, 317–53. Madrid: Ministerio de Defensa, 2007.

——. *Oficiales y soldados en el ejército de America*. Seville: Escuela de Estudios Hispano-Americanos, 1983.

Marichal, Carlos. *Bankruptcy of Empire: Mexican Silver and the Wars between Spain, Britain, and France, 1760–1810*. Cambridge: Cambridge University Press, 2007.

——. "Beneficios y costes fiscales del colonialismo: Las remesas americanas a España, 1760–1814." *Revista de Historia Económica* 15, no. 3 (Otoño–Invierno 1997): 475–505.

——. *De colonia a nación: Impuestos y política en México, 1750–1860*. Mexico: Colegio de México, 2001.

——. "Rethinking Negotiation and Coercion in an Imperial State." *The Hispanic American Historical Review* 88, no. 2 (May 2008): 211–18.

Marichal, Carlos, and Matilde Souto Mantecón. "Silver and Situados: New Spain and the Financing of the Spanish Empire in the Caribbean in the Eighteenth Century." *Hispanic American Historical Review*, 74, no. 4 (November 1994): 587–613.

Marks, Patricia H. "Confronting a Mercantile Elite: Bourbon Reformers and the Merchants of Lima, 1765–1796." *The Americas* 60, no. 4 (April 2004): 519–58.

——. *Deconstructing Legitimacy: Viceroys, Merchants, and the Military in Late Colonial Peru*. University Park: Pennsylvania State University Press, 2007.

Márquez Redondo, Ana Gloria. *Sevilla "ciudad y corte" (1729–1733)*. Seville: Servicio de Publicaciones del Ayuntamiento de Sevilla, 1994.

Marrero, Leví. *Cuba: Economía y sociedad, VI–IX, XI–XII*. Barcelona and Madrid: Editorial Playor and San Juan: Editorial San Juan, 1978–1985.

Marshall, Dorothy. *Eighteenth Century England*. London: Longman Group Limited, 1962.

Martínez Cardos, José. "Don José del Campillo y Cossío." *Revista de Indias*, no. 119–122 (1970): 501–42.

Martínez Shaw, Carlos. "El libre comercio y cataluña: Contribución a un debate." In *El "comercio libre" entre España y América (1765–1824)*, edited by Josep Fontana Lázaro, and Antonio Miguel Bernal, 43–51. Madrid: Fundación Banco Exterior, 1987.

Martínez Shaw, Carlos, and Marina Alfonso Mola. *Felipe V*. Madrid: Arlanza Ediciones, 2001.

McAlister, Lyle N. *The "Fuero Militar" in New Spain, 1764–1800*. Gainesville: University of Florida Press, 1957.

McFarlane, Anthony. *Colombia before Independence: Economy, Society, and Politics under Bourbon Rule*. Cambridge: Cambridge University Press, 1993.

——— "The Rebellion of the Barrios: Urban Insurrection in Bourbon Quito." *The Hispanic American Historical Review* 69, no. 2 (May 1989): 283–330.

McKay, Derek. *Allies of Convenience: Diplomatic Relations between Great Britain and Austria, 1714–1719*. New York: Garland Publishers, 1986.

McLachlan, Jean O. *Trade and Peace with Old Spain, 1667–1750*. Cambridge: Cambridge University Press, 1940.

McNeill, John Robert. *Atlantic Empires of France and Spain: Louisbourg and Havana, 1700–1763*. Chapel Hill: University of North Carolina Press, 1985.

——— *Mosquito Empires: Ecology and War in the Greater Caribbean, 1620–1914*. Cambridge: Cambridge University Press, 2010.

Meléndez, Santiago de Luxán, Ojanguren, Montserrat Gárate, and Rodríguez Gordillo, José Manuel, *Cuba-Canarias-Sevilla: El estanco español del Tabaco y Las Antillas, 1717-1817*. Las Palmas de Gran Canaria: Las Palmas de Gran Canaria Ediciones del Cabildo de Gran Canaria, 2012.

Menéndez Vives, Concepción and Carmen Torroja Menéndez. *Tratados Internacionalses suscritos por España . . . (siglos XII al XVII)*. Madrid: Dirección de Archivos Estatales, 1991.

Merino Navarro, José P., and Miguel M. Rodríguez Vicente, eds. *Relación histórica del viaje al América meridional de Jorge Juan y Antonio de Ulloa*. Madrid: Fundación Universitaria Española, 1978.

Mijares, Lucio. "Política exterior: La diplomacia." In *Historia general de España y América: América en el siglo XVIII, los primeros borbones*, edited by Luis Navarro García, 65–100. Madrid: Rialp, 1983.

Miller, Joseph C. *Way of Death: Merchant Capitalism and the Angolan Slave Trade, 1730–1830*. Madison: University of Wisconsin Press, 1988.

Mills, Kenneth. *Idolatry and Its Enemies: Colonial Andean Religion and Extirpation, 1640–1750*. Princeton, NJ: Princeton University Press, 1997.

Milton, Cynthia E. *The Many Meanings of Poverty: Colonialism, Social Compacts, and Assistance in Eighteenth-Century Ecuador*. Stanford, CA: Stanford University Press, 2007.

Minchom, Martin. *The People of Quito, 1690–1810: Change and Unrest in the Underclass*. Boulder, CO: Westview Press, 1994.

Molina Cortón, Juan. *Reformismo y neutralidad: José de Carvajal y la diplomacia de la España preilustrada.* Merida: Editora Regional de Extremadura, 2003.

Montgomery Keelan, Sandra. "The Bourbon Mining Reform in New Granada, 1784–1796." In *Reform and Insurrection in Bourbon New Granada and Peru,* edited by John R. Fisher, Allan J. Kuethe and Anthony McFarlane, 41–53. Baton Rouge: Louisiana State University Press, 1990.

Morales Folguera, José Miguel, and María Isabel Pérez de Colosía Rodríguez. *Los Gálvez de Macharaviaya.* Málaga: Benedicto Editores, 1991.

Morales Padrón, Francisco, ed. *The Journal of Don Francisco Saavedra De Sangronis, 1780–1783.* Gainesville: University of Florida Press, 1989.

Morales Valeiro, Francisco. "Secularización de doctrinas: ¿Fin de un modelo evangelizador en la Nueva España?" *Archivo Ibero-Americano: Revista Franciscana de Estudios Históricos* 52 (1992): 465–95.

Moreno Cebrián, Alfredo. "Acumulación y blanqueo de capitales del Marqués de Castelfuerte (1723–1763)." In *El "premio" de ser virrey: Los intereses públicos y privados del gobierno virreinal en el Perú de Felipe V,* edited by Alfredo Moreno Cebrián and Núria Sala i Vila, 233–63. Madrid: Consejo Superior de Investigaciones Científicas, 2004.

El Corregidor de indios y la economía peruana en el siglo XVIII. Madrid: Consejo Superior de Investigaciones Científicas, 1977.

"El regalismo borbónico frente al poder Vaticano: Acerca del estado de la iglesia en el Perú durante el primer tercio del siglo XVIII." *Revista de Indias* 63, no. 227 (2003): 223–74.

ed. *Relación y documentos de Gobierno del Virrey del Perú, José Manso de Velasco, Conde de Superunda (1745–1761).* Madrid: Consejo Superior de Investigaciones Científicas, Instituto Gonzalo de Oviedo, 1983.

Muñoz Pérez, J. "La publicación del Reglamento de Comercio Libre de Indias de 1778." *Anuario de estudios americanos* 4 (1947): 615–64.

Nava Rodríguez, Teresa. "Problemas y perpectivas (sic) de una historia social de la administración: Los secretarios del Despacho en la España del siglo XVIII." *Mélanges de la Casa de Vélazquez* 30 (1994): 151–66.

Navarro García, Luis. "Campillo y el nuevo sistema: Una atribución dudosa." *Temas americanistas* 2 (1983): 22–29.

Don José de Gálvez y la Comandancia General de las Provincias Internas del norte de Nueva España. Seville: Consejo Superior de Investigaciones Científicas, 1964.

"El primer proyecto reformista de José de Gálvez." In *Homenaje al Dr. José Antonio Calderón Quijano,* 378–402. Seville: Escuela de Estudios Hispano-Americanos, 1997.

Intendencias de Indias. Seville: Escuela de Estudios Hispano-Americanos, 1959.

La Casa de la Contratación en Cádiz. Cadiz: Instituto de Estudios Gaditanos, 1975.

La política Americana de José de Gálvez. Malaga: Editorial Algazara, 1998.

Las reformas borbónicas en América: El plan de intendencias y su aplicación. Seville: Universidad de Sevilla, 1995.

Nelson, George H. "Contraband Trade under the Assiento." *The American Historical Review* 51, no. 1 (October 1945): 55–67.

Noel, Charles C. "Clerics and Crown in Bourbon Spain, 1700–1808: Jesuits, Jansenists, and Enlightened Reformers." In *Religion and Politics in Enlightenment Europe*, edited by James E. Bradley and Dale K. Van Kley. 119–53. West Bend, IN: University of Notre Dame Press, 2001.

North, Douglas C. "Institutions and Economic Growth: An Historical Introduction." *World Development* 17, no. 9 (1989): 1319–32.

Nowell, Charles E. "The Defense of Cartagena." *The Hispanic American Historical Review* 42, no. 4 (November 1962): 477–501.

O'Donnell, Hugo. *El primer marqués de la Victoria, personaje silenciado en la reforma dieciochesca de la Armada*. Madrid: Real Academia de la Historia, 2004.

Ogelsby, J. C. M. "The British and Panama – 1742." *Caribbean Studies* 3, no. 2 (July 1963): 71–79.

"Havana Squadron and the Preservation of the Balance of Power in the Caribbean, 1740–1748." *The Hispanic American Historical Review* 49, no. 3 (August 1969): 473–88.

Olaechea, Rafael. "Política eclesiástica del gobierno de Fernando VI" In *La época de Fernando VI*, 139–225. Oviedo: Cátedra Feijo, 1981.

Olaechea, Rafael, and José Ferrer Benimeli. *El Conde de Aranda (Mito y realidad de un político aragonés)*,2 vols. Zaragoza: Librería General, 1978.

Oliva Melgar, José María. *Cataluña y el comercio privilegiado con América: La Real Compañía de Comercio de Barcelona a Indias*. Barcelona: Universitat de Barcelona, 1987.

"La Metrópoli sin territorio. ¿Crisis del comercio de Indias en el siglo XVII o pérdida del control del monopolio?" In *El sistema atlántico español (siglos XVII–XIX)*, edited by Carlos Martínez Shaw and José María Oliva Melgar, 19–73. Madrid: Marcial Pons, 2005.

Ortiz de la Tabla Ducasse, Javier. *Comercio exterior de Veracruz, 1778–1821: Crisis de dependencia*. Seville: Escuela de Estudios Hispano-Americanos, 1978.

Osante, Patricia. "Colonization and Control: The Case of Nuevo Santander," In *Choice, Persuasion and Coercion: Social Control on Spain's North American Frontiers*, edited by Jesús de la Teja and Ross Frank, 227–51. Albuquerque: University of New Mexico Press, 2005.

Orígenes del Nuevo Santander (1748–1772). Mexico: Universidad Autónoma de Tamaulipas, 1997.

Ozanam, Didier. *La diplomacia de Fernando VI: Correspondencia entre Carvajal y Huéscar, 1746–1749*. Madrid: Consejo Superior de Investigaciónes Científicas, 1975.

Palacio Atard, Vicente. *Introduction to Patiño en la política internacional de Felipe V by Antonio de Béthencourt Massieu*. Valladolid: Facultad de Filosofía y Letras de la Universidad de Valladolid, 1954.

Palmer, R. R. *The Age of Democratic Revolutions: A Political History of Europe and America, 1760–1800*. Princeton, NJ: Princeton University Press, 1959.

Paquette, Gabriel, ed. *Enlightened Reform in Southern Europe and Its Atlantic Colonies, c. 1750–1830*. Surry: Ashgate Publishing Limited, 2009.

Enlightenment, Governance, and Reform in Spain and Its Empire, 1759–1808. Basingstoke: Palgrave-MacMillan, 2008.

"State-Civil Society Cooperation and Conflict in the Spanish Empire: The Intellectual and Political Activities of the Ultramarine Consulados and Economic Societies, c. 1780–1810."*Journal of Latin American Studies* 39, no. 2 (May 2007): 263–98.

Parcero Torre, Celia María. *La pérdida de la Habana y las reformas borbónicas en Cuba (1760–1773)*. Valladolid: Junta de Castilla y León, Consejería de Educación y Cultura, 1998.

Pares, Richard. *War and Trade in the West Indies, 1739–1763*. Oxford: Oxford University Press, 1936.

Parry, John H. *The Spanish Seaborne Empire*. New York: Knopf, 1966.

Patch, Robert W. *Maya and Spaniard in Yucatán, 1648–1812*. Stanford: Stanford University Press, 1993.

Pearce, Adrian J. *British Trade with Spanish America, 1763–1808*. Liverpool: Liverpool University Press, 2007.

"Early Bourbon Government in the Viceroyalty of Peru, 1700–1759." PhD diss., University of Liverpool, 1998.

Peragallo, Edward. *Origin and Evolution of Double Entry Bookkeeping: A Study of Italian Practice from the Fourteenth Century*. New York: American Institute of Publishing Company, 1938.

Peralta Ruiz, Víctor. "Las razoznes de la fé: La iglesia y ilustraciónen el Perú, 1750–1800." In *Perú en el siglo XVIII: La era Borbónica*, edited by Scarlett O'Phelan Godoy, 177–204. Lima: Pontífica Universidad Católica del Perú, 2003.

Patrones, clientes y amigos. El poder burocrático indiano en la España del siglo XVIII. Madrid: Consejo Superior de Investigaciones Científicas, 2006.

Pérez Samper, María Angeles. *Isabel de Farnesio*. Barcelona: Editorial Juventud, 2003.

Pérez-Mallaína Bueno, Pablo Emilio. *La política española en el Atlántico, 1700–1715*. Seville: Escuela de Estudios Hispano-Americanos, 1982.

Los hombres del océano. Vida cotidiana de los tripulantes de las flotas de India, Siglo XVI. Seville: Escuela de Estudios Hispano-Americanos, 1992.

Retrato de una ciudad en crisis: La sociedad limeña ante el movimiento sísmico de 1746. Seville: Escuela de Estudios Hispano-Americanos, 2001.

Phelan, John Leddy. "El auge y la caída de los criollos en la Audiencia de Nueva Granada, 1700–1781." *Boletín de historia y antigüedades* 59 (1972): 597–618.

The People and the King: The Comunero Revolution in Colombia, 1781. Madison: University of Wisconsin Press, 1978.

Pieper, Renate. "Contiendas imperiales y política fiscal: España y Gran Bretaña en el siglo XVIII." In *Finanzas y política en el mundo iberoamericano: Del antiguo régimen a las naciones independientes, 1754–1850*, 63–76. Mexico: Universidad Autónoma de México, 2001.

Pietschmann, Horst, ed. *Atlantic History: History of the Atlantic System, 1580–1830*. Göttingen: Vandenhoeck & Ruprecht, 2002.

ed. *Las reformas borbónicas y el sistema de intendencias en Nueva España: Un estudio político administrativo*. Translated by Rolf Roland Meyer Misteli. Mexico City: Fondo de Cultura Económica, 1996.

Piho, Virve. *La secularización de las parroquias en la Nueva España y su repercusión en San Andrés Calpan.* Mexico: Instituto Nacional de Antropología e Historia, 1981.

Placer Cervera, Gustavo. *Inglaterra y La Habana: 1762.* Havana: Editorial Ciencias Sociales, 2007.

Pogonyi, Miklos. "The Search for Trade and Profits in Bourbon Colombia, 1765–1777." PhD diss., University of New Mexico, 1978.

Portuondo Zúñiga, Olga. *Una derrota británica en Cuba.* Santiago: Editorial Oriente, 2000.

Prados de la Escosura, Leandro. *De imperio a nación. Crecimiento y atraso económico en España (1780–1930).* Madrid: Alianza Editorial, 1988.

Priestley, Herbert Ingram. *José de Gálvez: Visitor-General of New Spain (1765–1771).* Berkeley: University of California Press, 1916.

Ramos Gómez, Luis J. *Noticias secretas de América de Jorge Juan y Antonio de Ulloa (1735–1745),* 2 vols. Madrid: Consejo Superior de Investigaciones Científicas, 1985.

Ramos-Kuethe, Lourdes, ed. *Romance anónimo sobre el sitio y la toma de La Habana por los ingleses en 1762.* Prague: Charles University Press, 2011.

Real Díaz, José Joaquín. *Estudio diplomático del documento indiano.* Madrid: Dirección de Archivos Estatales, 1991. Reprint, 2.

Las ferias de Jalapa. Seville: Escuela de Estudios Hispano-Americanos, 1959.

Reglamento y aranceles reales para el comercio libre de España a Indias de 12 de octubre de 1778. Seville: Escuela de Estudios Hispano-Americanos, 1977.

Renaut, Francis P. *Pacte de Famille et l'Amerique: La Politique Coloniale Franco-Espagnole de 1760 á 1792.* Paris: Leroux, 1922.

Ringrose, David R. *Madrid and the Spanish Economy, 1650–1850.* Berkeley: University of California Press, 1983.

Ríos Mazcarelle, Manuel. *Reinas de España.* Madrid: Alderaban, 1999.

Rishel, Joseph, and Suzanne Straton-Pruitt. *The Arts in Latin America, 1492–1820.* Philadelphia: Philadelphia Museum of Art, 2006.

Robles, Gregorio, de, ed. *América a fines del siglo XVII: Noticia de los lugares de contrabando.* Valladolid: Casa-Museo de Colón y Seminario Americanista de la Universidad, 1980.

Rodger, N. A. M. *The Command of the Ocean: A Naval History of Britain, 1649–1815.* London: W.W. Norton & Company, 2004.

Rodríguez, Laura. "The Riots of 1766 in Madrid." *European Studies Review* 3, no. 3 (1973): 232–37.

Rodríguez Casado, Vicente. "Comentarios al Decreto y Real Instrucción de 1765 regulando las relaciones comerciales de España e Indias." *Anuario de historia del derecho español* 13 (1936–1941): 100–35.

"El ejército y la marina en el reinado de Carlos III." *Boletín del Instituto Riva Agüero* 3 (1956–1957).

La política y los políticos en el reinado de Carlos III. Madrid: Ediciones Rialp, 1962.

Rodríguez Casado, Vicente, and Florentino Pérez Embid, eds. *Manuel de Amat y Junient, Virrey del Perú, 1761–1776: Memoria de Gobierno.* Seville: Escuela de Estudios Hispano-Americanos, 1947.

Rodríguez Villa, Antonio. *Don Cenón de Somodevilla.* Madrid: M. Murillo, 1878.

Patiño y Campillo: Reseña histórico-biográfica de estos dos ministros de Felipe V. Madrid: Sucesores de Rivadeneyra, 1882.

Rosenmüller, Christoph. *Patrons, Partisans, and Palace Intrigues: The Court Society of Colonial Mexico.* Calgary: University of Calgary Press, 2008.

Ruiz Rivera, Julián B. *El Consulado de Cádiz: Matrícula de comerciantes, 1730–1823.* Cádiz: Diputación Provincial de Cádiz, 1988.

Safier, Neil. *Measuring the New World: Enlightenment Science in South America.* Chicago: University of Chicago Press, 2008.

Sala i Vila, Núria. "Una Corona bien vale un Virreinato: El Marqués de Castelldosríus, Primer Virrey Borbónico del Perú." In *El "premio" de ser virrey: Los intereses públicos y privados del gobierno virreinal en el Perú de Felipe V,* edited by Alfredo Moreno Cebrián and Núria Sala i Vila, 17–150. Madrid: Consejo Superior de Investigaciónes Científicas, 2004.

Salvucci, Linda K. "Costumbres Viejas, 'hombres nuevos': José de Gálvez y la burocracia fiscal novohispana (1754–1800)." *Historia mexicana* 33 (October–December 1983): 224–60.

San Felipe, Marqués de. *Comentarios de la guerra de España e historia de su rey Felipe V, el animoso.* Vol. 99 of *Biblioteca de Autores Españoles.* Madrid: Atlas, 1957.

Sánchez Bella, Ismael. *Iglesia y estado en la América española.* Pamplona: Ediciones Universidad de Navarra, 1990.

Sánchez Blanco, Francisco. *El absolutismo y las luces en el reinado de Carlos III.* Madrid: Marcial Pons, 2002.

Sánchez Santiró, Ernest. "El nuevo orden parroquial de la ciudad de México: Población, etnia, y territorio (1768–1777)." *Estudios de historia novohispana* 30 (January–June 2004): 63–92.

Schwartz, Stuart B. *All Can Be Saved: Religious Tolerance and Salvation in the Iberian Atlantic World.* New Haven, CT: Yale University Press, 2008.

Seed, Patricia. *American Pentimento: The Invention of Indians and the Pursuit of Riches.* Minneapolis: University of Minnesota Press, 2001.

———. *Ceremonies of Possession: Europe's Conquest of the New World.* Cambridge: Cambridge University Press, 1995.

Serrano Álvarez, José Manuel. *Ejercito y fiscalidad en Cartagena de Indias: Auge y declive en la segunda mitad del siglo XVIII.* Bogotá: Áncora Editoriales, 2006.

———. *Fortificaciones y tropas: El gasto militar en Tierra Firme, 1700–1788.* Seville: Escuela de Estudios Hispano-Americanos, 2004.

———. "Situados y rentas en Cartagena de Indias durante el siglo XVIII." *Temas americanistas, núm.* 17 (2004).

Serrano Álvarez, José Manuel, and Allan J. Kuethe. "La familia O'Farrill y la élite habanera." In *Élites urbanas en Hispanoamérica,* edited by Luis Navarro García, 203–12. Seville: Universidad De Sevilla, 2005.

———. "La Texas colonial entre Pedro de Rivera y el marqués de Rubí, 1729–1772: Aportaciones económicas al sistema presidial." *Colonial Latin American Historical Review* 14 (Summer 2005): 281–311.

Serulnikov, Sergio. *Subverting Colonial Authority: Challenges to Spanish Rule in Eighteenth-Century Southern Andes.* Durham: Duke University Press, 2003.

Sevilla Soler, María Rosario. *Santo Domingo: Tierra de frontera (1750–1800).* Seville: Escuela de Estudios Hispano-Americanos, 1980.

Sharp, William F. *Slavery on the Spanish Frontier: The Colombian Chocó, 1680–1810*. Norman: University of Oklahoma Press, 1976.

Sierra Nava, Luis. "La cesión de Santo Domingo a Francia en la Paz de Bale: Trueque de intereses comerciales, en las correspondencias de Godoy con sus plenipotenciarios Iriarte e Iranda con una referencia a la devolución de las Vascongadas (1795)." In *Euskal Herria y el Nuevo Mundo: La contribución de los Vascos a la formación de las Américas*, edited by Ronald Escobedo Mansilla, Ana de Zaballa Beascoechea and Óscar Álvarez Gila, 319–37. Vitoria: Universidad del País Vasco, 1996.

Smith, Robert Sidney. "Origins of the Consulado of Guatemala." *The Hispanic American Historical Review* 26, no. 2 (May 1946): 150–160.

Socolow, Susan Migden. "Buenos Aires: Atlantic Port and Hinterland in the Eighteenth Century." In *Atlantic Port Cities: Economy, Culture, and Society in the Atlantic World, 1650–1850*, edited by Franklin W. Knight and Peggy K. Liss, 240–61. Knoxville: University of Tennessee Press, 1991.

The Merchants of Buenos Aires, 1778–1810. Cambridge: Cambridge University Press, 1978.

Souto Mantecón, Matilde. *Mar abierto: La política y el comercio del consulado de Veracruz o el ocaso del sistema imperial*. Mexico: Colegio de México, 2001.

Spalding, Karen. *Huarochirí: An Andean Society under Inca and Spanish Rule*. Stanford, CA: Stanford University Press, 1984.

Stavig, Ward. *The World of Túpac Amaru: Conflict, Community, and Identity in Colonial Peru*. Lincoln: University of Nebraska Press, 1999.

Stein, Barbara H., and Stanley J. Stein. "Concepts and Realities of Spanish Economic Growth, 1759–1789." *Historia ibérica* (1973): 103–19.

Stein, Stanley J. "Bureacracy and Business in the Spanish Empire, 1759–1804: Failure of a Bourbon Reform in Mexico and Peru." *The Hispanic American Historical Review* 61, no. 1 (February 1981): 2–28.

Stein, Stanley, J., and Barbara H. Stein. *Apogee of Empire: Spain and New Spain in the Age of Charles III, 1759–1789*. Baltimore and London: Johns Hopkins University Press, 2003.

The Colonial Heritage of Latin America: Essays in Economic Dependence in Perspective. Oxford: Oxford University Press, 1970.

Edge of Crisis: War and Trade in the Spanish Atlantic, 1789–1808. Baltimore: Johns Hopkins University Press, 2009.

Silver, Trade, and War: Spain and America in the Making of Early Modern Europe. Baltimore and London: Johns Hopkins University Press, 2000.

Suárez, Santiago-Gerardo, ed. *Las fuerzas armadas venezolanas en la colonia*. Caracas: Academia Nacional de la Historia, 1979.

Summerhill, William R. "Fiscal Bargains, Political Institutions, and Economic Performance." *The Hispanic American Historical Review* 88, no. 2 (May 2008): 219–33.

Tanck de Estrada, Dorothy. *Pueblos de Indios y educación en el México colonial, 1750–1821*. Mexico: Colegio de México, 1999.

Taylor, William B. *Magistrates of the Sacred: Priests and Parishioners in Eighteenth-Century Mexico*. Stanford, CA: Stanford University Press, 1996.

Tedde de Lorca, P. "Política financiera y política comercial en el reinado de Carlos III." In *Actas del Congreso internacional sobre Carlos III y la ilustración*, 139–217. Madrid: Ministerio de Cultura, 1989.

Téllez Alarcia, Diego. *El ministerio Wall: La <España discreta> del <ministro olvidado>*. Madrid: Fundación de Municipios Pablo Olavide y Marcial Pons Historia, 2012.

TePaske, John J. "La política española en el Caribe durante los siglos XVII y XVIII." In *La influencia de España en el Caribe, la Florida, y la Luisiana, 1500–1800*, edited by Juan Marchena Fernández and Antonio Acosta, 61–87. Madrid: Instituto de Cooperación Iberoamericana, 1983.

"New World Silver, Castile, and the Far East (1590–1750)." In *Precious Metals in the Later Medieval and Early Modern Worlds*, edited by John F. Richards, 425–45. Durham, NC: Duke University Press, 1983.

Thomas, Hugh. *Cuba: The Pursuit of Freedom*. New York: Da Capa Press, 1971.

Thomson, Sinclair. *We Alone Shall Rule: Native Andean Politics in the Age of Insurgency*. Madison: University of Wisconsin Press, 2002.

Torres Sánchez, Rafael. *La llave de todos los tesoros: La Tesorería General de Carlos III*. Madrid: Silez, 2012.

Tibesar, Antonine S. "The Suppression of the Religious Orders in Peru, 1826–1830 or the King Versus the Peruvian Friars: The King Won." *The Americas* 39, no. 2 (October 1982): 205–39.

Tietz, Manfred, ed. *Los jesuitas españoles expulsos: Su imagen y contribución al saber sobre el mundo hispánico en la Europa del siglo XVIII*. Frankfort and Madrid: Vervuert, 2001.

Tilley, John A. *The British Navy and the American Revolution*. Columbia: University of South Carolina Press, 1987.

Tjarks, Germán. *El Consulado de Buenos Aires y sus proyecciones en la historia del Río de La Plata*, Vol. 1. Buenos Aires: Universidad de Buenos Aires, 1962.

Torres Ramírez, Bibiano. *Alejandro O'Reilly en las Indias*. Seville: Escuela de Estudios Hispano-Americanos, 1969.

La Armada del Mar del Sur. Seville: Escuela de Estudios Hispano-Americanos, 1987.

La Compañía Gaditana de Negros. Seville: Escuela de Estudios Hispano-Americanos, 1973.

La marina en el gobierno y administración de Indias. Madrid: Mapfre, 1992.

Townsend Cummins, Light. *Spanish Observers and the American Revolution, 1775–1783*. Baton Rouge: Louisiana State University, 1991.

Twinam, Ann. *Miners, Merchants, and Farmers in Colonial Colombia*. Austin: University of Texas Press, 1982.

Public Lives, Private Secrets: Gender, Honor, Sexuality, and Illegitimacy in Colonial Spanish America. Stanford, CA: Stanford University Press, 1999.

Uribe-Uran, Víctor M. "The Birth of a Public Sphere in Latin America During the Age of Revolution." *Comparative Studies in Society and History* 42 (2000): 425–57.

Valle Menéndez, Antonio del. *Juan Francisco de Güemes y Horcasitas, Primer Conde de Revillagigedo, Virrey de México: La Historia de un Soldado (1681–1766)*. Santander: Ediciones de Librería Estudio, 1998.

Vargas Ugarte, Rubén. *Historia de la Compañía de Jesús*. Burgos: Imprenta de Aldecoa, 1965.

Vigón, Ana María. *Guía del Archivo Museo "D. Alvaro de Bazán."* Viso del Marqués: Instituto de Historia y Cultura Naval, 1985.

Vila Vilar, Enriqueta. "Algunas consideraciones sobre la creación del Consulado de Sevilla." *Congreso de Historia del Descubrimiento* 4 (1992): 53–65.

———. *Hispanoamérica y el comercio de esclavos*. Seville: Escuela de Estudios Hispano-Americanos, 1977.

———. "Las ferias de Portobelo: Apariencia y realidad del comercio con Indias." *Anuario de Estudios Americanos* 39 (1982): 275–340.

———. *Los Corzo y los Mañara: Tipos y arquetipos del mercader con América*. Sevilla: Escuela de Estudios Hispano-Americanos, 1991.

Vinson III, Ben. *Bearing Arms for His Majesty: The Free-Colored Militia in Colonial Mexico*. Stanford, CA: Stanford University Press, 2001.

Walker, Charles F. "Upper Classes and Their Upper Stories: Architecture and the Aftermath of the Lima Earthquake of 1746." *Hispanic American Historical Review* 83, no. 1 (February 2003): 53–82.

Walker, Geoffrey J. *Spanish Politics and Imperial Trade, 1700–1789*. Bloomington: Indiana University Press, 1979.

Washburn, Douglas Alan. "The Bourbon Reforms: A Social and Economic History of the Audiencia of Quito, 1760–1810." PhD diss., University of Texas at Austin, 1984.

Weber, David J. *Indios Bárbaros: Spaniards and Their Savages in the Age of Enlightenment*. New Haven, CT: Yale University Press, 2005.

Weddle, Robert S. *The San Sabá Mission: Spanish Pivot in Texas*. Austin: University of Texas, 1964.

Whatley Pierson, Jr., William. "The Establishment and Early Functioning of the 'Intendencia' of Cuba." In *Studies in Hispanic American History*, 113–33. Chapel Hill: University of North Carolina Press, 1927.

Whitaker, Arthur P. "The Elhúyar Mining Missions and the Enlightenment." *The Hispanic American Historical Review* 31, no. 4 (November 1951): 557–85.

Williams, Derek. "Who Induced the Indian Communities? The Los Pastos Uprising and the Politics of Ethnicity and Gender in Late-Colonial New Granada." *Colonial Latin American Historical Review* 10, no. 3 (Summer 2001): 292–94.

Winfield, Rif. *British Warships in the Age of Sail, 1793–1817*. London: Chatham Publishing, 2005.

Woodward, Ralph Lee. *Class Privilege and Economic Development: The Consulado de Comercio de Guatemala, 1793–1871*. Chapel Hill: University of North Carolina Press, 1966.

Wortman, Miles. "Bourbon Reforms in Central America, 1750–1786." *The Americas* 32, no. 2 (October 1975): 222–38.

Yalí Román, Alberto. "Sobre alcaldías mayores y corregimientos en Indias," *Jahrbuch fur Geschichte von Staat, Wirtsc haft, und Geselschaft Lateinamerikas, 9 (1974):* 1–39

Zaret, David. *Origins of Democratic Culture: Printing, Petitions, and the Public Sphere in Early-Modern England*. Princeton: Princeton University Press, 2000.

Index

89–96, 122, 128, 254–55; and military reform in Cuba, 89–95; and Royal Havana Company, 145–46; under Esquilache, 253–55; under Patiño, 122

Torija, Fernando, 276

Torreblanca, Marqués de, 125

Torrenueva, Marqués de, 136, 139–41

Torres, Rodrigo de, 140, 149, 152n90

Torres Sánchez, Rafael, 18

Townsend, Joseph, 316–17

Triple Alliance, 56–57, 59

Tupac Amaru II, 298–99

Tuy River frontier, 162–63

Ulloa, Antonio de, 8, 9, 10, 169–71, 173, 175, 192, 208, 261

Urbina, Andrés, 275

Ursins, Princess, 40–41, 42, 47, 61

Ustáriz, Casimiro de, 134

Utrecht, Treaties of (1713): benefits to Spanish monarchy under, 38–39; concessions under, 37–38, 72, 348; effects of, 2; impediments imposed by, 33; legacy of, 103–9; Spain forced to uphold pledges under, 62–63; and Triple Alliance, 56–57

Vadillo, Manuel, 43

Valdés y Bazán, Antonio, 319–20, 321*fig.*, 322, 327, 332–34

valimiento de Vigo, 76

Valparaíso, Conde de, 211, 217

van Loo, Louis Michael, 100, 101*fig.*

Varas y Valdés, Francisco, 63, 64n163, 79, 112, 205, 206, 212

Vaulgrenant, Compte de, 135

veguero uprisings, Cuba, 90–94

Velasco, Luis Vicente, 222

Velasco, Manuel, 76

Vendôme, Duke of, 2, 46–47

Venezuela: challenge to Bourbon rule in, 134; impact of termination of South Sea Company's *asiento* on, 162–65; and imperial free trade, 292, 330–31; and León's rebellion, 162–65. *See also* Caracas, captaincy general of, and Caracas Company

Vernon, Edward, 147–48, 149, 150–51, 152n90, 153

Victoria, Marqués de la, 153, 198, 215n120

Villalba y Angulo, Juan de, 247, 248, 249, 251, 253, 274

Villalengua, President, 324

Villalonga, Jorge, 87

Villarías, Marqués de, 136, 158n108, 160n117, 161, 243. *See also* Sebastián de la Cuadra

Vinson, Ben, 22

visitadores, 5, 306, 311, 351

von Nordenflicht, Thaddeus, 327

Wall, Ricardo: and accession of Charles III, 217; and downfall of Ensenada, 209, 211–12; and Seven Years' War, 233; shipbuilding under, 214; and Treaty of Madrid, 195

Walpole, Robert, 146–47

War of Jenkins' Ear: attack on Cartagena, 148–51; attack on Santiago de Cuba, 151; British defeat in, 151–52; causes of, 146–47; and curtailed autonomy of *Consulado* of Cádiz, 139; declaration of, 147–48; pressures on transatlantic trade during, 133–34; use of register ships during, 153–57, 166

War of the American Revolution, 301–3, 305, 306–7, 342

War of the Austrian Succession, 157–62, 352

War of the Polish Succession, 103, 111

War of the Quadruple Alliance: Bourbon defensive entente following, 81; causes and events of, 57–62; effects of, 66; maritime traffic halted during, 106; and Project of 1720, 62–66; and transfer of colonial trade apparatus to Cádiz, 76

War of the Spanish Succession, 1–2, 40, 45, 53, 91, 347

war(s): as constant theme in eighteenth-century Atlantic world, 354; funding, 342–43; impact of, on reform efforts, 344; as impediment to reform, 18; and implementation of Bourbon reform policies, 26

Wentworth, Thomas, 148, 150, 151, 152

woolen textile production, resuscitation of, in Quito, 325–26

yellow fever, 148, 152, 221, 236

Zuloaga, Gabriel José de, 163

Zúñiga, Baltasar, 102, 113